本书为国家社会科学基金青年项目"美国现代口述史学研究"（课题编号 09CSS001）研究成果

美国现代口述史学研究

Studies on American Modern Oral History

杨祥银 著

中国社会科学出版社

图书在版编目（CIP）数据

美国现代口述史学研究/杨祥银著 . —北京：中国社会科学出版社，2016. 12
ISBN 978 - 7 - 5161 - 9178 - 1

Ⅰ. ①美…　Ⅱ. ①杨…　Ⅲ. ①口述历史学 - 研究 - 美国　Ⅳ. ①K0

中国版本图书馆 CIP 数据核字（2016）第 261125 号

出 版 人	赵剑英
责任编辑	安　芳
特约编辑	席建海
责任校对	冯英爽
责任印制	李寡寡

出　　版	中国社会科学出版社
社　　址	北京鼓楼西大街甲 158 号
邮　　编	100720
网　　址	http://www.csspw.cn
发 行 部	010 - 84083685
门 市 部	010 - 84029450
经　　销	新华书店及其他书店

印刷装订	北京君升印刷有限公司
版　　次	2016 年 12 月第 1 版
印　　次	2016 年 12 月第 1 次印刷

开　　本	710 × 1000　1/16
印　　张	37. 5
字　　数	628 千字
定　　价	98. 00 元

凡购买中国社会科学出版社图书，如有质量问题请与本社营销中心联系调换
电话：010 - 84083683

目　　录

Contents

第一章 导论

现代口述史学（oral history）是 20 世纪中叶在美国率先兴起并发展的研究方法与学科领域，其标志性事件是 1948 年哥伦比亚大学（以下简称哥大）口述历史研究室（Columbia University Oral History Research Office）的创建。目前，世界各国一般都有全国性的口述历史组织，它们不仅频繁地召开各种学术会议与出版学术刊物和著述，而且近年来的国际合作与交流也不断得到加强和深化，其中最具代表性的就是国际口述历史协会（International Oral History Association）的活动重心逐渐从北美洲和欧洲向亚洲、非洲、澳洲和南美洲延伸。

概括而言，口述史学在当代的发展呈现一个相当明显的辐射走向，它发端于 20 世纪中叶的美国，20 世纪 60—70 年代兴起于英国和加拿大，而 20 世纪 80—90 年代以来逐步流行于世界各地。经过 60 多年的发展，口述史学不仅有助于历史学研究的不断深化与革新，同时也被广泛地应用于人文、社会与自然科学等众多领域，在推动跨学科应用与交叉研究中起到相当重要的作用。

本章将从口述史学简史、基本概念界定、美国口述史学研究的学术史回顾以及本书研究的基本思路与框架等方面做一导论性梳理与分析。

一 口述史学简史

一般而言，国际口述史学界普遍将美国著名历史学家、新闻记者阿兰·内文斯（Allan Nevins，1890—1971）于 1948 年创建哥大口述历史研究室视为现代口述史学诞生的标志。① 英国著名口述历史学家保罗·汤普森（Paul Thompson，1935—）曾援引美国口述历史协会（Oral History Association）官方记录指出："1948 年哥大历史学家阿兰·内文斯开始记录美国生活中重要人物的回忆，从那时起，口述历史作为一种获得历史文献（historical documentation）的现代手段而正式创立起来。"②

显然，口述史学的现代复兴与应用也不过是新近的事。但是，这并不意味着它没有自己的悠久历史，正如保罗·汤普森所说："事实上，口述历史就如历史一样悠久。它是历史的第一种形式。"③ 在文字产生之前，人类为了将先辈们的历史尽可能完整地传递下去，除一些简单的符号记忆（据记载，北美印第安人、非洲各部落等都曾经利用打结的绳头、贝壳、斑纹、图画等手段来记录他们的经历）之外，主要是依赖于口耳相传。在中华文化五千年的文明史上，迄今发现的最早文字是甲骨文，它产生于商朝先公示壬、示癸时期。④ 显然，之前的历史大部分都是通过口头世代相传。

而文字出现以后，文字史料逐渐成为历史学家研究的主要来源。即使如此，对于口述资料的应用从来没有停止过，只不过与文字资料

---

① 2011 年 6 月 1 日，该研究室正式更名为哥伦比亚大学口述历史中心（Columbia Center of Oral History）。此外，据现任哥大口述历史中心主任玛丽·克拉克（Mary Marshall Clark）2014 年 4 月 10 日给笔者的电子邮件显示，为区隔口述历史中心的研究与档案功能以及加强各自的发展，哥大又于 2013 年 11 月成立分别隶属于哥大文理学部（Faculty of Arts and Sciences）的哥大口述历史研究中心（Columbia Center for Oral History Research）和隶属于哥大图书馆善本与手稿部（Rare Book and Manuscript Division，Columbia Libraries）的哥大口述历史档案中心（Columbia Center for Oral History Archives）。详细内容访问该中心官方网站 http：//library. columbia. edu/locations/ccoh. html，2015 年 8 月 1 日访问。

② Paul Thompson，*The Voice of the Past：Oral History*，Oxford and New York：Oxford University Press，third edition，2000，p. 65. 关于哥大口述历史研究室的创建过程与早期发展，下文将有进一步论述。

③ Paul Thompson，*The Voice of the Past：Oral History*，Oxford and New York：Oxford University Press，third edition，2000，p. 25.

④ 于省吾：《略论甲骨文"自上甲六示"的庙号以及我国成文历史的开始》，《社会科学战线》1978 年第 1 期，第 333—335 页。

相比显得相形见绌。之所以说口述资料仍然受到历史学家的重视，这从"文献"一词的意义中也可以看出。"文献"一词最早可见于孔子（公元前551—前479）的《论语》："夏礼吾能言之，杞不足征也。殷礼吾能言之，宋不足征也。文献不足故也，足则吾能征之矣。"① 当然，这里孔子并没有明确指出"文献"都包含什么内容，也无从考证。后人对"文献"的理解尽管表述不一，不过其意思却很相近，即认为"文献"就是文字资料和口头（言论）资料的结合。② 宋代马端临（1254—1323）认为，"文"是经、史、历代会要以及百家传记之书；而"献"则是臣僚之奏疏、诸儒之评论、名流之燕谈、稗官之记录。③ 而清代刘宝楠（1791—1855）则说："文谓典策，献谓秉礼之贤士大夫。"④ 清代徐灏（1809—1879）指出："载诸典籍者文也，传诸其人者献也。"⑤

回顾中西史学史的发展历程，便可以发现很多历史学家很早就采用"口述历史"这种方法并对其有所研究。在中国，司马迁（公元前145—前90）的《史记》就被誉为久负盛名的"口述历史"著作，他在撰写《史记》过程中曾搜集大量的口述资料。而在西方，利用口头传说编撰而成的《荷马史诗》（*The Homeric Hymns*）与希罗多德（Herodotus，公元前484—前425）的《历史》（*The Histories*）和修昔底德（Thucydides，公元前460—前395）的《伯罗奔尼撒战争史》（*The History of the Peloponnesian War*）在西方口述史学上也是抹不去的一页。此后，尽管文献资料的地位在不断提升，但仍然有相当多的历史学家在实践着这种古老的历史研究方

---

① 《论语·八佾第三》。
② 王余光：《试论中国历史文献学研究中的几个问题》，《图书馆学研究》1985年第1期，第85页。
③ 《文献通考·自序》曰：凡叙事则本之经史，而参之以历代会要，以及百家传记之书，信而有证者从之，乖异传疑者不录，所谓"文"也。凡论事则先取常时臣僚之奏疏，次及近代诸儒之评论，以至名流之燕谈、稗官之纪录，凡一话一言可以订典故之得失，证史传之是非者，则采而录之，所谓"献"也。
④ 《论语正义》。
⑤ 《说文解字注笺》。

法。① 正如美国参议院历史办公室（United States Senate Historical Office）历史学家唐纳德·里奇（Donald A. Ritchie, 1945—）所说："直到19世纪晚期，同时参考口述与文献资料看上去仍然是合理的。"②

然而，随着历史学专业化的逐步发展，对于口述资料的质疑与批判与日俱增，很多历史学家以客观性为由抨击其作为一种史料的合法性。进入19世纪中叶以后，尤其是随着德国兰克（Leopold von Ranke, 1795—1886）学派的兴起，档案文献资料逐渐被看成唯一可靠的史料类型。兰克就认为在历史事件发生期间的记载才是最可靠的历史证据，在撰写《宗教改革时期的德意志史》的过程中，他从故纸堆中挖掘出大量珍贵资料，这使得他对文献资料深信不疑："我看到这样一个时期正在到来，那就是，我们在编写近代史时，甚至不再依靠当代史家的记载（除非是他们提出了原始知识的地方）。"③ 而随着兰克学术思想和方法的广泛传播，在德国、法国、英国和美国等地培养出一大批颇具影响的历史学家，因而也形成以"客观主义治史原则"著称的"科学历史学派"（school of scientific history）。兰克的追随者们致力于将历史由一种文学形式转变成一门依赖于严谨地利用证据的学科，并将口述资料贬低为民间传说和神话，认为口述证据过于主观。④ 法国著名历史杂志《史学评论》（*Revue Historique*）在其1876年《创刊词》中就说："本刊只接受以'原始资料为根据'的稿件，作者应采取'严格的科学表述方法，每个论断都必须有证据、有史料出处和引语'。"⑤

---

① 汤普森在《过去的声音：口述历史》一书中专门有一章"历史学家与口述历史"（Historians and Oral History）回顾了1948年以前世界各地历史学家对于这种方法的应用与思考。详细内容参阅 Paul Thompson, *The Voice of the Past: Oral History*, Oxford and New York: Oxford University Press, third edition, 2000, pp. 25-65. 此外还可参阅 Charles T. Morrissey, "Why Call It 'Oral History'? Searching for Early Usage of a Generic Term", *Oral History Review*, Vol. 8, 1980, pp. 20-48.

② Donald A. Ritchie, *Doing Oral History: A Practical Guide*, Oxford and New York: Oxford University Press, second edition, 2003, p. 20.

③ 转引自乔治·皮博迪·古奇《十九世纪历史学与历史学家》，耿淡如译，商务印书馆1989年版，第193页。

④ Donald A. Ritchie, *Doing Oral History: A Practical Guide*, Oxford and New York: Oxford University Press, second edition, 2003, p. 21.

⑤ 转引自罗凤礼主编《现代西方史学思潮评析》，中央编译出版社1996年版，第5页。

从此，口述资料便日益遭到冷落和诋毁。

在 20 世纪初，兰克学派的"历史科学规律"开始遭到不断挑战。首先是因为科学自身的进步，曾有学者指出："科学的进步使既定的科学规律或定律的精确性和绝对性的神话失去了魔力。"① 同时，由于新史学运动（new history movement）的兴起，传统史学研究方法已不适应历史学发展的新潮流，很多历史学家便重新提出发展口述史学的呼吁。而上述提到的内文斯早在 1938 年就提出开展口述历史访谈的倡导，他认为应该创立一个组织，系统地搜集和记录过去 60 年来参与国家政治、经济和文化生活的著名美国人的回忆。② 因为他担心随着电话、汽车和飞机等通讯和交通技术的发展，人们之间的面对面接触会逐步代替古老的信件来往，这有可能导致将来的历史学家缺乏信件等传统的文字记录。③ 正是如此，内文斯积极倡导通过口述历史来保存历史当事人和见证者的即将逝去的声音与历史记忆。而 10 年后，内文斯的理想终于成为现实，在哥大班克罗夫特基金（Bancroft Fund）的支持下，他率先开启这项影响深远和具有重要意义的现代口述史学试验（oral history experiment），于 1948 年在哥大创建美国历史上第一个口述历史机构，即上述提到的哥大口述历史研究室。

尽管这一举措也曾遭到那些认为口述历史不可靠的传统历史学家的极力反对与嘲讽，但口述史学凭借自身的独特价值与作用，在短短的时间内就取得令人瞩目的成绩。以美国为例，据统计，到 1965 年全美共有 89 个口述历史计划。④ 哥大口述历史研究室认为它们在口述史学领域引领了一场"真正的运动"，包括历史学会、大学（研究机构）、公司、图书馆、博物馆和专业

① 郭小凌：《西方史学史》，北京师范大学出版社 1995 年版，第 371—372 页。

② Allan Nevins, *The Gateway to History*, New York：D. C. Heath and Company, 1938, p. iv.

③ Columbia University, Oral History Research Office, *The Oral History Collection of Columbia University*, New York：Oral History Research Office, 1964, pp. 9—10.

④ Louis M. Starr, "Introduction", in Gary L. Shumway（ed.）, *Oral History in the United States：A Directory*, New York：Oral History Association, 1971, p. 3.

协会在内的不同机构都开展了相应的口述历史计划。① 同时，美国口述史学发展开始走向正规化和专业化，在内文斯的倡议下，美国第一届全国口述史学会议（National Colloquium on Oral History）于 1966 年 9 月 25—28 日在加利福尼亚州阿罗黑德湖（Lake Arrowhead）举行，包括档案工作者、图书管理员、历史学家和医生在内的近 100 位学者围绕口述历史的定义、应用与发展方向、口述历史访谈技巧以及专业目标和标准等问题展开激烈讨论。② 酝酿于第一届会议的全国性口述历史组织，美国口述历史协会也于 1967 年正式成立，其会员遍布全美与海外各地。③ 该协会除主办口述历史年会之外，还分别于 1967 年和 1973 年出版《口述历史协会通讯》（*Oral History Association Newsletter*）和学术杂志《口述历史评论》（*Oral History Review*）。④

与此同时，随着地方性口述历史组织和研究机构的不断创建，到 20 世纪 60 年代中期，口述史学在美国已经取得长足发展，而最能体现当时发展水平的标志是"口述历史"这一术语已经深入日常语言当中，《纽约时报》（*New York Times*）和《纽约每日新闻》（*New York Daily News*）等权威媒体都已经用小写字母来表示，而无须大写字母来特别提醒读者。正如内文斯学术继承人、哥大口述历史研究室第二任主任路易斯·斯塔尔（Louis M. Starr, 1917—1980）所说："不管喜欢与否，口述历史已经扎下根来。它已经自成一类。"⑤

---

① Columbia University, Oral History Research Office, *The Oral History Collection of Columbia University*, New York：Oral History Research Office, 1964, p. 10.

② Elizabeth I. Dixon and James V. Mink（eds.）, *Oral History at Arrowhead：The Proceedings of the First National Colloquium on Oral History*, Los Angeles：Oral History Association, 1967.

③ 有关该协会的详细信息可访问其官方网站 http：//www. oralhistory. org/, 2015 年 8 月 2 日访问。

④ *Oral History Association Newsletter*, Vol. 1, No. 1, 1967, p. 1；Samuel B. Hand, "Introduction", *Oral History Review*, Vol. 1, 1973, p. v.

⑤ Elizabeth I. Dixon, "Definitions of Oral History", in Elizabeth I. Dixon and James V. Mink（eds.）, *Oral History at Arrowhead：The Proceedings of the First National Colloquium on Oral History*, Los Angeles：Oral History Association, 1967, p. 14. 斯塔尔于 1956—1980 年期间担任哥大口述历史研究室主任，并于 1967—1968 年担任美国口述历史协会第二任主席。其生平经历与学术研究可参阅 Forrest Pogue, "Louis Starr：A Remembrance", *Oral History Review*, Vol. 8, 1980, pp. 93-97；"Louis Starr, Distinguished Oral Historian (1917-1980)", *Oral History Association Newsletter*, Vol. 14, No. 2, Spring 1977, pp. 3, 7；Thomas W. Ennis, "Louis M. Starr Dies, Oral History Head", *New York Times*, March 4, 1980.

而在美国的影响下，现代意义上的口述史学也在英国（1971）、法国、加拿大（1974）、澳大利亚（1978）、以色列、西班牙、马来西亚、新加坡、菲律宾、荷兰（1980）、新西兰（1986）、俄罗斯（苏联）、意大利（2005）、德国、比利时、波兰、瑞典、丹麦、挪威、芬兰、冰岛、瑞士、墨西哥（1996）、土耳其、巴西（1998）、津巴布韦（1988）、纳米比亚、葡萄牙、特立尼达和多巴哥、牙买加、多米尼加共和国、爱尔兰、南非（2004）、日本（2003）、中国（2004）、阿根廷（2005）、捷克（2007）、乌克兰（2007）、希腊（2012）和印度（2012）等地相继兴起与发展，它们大都拥有自己的专业协会与学术刊物。①

随着口述史学在欧美和世界各地的发展，各国口述历史学家感到有必要加强相互交流与合作，共同探讨口述史学的理论和方法问题。在保罗·汤普森的倡议和组织下，第一届国际口述历史大会（International Oral History Conference）于 1979 年 3 月 23—25 日在英国科尔切斯特（Colchester）的埃塞克斯大学（University of Essex）举行，此次会议由英国口述历史学会（Oral History Society）主办及埃塞克斯大学社会学系和历史系联合赞助。在为期三天的会期内，来自英国、美国、法国、西班牙、意大利、匈牙利、联邦德国、瑞典、荷兰、冰岛、挪威和墨西哥的将近 200 位与会者

---

① 括号中的年份表示这些国家的全国性口述历史组织的成立时间，由笔者根据各种资料整理而成，其余因信息不全而没有标示。目前，并没有有关国际口述史学发展历史的系统性研究，相关内容可参阅 Paul Thompson, *The Voice of the Past: Oral History*, Oxford and New York: Oxford University Press, third edition, 2000, pp. 65-117. 同时也可参考英国《口述历史》（*Oral History*）杂志各期有关国际口述史学进展的信息报道。另外可参阅一些相关文章 Leo La Clare, "Oral History in Canada: An Overview", *Oral History Review*, Vol. 1, 1973, pp. 66-76; Maclyn Burg, "An Oral Historian in Moscow: Some First-Hand Observations", *Oral History Review*, Vol. 2, 1974, pp. 10-23; David Lance, "Oral History in Britain", *Oral History Review*, Vol. 2, 1974, pp. 64-76; Modupeolu M. Faseke, "Oral History in Nigeria: Issues, Problems, and Prospects", *Oral History Review*, Vol. 18, No. 1, 1990, pp. 77-92; Luke S. K. Kwong, "Oral History in China: A Preliminary Review", *Oral History Review*, Vol. 20, No. 1/2, 1992, pp. 23-50; Mercedes Vilanova, "The Struggle for a History Without Adjectives: A Note on Using Oral Sources in Spain", *Oral History Review*, Vol. 24, No. 1, 1997, pp. 81-90; José Carlos Sebe Bom Meihy, "Oral History in Brazil: Development and Challenges", *Oral History Review*, Vol. 26, No. 2, 1999, pp. 127-136; Yang Liwen, "Oral History in China: Contemporary Topics and New Hurdles", *Oral History Review*, Vol. 26, No. 2, 1999, pp. 137-146.

围绕口述史学理论与方法以及口述史学在妇女史、家庭史、乡村史、劳工史、民主史和法西斯主义研究中的应用问题展开激烈讨论。① 而于 1996 年 6 月 13—16 日在瑞典歌德堡（Goteborg）举行的第九届国际口述历史大会上，国际口述历史协会正式宣告成立。此后，每两年举办一次国际口述历史大会，而第二十届大会将于 2018 年 6 月 18—21 日在芬兰于韦斯屈莱（Jyväskylä）举行。② 该协会除主办国际大会外，还分别于 1997 年和 1998

———————————

① 有关此次会议的相关信息可参阅 *Oral History*，Vol. 6，No. 2，1978，p. 8；Vol. 7，No. 2，1979，pp. 9，17-23.

② 第二届国际口述历史大会于 1980 年 10 月 24—26 日在荷兰阿姆斯特丹（Amsterdam）举行。不过，有关国际口述历史大会的届数问题，由于英国《口述历史》杂志在 1982 年和 1983 年的两期内容将 1982 年 9 月 24—26 日在法国普罗旺斯地区艾克斯（Aix-en-Provence）举行的同一次国际口述历史大会分别称为"第三届"和"第四届"，因此造成一定混淆。详细内容参阅 *Oral History*，Vol. 8，No. 1，1980，p. 5；Vol. 10，No. 1，1982，p. 4；Vol. 10，No. 2，1982，p. 9；Vol. 11，No. 1，1983，p. 18. 为核实该问题，笔者曾经发电子邮件向保罗·汤普森、罗纳德·格里（Ronald J. Grele）和意大利著名口述历史学家路易莎·帕萨里尼（Luisa Passerini）予以求证，他们都是早期国际口述历史大会的重要参与者与组织者。她们都认为造成这种混淆的主要原因是是否应该将 1976 年 12 月 16—18 日在意大利博洛尼亚（Bologna）举行的"人类学与历史学：口述资料"国际会议（International Conference on "Anthropology and History：Oral Sources"）计算在内，此次会议吸引了来自意大利、英国、法国、美国和波兰等国家的历史学家、人类学家和社会学家围绕口述资料在人类学和历史学中的应用问题展开激烈讨论，而汤普森和帕萨里尼也是与会者。会议详细信息参阅 *Oral History*，Vol. 5，No. 1，1977，pp. 21-32. 而在 1982 年法国艾克斯会议之前，一般都没有将 1976 年博洛尼亚会议视为国际口述历史大会，因此当时大部分报道和记载都认为 1979 年科尔切斯特会议才是第一届国际口述历史大会，据汤普森和帕萨里尼确认，大概在 1982 年艾克斯会议临近召开前或召开时有许多人主张应该将 1976 年博洛尼亚会议视为第一届国际口述历史大会，后来汤普森也不愿跟他们争辩，就接受了这些人的意见。因此，在 1982 年会议结束之后，《口述历史》杂志 1983 年第 1 期刊登的会议报道就将其称为"第四届"会议，以后依次命名。详细内容参阅汤普森（2013 年 2 月 25 日和 26 日回信）、格里（2013 年 2 月 23 日和 24 日回信）和帕萨里尼（2013 年 2 月 24 日回信）给笔者的电子邮件回信，在此深表感谢。不过，即使如此，在新近出版的很多研究成果中，仍然将 1979 年会议视为第一届国际口述历史大会。另外，第五至第十八届大会基本信息如下：1985 年西班牙巴塞罗那（Barcelona）、1987 年英国牛津（Oxford）、1990 年联邦德国埃森（Essen）、1993 年意大利锡耶纳和卢卡（Siena and Lucca）、1996 年瑞典歌德堡、1998 年巴西里约热内卢（Rio de Janeiro）、2000 年土耳其伊斯坦布尔（Istanbul）、2002 年南非彼得马里茨堡（Pietermaritzburg）、2004 年意大利罗马（Rome）、2006 年澳大利亚悉尼（Sydney）、2008 年墨西哥瓜达拉哈拉（Guadalajara）、2010 年捷克布拉格（Prague）、2012 年阿根廷布宜诺斯艾利斯（Buenos Aires）、2014 年西班牙巴塞罗那和 2016 年印度班加罗尔（Bengaluru）。另外，2018 年第二十届国际口述历史大会官方网站为 https：//www. jyu. filen/congress/ioha2018，2016 年 7 月 5 日访问。

年开始出版双语（英语和西班牙语）刊物《话语与沉默》（*Words and Si-lences*）和《国际口述历史协会通讯》（*International Oral History Association Newsletter*）。[①]

简言之，经过60多年的发展，尽管仍然遭到部分传统史学家的批判与质疑，不过在世界各地口述历史工作者的共同努力下，现代口述史学已经成为国际史学界一支不可忽视的新生力量。而体现口述史学在国际史学界影响力的重要标志之一就是早在1980年8月10—17日于罗马尼亚首都布加勒斯特（Bucharest）举行的第十五届国际历史科学大会（International Congress of Historical Sciences）就设有"口述史学的问题与方法"（Problems and Methods of Oral History）专场研讨会。此次研讨会持续一天，报告人来自尼日利亚、西班牙、塞内加尔、英国、挪威、匈牙利、比利时、加拿大和美国等国家，而与会者将近200人。[②] 而30年后于2015年8月23—29日在中国济南举行的第二十二届国际历史科学大会上，口述史学同样是重要议题。在8月24日举行的晚间会议上，来自美国、英国、捷克、南非、印度、芬兰与波兰等国家的多位口述历史学家围绕"价值的转变与转变的价值：口述史中全球视野下的社会变迁"（Change of Value-Value of Change：Transforming Societies in Global Perspective via Oral History）展开深入讨论。[③] 当然，在期间的历届国际历史科学大会以及相关的跨地区和全国性史学会议上，口述史学都是相当重要的议题。

更为重要的是，口述史学从诞生起就已经超越历史学的传统学科

---

① 有关该协会的详细信息可访问其官方网站（http：//www. iohanet. org/），2015年8月2日访问。

② 会议详细内容可参阅 *International Journal of Oral History*，Vol. 2，No. 1，1981，p. 76；*Oral History*，Vol. 9，No. 1，1981，pp. 17-18.

③ 相关议程和会议报道可访问 http：//cn. ichschina2015. org/cms/richenganpainew/1071. jhtml 和 http：//jds. cass. cn/Item/31456. aspx，2015年8月26日访问。

界限，其自身发展呈现极其鲜明的跨学科特征。概括而言，口述史学的跨学科性主要体现在两个方面。首先，口述史学本身的方法与理论来源是高度跨学科的，在某种程度上，它几乎涵盖了全部的人文与社会科学。口述历史访谈需要新闻学的采访技巧；受访者的选择需要社会学的社会调查和统计方法；口述资料的转录和编辑需要语言学和文学的表达方式；口述历史的解释需要诠释学和心理学理论；口述历史资料的收藏需要图书馆学和档案学的编目和保存知识；口述历史资料的传播需要掌握现代各种媒体的操作方法；而口述历史的著作权、隐私权和名誉权则涉及复杂的法律问题。尤其是受到 20 世纪 70 年代以来西方史学"记忆转向"、"叙事转向"（语言学转向）和"文化转向"等重要理论与学术思潮的影响，口述史学的研究与诠释视角因人类学、民族志、叙事学、文本理论、批判理论、交际理论、记忆研究和文化研究等相关学科理论的影响而不断深化与革新。

其次，口述史学也引起其他学科与研究领域的广泛关注，并在推动与促进跨学科研究与应用中起到相当重要的作用。美国著名口述历史学家戴维·杜纳威（David K. Dunaway）就将 20 世纪 90 年代以口述史学发展的特征描述为对于跨学科性的日益兴起。他进一步指出，随着口述史学对于研究生和公共历史（public history）计划重要性的加强，它的最大作用可能就在于它的跨学科应用。① 综观口述史学在世界各地的发展历史与现状，可以发现它已经被广泛地应用于图书馆学、档案学、社会学（社区研究）、人类学、民俗学、教育学、文学、艺术学、民族志、性别研究、族裔研究、移民研究、医学（临床医学与健康护理）、心理学、赋权研究（政治和解、社会正

---

① David K. Dunaway, "The Interdisciplinarity of Oral History", in David K. Dunaway and Willa K. Baum（eds.）, *Oral History: An Interdisciplinary Anthology*, Walnut Creek: AltaMira Press, second edition, 1996, pp. 9-10.

义、法律诉讼、残障研究)、传记研究、灾难研究、文化研究、LG-BTQ 研究(同性恋、双性恋和跨性别研究)与媒体研究等人文、社会和自然科学等众多领域。在这些跨学科应用中,口述史学不仅被用来搜集和保存相关学科本身发展的历史,同时也直接影响这些学科的研究方法、理论和视角。

举例而言,在医学领域,已经有众多学者将口述史学用于老年医学与怀旧治疗等临床医学与社会护理等领域,希望通过口述历史为那些经历老年失忆与心理创伤的患者提供医学治疗,甚至逐渐发展出一门新兴学科——叙事医学(narrative medicine)。① 近十年来,口述史学在艾滋病等疾病治疗与护理中的应用也日渐受到重视。② 在妇女、农民、土著以及同性恋等弱势群体研究中,口述史学不仅被用来挖掘他(她)们的沉默声音,同时也逐渐成为他们要求获得社会认可和提高政治经济权利的极其重要的赋权(empowerment)工具,其政治性日益突显。③ 而在灾难研究领域,近年来,口述史学也成为记录、理解与反思灾难事件与灾难记忆的重要手段。正是如此,1999 年中国台湾"9·21"大地震、2001 年美国"9·11"事件、2005 年美国卡特里娜

---

① 具体内容参阅 Raymond Harris and Sara Harris, "Therapeutic Uses of Oral History Techniques in Medicine", *International Journal of Aging and Human Development*, Vol. 12, No. 1, 1980-1981, pp. 27-34; Willa Baum, "Therapeutic Value of Oral History", *International Journal of Aging and Human Development*, Vol. 12, No. 1, 1980-1981, pp. 49-52; Mary Marshall Clark, "Holocaust Video Testimony, Oral History and Narrative Medicine: The Struggle Against Indifference", *Literature and Medicine*, Vol. 24, No. 2, 2005, pp. 266-282; Joanna Bornat and Josie Tetley (eds.), *Oral History and Ageing*, London: Centre for Policy on Ageing, 2010.

② Ronald Bayer and Gerald M. Oppenheimer, *AIDS Doctors: Voices from the Epidemic: An Oral History*, Oxford and New York: Oxford University Press, 2000; Gerald M. Oppenheimer and Ronald Bayer, *Shattered Dreams? An Oral History of the South African AIDS Epidemic*, Oxford and New York: Oxford University Press, 2007.

③ 作为加拿大土著人争取其土地索偿(land claim)等政治、经济权利的重要努力,从 1997 年开始,土著口述历史(口头传统)已经成为加拿大法院的合法证词。具体内容参阅 Bruce Granville Miller, *Oral History on Trial: Recognizing Aboriginal Narratives in the Courts*, Vancouver: University of British Columbia Press, 2011.

飓风（Katrina Hurricane）和 2008 年汶川"5·12"大地震等重大灾难发生后，相关部门都随即开展相应的口述历史计划。同时，灾难口述历史研究也受到学术界的积极关注，近年来，美国主流史学杂志《美国历史杂志》和《口述历史评论》都频繁刊登相关研究成果，而讨论焦点大都集中于灾难记忆，甚至思考口述历史对于治疗创伤记忆的医疗价值。[①]

就中国而言，如上所述，中国史学界同样具有相当悠久的口述历史传统，而现代意义上的西方口述史学概念则是从 20 世纪 80 年代开始传入中国。不过，直到 20 世纪 90 年代末期以后，中国口述史学才开始真正有所发展，2004 年中华口述历史研究会的成立则是中国口述史学开始走向正规化和专业化发展的重要标志。目前，口述史学在中国日益流行，其发展甚至呈现出"火爆"趋势，主要体现在以下几个方面：（1）口述史学受到越来越多的历史学家和其他学科相关学者的日益认可与重视，同时国内外口述史学界的相互交流也日渐频繁；（2）有关口述史学理论与方法研究的著作、学术论文与全国性学术会议不断增多，而高层次的口述历史科研项目也不断获得国家和省部级立项；（3）以纸质出版、电视节目、纪录片和网络（门户网站、博客、微博、微信）呈现为依托的口述历史作品与成果不断问世，部分作品逐渐赢得公众的认可与好评；（4）一大批口述历史计划如雨后春笋般地展开，其发起和组织者包括学校与科研机构、政府机构、图书馆与档案机构、媒体机构、基金会、公司与企业、非营利组织、社会团体、学生组织以及从事不同工作的个体，在此基础上，国内高校也开始

---

① Mark Klempner, "Navigating Life Reviews: Interviews with Survivors of Trauma", *Oral History Review*, Vol. 27, No. 2, 2000, pp. 67-83; Mary Marshall Clark, "The September 11, 2001, Oral History Narrative and Memory Project: A First Report", *Journal of American History*, Vol. 89, No. 2, 2002, pp. 569-579.

出现一批专业的口述历史研究机构。①

二 基本概念界定

要理解什么是"口述史学",其前提是理解什么是"口述历史"。所谓"口述历史"就是指口头的、有声音的历史。简单而言,就是通过传统的

---

① 有关中国口述史学发展的综述文章可参阅钟少华《中国口述历史研究的探索》,《自然辩证法通讯》1986 年第 5 期,第 77—79 页;钟少华《中国口述史学漫谈》,《学术研究》1997 年第 5 期,第 46—51 页;布鲁斯·M. 斯蒂文《中国口述史学的调查》,《当代中国史研究》1998 年第 1 期,第 83—91 页;杨祥银《当代中国口述史学透视》,《当代中国史研究》2000 年第 3 期,第 47—58 页;周新国《构建中国特色、中国风格和中国气派的中国口述史学——关于口述史料与口述史学的若干问题》,《当代中国史研究》2004 年第 4 期,第 101—106 页;王艳勤《中国的口述史学研究》,《湖北大学学报》(哲学社会科学版)2004 年第 5 期,第 592—596 页;姚力《我国口述史学发展的困境与前景》,《当代中国史研究》2005 年第 1 期,第 96—100 页;徐国利、王志龙《当代中国的口述史学理论研究》,《史学理论研究》2005 年第 1 期,第 118—125 页;周新国《中国口述史学之回顾与展望》,《扬州大学学报》(人文社会科学版)2005 年第 2 期,第 24—27 页;胡鸿保、韩俊红《当代中国的口述史研究》,《内蒙古大学艺术学院学报》2005 年第 2 期,第 9—13 页;左玉河《方兴未艾的中国口述历史研究》,《中国图书评论》2006 年第 5 期,第 4—10 页;宋学勤《当代中国史研究与口述史学》,《史学集刊》2006 年第 5 期,第 70—75 页;沈飞德《当代中国的口述历史:前景和问题》,《探索与争鸣》2008 年第 8 期,第 76—80 页;王军《中国大陆口述历史研究现状综述》,《文化艺术研究》2009 年第 3 期,第 39—42 页;闫茂旭《当代中国史研究中的口述史问题:学科与方法》,《唐山学院学报》2009 年第 4 期,第 16—20 页;左玉河《近年来的中国口述历史研究》,《中国科技史杂志》2009 年第 3 期,第 277—281 页;姚力《再论国史研究与口述历史》,《中国科技史杂志》2009 年第 3 期,第 282—286 页;章玉钧《从中国大陆口述史发展态势、动因展望未来之路》,《中华文化论坛》2011 年第 1 期,第 31—35 页;左玉河《热点透视与学科建设:近年来的中国口述历史研究》,《中华文化论坛》2011 年第 1 期,第 36—45 页;王宇英《口述历史四问——对近年来中国大陆口述历史发展现状的反思》,《首都师范大学学报》(社会科学版)2011 年第 5 期,第 1—5 页;王宇英《近年来口述史研究的热点审视及其态势》,《重庆社会科学》2011 年第 5 期,第 107—110 页;周新国《中国大陆口述历史的兴起与发展态势》,《江苏社会科学》2013 年第 4 期,第 189—194 页;左玉河《中国口述史研究现状与口述历史学科建设》,《史学理论研究》2014 年第 4 期,第 61—67 页。此外,有关中国口述史学理论与方法研究的代表性作品可参阅杨祥银《与历史对话:口述史学的理论与实践》,中国社会科学出版社 2004 年版;周新国主编《中国口述史的理论与实践》,中国社会科学出版社 2005 年版;当代上海研究所编《口述历史的理论与实务:来自海峡两岸的探讨》,上海人民出版社 2007 年版;陈旭清《口述史研究的理论与实践》,中国社会出版社 2010 年版;李向平、魏扬波《口述史研究方法》,上海人民出版社 2010 年版;定宜庄、汪润主编《口述史读本》,北京大学出版社 2011 年版;王宇英《当代中国口述史:为何与何为》,中国大百科全书出版社 2012 年版;陈墨《口述历史门径(实务手册)》,人民出版社 2013 年版;李卫民《本土化视域下的口述历史理论研究》,上海人民出版社 2014 年版;杨祥银主编《口述史研究》(第一辑),社会科学文献出版社 2014 年版。

笔录或者录音和录影等现代技术手段的使用，进而记录历史事件当事人或目击者的回忆而保存的口述证词（oral testimony）。然而，对于什么是"口述历史"，在口述史学界也存在诸多分歧。路易斯·斯塔尔就认为："口述历史是通过有准备的、以录音机为工具的访谈，记录人们口述所得的具有保存价值和迄今尚未获得的原始资料（primary source material）。"① 唐纳德·里奇在其经典著作《大家来做口述历史》中则指出："简单而言，口述历史就是通过记录访谈（recorded interviews）来收集具有历史意义的记忆与个人评论（personal commentaries）。"② 而保罗·汤普森认为："口述历史是关于人们生活的询问和调查，包括对他们口头叙述（oral accounts）的记录。"③

对于何谓"口述历史"，中国学者也做出不同的回答。钟少华认为："口述历史是受访者与历史工作者合作的产物，利用人类特有的语言，利用科技设备，双方合作谈话的录音都是口述史料，将录音整理成文字稿，再经研究加工，可以写成各种口述历史专著。"④ 显然，钟少华强调口述历史必须以录音为依据，以口述史料为主。而杨立文则认为："口述历史最基本的含意，是相对于文字资料而言，就是收集当事人或知情人的口头资料。它的基本方法就是调查访问，采用口述手记的方式收集资料，经与文本文件核实，整理成为文字稿。"⑤ 当然，杨立文也并不否认录音机与摄影机等记录技术手段的使用。

上述定义可以看出两点较为重要的分歧原因与差异所在，首先是关于

---

① Louis Starr, "Oral History", *Encyclopedia of Library and Information Sciences*（Vol. 20）, New York: Marcel Dekker, 1977, p. 440.

② Donald A. Ritchie, *Doing Oral History: A Practical Guide*, Oxford and New York: Oxford University Press, second edition, 2003, p. 19.

③ 汤普森关于口述历史的这个定义首次发表于 1985 年 4 月 17 日在北京举行的一次口述历史研讨会上，详细内容参阅 Yang Liwen, "Oral History in China", *Oral History*, Vol. 15, No. 1, 1987, p. 22.

④ 钟少华：《进取集：钟少华文存》，中国国际广播出版社 1998 年版，第 414 页。

⑤ 杨立文：《论口述史学在历史学中的功用和地位》，《北大史学》（第 1 辑），1993 年，第 120 页。

口述历史访谈的记录手段问题。显然，斯塔尔、里奇和钟少华都认为必须使用录音机等现代记录手段；而汤普森和杨立文则着眼于资料收集角度来理解，他们甚至认为笔录都可以。当然，使用录音机等设备有其自身优势，它不仅能够记录访谈者和受访者之间的交流内容，而且能够将双方的口音和语调等信息都完整记录下来。而且，口述历史录音也改变了传统的接受历史的文字阅读方式，进而可以通过声音来倾听历史。实际上，在摄影机等新式记录技术出现之后，大部分口述历史工作者都主张要使用口述历史录影，因为它能进一步记录和发挥口述历史的视觉信息与价值。基于此，笔者以为不应该以记录手段来判断一项访谈活动是否可以被看成口述历史，可以预见的是，技术的不断发展将挑战口述历史的记录与呈现形式以及我们对于口述历史的传统理解。比如，随着网络技术的发展，口述历史工作者开始通过网络摄像机、网络视频会议系统和网络移动应用程序等手段进行跨越地理障碍的"跨空间访谈"，甚至无须访谈者的提问与互动。正是由于这些数字化技术的革命性影响，笔者也曾指出，在最基本的术语使用问题上，"数字化讲故事"（digital storytelling）也可能逐渐代替"口述历史"这一传统术语。[①]

其次是口述历史研究对象与内容的差异，这一点突出地体现在英美口述史学发展初期的访谈对象上，美国尤其关注重大历史事件的重要参与者与见证者，而英国则侧重于社会史范畴，尤其关注普通民众的生活故事。而这种差异很大程度上也是由口述历史不同实践者和研究者的专业身份或学科背景所决定，很显然，历史学家、传记作家、人类学家、民俗学家、社会学家、档案工作者和老年医学家在各自利用口述史学这一方法时，其

---

① 杨祥银：《口述史学的数字化转型》，《人民日报》2015 年 9 月 21 日第 20 版。当然，就目前而言，绝大部分口述史学家都认可口述历史访谈是访谈者和受访者之间有意识的（即预先准备好的）互动产物，即伴随着问答形式。基于此，有学者警告，口述历史不包括演讲和窃听录音、个人录音日记或其他不是经由访谈者和受访者会话的声音记录。详细参阅 Donald A. Ritchie, *Doing Oral History: A Practical Guide*, Oxford and New York: Oxford University Press, second edition, 2003, p. 19.

关注点和侧重点都有所不同。① 需要指出的是，这些差异不应该成为口述史学界相互争论或攻击的焦点，因为给口述历史下一个普遍认同或接受的定义不仅很难，而且也没有必要。而笔者认为关键在于如何把握口述历史的精髓，即它的核心价值——保存即将逝去的声音，并进而实现过去与现在的对话。创建于 1954 年的加州大学伯克利分校地区口述历史办公室（Regional Oral History Office，University of California，Berkeley）在主题为《捕捉历史的瞬间：从谈话到打印》的网站序言中就曾写道："口述历史对理解过去、呈现当前以及保存即将逝去的声音都是一种理想的方法。"② 显然，口述历史的价值不仅仅在于记录和保存过去的经历，而且赋予我们在当下如何重新思考与评价过去的机会。正是如此，以唐纳德·里奇为代表的口述史学家强调口述历史访谈所挖掘与呈现的内容主要是基于个体记忆的评论与理解。

再次，就"口述历史"这个概念而言，它既可以被理解为口述历史实践过程的具体"结果"（product），也可以指口述历史实践的具体"过程"（process）。就前者而言，笔者强调口述历史一般有四种存在形式：（1）口述历史访谈过程的原始录音（录影）；（2）经过转录、整理、修订和保存的口述历史抄本；（3）考虑受众市场而几经修改（甚至删除访谈者提问）的口述历史抄本的公开出版物；（4）主要利用口述历史资料作为研究来源的研究性作品。到底何者才是真正的"口述历史"？显然，在不同专业实践者看来，他们的答案也是各不相同。而事实上，读者在市场上更多看到的是后面两种，比如斯塔兹·特克尔（Studs Terkel，1912—2008）的系列

---

① 也正是如此，就术语本身而言，口述历史与生活史（life history）、生活故事（life stories）、生平回顾（life review）、个人叙事（personal narrative）、口述自传（oral autobiography）、录音回忆录与深度访谈（in-depth interview）等术语存在诸多交叉与互用。详细参阅 Valerie Raleigh Yow，*Recording Oral History: A Guide for the Humanities and Social Sciences*，Walnut Creek：AltaMira Press，second edition，2005，pp. 3-4.

② Regional Oral History Office，"Capturing the Historical Moment: From Talk To Type"，https://web. archive. org/web/19990224084844/http://library. berkeley. edu/BANC/ROHO/about. html. 需要指出的是，这里笔者访问的是 1999 年的页面。目前网站已经更新为 http://bancroft. berkeley. edu/ROHO/。上述访问时间为 2015 年 8 月 26 日。

口述历史作品①、台湾"中央研究院"近代史研究所的《口述历史丛书》②以及一些国际知名出版社出版的"口述历史系列"（*Oral History Series*）③。对于那些倾向于使用较为原始的口述历史资料的研究者来说，他们可能更加认可前面两种；对于人类学家、民俗学家和剧作家来说，他们主张第一种才是真正的口述历史，因为它不仅记录了访谈的言语内容，而且还有助于保存叙述者的口音、语调、身体动作、面部表情以及当中的细微变化。

而就"过程"而言，越来越多的实践者与研究者主张应该通过口述历史来呈现其中所发生的回忆、叙事、表演与意义诠释等复杂过程，并以此分析背后所隐含的影响个人与群体的政治、社会、文化与意识形态等多元因素。在有关保罗·汤普森《爱德华时代的人：英国社会的重塑》一书的评论中，该评论者相当生动地描绘了口述历史的这种动态性特征："归根结底，他那些'爱德华时代的人'活下来变成了'乔治时代的人'，而现在又成了'伊莉萨白时代的人'。经历了这些岁月，一些往事在记忆中消失了，或至少关于这些往事的回忆也会受到后来经历的影响。其实，他们童年时期的往事有多少是他们的长者对他们提起的呢？在那以后他们可能读了哪些自传或小说，使他们加深一些印象而冲淡另一些印象呢？哪些电影或电视节目对他们的意识发生了影响呢？"④ 在某种程度上，尽管口述历史原本记录的"过去的声音"也成为"现在的声音"，并因此直接影响口述资料的客观性与真实性；但它却有助于我们了解这些变迁背后的

---

① 关于特克尔的口述历史作品与研究经历，请参阅第四章。

② 该丛书自 1982 年出版以来，到 2015 年 9 月为止共有 97 种，而且部分作品由中国大百科全书出版社和九州出版社出版。详细内容访问 http://www.mh.sinica.edu.tw/Historicalsources.aspx? minor=3&pageNumber=1，2015 年 10 月 2 日访问。此外，作为《口述历史丛书》的重要补充，该所还于 1989—2004 年出版《口述历史》杂志 12 期，并于 2013 年复刊。

③ 目前较有影响的包括：特韦恩（Twayne Publishers）、阿尔塔米拉（AltaMira Press）、帕尔格雷夫·麦克米伦（Palgrave Macmillan）和牛津大学出版社（Oxford University Press）等出版社出版的口述历史系列。

④ 约翰·托什：《口述的历史》，雍恢译，《史学理论》1987 年第 4 期，第 85 页。该书详细内容参阅 Paul Thompson, *The Edwardians*: *The Remaking of British Society*, London: Weidenfeld & Nicolson, 1975.

故事、记忆、社会时代与情感因素。基于此，有学者指出，正是因为故事讲述者（story-teller）与故事倾听者（story-hearer）之间的互动关系，口述历史能够探索个体如何解释他们的环境以及他们的理解发生变化的方式。①

另外一个需要界定的重要概念是公共史学（public history）以及它与口述史学之间的紧密关系。美国公众史学创始人之一罗伯特·凯利（Robert Kelley）教授从"应用主义"的角度给公共史学下了一个定义："从最简单的意义上而言，公共史学是指历史学家的就业和将历史方法应用于学院之外的诸多领域的学问，包括政府、私人公司、新闻媒体、历史学会和博物馆乃至私人领域。公众史学家无时不在工作，他们凭借自己的专业能力而成为公共进程的一部分。当某个问题需要解决，一项政策必须制定，资源使用或行动方向必须更为有效地规划时，历史学家会应召而来：这就是公共史学。"② 而作为一种基于主要公众利益（public benefits）的历史分支学科，美国公共史学另一位创始人小卫斯理·约翰逊（G. Wesley Johnson, Jr.）列举了历史学家可以发挥作用的 8 个公共领域：政府机构；商业机构；研究机构；媒体；历史保护；历史解释（历史学会与博物馆）；档案与资料管理部门与公共历史教学。③ 通常而言，对于公共史学家来说，他们是以客户的需求为目的，其客户包括联邦和地方政府、公司、博物馆、档案馆、地方历史学会、历史遗址或个人。而笔者则更加倾向于将公共史学家定位为"契约史学家"（contract historians），即根据客户需求提供相关的历史服务。当然，在这种契约式的历史服务中，公共史学工作者尤其需要处理好他们对于历史本身的专业伦理与对于客户的职业伦理之间

---

① Carolyn Lunsford Mears, *Interviewing for Education and Social Science Research*, New York: Palgrave Macmillan, 2009, p. 56.

② Robert Kelley, "Public History: Its Origins, Nature, and Prospects", *The Public Historian*, Vol. 1, No. 1, 1978, p. 16.

③ G. Wesley Johnson, Jr., "Editor's Preface", *The Public Historian*, Vol. 1, No. 1, 1978, pp. 4-10.

的平衡关系。①

　　至于口述史学与公共史学的关系，美国大部分口述史学家和公共史学家认为，从方法论上而言，口述史学是公共史学的一个重要手段。正如唐纳德·里奇所说："公共史学是有组织性的工作，它为公众提供既准确又富有意义的历史，而口述史学是实现这个目标的最当然的工具。"而从学科分类或学位设置而言，口述史学通常是公共史学学位课程的一部分。在美国一些大学中，一般都颁发公共史学硕士和博士学位，相对来说则较少设置口述史学硕士和博士学位。当然，口述史学并不是公共史学家的专利，很多学院史学家同样把口述史学作为学术研究的重要方法，而公共史学家也可能同时从事学院史学（academic history）研究。

　　综上所述，口述史学促使历史学家与实践者从故纸堆中解放出来，深入现实生活之中，并直接倾听来自历史行动者的真实心声。保罗·汤普森曾有一段相当精彩的论述，足以精辟地总结和概括口述史学的基本特征与主要价值。他在其经典作品《过去的声音：口述历史》一书中指出："口述历史是一种围绕人民所建构的历史。它为历史本身注入了活力，并拓宽了其视野。它不仅允许英雄来自领袖，而且还包括不被人知晓的大多数人。它鼓励教师与学生成为工作伙伴。它将历史带入社群，又从中引出历

---

　　① 国内学者对于"public history"的翻译存在争论，不过主流翻译是"公共史学（历史）"或"公众史学（历史）"。相关研究参阅 Enid H. Douglass, "Oral History and Pubic History", *Oral History Review*, Vol. 8, 1980, pp. 1-5; Barbara J. Howe and Emory L. Kemp (eds.), *Public History: An Introduction*, Malabar: Krieger Publishing Company, 1986; Jo Blatti, "Public History and Oral History", *Journal of American History*, Vol. 77, No. 2, 1990, pp. 615-625; Phyllis K. Leffler and Joseph Brent (eds.), *Public History Readings*, Malabar: Krieger Publishing Company, 1992; James B. Gardner and Peter S. LaPaglia (eds.), *Public History: Essays from the Field*, Malabar: Krieger Publishing Company, 1999; 杨祥银：《美国公共历史学综述》，《国外社会科学》2001 年第 1 期，第 33—37 页；王希：《谁拥有历史——美国公共史学的起源、发展与挑战》，《历史研究》2010 年第 3 期，第 34—47 页；Hilda Kean and Paul Martin (eds.), *The Public History Reader*, London and New York: Routledge, 2013; 李娜：《美国模式之公众史学在中国是否可行——中国公众史学的学科建构》，《江海学刊》2014 年第 2 期，第 149—156 页；Faye Sayer, *Public History: A Practical Guide*, New York: Bloomsbury Academic, 2015; 李娜：《公众史学与口述历史：跨学科的对话》，《史林》2015 年第 2 期，第 195—203 页。

史。它帮助较少有特权者（尤其是老人）获得尊严与自信。它有助于社会阶级、代际的接触，以及由此而来的理解。对于个别历史学家和其他人来说，由于其共享意义，口述历史能够给予一种地点或时间的归属感。总之，它有助于人类变得更加充实。同样，口述历史向公认的历史神话以及历史传统中所固有的权威判断发出挑战。它为实现历史的社会意义的根本转变提供了一种手段。"①

基于此，笔者主张应该将口述历史视为"复合概念"和开放性学科，充分发挥口述历史作为收集原始资料、拓宽研究视野、更新研究方法、加强公众互动、促进跨学科应用、推动教育改革、促进社会正义以及实现政治和解的独特价值与功能。

三　学术史回顾

作为 20 世纪中叶在美国兴起的一种重要的研究方法与学科领域，口述史学以其在挖掘史料与再现底层声音方面的独特优势而迅速引起美国史学界和相关领域的关注，成为推动美国史学革新与跨学科发展的重要力量。目前，口述史学在美国已经形成一套集专业学术组织、学术年会、学术刊物、学术规范、学术指南、教育与培训、研究机构与计划以及在线"口述历史论坛"（H-OralHist）为一体的相当完善的发展体系。

就专业学术组织而言，除成立于 1967 年的美国口述历史协会之外，还有密歇根口述历史协会（Michigan Oral History Association）、德克萨斯口述历史协会（Texas Oral History Association）、新英格兰口述历史协会（New England Association for Oral History）、西南口述历史协会（Southwest Oral

---

① Paul Thompson, *The Voice of the Past: Oral History*, Oxford and New York: Oxford University Press, third edition, 2000, pp. 23-24.

History Association）、中大西洋地区口述历史联盟（Oral History Mid-Atlantic Region）和中西部口述历史组织（Midwest Oral History Group）等6个地区性专业组织。就学术会议而言，从1966年举办首届全国口述史学会议以来，口述历史协会一直坚持举办年会，第五十届年会于2016年10月重回首届会议举办地加利福尼亚州举行。而在出版方面，除学术刊物和通讯——《口述历史评论》和《口述历史协会通讯》之外，还出版多本涉及法律和伦理问题、家庭史、社区史与课堂教学等主题的口述历史"小册子系列"（pamphlet series）。而为规范口述历史实践，口述历史协会还分别于1968年、1979年、1989年、2000年和2009年对其原则、标准与评估指南进行多次制订与修改，而每次修改都充分反映了口述历史实践的最新变革与发展趋势。而作为口述历史资料收集、保存与研究的重要基地，各种类型的口述历史机构（计划）和规模不等的口述历史馆藏遍布全美各地。此外，在口述历史协会教育委员会（Education Committee）的组织与协调下，美国中小学、大学乃至社区继续教育中都设置了相关的口述历史培训或学位课程，培养了一大批来自历史学和相关领域的口述历史工作者。① 而作为以网站为基础的在线论坛，经过将近20年的发展，"口述历史论坛"已经成为美国乃至国际口述史学界最具规模和权威的网络交流平台。②

就本书的学术史而言，国外学术界对于美国口述史学本身发展历史的研究主要集中于美国和英国学者当中。自1948年美国现代口述史学诞生之后，当时的相关论文都是局限于具体口述历史计划的介绍与评价。20世纪五六十年代，在当时美国口述史学档案实践导向的影响下，《美国档案工作者》（American Archivist）、《图书馆杂志》（Library Journal）、《图书馆历史杂志》（Journal of Library History）和《威尔逊图书馆公告》（Wilson

---

① 上述相关信息可访问美国口述历史协会官方网站（http：//www.oralhistory.org/），2015年8月10日访问。

② 具体内容访问论坛网站（https：//networks.h-net.org/h-oralhist），2015年8月10日访问。

Library Bulletin）等杂志发表了多篇有关美国口述史学起源与现状的简短论文。[①]

结合当时美国口述史学的发展现状与趋势，在20世纪70年代，路易斯·斯塔尔、维拉·鲍姆（Willa K. Baum）、查尔斯·克劳福德（Charles W. Crawford）、塞缪尔·普罗克特（Samuel Proctor）、威廉·莫斯（William W. Moss）、小沃尔特·兰德尔（Walter Rundell, Jr.）和威廉·怀亚特（William R. Wyatt）等美国学者和保罗·汤普森等英国学者继续对这一问题进行探讨。其中以斯塔尔的研究最具代表性，在《口述史学：问题与希望》和《口述史学》两篇文章中，他对20世纪70年代末之前的美国口述史学做了全方位考察与分析，内容涉及起源、发展阶段、学科地位、理论和方法建设以及具体应用等问题。[②]

在口述史学理论反思与跨学科应用方面，罗纳德·格里的研究具有相当重要的贡献。在1975年发表的《倾听他们的声音：口述历史访谈解释的两个个案研究》一文中，作者旨在探求口述历史访谈中展现的特定的历史视野、概述口述历史访谈的结构以及思考这种视野与结构的意义；并且说明口述历史如何帮助我们理解受访者和他们的历史观，以及如何理解访谈作为一种历史叙述和这种叙述所具有的深层次

---

① Owen W. Bombard, "A New Measure of Things Past", *American Archivist*, Vol. 18, No. 2, 1955, pp. 123-132; Elizabeth I. Dixon, "Oral History: A New Horizon", *Library Journal*, Vol. 87, 1962, pp. 1363-1365; Allan Nevins, "Oral History: How and Why It Was Born", *Wilson Library Bulletin*, Vol. 40, 1966, pp. 600-601; Elizabeth I. Dixon, "Oral History: Something New Has Been Added", *Journal of Library History*, Vol. 2, No. 1, 1967, pp. 68-72.

② 详细内容参阅 Louis M. Starr, "Oral History: Problems and Prospects", *Advances in Librarianship*, Vol. 2, 1971, pp. 275-304; Willa K. Baum, "Oral History in the United States", *Oral History*, Vol. 1, No. 3, 1972, pp. 15-29; Charles W. Crawford, "Oral History-The State of the Profession", *Oral History Review*, Vol. 2, 1974, pp. 1-9; Samuel Proctor, "Oral History Comes of Age", *Oral History Review*, Vol. 3, 1975, pp. 1-4; William W. Moss, "The Future of Oral History", *Oral History Review*, Vol. 3, 1975, pp. 5-15; Paul Thompson, "Oral History in North America", *Oral History*, Vol. 3, No. 1, 1975, pp. 26-40; Walter Rundell, Jr., "Main Trends in U. S. Historiography since the New Deal: Research Prospects in Oral History", *Oral History Review*, Vol. 4, 1976, pp. 35-47; William R. Wyatt, "OHA: The Road Ahead", *Oral History Review*, Vol. 5, 1977, pp. 1-6; Louis Starr, "Oral History", *Encyclopedia of Library and Information Sciences*(Vol. 20), New York: Marcel Dekker, 1977, pp. 440-463.

意义。① 在1975年发表的《一种可推测的多样性：跨学科性和口述历史》中，格里从多学科视角总结了有关访谈的最新成果，并强调这些跨学科理论与方法可以应用口述史学研究，包括民族志学、民俗学、人类学、语言学、交际理论、心理学、法学和精神病学等。② 而在哥大口述历史研究室成立30周年之际，格里于1978年发表的《超过30岁的人能相信吗？关于口述历史的友好批评》一文则全面回顾了美国口述史学30年的发展历程，在充分肯定其成果的基础上，他深刻地反思了口述史学发展过程中存在的深层次问题，比如历史记忆的真实性、会话叙述的语言和认知结构等。③

　　进入20世纪80年代，以1984年戴维·杜那威和维拉·鲍姆主编的《口述史学：跨学科文集》一书最具代表性，该书除回顾美国现代口述史学的起源与发展过程之外，着重探讨了口述史学在历史学分支学科和其他领域中的应用问题。④ 此外，罗纳德·格里分别在1990年和1996年的论文中对美国口述史学的历史与发展阶段做了比较详细的考察与分析，其中他非常关注口述史学的跨学科关系与应用，不过并没有展开详细讨论。⑤ 作为对半个世纪以来美国口述史学发展历程的总结性反思，美国著名口述

---

① Ronald J. Grele, "Listen to Their Voices: Two Case Studies in the Interpretation of Oral History Interviews", *Oral History*, Vol. 7, No. 1, 1975, pp. 33-42.

② Ronald J. Grele, "A Surmisable Variety: Oral History and Interdisciplinarity", *American Quarterly*, Vol. 27, No. 3, 1975, pp. 275-295.

③ Ronald Grele, "Can Anyone over Thirty Be Trusted: A Friendly Critique of Oral History", *Oral History Review*, Vol. 6, 1978, pp. 36-44.

④ David K. Dunaway and Willa K. Baum (eds.), *Oral History: An Interdisciplinary Anthology*, Nashville: American Association for State and Local History, 1984. 需要指出的是，其中很多文章是在20世纪六七十年代发表的，而且由于是论文集，该书对于美国现代口述史学发展历史的探讨缺乏系统性。

⑤ Ronald J. Grele, "The Development, Cultural Pecularities and State of Oral History in the United States", *BIOS: Zeitschrift für Biographieforschung und Oral History*, special issue, 1990, pp. 3-15; Ronald J. Grele, "Directions for Oral History in the United States", in David K. Dunaway and Willa K. Baum (eds.), *Oral History: An Interdisciplinary Anthology*, Walnut Creek: AltaMira Press, second edition, 1996, pp. 62-84. 据作者交代，第二篇文章是在第一篇文章基础上修改而成，反映了20世纪90年代以来的发展特征与趋势。

历史学家肖娜·格拉克（Sherna Berger Gluck）和布雷特·艾农（Bret Eynon）在 1999 年的《口述历史评论》上分别以个人的研究经历为基础回顾与总结了美国口述史学 50 年来的发展历程、特点、存在的问题以及未来趋势。① 而澳大利亚口述历史学家阿利斯泰尔·汤姆森（Alistair Thomson）在 1998 年发表的《口述史学 50 年国际展望》一文中也以相当的笔墨分析了美国口述史学的相关问题，其中尤其强调美国口述史学在国际上的先驱地位。②

进入 21 世纪，包括罗纳德·格里和阿利斯泰尔·汤姆森在内的英美学者继续对美国口述史学的历史、理论、方法和应用等问题进行探讨。在 2006 年发表的《作为证据的口述历史》一文中，格里详细地考察了美国口述史学发展的阶段性特征以及跨学科关系与应用。③ 而在 2007 年发表的《口述史学的四种范式转换》一文中，汤姆森则借用库恩的"范式"理论来分析过去 60 年来国际口述史学的研究模式，其中相当一部分是基于对于美国口述史学发展历程与特点的总结。④

当然，在过去 60 多年间，英美出版的一些有关口述史学理论与方法的重要著作也都部分涉及美国口述史学的发展历史问题，其中比较有代表性的包括保罗·汤普森的《过去的声音：口述历史》⑤、唐纳德·里奇的《大

---

① Sherna Berger Gluck，"From First Generation Oral Historian to Fourth and Beyond"，*Oral History Review*，Vol. 26，No. 2，1999，pp. 1-9；Bret Eynon，"Oral History and the New Century"，*Oral History Review*，Vol. 26，No. 2，1999，pp. 16-27.

② Alistair Thomson，"Fifty Years On：An International Perspective on Oral History"，*Journal of American History*，Vol. 85，No. 2，1998，pp. 581-595.

③ Ronald J. Grele，"Oral History as Evidence"，in Thomas L. Charlton，Lois E. Myers，and Rebecca Sharpless（eds.），*Handbook of Oral History*，Walnut Creek：AltaMira Press，2006，pp. 43-101.

④ Alistair Thomson，"Four Paradigm Transformations in Oral History"，*Oral History Review*，Vol. 34，No. 1，2007，pp. 49-70.

⑤ Paul Thompson，*The Voice of the Past：Oral History*，Oxford and New York：Oxford University Press，1978，1988 and 2000.

家来做口述历史》①、罗伯特·佩克斯（Robert Perks）和阿利斯泰尔·汤姆森主编的《口述史学读本》②、托马斯·查尔顿（Thomas L. Charlton）等人主编的《口述史学手册》③ 和唐纳德·里奇主编的《牛津口述史学手册》④ 等。需要特别指出的是，这些研究成果都是针对具体理论与方法问题，而且通常是围绕国际口述史学总体发展来考察，因而并不是着眼于美国口述史学本身的发展历程。

随着现代意义上的西方口述史学概念从 20 世纪 80 年代开始传入中国，⑤ 国内学术界对于美国口述史学的关注与研究也逐渐兴起。侯成德在 1981 年的一篇文章中对美国口述史学的兴起原因、发展过程、特点以及相关应用进行了比较详细的考察。⑥ 由于各种原因，在此后相当长的时间内，国内学术界都没有专门探讨美国口述史学问题的研究成

---

①　Donald A. Ritchie, *Doing Oral History*, New York: Twayne Publishers, 1995; Donald A. Ritchie, *Doing Oral History: A Practical Guide*, Oxford and New York: Oxford University Press, second edition, 2003; Donald A. Ritchie, *Doing Oral History*, Oxford and New York: Oxford University Press, third edition, 2014.

②　Robert Perks and Alistair Thomson（eds.）, *The Oral History Reader*, London and New York: Routledge, 1998, 2006 and 2015.

③　Thomas L. Charlton, Lois E. Myers, and Rebecca Sharpless（eds.）, *Handbook of Oral History*, Walnut Creek: AltaMira Press, 2006. 该书被拆分成两本书分别于 2007 年和 2008 年出版，详细参阅 Thomas L. Charlton, Lois E. Myers and Rebecca Sharpless（eds.）, *History of Oral History: Foundations and Methodology*, Walnut Creek: AltaMira Press, 2007; Thomas L. Charlton, Lois E. Myers and Rebecca Sharpless（eds.）, *Thinking about Oral History: Theories and Applications*, Walnut Creek: AltaMira Press, 2008.

④　Donald A. Ritchie（ed.）, *The Oxford Handbook of Oral History*, Oxford and New York: Oxford University Press, 2011.

⑤　相关文章可参阅 P. 汤普逊《过去的声音，口头历史》，董进泉摘译，《现代外国哲学社会科学文摘》1980 年第 1 期，第 77—78 页；J. 福克斯《面向过去之窗：口述历史入门》，黄育馥译，《国外社会科学》1981 年第 1 期，第 41—42 页；M. 海德《哲学诠释学和经历的交流——口述历史的范型》，朱小红译，《国外社会科学》1981 年第 1 期，第 42—43 页；胡佛《美国的口述史》，正一译，《现代外国哲学社会科学文摘》1982 年第 11 期，第 21—25 页；正一译《口述史》，《现代外国哲学社会科学文摘》1982 年第 11 期，第 58 页；汤普逊《口述史与历史学家》，方任译，《现代外国哲学社会科学文摘》1984 年第 6 期，第 9—11 页。

⑥　侯成德：《美国口碑史料学三十年》，《世界史研究动态》1981 年第 9 期，第 4—8 页。

果。直到进入 21 世纪，对于该问题的关注度才逐渐提高。在 2002 年发表的《口述历史在美国刍议》一文中，齐小新对美国口述史学的发展现状进行了初步探讨，其中尤其强调美国口述史学对于重建大众记忆和实现社会变革的作用。① 而在 2009 年的一篇硕士学位论文中，黄敬品对美国口述历史教学问题做了综述性考察与分析。② 王子舟和尹培丽则以加州大学班克罗夫特图书馆为例来分析该校地区口述历史办公室的口述历史传统与发展过程。③ 而冯云和王玉龙则主要基于美国口述史学发展的经验出发，分别探讨了口述历史伦理审查机制与著作权保护问题。④ 在其余并不丰富的论文中，有关美国口述史学问题的考察主要是基于一些简单的口述历史中心和馆藏资源介绍或粗略的经验反思。⑤

此外，由于美国是现代口述史学的起源地，因而国内学者所撰写的相

---

① 齐小新：《口述历史在美国刍议》，《北京大学学报》（哲学社会科学版）2002 年第 5 期，第 69—74 页。他曾出版一本口述历史作品，详细参阅齐小新《口述历史分析：中国近代史上的美国传教士》，北京大学出版社 2003 年版。

② 黄敬品：《美国口述历史教学研究》，硕士学位论文，华东师范大学，2009 年。

③ 王子舟、尹培丽：《口述资料采集与收藏的先行者--美国班克罗夫特图书馆》，《中国图书报》2013 年第 1 期，第 1—10 页。

④ 冯云：《美国口述历史伦理审查机制研究》，《图书馆建设》2015 年第 2 期，第 88—91、95 页；王玉龙：《口述档案的著作权保护：基于英美口述史法律伦理指南的分析》，《浙江档案》2015 年第 2 期，第 12—15 页。

⑤ 具体可参阅刘维荣、林挺《美国总统图书馆的口述历史档案》，《湖南档案》2001 年第 2 期，第 35 页；赵杰《张学良与美国哥伦比亚大学"口述历史中心"》，《百年潮》2001 年第 12 期，第 37—40 页；刘维荣、吴德正《美国总统图书馆的口述档案》，《云南档案》2002 年第 1 期，第 39 页；刘维荣《美国总统图书馆收藏的口述档案》，《山东图书馆季刊》2002 年第 4 期，第 106—108 页；刘维荣《口述历史档案管理在欧美》，《浙江档案》2003 年第 9 期，第 33—34 页；何品《美国哥伦比亚大学口述史研究管窥》，《档案与史学》2004 年第 1 期，第 85—89 页；李群、刘维荣《美国总统图书馆收藏的口述档案扫描》，《档案时空》2010 年第 8 期；黄迎风《美国现代口述史学考察印象》，《北京党史》2012 年第 5 期，第 57—58 页；艾琦《美国口述史发展与经验及对中国档案部门的启示》，《北京档案》2013 年第 11 期，第 33—35 页。

关论文或专书中的某些章节也一般都会涉及美国口述史学问题。① 综上所述，国内对于该问题的研究基本上是限于简单的介绍与分析，而且笔者发现对于美国口述史学发展历史的众多论述都有史实性错误，究其原因还是缺乏对于一手资料或重要相关文献的了解与掌握。当然，最后需要指出的

---

① 　具体可参阅箐舜《口碑史学方法评析》，《西北大学学报》（哲学社会科学版）1986 年第 3 期，第 103—109 页；孟庆顺《口碑史学略述》，《国外社会科学》1987 年第 1 期，第 51—54 页；杨雁斌《口述史的基本理论面面观——历史学家眼中的口述史学》，《国外社会科学》1993 年第 7 期，第 39—42 页；荣维木《口碑史料与口述历史》，《苏州大学学报》1994 年第 1 期，第 87—91 页；沈固朝《与人民共写历史——西方口述史的发展特点及对我们的启发》，《史学理论研究》1995 年第 2 期，第 98—207 页；宋瑞芝《口述史学在史学研究中的功用》，《史学理论研究》1995 年第 3 期，第 93—98 页；杨雁斌《口述史学百年透视（上）》，《国外社会科学》1998 年第 2 期，第 2—6 页；杨雁斌《口述史学百年透视（下）》，《国外社会科学》1998 年第 3 期，第 2—7 页；杨雁斌《面向大众的历史学——口述史学的社会含义辨析》，《国外社会科学》1998 年第 5 期，第 27—32 页；庞玉洁《从往事的简单再现到大众历史意识的重建——西方口述史学方法述评》，《世界历史》1998 年第 6 期，第 74—81 页；鲍晓兰《西方女性主义口述史发展初探》，《浙江学刊》1999 年第 6 期，第 85—90 页；熊月之《口述史的价值》，《史林》2000 年第 3 期，第 1—7 页；邬情《口述历史与历史的重建》，《学术月刊》2003 年第 6 期，第 77—82 页；陈献光《口述史二题：记忆与诠释》，《史学月刊》2003 年第 7 期，第 78—83 页；张广智《论口述史学的传统及其前景》，《江西师范大学学报》2003 年第 3 期，第 16—20 页；张广智《"把历史交还给人民"——口述史学的复兴及其现代回响》，《学术研究》2003 年第 9 期，第 101—106 页；朱志敏《现代口述史的产生及相关几个概念的辨析》，《史学史研究》2007 年第 2 期，第 68—74 页；李宝梁《现代口述史的兴起与研究述要》，《社科纵横》2007 年第 7 期，第 113—114 页；梁景和、王胜《关于口述史的思考》，《首都师范大学学报》（社会科学版）2007 年第 5 期，第 10—15 页；傅光明《口述史：历史、价值与方法》，《甘肃社会科学》，2008 年第 1 期，第 77—81 页；李小沧《现代口述史的时代性刍议》，《山西大学学报》（哲学社会科学版）2010 年第 6 期，第 77—80 页；王军《英美口述史实践及研究综述》，《华侨大学学报》（哲学社会科学版）2011 年第 2 期，第 110—115 页；王宇英《近年来口述史研究的热点审视及其态势》，《重庆社会科学》2011 年第 5 期，第 107—110 页；刘平平《现代口述史研究的理论与方法综述》，《传奇·传记文学选刊》（理论研究）2011 年第 4 期，第 92—94 页；李洁《口述史与女性主义研究的亲缘性》，《中华女子学院学报》2012 年第 3 期，第 94—97 页；岳庆平《关于口述史的五个问题》，《中国高校社会科学》2013 年第 5 期，第 81—93 页；李娜《公众史学与口述历史：跨学科的对话》，《史林》2015 年第 2 期，第 195—203 页。专书中的某些章节可参阅"历史的回声：口碑史学"，彭卫、孟庆顺：《历史学的视野：当代史学方法概述》，陕西人民出版社 1987 年版，第 265—301 页；"英美的'新社会史'与'口述史'"，陆象淦：《现代历史科学》，重庆出版社 1991 年版，第 246—262 页；"从人们记忆中追踪往昔的历程——当代西方口述史学方法"，庞卓恒主编：《西方新史学述评》，高等教育出版社 1992 年版，第 469—506 页；"口述史"，杨豫：《西方史学史》，江西人民出版社 1993 年版，第 486—494 页；"口述史"，杨豫、胡成：《历史学的思想和方法》，南京大学出版社 1996 年版，第 211—219 页；"口述史学"，于沛主编：《现代史学分支学科概论》，中国社会科学出版社 1998 年版，第 228—248 页；"口述史学方法"，庞卓恒、李学智、吴英：《史学概论》，高等教育出版社 2006 年版，第 288—299 页；"口述史学"，张广智主编：《西方史学通史》（第 6 卷 现当代时期），复旦大学出版社 2011 年版，第 194—200 页。

是，保罗·汤普森和唐纳德·里奇的两本经典口述史学的中文译著也是中国学术界了解西方口述史学发展历史、具体实践与理论研究的重要来源。①

四 研究思路与基本框架

综观国内外学术界有关该课题的研究现状，尽管已经发表许多相当有价值的论文研究成果，不过到目前为止，国内外学术界都还没有出版过关于美国口述史学发展史的学术专著，而本书则希望为弥补这方面的不足做出一些尝试与努力。需要指出的是，本书是笔者从事口述史学研究的另外一个阶段性成果，大约在 10 年前，笔者出版了国内较早的以口述史学基本理论、方法与发展现状为主要内容的口述史学专著，而其中也较为粗线条地梳理了美国现代口述史学的基本发展历程。考虑到美国是现代口述史学的发源地与发展水平最高的国家，因此对于美国口述史学的系统研究也就具有相当的代表性与典型性，而这也是笔者选择本书的重要原因所在。基于此，本书试图对美国现代口述史学的起源、发展历程、国际背景、基本特征、理论研究、跨学科应用与面临的主要挑战等问题进行较为全面和系统的梳理与研究，并希望为方兴未艾的中国口述史学的发展与建设提供某些借鉴与参考。概括而言，本书研究主要基于以下基本思路与原则。

第一，研究视角注重编年史脉络。作为一种史学史的研究路径，本书特别注重从编年史的角度来梳理与分析美国口述史学在不同阶段的发展概况、基本特征以及理论与方法建设。就发展阶段而言，本书认为美国现代

---

① 汤普森中文译本根据 1988 年英文版翻译，具体参阅保尔·汤普逊《过去的声音：口述史》，覃方明、渠东、张旅平译，香港：牛津大学出版社 1999 年；辽宁教育出版社 2000 年版。而里奇著作的繁体和简体中文译本分别根据英文版第一版和第二版翻译，具体参阅唐诺·里奇《大家来做口述历史》，王芝芝译，台源流出版公司 1997 年版；唐纳德·里奇《大家来做口述历史：实务指南（第二版）》，王芝芝、姚力译，当代中国出版社 2006 年版。

口述史学主要经历"起源与诞生"、"作为档案实践的口述史学"、"口述史学的新社会史转向"、"口述史学的理论转向与反思"与"数字化时代的口述史学"等五个相互分离而又重叠的阶段。在每一个阶段,笔者又试图从编年史发展脉络来呈现美国口述史学的具体实践与应用历程。

第二,研究资料强调全面而新颖。为做到上述一点,本书在研究过程中搜集到大量能够反映美国口述史学发展历程的重要资料,其中包括美国重要口述历史机构出版的重要报告与收藏目录、1966 年至 1972 年美国全国口述史学会议论文集、1967 年创刊以来的所有《口述历史协会通讯》①、1973 年创刊以来的所有《口述历史评论》以及 1948 年以来美国大部分主流报纸有关"oral history"的相关报道。此外,为了解美国和国际口述史学的发展历程与最新研究现状,笔者还通过各种渠道搜集到绝大部分重要研究论文与专著,其中包括《国际口述历史杂志》(*International Journal of Oral History*)和《话语与沉默》以及英国、加拿大、澳大利亚、新西兰等国家出版的官方口述史学刊物。正是如此,为了让感兴趣的读者了解更多背景信息和研究资料,笔者在写作过程中特意将重要资料以大量注释方式呈现出来。

第三,研究视野强调前沿性与跨学科性。由于美国当代口述史学本身的发展是处于现在进行时状态,为更加深刻理解其发展过程与最新动态,本书特别注重与美国和国际知名口述史学家的直接互动与交流,以尽可能掌握最新学术前沿。② 他们不仅为笔者提供众多重要的研究资料,而且为本书中所遇到的一些问题提供诸多建设性的参考意见。同时,考虑到美国口述史学发展的跨学科特征,本书在研究过程中也试图借鉴和学习尽可能

---

① 该刊详细记录美国口述史学发展过程中的重要事件,因而对本书研究至关重要。自 1999 年以来,美国口述历史协会已经将该刊电子版发布到网站上,而之前的资料因为没有一个图书馆有完整保存,笔者通过几年时间分别从哈佛大学图书馆、密歇根州立大学图书馆、澳大利亚悉尼大学图书馆和香港中文大学图书馆等多个图书馆才搜集完整。

② 过去 17 年来,笔者与世界各地的口述历史工作者(最多时达到 100 多人)建立了非常广泛和紧密的学术联系,其中包括当代最知名和活跃的口述历史学家:保罗·汤普森、罗纳德·格里、唐纳德·里奇、阿利桑乔·波特利、迈克尔·弗里斯科、琳达·肖普思和罗伯特·佩克斯等。

多的相关学科的理论与方法。

第四，研究方法坚持理论与实践相结合。相对于其他历史学分支学科或研究方法而言，口述史学特别注重具体实践与操作，因为其资料完全依赖于以计划为导向的口述历史访谈过程。而实践很大程度上有助于深化对于口述史学理论问题的思考与理解，基于此，过去8年来，在笔者主持下，我们的研究团队总共完成80多人的口述历史访谈工作，搜集了大量的口述历史访谈稿、录音和视频资料以及照片、手稿、证书等众多实物资料。① 而为加强国内外口述史学研究成果的交流与信息互动，笔者还于2014年创办国内首份口述史学理论研究中文学术集刊《口述史研究》，并于同年开通微信公众平台"口述历史"，这两项做法都受到国内同行的较高评价与认可。这两项做法都受到国内同行的较高评价与认可。此外，笔者从2008年开始在本科生当中开设"口述史学概论"课程，同时，过去几年来曾受众多单位邀请为来自高校、政府部门、媒体领域与社会组织的口述历史工作者提供各种培训工作或举办学术报告会。而上述这些充分结合理论研究与实践反思的机会与平台对于本书的深入研究具有相当重要的意义。

基于上述考虑，本书以美国现代口述史学发展的基本脉络与主流趋势为主线，同时也重点考察美国口述历史教育的兴起与发展以及所面临的法律与伦理问题，其基本写作框架包括以下几个部分。第一章"导论"部分将对口述史学简史、基本概念界定、美国口述史学研究的学术史回顾以及本书的基本思路与框架等内容做一导论性梳理与分析。

第二章"美国现代口述史学的起源与诞生"将回顾与追溯1948年以前"oral history"（口述历史）这个术语在美国的起源与早期使用，并以个别具体例子来分析美国学者（并不局限于历史学家）和机构对于口述访谈方法的早期倡导与实践。同时，将重点介绍与分析阿兰·内文斯与哥大口

---

① 目前，我们团队维持每年10—15人的口述历史访谈规模，而且与相关部门达成定期委托合作协议。

述历史研究室的创建过程及其早期发展。

第三章"精英主义、档案实践与美国口述史学"将主要侧重于介绍与分析 20 世纪 70 年代之前基于哥大口述历史研究室精英访谈模式的主要口述历史计划，并在此基础上考察与分析美国口述史学早期发展的基本特征、核心功能与主要争论。这种精英访谈模式也反映了美国现代口述史学兴起与发展的最初动力，即基于精英人物的口述历史访谈而获得具有保存价值的原始资料，以填补现存文献记录的空白或者弥补其不足。简单而言，这种模式强调口述史学的档案功能与史料价值。

第四章"美国口述史学与'新社会史转向'"将首先分析美国新社会史的兴起与发展，并以斯塔兹·特克尔口述历史系列作品为例来探讨非精英（民间）口述历史在美国的逐渐发展过程。同时，本章将重点介绍与探讨美国口述史学在少数族裔史、女性史、劳工史与同性恋史等新社会史领域的具体应用。所谓美国口述史学的"新社会史转向"是指口述历史实践者将口述历史视为非传统资料的一种重要来源，而且利用口述史学方法来描述与赋权于那些没有文字记录和在历史上被剥夺话语权力的人群，进而超越第一代口述史学家所主导的精英访谈模式而扩展口述历史的搜集范围与视野。简而言之，在新的社会与学术思潮的影响下，深具档案实践功能的口述史学为挖掘与呈现那些没有文献记录的经历提供了重要途径，并因此恢复和拯救了那些边缘人物与弱势群体的"隐藏的历史"。

第五章"美国口述史学的理论转向与反思"将从"记忆转向"、"叙事转向"与"'共享（的）权威'：口述历史关系反思"三个角度来分析和论述美国口述史学的理论转向与反思。综观 20 世纪 70 年代末之前的美国口述史学的主要发展趋势，不管是"档案实践模式"还是"新社会史转向"都着重强调口述史学的档案功能与史料价值。而进入 20 世纪 70 年代末以来，一些更具理论导向的口述历史学家呼吁重新思考口述历史的实践与解释方式。

第六章"数字化革命与美国口述史学"将从数字化记录、数字化管理以及数字化传播与交流等三个方面来分别阐述数字化革命与美国口述史学之间的紧密关系。概括而言,数字化革命对于美国口述史学的影响是全方位的,它不仅极大地促进了更为广泛而深入的国际交流,更为重要的是,它也改变着记录、保存、编目、索引、检索、解释、分享与呈现口述历史的方式与内容,这些都将严重挑战以书写抄本为基础的美国口述史学的传统模式。

第七章"美国口述历史教育的兴起与发展"将在考察美国口述历史教育兴起与发展过程的基础上,对当代(尤其是20世纪90年代以来)美国口述历史教育发展的基本特征做一概括性总结与评价。经过将近半个世纪的发展与探索,口述历史教育在美国已经步入一个良性的发展轨道。它或许不是摆脱现代教育困境的灵丹妙药,可是对于那些实践者来说,口述历史教育确实是一种值得尝试和努力探索的改革方向。

第八章"美国口述史学的法律与伦理问题"将以分别发生于1986年和2011年的两个涉及法律与伦理纠纷的美国口述历史案件为例,来分析美国口述史学的法律与伦理问题,主要包括著作权、诽谤与隐私权侵犯、法律挑战与"学者特权"、口述历史伦理审查机制以及口述历史参与者之间基于专业伦理的权责关系等。需要指出的是,随着美国口述史学日益关注和重视战争与冲突、突发事件(比如自然灾难与恐怖袭击)、犯罪问题(如毒品贸易与非法移民)、特殊疾病(比如艾滋病)以及多元性取向(LGBTQ)等具有当代性、敏感性与隐私性的议题,同时也因为数字化技术的发展使得口述历史资料的网络传播与应用变得更为容易与便捷,这些因素都导致口述历史工作所面临的法律与伦理风险进一步加剧。

结语部分将以时间跨度近100年的两个经典口号——"我们时代的口述历史"(An Oral History of Our Time)和"口述历史的时代"(The Age of Oral Histories)来总结美国口述史学发展过程所体现的时代与历史的互动关系。

　　最后需要说明的是，由于笔者才疏学浅与时间所限，本书在对美国口述史学的总体把握、主题设计与材料取舍和应用等方面肯定存在诸多不足。尤其是美国口述史学理论研究涉及众多跨学科概念与理论，对它们的理解与研究还需进一步深化。同时，由于美国口述史学是一门正在发展与不断演进的新兴学科，许多专业术语与概念尚未规范，再加上语言水平的限制，肯定存在对外文资料理解与中文表达不准确的问题。学无止境，笔者希望在后续研究中能够进一步拓展与深化对于美国乃至国际口述史学的认识与研究。

第二章 美国现代口述史学的起源与诞生

如上所述，学术界和公众一般都将内文斯于 1948 年在哥伦比亚大学创建口述历史研究室作为美国现代口述史学诞生的标志。而作为当代国际口述史学发展的先驱与重镇，事实上，"oral history"（口述历史）这个术语在美国诞生于 1948 年之前，而且本身就有着较为广泛和悠久的实践传统。本章试图回顾与追溯 1948 年以前该术语在美国的起源与早期使用，并以个别具体例子来分析美国学者（并不局限于历史学家）和机构对于口述访谈方法的早期倡导与实践。[①] 同时，也将重点介绍与分析阿兰·内文斯与哥大口述历史研究室的创建过程及其早期发展。

一 "口述历史"术语的产生

很大程度上，一个学术术语的起源、发展与普及能够反映一个学科被逐渐接受与认可的过程。事实上，作为口述历史核心的"口述"与"访谈式记录"方法一直以来就被不同学科和领域的学者所采用，当然如果某一

---

① 关于"口述历史"这一通用术语的早期使用，美国著名口述历史学家查尔斯·莫里斯（Charles T. Morrissey）已经做了较为完整的梳理，本章写作颇受他的启发。详细内容参阅 Charles T. Morrissey, "Why Call It 'Oral History'? Searching for Early Usage of a Generic Term", *Oral History Review*, Vol. 8, 1980, pp. 20-48.

术语能够作为"通用术语"被普遍性应用则意味着它的学科地位的逐步确立。基于此，为了了解美国现代口述史学的最初起源，有必要首先追溯"口述历史"这个术语的出现与发展过程。

笔者利用"Google 图书"（Google Books）查询关键词"oral history"①，发现最早出现"oral history"一词的记录是英国著名作家、小说家丹尼尔·笛福（Daniel Defoe，1660-1731）于 1725 年出版的《英伦全岛之旅》（第Ⅱ卷）。② 在该书中，他谈到了自己在廷塔哲城堡（Tintagel Castle，现在位于英国康沃尔郡廷塔哲沿岸）旅行时所听到的只以口述历史方式呈现的有关亚瑟王（King Arthur）出生与被杀的传说。③ 在 1763 年出版的《吕底亚或孝心：一部小说》当中，英国作家约翰·夏比尔（John Shebbeare，1709—1788）也提到"口述历史"一词，内容是指保存在古老部落中的由男性祖先传给儿子的口述历史。④ 同笛福一样，英国博物学者、作家托马斯·彭南特（Thomas Pennant，1726—1798）在其 1776 年出版的旅行游记《苏格兰之旅与赫布里底群岛之行》当中也使用了"口述历史"这个术语，当描述在阿蓝岛（Arran，英国苏格兰西南部岛屿）的旅行经历时，他谈到

---

① "Google 图书"是一个由 Google 研发的图书搜寻和浏览工具（部分图书提供下载功能），通过与哈佛大学图书馆、密歇根大学图书馆、纽约公共图书馆、牛津大学图书馆与斯坦福大学图书馆等全球知名图书馆的合作，它积极致力于推动图书的数字化发展与呈现。据统计，到 2013 年 4 月截止，扫描书籍数量达到三千万册，尤其是 20 世纪 20 年代以前的大部分书籍都可以实现在线检索与全文阅览（部分可下载）。详细内容参阅"Google Books"，from Wikipedia，https：// en. wikipedia. org/wiki/Google_ Books，2015 年 8 月 10 日访问。

② 需要强调的是，通过"Google 图书"搜寻未必能确保找到所有出现"oral history"这一术语的文献记录，只是希望通过这种方式来呈现该术语在不同历史时代与背景中的大概使用情况。

③ 原文如下：Tintagel Castle lies upon this coast a little farther, a mark of great antiquity, and every Writer has mentioned it；but as an antiquity is not my work, I leave the ruins of Tintagel to those that search into antiquity；little or nothing, that I could hear, is to be seen at it；and as for the story of King Arthur being both born and killed there,' tis a piece of tradition, only on oral history, and not any authority to be produced for it. 详细内容参阅 Daniel Defoe, "Letter I", in Daniel Defoe, *A Tour through the Whole Island of Great Britain*（Vol.Ⅱ），London：G. Strahan, 1725, p. 6.

④ 原文如下：In all the oral history of this antient race delivered down from sire to son, no instance is to be found of broken faith with other nations, no anecdote of friends betrayed, or allied deserted in the hour of danger and distress；their words are sacredly preserved, their lives offered up in battle the proof of it. 详细内容参阅 John Shebbeare, *Lydia, or Filial Piety：A Novel*, Dublin：Sarah Cotter, 1763, p. 1.

除了有关该岛的口述历史之外没有发现任何东西。① 而该书有关阿蓝岛的描述也成为 1797 年出版的《大英百科全书》词条"阿蓝岛"的重要内容来源，这也应该是《大英百科全书》（最早于 1768—1771 年间出版）中有关"口述历史"这个术语的最早记录。② 根据笔者详细查询发现，从 19 世纪开始，在一些作家的游记中还是不断出现有关"口述历史"一词的相关记录，而其意义同上述几位作家所呈现的内容都是差不多的。而笔者研究发现，他们所使用的"口述历史"概念更加接近于今天学术界所理解的"口头传统"（oral tradition），即那些通过口头世代传承的历史记忆与传说。③

　　至于"口述历史"这个术语在美国最早何时出现，莫里斯认为该术语于 1863 年就被正式杜撰出来。他研究发现，历史学家温斯洛·沃森（Winslow C. Watson, 1803—1884）于 1863 年 10 月 20 日在佛蒙特州历史学会（Vermont Historical Society）的一次题为《理查德·斯金纳的生活与性格》（*The Life and Character of the Hon. Richard Skinner*）的演讲中就曾谈到"口述历史"这一术语，他说："在我自己的地方研究中，通过观察一个社区中的口述历史源泉在仅仅十年中所遭受的破坏，我就感到很震惊。"基于此，他强调我们要勤勉尽责和具有预见性，去收集那些可能永远消失

---

　　① 原文如下：Here are still traditions of the hero Fingal, or Fin-mac-coul, who is supposed here to have enjoyed the pleasures of the chace; and many places retain his name: but I can discover nothing but oral history that relates to the island, till the time of Magnus the barefooted, the Norwegian victor, who probably included Arran in his conquests of Cantyre. 详细内容参阅 Thomas Pennant, *A Tour in Scotland, and Voyage to the Hebrides*, 1772 (Part Ⅰ), London: Benj. White, second edition, 1776, p. 196.

　　② "Arran", in *Encyclopaedia Britannica*; *or, A Dictionary of Arts, Sciences, and Miscellaneous Literature* (Vol. Ⅱ), Edinburgh: A. Bell and C. Macfarquhar, 1797, p. 349.

　　③ 有关口头传统的相关研究可参阅 1986 年出版至今的专业刊物《口头传统》（*Oral Tradition*），其他相关研究还包括 Jan Vansina, *Oral Tradition: A Study in Historical Methodology*, Chicago: Aldine Publishing Company, 1965 (Harmondsworth: Penguin Books, 1973; New Brunswick: Aldine Transaction, 2006); Jan Vansina, *Oral Tradition as History*, London: James Currey, 1985; Hassimi Oumarou Maïga, *Balancing Written History with Oral Tradition: The Legacy of the Songhoy People*, London and New York: Routledge, 2010; John Miles Foley, *Oral Tradition and the Internet: Pathways of the Mind*, Urbana: University of Illinois Press, 2012.

的事实和事件。同时，他还盛赞佛蒙特州历史学会通过收集杰出人物的真实传奇和保存他们的记录为未来历史学家的研究提供了丰富的宝藏。① 显然，这里他所谈到的"口述历史"含义已经相当接近于现代意义上的口述历史概念。

不过，笔者研究发现早在 1818 年出版的《美国杂志月刊和评论》（*American Monthly Magazine and Critical Review*）的有关纽约州古迹的文章中也曾明确提到"口述历史"这个术语，文章指出："我们能够依赖的自信是野蛮人流传给我们的口述历史。"② 而另外一条较早记录则是美国著名地理学家、地质学家、人种志学者亨利·斯库尔克拉夫特（Henry Rowe Schoolcraft，1793—1864）在 1834 年出版的《从密西西比河上游到伊塔斯加湖的探险经历》一书中谈到口述历史的不确定性。③

限于篇幅，这里不再详细罗列"口述历史"这个术语的具体应用历史，有兴趣读者可以通过"Google 图书"查询建立一种较为完整的学术史脉络。当然，需要强调的是，在美国学术史上，尽管很多学者没有明确提出"口述历史"这个术语，但他们已经在具体实践中践行着口述历史的某些基本精髓。

---

① Charles T. Morrissey, "Why Call It 'Oral History'? Searching for Early Usage of a Generic Term", *Oral History Review*, Vol. 8, 1980, pp. 21-22. 有关该演讲内容全文可参阅 Winslow C. Watson, *The Life and Character of the Hon. Richard Skinner*: A Discourses Read Before and at the Request of the Vermont Historical Society, Montpelier, October 20, 1863.

② "Antiquities of the State of New-York", *American Monthly Magazine and Critical Review*, Vol. 4, No. 1, November 1818, p. 43. 有关这篇文章的全文可参阅 De Witt Clinton, *A Memoir on the Antiquities of the Western Parts of the State of New-York*: *Read before the Literary and Philosophical Society of New-York*, Albany: E. & E. Hosford, 1820. 当然，这里笔者并不是说这篇文章就是美国出现"口述历史"术语的最早记录。

③ Henry Rowe Schoolcraft, *Narrative of an Expedition through the Upper Mississippi to Itasca Lake*, New York: Harper & Brothers, 1834, p. 92.

二 美国学者的早期倡导与实践

美国口述历史学界一般认为美国口述历史的最早实践者可以追溯到夏威夷传教士谢尔登·迪布尔（Sheldon Dibble，1809—1845），他从 1836 年开始从他的神学院学生中组织一个团队通过问卷调查和访谈方法来收集那些来自所在社区的酋长和老人们的回忆，试图记录和保存那些很快被遗忘和消失的夏威夷历史中的重要事件。① 而在 19 世纪 60—70 年代，两位美国历史学家莱曼·德拉佩（Lyman Copeland Draper，1815—1891）和休伯特·班克罗夫特（Hubert Howe Bancroft，1832—1918）都在其各自所在地区进行大规模的访谈收集工作。作为威斯康星州历史学会（Wisconsin Historical Society）的长期通讯秘书（1854—1886），德拉佩被称为"不知疲倦的威斯康星收藏者"②，除收集文献资料之外，从 19 世纪 60 年代开始，他还与那些来自该州的开拓者、昔日印第安战士（Indian fighters）以及他们的后裔进行广泛访谈，从这些老者的记忆中提取出大量的宝贵信息。正是如此，他所进行的这些系列访谈与记录工作也被其他学者称为是美国首个口述历史计划；③ 因为他在该领域的开拓性贡献，德拉佩还被某些学者誉为"美

---

① "Sheldon Dibble", from Wikipedia, https：//en. wikipedia. org/wiki/Sheldon_ Dibble，2015 年 8 月 10 日访问。更多内容可参阅 Sheldon Dibble，*History of the Sandwich Islands*，Lahainaluna：Press of the Mission Seminary，1843.

② Charles T. Morrissey，"Why Call It 'Oral History'? Searching for Early Usage of a Generic Term"，*Oral History Review*，Vol. 8，1980，p. 30.

③ William B. Hesseltine，"Lyman Draper and the South"，*Journal of Southern History*，Vol. 19，No. 1，1953，p. 23.

国口述历史之父"①。

　　而作为美国著名历史学家和图书收藏者，从 19 世纪 60—70 年代开始，为保存那些即将消逝的活生生的历史参与者的记忆，班克罗夫特和他的助手访谈大量美国西部的早期拓荒者，并为他们创作自传，经由口述而整理的资料最终形成几页甚至 5 卷本的回忆录。② 有学者认为，班克罗夫特的口述方法已经基本具备现代意义上的口述历史项目的特征，主要体现在四个方面：（1）将口述内容尽可能整理成逐字抄本；（2）口述内容涉及广泛的主题，而不仅仅是单一的历史研究主题；（3）尽管搜集的信息是由班克罗夫特及其助手所使用，不过也是为未来的历史学家而保存；（4）同时也会搜集诸如私人文件、法庭记录和新闻报纸等各种补充资料。③ 后来，这些资料也成为以其名字命名的班克罗夫特图书馆（Bancroft Library）的核心收藏，而它们也深受后世学者的高度评价，1942 年美国著名藏书家亨利·瓦格纳（Henry Raup Wagner，1862—1957）在其著作中就曾指出："今天图书馆的巨大价值不在于它所收藏的书籍，而在于班克罗夫特先生从年老的加州要人（grandees）那里所获得的丰富的手稿和印刷资料，以

---

①　Charles William Conaway，"Lyman Copeland Draper，'Father of American Oral History'"，*Journal of Library History*，Vol. 1，No. 4，1966，pp. 234-235，238-241，269. 有关德拉佩的详细资料可参阅 "Lyman Draper"，from Wikipedia，https：//en. wikipedia. org/wiki/Lyman_ Draper，2015 年 8 月 10 日访问；Louise Phelps Kellogg，"The Services and Collections of Lyman Copeland Draper"，*The Wisconsin Magazine of History*，Vol. 5，No. 3，1922，pp. 244-263；Josephine L. Harper，"Lyman C. Draper and Early American Archives"，*The American Archivist*，Vol. 15，No. 3，1952，pp. 205-212；William B. Hesseltine，"Lyman Copeland Draper，1815-1891"，*The Wisconsin Magazine of History*，Vol. 35，No. 3，1952，pp. 163-166，231-234.

②　Willa K. Baum，Kathryn Anderson，and Mary Ellen Leary，"History on Tape：The Regional Oral History Office at The Bancroft Library"，*California Historical Quarterly*，Vol. 54，No. 1，1975，p. 77；Rebecca Sharpless，"The History of Oral History"，in Thomas L. Charlton，Lois E. Myers，and Rebecca Sharpless（eds.），*Handbook of Oral History*，Walnut Creek：AltaMira Press，2006，p. 20；王子舟、尹培丽：《口述资料采集与收藏的先行者：美国班克罗夫特图书馆》，载杨祥银主编《口述史研究》（第一辑），社会科学文献出版社 2014 年版，第 45—47 页。有关班克罗夫特的详细资料可参阅 "Hubert Howe Bancroft"，from Wikipedia，https：//en. wikipedia. org/wiki/Hubert_ Howe_ Bancroft，2015 年 8 月 10 日访问。

③　Willa Klug Baum，"Oral History：A Revived Tradition at the Bancroft Library"，*Pacific Northwest Quarterly*，Vol. 58，No. 2，1967，p. 57.

及向其代理人（agents）所口述的拓荒者的个人回忆。"① 经过 40 多年的发展，1905 年班克罗夫特先生将图书馆出售给加州大学伯克利分校（University of California，Berkeley），其前提条件之一是保持图书馆名称不变。②

此外，莫里斯还提到几位曾经利用访谈方法的美国作家或历史学家，其中包括教会历史学家安德鲁·詹森（Andrew Jenson，1850—1941），他从 19 世纪 80—90 年代开始采访了很多美国教会的创始人。③ 另外一位是美国著名铁路专家、作家和历史研究者沃尔特·坎普（Walter Mason Camp，1867—1925），他采访了几百位曾经参与 19 世纪下半叶北美印第安战争（American Indian Wars，美国拓荒者和联邦政府与印第安人在美国独立战争前后的一系列冲突）的美国白人与印第安人。他的这些访谈笔记已经成为重要的原始资料，尤其对于那些从事小大角战役（Battle of the Little Bighorn）的研究者来说更具价值，其中涉及 150 位苏族印第安人的访谈。④第三位则是有点技术天赋的农场主乔纳斯·伯格雷恩（Jonas Bergren），他定居于伊利诺伊州主教山（Bishop Hill）的一个瑞典人定居点，他仿效爱迪生设计的留声机并于 19 世纪末 20 世纪初发明了他自己的"谈话机器"（talking machine）。随后，他就利用这台机器记录了他所在社区的早期定居者的生活经历，而这些记录也被一些学者认为是世界上最古老的录音访谈

---

① Henry Raup Wagner, *Bullion to Books*：*Fifty Years of Business and Pleasure*, Los Angeles：The Zamorano Club, 1942, p. 251.

② 现有资料无法确定班克罗夫特图书馆创建的准确时间，不过大概是在 1858—1863 年期间。详细内容可参阅 "Bancroft Library", from Wikipedia, https：//en. wikipedia. org/wiki/Bancroft_ Library；The Bancroft Library, " Building Bancroft：The Evolution of a Library ", http：// bancroft. berkeley. edu/Exhibits/bancroft/. 上述访问时间为 2015 年 8 月 10 日访问。

③ "Andrew Jenson", from Wikipedia, https：//en. wikipedia. org/wiki/Andrew_ Jenson, 2015 年 8 月 10 日访问。

④ "Walter Mason Camp", from Wikipedia, https：//en. wikipedia. org/wiki/Walter _ Mason _ Camp, 2015 年 8 月 10 日访问；Walter Mason Camp, *Camp, Custer, and the Little Bighorn*：*A Collection of Walter Mason Camp's Research Papers*, edited by Richard G. Hardorff, El Segundo：Upton and Sons, 1997；Debra Buchholtz, *The Battle of the Greasy Grass/Little Bighorn*：*Custer's Last Stand in Memory, History, and Popular Culture*, London and New York：Routledge, 2012, p. 146.

(recorded interviews) 之一。① 需要强调的是，随着留声机技术的改进，其实从 19 世纪 80 年代末期开始，包括民俗学、人类学与民族学等相关学科的美国田野工作者已经利用录音技术来记录他们所需的资料。事实上，美国当代口述史学的发展历史也足以证明录音（录影）技术对于该学科领域的重要性，显然这些早期实践者都为后来的发展奠定了一定基础。②

三　约瑟夫·古尔德与《我们时代的口述历史》

上述主要从学术界对于"口述历史"术语及其方法的应用来呈现美国现代口述史学的最初雏形，而真正推动美国公众乃至学术界认识"口述历史"这个术语与概念的传奇人物是美国著名流浪约瑟夫·古尔德（Joseph Ferdinand Gould，1889—1957），他因经常在酒吧给人朗诵诗歌或者学海鸥的叫声（以此换取酒钱）而又被称为"海鸥教授"（Professor Seagull）。他之所以跟美国口述史学有着非常紧密的关系，是因为他在 1917 年就声称自己正在创作一部巨著《我们时代的口述历史》（*An Oral History of Our Time*，又名 *An Oral History of the Contemporary World*），记录他在街头巷尾所听到的人们的闲谈和自己在村里生活的经历与感受，总字数将达 900 万字。③

古尔德于 1889 年出生于波士顿的一个医生世家，即使家里希望他能够成为一位医生，也将他送进哈佛大学，可是他却宁愿选择文学专业。1911

---

① Charles T. Morrissey, "Why Call It 'Oral History'? Searching for Early Usage of a Generic Term", *Oral History Review*, Vol. 8, 1980, pp. 30-31.

② 有关录音（录影）技术的发展以及与美国口述史学之间的关系，请参阅第六章"数字化革命与美国口述史学"。

③ Ross Wetzsteon, "Joe Gould: The Last of the Last Bohemians", in Ross Wetzsteon, *Republic of Dreams: Greenwich Village: The American Bohemia, 1910-1960*, New York: Simon & Schuster, 2002, p. 419; Kenneth Goldsmith, *Uncreative Writing: Managing Language in the Digital Age*, New York: Columbia University Press, 2011, p. 160.

年毕业之后，他曾去加拿大游历，后来回到波士顿。1915 年为纽约冷泉港（Cold Spring Harbor）的优生学档案室（Eugenics Record Office）做田野调查。随后又到北达科他州（North Dakota）研究齐佩瓦族（Chippewa）和曼丹族（Mandan）文化，同时也学会了骑马、跳舞和唱歌。1916 年古尔德再次回到纽约，并于翌年在《纽约晚邮报》（*New York Evening Mail*）担任新闻记者，正是这时候他声称要撰写巨著《我们时代的口述历史》。① 古尔德传记作者、美国著名作家约瑟夫·米切尔（Joseph Mitchell，1908—1996）曾非常生动地描述了他的这一突发奇想："在 1917 年夏天的一个早上，我正坐在警察局总部后面的台阶上晒太阳，为了能够从宿醉中清醒。在一家二手书店中，我最近碰到并阅读了一本由伟大的爱尔兰农民作家威廉·卡尔顿（William Carleton）撰写的故事小书，该书于 80 年代在伦敦出版并由威廉·叶芝（William Butler Yeats）作序，而叶芝序言中的一句话让我留下深刻印象：'一个国家的历史不是在议会和战场中，而存在于人们在集会日和节日中相互所说的话当中，以及他们怎么种田、吵架和朝拜。'突然，我就有了口述历史这个想法：我将用我的余生去城市聆听人们--如果有必要的话也可以偷听--并写下我所听到的任何对我具有启迪作用的东西，不管对于其他人来说可能是无聊的、愚蠢的、粗俗的或淫秽的。……当我有口述历史这个想法的时候正好是十点半。而在大约十点四十五的时候，我就起身去打电话辞掉我的工作。"②

最初，古尔德的一些口述历史短文也逐渐通过报刊进行发表，其中 1929 年文学杂志《刻度盘》（*The Dial*）就以《来自约瑟夫·古尔德的口述历史》（*From Joe Gould's Oral History*）为题刊登了两篇有关"婚姻"

---

① "Joe Gould（bohemian）", from Wikipedia, https：//en. wikipedia. org/wiki/Joe ＿ Gould＿（bohemian），2015 年 8 月 10 日访问。

② Joseph Mitchell, "Profiles：Joe Gould's Secret-I", *The New Yorker*, September 19, 1964, p. 99.

（Marriage）和"文明"（Civilization）的文章。而两年之后，《异教》（*The Pagany*）杂志以《我的执行：约瑟夫·古尔德口述历史选集》（Me Tempore：A Selection From Joe Gould's Oral History）为题发表了"精神病"（Insanity）与"自由"（Freedom）两篇文章。① 紧接着，《纽约论坛先驱报》（*New York Herald Tribune*）分别于1934年3月2日和1937年4月10日专题报道古尔德的口述历史工作，并称他所搜集的口述历史资料已经分别达到730万字和880万字。而 *PM*（具体信息未详）于1941年8月24日报道指出，古尔德所撰写的口述历史手稿堆起来已经超过7英尺，而他的身高只有5.4英尺。②

真正让古尔德（尤其是他所宣称的口述历史工作）产生极大影响的是米切尔为其撰写的于1942年发表于《纽约客》（*The New Yorker*）杂志的传记文章《海鸥教授》。③ 这篇文章在纽约乃至全美引起轰动，令古尔德一夜之间成为名人，很多人给他写信，而且有些信中夹着支票或现金，甚至有人匿名为他提供长期生活资助。尽管获得美国大众的热切期待和慷慨相助，不过遗憾的是，古尔德并没有完成它所说的口述历史巨著。直到1957年去世，他所谓的这本巨著仍然杳无踪影，这也导致米切尔和其他美国公众不断质疑他的诚信。④ 基于此，米切尔分别于1964年9月19日和26日在《纽约客》刊登长文《约瑟夫·古

① Joseph Mitchell， "Profiles：Joe Gould's Secret-I"， *The New Yorker*， September 19，1964，pp. 104-105，121，125；Charles T. Morrissey， "Why Call It 'Oral History'？Searching for Early Usage of a Generic Term"， *Oral History Review*， Vol. 8，1980，pp. 26-27.

② Joseph Mitchell， "Profiles：Joe Gould's Secret-II"， *The New Yorker*， September 26，1964，p. 68.

③ Joseph Mitchell， "Profiles：Professor Sea Gull"， *The New Yorker*， December 12，1942，pp. 28-39.

④ 直到2000年才终于发现古尔德的部分手稿，不过只是些零散的日记而已，记录的也是吃饭、洗澡这类毫无价值的琐事。相关资料参阅朱诺《"海鸥教授"》，《万象》2009年2月号，第32—41页；王瑞芸《走运的"海鸥教授"》，雅昌艺术网，2009年7月2日；Jill Lepore， "Joe Gould's Teeth：The Long-Lost Story of the Longest Book Ever Written"， *The New Yorker*， July 27，2015.

尔德的秘密》，除了介绍其生平经历之外，他还详细回顾了与古尔德的交往经历，尤其是围绕他宣称的口述历史工作。不过，令他沮丧和难过的是，他的传记文章《海鸥教授》因为未经任何验证就向读者介绍了古尔德根本子虚乌有的口述历史巨著，因而觉得自己在一定程度上帮助他实施了欺骗。①

尽管古尔德所宣称的《我们时代的口述历史》最终是一场"骗局"，但是经由《纽约论坛先驱报》、《纽约客》、《纽约阿姆斯特丹新闻》（*New York Amsterdam News*）与《纽约时报》（*New York Times*）等美国主流报纸杂志的大量报道，② "口述历史"这个术语却被美国学界与公众所广泛了解。斯塔尔就认为是古尔德杜撰了"口述历史"这个术语，他指出："古尔德命名了一种他可能或可能不从事的活动，给世界带来一个现在深深根植于语言当中的误称（misnomer）"，甚至他推测内文斯之所以将他在哥大的访谈计划称为"口述历史"也可能受到古尔德的影响。③ 而唐纳德·里奇也坦言，尽管沃森在 1863 年就明确提出"口述历史"这个术语，可是他没有产生像古尔德那样的全国影响力。④

---

① Joseph Mitchell, "Profiles：Joe Gould's Secret-I", *The New Yorker*, September 19, 1964, pp. 61-125; Joseph Mitchell, "Profiles：Joe Gould's Secret-II", *The New Yorker*, September 26, 1964, pp. 53-159. 1965 年米切尔将发表于《纽约客》杂志上的三篇文章集结出版，详细参阅 Joseph Mitchell, *Joe Gould's Secret*, New York：Viking Press, 1965; New York：Modern Library, 2000. 关于米切尔的更多内容可参阅 Thomas Kunkel, *Man in Profile：Joseph Mitchell of the New Yorker*, New York：Random House Publishing Group, 2015.

② Constance H. Curtis, "About Books", *New York Amsterdam News*, October 2, 1943; Lincoln Barnett, "Nostalgic Portraits of the Lunatic Fringe", *New York Times*, July 25, 1943; Al Hirschfeld, "Counter-Revolution in the Village", *New York Times*, April 23, 1944; "People Who Read and Write", *New York Times*, April 18, 1948; "Joe Gould Dead；'Last Bohemian'", *New York Times*, August 20, 1957; D. L. Harley, "Oral History's Fate", *The Washington Post and Times Herald*, September 4, 1957.

③ Louis Starr, "Oral History", *Encyclopedia of Library and Information Sciences* (Vol. 20), New York：Marcel Dekker, 1977, p. 444.

④ Donald A. Ritchie, *Doing Oral History*, Oxford and New York：Oxford University Press, third edition, 2014, p. 282.

四　联邦作家计划：美国人生活史访谈和奴隶叙述计划

上述侧重于从"口述历史"术语和概念角度强调美国现代口述史学发展的历史基础，而启动于20世纪30年代的联邦作家计划（Federal Writers' Project）对于当代美国口述史学的发展具有更为直接的实践意义。尽管其价值直到20世纪60年代以后才逐渐被美国口述历史学界所认可，但是越来越多的学者强调它在美国口述史学史上的特殊地位。正如杰罗尔德·赫希（Jerrold Hirsch）所说："联邦作家计划和哥伦比亚大学口述历史项目的开端在美国口述历史研究史上都是重要的事件。……将联邦作家计划视为当前口述历史工作的始祖是一项非常吸引人的策略。不只是内文斯在哥伦比亚大学的努力，联邦作家计划似乎与我们当前的研究趋势连接在一起。很显然，口述历史研究不再仅仅关注那些著名的与有影响力的人物，而哥伦比亚大学口述历史项目在创建之后的将近20年间都是侧重于这些人物。"[1] 事实上，大部分当代学者在重新研究联邦作家计划所开展的访谈计划时，都将它们看成现在所理解的口述历史概念，只不过是当时的实践者并不熟悉"口述历史"这个术语。[2] 而且，美国口述历史协会官方刊物《口述历史评论》和英国口述历史学会（Oral History Society）官方

① Jerrold Hirsch, "Before Columbia: The FWP and American Oral History Research", *Oral History Review*, Vol. 34, No. 2, 2007, p. 3.

② George T. Blakey, "Oral History", in George T. Blakey, *Creating a Hoosier Self-portrait: The Federal Writers' Project in Indiana, 1935-1942*, Bloomington: Indiana University Press, 2005, pp. 107-129; Peggy A. Bulger, "Foreword", in Federal Writers' Project, *Missouri Slave Narratives: A Folk History of Slavery in Missouri from Interviews with Former Slaves*, Bedford: Applewood Books, 2006; James R. Dow, Roger L. Welsch, and Susan D. Dow (eds.), *Wyoming Folklore: Reminiscences, Folktales, Beliefs, Customs, and Folk Speech*, Lincoln: University of Nebraska Press, 2010, p. 2; Mary Kay Quinlan, "The Dynamics of Interviewing", in Donald A. Ritchie (ed.), *The Oxford Handbook of Oral History*, Oxford and New York: Oxford University Press, 2011, p. 32.

刊物《口述历史》（*Oral History*）也发表多篇相关论文，[①] 甚至有些学者将联邦作家计划所搜集的访谈资料重新编辑出版时直接在标题中冠以口述历史。[②]

联邦作家计划是富兰克林·罗斯福（Franklin Delano Roosevelt，1882—1945；总统任期为1933—1945年）总统于1935年7月27日发起的一项旨在为职业作家、新闻工作者和研究人员提供资金和政策支持的新政计划，以解决他们在大萧条时期的就业问题，其具体工作由公共事业振兴署（Works Progress Administration）负责监管和指导。联邦作家计划在各州都设立一个非救助性的编辑部，从当地失业人员中挑选组建一支更大规模的专业人员队伍。据统计，该计划共雇佣作家、编辑、历史学家、研究人员、评论家、考古学家、地质学家和制图师等6600人左右。联邦作家计划先后由新闻记者、戏剧制作人亨利·阿尔斯贝格（Henry Alsberg，1881—1970）和约翰·纽瑟姆（John D. Newsome）担任主任，主要开展编撰地方史、口述历史、民族志以及儿童读物等工作。随着失业危机的逐渐缓和以及政府将焦点转向第二次世界大战问题，联邦政府于1939年停止对该计划的资助，而随着

---

① Thomas F. Soapes, "The Federal Writers' Project Slave Interviews: Useful Data or Misleading Source", *Oral History Review*, Vol. 5, 1977, pp. 33-38; Leonard Rapport, "How Valid Are the Federal Writers' Project Life Stories: An Iconoclast among the True Believers", *Oral History Review*, Vol. 7, 1979, pp. 6-17; Tom E. Terrill and Jerrold Hirsch, "Replies to Leonard Rapport's 'How Valid Are the Federal Writers' Project Life Stories: An Iconoclast among the True Believers'", *Oral History Review*, Vol. 8, 1980, pp. 81-89; Leonard Rapport, "Comment: Replies to Leonard Rapport's 'How Valid Are the Federal Writers' Project Life Stories: An Iconoclast among the True Believers'", *Oral History Review*, Vol. 8, 1980, pp. 89-92; Lynda M. Hill, "Ex-Slave Narratives: The WPA Federal Writers' Project Reappraised", *Oral History*, Vol. 26, No. 1, 1998, pp. 64-72; Jerrold Hirsch, "Before Columbia: The FWP and American Oral History Research", *Oral History Review*, Vol. 34, No. 2, 2007, pp. 1-16; Bruce M. Stave, "'The Doctor Told Us What He Wanted': Sam Koenig's Instructions to WPA Ethnic Group Survey Interviewers", *Oral History Review*, Vol. 34, No. 2, 2007, pp. 17-26.

② Belinda Hurmence (ed.) *Before Freedom, When I Just Can Remember: Twenty-Seven Oral Histories of Former South Carolina Slaves*, Winston-Salem: John F. Blair, Publisher, 1989; Theda Perdue, *Nations Remembered: An Oral History of the Cherokees, Chickasaws, Choctaws, Creeks, and Seminoles*, Norman: University of Oklahoma Press, 1993.

1943 年公共事业振兴署的宣告解散，联邦作家计划也最终退出历史舞台。①

　　而联邦作家计划中跟访谈相关的内容主要包括美国人生活史访谈（American Life Stories Interviews）与奴隶叙述计划（Slave Narratives Project）两部分。② 在 1936—1940 年间，通过笔记访谈方式，超过 300 位联邦作家在 24 个州收集了 2900 份有关美国人生活史的访谈资料。这些资料主要涉及美国人对于他们自己生活中的重要事件的回忆，可以说是对美国乡村和城市的日常生活的充分展现，其时间范围涵盖内战结束到大萧条时期。而且，访谈主题也相当丰富，主要包括以下几个方面：（1）美国拓荒者所经历的戏剧性的艰难故事；（2）移民美国的故事（主要集中于 1840—1920 年间）；（3）冒险故事（比如犯法、遭遇印第安人、抗击大自然、火灾）；（4）战争故事（内战、美西战争与第一次世界大战）；（5）美国内战前后非裔美国人的生活故事与他们面对困难的毅力；（6）工作条件与工业化对于美国人的影响；（7）大萧条时期的艰难经历。③

---

① "Federal Writers, Project", from Wikipedia, https://en. wikipedia. org/wiki/Federal _ Writers'_ Project，2015 年 8 月 10 日访问。有关该计划的相关研究可参阅 Jerre Mangione, *The Dream and the Deal：the Federal Writers'Project, 1935-1943*, Boston：Little, Brown and Company, 1972；Monty Noam Penkower, *The Federal Writers'Project：A Study in Government Patronage of the Arts*, Urbana：University of Illinois Press, 1976；Jeutonne P. Brewer, *The Federal Writers' Project：A Bibliography*, Metuchen：Scarecrow Press, 1994；Christine Bold, *The WPA Guides：Mapping America*, Jackson：University Press of Mississippi, 1999；Jerrold Hirsch, *Portrait of America：A Cultural History of the Federal Writers' Project*, Chapel Hill：University of North Carolina Press, 2003；David A. Taylor, *Soul of a People：The WPA Writers' Project Uncovers Depression America*, Hoboken：Wiley & Sons, 2009.

② 有关联邦作家计划的完整资料信息，可以参阅 Library of Congress, "Federal Writers' Project", http：//www. loc. gov/rr/program/bib/newdeal/fwp. html，2015 年 8 月 11 日访问。

③ 美国人生活史访谈资料已经由美国国会图书馆（Library of Congress）进行数字化处理并提供上网查询、浏览与下载服务，详细内容参阅 Library of Congress, "American Life Histories：Manuscripts from the Federal Writers' Project, 1936-1940", http：//www. loc. gov/collections/federal-writers-project/about-this-collection/和 http：//www. loc. gov/teachers/classroommaterials/connections/american-life-hist/，2015 年 8 月 11 日访问。

这些生活史资料从 1939 年开始就逐渐公开披露，时任北卡罗来纳大学出版社（University of North Carolina Press）社长和联邦作家计划南方地区（Federal Writers' Project in the South）主任的威廉·考奇（William T. Couch，1926—1988）编辑出版了《我们的生活》一书。该访谈集很明显就是为了呈现弱势群体的声音，正如考奇在序言中所说："其想法就是为了获得生活史，它们是活生生的人们（living persons）的可阅读的和忠实的再现，总之，它将呈现一种社会结构和活动的合理图景。……在撰写生活史过程中，首要原则就是让人们讲述他们自己的故事。"① 随后，又有不同学者从中选取部分访谈资料编辑出版。② 当然，对于那些从事美国内战至大萧条时期的历史、民俗与文化研究者而言，它们也是非常宝贵的原始资料。③ 而如上所述，为提高这些资料的使

① William T. Couch, "Preface", in Federal Writers' Project, *These Are Our Lives: As Told by the People and Written by Members of the Federal Writers' Project of the Works Progress Administration in North Carolina, Tennessee and Georgia*, Chapel Hill: University of North Carolina Press, 1939, pp. ix-x; Christine Bold, *The WPA Guides: Mapping America*, Jackson: University Press of Mississippi, 1999, p. 123.

② 比如 Tom E. Terrill and Jerrold Hirsch (eds.), *Such As Us: Southern Voices of the Thirties*, Chapel Hill: University of North Carolina Press, 1978; Ann Banks (ed.), *First Person America*, New York: Random House, 1980; James Seay Brown (ed.), *Up Before Daylight: Life Histories from the Alabama Writers' Project, 1938-1939*, Tuscaloosa: University of Alabama Press, 1982; Charles Stewart Doty (ed.), *The First Franco-Americans: New England Life Histories from the Federal Writers' Project, 1938-1939*, Orono: University of Maine at Orono Press, 1985; David Steven Cohen (ed.), *America, the Dream of My Life: Selections from the Federal Writers' Project's New Jersey Ethnic Survey*, New Brunswick: Rutgers University Press, 1990.

③ 比如 Jerrold Hirsch, "Grassroots Environmental History: The Southern Federal Writers' Project Life Histories as a Source", *Southern Cultures*, Vol. 2, No. 1, 1995, pp. 129-136; Martin Henry Blatt and Martha K. Norkunas (eds.), *Work, Recreation, and Culture: Essays in American Labor History*, London: Taylor & Francis, 1996; Stewart Emory Tolnay, *The Bottom Rung: African American Family Life on Southern Farms*, Urbana: University of Illinois Press, 1999; Julie Husband and Jim O' Loughlin, *Daily Life in the Industrial United States, 1870-1900*, Westport: Greenwood Publishing Group, 2004; Kolan Thomas Morelock, *Taking the Town: Collegiate and Community Culture in the Bluegrass, 1880-1917*, Lexington: University Press of Kentucky, 2009; Rebecca Sharpless, *Cooking in Other Women's Kitchens: Domestic Workers in the South, 1865-1960*, Chapel Hill: University of North Carolina Press, 2010; David A. Taylor, *Soul of a People: The WPA Writers' Project Uncovers Depression America*, Chichester: John Wiley & Sons, 2010.

用率，它们已经由国会图书馆全部上线并免费提供查询、浏览与下载服务。

当然，需要指出的是，奴隶叙述计划与美国人生活史访谈并非完全割裂的，它是联邦作家计划旨在实现让普通美国人讲述他们自己的生活故事这一目的的自然延伸。在1936—1938年间，联邦作家们通过与昔日奴隶（former slaves）的访谈，总共搜集超过2300份有关奴隶生活及其感受的第一人称叙述资料，同时还包括500张左右的黑白照片。① 这些访谈为那些年长的昔日奴隶提供了一个前所未有的机会让她们讲述在"特殊制度"下的生活经历，用她们自己的语言来描述在美国做一个奴隶的感受。② 联邦作家计划于1939年失去联邦政府经费资助之后，各州搜集的大部分访谈及其相关资料都转移到国会图书馆，而后续编辑、索引与整理工作则由美国著名民俗学家、时任联邦作家计划民俗编辑本杰明·博特金（Benjamin A. Botkin，1901—1975）负责，其初步成果是1941年编辑整理的17卷本《奴隶叙述》。③ 博特金还于1945年编辑出版了《如释重负：奴隶民间史》，他在该书前言中写道："从昔日奴隶的记忆与口中获得了只有她们才能回答的答案，而

---

① 事实上，在联邦紧急救济总署计划（Federal Emergency Relief Administration Program）的资助下，菲斯克大学（Fisk University）研究生劳伦斯·雷迪克（Lawrence Reddick，1910—1995）从1932年开始就致力于收集肯塔基州和印第安纳州昔日奴隶的回忆，而在1937年他为联邦作家计划采访佐治亚州的黑人。详细参阅 Jacqueline Goggin，*Carter G. Woodson*：*A Life in Black History*，Baton Rouge：Louisiana State University Press，1993，p. 121；Elinor Des Verney Sinnette，"Oral History"，in Evelyn Brooks Higginbotham，Leon F. Litwack，Darlene Clark Hine，and Randall K. Burkett（eds.），*The Harvard Guide to African-American History*，Cambridge：Harvard University Press，2001，p. 114.

② Norman R. Yetman，"An Introduction to the WPA Slave Narratives"，http：//memory. loc. gov/ammem/snhtml/snintro00. html，2015年8月11日访问。有关奴隶叙述计划的详细内容还可参阅 Norman R. Yetman，"The Background of the Slave Narrative Collection"，*American Quarterly*，Vol. 19，No. 3，1967，pp. 534-553；Norman R. Yetman，"Ex-Slave Interviews and the Historiography of Slavery"，*American Quarterly*，Vol. 36，No. 2，1982，pp. 181-210.

③ Federal Writers' Project，*Slave Narratives*：*A Folk History of Slavery in the United States from Interviews with Former Slaves*，Washington：Library of Congress Project，1941. 有关博特金的研究可参阅 Lawrence R. Rodgers and Jerrold Hirsch（eds.），*America's Folklorist*：*B. A. Botkin and American Culture*，Norman：University of Oklahoma Press，2014.

这些也是美国人仍然在问的：作为一个奴隶意味着什么？自由意味着什么？而且，那到底是什么感觉？"①

　　同美国人生活史访谈资料一样，这些奴隶叙述的原始资料也由后来学者不断编辑出版，其中比较有代表性的是诺曼·耶特曼（Norman R. Yetman）于1970年编辑出版的《奴隶声音》与乔治·拉威克（George P. Rawick）于1972—1979年间编辑出版的多卷本《美国奴隶》系列。② 由于这项计划涉及美国许多州，因此也编辑出版了大量以州为单位的奴隶叙述资料集。③ 需要指出的是，这些原始资料也已经由美国国会图书馆进行数字化处理并提供上网查询、浏览与下载服务，同时该网站还提供相当丰富的参考资料信息与网站资源链接。④ 当然，它们也成为众多学者研究美国奴隶制与黑人历史文化等相关问题的重要原始资料来源，而且出版了大

---

① Benjamin A. Botkin（ed.），*Lay My Burden Down*：*A Folk History of Slavery*，Chicago：University of Chicago Press，1945，p. ix.

② Norman R. Yetman（ed.），*Voices from Slavery*，New York：Holt，Rinehart and Winston，1970；George P. Rawick（ed.），*The American Slave*：*A Composite Autobiography*，Westport：Greenwood Press，1972-1976；George P. Rawick，Jan Hillegas，and Ken Lawrence（eds.），*The American Slave*：*A Composite Autobiography*（Supplement Series 1），Westport：Greenwood Press，1977；George P. Rawick（ed.），*The American Slave*：*A Composite Autobiography*（Supplement Series 2），Westport：Greenwood Press，1979. 其他代表性成果可参阅 Paul D. Escott（ed.），*Slavery Remembered*：*A Record of Twentieth-Century Slave Narratives*，Chapel Hill：University of North Carolina Press，1979；Ira Berlin，Marc Favreau，and Steven F. Miller（eds.），*Remembering Slavery*：*African Americans Talk About Their Personal Experiences of Slavery and Freedom*，New York：The New Press，1998；Spencer Crew，Lonnie Bunch III，and Clement Price（eds.），*Slave Culture*：*A Documentary Collection of the Slave Narratives from the Federal Writers' Project*，Santa Barbara：ABC-CLIO，LLC，2014.

③ 比如 Ronnie C. Tyler Lawrence R. Murphy（eds.），*The Slave Narratives of Texas*，Austin：Encino Press，1974；T. Lindsay Baker and Julie P. Baker（eds.），*The WPA Oklahoma Slave Narratives*，Norman：University of Oklahoma Press，1996；George E. Lankford，*Bearing Witness*：*Memories of Arkansas Slavery Narratives from the 1930s WPA Collections*，Fayetteville：University of Arkansas Press，2003；Federal Writers' Project，*Kentucky Slave Narratives*：*A Folk History of Slavery in Kentucky from Interviews with Former Slaves*，Bedford：Applewood Books，2006（该出版社以州为单位于2006年再版所有奴隶叙述资料，这里仅举一例）。

④ Library of Congress，"Born in Slavery：Slave Narratives from the Federal Writers' Project，1936-1938"，http：//memory. loc. gov/ammem/snhtml/，2015 年 8 月 12 日访问。

量研究成果。[1]

　　显然，上述联邦作家计划所实施的两个访谈计划都侧重于记录美国普通人物或弱势群体的生活故事与经历，而这种具有新政民粹主义（New Deal populism）特征并试图撰写"自下而上的历史"（history from the bottom up）的努力与 20 世纪 60 年代兴起的美国新社会史（new social history）有诸多共同之处。[2] 在某种程度上，这也能解释为什么联邦作家计划的意义与价值到 20 世纪 60 年代才逐渐被美国学术界（尤其是那些将焦点转向普通人物或弱势群体的口述历史学家）所发现与认可。

---

　　[1] 比如 Stanley M. Elkins, *Slavery: A Problem in American Institutional and Intellectual Life*, Chicago: University of Chicago Press, 1959; Eugene D. Genovese, *Roll, Jordan, Roll: The World the Slaves Made*, New York: Pantheon Books, 1974; C. Vann Woodward, "History from Slave Sources", *American Historical Review*, Vol. 79, No. 2, 1974, pp. 470-481; John W. Blassingame, "Using the Testimony of Ex-Slaves: Approaches and Problems", *Journal of Southern History*, Vol. 41, No. 4, 1975, pp. 473-492; Randolph B. Campbell, *An Empire for Slavery: The Peculiar Institution in Texas, 1821-1865*, Baton Rouge: Louisiana State University Press, 1989; Ira Berlin, *Cultivation and Culture: Labor and the Shaping of Slave Life in the Americas*, Charlottesville: University of Virginia Press, 1993; Patricia Morton, *Discovering the Women in Slavery: Emancipating Perspectives on the American Past*, Athens: University of Georgia Press, 1996; Donna J. Spindel, "Assessing Memory: Twentieth-Century Slave Narratives Reconsidered", *Journal of Interdisciplinary History*, Vol. 27, No. 2, 1996, pp. 247-261; Saidiya V. Hartman, *Scenes of Subjection: Terror, Slavery, and Self-Making in Nineteenth-Century America*, London and New York: Oxford University Press, 1997; Jessica Adams, *Wounds of Returning: Race, Memory, and Property on the Post Slavery Plantation*, Chapel Hill: University of North Carolina Press, 2007; Lynette D. Myles, *Female Subjectivity in African American Women's Narratives of Enslavement: Beyond Borders*, New York: Palgrave Macmillan, 2009; Kathleen Fitzgerald, *Recognizing Race and Ethnicity: Power, Privilege, and Inequality*, Boulder: Westview Press, 2014; John Ernest (ed.), *The Oxford Handbook of the African American Slave Narrative*, Oxford and New York: Oxford University Press, 2014.
　　[2] Ronald J. Grele, "Directions for Oral History in the United States", in David K. Dunaway and Willa K. Baum (eds.), *Oral History: An Interdisciplinary Anthology*, Walnut Creek: AltaMira Press, second edition, 1996, p. 64.

五　第二次世界大战中的美国战地史学家与战地访谈

当美国卷入第二次世界大战（World War Ⅱ）之后，军事史学家也将其目光转向战事本身，他们通过与参战军官和普通士兵的战地访谈（field interviewing），[①] 记录和保存了大量宝贵的有关第二次世界大战亲历者的口述资料。当然，这跟美国政府与军队的重视有很大关系，1942 年罗斯福总统通过预算局（Bureau of the Budget）要求政府所有民事与军事部门都要保存有关战时经历的历史记录，其目的不仅是为撰写战后历史（postwar history）做准备，而且也是为出版一系列鼓舞士气的《美军在行动》（*American Forces in Action*）小册子提供素材。其中，美国陆军（United States Army）扮演相当重要的作用，在陆军参谋长乔治·马歇尔（George C. Marshall，1880—1959）将军的直接领导与罗斯福总统的全力支持下，陆军专门设立一个计划负责保存和收集相关文献资料，并且招募许多受过专业训练的历史学家参与其中。不过，他们很快意识到需要通过访谈来补充官方文献记录的不足。[②] 正是如此，在第二次世界大战期间，美国陆军派遣大量历史学家深入战场进行大规模战地访谈，而其中做出重要贡献的是两位著名战地史学家（combat historian）塞缪尔·马歇尔（Samuel L. A. Marshall，1900—1977）与福雷斯

---

① 战地访谈也可以称为战事后访谈（post-combat interviewing, post-action interviewing），简单而言，就是指在每场战事结束之后进行访谈。当然，到底是在战事结束之后多久进行访谈并不统一，也需要视战争具体情况而定，不过一般是在战事结束之后的几小时到几周不等。详细参阅 Frederick Deane Goodwin Williams, *SLAM, the Influence of S. L. A. Marshall on the United States Army*, Fort Monroe: Office of the Command Historian, U. S. Army Training and Doctrine Command, 1994, p. 25.

② Stephen E. Everett, *Oral History: Techniques and Procedures*, Washington: Center of Military History, United States Army, 1992, p. 5; Donald A. Ritchie, *Doing Oral History*, Oxford and New York: Oxford University Press, third edition, 2014, p. 4. 有关美国陆军开展的历史工作可参阅 Stetson Conn, *Historical Work in the United States Army, 1862-1954*, Washington: Center of Military History, United States Army, 1980.

特·波格（Forrest C. Pogue，1912—1996），尤其是马歇尔开启了美国陆军的口述历史事业。①

马歇尔于 1900 年出生于纽约并在加州和德克萨斯州长大，1917 年加入美国陆军并参加第一次世界大战（World War Ⅰ）。在 20 世纪 20 年代初，他先后成为《厄尔巴索先驱报》（*El Paso Herald*）和《底特律新闻》（*The Detroit News*）的新闻记者与编辑。作为记者，他因为报道包括西班牙内战（Spanish Civil War）在内的拉丁美洲和欧洲战事而蜚声全国。其职业生涯中最为耀眼的经历是在第二次世界大战与朝鲜战争（Korean War）期间担任美国陆军作战历史学家主管，并因此出版大约 30 本有关战争的书籍。②

1943 年秋，作为陆军中校（Lieutenant Colonel）的马歇尔以历史学家身份被派往太平洋战区（Pacific theater），负责记录和报道美国陆军第七步兵师（7th Infantry Division）的岛屿战。马歇尔利用自己作为新闻记者的经验发展了他所谓的战地访谈方法，即在每场战事结束之后不久（通常是几个小时内）就召集参战人员进行集体访谈（group interviews），试图尽可能生动和全面地重建战事经过。马歇尔具有一种非凡的提问能力，他能够循序渐进地引导士兵讲述他们在战争中的个人经历与详细信息。他的访谈与叙述风格以人情味（human interest）和战场现实主义而著称，因此其方法被所有战区的历史学家所采用。据记录，马歇尔的首次访谈是在发生于 1943 年 11 月 20—23 日的吉尔伯特群岛（Gilbert Islands）马金环礁（Markin Atoll）的一场激烈夜战之后，他采访了美国陆军第 165 步兵师第 3 营

---

① Arnold Kransdorff, *Corporate DNA*: *Using Organizational Memory to Improve Poor Decision-Making*, Burlington: Gower Publishing, Ltd., 2006, p. 136; "D-Day: Diaries of Forrest C. Pogue", in Priscilla Roberts (ed.), *Voices of World War Ⅱ*: *Contemporary Accounts of Daily Life*, Santa Barbara: ABC-CLIO, LLC, 2012, pp. 80-81; Mark Cave, "Introduction: What Remains: Reflections on Crisis Oral History", in Mark Cave and Stephen M. Sloan (eds.), *Listening on the Edge*: *Oral History in the Aftermath of Crisis*, Oxford and New York: Oxford University Press, 2014, pp. 6-7.

② "S. L. A. Marshall", from Wikipedia, https://en.wikipedia.org/wiki/S. L. A. _ Marshall, 2015 年 8 月 12 日访问。有关他的回忆录可参阅 S. L. A. Marshall, *Bringing Up the Rear*, *A Memoir*, San Rafael: Presidio Press, 1979.

（3rd Battalion，165th Infantry Division）的参战人员。几个月之后，马歇尔利用相同方法采访了参与夸贾林环礁战役（The Battle of Kwajalein Atoll，发生于 1944 年 1 月 31 日—2 月 3 日）的第七步兵师，为其后来出版《岛屿胜利》（*Island Victory*）搜集了大量宝贵一手资料。1944 年马歇尔带领一批历史学家赶赴欧洲战区继续战地访谈工作，在 1944 年 6 月 6 日诺曼底登陆日（D-Day）之后，他随即奔赴诺曼底采访美国第 82 和第 101 空降师（82d and 101st Airborne Divisions）的参战人员。这些访谈资料成为空降突袭的基本记录，因为分布广泛和困难重重的空降部队很少保存文字记录。六个月之后，在坦克大决战（The Battle of the Bulge，又称"突出部战役"）中，马歇尔与他的助手采访了在比利时巴斯托涅（Bastogne）的第101 空降师及其附属部队的参战人员，而他们共同搜集的口述历史与官方记录也成为后来马歇尔撰写《巴斯托涅》（*Bastogne*）的核心资料。①

在后来的朝鲜战争与越南战争（Vietnam War）期间，他也利用相同方法进行广泛的战地访谈。尽管马歇尔的战地访谈方法以及由此搜集的口述历史资料与出版的作品受到一部分学者的质疑与批判，② 但是其贡献还是无可置疑的。有学者指出，马歇尔和其他战地史学家的工作巩固了军事史在美国陆军当中的地位，为军事史（尤其是口述历史）的发展提供了制度

---

① 详细内容可参阅 S. L. A. Marshall，*Island Victory：The Battle of Kwajalein Atoll*，Washington：Infantry Journal，1945；S. L. A. Marshall（assisted by John G. Westover and A. Joseph Webber），*Bastogne：The Story of the First Eight Days in Which the 101st Airborne Division Was Closed Within the Ring of German Forces*，Washington：Infantry Journal Press，1946；Richard A. Hunt，"The Military History Detachment in the Field"，in John E. Jessup，Jr. & Robert W. Coakley（eds.），*A Guide to the Study and Use of Military History*，Washington：Center of Military History，United States Army，1979，p. 313；Robert K. Wright，Jr.，"Clio in Combat：The Evolution of the Military History Detachment"，*The Army Historian*，No. 6，1985，p. 3；Stephen E. Everett，*Oral History：Techniques and Procedures*，Washington：Center of Military History，United States Army，1992，pp. 5-6；Joseph G. Dawson Ⅲ，"Foreword"，in S. L. A. Marshall，*Island Victory：The Battle of Kwajalein Atoll*，Lincoln：University of Nebraska Press，2010，pp. xxi-xxv；Jerome Corsi，*No Greater Valor：The Siege of Bastogne and the Miracle That Sealed Allied Victory*，Nashville：Thomas Nelson，2014，pp. xxi-xxii.

② Roger J. Spiller，"S. L. A. Marshall and the Ratio of Fire"，*Royal United Services Institution Journal*，Vol. 133，No. 4，1988，pp. 63-71；Frederic Smoler，"The Secret of the Soldiers Who Didn't Shoot"，*American Heritage*，Vol. 40，No. 2，1989，pp. 36-45.

支持，同时通过借鉴有关战事性质的重要经验教训为陆军提供了一种有用的历史。[①] 需要指出的是，他不仅为其他人做了大量的口述历史工作，在去世两年前，他也作为受访者接受别人的口述历史访谈，目前这些口述历史资料保存在德克萨斯大学厄尔巴索分校口述历史研究所（Institute of Oral History，University of Texas at El Paso）。[②]

　　另外一位在第二次世界大战期间对战地访谈工作做出重要贡献的军事历史学家是曾为马歇尔下属的波格，更值一提的是，他为推动战后美国现代口述史学运动的发展颇有贡献，更有学者称其为"口述历史先驱"[③]。波格于 1912 年出生于肯塔基州，先后获得莫瑞州立学院（Murray State College）和肯塔基大学（University of Kentucky）学士和硕士学位（欧洲史方向）。1933 年他回到莫瑞州立学院任教，三年之后申请到克拉克大学（Clark University）攻读欧洲史博士学位并于 1939 年获得学位，还于 1937—1938 年在法国巴黎大学（University of Paris）学习国际关系和外交学。波格于 1942 年加入美国陆军，随后被指派到陆军第二军团（The Second Army）总部协助历史学家贝尔·威利（Bell I. Wiley，1906—1980）撰写该军团的训练历史。经威利推荐，波格于 1944 年春成为战地史学家小组成员并随诺曼底登陆部队赶赴英国，而他也是参与采访诺曼底登陆士兵的三位历史学家之一。在诺曼底登陆日当天，波格就在一只医疗船上待命，第二天开始正式

---

　　① G. Kurt Piehler, "Veterans Tell Their Stories and Why Historians and Others Listened", in G. Kurt Piehler and Sidney Pash（eds.）, *The United States and the Second World War*: *New Perspectives on Diplomacy*, *War*, *and the Home Front*, New York: Fordham University Press, 2010, p. 217.

　　② Interview with S. L. A. Marshall by Richard Estrada, July 5, 7, 9, 11 and 19, 1975, "Interview No. 181", Institute of Oral History, University of Texas at El Paso, http://digitalcommons. utep. edu/interviews/181/, 2015 年 8 月 12 日访问。

　　③ 有学者评论指出，尽管马歇尔最后成为陆军准将（Brigadier General）而在陆军当中具有一定的影响力，不过身为其下属之一的波格却成为口述历史领域的一个更为重要的人物。详细参阅 Edward M. Coffman, "Talking about War: Reflections on Doing Oral History and Military History", *Journal of American History*, Vol. 87, No. 2, 2000, p. 583; Edward M. Coffman, "Memories of Forrest C. Pogue, Oral History Pioneer and One of Kentucky's Greatest Historians", *The Register of the Kentucky Historical Society*, Vol. 104, No. 3/4, 2006, pp. 675-684.

采访参与登陆战的受伤士兵，不过直到 6 月 8 日他才登岸继续访谈工作。在 1945 年 5 月欧战结束之前，除 1944 年夏天在巴黎从事短暂的访谈编辑工作之外，波格一直随美军行动，其间经历许特根森林战役（The Huertgen Forest Battle）、坦克大决战以及苏联红军与美军易北河（Elber River）会师等重大历史事件并进行大量访谈工作。欧战结束之后，他又被重新召回巴黎整理他们所搜集的访谈资料并撰写欧洲战区的历史。尽管他于 1945 年 10 月退役，不过还是以平民历史学家（civilian historian）身份被美国陆军部（Department of the Army）雇用，在 1945—1952 年期间主要致力于撰写与研究盟国远征军最高统帅部（Supreme Headquarters，Allied Expeditionary Force）的历史。当然，除了利用官方文献记录之外，波格还是积极发挥他的优势，相继采访了包括伯纳德·蒙哥马利（Bernard Law Montgomery，1887—1976）和夏尔·戴高乐（Charles Marie de Gaulle，1890—1970）在内的许多英法指挥官。而在 1952—1954 年期间，他以契约历史学家（contract historian）身份加入美国陆军作战研究办公室（Operations Research Office），并被指派到位于德国海德堡（Heidelberg）的总部担任作战研究分析师。①

波格的战地访谈以及据此撰写的有关战事经历的作品之所以如此具有

---

① 详细内容可参阅 Forrest C. Pogue, *The Supreme Command*, Washington：Office of the Chief of Military History, Department of the Army, 1954；"Forrest C. Pogue Oral History Pioneer", *Oral History Association Newsletter*, Vol. 11, No. 3, Summer 1977, p. 1；H. Lew Wallace, "Forrest C. Pogue：A Biographical Sketch", *The Filson Club History Quarterly*, Vol. 60, No. 3, 1986, pp. 373-402；James Russell Harris, "Profile：Oral History Pioneer Dr. Forrest C. Pogue", *Bulletin of the Kentucky Historical Society*, Vol. 14, 1988, p. 4；Forrest C. Pogue and Holly C. Shulman, "Forrest C. Pogue and the Birth of Public History in the Army", *The Public Historian*, Vol. 15, No. 1, 1993, pp. 27-46；Wolfgang Saxon, "Forrest C. Pogue, 84；Wrote an Epic Study of General Marshall", *New York Times*, October 8, 1996；Bart Barnes, "Forrest C. Pogue Dies at 84；Army Historian, Biographer", *The Washington Post*, October 8, 1996；Donald A. Ritchie, "Remembering Forrest Pogue", *Oral History Association Newsletter*, Vol. 31, No. 1, Winter 1997, pp. 7-8；Forrest C. Pogue, *Pogue's War：Diaries of a WWII Combat Historian*, Lexington：University Press of Kentucky, 2001.

吸引力，这完全得益于他总是试图能够在战争第一线采访参战士兵，正如他所说："美国陆军需要一部活生生的历史和一位活生生的历史学家。"也正是因为他的"前线访谈"（front line interviewing），波格因此获得青铜勋章（Bronze Star）和英勇十字勋章（French Croix de Guerre）。[1] 而美国当代著名历史学家、传记作家斯蒂芬·安布罗斯（Stephen E. Ambrose，1936—2002）也曾给予高度评价："与他的同事一起，他们创作了有关一场战争书写的最完美的历史，正如马歇尔将军所希望的。"[2]

综上所述，马歇尔、波格与其他战地史学家在第二次世界大战期间搜集了大量有价值的原始资料，它们详细生动地记录了战争进程以及参战人员的心理感受与自我反思。据统计，就数量而言，到第二次世界大战结束为止，单单欧洲战区历史学家所搜集的访谈资料就达到2000多份。尽管这些访谈资料的质量各有差异，而学者在利用时也需要相当谨慎，不过毫无疑问它们仍然是历史学家所能获得的有关第二次世界大战的最为宝贵的信息来源之一。[3] 而对于美国口述史学来说，他们为战后口述历史方法在军事史研究当中的迅速发展奠定坚实基础，而这些发展也进一步提升了口述史学在美国的学术声誉与认可度。[4]

---

① H. Lew Wallace, "Forrest C. Pogue: A Biographical Sketch", *The Filson Club History Quarterly*, Vol. 60, No. 3, 1986, p. 384.

② Stephen E. Ambrose, "Foreword", in Forrest C. Pogue, *Pogue's War: Diaries of a WWII Combat Historian*, Lexington: University Press of Kentucky, 2001, p. ix.

③ Stephen E. Everett, *Oral History: Techniques and Procedures*, Washington: Center of Military History, United States Army, 1992, p. 7.

④ Wendell P. Holbrook, "Oral History and the Nascent Historiography for Africa and World War II: A Focus on Ghana", *International Journal of Oral History*, Vol. 3, No. 3, 1982, pp. 148-166; Roger Horwitz, "Oral History and the Story of America and World War II", *Journal of American History*, Vol. 82, No. 2, 1995, pp. 617-624; Edward M. Coffman, "Talking about War: Reflections on Doing Oral History and Military History", *Journal of American History*, Vol. 87, No. 2, 2000, pp. 582-592; Stephen J. Lofgren, "The Status of Oral History in the Army: Expanding a Tradition", *Oral History Review*, Vol. 30, No. 2, 2003, pp. 81-97.

六 阿兰·内文斯与美国现代口述史学的诞生

之所以将内文斯于 1948 年创建哥大口述历史研究室作为美国现代口述史学诞生的标志，很大程度上是因为该研究室是美国乃至国际上首个正式以口述历史命名的收集、保存与研究机构。[①] 以下将重点介绍与分析内文斯与哥大口述历史研究室的创建过程及其早期发展。

内文斯于 1890 年出生于伊利诺伊州，在获得伊利诺伊大学（University of Illinois）英语学士与硕士学位之后，从 1913 年开始在《纽约晚邮报》（*New York Evening Post*）、《纽约太阳报》（*New York Sun*）和《纽约世界报》（*New York World*）担任新闻记者与编辑。他从 1928 年开始在哥伦比亚大学历史系任教，并于 1939 年荣升为迪威特·克林顿历史学讲座教授（DeWitt Clinton Professor of History），[②] 1958 年于哥大退休之后担任亨廷顿图书馆（Huntington Library）资深研究员。此外，他还是 1959 年美国历史协会（American History Association）主席和著名历史通俗杂志《美国遗

---

① 瓦拉利·姚（Valerie Raleigh Yow）认为它是第一个有组织的口述历史计划，而里奇称其为"第一座现代口述历史档案馆"（Oral History Archives），并且尤其强调是对录音口述历史访谈（taped-recorded oral history interviews）的系统收集与档案保存。详细参阅 Valerie Raleigh Yow, *Recording Oral History: A Practical Guide for Social Scientists*, Thousand Oaks: Sage Publications, 1994, p. 3; Donald A. Ritchie, *Doing Oral History*, New York: Twayne Publishers, 1995, p. 3; Donald A. Ritchie, "Oral History", in David Herman, Manfred Jahn, and Marie-Laure Ryan (eds.), *Routledge Encyclopedia of Narrative Theory*, London and New York: Routledge, 2005, p. 411. 其他类似观点可参阅 Richard D. Challener and John M. Fento, "Recent Past Comes Alive in Dulles 'Oral History'", *Princeton Alumni Weekly*, March 14, 1967, 14; Charles T. Morrissey, "Oral History and Local History: Opportunities for Librarians", *Journal of Library History*, Vol. 4, No. 4, 1969, p. 341; Paul Thompson, "Oral History in North America", *Oral History*, Vol. 3, No. 1, 1975, p. 27; Robert Perks and Alistair Thomson, "Critical Developments: Introduction", in Robert Perks and Alistair Thomson (eds.), *The Oral History Reader*, London and New York: Routledge, 1998, p. 1.

② 有很多资料认为内文斯荣升为迪威特·克林顿历史学讲座教授的时间是 1931 年，不过通过比较各种资料的合理性，笔者更加倾向于是 1939 年，尤其是哥大官方网站也认为是 1939 年。详细参阅 "Allan Nevins", http://c250.columbia.edu/c250_ celebrates/remarkable_ columbians/allan_ nevins.html, 2015 年 8 月 13 日访问。

产》（*American Heritage*）创始人之一。作为美国著名的历史学家、新闻记者与传记作家，内文斯总共出版60多本书，其作品以美国内战史、经济史与美国政治和商业人物传记著称，其中两本传记《克利夫兰传》（*Grover Cleveland: A Study in Courage*，1932）和《菲什传》（*Hamilton Fish: The Inner History of the Grant Administration*，1936）都获得普利策奖（*Pulitzer Prize*）。① 而就口述史学来说，他因为于1948年创建哥大口述历史研究室（并于1948—1956年间担任首任主任）而被公认为是真正意义上的"口述历史之父"②，尽管有许多学者将口述史学的起源追溯得越来越早。

如上所述，莫里斯和斯塔尔都曾推测内文斯之所以将他在哥大的访谈

① 有关内文斯的生平经历与学术研究，可参阅 "Nevins Retiring from Columbia: 8-Year-Old Historian to Go to Huntington Library as Senior Researcher"，*New York Times*，May 13，1958；Louis M. Starr，"Allan Nevins at Eighty"，*Columbia Library Columns*，Vol. 20，No. 1，1970，pp. 3-9；Allan Nevins，"Historian, Dies; Winner of Two Pulitzer Prizes"，*New York Times*，March 6，1971；Ellen Hoffman，"Historian Allan Nevins, 80, Dies"，*The Washington Post*，March 6，1971；"Allan Nevins, Honorary Chairman of OHA, Dies at 80"，*Oral History Association Newsletter*，Vol. 5，No. 2，April 1971，p. 1，11；Donald F. Tingley，"Allan Nevins: A Reminiscence"，*Journal of the Illinois State Historical Society*，Vol. 66，No. 2，1973，pp. 177-86；Ray Allen Billington（ed.），*Allan Nevins on History*，New York: Scribner，1975；Gerald L. Fetner，*Immersed in Great Affairs: Allan Nevins and the Heroic Age of American History*，Albany: State University of New York Press，2004；"Allan Nevins"，from Wikipedia，https://en. wikipedia. org/wiki/Allan_ Nevins，2015年8月13日访问。

② Allan Nevins，"The Uses of Oral History"，in Elizabeth I. Dixon and James V. Mink（eds.），*Oral History at Arrowhead: The Proceedings of the First National Colloquium on Oral History*，Los Angeles: Oral History Association，1967，p. 25（斯塔尔在1966年美国口述历史协会会议上介绍内文斯时就称其为"现代口述历史之父"）；Donald H. Mugridge，"Book Review: The Oral History Collection of Columbia University"，*American Archivist*，Vol. 24，No. 1，1961，p. 93；Louis Shores，"Epitome"，*Journal of Library History*，Vol. 2，No. 1，1967，p. 6；Richard D. Curtiss，Gary L. Shumway and Shirley E. Stephenson（eds.），*A Guide for Oral History Programs*，Fullerton: Oral History Program，California State University，Fullerton，1973，p. 8；Arlene Weber，"Oral History: Mining the Nuggets of the Past or, Oral History Observed"，*Journal of Library History*，Vol. 6，No. 3，1971，p. 277；Allan Nevins，"Oral History: How and Why It Was Born, The Uses of Oral History"，in David K. Dunaway and Willa K. Baum（eds.），*Oral History: An Interdisciplinary Anthology*，Nashville: American Association for State and Local History，1984，p. 27（这里是两位主编对于内文斯的评价）；J. C. Hurewitz，"The Education of J. C. Hurewitz"，in Thomas Naff（ed.），*Paths to the Middle East: Ten Scholars Look Back*，Albany: State University of New York Press，1993，p. 60；Sandy Polishuk，*Sticking to the Union: An Oral History of the Life and Times of Julia Ruuttila*，New York: Palgrave Macmillan，2003，p. 8. 内文斯好友、美国著名历史学家亨利·康马格（Henry Steele Commager）认为内文斯的最大贡献在于创造（复兴）和实现口述历史的现代化、系统化和制度化。详细参阅 Henry Steele Commager，"Allan Nevins"，*American Historical Review*，Vol. 77，No. 3，1972，p. 871.

计划称为"口述历史"有可能受到《纽约客》杂志上有关古尔德报道文章的影响。不过,事实上,内文斯有关通过大规模访谈计划为当前和未来学者提供研究资料的想法可以追溯到 1931 年,当时他正在撰写美国总统格罗弗·克利夫兰(Grove Cleveland, 1837—1908)的传记。① 内文斯为没有人采访克利夫兰总统和他的同僚而感到痛惜,他们当中的大部分人到去世也没有为历史学家留下任何类型的遗产。内文斯曾回忆指出,当他看到《纽约时报》等报章上的讣告栏时就有一种感叹,"人们的记忆被完全遗忘,它们是丢失得多么彻底"②。在 1935 年前后,他与哥伦比亚大学法学院教授阿道夫·贝利(Adolf A. Berle, 1895—1971)和商学院教授埃德温·盖伊(Edwin F. Gay, 1867—1946)等朋友讨论其想法是否可行和如何实施。③ 而在 1938 年出版的《通向历史之路》序言中,内文斯首次公开提出开展口述历史访谈的呼吁。他认为要让美国的历史研究变得富有生命力和活力必须做到两点,除创办一份大众历史杂志(月刊)之外,还应该"创立某个组织,从那些引领重要生活的活生生的美国人的唇边和文件(lips and papers)中系统地获得一种有关他们过去 60 年来参与政治、经济与文化生活的更为完整的记录"。他继续强调,缺乏这些可能很容易创建和应当相当成功的机构本身就是令人遗憾的,而这种遗憾也是对历史普遍漠视的一种象征。④

　　需要指出的是,内文斯之所以强调通过访谈来记录和保存美国重要人士的生活经历,很大程度上是因为他担心随着电话、汽车和飞机等通讯和

---

① Allan Nevins, *Grover Cleveland: A Study in Courage*, New York: Dodd, Mead & Company, 1932.

② Allan Nevins, "The Uses of Oral History", in Elizabeth I. Dixon and James V. Mink (eds.), *Oral History at Arrowhead: The Proceedings of the First National Colloquium on Oral History*, Los Angeles: Oral History Association, 1967, p. 31.

③ Doyce B. Nunis, Jr., "Oral History and the History of Technology", *Technology and Culture*, Vol. 4, No. 2, 1963, p. 150; Louis Starr, "Oral History", *Encyclopedia of Library and Information Sciences* (Vol. 20), New York: Marcel Dekker, 1977, pp. 444-445.

④ Allan Nevins, *The Gateway to History*, New York: D. C. Heath and Company, 1938, pp. iv-v.

交通技术的发展以及生活节奏的日益加快，原本可以通过信件和日记等形式所保存的信息在不断丢失，这也是内文斯所说的技术变迁所造成的历史记录的重大缺漏。[1] 当然，需要强调的是，技术发展同时也带来书写记录（written record）的不断增加，可是这些公共记录（public documents）的价值不断受到历史学家的质疑。正如美国著名历史学家小阿瑟·斯莱辛格（Arthur M. Schlesinger, Jr., 1917—2007）所说："作为一个权利问题，对于官方文件应该立即向学者开放得越来越多的坚决主张导致书写记录的稀释和歪曲。因为担心未来十年以后的研究生、公职人员不愿意写下他们某些行动背后的真实原因。"[2] 正是如此，内文斯等历史学家积极倡导通过口述历史方法来记录和保存重要历史当事人与亲历者的即将逝去的历史记忆，以弥补个人书写记录的日益缺失。

不过直到十年后，内文斯的理想才终于成为现实，在哥大班克罗夫特基金（Bancroft Fund）的支持下，他率先开启这项影响深远的现代口述史学试验（oral history experiment）。1948 年 5 月 18 日，内文斯带着他的研究生助理迪恩·艾伯森（Dean Albertson）帮助他进行第一次访谈，采访对象是纽约公民领袖乔治·麦卡内尼（George McAneny, 1869—1953）。由于没有录音设备，整个访谈过程由艾伯森以速记方法记录，访谈结束之后就立即回去凭借笔录和记忆将访谈内容用打字机打印出来。通过这种相当费劲

---

① Meyer Berger, *Meyer Berger's New York*, New York, Random House, 1960, p. 245; Columbia University, Oral History Research Office, *The Oral History Collection of Columbia University*, New York: Oral History Research Office, 1964, pp. 9-10; Ray Allen Billington (ed.), *Allan Nevins on History*, New York: Scribner, 1975, p. xxiii; David L. Nass, "MHS Collections: An Interview from the Oral History Collection of the Southwest Minnesota Historical Center Recollections of Rural Revolt", *Minnesota History*, Vol. 44, No. 8, 1975, p. 304; Trevor Lummis, *Listening to History: The Authenticity of Oral Evidence*, London: Hutchinson Education, 1987, p. 17. 内文斯甚至认为名人们不愿意留下历史记录的原因可能是工作压力、谦逊或仅仅是懒惰。详细参阅 "History Recorded by Wire and Film: Current 'History in the Making' Documented at Columbia", *New York Times*, January 13, 1950; "History on a Sound Track", *New York Times*, January 14, 1950.

② Arthur Schlesinger, Jr., "On the Writing of Contemporary History", *The Atlantic Monthly*, Vol. 219, No. 3, March 1967, p. 71.

的方式，到 1948 年底，哥大口述历史研究室总共完成三位受访者的口述历史访谈工作，并以自传（memoir）形式进行整理和编辑。而录音技术的发展可以说拯救和推动了口述历史研究室刚刚兴起的口述历史事业，据记录，它在创建之后不久的 1949 年 1 月 21 日的一次与勒恩德·汉德（Learned Hand，1872—1961）法官的口述历史访谈中首次使用钢丝录音机（wire recorder）。而在几个月之后，内文斯和艾伯森又很快以刚刚上市的磁带录音机（tape recorder）代替笨重的钢丝录音机。同时加上录音转录设备的应用，使口述历史访谈者与整理者的工作任务不断减轻。正是如此，口述历史研究室围绕着在美国历史上扮演重要角色的知名人物进行一系列访谈工作，其受访对象来自政治、经济、医学、法律、社会福利与文化艺术等众多领域，其中包括美国前国务卿亨利·史汀生（Henry L. Stimson，1867—1950）和班布里奇·科尔比（Bainbridge Colby，1869—1950）、纽约州前州长赫伯特·莱曼（Herbert H. Lehman，1878—1963）、美国外交官詹姆斯·杰勒德（James W. Gerard，1867—1951）、洛克菲勒基金会（Rockefeller Foundation）前主席雷蒙德·福斯迪克（Raymond B. Fosdick，1883—1972）、美国社会学家霍默·福克斯（Homer Folks，1867—1963）和美国神经学家约瑟夫·柯林斯（Joseph Collins，1866-1950）等。①

除上述以个别人物生平访谈为基础的口述自传模式之外，口述历史研究室还发展了一系列主题性的特别口述历史计划。这些早期计划所涉及的主题包括政治与外交事务、广播电视业、福特汽车公司、石油钻探、森林与木材业、医学、法律、音乐、文学和建筑学等。其中第一个特别计划是

----

① Dean Albertson, "History in the Deep-Freeze: The Story of Columbia's Oral History Project", *Columbia Library Columns*, Vol. 2, No. 2, 1953, pp. 2-11; Allan B. Holbert, "Personal History on Tape", *Senior Scholastic* (Teachers Edition), Vol. 65, 1960, pp. 6-T; "Columbia Seeks Million for Oral History Project", *New York Times*, June 23, 1963; "The Oral History Collection, Columbia University", *Wilson Library Bulletin*, Vol. 38, 1964, p. 716; Louis M. Starr, "Oral History: Problems and Prospects", *Advances in Librarianship*, Vol. 2, 1971, p. 279; Willa K. Baum, "Oral History in the United States", *Oral History*, Vol. 1, No. 3, 1972, p. 17.

于 1950 年启动的 "广播先驱者计划"（Radio Pioneers Project），该计划由当时广播先驱者全国组织——二十年俱乐部（The Twenty Year Club，1957年更名为 The Broadcast Pioneers）委托并提供经费支持，内文斯聘任其同事弗兰克·希尔（Frank Ernest Hill，1888—1969）担任计划主任并负责访谈工作，对广播员、节目导演、技术员、监管与行政主管等行业先驱（后来也扩展至电视领域）进行广泛访谈。该计划一直持续到 1974 年，整理的访谈抄本资料达到 4795 页。① 而第二个具有深远影响的特别计划是内文斯与福特汽车公司档案馆（Ford Motor Company Archives）亨利·埃德蒙兹（Henry E. Edmonds，1912—1982）于 1951 年共同发起的 "福特汽车公司档案馆口述历史计划"（Ford Motor Company Archives Oral History Project），该计划最初主要是为内文斯和希尔撰写有关福特公司的三卷本书收集资料。② 不过，该计划后来发展成为一个大型的工业口述历史计划，由哥大口述历史研究室的欧文·邦巴德（Owen W. Bombard，1922—2007）负责主持。到 1958 年为止，该计划对公司创始人亨利·福特（Henry Ford，1863—1947）的家人、朋友、同事以及公司发展重要参与者等 434 人进行采访，访谈抄本资料总共达到 2.6 万页左右。与其他计划不同的是，该计划所收集的所有口述历史资料并不是保存在哥大口述历史研究室，而是通过专门成立口述历史部（Oral History Section）保存在福特汽车公司档案馆。正是如此，该计划也被斯塔尔看成口述历史在哥伦比亚大学之外的另

---

① "Radio Study: Progress Reported by Hill", *Broadcasting*, November 19, 1951, p. 62; Michele Hilmes（ed.）, *NBC: America's Network*, Berkeley: University of California Press, 2007, pp. 313-314; Shawn Gary VanCour, "The Sounds of 'radio': Aesthetic Formations of 1920s American Broadcasting", Ph. D. dissertation, University of Wisconsin-Madison, 2008, p. 77; Columbia Center for Oral History, "Radio Pioneers Project: Oral History, 1950-1974", https://clio. columbia. edu/catalog/4072581, 2015 年 8 月 14 日访问。

② Allan Nevins and Frank Ernest Hill, *Ford: The Times, The Man, The Company*, New York: Charles Scribner's Sons, 1954; Allan Nevins and Frank Ernest Hill, *Ford: Expansion and Challenge, 1915-1933*, New York: Charles Scribner's Sons, 1957; Allan Nevins and Frank Ernest Hill, *Ford: Decline and Rebirth, 1933-1962*, New York: Charles Scribner's Sons, 1963.

外一个地方首次立足。①

总体而言,这些特别计划发展很快,据统计,到 1960 年就已经达到 15 个,而到 1964 年则迅速增加到 38 个。② 之所以选择这些计划,很大程度上是出于经费考虑,因为这些计划所在的公司和个人愿意提供经费支持。正是如此,这些特别计划的访谈对象也大都集中于相关领域的精英人物。

尽管口述历史研究室在短短十多年间就取得相当大的进展与成绩,不过它的创建与运作并非像内文斯于 1938 年所说的那样容易,其早期发展可谓困难重重,甚至差一点被解散。概括而言,其困难与挑战主要来自两个方面:(1)经费紧张与筹措压力;(2)哥大对口述历史研究室的认可度不高。如上所述,口述历史研究室的创建经费来自班克罗夫特基金的支持,该基金是内文斯的朋友弗雷德里克·班克罗夫特(Frederic Bancroft, 1860—1945)在 1945 年去世后捐赠给哥大用于支持历史研究的,其总数是 200 万美元。③ 班克罗夫特毕业于哥大(获历史学博士学位)并在哥大担任一年讲师,后于 1888—1892 年担任美国国务院(State Department)图书管理员。他哥哥埃德加·班克罗夫特(Edgar A. Bancroft, 1857—1925)于 1925 年去世之后便将所有遗产留给他,而随着班克罗夫特的逐渐年老,当时内文斯和同事兼好友康马格就积极劝说班克罗夫特将遗产捐赠给哥大,这样就有机会帮助他实现开展口述历史计划的理想。康马格还曾用"诱

---

① Owen W. Bombard, *Speaking of Yesterday: An Explanation of the Ford Motor Company Archives Oral History Project*, Dearborn: The Archives, 1952; Henry E. Edmunds, "The Ford Motor Company Archives", *American Archivist*, Vol. 15, No. 2, 1952, pp. 99-104; Louis Starr, "Oral History", *Encyclopedia of Library and Information Sciences*(Vol. 20), New York: Marcel Dekker, 1977, p. 445; Ford R. Bryan, *Clara: Mrs. Henry Ford*, Dearborn: Ford Books, 2001, p. 13. 目前这些资料都可以在线浏览和查询,详细参阅 Benson Ford Research Center, "Ford Reminiscences Oral Histories", http://cdm15889. contentdm. oclc. org/cdm/landingpage/collection/p15889coll2, 2015 年 8 月 14 日访问。

② Columbia University, Oral History Research Office, *The Oral History Collection of Columbia University*, New York: Oral History Research Office, 1960 and 1964.

③ 有关班克罗夫特的研究可参阅 Jacob Ernest Cooke, *Frederic Bancroft, Historian*, Norman: University of Oklahoma Press, 1957.

骗"这个词来形容当时他们所采用的游说方法，尽管班克罗夫特并没有当面明确答复他们，不过在他去世之后，内文斯和康马格发现 200 万美元都已经捐赠给哥大。显然，这其中跟他们两位的努力是分不开的，因为当时还有其他机构也不断向班克罗夫特游说。内文斯坦言，当时他就想着如何利用这些捐赠，其中之一就是要创建口述历史研究室。①

不过令内文斯始料不及的是，班克罗夫特基金只向口述历史计划提供 3000 美元的启动经费。至于后续经费如何拨付并不清楚，但是从相关资料可以发现该基金支持口述历史的经费只占捐赠总数的极小部分。据艾柏森回忆，在 1953 年年初，口述历史研究室获得班克罗夫特基金的原始津贴维持在 9000 美元。而面对庞大的支出，艾柏森也直言经费筹措是研究室面临的最大障碍。② 正是如此，他们除开展上述特别计划获得委托服务之外，还需要积极申请各种基金会支持。据记录，1949 年研究室从卢修斯·李奈特基金会（Lucius N. Littauer Foundation）获得一项 6000 美元的资助，随后分别于 1951 年和 1952 年获得奥多明尼昂基金会（Old Dominion Foundation）和威廉·惠特尼基金会（William C. Whitney Foundation）的资助。③ 尽管如此，口述历史研究室的经费运行还是面临赤字，而哥大行政主管也没有提供相应的支持与帮助。据斯塔尔回忆，在 1954 年的某一天，哥大副校长和财务主管曾召集口述历史研究室举行会议，而在内文斯慷慨激昂的恳请下，哥大同意暂缓一年解散。而最后挽救口述历史研究室的是纽约卡内基基金会（Carnegie Corporation of New York），该基金会同意从 1955 年

---

① Allan Nevins, "The Uses of Oral History", in Elizabeth I. Dixon and James V. Mink (eds.), *Oral History at Arrowhead: The Proceedings of the First National Colloquium on Oral History*, Los Angeles: Oral History Association, 1967, pp. 25-26; Neil Jumonville, *Henry Steele Commager: Midcentury Liberalism and the History of the Present*, Chapel Hill: University of North Carolina Press, 1999, p. 60.

② Dean Albertson, "History in the Deep-Freeze: The Story of Columbia's Oral History Project", *Columbia Library Columns*, Vol. 2, No. 2, 1953, pp. 10-11.

③ "History Recorded by Wire and Film: Current 'History in the Making' Documented at Columbia", *New York Times*, January 13, 1950; Columbia University, Oral History Research Office, *The Oral History Collection of Columbia University*, New York: Oral History Research Office, 1960, p. 6.

开始提供一项为期 5 年的资助。① 作为口述历史研究室的创始人与首任主任，内文斯深感经费问题对于口述历史发展的重要性，在 1966 年举行的美国第一届全国口述史学会议上，内文斯发言首先谈的就是经费问题。正如他所说："我们开始于经费资助，但有时候也会因为没有经费而结束。"②他向与会者讲述了口述历史研究室的经费筹措经验，这对于当时正在蓬勃兴起的其他美国口述历史机构或计划来说具有相当重要的借鉴意义。

至于第二点，艾柏森曾回忆指早期的口述历史研究室在哥大是一个"问题小孩"（problem child），③ 而斯塔尔也指出它在校园中总是遭受各种怀疑、冷漠乃至偶尔的敌意。概括而言，斯塔尔主要列举了以下几个方面：（1）年轻的教授尽管不愿意冒犯内文斯，可是并不理会内文斯希望他们担任访谈员的要求；（2）受薪访谈员难以留用，一般 1 年或 2 年就会离任，斯塔尔坦言最初之所以加入研究室也主要是为了迎合身为其导师的内文斯教授；（3）当时的哥大历史系主任认为口述历史完全是一项浪费时间和金钱的工作；（4）考虑到经费赤字问题，大学行政主管曾考虑解散研究室；（5）哥大图书馆管理人员并不认可口述历史资料的独特价值，尤其是在 1959 年出版的《哥大图书馆手稿收藏》（*Manuscript Collections in the Columbia Libraries*）中，只是将研究室的口述历史收藏简略地描述为两份模糊的通信集。④

---

① Louis M. Starr, "Oral History: Problems and Prospects", *Advances in Librarianship*, Vol. 2, 1971, p. 279.

② Allan Nevins, "The Uses of Oral History", in Elizabeth I. Dixon and James V. Mink (eds.), *Oral History at Arrowhead: The Proceedings of the First National Colloquium on Oral History*, Los Angeles: Oral History Association, 1967, p. 25.

③ Dean Albertson, "History in the Deep-Freeze: The Story of Columbia's Oral History Project", *Columbia Library Columns*, Vol. 2, No. 2, 1953, p. 6.

④ Louis M. Starr, "Oral History: Problems and Prospects", *Advances in Librarianship*, Vol. 2, 1971, pp. 279-281; "The Oral History Project of Columbia University", *American Heritage*, Vol. 6, No. 4, 1954, pp. 73-84; Louis M. Starr, "History, Warm", *Columbia University Forum*, Vol. 5, No. 4, 1962, pp. 27-30; Louis M. Starr, "Up to Now", in Gould P. Colman (ed.), *The Third National Colloquium on Oral History*, New York: Oral History Association, 1969, pp. 1-3.

基于上述偏见与不理解，口述历史研究室意识到需要让学校各方乃至更为广泛的学术界充分了解其工作价值。于是，时任研究室主任斯塔尔（任期为 1956—1980 年）决定编辑出版一本能够全面反映研究室口述历史收藏的详细目录。同时，又因为得到卡内基基金会为期 5 年的新一轮资助，最终促使《哥伦比亚大学口述历史收藏》于 1960 年正式出版。而在 20 世纪 70 年代之前，研究室还于 1964 年出版新版《哥伦比亚大学口述历史收藏》，此外还分别于 1962 年、1966 年和 1968 年出版《哥伦比亚大学口述历史收藏（补编）》。[①] 这些目录可以说极大地提升了研究室的知名度，而保存在哥大图书馆特藏部的口述历史收藏也很快成为该部中最为频繁使用的资源，尤其是越来越多的学者在他们的研究成果中大量利用这些口述历史资料。事实上，从 20 世纪 50 年代初开始，一些著名学者就已经开始在公开出版物中利用这些资料。除上述内文斯和希尔有关福特及其公司的 3 卷本书之外，其中比较有代表性的还包括路易斯·韦勒（Louis B. Wehle，1880—1959）、阿瑟·沃尔沃思（Arthur Walworth，1903—2005）、乔治·凯南（George F. Kennan，1904—2005）、小阿瑟·斯莱辛格、弗兰克·弗赖德尔（Frank Freidel，1916—1993）与詹姆斯·伯恩斯（James MacGregor Bruns，1918—2014）等美国著名历史学家和传记作家有关伍德罗·威尔逊（Woodrow Wilson，1856—1924）和富兰克林·罗斯福

---

① Columbia University, Oral History Research Office, *The Oral History Collection of Columbia University*, New York: Oral History Research Office, 1960 and 1964; Columbia University, Oral History Research Office, *A Supplement to the Oral History Collection of Columbia University*, New York: Oral History Research Office, 1962; Columbia University, Oral History Research Office, *The Oral History Collection*; *Recent Acquisitions and A Report for 1966*, New York: Oral History Research Office, 1966; Columbia University, Oral History Research Office, *Oral History, The First Twenty Years: Published Use 1948-1968, Recent Acquisitions Available for Use*, New York: Oral History Research Office, 1968; Columbia University, Oral History Research Office, *Oral History: Prospects in the 1970's: A Test: 100 Americans in the Oral History Collection: Review of 1968-1969*, New York: Oral History Research Office, 1969. 事实上，1957 年已经出版一份哥大口述历史收藏摘要。详细参阅 Columbia University, Oral History Research Office, *Compendium of the Columbia University Oral History Collection to August 1, 1957*, New York: Oral History Research Office, 1957.

总统及其时代以及美国国际关系的研究。①

综上所述，经过将近 20 年的艰辛努力，口述历史研究室逐渐发展成为美国乃至世界著名的口述历史收藏机构，它甚至成为哥大的一个特色品牌，这或许是当初那些试图解散研究室的哥大行政主管所没有预见到的。当然，更需要指出的是，口述历史研究室的示范意义与辐射效应远比它在哥大获得立足之地的时间要早得多，在其创建之后不久，就陆续出现众多口述历史计划或口述历史机构。到 20 世纪 60 年代中期，哥大口述历史研究室所开创的口述史学试验已经发展成为一场席卷美国各地和不同领域的口述史学运动（oral history movement），其口述历史收藏的价值也逐渐得到学术界的认可与赞赏。②

---

① Louis B. Wehle, *Hidden Threads of History: Wilson Through Roosevelt*, New York: Palgrave Macmillan, 1953; Arthur Walworth, *Woodrow Wilson* (Vol. 2: World Prophet), New York: Longmans & Green, 1958; George Frost Kennan, *Soviet-American Relations, 1917-1920* (Vol. 2: The Decision to Intervene), Princeton: Princeton University Press, 1958; Arthur M. Schlesinger, Jr., *The Age of Roose-velt* (Vol. 1: The Crisis of the Old Order, 1919-1933; Vol. 2: The Coming of the New Deal), Boston: Houghton Mifflin, 1957 and 1959; Frank Freidel, *Franklin D. Roosevelt* (Vol. 2: The Ordeal; Vol. 3: The Triumph), Boston: Little, Brown and Company, 1954 and 1956; James MacGregor Bruns, *Roose-velt: The Lion and The Fox*, New York: Harcourt, Brace, 1956. 此外，在 20 世纪 60 年代中期之前，较多利用哥大口述历史收藏的代表性研究成果还有 Howard Zinn, *LaGuardia in Congress*, Ithaca: Cornell University Press, 1959; Wallace Sayre and Herbert Kaufman, *Governing New York City: Politics in the Metropolis*, New York: Russell Sage Foundation, 1960; Roy Lubove, *The Progressives and the Slums: Tenement House Reform in New York City, 1890-1917*, Pittsburgh: University of Pittsburgh Press, 1962; Erik Barnouw, *A History of Broadcasting in the United States* (Vol. 1: A Tower in Babel; to 1933), New York: Oxford University Press, 1966; George Brown Tindall, *The Emergence of the New South, 1913-1945*, Baton Rouge: Louisiana State University Press, 1967.

② 据统计，截止到 1965 年，全美共有 89 个口述历史计划。详细参阅 Louis M. Starr, "Intro-duction", in Gary L. Shumway (ed.), *Oral History in the United States: A Directory*, New York: Oral History Association, 1971, p. 4.

第三章　精英主义、档案实践与美国口述史学

美国现代口述史学兴起与发展的最初动力是基于精英人物的口述历史访谈而获得具有保存价值的原始资料，以填补现存文献记录的空白或者弥补其不足，即强调口述史学的档案功能与史料价值。正如戴维·杜那威（David K. Dunaway）和维拉·鲍姆（Willa K. Baum, 1926—2006）所说，由内文斯和斯塔尔所引领的美国第一代口述历史学家将口述历史视为撰写口述传记和自传（oral biography and autobiography）的一种工具，以及作为将来的历史学家搜集和保存重要原始史料的一种手段。① 正是这种以搜集和保存史料为首要目标的档案实践（archival practices）主导了美国口述史学在 20 世纪 70 年代以前的主要发展趋势，同时它也使早期美国口述史学理论与方法研究的焦点集中于思考口述历史作为一种历史证据的客观性与真实性问题，并积极探索推广口述历史资源与发挥其史料价值的重要方式。

需要指出的是，不管是在美国口述史学发展的早期还是当代，档案考量（archival considerations）始终是口述历史实践的最基本特征与目的。②

---

① David K. Dunaway and Willa K. Baum, "Preface", in David K. Dunaway and Willa K. Baum (eds.), *Oral History: An Interdisciplinary Anthology*, Nashville: American Association for State and Local History, 1984, p. xiii.

② Robyn Russell, "Archival Considerations for Librarians and Oral Historians", *Oral History Association Newsletter*, Vol. 38, No. 1, Spring 2004, pp. 4-5. 当然，这并不局限于美国，档案考量是口述历史实践本身的最基本特征和目的，其区别在于不同地区和不同时期所侧重的口述历史访谈对象的差异。

本章将主要侧重于介绍与分析 20 世纪 70 年代之前基于哥大精英访谈模式的主要口述历史计划，并在此基础上考察与分析美国口述史学早期发展的基本特征、核心功能与主要争论。

一　口述历史计划的初创与发展

在哥大口述历史研究室的影响与推动下，其他口述历史计划和机构也相继应运而生。除上述 1951 年启动的"福特汽车公司档案馆口述历史计划"成为首个效仿计划之后，1952 年德克萨斯大学档案馆（University of Texas Archives，1967 年"University of Texas"的官方名称更名为"University of Texas at Austin"）启动"德克萨斯石油工业口述历史计划"（Oral History of the Texas Oil Industry Project），该计划由哥伦比亚大学威廉·欧文斯（William A. Owens，1905—1990）和德克萨斯大学莫迪·博特赖特（Mody C. Boatright，1896—1970）担任主任和主要访谈者。事实上，该计划很大程度上也是由于哥大口述历史研究室特别计划的影响，1951 年内文斯和希尔曾启动一项有关德克萨斯石油勘探历史的口述历史计划——"本尼德和石油工业计划"（Benedum and the Oil Industry Project），主要致力于收集美国著名石油开发商迈克尔·本尼迪（Michael Late Benedum，1869—1959）及其同僚的经历。[①]"德克萨斯石油工业口述历史计划"最初酝酿于 1951 年，当时正值纪念德克萨斯州博蒙特（Beaumont）的斯平德尔托普卢卡斯油井（Lucas Gusher，Spindletop）发现 50 周年。受到纪念会上石油开采先驱者交谈的启发，身为先驱之一的沃尔特·夏普（Walter Benona Sharp，1870—

---

① 详细资料可参阅 Columbia Center for Oral History，"Benedum and the Oil Industry Project：Oral History，1951"，https：//clio. columbia. edu/catalog/4072325，2015 年 8 月 14 日访问。

1912）的妻子埃斯特尔·夏普（Estelle B. Sharp，1883—1965）开始意识到有必要在这些先驱者去世之前能够很好地记录和保存他们的回忆。通过与德克萨斯大学档案馆维尼·艾伦（Winnie Allen，1895-1985）长达一年多的讨论与协商，该计划最后在夏普和她的儿子达德利·夏普（Dudley Sharp，1905—1987）的资助下于1952年6月正式启动。该计划主要有三个目标：（1）尽可能多地录音记录德克萨斯石油先驱者的回忆；（2）搜集与德克萨斯石油工业相关的记录与照片；（3）撰写一部德克萨斯石油先驱者的历史。通过学校各方（包括档案馆、图书馆、英语系和历史系）与两位计划主任的共同努力，在1952—1958年间，该计划取得丰硕成果，单单口述历史访谈就达到218份（共使用325卷盘式录音带）；而作为口述历史资料的重要补充，额外搜集到的与德克萨斯石油工业相关的手稿与照片等资料就达到20直线英尺。① 值得一提的是，这些口述历史资料很快成为学者研究的重要资料来源，欧文斯与博特赖特分别于1958年和1963年出版的两本著作就是很好的例证。②

---

① Ray O. Stephens，"The Oral History of Texas Oil Pioneers"，*Library Chronicle of the University of Texas*，Vol. 7，1961，pp. 35-39；Chester V. Kielman，"The Texas Oil Industry Project"，*Wilson Library Bulletin*，Vol. 40，1966，pp. 616-618；Mody C. Boatright and William A. Owens，*Tales from the Derrick Floor: A People's History of the Oil Industry*，Garden City：Doubleday，1970. 经过整理、编辑和索引之后，目前这些资料保存在德克萨斯大学奥斯汀分校道尔夫·布里斯科美国历史中心（Dolph Briscoe Center for American History，University of Texas at Austin），详细指南可参阅 "A Guide to the Oral History of the Texas Oil Industry Collection，1952-1958"，http：//www. lib. utexas. edu/taro/utcah/00282/cah-00282. html，2015年8月15日访问。这些资料之前保存在该校尤金·巴克德克萨斯历史中心（Eugene C. Barker Texas History Center），1991年该中心并入道尔夫·布里斯科美国历史中心。

② William A. Owens，*Fever in the Earth*，New York：Putnam，1958；Mody C. Boatright，*Folklore of the Oil Industry*，Dallas：Southern Methodist University Press，1963. 其他代表性研究成果可参阅 David G. McComb，*Texas: A Modern History*，Austin：University of Texas Press，1989；Lawrence Goodwyn，*Texas Oil，American Dreams: A Study of the Texas Independent Producers and Royalty Owners Association*，Austin：Center for American History，Texas State Historical Association，1996；Diana Davids Hinton and Roger M. Olien，*Oil in Texas: The Gusher Age，1895-1945*，Austin：University of Texas Press，2002；Bobby D. Weaver，*Oilfield Trash: Life and Labor in the Oil Patch*，College Station：Texas A&M University Press，2010；Brian Frehner，*Finding Oil: The Nature of Petroleum Geology，1859-1920*，Lincoln：University of Nebraska Press，2011；David G. McComb，*The City in Texas: A History*，Austin：University of Texas Press，2015.

同在 1952 年，在埃尔伍德·蒙德（Elwood R. Maunder，1917—2011）的主持下，森林历史学会（Forest History Society）正式启动"森林历史口述历史计划"（Forest History Oral History Project）。事实上，作为森林历史学会的前身——林产历史基金会（Forest Products History Foundation，1955 年更名为"Forest History Foundation"，1959 年正式更名为"Forest History Society"）从 1946 年创建开始就利用笔录方式记录林产业先驱者的回忆。而从 1952 年开始，该学会正式利用录音机启动口述历史计划，其内容主要涉及受访者对于 19 世纪末 20 世纪初影响美国林产业发展的重要政策变迁的第一手叙述。而从 20 世纪 60 年代开始，随着森林历史向相关的保育和环境历史等领域的扩展，口述历史访谈对象也不断扩大，包括森林教育者与研究者、保育主义者、负责自然资源管理的政府雇员等更为广泛的林产从业者。[1] 该计划一直持续到 21 世纪，据森林历史学会官方网站统计，截至 2008 年，整个口述历史收藏总共超过 250 份访谈。[2] 目前，学会也将该口述历史收藏的注释指南及部分访谈抄本全文上传到其官方网站，并提供在线查询功能。[3] 利用该学会于 1957 年正式出版的专业刊物《森林历史通讯》（*Forest History Newslet-*

---

① "Project News", *Oral History Association Newsletter*, Vol. 1, No. 1, June 1967, p. 14; "Forest History Society Marks 25th Anniversary with Tribute to Oral History", *Oral History Association Newsletter*, Vol. 6, No. 3/4, July 1972, p. 1; Harold K. Steen and Susan R. Schrepfer, "Why Oral History?" *Forest History*, Vol. 16, No. 3, 1972, pp. 4-5; Barbara D. Holman, *Oral History Collection of the Forest History Society: An Annotated Guide*, Santa Cruz: Forest History Society, 1977; K. Peter Harder, "Forestry, 8. 0", in David O. Whitten and Bessie E. Whitten (eds.), *Handbook of American Business History* (Vol. 2: Extractives, Manufacturing, And Services: A Historiographical and Bibliographical Guide), New York: Greenwood Press, 1997, p. 56; Steven Anderson, "Changing Roles of the Forest History Society: New Approaches to Environmental History in North America", in Mauro Agnoletti and Steven Anderson (eds.), *Methods and Approaches in Forest History*, New York: CABI Publishing, 2000, pp. 21-28.

② Forest History Society, "Inventory of the Forest History Society Oral History Interviews, 1940-2008", http://www. foresthistory. org/ead/FHS_ Oral_ Histories. html, 2015 年 8 月 15 日访问。

③ Forest History Society, "Annotated Guide to Oral History Interviews of the Forest History Society", http://www. foresthistory. org/research/ohisrch. html, 2015 年 8 月 15 日访问。

ter），1959 年更名为 *Forest History*，1974 年更名为 *Journal of Forest History*，1990 年更名为 *Forest & Conservation History*。该计划所收集的口述历史摘录和相关信息都能及时发布，因而也很快为研究者所了解和利用。此外，部分口述历史访谈资料除了被学会编辑出版之外，[1] 它们也为相关领域的研究者所广泛利用。[2]

1954 年，加州大学伯克利分校班克罗夫特图书馆创建地区口述历史办公室（Regional Oral History Office），这是继哥大口述历史研究室之后所创建的美国第二个综合性口述历史机构。如上所述，作为班克罗夫特图书馆的创始人，班克罗夫特从 19 世纪 60—70 年代开始就致力于搜集美国西部地区早期拓荒者的口述资料，因而地区口述史办公室的创建被认为是一种"传统的复兴"。而这种传统在加州大学伯克利分校的复兴可以追溯到 1943 年，当时作为英语系教授、历史学家和知名作家的乔治·斯图尔特（George R. Stewart，1895—1980）因为受到班克罗夫特口述资料与内文斯相关著述的影响，他突然意识到需要继续班克罗夫特的访谈工作。而在他于 1945—1946 年担任图书馆委员会（Library Committee）主席期间，斯图尔特更是积极与各方协调希望能够落实该项工作，不过最终没有取得实际进展。直到 20 世纪 50 年代

---

① Forest History Society, "Selected FHS Oral History Interviews Available for Purchase", http：// www. foresthistory. org/Publications/oralhist. html，2015 年 8 月 15 日访问。

② 代表性成果有 Harold K. Steen，*The U. S. Forest Service*：*A History*，Seattle：University of Washington Press，1976；Richard C. Davis（ed.），*North American Forest History*：*A Guide to Archives and Manuscripts in the United States and Canada*，Santa Barbara：Clio Books，1977；Paul W. Hirt，*A Conspiracy of Optimism*：*Management of the National Forests Since World War Two*，Lincoln：University of Nebraska Press，1994；Richard A. Rajala，*Clearcutting the Pacific Rain Forest*：*Production*，*Science*，*and Regulation*，Vancouver：University of British Columbia Press，1998；Robert B. Outland，*Tapping the Pines*：*The Naval Stores Industry in the American South*，Baton Rouge：Louisiana State University Press，2004；Sara Witter Connor，*Wisconsin's Flying Trees in World War II*：*A Victory for American Forest Products and Allied Aviation*，Charleston：The History Press，2014；James E. Fickle，*Green Gold*：*Alabama's Forests and Forest Industries*，Tuscaloosa：The University of Alabama Press，2014.

初，随着较易操作和相对经济的磁带录音机的问世及哥大口述历史研究室的影响，班克罗夫特图书馆于 1952—1953 年间率先启动一项小型口述历史试点计划，由图书馆手稿部主管罗伯特·伯克（Robert E. Burke，1921—1998）负责。随后，在英语系教授詹姆斯·哈特（James D. Hart，1911—1990，他于 1969—1990 年担任班克罗夫特图书馆馆长）的具体主持下，对旅居法国的美国女作家爱丽丝·托克勒斯（Alice B. Toklas，1877—1867）与居住在加州卡梅尔（Carmel）小镇的美国流行作家詹姆斯·霍普（James M. Hopper，1897—1952）进行了一系列访谈。由于这些访谈计划被证明是相当成功的，于是，班克罗夫特图书馆于 1954 年正式启动一项名为"地区文化历史计划"（Regional Cultural History Project）的口述历史计划，并随后更名为地区口述历史办公室。①

地区口述历史办公室主要致力于通过口述历史访谈记录美国西部的历史，不过也有相当的口述历史计划涉及全国性乃至世界性议题。自 1954 年创建至今，该办公室所搜集的口述历史资料达到 4000 多份，主题涉及艺术与文化、商业、社区历史、食品与酒业、法律与法学、自然资源（土地和环境）、政治与政府、科学技术（医学）、社会运动及加州大学历史等。而这些口述历史访谈作为原始资料也被广泛地应用于专著、书籍、论文、舞台作品、广播节目、视频和电影纪录片、

---

① Corinne Lathrop Gilb, "Tape-Recorded Interviewing: Some Thoughts From California", *American Archivist*, Vol. 20, No. 4, 1957, pp. 335-344; Willa Klug Baum, "Oral History: A Revived Tradition at the Bancroft Library", *Pacific Northwest Quarterly*, Vol. 58, No. 2, 1967, pp. 57-64; Willa K. Baum, Kathryn Anderson and Mary Ellen Leary, "History on Tape: The Regional Oral History Office at The Bancroft Library", *California Historical Quarterly*, Vol. 54, No. 1, 1975, pp. 77-84; James D. Hart, "Foreword", in Suzanne B. Riess and Willa Baum (eds.), *Catalogue I of the Regional Oral History Office, 1954-1979*, Berkeley: Bancroft Library, University of California, Berkeley, 1980, p. 3.

网站、博客和学位论文等。① 而为进一步扩大其影响力和满足远程客户的需求，目前办公室已经将大部分访谈抄本上传到官方网站，并提供浏览与下载功能。同时，为提升其教育功能，办公室还从 2002 年开始举办年度口述历史高级暑期学院（Advanced Oral History Summer Institute）与不定期的口述历史工作坊。②

---

① 利用口述历史收藏的相关研究成果可参阅 Myron Edward Krueger, Amelia R. Fry, and Richard A. Colgan, *Forestry and Technology in Northern California, 1925-1965*, Berkeley: Regional Oral History Office, 1968; Norris Hundley, Jr., *The Great Thirst: Californians and Water, 1770s-1990s*, Berkeley: University of California Press, 1992; Marilynn S. Johnson, *The Second Gold Rush: Oakland and the East Bay in World War II*, Berkeley: University of California Press, 1993; Mark W. T. Harvey, *A Symbol of Wilderness: Echo Park and the American Conservation Movement*, Albuquerque: University of New Mexico Press, 1994; Ed Cray, *Chief Justice: A Biography of Earl Warren*, New York: Simon & Schuster, 1997; Megan Benton, *Beauty and the Book: Fine Editions and Cultural Distinction in America*, New Haven: Yale University Press, 2000; Shirley Ann Wilson Moore, *To Place Our Deeds: The African American Community in Richmond, California, 1910-1963*, Berkeley: University of California Press, 2000; Robert Cohen and Reginald E. Zelnik, *The Free Speech Movement: Reflections on Berkeley in the 1960s*, Berkeley: University of California Press, 2002; Jo Freeman, *At Berkeley in the Sixties: The Education of an Activist, 1961-1965*, Bloomington: Indiana University Press, 2004; Chris Rhomberg, *No There There: Race, Class, and Political Community in Oakland*, Berkeley: University of California Press, 2004; Thomas Pinney, *A History of Wine in America: From Prohibition to the Present*, Berkeley: University of California Press, 2005; Jim Newton, *Justice for All: Earl Warren and the Nation He Made*, New York: Riverhead Books, 2006; Beret E. Strong, *Seeking the Light: The Lives of Phillips and Ruth Lee Thygeson, Pioneers in the Prevention of Blindness*, Jefferson: McFarland & Co., 2008; Sebastian Fichera, *Italy on the Pacific: San Francisco's Italian Americans*, New York: Palgrave Macmillan, 2011; Thomas Pinney, *The Makers of American Wine: A Record of Two Hundred Years*, Berkeley: University of California Press, 2012; Fred Pelka, *What We Have Done: An Oral History of the Disability Rights Movement*, Amherst: University of Massachusetts Press, 2012; Seth Rosenfeld, *Subversives: The FBI's War on Student Radicals, and Reagan's Rise to Power*, New York: Farrar, Straus and Giroux, 2012; Matthew Partington and Linda Sandino (eds.), *Oral History in the Visual Arts*, London: Bloomsbury, 2013; Sally Smith Hughes, *Genentech: The Beginnings of Biotech*, Chicago: University of Chicago Press, 2013; Jill Diane Zahniser and Amelia R. Fry, *Alice Paul: Claiming Power*, Oxford and New York: Oxford University Press, 2014; Marta Gutman, *A City for Children: Women, Architecture, and the Charitable Landscapes of Oakland, 1850-1950*, Chicago: University of Chicago Press, 2014; Tom Turner, *David Brower: The Making of the Environmental Movement*, Berkeley: University of California Press, 2015.

② 详细资料可以访问地区口述历史办公室官方网站 http://bancroft.berkeley.edu/ROHO/index.html, 2015 年 8 月 16 日访问。此外，有关 1954—1997 年的口述历史收藏目录可参阅 Suzanne B. Riess and Willa Baum (eds.), *Catalogue I of the Regional Oral History Office, 1954-1979*, Berkeley: Bancroft Library, University of California, Berkeley, 1980; Suzanne B. Riess and Willa Baum (eds.), *Catalogue II of the Regional Oral History Office, 1980-1997*, Berkeley: Bancroft Library, University of California, Berkeley, 1997.

而与地区口述历史办公室同属加州大学体系的另外一个著名综合性口述历史机构是加州大学洛杉矶分校（University of California, Los Angeles）口述历史项目（Oral History Program），在当时该校历史学家、图书管理员和其他同事的力促下，该项目由大学董事会于 1959 年创建，并于 2005 年更名为口述历史研究中心（Center for Oral History Research）。① 作为加州大学洛杉矶分校图书馆特藏部（Department of Special Collections）的一个部门，该项目主要致力于通过口述历史访谈来记录加州和加州大学洛杉矶分校的历史，同时也会涉及一些具有全国性和国际性主题的口述历史计划。作为美国最为悠久和大型的口述历史计划之一，该项目记录和保存的口述历史资料的主题相当广泛，主要包括非裔美国人、建筑学、视觉艺术、图书与印刷、公民权利、劳工、文学与艺术（音乐、电影）、政治与政府、生物医学、社区历史及加州大学历史等。这些口述历史收藏很好地补充了加州大学洛杉矶分校和其他分校图书馆和档案馆的现存收藏的不足，同时通过口述历史访谈也能够额外搜集大量与访谈相关的个人与机构文件。而为进一步完善口述历史收藏结构，该项目的一个重要特色是相当重视接受其他机构或个人捐赠的口述历史录音和抄本资料，并进行相应整理和编目。而为进一步扩大其影响力和满足远程客户的需求，目前口述历史研究

---

① Doyce B. Nunis, Jr., "Time for Taping", *Educational Theatre Journal*, Vol. 14, No. 3, 1962, pp. 236-239; Elizabeth I. Dixon, "Early San Fernando: Memoirs of Mrs. Catherine Dace", *Southern California Quarterly*, Vol. 44, No. 3, 1962, p. 221; "Oral History Colloquium", *University Bulletin: A Weekly Bulletin for the Staff of the University of California*, Vol. 14, No. 37, May 23, 1966, pp. 233-234; "New Oral History Catalog Available for Purchase", *University Bulletin: A Weekly Bulletin for the Staff of the University of California*, Vol. 31, No. 31, June 6-10, 1983, p. 119; Jacqueline R. Braitman, "History by Word of Mouth: The UCLA Oral History Program", *UCLA Historical Journal*, Vol. 6, 1985, pp. 136-138; Dale Treleven and James V. Mink, "An Interview with James V. Mink", *Oral History Review*, Vol. 27, No. 1, 2000, pp. 122-127; UCLA Library Special Collections, *Oral History Program Publications, 1966-1975*, Los Angeles: Charles E. Young Research Library, UCLA, 2013.

中心也已经将大部分访谈抄本上传到官方网站，并提供浏览与下载功能。① 当然，在过去 50 多年里，这些丰富的口述历史资料已经成为不同学者研究的重要资料来源。②

　　除上述大学之外，到 20 世纪 60 年代初，还有一些美国高校纷纷设立规模大小不等的口述历史计划，其中包括印第安纳大学（Indiana University）、西弗吉尼亚大学（West Virginia University）、海斯堡堪萨斯州立学院（Fort Hays Kansas State College）、新泽西州卑尔根社区学院（Bergen Com-

---

　　① 详细资料可以访问口述历史研究中心官方网站 http：//oralhistory. library. ucla. edu/，2015 年 8 月 16 日访问。相关口述历史收藏目录可参阅 Elizabeth I. Dixon（ed.），*The Oral History Program at UCLA：A Bibliography*，Los Angeles：University of California Library，1966；Constance S. Bullock and Saundra Taylor（eds.），*The UCLA Oral History Program：Catalog of the Collection*，Los Angeles：Regents of the University of California，1982；Vimala Jayanti（ed.），*The UCLA Oral History Program：Catalog of the Collection*，Los Angeles：Oral History Program，Department of Special Collections，UCLA，second edition，1992；Teresa Barnett（ed.），*The UCLA Oral History Program：Catalog of the Collection*，Los Angeles：Oral History Program，Department of Special Collections，UCLA，third edition，1999.

　　② 相关研究成果可参阅 Roger L. Geiger，*Research and Relevant Knowledge：American Research Universities Since World War II*，Oxford and New York：Oxford University Press，1993；Stephen Kresge and Leif Wenar（ed.），*Hayek on Hayek：An Autobiographical Dialogue*，London and New York：Routledge，1994；Alan Ebenstein，*Friedrich Hayek：A Biography*，New York：St. Martin's Press，2000；John Allswang，*The Initiative and Referendum in California：1898-1998*，Stanford：Stanford University Press，2000；Matthew Dallek，*The Right Moment：Ronald Reagan's First Victory and the Decisive Turning Point in American Politics*，New York：Free Press，2000；Richard G. Hovannisian，*Looking Backward，Moving Forward：Confronting the Armenian Genocide*，New Brunswick：Transaction Publishers，2003；Douglas Flamming，*Bound for Freedom：Black Los Angeles in Jim Crow America*，Berkeley：University of California Press，2005；Shirley Jennifer Lim，*A Feeling of Belonging：Asian American Women's Public Culture，1930-1960*，New York：New York University Press，2006；Steven L. Isoardi，*The Dark Tree：Jazz and the Community Arts in Los Angeles*，Berkeley：University of California Press，2006；Margaret Leslie Davis，*The Culture Broker：Franklin D. Murphy and the Transformation of Los Angeles*，Berkeley：University of California Press，2007；Robert Bauman，*Race and the War on Poverty：From Watts to East L. A.*，Norman：University of Oklahoma Press，2008；Marina Dundjerski，*UCLA：The First Century*，Los Angeles：The Regents of the University of California，2011；Natalie M. Fousekis，*Demanding Child Care：Women's Activism and the Politics of Welfare，1940-1971*，Urbana：University of Illinois Press，2011；Jacqueline R. Braitman and Gerald F. Uelmen，*Justice Stanley Mosk：A Life at the Center of California Politics and Justice*，Jefferson：McFarland & Co.，2013；William Hackman，*Out of Sight：The Los Angeles Art Scene of the Sixties*，New York：Other Press，2015.

munity College）、杜兰大学（Tulane University）①、西密歇根大学（Western Michigan University）、明尼苏达大学（University of Minnesota）、德克萨斯理工大学（Texas Tech University）、爱达荷大学（University of Idaho）、密歇根大学安娜堡分校（University of Michigan，Ann Arbor）、韦恩州立大学（Wayne State University）、北卡罗来纳教堂山分校（University of North Carolina at Chapel Hill）、杨百翰大学（Brigham Young University）、克莱蒙特研究学院（Claremont Graduate School）②、南加州大学（University of Southern California）、纽约州立农业学院（New York State College of Agriculture）、康奈尔大学（Cornell University）③ 和加州大学圣克鲁兹分校（University of California，Santa Cruz）④ 等。⑤ 至此，美国口述史学基本形成以首批大学口述历史计划为基础的早期发展格局。

当然，在 20 世纪 60 年代末之前，美国口述历史计划的发起单位还包

---

① 杜兰大学于 1958 年创建新奥尔良爵士乐档案馆（Archives of New Orleans Jazz，现更名为 "Hogan Jazz Archive"），主要致力于搜集新奥尔良爵士乐音乐家及其相关人士的口述历史访谈。详细内容参阅 "＄2,666,958 Given for U. S. Culture, Ford Gifts Include ＄75,000 to Amass Oral History of New Orleans Jazz", *New York Times*，April 4，1958；Richard B. Allen，"The New Orleans Jazz Archive at Tulane"，*Wilson Library Bulletin*，Vol. 40，1966，pp. 619-623. 另外，也可以访问其官方网站 http：//jazz. tulane. edu/collections/oral-history，2015 年 8 月 17 日访问。

② 克莱蒙特研究学院（现更名为 "Claremont Graduate University"）口述历史项目创建于 1962 年，它所展开的一个重要项目是由亨利·鲁斯基金会（Henry Luce Foundation）赞助并于 1968 年启动的 "中国传教士口述历史计划"（China Missionaries Oral History Project）。详细内容参阅 Claremont Graduate School，*Claremont Graduate School Oral History Program：A Bibliography*，Claremont：Claremont University Center，1978. 另外，也可访问其官方网站 "Oral History Program Archive"，http：//cgu. edu/pages/663. asp，2015 年 8 月 17 日访问。

③ 康奈尔大学口述历史项目创建于 1962 年，详细内容参阅 Gould P. Colman，"Oral History at Cornell"，*Wilson Library Bulletin*，Vol. 40，1966，pp. 624-628.

④ 加州大学圣克鲁兹分校地区历史计划（Regional History Project）创建于 1963 年，它主要致力于通过口述史访谈来记录加州中部海岸地区和圣克鲁兹分校的历史。详细内容参阅 Regional History Project，*Oral History Collection：Bibliography*，Santa Cruz：McHenry Library，University of California，Santa Cruz，1988. 另外，也可访问其官方网站 http：//library. ucsc. edu/regional-history-project，2015 年 8 月 17 日访问。

⑤ 上述大学口述历史计划信息总结自 Gary L. Shumway（ed.），*Oral History in the United States：A Directory*，New York：Oral History Association，1971. 根据作者提供的信息，很难确定这些计划的具体创建时间。

括专业学会、图书馆（公共和专业图书馆）、档案馆、博物馆、基金会、公司、政府机构与专业研究机构等。以专业学会为例，其中包括内布拉斯加州历史学会（Nebraska State Historical Society）、美国西班牙裔学会（Hispanic Society of America）、威斯康星州历史学会（State Historical Society of Wisconsin）、洛杉矶心理分析学会（Los Angeles Psychoanalytic Society）、美国微生物学学会（American Society for Microbiology）、美国土木工程师学会（American Society of Civil Engineers）和美国航空历史学会（American Aviation Historical Society）等。而基金会方面则包括迈阿密皮肤科基金会（Dermatology Foundation of Miami）、商业与职业妇女基金会（Business and Professional Women's Foundation）、梅约诊所基金会（Mayo Clinic Foundation）和旧金山中国文化基金会（Chinese Culture Foundation of San Francisco）等。在公司方面，除上述谈到的福特汽车公司之外，通用汽车公司（General Motors Corporation）、国际商用机器公司（International Business Machines Corporation）和菲尔德公司（Field Enterprises, INC.）等企业也有相应的口述历史计划。此外，还包括美国国家航空航天局（National Aeronautics and Space Administration）、国家公园管理局（National Park Service）、美国国家卫生研究院（National Institute of Health）、美国社会保障事务管理局（Social Security Administration）与美国海军陆战队（United States Marine Corps)[1] 等政府机构。不过，除大学之外，在众多口述历史计划发起单位当中，占据主要部分的还是各种类型的图书馆、档案馆或博物馆（不包括大学所属）。[2] 比如，创建于 1954 年的美国艺术档案馆（Archives of American Art）就一直致力于搜集美国视觉艺术领域的艺术家、收藏者、商人与博物馆人员的口述历史资料，该馆于 1970 年正式加入史密森学会

---

① "Marine Corps Continues to Collect Oral History Interviews", *Oral History Association Newsletter*, Vol. 2, No. 4, October 1968, p. 2.

② 上述内容总结自 Gary L. Shumway（ed.），*Oral History in the United States：A Directory*, New York：Oral History Association, 1971.

（Smithsonian Institution）。① 而在波格于 1956 年被乔治·马歇尔研究基金会（George G. Marshall Research Foundation）聘任为乔治·马歇尔研究图书馆（George G. Marshall Research Library）馆长之后，他随即于同年启动一项口述历史计划，主要采访马歇尔将军及其同僚。② 这些口述历史资料连同相关的手稿与文件成为该图书馆的核心收藏，而且它们也成为众多研究成果的重要资料来源。③ 不过，在非大学图书馆（档案馆、博物馆）体系中，对于推动美国早期乃至当代口述史学发展做出重要贡献的是总统图书馆，1961 年哈里·杜鲁门总统图书馆（Harry S. Truman Presidential Library）率先启动口述历史计划。④ 而到目前为止，总统图书馆口述历史计划仍然是唯一一项由美国联邦政府持续倡导和负责管理的项目，足见其重要性。

---

① "The Archives of American Art Oral History Program：A Preliminary Guide to Tape-Recorded Interviews"，*Archives of American Art Journal*，Vol. 8，No. 1，1968，pp. 1-9；"The Archives of American Art Oral History Program：A Preliminary Guide to Tape-Recorded Interviews：II"，*Archives of American Art Journal*，Vol. 9，No. 1，1969，pp. 1-10；Garnett McCoy，"A Guide to the Archives of American Art Oral History Program"，*Archives of American Art Journal*，Vol. 11，No. 1/4，1971，pp. 1-38；Paul Cummings，"The Oral History Program"，*Archives of American Art Journal*，Vol. 14，No. 1，1974，pp. 20-21. 具体内容可访问美国艺术档案馆官方网站 http：//www. aaa. si. edu/collections/interviews，2015 年 8 月 17 日访问。

② Forrest C. Pogue，"The George C. Marshall Oral History Project"，*Wilson Library Bulletin*，Vol. 40，1966，pp. 607-615；Forrest C. Pogue，"The George C. Marshall Project"，in Louis M. Starr（ed.），*The Second National Colloquium on Oral History*，New York：Oral History Association，1968，pp. 82-94；Donald A. Ritchie，"Remembering Forrest Pogue"，*Oral History Association Newsletter*，Vol. 31，No. 1，Winter 1997，pp. 7-8.

③ Larry I. Bland，Joellen K. Bland，and Sharon Ritenour Stevens（eds.），*George C. Marshall：Interviews and Reminiscences for Forrest C. Pogue*，Lexington：George C. Marshall Research Foundation，revised edition，1991. 而波格所写的马歇尔将军四卷本传记就曾大量利用这些口述历史资料，详细参阅 Forrest C. Pogue，*George C. Marshall：Education of A General*，*1880-1939*，New York：Viking Press 1963；Forrest C. Pogue，*George C. Marshall：Ordeal and Hope*，*1939-1942*，New York：Viking Press 1966；Forrest C. Pogue，*George C. Marshall：Organizer of Victory*，*1943-1945*，New York：Viking Press 1973；Forrest C. Pogue，*George C. Marshall：Statesman*，*1945-1959*，New York：Viking Press 1987. 目前这些口述历史资料都已经被上传到基金会官方网站，具体内容可访问 http：//marshallfoundation. org/library/results/#! /format = 5，2015 年 8 月 17 日访问。

④ Richard S. Kirkendall，"A Second Look at Presidential Libraries"，*American Archivist*，Vol. 29，No. 3，1966，pp. 371-386；Louis Starr，"Oral History"，*Encyclopedia of Library and Information Sciences*（Vol. 20），New York：Marcel Dekker，1977，p. 448.

二　美国总统图书馆与口述历史计划[①]

在美国，作为致力于收集和保存与总统相关的各种档案、文件、手稿及相关记录的历史资料馆藏，目前的总统图书馆体系是一个由 13 个总统图书馆所组成的全国网络，它们由美国国家档案和记录管理局（National Archives and Records Administration）下属的总统图书馆办公室（Office of Presidential Libraries）负责管理与维护。[②] 鉴于历任总统相关文件与记录的保存与管理一直缺乏一套有效的规章制度，罗斯福总统于 1938 年正式提出创建总统图书馆的建议，并得到国会批准，他也随即于 1941 年发布建设自己图书馆的正式委任。1946 年，坐落于纽约海德公园（Hyde Park）的美国首个总统图书馆——罗斯福总统图书馆正式对外开放。在其影响下，目前，自美国第 31 任总统赫伯特·胡佛（Herbert Hoover，1874—1964；总统任期为 1929—1933 年）到第 43 任总统乔治·沃克·布什（George W. Bush，1946—，总统任期为 2001—2009 年），历任总统都设有总统图书馆。[③] 而为加强对总统图书馆的管理，美国国会还于 1955 年通过《总统图书馆法案》（*Presidential Libraries Act*），并于 1978 年和 1986 年进行修改，可以说为总统图

---

① 为保证完整性，这里将介绍与分析现有全部总统图书馆的口述历史计划。

② 需要指出的是，除这 13 个由国家档案与文件管理局负责管理与维护的总统图书馆之外，在胡佛总统之前，还有大约 9 位总统也设有相应的总统图书馆。详细内容参阅 "Presidential Library"，from Wikipedia，https：//en. wikipedia. org/wiki/Presidential_ library，2015 年 8 月 18 日访问。

③ Cynthia J. Wolff，"Necessary Monuments：The Making of the Presidential Library System"，*Government Publications Review*，Vol. 16，No. 1，1989，pp. 47-62；Don W. Wilson，"Presidential Libraries：Developing to Maturity"，*Presidential Studies Quarterly*，Vol. 21，No. 4，1991，pp. 771-779；Richard J. Cox，"America's Pyramids：Presidents and Their Libraries"，*Government Information Quarterly*，Vol. 19，No. 1，2002，pp. 45-75；"Presidential Library"，from Wikipedia，https：//en. wikipedia. org/wiki/Presidential_ library，2015 年 8 月 18 日访问。

书馆的有效管理与维护提供了法律保障。① 需要指出的是，总统图书馆与一般图书馆不同，其藏品不仅包括总统任内各种文献、手稿、档案、书籍和纪念品，同时还包括与总统及其家人和重要同僚等生平相关的各类资料（包括口述历史）。因此，总统图书馆实际上是集图书馆、档案馆与博物馆于一体的多功能机构。②

正如有学者指出，哥大口述历史研究室是最初启动的总统图书馆口述历史计划的"范型"，尽管各有差异，不过所有计划都具有一个共同目标，即不是为了赞美总统、第一夫人或他们的家庭，而是为了通过口述历史访谈来保存那些即将消失的信息以补充文字记录。一般而言，其访谈者都是训练有素的历史学家或档案工作者，而受访者则包括总统、家族成员、朋友、白宫工作人员、政府内阁成员及其他重要相关人士。而就访谈内容而言，除侧重于总统任期的重要事件之外，也会涉及受访者的生平经历与职业生涯。③ 以下将根据各位总统任期时间的先后顺序来介绍与分析各自的口述历史计划。

赫伯特·胡佛总统图书馆（Herbert Hoover Presidential Library）和斯坦福大学胡佛研究所（Hoover Institution, Stanford University）于1965 年（也有一说是 1966 年）共同启动赫伯特·胡佛口述历史项目（Herbert Hoover Oral History Program），由雷蒙德·亨利（Raymond Z. Henle，1899—1974）担任主任和主要访谈者，其主要目的是补充和丰富总统图书馆和胡佛研究所档案馆的收藏。该项目的主要受访者包

---

① Wendy R. Gingberg and Erika K. Lunder, "The Presidential Libraries Act and the Establishment of Presidential Libraries", *CRS Report for Congress*, December 1, 2010.

② 正是如此，目前各个总统图书馆的全称一般都是"××总统图书馆和博物馆"（×× Library and Museum）。而为行文方便，这里统一表述为"××总统图书馆"。详细内容参阅"Presidential Libraries and Museums", http://www.archives.gov/presidential-libraries/, 2015 年 8 月 18 日访问。

③ Regina Greenwell, "The Oral History Collections of the Presidential Libraries", *Journal of American History*, Vol. 84, No. 2, 1997, p. 597.

括政治领袖、商人、军事官员、新闻记者、作家以及胡佛的医生、秘书、助手、朋友、同僚及其家人，目前图书馆所收藏的口述历史访谈总共达到 443 份。① 需要指出的是，其中部分访谈是由其他机构完成的，包括哥大口述历史研究室②、爱荷华大学图书馆（University of Iowa Libraries）、普林斯顿大学约翰·杜勒斯口述历史计划（John Foster Dulles Oral History Project，Princeton University）③、美国参议院历史办公室（United States Senate Historical Office）④、加州大学伯克利分校地区口述历史办公室和加州大学洛杉矶分校口述历史项目。为方便读者查询，图书馆还将口述历史收藏的索引指南信息上传到官方网站，⑤ 目前有 42 份口述历史访谈的完整抄本可以通过弗吉尼亚大学米勒公共事务中心（Miller

---

① "Hoover Project Devises a Quick Way for Handling Legal Agreements", *Oral History Association Newsletter*, Vol. 2, No. 3, July 1968, p. 4; "Hoover Interviews are Deposited at West Branch and Stanford", *Oral History Association Newsletter*, Vol. 3, No. 3, July 1969, p. 2; Dale C. Mayer and Dwight M. Miller (eds.), *Historical Materials in the Herbert Hoover Presidential Library*, West Branch: Herbert Hoover Presidential Library, 1996; Rebecca J. Mead (ed.), *Register of the Herbert Hoover Oral History Program Interviews 1966-1973*, Stanford: Hoover Institution Archives, Stanford University, 1999; Rebecca Sharpless, "The History of Oral History", in Thomas L. Charlton, Lois E. Myers, and Rebecca Sharpless (eds.), *Handbook of Oral History*, Walnut Creek: AltaMira Press, 2006, p. 23; Herbert Hoover Presidential Library, "Historical Materials: Introduction", http://www.ecommcode2.com/hoover/research/historicalmaterials/oral.html, 2015 年 8 月 18 日访问。

② 比如，胡佛总统曾于 1950 年接受内文斯和希尔的口述历史访谈，详细参阅 Columbia Center for Oral History, "Reminiscences of Herbert Clark Hoover: Oral History, 1950", https://clio.columbia.edu/catalog/4074949, 2015 年 8 月 18 日访问。

③ 该计划启动于 1963 年，详细参阅 James H. Rubin, "Dulles Oral History Project", *Princeton Alumni Weekly*, Vol. 65, No. 8, November 10, 1964, pp. 6-7; Richard D. Challener and John M. Fenton, "Recent Past Comes Alive in Dulles 'Oral History'", *Princeton Alumni Weekly*, Vol. 67, No. 21, March 14, 1967, pp. 11-17, 37-42; Philip A. Crowl, "The Dulles Oral History Project: Mission Accomplished", *American Historical Association Newsletter*, Vol. 5, February 1967, pp. 6-10; "Dulles Oral History", *New York Times*, May 27, 1968; Philip A. Crowl, "The John Foster Dulles Project", in Louis M. Starr (ed.), *The Second National Colloquium on Oral History*, New York: Oral History Association, 1968, pp. 73-81.

④ 该办公室口述历史计划（Oral History Project）启动于 1976 年，著名口述历史学家唐纳德·里奇就曾长期参与和负责该计划。详细访问 http://www.senate.gov/history/oralhistory.htm, 2015 年 8 月 18 日访问。

⑤ Herbert Hoover Presidential Library, "Historical Materials: Oral History Transcripts", http://www.ecommcode2.com/hoover/research/historicalmaterials/oral.html, 2015 年 8 月 18 日访问。

Center of Public Affairs, University of Virginia）官方网站进行浏览和下载。① 当然，这些丰富的口述历史资料已经成为胡佛总统时代的美国政治史、外交史、经济史与社会史等相关研究的重要资料来源。②

富兰克林·罗斯福总统图书馆（Franklin D. Roosevelt Presidential Library）尽管是美国创建的首个总统图书馆，不过其口述历史计划的开展却相对迟缓。在罗斯福于 1945 年去世之前，美国现代意义上的口述史学还没有诞生，因此他并没有像其前任胡佛那样接受过任何正式的口述历史访谈。不过，在哥大口述历史研究室等其他机构所开展的口述历史计划当中，有相当的受访者都详细谈到他们在罗斯福总统任期内的经历或者他们对于总统本人的回忆。③ 直到 20 世纪 70 年代晚期，图书馆才正式启动自己的口述历史计划，主要致力于收集与罗斯福夫人埃利诺·罗斯福（Eleanor Roosevelt，1884—1962）

---

① Miller Center, "Herbert Hoover Oral History", http://millercenter. org/scripps/archive/oral-histories/hoover, 2015 年 8 月 18 日访问。

② 相关研究成果可参阅 Lawrence Emerson Gelfand (ed.), *Herbert Hoover: The Great War and Its Aftermath, 1914-23*, Iowa City: University of Iowa Press, 1979; Carl E. Krog and William R. Tanner (eds.), *Herbert Hoover and the Republican Era: A Reconsideration*, Lanham: University Press of America, 1984; Donald J. Lisio, *The President and Protest: Hoover, MacArthur, and the Bonus Riot*, New York: Fordham University Press, second edition, 1994; Louis Liebovich, *Bylines in Despair: Herbert Hoover, the Great Depression, and the U. S. News Media*, Westport: Greenwood Publishing Group, 1994; W. Dale Nelson, *Who Speaks for the President?: The White House Press Secretary from Cleveland to Clinton*, Syracuse: Syracuse University Press, 1998; Anne Beiser Allen, *An Independent Woman: The Life of Lou Henry Hoover*, Westport: Greenwood Publishing Group, 2000; Timothy Walch, *Uncommon Americans: The Lives and Legacies of Herbert and Lou Henry Hoover*, Westport: Greenwood Publishing Group, 2003; Lee Nash, *Herbert Hoover and World Peace*, Lanham: University Press of America, 2010; George H. Nash, *Freedom Betrayed: Herbert Hoover's Secret History of the Second World War and Its Aftermath*, Stanford: Hoover Institution Press, 2011.

③ 通过哥大口述历史中心（Columbia Center for Oral History）"口述历史在线门户"（Oral History Portal, http://library. columbia. edu/find/oral-history-portal. html）查询关键词 "Franklin D. Roosevelt" 可以检索到与罗斯福总统相关的口述历史访谈达到 54 份，其中包括美国著名作家沃尔特·李普曼（Walter Lippmann, 1889—1974）和罗斯福总统女儿安娜·霍尔斯特德（Anna Roosevelt Halsted, 1906—1975）的访谈资料。

相关的口述历史访谈资料。① 而在埃利诺·罗斯福基金会（Eleanor Roosevelt Foundation）的资助下，该计划在 1977—1980 年间总共访谈 70 余位受访者。② 目前，罗斯福总统图书馆并没有将其口述历史收藏的目录或访谈抄本上传到官方网站，不过这并不影响学者对于这些珍贵资料的广泛使用，而以口述历史资料为重要资料来源的研究成果也相当丰富。③

---

① 早在 1957 年，埃利诺·罗斯福就曾接受哥大口述历史研究室的访谈，详细参阅 Columbia Center for Oral History，"Reminiscences of Eleanor Roosevelt: Oral History, 1957"，https: //clio. columbia. edu/catalog/4072968，2015 年 8 月 18 日访问。

② Roger Daniels （ed.），*The Eleanor Roosevelt Oral History Collection of the Franklin D. Roosevelt Library*，Westport: Meckler, 1991；"Eleanor Roosevelt Oral History Transcripts"，*Historical Materials in the Franklin D. Roosevelt Presidential Library*，Hyde Park: Franklin D. Roosevelt Presidential Library and Museum，National Archives and Records Administration，2011.

③ 相关研究成果可参阅 James E. Sargent，"Oral History, Franklin D. Roosevelt, and the New Deal: Some Recollections of Adolf A. Berle, Jr., Lewis W. Douglas, and Raymond Moley"，*Oral History Review*，Vol. 1，1973，pp. 92-109；John B. Kirby，*Black Americans in the Roosevelt Era: Liberalism and Race*，Knoxville: University of Tennessee Press, 1980；David Milton，*The Politics of U. S. Labor: From the Great Depression to the New Deal*，New York: Monthly Review Press，1982；Nancy Joan Weiss，*Farewell to the Party of Lincoln: Black Politics in the Age of FDR*，Princeton: Princeton University Press, 1983；Maurine Hoffman Beasley，*Eleanor Roosevelt and the Media: A Public Quest for Self-fulfillment*，Urbana: University of Illinois Press, 1987；Robert Dallek，*Franklin D. Roosevelt and American Foreign Policy，1932-1945: With a New Afterword*，Oxford and New York: Oxford University Press, 1995；Mark J. Rozell and William D. Pederson （eds.），*FDR and the Modern Presidency: Leadership and Legacy*，Westport: Praeger Publishers, 1997；Kati Marton，*Hidden Power: Presidential Marriages That Shaped Our History*，New York: Pantheon Books，2001；Steven Casey，*Cautious Crusade: Franklin D. Roosevelt, American Public Opinion, and the War against Nazi Germany*，Oxford and New York: Oxford University Press, 2001；Thomas Fleming，*The New Dealers' War: Franklin D. Roosevelt and the War Within World War II*，New York: Basic Books, 2001；Michael Janeway，*The Fall of the House of Roosevelt: Brokers of Ideas and Power from FDR to LBJ*，New York: Columbia University Press, 2004；Julie M. Fenster，*FDR's Shadow: Louis Howe, The Force That Shaped Franklin and Eleanor Roosevelt*，New York: Palgrave Macmillan，2009；James Tobin，*The Man He Became: How FDR Defied Polio to Win the Presidency*，New York: Simon & Schuster, 2013.

如上所述，哈里·杜鲁门总统图书馆是美国第一个率先启动口述历史计划的总统图书馆，于1961年（也有一说是1963年）由时任图书馆馆长菲利普·布鲁克斯（Philip C. Brooks, 1906—1977）负责主持，其主要目的是为了填补有关哈里·杜鲁门（Harry S. Truman, 1884—1972；总统任期为1945—1953年）总统生平及其时代的文献记录的空白或弥补其不足。① 目前，图书馆所收藏的口述历史访谈数量达到500份左右，访谈抄本页数从几页到1000多页不等，不过大部分都在20—200页。② 值得一提的是，由于杜鲁门总统实施的马歇尔计划（Marshall Plan）在欧洲影响深远，因此口述历史计划中有许多受访者是来自欧洲的领导人，比如联邦德国首任总理康拉德·阿登纳（Konrad Adenauer, 1876—1967）和法国欧洲经济合作组织（Organization for European Economic Cooperation）秘书长罗伯特·马若兰（Robert Marjolin, 1911—1986）等。而在数字化在线传播方面，杜鲁门总统图书馆则走在其他总统图书馆前面，目前已经将口述历史资料的所有索引指南信息（按照受访者分类）和绝大部分访谈抄本全文都上传到其官方

① Philip C. Brooks, "The Harry S. Truman Library-Plans and Reality", *American Archivist*, Vol. 25, No. 1, 1962, pp. 25-37; Charles T. Morrissey, "Truman and the Presidency: Records and Oral Recollections", *American Archivist*, Vol. 28, No. 1, 1965, pp. 53-61; Forrest C. Pogue, "Philip Brooks and Oral History", *Oral History Association Newsletter*, Vol. 11, No. 4, Fall 1977, p. 6; Harry S. Truman Library, *Historical Materials in the Harry S. Truman Library*, Independence: Harry S. Truman Library, 1982, p. 2; Jonathan Soffer, "Oral History and the History of American Foreign Relations", *Journal of American History*, Vol. 82, No. 2, 1995, p. 607; Regina Greenwell, "The Oral History Collections of the Presidential Libraries", *Journal of American History*, Vol. 84, No. 2, 1997, p. 598. 不过，杜鲁门本人的口述历史访谈并非由总统图书馆执行，他曾于1959年和20世纪60年代接受莫尔·米勒（Merle Miller）等人的多次口述历史访谈，相关成果可以参阅 Merle Miller, *Plain Speaking: An Oral Biography of Harry S. Truman*, New York: Berkley Publishing Corporation, 1974; Ralph Edward Weber (ed.), *Talking with Harry: Candid Conversations with President Harry S. Truman*, Wilmington: Scholarly Resources, 2001.

② 需要指出的是，其中也有相当一部分口述历史资料是由其他机构完成的，包括国家公园管理局（National Park Service）、孟菲斯州立大学口述历史研究室（Memphis State University Oral History Research Office）、威廉诸维尔学院口述历史计划（William Jewell College Oral History Project）和参议院历史办公室等。

网站。① 同样，这些极其丰富的口述历史资料也是研究杜鲁门总统时代的美国政治史、外交史、经济史与社会史等相关领域及撰写人物传记的重要资料来源。②

德怀特·艾森豪威尔总统图书馆（Dwight D. Eisenhower Presidential Library）同罗斯福总统图书馆一样，其口述历史收藏有相当一部分来自与其他机构的合作或捐赠。在美国国家人文科学基金会（National Endowment for the Humanities）与国家档案和记录管理局的部分资助下，哥大口述历史研究室于 1962—1972 年间启动"艾森豪威尔政府口述历史计划"（Eisenhower Administration Oral History Project），主要致力于收集那些在艾森豪威尔政府时期扮演重要角色的亲历者的第一手证词。除德怀特·艾森豪威尔（Dwight D. Eisenhower, 1890—1969；总统任期为 1953—1961 年）及其家族成员之外，受访者还包括白宫职员、内阁成员、政治顾问、国会议员、行政管理人员、科学家、新闻记者、

---

① Harry S. Truman Library, "Oral History Interviews", http：//www. trumanlibrary. org/oral-hist/oral_ his. htm, 2015 年 8 月 19 日访问。

② 相关研究成果可参阅 Robert J. Donovan, *Tumultuous Years*：*The Presidency of Harry S. Truman*, *1949-1953*, New York：Norton, 1982；Nancy Bernkopf Tucker, *Patterns in the Dust*：*Chinese-American Relations and the Recognition Controversy*, *1949-1950*, New York：Columbia University Press, 1983；June M. Grasso, *Truman's Two-China Policy*：*1948-1950*, Armonk：M. E. Sharpe, 1987；Michael J. Hogan, *The Marshall Plan*：*America*, *Britain and the Reconstruction of Western Europe*, *1947-1952*, Cambridge：Cambridge University Press, 1987；Rosemary Foot, *A Substitute for Victory*：*The Politics of Peacemaking at the Korean Armistice Talks*, Ithaca：Cornell University Press, 1990；David McCullough, *Truman*, New York：Simon & Schuster, 1992；Melvyn P. Leffler, *A Preponderance of Power*：*National Security*, *the Truman Administration*, *and the Cold War*, Stanford：Stanford University Press, 1992；Robert H. Ferrell, *Harry S. Truman*：*A Life*, Columbia：University of Missouri Press, 1994；Sean J. Savage, *Truman and the Democratic Party*, Lexington：University Press of Kentucky, 1997；Franklin D. Mitchell, *Harry S. Truman and the News Media*：*Contentious Relations*, *Belated Respect*, Columbia：University of Missouri Press, 1998；Michael R. Gardner, *Harry Truman and Civil Rights*：*Moral Courage and Political Risks*, Carbondale：Southern Illinois University Press, 2002；Robert H. Ferrell, *Harry S. Truman and the Cold War Revisionists*, Columbia：University of Missouri Press, 2006；Michael J. Devine, *Harry S. Truman*, *the State of Israel*, *and the Quest for Peace in the Middle East*, Kirksville：Truman State University Press, 2009；Donald A. Ritchie (ed.), *Congress and Harry S. Truman*：*A Conflicted Legacy*, Kirksville：Truman State University Press, 2011.

大使及军事和民事专家等。该计划总共收集口述历史访谈 369 份，整理而成的访谈抄本达到 35695 页。① 最后，通过双方的合作安排，哥大口述历史研究室将全部访谈抄本捐赠给艾森豪威尔总统图书馆。而艾森豪威尔总统图书馆自己的口述历史项目于 1963 年（也有一说是 1967 年）开始，② 在哥大计划的基础上，其访谈对象则进一步扩大以更加完整地呈现艾森豪威尔总统的生平及其时代。而在数字化方面，图书馆目前已经将口述历史资料的所有索引指南信息（按照受访者分类）和少部分访谈抄本上传到其官方网站。③ 同样，这些口述历史资料也是深受众多学者的欢迎和重视，并有大量相关研究成果问世。④

① 详细内容参阅 Columbia Center for Oral History, "Eisenhower Administration Project: Oral History, 1962—1972", https: //clio. columbia. edu/catalog/4074583, 2015 年 8 月 19 日访问。另外，艾森豪威尔总统的口述历史访谈可参阅 Columbia Center for Oral History, "Reminiscences of Dwight David Eisenhower: Oral History, 1967", https: //clio. columbia. edu/catalog/4074245, 2015 年 8 月 19 日访问。"Eisenhower and Stevenson Projects at Columbia Receive a Decrease in Funding, But the Carnegie Corporation Extends Its One-Year Project to Two", *Oral History Association Newsletter*, Vol. 2, No. 2, April 1968, p. 2; John E. Wickman, "Dwight D. Eisenhower Library", *Encyclopedia of Library and Information Sciences* (Vol. 37), New York: Marcel Dekker, 1984, pp. 77-78.

② 《艾森豪威尔总统图书馆历史资料》在"前言"中指出，图书馆与哥大口述历史研究室合作的口述历史计划的起止时间是 1960—1973 年，而如上所述，哥大记录则是 1962—1972 年。详细参阅 Dwight D. Eisenhower Library, *Historical Materials in the Dwight D. Eisenhower Library*, Abilene: Dwight D. Eisenhower Library, 1999, https: //web. archive. org/web/20060718175024/http://www. kansasheritage. org/abilene/holdings. html, 2015 年 8 月 19 日访问; Rebecca Sharpless, "The History of Oral History", in Thomas L. Charlton, Lois E. Myers, and Rebecca Sharpless(eds.), *Handbook of Oral History*, Walnut Creek: AltaMira Press, 2006, p. 23.

③ 详细内容参阅 Dwight D. Eisenhower Library, "Oral Histories", http: //www. eisenhower. archives. gov/research/oral_ histories. html, 2015 年 8 月 19 日访问。

④ 相关研究成果可参阅 Herbert S. Parmet, *Eisenhower and the American Crusades*, New York: Palgrave Macmillan, 1972; Elmo R. Richardson, *The Presidency of Dwight D. Eisenhower*, Lawrence: Regents Press of Kansas, 1979; Blanche W. Cook, *The Declassified Eisenhower: A Divided Legacy*, Garden City: Doubleday, 1981; Joann P. Krieg, *Dwight D. Eisenhower: Soldier, President, Statesman*, New York: Greenwood Press, 1987; Stephen G. Rabe, *Eisenhower and Latin America: The Foreign Policy of Anticommunism*, Chapel Hill: University of North Carolina Press, 1988; Rosemary Foot, *A Substitute for Victory: The Politics of Peacemaking at the Korean Armistice Talks*, Ithaca: Cornell University Press, 1990; John Lewis Gaddis, *Cold War Statesmen Confront the Bomb: Nuclear Diplomacy Since 1945*, Oxford and New York: Oxford University Press, 1999; Matthew F. Holland, *Eisenhower Between the Wars: The Making of a General and Statesman*, Westport: Praeger, 2001; Michael D. Bowen, *The Roots of Modern Conservatism: Dewey, Taft, and the Battle for the Soul of the Republican Party*, Chapel Hill: University of North Carolina Press, 2011; Douglas E. Clark, *Eisenhower in Command at Columbia*, Lanham: Lexington Books, 2013; Richard M. Filipink Jr. , *Dwight Eisenhower and American Foreign Policy during the 1960s: An American Lion in Winter*, Lanham: Lexington Books, 2015.

在约翰·肯尼迪（John F. Kennedy，1917—1963；总统任期为 1961-1963年）于 1963 年 11 月遇刺身亡之后不久，约翰·肯尼迪总统图书馆（John F. Kennedy Presidential Library）的筹建工作随即展开。而在卡内基基金会的资助下，总检察长罗伯特·肯尼迪（Robert F. Kennedy，1925—1968）于 1964 年 1 月宣布启动一项口述历史计划，其主要对象是肯尼迪政府职员、国内外政治家及总统朋友和家人，而当时的访谈者主要是来自肯尼迪政府时期的工作人员。从 1965 年开始，国家档案和记录管理局接管该项目，并聘请训练有素的历史学家负责访谈工作。而从 1970 年开始，该口述历史项目则正式转移到肯尼迪总统图书馆，并且不断扩展访谈对象，包括新闻记者、大使及商界与劳工界领袖等。[1] 目前，图书馆口述历史收藏总共达到 1600 多份，其中罗伯特·肯尼迪口述历史收藏大概有 300 多份。而在数字化方面，图书馆取得重大进展，除将所有口述历史访谈资料的详细索引指南信息（按照受访者分类）发布到官方网站之外，还提供大约 800 份访谈抄本的全文浏览与下载服务，而最终目标是尽可能将所有抄本在线上传。[2] 在资料使用方面，除将这些口述历史访谈抄本作为相关研究的重要

[1]　Anthony Lewis, "Taped Oral History of Kennedy to Go in Projected Library", *New York Times*, January 14, 1964; "Kennedy Library Adds Oral History Project on RFK", *Oral History Association Newsletter*, Vol. 6, No. 3/4, July 1972, p. 3; Dan H. Fenn, Jr., "Launching the John F. Kennedy Library", *American Archivist*, Vol. 42, No. 4, 1979, pp. 429-442; Robert E. Lester (ed.), *The John F. Kennedy Presidential Oral History Collection*, Frederick: University of Publications of America, 1988; Regina Greenwell, "The Oral History Collections of the Presidential Libraries", *Journal of American History*, Vol. 84, No. 2, 1997, p. 598; "John F. Kennedy Presidential Library and Museum", from Wikipedia, https://en.wikipedia.org/wiki/John_ F. _ Kennedy _ Presidential _ Library _ and _ Museum, 2015 年 8 月 20 日访问。

[2]　John F. Kennedy Library, "Oral History Program", http://www.jfklibrary.org/Research/About-Our-Collections/Oral-history-program. aspx, 2015 年 8 月 20 日访问。

资料来源之外；① 近年来，图书馆所保存的口述历史录音资料也被制作成广播纪录片（radio documentary），以充分展示口述历史的声音特征。②

由于林登·约翰逊（Lyndon B. Johnson，1908-1973；总统任期为1963—1969年）总统并不像其他某些总统那样喜欢用文字广泛记录其工作与生活经历，因此口述历史方法对于记录约翰逊生平及其时代就显得至关重要。总体而言，林登·约翰逊总统图书馆（Lyndon B. Johnson Presidential Library）的口述历史收藏主要来自四个机构所完成的口述历史计划，它们包括国家档案和记录管理局、约翰逊政府时期的白宫（White House）、德克萨斯大学奥斯汀分校和约翰逊总统图书馆。在图书馆正式启动口述历史计划之前，就有白宫工作人员、新闻记者和专业历史学家对林登·约翰逊进行了一系列访谈，其中以德克萨斯大学奥斯汀分校的乔·弗兰兹（Joe B. Frantz，1917—1993）教授最具代表性。在1967—1974年，作为德克萨斯大学奥斯汀分校约翰逊口述历史计划主任，他领导一个历史学家团队对约翰逊漫长职业生涯的每个阶段进行一系列访谈。③ 最后，该计划移交给

---

① 相关研究成果可参阅 Arthur M. Schlesinger, Jr., *Robert Kennedy and His Times*, Boston: Houghton Mifflin, 1978; Richard E. Welch, *Response to Revolution: The United States and the Cuban Revolution, 1959-1961*, Chapel Hill: University of North Carolina Press, 1985; Gordon H. Chang, *Friends and Enemies: The United States, China, and the Soviet Union, 1948-1972*, Stanford: Stanford University Press, 1990; Irving Bernstein, *Promises Kept: John F. Kennedy's New Frontier*, Oxford and New York: Oxford University Press, 1991; Gerald S. Strober and Deborah H. Strober, *"Let Us Begin Anew": An Oral History of the Kennedy Presidency*, New York: HarperCollins Publishers, 1993; Larry A. Sneed, *No More Silence: An Oral History of the Assassination of President Kennedy*, Denton: University of North Texas Press, 1998; David Niven, *The Politics of Injustice: The Kennedys, the Freedom Rides, and the Electoral Consequences of a Moral Compromise*, Knoxville: University of Tennessee Press, 2003; Philip A. Goduti, Jr., *Kennedy's Kitchen Cabinet and the Pursuit of Peace: The Shaping of American Foreign Policy, 1961-1963*, Jefferson: McFarland & Co., 2009; Edward R. Schmitt, *President of the Other America: Robert Kennedy and the Politics of Poverty*, Amherst: University of Massachusetts Press, 2010; Alice L. George, *The Assassination of John F. Kennedy: Political Trauma and American Memory*, London and New York: Routledge, 2013; Paul H. Santa Cruz, *Making JFK Matter: Popular Memory and the Thirty-Fifth President*, Denton: University of North Texas Press, 2015.

② Public Radio Exchange, *We Knew JFK: Unheard Stories from the Kennedy Archive*, http://weknewjfk.org/, 2015 年 8 月 20 日访问。

③ David G. Mccomb, "Joe B. Frantz", in Patrick L. Cox and Kenneth E. Hendrickson, Jr. (eds.), *Writing the Story of Texas*, Austin: University of Texas Press, 2013, pp. 211-222.

约翰逊总统图书馆，并由口述历史学家迈克尔·吉利特（Michael Gillette）和历史学家特德·吉特廷格（Ted Gittinger）主持。该计划主要集中于那些文献记录相对缺乏和不完整的主题和事件，比如约翰逊所领导的新政时期的国家青年局（National Youth Administration）、约翰逊的参议员生涯、越南战争及贫困宣战计划等。目前，图书馆口述历史收藏总共达到1234份左右，受访人数超过1000人（有些人接受不同机构的口述历史访谈）。而在数字化方面，图书馆已经将口述历史资料的所有索引指南信息（按照受访者分类）和少部分访谈抄本（只有大约90份）上传到其官方网站，该网站还提供在线访谈抄本的全文检索功能。① 不过，值得一提的是，目前已有1161份口述历史访谈的完整抄本可以通过弗吉尼亚大学米勒公共事务中心官方网站进行浏览和下载。② 当然，这些极其丰富的口述历史资料已经成为研究约翰逊总统时代的美国政治史、外交史、经济史与社会史等相关领域及撰写人物传记的重要资料来源。③

理查德·尼克松总统图书馆（Richard Nixon Presidential Library）直到

---

① Lyndon B. Johnson Library, *Historical Materials in the Lyndon B. Johnson Library*, Austin：Lyndon B. Johnson Library, 1977；Robert E. Lester（ed.）, *Oral Histories of the Johnson Administration, 1963-1969*, Frederick：University of Publications of America, 1988；Regina Greenwell, "The Oral History Collections of the Presidential Libraries", *Journal of American History*, Vol. 84, No. 2, 1997, pp. 598-599；Lyndon B. Johnson Library, "Oral Histories", http：//www. lbjlibrary. net/collections/oral-histories/, 2015年8月20日访问。

② Miller Center, "Lyndon Johnson Oral History", http：//millercenter. org/scripps/archive/oral-histories/lbj, 2015年8月20日访问。

③ 相关研究成果可参阅 Merle Miller, *Lyndon：An Oral Biography*, New York：Putnam, 1980；Robert A. Divine, *The Johnson Years：Foreign policy, the Great Society, and the White House*, Lawrence：University Press of Kansas, 1987；John P. Burke and Fred L. Greenstein, *How Presidents Test Reality：Decisions on Vietnam, 1954 and 1965*, New York：Russell Sage Foundation, 1989；Michael L. Gillette, *Launching the War on Poverty：An Oral History*, New York：Twayne Publishers, 1996；Robert Dallek, *Flawed Giant：Lyndon Johnson and His Times, 1961-1973*, Oxford and New York ：Oxford University Press, 1998；Eric Alterman, *When Presidents Lie：A History of Official Deception and Its Consequences*, New York：Viking, 2004；Robert Mann, *When Freedom Would Triumph：The Civil Rights Struggle in Congress, 1954-1968*, Baton Rouge：Louisiana State University Press, 2007；Michael L. Gillette, *Lady Bird Johnson：An Oral History*, Oxford and New York：Oxford University Press, 2012；Gary A. Donaldson, *The Secret Coalition：Ike, LBJ, and the Search for a Middle Way in the 1950s*, New York：Carrel Books, 2014；Godfrey Hodgson, *JFK and LBJ：The Last Two Great Presidents*, New Haven：Yale University Press, 2015.

2007 年才成为联邦资助和管理的第 12 个总统图书馆，在此之前，美国国会（United States Congress）于 2004 年 1 月通过立法要求创建一个由联邦管理的尼克松总统图书馆。而其前身则是创建于 1990 年并由理查德·尼克松基金会（Richard Nixon Foundation）负责管理的理查德·尼克松图书馆和故居（Richard Nixon Library & Birthplace），目前尼克松故居由国家档案和记录管理局与尼克松基金会共同管理。① 与理查德·尼克松（Richard M. Nixon，1913—1994；总统任期为 1969—1974 年）相关的访谈工作开始于白宫工作人员的离职访谈（exit interviews），而离职访谈作为一种惯例也正是始于尼克松政府时期。② 基于此，国家档案和记录管理局创建尼克松总统资料办公室（Nixon Presidential Materials Staff）负责此项访谈工作，并由雷蒙德·格赛尔布拉赫特（Raymond H. Geselbracht）、弗雷德里克·格拉博斯克（Frederick J. Graboske）和保罗·施密特（Paul A. Schmidt）等人担任访谈者，他们于 1987 年和 1988 年对尼克松政府时期的多位白宫职员进行口述历史访谈（总共收集到 22 份访谈资料）。而新建尼克松总统图书馆的口述历史计划则由提摩西·纳夫塔利（Timothy Naftali）馆长于 2006 年启动，其目的是通过视频口述历史访谈来记录与保存尼克松政府时期的重要官员与相关人士的记忆与反思。到目前为止，该计划总共收集到大约 130 份访谈资料，占图书馆整个口述历史收藏（大约 150 多份）的绝大部分。而在数字化方面，尼克松总统图书馆也有所创新，除在线上传所有访谈资料的索引指南信息（按照受访者分类）和绝大部分访谈抄本之外，图书馆也尝试通过美国国家卫生研究院（National Institute of Health）的视频播放与播客系统（Videocasting and Podcasting）和 YouTube 网站来在线播放

---

① "Richard Nixon Presidential Library and Museum", from Wikipedia, https：// en. wikipedia. org/wiki/Richard_ Nixon_ Presidential_ Library_ and_ Museum, 2015 年 8 月 20 日访问。

② Regina Greenwell, "The Oral History Collections of the Presidential Libraries", *Journal of American History*, Vol. 84, No. 2, 1997, pp. 599-600.

口述历史视频资料。① 除此之外，加州州立大学富尔顿分校口述历史项目（Oral History Program, California State University, Fullerton）和惠特学院（Whittier College）在 20 世纪 60 年代末和 70 年代初期各自启动一项有关尼克松的口述历史计划，主要通过采访其家人、朋友和同僚来收集尼克松任总统之前的生活与工作经历，其中前者的访谈数量超过 190 份，而后者也达到 300 多份。② 作为记录和呈现尼克松生平与时代的重要资料，上述口述历史资料也是受到众多相关学者的高度重视与积极利用。③

杰拉尔德·福特总统图书馆（Gerald R. Ford Presidential Library）始建于 1979 年，并于 1981 年正式对外开放。④ 1980 年，国家档案和记录管理局工作人员启动一项"大急流城口述历史收藏计划"（Grand Rapids Oral History Collection Project），该计划主要采访杰拉尔德·福特（Gerald

---

① Richard Nixon Library, "Oral Histories", http：//www. nixonlibrary. gov/forresearchers/find/histories. php, 2015 年 8 月 20 日访问。

② Henry Raymont, "Whittier College to Produce Oral History of Nixon", *New York Times*, July 21, 1970; "Director Named for Nixon Oral History Project", *Oral History Association Newsletter*, Vol. 5, No. 3, July 1971, p. 2; Keith Takahashi, "Whittier Professor to Direct Nixon Research", *Los Angeles Times*, June 24, 1971; "Whittier College Richard Nixon Oral History Project", *Oral History Association Newsletter*, Vol. 8, No. 2, Summer 1974, p. 7; James L. Ash, Jr., "Nixon Oral History", *Los Angeles Times*, July 18, 1994; Renée K. Schulte (ed.), *The Young Nixon: An Oral Inquiry*, Fullerton: Oral History Program, CSUF, 1978; Joseph Dmohowski, "The Pre-Political Years, 1913-1945", in Melvin Small (ed.), *A Companion to Richard M. Nixon*, Malden: Wiley Blackwell, 2011, pp. 35-36.

③ 相关研究成果可参阅 Hal Bochin, *Richard Nixon: Rhetorical Strategist*, New York: Greenwood Press, 1990; Leon Friedman and William F. Levantrosser, *Watergate and Afterward: The Legacy of Richard M. Nixon*, Westport: Greenwood Press, 1992; Gerald S. Strober and Deborah H. Strober, *Nixon: An Oral History of His Presidency*, New York: HarperCollins, 1994; Blema S. Steinberg, *Shame and Humiliation: Presidential Decision Making on Vietnam*, Pittsburgh: University of Pittsburgh Press, 1996; Vamik D. Volkan, Norman Itzkowitz, and Andrew W. Dod, *Richard Nixon: A Psychobiography*, New York: Columbia University Press, 1997; Dean J. Kotlowski, *Nixon's Civil Rights: Politics, Principle, and Policy*, Cambridge: Harvard University Press, 2001; David Greenberg, *Nixon's Shadow: The History of an Image*, New York: W. W. Norton, 2003; Tim Weiner, *One Man Against the World: The Tragedy of Richard Nixon*, New York : Henry Holt and Company, 2015.

④ "Gerald R. Ford Presidential Library", from Wikipedia, https: //en. wikipedia. org/wiki/Gerald_ R. _ Ford_ Presidential_ Library, 2015 年 8 月 21 日访问。

R. Ford，1913—2006；总统任期为 1974—1977 年）在大急流城时期的 7 位同僚，访谈主题涉及他们的相识过程、20 世纪 30—40 年代的大急流城政治及 1948 年福特国会竞选活动等。① 随后，在杰拉尔德·福特基金会（Gerald R. Ford Foundation）资助下，福特总统图书馆于 1981 年启动自己的口述历史计划，由其工作人员对福特政府时期的官员、白宫职员、新闻记者及其他重要人士进行系列访谈。到目前为止，该计划总统访谈 40 余人，因而相对其他图书馆来说，福特图书馆的规模则是相当小的。② 另外，在 2008—2013 年，杰拉尔德·福特基金会独立启动"杰拉尔德·福特口述历史计划"（Gerald R. Ford Oral History Project），通过对福特家族成员、福特及其夫人朋友、福特政府时期的内阁成员及白宫工作人员等众多相关人士的口述历史访谈，从而记录和保存福特的持久遗产。③ 不过事实上，福特图书馆口述历史收藏的主要内容还是来自新闻记者、历史学家、政治科学家、传记作家、独立作家及美国海军陆战队和国家航空航天局等个人和机构的捐赠。而在数字化方面，福特图书馆的努力也是相对迟缓的，除完整在线上传"大急流城口述历史收藏"的 7 个访谈抄本之外，其他访谈资料则仅仅提供较为详细的索引指南信息（按照受访者分类）。④ 尽管如此，这些相当宝贵的口述历史资料仍然是研究福特生平及其时代的重要资

---

① Gerald R. Ford Library，"Grand Rapids Oral History Collection"，http：//www. fordlibrarymu-seum. gov/library/guides/findingaid/Grand_ Rapids_ -_ Oral_ Histories. asp，2015 年 8 月 21 日访问。

② Gerald R. Ford Library，"Gerald R. Ford Library Oral History Projects"，http：//www. fordlibrarymuseum. gov/library/guides/findingaid/grfliboh. asp，2015 年 8 月 21 日访问；Cathy Lu-bin，"Gerald F. Ford Library：Archives of a President"，*Michigan Ensian*，Vol. 85，1981，pp. 106-107.

③ 该计划总共收集 160 多份访谈资料，目前大部分抄本都已经上网。详细内容访问"Gerald R. Ford Oral History Project"，http：//geraldrfordfoundation. org/centennial/oralhistory/，2015 年 8 月 21 日访问。

④ Gerald R. Ford Library，"Oral Histories in the Gerald R. Ford Library"，http：//www. fordlibrarymuseum. gov/library/oralhist. asp，2015 年 8 月 21 日访问；David A. Horrockes（ed.），*Guide to Historical Material in the Gerald R. Ford Presidential Library*，Ann Arbor：Gerald R. Ford Library，2009.

料来源。①

吉米·卡特总统图书馆（Jimmy Carter Presidential Library）始建于 1984 年，并于 1986 年正式对外开放。② 有关吉米·卡特（Jimmy Carter，1924—，总统任期为 1977—1981 年）总统的口述历史工作也是始于离职访谈，国家档案和记录管理局专门设立一个联络办公室负责此项工作，并由玛丽·艾伦（Marie Allen）、戴维·阿尔索布鲁克（David Alsobrook）和艾米丽·索佩斯（Emily W. Soapes）等人担任主要访谈者，他们于 1977-1981 年对卡特政府时期的多位白宫职员（包括高级总统顾问）进行口述历史访谈，总共收集到 163 份访谈资料。国家档案和记录管理局工作人员还于 1978—1980 年启动"卡特/斯密斯家族口述历史计划"（Carter/Smith Family Oral History Project），该计划主要通过采访卡特总统和第一夫人的家族成员以集中记录卡特总统和第一夫人的早期生活，总共收集到 19 份访谈资料。不过，卡特总统图书馆自己的口述历史计划则直到 2000 年才开始，而且到目前为止也只收集到 10 份访谈资料，其中部分访谈得益于卡特中心（Carter Center）的支持。③ 此外，图书馆还积极通过获得其他机构的捐赠等渠道来增加口述历史收藏。作为弗吉尼亚大学米勒公共事务中心的首个总统口述历史计划，该中心于 1981 年启动"吉米·卡特口述历史计划"（Jimmy Carter Oral History Project）。在弗吉尼亚大学政治学教授、班克罗

---

① 相关研究成果可参阅 James Reichley, *Conservatives in an Age of Change：The Nixon and Ford Administrations*, Washington：Brookings Institution, 1981；James M. Cannon, *Time and Chance：Gerald Ford's Appointment with History*, New York：HarperCollins, 1994；John Robert Greene, *The presidency of Gerald R. Ford*, Lawrence：University Press of Kansas, 1995；Kenneth E. Collier, *Between the Branches：The White House Office of Legislative Affairs*, Pittsburgh：University of Pittsburgh Press, 1997；Arthur J. Dommen, *The Indochinese Experience of the French and the Americans：Nationalism and Communism in Cambodia, Laos, and Vietnam*, Bloomington：Indiana University Press, 2001；Nancy Gibbs and Michael Duffy, *The Presidents Club：Inside the World's Most Exclusive Fraternity*, New York：Simon & Schuster, 2012.

② "Jimmy Carter Library and Museum", from Wikipedia, https：//en. wikipedia. org/wiki/Jimmy_ Carter_ Library_ and_ Museum, 2015 年 8 月 21 日访问。

③ Jimmy Carter Library, "Oral Histories at the Jimmy Carter Library", http：//www. jimmycarterlibrary. gov/library/oralhist. phtml, 2015 年 8 月 21 日访问。

夫特奖（Bancroft Prize）获得者詹姆斯·杨格（James Sterling Young, 1927—2013）的领导下，在 1981—1985 年，该中心学者完成 50 多位卡特政府时期重要成员（包括卡特总统本人）的口述历史访谈，而目前已有一半左右（23 份）的口述历史访谈抄本上传到官方网站。[①] 而国家公园管理局也曾于 1985—1990 年间启动"普莱恩斯计划口述历史"（Plains Project Oral Histories）项目，它主要通过与卡特和夫人罗莎琳·卡特（Rosalynn Carter, 1927— ）的口述历史访谈来帮助吉米·卡特国家历史公园（Jimmy Carter National Historical Park）的规划者与设计者更好地理解卡特的童年家乡生活对于其政治和人权思想发展的重要性。为更好地记录和保存卡特的早年生活经历，该项目还对普莱恩斯的居民、家乡教堂的牧师以及卡特的同学、老师、亲戚及邻居进行系列访谈，总共收集到 25 份访谈资料。[②] 而在数字化方面，卡特总统图书馆将其口述历史收藏的所有简单目录（按照受访者分类）和部分访谈抄本上传到官方网站。[③] 当然，对于卡特生平及其时代的研究者来说，上述口述历史资料毫无疑问是补充文献记录的重要资料来源。[④]

[①] Miller Center, "Jimmy Carter Oral Histories", http：//millercenter. org/president/carter/oral-history, 2015 年 8 月 21 日访问。

[②] Lu Ann Jones（ed.）, *A Directory of Oral History in the National Park Service*, Washington：National Park Service, U. S. Department of the Interior, third edition, 2015, pp. 39-40.

[③] Jimmy Carter Library, "Oral Histories at the Jimmy Carter Library", http://www. jimmycarterlibrary. gov/library/oralhist. phtml, 2015 年 8 月 21 日访问。

[④] 相关研究成果可参阅 Erwin C. Hargrove, *Jimmy Carter as President：Leadership and the Politics of the Public Good*, Baton Rouge：Louisiana State University Press, 1988；Charles O. Jones, *The Trustee Presidency：Jimmy Carter and the United States Congress*, Baton Rouge：Louisiana State University Press, 1988；Robert P. Grathwol, Donita M. Moorhus, and Douglas J. Wilson, *Oral History and Postwar German-American Relations：Resources in the United States*, Washington：German Historical Institute, 1997；Kenneth E. Morris, *Jimmy Carter, American Moralist*, Athens：University of Georgia Press, 1996；Robert A. Strong, *Working in the World：Jimmy Carter and the Making of American Foreign Policy*, Baton Rouge：Louisiana State University Press, 2000；Robert Schlesinger, *White House Ghosts：Presidents and Their Speechwriters*, New York：Simon & Schuster, 2008；Scott A. Frisch, *Jimmy Carter and the Water Wars*, Amherst：Cambria Press, 2008；Erica J. Seifert, *The Politics of Authenticity in Presidential Campaigns, 1976-2008*, Jefferson：McFarland & Co. , 2012；William Steding, *Presidential Faith and Foreign Policy：Jimmy Carter the Disciple and Ronald Reagan the Alchemist*, New York：Palgrave Macmillan, 2014.

罗纳德·里根总统图书馆（Ronald Reagan Presidential Library）始建于1988 年，并于 1991 年正式对外开放。① 到目前为止，里根总统图书馆的口述历史收藏主要来自离职访谈和其他机构的捐赠。在 1981—1988 年，白宫记录管理办公室（Office of Records Management）与国家档案和记录管理局的工作人员对罗纳德·里根（Ronald W. Reagan，1911—2004；总统任期为 1981—1989 年）政府时期的离职白宫职员进行口述历史访谈，总共收集到 201 份录音访谈。由于里根图书馆是受《1978 年总统记录法案》（*Presidential Records Act of 1978*）管理的首个总统图书馆，根据其规定，上述的离职访谈属于总统记录而并非捐赠的历史资料，因而受到信息自由法案（*Freedom of Information Act*，"FOIA"）的保护与约束。如果要获得这些访谈资料（只有录音带资料），必须依据标准程序向图书馆提出信息自由法案请求（FOIA request）。② 正是如此，里根总统图书馆也只是将这些离职访谈的较为详细的索引指南信息（按照受访者分类）上传到其官方网站，而且其中部分录音资料仍然不能对外开放。③ 目前，里根总统图书馆受赠的口述历史收藏主要来自加州大学伯克利分校地区口述历史办公室和战略防御计划组织（Strategic Defense Initiative Organization），该部分访谈资料达到 116 份左右，它们主要完成于 20 世纪 80 年代至 21 世纪初。④ 不过，有关里根的最具系统性的口述历史工作还是弗吉尼亚大学米勒公共事务中心于 2001 年启动的"罗纳德·里

---

① 早在 1984 年就曾决定在斯坦福大学建造里根图书馆，不过该规划于 1987 年被取消。详细参阅 Robert Lindsey，"Plan for Reagan Library at Stanford Is Dropped"，*New York Times*，April 24，1987；"Ronald Reagan Presidential Library"，from Wikipedia，https://en. wikipedia. org/wiki/Ronald_ Reagan_ Presidential_ Library，2015 年 8 月 21 日访问。

② "White House Staff Exit Interviews"，in Ronald Reagan Presidential Library，*Preliminary List of Holdings of Presidential Records and Historical Materials in the Ronald Reagan Presidential Library*，Simi Valley：Ronald Reagan Presidential Library，2014，pp. 164-173.

③ White House Office of Records Management，"White House Staff Exit Interviews，Reagan Library Collections"，http：//www. reagan. utexas. edu/archives/textual/smof/whormexi. htm，2015 年 8 月 21 日访问。

④ "Personal Records"，in Ronald Reagan Presidential Library，*Preliminary List of Holdings of Presidential Records and Historical Materials in the Ronald Reagan Presidential Library*，Simi Valley：Ronald Reagan Presidential Library，2014，pp. 173-178.

根口述历史计划"（Ronald Reagan Oral History Project）。在与里根总统图书馆的合作下（提供档案支持），该中心于2001—2004年总共完成45份里根政府时期重要成员的口述历史访谈，目前大部分访谈抄本（36份）都已经上传到官方网站（2006年1月首次对外开放）。该计划也得到里根夫人南希·里根（Nancy Reagan，1921— ）的高度赞赏，她指出："米勒中心已经成为我们生活的一个宝贵部分，因为它与里根总统图书馆紧密合作以创建一个有关里根总统任期的最终的口述历史。……我知道罗尼（笔者注：南希对里根的昵称）一定很高兴看到这八年的历史能够为后代而记录。"① 同其他总统图书馆口述历史收藏一样，上述口述历史资料也是学者研究的重要资料来源。②

　　乔治·赫伯特·沃克·布什（以下简称"老布什"）总统图书馆（George Bush Presidential Library）于1997年正式对外开放，并于2007年整修之后重新开放。③ 从其2011年更新的图书馆收藏指南来看，除提到弗吉尼亚大学米勒公共事务中心口述历史计划收藏（Miller Center Oral History Project Collection）之外，并没有发现图书馆还有其他任何口述历史资料。④

---

① 详细内容参阅 Miller Center, *Ronald Reagan Oral History Project*, Charlottesville: Miller Center of Public Affairs, University of Virginia, 2006; Miller Center, "Ronald Reagan Oral Histories", http://millercenter. org/president/reagan/oralhistory, 2015年8月21日访问。还可参阅 Melanie Mayhew, "UVa Presents Reagan Through Interviews", *Daily Progress*, February 5, 2006; Dan Balz, "Oral Histories of Reagan Offer Glimpse of President", *Washington Post*, February 20, 2006.

② 相关研究成果可参阅 Earl W. Brian (ed.), *Governor Reagan's Cabinet and Agency Administration: Interviews*, Berkeley: Regional Oral History Office, University of California, Berkeley, 1986; William E. Pemberton, *Exit with Honor: The Life and Presidency of Ronald Reagan*, Armonk: M. E. Sharpe, 1997; Matthew Dallek, *The Right Moment: Ronald Reagan's First Victory and the Decisive Turning Point in American Politics*, New York: Free Press, 2000; Bob Colacello, *Ronnie and Nancy: Their Path to the White House, 1911 to 1980*, New York: Warner Books, 2004; Charles W. Dunn (ed.), *The Enduring Reagan*, Lexington: University Press of Kentucky, 2009; Margot Morrell, *Reagan's Journey: Lessons From a Remarkable Career*, New York: Simon & Schuster, 2011; Seth Rosenfeld, *Subversives: The FBI's War on Student Radicals, and Reagan's Rise to Power*, New York: Farrar, Straus and Giroux, 2012; James H. Broussard, *Ronald Reagan: Champion of Conservative America*, London and New York: Routledge, 2015; Jeffrey L. Chidester and Paul Kengor (eds.), *Reagan's Legacy in a World Transformed*, Cambridge: Harvard University Press, 2015.

③ "George Bush Presidential Library", from Wikipedia, https://en. wikipedia. org/wiki/George _ Bush_ Presidential _ Library, 2015年8月21日访问。

④ George Bush Presidential Library, *Guide to Holdings*, http://bush41library. tamu. edu/files/guide_ to_ holdings. pdf, 2015年8月21日访问。

显然，与上述其他总统图书馆不同，老布什总统图书馆并没有独立开展或合作参与任何类型的口述历史计划。① 而这个缺憾则由米勒公共事务中心弥补，1999 年该中心与老布什总统图书馆基金会（George H. W. Bush Presidential Library Foundation）合作启动"老布什口述历史计划"（George H. W. Bush Oral History Project），② 旨在通过口述历史来记录与保存老布什（George H. W. Bush，1924—　；总统任期为 1989—1993 年）政府时期关键人物的回忆与反思。在 1999—2011 年，该计划总共完成 44 份口述历史访谈（总时长大约 425 小时），目前大部分访谈抄本（31 份）都已经上传到官方网站。对于该计划，老布什也曾给予高度评价，他指出："幸运的是，米勒中心总是理解和尊重公共服务的目标。这体现在中心的学术工作中，正如这项有耐心的、持续的记录我的总统任期故事的计划。文献记录是重要的，但是你们的学者也增加了那些文件所无法捕捉的人文面向（human side）。对于我的总统任期和其他人来说，米勒中心是一个获得历史并为后代保存历史的地方。"③ 这些口述历史资料于 2011 年 10 月正式对外开放之后，④ 也很快引

① 有学者指老布什总统图书馆收藏中有 47 份离职访谈录音资料。详细参阅 Regina Greenwell，"The Oral History Collections of the Presidential Libraries"，*Journal of American History*，Vol. 84，No. 2，1997，p. 600. 老布什总统图书馆档案工作人员黛博拉·惠勒（Deborah Wheeler）于 2015 年 9 月 2 日给笔者的电子邮件回复中也表示，目前图书馆并没有任何开展有关老布什总统任期的口述历史计划。

② 需要指出的是，老布什总统图书馆基金会是一个成立于 1991 年的非政府组织，它主要致力于保存和维护老布什总统的历史遗产。除赞助它自己的项目之外，基金会也为老布什图书馆中心（George Bush Presidential Library Center）提供项目和经费支持，而老布什图书馆中心则包括老布什总统图书馆（博物馆）和德克萨斯州农工大学（Texas A&M University）布什政府与公共服务学院（Bush School of Government and Public Service）。详细内容访问 http：//bush41. org/presidential-library-foundation，2015 年 8 月 21 日访问。

③ Miller Center，*George H. W. Bush Oral History Project*，Charlottesville：Miller Center of Public Affairs，University of Virginia，2011；Miller Center，"George H. W. Bush Oral Histories"，http：//millercenter. org/president/bush/oralhistory，2015 年 8 月 21 日访问。需要指出的是，尽管老布什支持这项口述历史计划，不过他本人并不愿意接受访谈。详细参阅 Timothy Naftali，*George H. W. Bush*，New York：Times Books，2007，p. 163.

④ Kim Curtis，"U. Va. 's Miller Center Releases George H. W. Bush Oral History"，*UVA Today*，October 14，2011.

起学术界的高度关注与积极利用。①

威廉·克林顿总统图书馆（William J. Clinton Presidential Library）始建于 2001 年，并于 2004 年正式对外开放。② 从其最新发布的图书馆收藏指南来看，笔者也没有发现任何类型的口述历史资料。③ 显然，同老布什总统图书馆一样，克林顿总统图书馆也没有独立开展或合作参与任何类型的口述历史计划。④ 而有关克林顿（William J. Clinton，1946— ；总统任期为 1993—2001 年）总统任期的口述历史工作还是由弗吉尼亚大学米勒公共事务中心负责。2001 年，该中心与阿肯色大学费耶特维尔分校（University of Arkansas at Fayetteville）戴维/芭芭拉·普莱尔阿肯色口述与视觉历史中心（David and Barbara Pryor Center for Arkansas Oral and Visual History）共同合作启动"威廉·克林顿总统历史计划"（William J. Clinton Presidential History Project），该计划还得到克林顿基金会（Clinton Foundation）的合作与支持。⑤ 最终，该计划总共收集到 134 份口述历史访谈（平均访谈时长是 9—12 小时），其访谈对象包括克林顿政府时期的高级白宫职员、内阁成员、竞选和政治顾问、国会议员及国外政要等众多重要人士。自 2014 年

---

① 相关研究成果可参阅 Samuel L. Popkin，*The Candidate：What it Takes to Win，and Hold the White House*，Oxford and New York：Oxford University Press，2012；Jeffrey Engel，*Into the Desert：Reflections on the Gulf War*，Oxford and New York：Oxford University Press，2013；Michael Nelson and Barbara A. Perry（eds.），*41：Inside the Presidency of George H. W. Bush*，Ithaca：Cornell University Press，2014；Spencer D. Bakich，*Success and Failure in Limited War：Information and Strategy in the Korean，Vietnam，Persian Gulf，and Iraq Wars*，Chicago：University of Chicago Press，2014.

② "Clinton Presidential Center"，from Wikipedia，https：//en. wikipedia. org/wiki/Clinton_ Presidential_ Center，2015 年 8 月 22 日访问。克林顿总统中心包括克林顿图书馆（博物馆）、克林顿基金会办公室和阿肯色大学克林顿公共服务学院（Clinton School of Public Service）。

③ William J. Clinton Presidential Library，*Guide to Textual Holdings and Audiovisual Holdings*，http：//www. clinton library. gov/textual-research. html，2015 年 8 月 22 日访问。

④ 克林顿总统图书馆档案工作人员朗达·杨格（Rhonda Young）于 2015 年 9 月 1 日给笔者的电子邮件回复中也表示，图书馆没有对克林顿政府时期的内阁成员或其他官员做过任何口述历史访谈，而且也没有发起此项工作的任何计划。

⑤ 有关该计划的具体情况，可以参阅 Russell L. Riley，"*Presidential Oral History*：The Clinton Presidential History Project"，*Oral History Review*，Vol. 34，No. 2，2007，pp. 81-106；Russell L. Riley，"The White House as a Black Box：Oral History and the Problem of Evidence in Presidential Studies."*Political Studies*，Vol. 57，No. 1，2009，pp. 187-206.

11 月正式对外开放以来，这些口述历史资料的部分访谈抄本（66 份）已经上传到官方网站，① 而且也逐渐成为相关学者研究的重要资料来源。②

乔治·沃克·布什（以下简称"小布什"）总统图书馆（George W. Bush Presidential Library）始建于 2010 年，并于 2013 年正式对外开放。③ 同样，小布什总统图书馆也没有独立开展或合作参与任何类型的口述历史计划。而有关小布什总统任期的口述历史工作也是由弗吉尼亚大学米勒公共事务中心负责，在小布什总统卸任（2009 年 1 月 20 日）不到一年之内，小布什基金会（George W. Bush Foundation）于 2009 年 11 月 12 日宣布小布什总统已经选择米勒中心来执行其总统任期的口述历史计划。小布什指出："我很高兴的是，米勒中心将为了历史而记录我们政府关键成员的详细访谈。这个口述历史计划将帮助后代全面审视这个国家是怎样经历和面对某些特殊的挑战。"据了解，该计划的目标是收集大约 100 份口述历史访谈，受访者主要是白宫和内阁关键成员、政治顾问、国会议员和外国政要等重要人士。目前，该计划正在进行当中，等全部完成之后，相关资料也会像其他口述历史计划一样对外开放（包括网络访问），而且访谈抄本副本也将会保存在小布什总统图书馆。④

综观上述 13 个总统图书馆（或总统任期）口述历史计划（收藏）的基本情况，可以看到一个相当明显的特征，即从 20 世纪 60 年代开始，总

---

① Kristy Schantz and H. Brevy Cannon, "U. Va. Miller Center to Begin Releasing Clinton Presidential History Project Friday", *UVA Today*, November 13, 2014; Miller Center, "William J. Clinton Presidential History Project", http://millercenter.org/president/clinton/oralhistory, 2015 年 8 月 22 日访问。需要指出的是，这些口述历史访谈抄本副本也将保存在克林顿图书馆和戴维/芭芭拉·普莱尔阿肯色口述与视觉历史中心。

② 相关研究成果可参阅 Nicolas Bouchet, *Democracy Promotion as US Foreign Policy: Bill Clinton and Democratic Enlargement*, London and New York: Routledge, 2015.

③ "George W. Bush Presidential Center", from Wikipedia, https://en.wikipedia.org/wiki/George_W._Bush_Presidential_Center, 2015 年 8 月 22 日访问。小布什总统中心包括小布什总统图书馆（博物馆）、小布什政策研究所（George W. Bush Policy Institute）和小布什基金会办公室。

④ Kim Curtis, "Bush Selects U. Va.'s Miller Center to Conduct His Official Oral History", *UVA Today*, November 12, 2009; Miller Center, "George W. Bush Oral Histories", http://millercenter.org/president/gwbush/oralhistory, 2015 年 8 月 22 日访问。

统图书馆口述历史计划呈现迅速发展态势，其中尤以肯尼迪和约翰逊总统图书馆口述历史收藏的规模最为庞大。而从 20 世纪 80 年代开始，总统图书馆口述历史计划（收藏）的规模日益缩小，甚至从老布什总统图书馆开始已经没有独立开展或合作参与任何类型的口述历史计划。有学者认为，除经费问题之外，造成这种趋势的主要原因还在于两个方面：（1）越来越多的机构（以弗吉尼亚大学米勒公共事务中心最具代表性）和研究者开展与总统相关的口述历史计划，而总统图书馆也倾向于直接获取这些机构或研究者完成的口述历史资料副本；（2）口述历史访谈适合于记录那些已经过去一段时间的事件，所以新卸任政府任期的口述历史计划相对而言就比较难开展（尤其是很多当事人不愿意接受访谈），而这也是那些新建总统图书馆没有较早启动口述历史计划的重要原因所在。① 尽管如此，总统图书馆口述历史收藏的价值还是深受相关研究者的重视和好评，而上述所列的代表性研究成果就是很好的例证。

三　精英口述历史、档案实践与史料价值

综上所述，基于哥大开创的口述历史模式，从 1948 年到 20 世纪 70 年代初，口述史学在美国的发展呈现爆发式快速增长趋势。据统计，到 1965 年全美共有 89 个口述历史计划，而在 1971 年和 1973 年则分别达到 230 个和 316 个。② 正是如此，哥大口述历史研究室也认为它们在美国口述史学领域引领了一场"真正的运动"（veritable movement），大学（学院）、图书馆（档案馆、博物馆）、历史学会、专业协会、联邦机构、公司、医疗卫生机构

① Regina Greenwell, "The Oral History Collections of the Presidential Libraries", *Journal of American History*, Vol. 84, No. 2, 1997, pp. 600-601.

② Columbia University, Oral History Research Office, *Oral History in the United States*, New York: Oral History Research Office, 1965; Gary L. Shumway (ed.), *Oral History in the United States: A Directory*, New York: Oral History Association, 1971, p. 3; Louis Starr, "Oral History", *Encyclopedia of Library and Information Sciences* (Vol. 20), New York: Marcel Dekker, 1977, p. 451.

以及校友组织等不同机构和独立研究者都相当积极地开展各自的口述历史计划。[①]

总体而言，到 20 世纪 70 年代初之前，以哥大口述历史研究室为主要效仿模式的美国口述史学呈现出极强的精英主义特征与档案实践导向，其根本目的是基于精英人物的口述历史访谈而获得具有保存价值的原始资料以填补现有文献记录的空白或弥补其不足。正如迈克尔·弗里斯科（Michael Frisch）在 20 世纪 70 年代初所指出的，"美国口述史学通过阿兰·内文斯在哥大的计划而逐渐得到发展，其主要焦点是政治史和外交史，其主要工作是让那些大人物（Great Men）在去世之前进行'汇报'（de-briefing）。它的性质显然是档案的、信息的和精英主义的（archival, informational, and elitist）"[②]。这种口述历史起源与发展模式也被某些学者称为"精英口述历史"（elite oral history），其核心特征是以某一地区或领域的知名、重要或权势人物为主要访谈对象。[③]

---

① Columbia University, Oral History Research Office, *The Oral History Collection of Columbia University*, New York: Oral History Research Office, 1964, p10; "Voices of History", *Newsweek*, Vol. 66, 1965, p. 72; Ann Mozley, "Oral History", *History Studies*, Vol. 12, No. 48, 1967, pp. 571-578; James E. Bylin, "Schools, Firms Launch Oral History Projects For Later Research", *Wall Street Journal*, January 6, 1967; Louis M. Starr, "Oral History: A Term Becomes a Movement", *George C. Marshall Research Library Newsletter*, Vol. 8, No. 1, Fall 1969; Marjie Driscoll, "Scholars Give Oral History Permanence", *Los Angeles Times*, March 19, 1970; Raymond Walters, Jr., "The Last Word: Call It Oral History", *New York Times*, January 2, 1972; Alice M. Hoffman, "Oral History in the United States", *Journal of Library History*, Vol. 7, No. 3, 1972, pp. 277-285; Columbia University, Oral History Research Office, *Oral History*, Annual Report, New York: Oral History Research Office, 1975, p. 4.

② Michael Frisch, "Oral History and *Hard Times*: A Review Essay", *Oral History Review*, Vol. 7, 1979, p. 73. 该文最初发表于 *Red Buffalo: A Journal of American Studies*, Vol. 1, No. 2/3, 1972, pp. 217-231.

③ Lewis A. Dexter (ed.), *Elite and Specialized Interviewing*, Evanston: Northwestern University Press, 1970; Anthony Seldon and Joanna Pappworth, *By Word of Mouth: 'Elite' Oral History*, London: Methuen, 1983; Eva M. McMahan, *Elite Oral History Discourse: A Study of Cooperation and Coherence*, Tuscaloosa: University of Alabama Press, 1989; William Schneider, *Living with Stories: Telling, Re-Telling, and Remembering*, Logan: Utah State University Press, 2008, p. 4; Per Lundin, *Computers in Swedish Society: Documenting Early Use and Trends*, London: Springer-Verlag London, 2012, pp. 21-22; Ylva Waldemarson, "Openness and Elite Oral History: The Case of Sweden", in Norbert Götza and Carl Marklund (eds.), *The Paradox of Openness: Transparency and Participation in Nordic Cultures of Consensus*, Leiden and Boston: Brill, 2015, pp. 173-189.

如上所述，内文斯于 1938 年提出的开展口述历史工作的呼吁就明确强调其记录对象是那些参与美国政治、经济与文化生活的重要人士。而在其担任首任主任的 8 年间，不管是以个别人物生平访谈为基础的口述自传模式，还是一系列主体性的特别口述历史计划，哥大口述历史研究室所围绕的访谈对象绝大部分都是美国政治、经济、社会、文化艺术、医学与法律等领域的知名人士。① 而且，因为受访对象的族裔与性别身份问题，内文斯所代表的哥大口述历史模式更是被某些学者称为是口述史学的"伟大白人男性"（great white men）学派。② 而在内文斯退休之后的很长一段时间内，尽管哥大口述历史研究室的访谈主题不断扩展，但是其受访对象仍然集中于法官、内阁成员、参议员、出版商、企业家和公民领袖。③

同样，加州大学伯克利分校地区口述历史办公室在创建初期也强调其受访对象集中于那些对美国西部发展做出重要贡献的人。正如鲍姆（于 1958—2000 年间担任地区口述历史办公室主任）所说："根据这个任务，我们尽量局限于那些主导者（prime movers）本人，即使我们偶尔也会依赖诸如妻子或秘书等合适的目击者。"④ 而从 20 世纪 70

① Allan Nevins, "Oral History: How and Why It was Born", *Wilson Library Bulletin*, Vol. 40, 1966, pp. 600-601.

② Mary A. Larson, "Research Design and Strategies", in Thomas L. Charlton, Lois E. Myers, and Rebecca Sharpless（eds.）, *Handbook of Oral History*, Walnut Creek: AltaMira Press, 2006, p. 112; Staughton Lynd, "Oral History from Below", *Oral History Review*, Vol. 21, No. 1, 1993, p. 1.

③ Donald A. Ritchie, *Doing Oral History*, Oxford and New York: Oxford University Press, third edition, 2014, p. 6. 有关 20 世纪 70 年代初之前哥大口述历史研究室的受访者信息，可参阅 Elizabeth B. Mason and Louis M. Starr（eds.）, *The Oral History Collection of Columbia University*, New York: Oral History Research Office, 1973. 据笔者查询，1997 年哥大口述历史研究室官方主页的"研究室简介"仍然强调其目的是为了保存历史、政治和文化等许多领域的领导者（leaders）的知识、经历与回忆。详细访问"About the Oral History Research Office", https://web.archive.org/web/19970607165007/http://www.columbia.edu/cu/libraries/indiv/oral/brief.html, 2015 年 8 月 23 日访问。

④ Willa Klug Baum, "Oral History: A Revived Tradition at the Bancroft Library", *Pacific Northwest Quarterly*, Vol. 58, No. 2, 1967, p. 58.

年代开始，在其出版的口述历史访谈中有关办公室的简介时仍然强调口述历史的访谈对象是那些主要事件的主要参与者。该简介首句就指出："自 1954 年以来，地区口述历史办公室一直采访那些经历北加州、西部乃至美国发展的主要事件的主要参与者（leading participants）或合适目击者。"①

而上述详细介绍的美国总统图书馆（或总统任期）口述历史计划的精英主义特征就表现得更为突出，其访谈对象除总统本人及其家族成员和亲戚朋友之外，主要包括高级白宫工作人员、内阁成员、政治顾问、国会议员、驻外大使、国外政要及知名科学家和新闻记者等重要人士。② 此外，在 20 世纪 70 年代初之前，美国还有大量以政治家（比如国务卿、州长、参议员）、军事家、科学家、企业家、艺术家与医生等各领域精英人物为主题的专题性口述历史计划。事实上，在当时那些并不认可口述历史价值的传统美国史学家看来，口述历史唯一值得记录的就是那些所谓的首脑人物。正如美国著名历史学家、新闻记者芭芭拉·塔奇曼（Barbara W. Tuchman，1912—1989）所说："各种各样的人只是被邀请张开他们的嘴巴，在口述历史助手的日常督促下，并在录音机前面毫不费力和无休止地絮絮叨叨，少许有价值的和大量的垃圾被保存下来，否则它们都将化成灰尘。我们正在将我们自己淹没在不需要的信息当中。这里我应当急忙补充一点，其中我发现

---

① "Introductory Materials", in Paul Schuster Taylor, *California Social Scientist，an interview conducted in 1970 by Suzanne B. Riess*, Regional Oral History Office, The Bancroft Library, University of California, Berkeley, 1973. 该访谈全文可访问 http：//www. oac. cdlib. org/view？docId = ft5 q2 nb29 x&brand = oac4&doc. view = entire_ text，2015 年 8 月 23 日访问。

② 弗吉尼亚大学米勒公共事务中心总统口述历史项目（Presidential Oral History Program）联合主席拉塞尔·赖利（Russell L. Riley）就曾指出，该中心在杨格教授领导下并于 1981 年启动的总统口述历史项目主要是通过与那些在白宫和内阁中担任高级职位的重要人士的深度精英口述历史访谈（in-depth elite oral history interviews）而记录与保存有关总统及其时代的回忆。详细参阅 Russell L. Riley，"Preface"，in Russell L. Riley（ed.），*Bridging the Constitutional Divide：Inside the White House Office of Legislative Affairs*，College Station：Texas A&M University Press，2010，p. xiii.

的最为有用和夺人眼目的资料来源是陆军史学家在 1949 年与马歇尔将军所做的两份录音访谈。然而，马歇尔是值得记录的首脑人物（summit figure），这可比最近几年所积累的那些成架成堆的口述抄本（oral transcripts）更具价值。"①

显然，美国现代口述史学兴起与早期发展的这种精英主义模式与英国有着相当大的区别，在 20 世纪 50、60 年代，英国现代口述史学先驱则更加关注那些所谓的普通人物与边缘（弱势）群体。比如，英国著名民俗学家、口述史学先驱乔治·埃文斯（George Ewart Evans，1909—1988）从 20 世纪 50 年代开始就致力于搜集东英吉利（East Anglian）农村地区的口述历史与口头传统，并以这些口述资料为基础出版多本著作，其中以 1956 年出版的《问问那些割草的同伴》（Ask The Fellows Who Cut The Hay）最具代表性。该书通过对农村劳动者的生活及其时代的口述历史访谈，将农业史、经济史、文化研究及个人生活故事巧妙结合起来，它被称为是口述历史应用于农村社会史研究的典范之作。② 此外，在一系列有关英国农村（乡村）史、城市史与社会史的研究中，口述历史成为挖掘与呈现普通人物与边缘（弱势）群体的声音与记忆的重要手段，其中包括英国著名作家罗纳德·布莱斯（Ronald Blythe）有关阿肯菲尔德（Akenfield）乡村的研究、英国著名马克思主义史学家拉斐尔·塞缪尔（Raphael Samuel，1934—1996）有关黑丁顿采石场（Headington Quarry）的研究、保罗·汤普森有关爱德

---

① Barbara Tuchman, "Distinguish the Significant from the Insignificant", in David K. Dunaway and Willa K. Baum（eds.）, *Oral History: An Interdisciplinary Anthology*, Nashville: American Association for State and Local History, 1984, p.76. 该文最初发表于 *Radcliffe Quarterly*, Vol. 56, No. 4, 1972, pp. 9-10. 塔奇曼有关口述史学的其他论述可参阅 Barbara Tuchman, "Ventures in Oral History", in Gould P. Colman（ed.）, *The Fourth National Colloquium on Oral History*, New York: Oral History Association, 1970, pp. 128-142.

② George Ewart Evans, *Ask The Fellows Who Cut The Hay*, London: Faber and Faber, 1956. 相关研究还可参阅 Alun Howkins, "Inventing Everyman: George Ewart Evans, Oral History and National Identity", *Oral History*, Vol. 22, No. 2, 1994, pp. 26-32.

华时代的英国普通人的社会史研究以及英国著名历史学家杰里·怀特
（Jerry White）有关伦敦城市街区的研究。① 这种以非精英人物为主要
访谈对象的"来自下层历史"（history from below）的英国口述史学模
式深刻地反映了其兴起与早期发展的马克思主义史学与社会史传统，
而它与美国口述史学兴起与早期发展的政治史或精英人物传记传统形
成鲜明对比。②

　　这种精英主义模式与美国现代口述史学兴起与早期发展的档案实践导
向有着非常紧密的联系，其根本目的是基于精英人物的口述历史访谈而获
得具有保存价值的原始资料以填补现有文献记录的空白或弥补其不足。如
上所述，内文斯之所以倡导和开展口述历史计划，其主要原因是担心随着

---

① Ronald Blythe, *Akenfield: Portrait of an English Village*, London: Allen Lane The Penguin
Press, 1969; Raphael Samuel, "Headington Quarry: Recording a Labouring Community", *Oral
History*, Vol. 1, No. 4, 1972, pp. 107-122; Raphael Samuel, "Local History and Oral History",
History Workshop, No. 1, Spring 1976, pp. 191-208; Paul Thompson, *The Edwardians: The Re-
making of British Society*, London: Weidenfeld and Nicolson, 1975; Jerry White, *Rothschild Build-
ings: Life in an East End Tenement Block, 1887-1920*, London: Routledge and Kegan Paul, 1980.
有关英国现代口述史学的早期发展，可参阅 Alice M. Hoffman, "Oral History in Great Britain",
Journal of Library History, Vol. 7, No. 3, 1972, pp. 275-277; Paul Thompson, *The Voice of the
Past: Oral History*, Oxford and New York: Oxford University Press, third edition, 2000, pp. 82-
117; John Tosh, *The Pursuit of History: Aims, Methods and New Directions in the Study of History*,
London and New York: Routledge, sixth edition, 2015, pp. 263-267.

② Jeremy Brecher, *History from Below: How to Uncover and Tell the Story of Your Community,
Association, or Union*, New Haven: Commonwork Pamphlets, 1986; Robert Perks, *Oral History:
Talking about the Past*, London: The Historical Association and Oral History Society, second and revised edition, 1995, pp. 9-11; Alistair Thomson, "Unreliable Memories? The Use and Abuse of
Oral History", in William Lamont (ed.), *Historical Controversies and Historians*, London: University College London Press, 1998, p. 24; Daniel. R. Woolf, "Oral History", in Daniel. R. Woolf
(ed.), *A Global Encyclopedia of Historical Writing*, New York: Garland Publishing, 1998,
pp. 671-676; Máirtín Mac Con Iomaire, "Hidden Voices from the Culinary Past: Oral History as a
Tool for Food Historians", in Richard Hosking (ed.), *Food and Language: Proceedings of the Oxford Symposium on Food and Cookery 2009*, Totnes: Prospect Books, 2010, pp. 218; Donald
A. Ritchie, "Introduction: The Evolution of Oral History", in Donald A. Ritchie (ed.), *The Oxford Handbook of Oral History*, Oxford and New York: Oxford University Press, 2011, pp. 4-5; Peter Claus and John Marriott, *History: An Introduction to Theory, Method and Practice*, London and
New York: Routledge, 2012, pp. 413-415; Staughton Lynd, *Doing History from the Bottom Up:
On E. P. Thompson, Howard Zinn, and Rebuilding the Labor Movement from Below*, Chicago: Haymarket Books, 2014.

电话、汽车和飞机等通讯和交通技术的发展，那些重要人物原本可以通过信件、日记或会议记录等形式加以记录和保存的信息在不断丢失，因此需要通过口述历史访谈来挖掘与记录保留在他们大脑中的记忆，并以此补充现有文献记录的空白或缺憾。① 而这种档案实践导向也直接影响了美国早期口述历史学家对于口述历史概念的定义，正如斯塔尔所说："口述历史是通过有准备的、以录音机为工具的访谈，记录人们口述所得的具有保存价值和迄今尚未获得的原始资料（primary source material）。"② 正是由于哥大口述历史学术传统的影响，大部分美国早期实践者都相信口述历史主要是一种挖掘原始资料和补充文献资料空白或不足的方法。③ 在 1966 年举行的美国第一届全国口述史学会议上，杜鲁门总统图书馆馆长菲利普·布鲁克斯就坦言："口述历史是一种补充的方法——不是代替，而是补充——文献记录、信件、日记与档案等任何可能已经存在的资料。……对于我们

---

① "Oral History: Columbia's Library on Tape", *Library Journal*, Vol. 85, 1960, pp. 36-37; Frederick J. Stielow, *The Management of Oral History Sound Archives*, Westport: Greenwood Press, 1986, p. 18; Columbia University, Oral History Research Office, *Oral History: Oral History at Columbia American Craftspeople Project, Projects and Interviews, 1987-1992*, New York: Oral History Research Office, 1992, p. 1; Trevor Lummis, "Oral History", in Richard Bauman (ed.), *Folklore, Cultural Performances, and Popular Entertainments: A Communications-centered Handbook*, Oxford and New York: Oxford University Press, 1992, pp. 93-94; Sucheng Chan (ed.), *Not Just Victims: Conversations with Cambodian Community Leaders in the United States*, Urbana: University of Illinois Press, 2003, pp. xiii-xiv; Geertje Boschma, Margaret Scaia, Nerrisa Bonifacio, and Erica Roberts, "Oral History Research", in Sandra B. Lewenson and Eleanor Krohn Herrmann (eds.), *Capturing Nursing History: A Guide to Historical Methods in Research*, New York: Springer Publishing, 2008, pp. 81-82; Linda Shopes, "Oral History", in Norman K. Denzin and Yvonna S. Lincoln (eds.), *Collecting and Interpreting Qualitative Materials*, Thousand Oaks: Sage Publications, fourth edition, 2013, pp. 124-125.

② Louis Starr, "Oral History", *Encyclopedia of Library and Information Sciences* (Vol. 20), New York: Marcel Dekker, 1977, p. 440; 事实上，斯塔尔早在 1966 年举行的美国第一届全国口述史学会议上就将口述历史界定为是一种 "原始资料"。详细参阅 Elizabeth I. Dixon, "Definitions of Oral History", in Elizabeth I. Dixon and James V. Mink (eds.), *Oral History at Arrowhead: The Proceedings of the First National Colloquium on Oral History*, Los Angeles: Oral History Association, 1967, p. 13.

③ Nancy Whistler, *Oral History: Workshop Guide*, Denver: Denver Public Library, 1979, p. 1; Lila Johnson Goff and James E. Fogerty (eds.), *The Oral History Collections of the Minnesota Historical Society*, St. Paul: Minnesota Historical Society Press, 1984, p. vii; Janet Elaine Rasmussen, *New Land, New Lives: Scandinavian Immigrants to the Pacific Northwest*, Seattle: University of Washington Press, 1993, pp. 8-9.

来说，口述历史是搜集历史证据的方法之一。"① 此外，对于更为主流的美国历史学家来说，口述历史同样被理解为是对传统原始资料的补充。美国著名历史学家弗兰克·弗赖德尔在其主编的《哈佛美国历史指南》（*Harvard Guide to American History*）就曾指出："一种补充传统原始资料的相对新的发展是口述历史。作为额外原始资料的一种有意识的创建，它是一种历史记录类型和一种档案形式。……随着技术发展的逐渐标准化，口述历史被更为有效地用来填补更为常见的历史原始资料的空白之处。"② 另外一位美国著名历史学家小阿瑟·施莱辛格也认为口述历史的价值在于它本质上是一种补充的证据（supplementary evidence）。③

相对而言，口述历史的这种补充价值在有关总统等更为精英人物的口述历史计划中显得更为突出，因为对于他们来说，本身就存在大量相关的文献记录。正是如此，不管是 20 世纪 80 年代以前各个总统图书馆开展的口述历史计划，④ 还是弗吉尼亚大学米勒公共事务中心最新开展的总统口述历史项目，其根本宗旨仍然是强调通过口述历史来弥补文献记录的空白或不足。该中心在总统口述历史项目简介中指出："它们（口述历史抄本）通过提供个人证词（personal testimony）来充当文献记录的一种宝贵补充，这些证词能够阐释文献记录书写的背景、

---

① Elizabeth I. Dixon, "Definitions of Oral History", in Elizabeth I. Dixon and James V. Mink (eds.), *Oral History at Arrowhead: The Proceedings of the First National Colloquium on Oral History*, Los Angeles: Oral History Association, 1967, pp. 5-6.

② Frank Freidel (ed.), *Harvard Guide to American History*, Cambridge: Belknap Press of Harvard University Press, revised edition, 1974, p. 107.

③ Lynn A. Bonfield and Arthur M. Schlesinger Jr., "Conversation with Arthur M. Schlesinger, Jr.: The Use of Oral History", *American Archivist*, vol. 43, No. 4, 1980, p. 466. 当然，除补充价值之外，也有学者认为通过口述历史获得的个人叙述也能够交叉验证文献记录中的偏见信息。详细参阅 Diana Kapiszewski, Lauren M. MacLean, and Benjamin L. Read, *Field Research in Political Science: Practices and Principles*, Oxford and New York: Oxford University Press, 2015, p. 197.

④ 比如，肯尼迪总统图书馆在其口述历史项目简介中就指出："录音带和抄本旨在补充我们的档案收藏，并且最好与那些资料结合起来使用。"详细参阅 John F. Kennedy Library, "Oral History Program", http://www.jfklibrary.org/Research/About-Our-Collections/Oral-history-program.aspx, 2015 年 8 月 24 日访问。

那些文献记录书写者的想法，以及文献记录与它们的接收者之间的关系。"①

正是这样一种以保存原始资料和补充文献记录不足为目的的档案实践导向，也决定了早期美国口述历史计划或机构大部分都设立在图书馆或档案馆中，而较少设在历史系或其他相关院系。② 除上述提到的总统图书馆和其他公共图书馆的口述历史计划之外③，以大学为基础的口述历史计划或机构也基本上都是设立在大学图书馆或档案馆中。比如，哥大口述历史研究室和加州大学伯克利分校地区口述历史办公室就分别设在巴特勒图书馆和班克罗夫特图书馆。据笔者统计，以 1971 年出版的《美国口述历史目录》为例，在该目录所罗列的 200 个口述历史计划或机构当中，由大学（学院）主办的共有 104 个，而其中有 50 个设在大学图书馆或档案馆中，而只有 24 个设在大学历史系当中。④ 正是如此，从事口述历史工作的实践者与研究者并不都是历史学家，而有相当一部分则是图书管理员或档案工作者。而他们对于口述历史的关注也主要集中于那些由图书馆和档案馆工作者提出的问题，比如：如何执行和处理口述历史访谈、口述历史如何被编目和保存、口述历史资料的使用问题、口述历史的著作权问

---

① 详细参阅 Miller Center，"Program Description of the Presidential Oral History Program"，http：//millercenter. org/oralhistory/programdescription，2015 年 8 月 24 日访问。其他参阅 Vivian Perlis and Libby Van Cleve，*Composers Voices from Ives to Ellington*：*An Oral History of American Music*，New Haven：Yale University Press，2005，p. xviii；John D' Emilio，"Afterword"，in Nan Alamilla Boyd and Horacio N. Roque Ramírez（eds.），*Bodies of Evidence*：*The Practice of Queer Oral History*，Oxford and New York：Oxford University Press，2012，p. 270.

② Daniel Chew，"Oral History Methodology：The Life History Approach"，in P. Lim Pui Huen，James H. Morrison，and Kwa Chong Guan（eds.），*Oral History in Southeast Asia*：*Theory and Method*，Singapore：National Archives of Singapore and Institute of Southeast Asian Studies，1998，p. 53；Ronald J. Grele，"Oral History as Evidence"，in Thomas L. Charlton，Lois E. Myers，and Rebecca Sharpless（eds.），*Handbook of Oral History*，Walnut Creek：AltaMira Press，2006，p. 45.

③ 有关 20 世纪 80 年代中期以前美国公共图书馆口述历史计划的情况，可参阅 Joseph W. Palmer，*Oral History in Public Libraries*，Urbana：University of Illinois Graduate School of Library and Information Science，1984.

④ 其中有 5 个是图书馆和历史系共同主办。上述信息总结自 Gary L. Shumway（ed.），*Oral History in the United States*：*A Directory*，New York：Oral History Association，1971.

题以及口述历史与其他历史资料类型之间的关系问题等。① 而这些问题也成为早期美国口述史学方法论研究的核心问题，即如何更好地通过口述历史访谈而获得具有保存价值并能够为其他研究者所使用的原始资料。

为满足上述需求，从 20 世纪 60 年代中期开始，美国口述历史学界开始出版相关的口述历史实践手册或指南。② 不过较早出版的与口述历史相关的实践手册并不是来自口述历史学界，而是由美国州与地方历史协会（American Association for State and Local History）于 1966 年出版的小册子《地方史的录音记录》，其作者是纽约州历史委员会（New York State Historical Commission）的威廉·泰瑞尔（William G. Tyrrell）。③ 而就口述历史学界来说，美国最早的口述历史实践手册是加州大学洛杉矶分校口述历史项目于 1968 年出版的《口述历史入门》，该手册主要介绍了一项口述历史计划的基本程序。④ 而在 20 世纪 70 年代之前，美国最为经典的口述历史实践指南则是鲍姆于 1969 年首次出版的《地方历史学会口述历史指南》，该指南包括"何谓口述历史"、"为什么做口述历史"、"如何启动一项口述历史项目"、"设备与录音带"、"访谈过程"、"应当访谈谁"、"访谈者小贴士"、"索引"、"使用协议"、"口述历史伦理问题"、"录音带的保存问题"、"转录问题"、"鼓励使用口述历史资料"和"培养专业能力"等丰富内容。由于该指南是鲍姆结合自己和加州大学伯克利分校地区口述历史办公室的实践经验撰写而成，因此具有相当重要的借鉴和

---

① Ronald J. Grele, "Directions for Oral History in the United States", in David K. Dunaway and Willa K. Baum（eds.）, *Oral History: An Interdisciplinary Anthology*, Walnut Creek: AltaMira Press, second edition, 1996, pp. 65-66.

② Marianna Trekell, "Oral History Research: Growth and Guidelines", *Journal of Health, Physical Education & Recreation*, Vol. 40, 1969, pp. 87-88.

③ William G. Tyrrell, *Tape-Recording Local History*, Nashville: American Association for State and Local History, 1966.

④ Hilda Clarke Gallaghan, *An Introduction to Oral History*, Los Angeles: Oral History Program, UCLA, 1968.

参考价值。①

　　此后，还有越来越多的口述历史机构和实践者在结合各自经验的基础上出版各种各样的手册或指南，其中加州州立大学富尔顿分校口述历史项目于 1973 年同时出版《口述历史初级读本》和《口述历史项目指南》，其内容涉及经费资助到编目的整个口述历史过程。② 而于 1974 年出版的《口述历史项目手册》，则是威廉·莫斯（William W. Moss）结合自己担任肯尼迪总统图书馆口述历史计划主任和访谈者的实践经验而撰写的，其内容除了包括肯尼迪图书馆口述历史计划简史之外，还包括"一般观察"、"启动一项口述历史项目"、"访谈技巧"、"访谈处理"、"口述历史录音带和抄本的研究性使用"、"记录处理"及"人员与设备问题"等内容。③ 另

　　① Willa K. Baum, *Oral History for the Local Historical Society*, Stockton: Conference of California Historical Societies, 1969. 该书深受美国口述历史学界高度评价，正是如此，它于 1971 年、1987 年和 1995 年多次再版。具体参阅 Willa K. Baum, *Oral History for the Local Historical Society*, Nashville: American Association for State and Local History by Special Arrangement with the Conference of California Historical Societies, new edition, 1971; Willa K. Baum, *Oral History for the Local Historical Society*, Nashville: American Association for State and Local History by Special Arrangement with The Conference of California Historical Societies, third edition, revised, 1987; Willa K. Baum, *Oral History for the Local Historical Society*, Walnut Creek: AltaMira Press, third edition, revised, 1995. 有关书评可参阅 Paige E. Mulhollan, "Book Review: *Oral History for the Local Historical Society*", *The Southwestern Historical Quarterly*, Vol. 73, No. 4, 1970, p. 578; John J. Fox, "Book Review: *Oral History for the Local Historical Society*, *The Practice of Oral History*: *A Hand-Book*, *A Manual for Field Workers*, *Oral History Program Manual*, *Oral History as a Teaching Approach*, *An Oral History Primer*", *Oral History Review*, Vol. 4, 1976, pp. 70-72; Larry J. Hackman, "Book Review: *Envelopes of Sound* and *Oral History for the Local Historical Society*", *American Archivist*, Vol. 39, No. 2, 1976, pp. 208-209; Eleanor Arnold, "Book Review: *Oral History for the Local Historical Society*", *Indiana Magazine of History*, Vol. 85, No. 2, 1989, pp. 189-190.

　　② Gary L. Shumway and William G. Hartley, *An Oral History Primer*, Salt Lake City: Primer Publications, 1973; Gary L. Shumway, Richard D Curtiss, and Shirley E. Stephenson (eds.), *A Guide for Oral History Programs*, Fullerton: California State University and Southern California Local History Council, 1973.

　　③ William W. Moss, *Oral History Program Manual*, New York, Praeger Publishers, 1974. 有关书评可参阅 Willa Baum and Amelia Fry, "Book Review: *Oral History Program Manual*", *American Archivist*, Vol. 37, No. 4, 1974, pp. 583-586; Maclyn P. Burg, "Book Review: *Oral History Program Manual*", *Oral History Association Newsletter*, Vol. 8, No. 3/4, Fall 1974, pp. 10-11; David Lance, "Book Review: *Oral History Program Manual*", *Oral History*, Vol. 3, No. 1, 1975, pp. 94-95.

外，由美国缩微公司（Microfilming Corporation of America）于 1975 年出版
的《口述历史实践指南》则是来自南达科他大学（University of South Dako-
ta）的四位教授从事美国印第安人研究计划（American Indian Research Pro-
ject）和南达科他口述历史计划（South Dakota Oral History Project）的经验
总结，其内容涉及口述历史计划的完整过程，并附录非常实用的法律授权
书（release form）和各种相关表格。① 而 1976 年出版的《口述历史程序》
与《口述历史：通向过去之窗》除介绍口述历史计划的完整程序之外，还
重点分析了口述历史的功用及其价值。② 而在 20 世纪 70 年代末之前，深
受美国口述历史学界好评的实践指南则是美国图书馆协会（American Library Association）于 1977 年出版的《口述历史：从录音带到打印稿》，该
书包括"理解口述历史"、"收集口述历史"、"处理口述历史"、"传播口
述历史"与"管理口述历史"等详细内容，并附录相当实用的涉及口述历
史资料整理与编辑的"样式规则"（rules of style）。③

　　上述口述历史实践手册或指南基本都涉及一项口述历史计划的完整过
程，不过，当时美国口述历史学界也出版了一些针对口述历史特定程序的实
践指南，比如玛丽·迪灵（Mary Jo Deering）和芭芭拉·波默罗伊（Barbara
Pomeroy）的《无泪转录：口述历史转录和编辑指南》、鲍姆的《口述历史转
录和编辑》及雪莉·斯蒂芬森（Shirley E. Stephenson）的《编辑与索引：口

---

① Ramon I. Harris, Joseph H. Cash, Herbert T. Hoover, and Stephen R. Ward, *The Practice of O-ral History: A Handbook*, Glen Rock: Microfilming Corporation of America, 1975. 有关南达科他口述历史计划的相关情况，可参阅 Stephen R. Ward, "An Early Assessment of the South Dakota Oral History Project", *South Dakota History*, Vol. 1, No. 1, 1970, pp. 73-78.

② David Kay Strate, *The Process of Oral History*, Dodge City: Cultural Heritage and Arts Center, 1976; John J. Fox, *Oral History: Window to the Past*, Salem: Salem State College, 1976.

③ Cullom Davis, Kathryn Back and Kay MacLean, *Oral History: From Tape to Type*, Chicago: A-merican Library Association, 1977. 有关书评可参阅 Elizabeth I. Dixon, "Book Review: *Oral History: From Tape to Type* and *Transcribing and Editing Oral History*", *Library Quarterly*, Vol. 48, No. 3, 1978, pp. 331-332; Gould P. Colman, "Book Review: *Oral History: From Tape to Type*", *American Archivist*, Vol. 41, No. 1, 1978, pp. 50-51; Doris Dale, "Book Review: *Oral History: From Tape to Type*", *Journal of Library History*, Vol. 13, No. 2, 1978, pp. 231-232.

述历史指南》。① 需要指出的是，在 20 世纪 70 年代末之前，由于美国口述历史学界本身的实践手册或指南相对稀缺，因而口头传统、新闻与民俗学领域等相关的访谈与田野方法也成为早期口述历史实践者的重要参考指南。②

也正是由于这种档案实践导向，在 20 世纪 70 年代之前，美国口述历史学界有关方法论与理论研究的论文基本都刊登在图书馆学与档案学相关的刊物和杂志上，其中包括《美国档案工作者》（*American Archivist*）、《威尔逊图书馆公告》（*Wilson Library Bulletin*）、《图书馆杂志》（*Library Journal*）、《图书馆历史杂志》（*Journal of Library History*）、《加州图书管理员》（*California Librarian*）、《图书馆趋势》（*Library Trends*）与《大学与研究图书馆》（*College and Research Libraries*）等主流学术刊物。相对而言，在 1973 年美国口述历史协会主办的《口述历史评论》正式创刊之前，很少有美国主流史学杂志刊登有关口述史学方面的论文，而于 1966 年开始的全国口述史学年会及随后

---

① Mary Jo Deering and Barbara Pomeroy, *Transcribing without Tears: A Guide to Transcribing and Editing Oral History*, Washington: Oral History Program, George Washington University Library, 1976; Willa K. Baum, *Transcribing and Editing Oral History*, Nashville: American Association for State and Local History, 1977 and 1991; Shirley E. Stephenson, *Editing and Indexing: Guidelines for Oral History*, Fullerton: Oral History Program, California State University, Fullerton, 1978. 其中，鲍姆的《口述历史转录和编辑》还于 1995 年由其他出版社再版，详细参阅 Willa K. Baum, *Transcribing and Editing Oral History*, Walnut Creek: AltaMira Press, 1995. 有关书评可参阅 Mary Jo Deering, "Book Review: Transcribing and Editing Oral History", *Oral History Review*, Vol. 7, 1979, pp. 92-93.

② 可参阅 Kenneth S. Goldstein, *A Guide for Field Workers in Folklore*, Hatboro: Folklore Associates, 1964; Jan Vansina, *Oral Tradition: A Study in Historical Methodology*, Chicago: Aldine Publishing Company, 1965; Alfred Benjamin, *The Helping Interview*, Boston: Houghton Mifflin, 1969; Raymond L. Gorden, *Interviewing: Strategy, Techniques, and Tactics*, Homewood: The Dorsey Press, 1969; Lewis A. Dexter (ed.), *Elite and Specialized Interviewing*, Evanston: Northwestern University Press, 1970; William H. Banaka, *Training in Depth Interviewing*, New York: Harper and Row, 1970; Ruth Finnegan, *Oral Literature in Africa*, Oxford: The Clarendon Press, 1970; Edward D. Ives, *A Manual for Field Workers*, Orono: Northeast Folklore Society, 1974; John Brady, *The Craft of Interviewing*, New York: Vintage Books, 1976; Neil V. Rosenberg (ed.), *Folklore and Oral History*, St. John's: Memorial University of Newfoundland, 1978.

出版的会议论文集则成为当时美国口述历史学界的主要探讨平台。①

概括而言，上述刊登在图书馆学和档案学杂志上的论文除探讨口述历史的基本定义与方法论问题之外，主要是强调口述历史资料对于填补现有历史记录的空白或弥补其不足的文献价值（documentary value）。而口述历史作为一种新的馆藏来源，需要图书管理员和档案工作者突破与更新传统的档案理论与实践模式，尤其是重新评估和衡量他们作为档案记录管理者（curator）与创造者（creator）的角色问题。② 正是如此，从 20 世纪 50 年代中期开始，《美国档案工作者》等杂志开始发表系列文章呼吁图书馆与档案馆要重视口述历史的史料与档案价值，并总结口述历史在未来可能影响图书馆与档案馆的主要方式。③

---

① 1973 年《口述历史评论》创刊之后，口述史学年会论文集就不再公开出版。详细内容参阅 Elizabeth I. Dixon and James V. Mink（eds.），*Oral History at Arrowhead：The Proceedings of the First National Colloquium on Oral History*，Los Angeles：Oral History Association，1967；Louis M. Starr（ed.），*The Second National Colloquium on Oral History*，New York：Oral History Association，1968；Gould P. Colman（ed.），*The Third National Colloquium on Oral History*，New York：Oral History Association，1969；Gould P. Colman（ed.），*The Fourth National Colloquium on Oral History*，New York：Oral History Association，1970；Peter D. Olch and Forrest C. Pogue（eds.），*Selections from the Fifth and Sixth National Colloquia on Oral History*，New York：Oral History Association，1972.

② Martha Jane K. Zachert，"The Implications of Oral History for Librarians"，*College and Research Libraries*，Vol. 29，No. 2，1968，pp. 101-103.

③ 代表性成果可参阅 Owen W. Bombard，"A New Measure of Things Past"，*American Archivist*，Vol. 18，No. 2，1955，pp. 123-132；Vaughn Davis Bornet，"Oral History Can Be Worthwhile"，*American Archivist*，Vol. 18，No. 3，1955，pp. 241-254；Robert A. Shiff，"The Archivist's Role in Records Management"，*American Archivist*，Vol. 19，No. 2，1956，pp. 111-120；Helen M. White，"Thoughts on Oral History"，*American Archivist*，Vol. 20，No. 1，1957，pp. 19-30；Corinne Lathrop Gilb，"Tape-Recorded Interviewing：Some Thoughts from California"，*American Archivist*，Vol. 20，No. 4，1957，pp. 335-344；John E. Caswell，"Archives for Tomorrow's Historians"，*American Archivist*，Vol. 21，No. 4，1958，pp. 409-418；Doyce B. Nunis，Jr.，"The Library and Oral History"，*California Librarian*，Vol. 22，1961，pp. 139-144；Saul Benison，"Oral History and Manuscript Collecting"，*Isis*，Vol. 53，No. 1，1962，pp. 113-117；Elizabeth I. Dixon，"Oral History：A New Horizon"，*Library Journal*，Vol. 87，1962，pp. 1363-1365；Charles T. Morrissey，"Truman and the Presidency：Records and Oral Recollections"，*American Archivist*，Vol. 28，No. 1，1965，pp. 53-61；Donald Swain，"Problems for Practitioners of Oral History"，*American Archivist*，Vol. 28，No. 1，1965，pp. 63-69；Saul Benison，"Reflections on Oral History"，*American Archivist*，Vol. 28，No. 1，1965，pp. 71-77；Gould P. Colman，"Oral History-An Appeal for More Systematic Procedures"，*American Archivist*，Vol. 28，No. 1，1965，pp. 79-83；Elizabeth I. Dixon，"The Implications of Oral History in Library History"，*Journal of Library History*，Vol. 1，No. 1，1966，pp. 59-62，74；Elizabeth I. Dixon，"Oral History：Something New Has Been Added"，*Journal of Library History*，Vol. 2，No. 1，1967，pp. 68-72；Louis Shores，"The Dimensions of Oral History"，*Library Journal*，Vol. 92，1967，pp. 979-983；A. Ray Stephans，"Oral History and Archives"，*Texas Librarian*，Vol. 29，1967，pp. 203-214.

如上所述，由于在早期美国口述历史学家当中有很多人同时是档案工作者或图书管理员，而且查尔斯·莫里斯和威廉·莫斯等人都曾同时在美国口述历史协会和美国档案工作者学会（Society of American Archivists）当中担任重要角色，因而可以很好地成为两个机构之间的沟通桥梁。而美国档案工作者学会也于 1969 年成立口述历史委员会（Committee on Oral History），并且澄清和明确了档案工作与口述历史之间的共同兴趣点：作为手稿的口述历史、口述历史录音带和手稿的开放问题、口述历史抄本的租借问题、口述历史和诽谤问题以及口述历史学家的培训问题等。① 而 1973 年的一份调查也显示，档案工作者开始更加赞同和认可口述历史，在所有接受问卷调查的档案工作者学会会员中，有 73% 的人相信口述历史应当被看成一项常规的档案活动。② 而从 1981 年开始，口述历史委员会成为美国档案工作者学会的一个专业附属团体，并于 1983 年正式成立口述历史部（Oral History Section）。③ 此外，档案工作者学会还与美国历史协会（American Historical Association）和口述历史协会积极合作参与 1989 年颁布实施的《为历史记录所做访谈的声明》（Statement on Interviewing for Historical Documentation）这一重要文件的起草与讨论工作。④

与此同时，正是随着美国档案工作者学会与相关图书馆组织对于口述历史工作的专业认可，《美国档案工作者》与《图书馆历史杂志》等刊物从 20 世纪 60 年代末开始持续刊登口述史学相关的学术论文与活动消息。事实上，从 20 世纪 70 年代末开始，尽管美国口述史学发展的理论化趋势

① "Society of American Archivists Creates an Oral History Committee", *Oral History Association Newsletter*, Vol. 4, No. 2, April 1970, p. 1.

② Ellen D. Swain, "Oral History in the Archives: Its Documentary Role in the Twenty-first Century", *American Archivist*, Vol. 66, No1, 2003, p. 141; Committee on Oral History of the Society of American Archivists, "Oral History and Archivists: Some Questions to Ask", *American Archivist*, Vol. 36, No. 3, 1973, pp. 361-365.

③ Society of American Archivists, "Oral History Section", http://www2. archivists. org/groups/oral-history-section, 2015 年 8 月 25 日访问。

④ "AHA Adopts Statement on Interviewing for Historical Documentation", *Oral History Association Newsletter*, Vol. 23, Fall 1989, p. 3; "Statement on Interviewing for Historical Documentation", *Journal of American History*, Vol. 77, No, 2, 1990, pp. 613-614.

日益凸显，不过作为口述历史的核心特征，其档案实践导向与史料价值功能仍然为档案和图书馆学界所重视。① 只不过，档案工作者与图书管理员更多的是从数字化角度探讨口述历史资料的多元化编目、索引、保

---

① Amelia R. Fry, "Oral History: The Nine Commandments of Oral History", *Journal of Library History*, Vol. 3, No. 1, 1968, pp. 63-73; Amelia R. Fry, "Persistent Issues in Oral History", *Journal of Library History*, Vol. 4, No. 3, 1969, pp. 265-267; Martha Jane K. Zachert, "Personal Records as Historical Sources", *Journal of Library History*, Vol. 4, No. 4, 1969, pp. 337-340; Charles T. Morrissey, "Oral History and Local History: Opportunities for Librarians", *Journal of Library History*, Vol. 4, No. 4, 1969, pp. 341-346; Amelia R. Fry and Willa Baum, "A Janus Look at Oral History", *American Archivist*, Vol. 32, No. 4, 1969, pp. 319-326; Alfred B. Rollins, Jr., "The Historian and the Archivist", *American Archivist*, Vol. 32, No. 4, 1969, pp. 369-374; Martha Jane K. Zachert, "Oral History Interviews", *Journal of Library History*, Vol. 5, No. 1, 1970, pp. 80-87; Ruth Teiser, "Oral History: Transcribers' Fancies", *Journal of Library History*, Vol. 5, No. 2, 1970, pp. 182-183; Willa K. Baum, "Oral History, the Library, and the Genealogical Researcher", *Journal of Library History*, Vol. 5, No. 4, 1970, pp. 359-371; Willa K. Baum, "Building Community Identity Through Oral History: A New Role for the Local Library", *California Librarian*, Vol. 31, 1970, pp. 271-284; Elizabeth Bauer, "Prytanean Oral History", *Journal of Library History*, Vol. 6, No. 2, 1971, pp. 163-168; Arlene Weber, "Oral History: Mining the Nuggets of the Past or, Oral History Observed", *Journal of Library History*, Vol. 6, No. 3, 1971, pp. 275-281; Gould P. Colman, "Making Library History", *Journal of Library History*, Vol. 7, No. 2, 1972, pp. 130-140; Carlos B. Hagen, "The Struggle of Sound Archives in the United States", *Library Trends*, Vol. 21, 1972, pp. 29-52; Hoyle Norman, "Oral History", *Library Trends*, Vol. 21, 1972, pp. 60-82; Committee on Oral History of the Society of American Archivists, "Oral History and Archivists: Some Questions to Ask", *American Archivist*, Vol. 36, No. 3, 1973, pp. 361-365; Ronald Filippelli, "Oral History and the Archives", *American Archivist*, Vol. 39, No. 4, 1976, pp. 479-483; Willa K. Baum, "The Expanding Role of the Librarian in Oral History", *Louisiana State University Library Lecture Series*, Vol. 34, 1976, pp. 33-43; William W. Moss, "Oral History: An Appreciation", *American Archivist*, Vol. 40, No. 4, 1977, pp. 429-439; Mary Jo Pugh, "Oral History in the Library: Levels of Commitment", *Drexel Library Quarterly*, Vol. 15, 1979, pp. 12-28; Irene Cortinovis, "Augmenting Manuscript Collections through Oral History", *American Archivist*, Vol. 43, No. 3, 1980, pp. 367-369; Lynn A. Bonfield and Arthur M. Schlesinger Jr., "Conversation with Arthur M. Schlesinger, Jr.: The Use of Oral History", *American Archivist*, Vol. 43, No. 4, 1980, pp. 461-472; James E. Fogerty, "Filling the Gap: Oral History in the Archives", *American Archivist*, Vol. 46, No. 2, 1983, pp. 148-157; Graham Eeles and Jill Kinnear, "Archivists and Oral Historians: Friends, Strangers, or Enemies?" *Journal of the Society of Archivists*, Vol. 9, No. 4, 1988, pp. 188-189; Dale Treleven, "Oral History and the Archival Community: Common Concerns about Documenting Twentieth-Century Life", *International Journal of Oral History*, Vol. 10, No. 1, 1989, pp. 50-58; Bruce H. Bruemmer, "Access to Oral History: A National Agenda", *American Archivist*, Vol. 54, No. 4, 1991, pp. 494-501.

存、检索、访问与利用等问题。①

　　尽管如此，在 20 世纪 70 年代末之前，美国口述史学还是遭到许多实证主义社会科学家、传统文献史学家和档案工作者的严重质疑与尖锐批评。其核心理由是强调口述历史主要是依赖于主观乃至错误的人类记忆，而且他们还认为受访者的个人动机与身份认同都极有可能影响其叙述的真实性与可靠性。② 而为了回应他们的质疑与批评，美国早期口述历史实践者同样基于档案实践考虑而试图通过倡导一种科学的访谈模式来宣称口述历史的客观性与真实性，并且主张作为口述历史学家的访谈者在意识形态上是完全客观和中立的记录者。③ 正是如此，当时大部分口述历史学家都认同应该遵循历史学的基本方法来从事口述历史工作，而其中以布鲁克斯的观点最具代表性，他于 1966 年曾指出：“对于我来说，口述历史是历史这样一个事实足够意味着它应该很好地成为定义的一部分；同时也意味着口述历史应当根据历史学研究的传统信条来实践。这主要包括客观性（objectivity）；它还包括准确性（accuracy）、全面性（thoroughness）以及我们应该在研究

---

　　① Ellen D. Swain, "Oral History in the Archives: Its Documentary Role in the Twenty-first Century", *American Archivist*, Vol. 66, No. 1, 2003, pp. 139-158; James E. Fogerty, "Oral History Archives: Documenting Context", in Thomas L. Charlton, Lois E. Myers, and Rebecca Sharpless (eds.), *Handbook of Oral History*, Walnut Creek: AltaMira Press, 2006, pp. 207-236.

　　② "Is Oral History Really Worthwhile?" in Clifford Lord (ed.), *Ideas In Conflict: A Colloquium on Certain Problems in Historical Society Work in the United States and Canada*, Harrisburg: American Association for State and Local History, 1958, pp. 17-57; William E. Leuchtengurg, Frank Freidel, Cornelius Ryan, and James McGregor Burns, "A Panel of Historians Discuss Oral History", in Louis M. Starr (ed.), *The Second National Colloquium on Oral History*, New York: Oral History Association, 1968, pp. 1-20; Nathan Reingold, "A Critic Looks at Oral History", in Gould P. Colman (ed.), *The Fourth National Colloquium on Oral History*, New York: Oral History Association, 1970, pp. 213-227; Ron Grele, "Can Anyone over Thirty Be Trusted: A Friendly Critique of Oral History", *Oral History Review*, Vol. 6, 1978, pp. 36-44; Donald A. Ritchie, "Oral History", in David Herman, Manfred Jahn, and Marie-Laure Ryan (eds.), *Routledge Encyclopedia of Narrative Theory*, London and New York: Routledge, 2005, p. 412.

　　③ Ronald J. Grele, "Directions for Oral History in the United States", in David K. Dunaway and Willa K. Baum (eds.), *Oral History: An Interdisciplinary Anthology*, Walnut Creek: AltaMira Press, second edition, 1996, pp. 65-66.

生院学习的其他许多东西，不过主要还是客观性。"① 而于 1968 年 11 月 25
日由美国口述历史协会一致采纳的《目标与指南》（*Goals and Guidelines*）
也强调："重要的是，所有的访谈都应当基于客观和学术诚信的精神并根
据事先达成的约定进行。"② 而为保证口述历史的客观性与真实性，美国早
期口述历史工作者在结合实践的基础上，探索了一系列记录、转录、编
辑、保存和利用口述历史的技巧与程序。③ 经过他们的不断努力，作为一
种原始史料，口述历史也同其他文献资料一样开始逐渐得到大部分专业历
史学家和档案工作者为的认可，尽管还有人对其功能与价值保持谨慎与怀
疑态度。

　　同时，这种档案实践模式也主导了早期美国口述历史学界对于什么是口
述历史的最终产物的争论方向，即到底是录音带（tape）还是抄本（tran-
script）？出于使用和保存方便及经济问题的考虑，以哥大口述历史研究室为
代表的早期口述历史计划大部分都没有保存它们的录音带（这种做法一直持
续到 20 世纪 60 年代），而是将录音带直接转录（消除后重复录音）并整理
编辑成抄本，进而根据个人文件或手稿等文献记录的传统标准来管理与保存

---

① Elizabeth I. Dixon, "Definitions of Oral History", in Elizabeth I. Dixon and James V. Mink
(eds.), *Oral History at Arrowhead*: *The Proceedings of the First National Colloquium on Oral History*, Los
Angeles: Oral History Association, 1967, p. 5.

② Oral History Association, "Goals and Guidelines", *Oral History Association Newsletter*, Vol. 3,
No. 1, January 1969, p. 4.

③ Charles T. Morrissey, "The Case for History", *Vermont History*, Vol. 31, No. 3, 1963,
pp. 145-155; Charles T. Morrissey, "Oral History and The Mythmakers", *Historical Preservation*,
Vol. 16, No. 6, 1964, pp. 232-237; George Blanksten, Ronald Cohen and Raoul Naroll, "Social Science Methodology and the Oral History Project", *African Studies Bulletin*, Vol. 8, No. 2, 1965, pp. 15-
23; Gould Colman, "Theoretical Models and Oral History Interviews", *Agricultural History*, Vol. 41,
No. 3, 1967, pp. 255-266; Peter D. Olch, "Oral History: Problems and Potentials", *American Journal
of Psychiatry*, Vol. 124, No. 8, 1968, pp. 1114-1115; William W. Cutler III, "Accuracy in Oral History
Interviewing", *Historical Methods Newsletter*, Vol. 3, No. 3, 1970, pp. 1-7; David F. Musto and Saul
Benison, "Studies on the Accuracy of Oral Interviews", in Gould P. Colman (ed.), *The Fourth National
Colloquium on Oral History*, New York: Oral History Association, 1970, pp. 167-181; Brooke Workman,
"Challenges of Oral History", *The Clearing House*, Vol. 46, No. 6, 1972, pp. 380-381; Alice Hoffman,
"Reliability and Validity in Oral History", *Today's Speech*, Vol. 22, No. 1, 1974, pp. 23-27; "Oral
History Reliability Is Under Question", *Library Journal*, Vol. 105, 1980, pp. 1350-1351.

口述历史抄本。① 在很大程度上，其原因是因为使用者对于抄本的明显偏好。据统计，那些提倡抄本与提倡录音带的比率是 1000:1 或更高。② 正是如此，当时大部分口述历史手册或指南也都倡导应该将录音带转录并整理编辑成易于保存和利用的口述历史抄本。③ 当然，也有少数学者主张录音带才是真正的原始资料，佛罗里达州立大学（Florida State University）路易斯·肖斯（Louis Shores）曾指出："我恳请的第一个问题是需要更严肃地考虑将录音带本身作为一种原始资料。我强烈建议我们所有创建口述历史收藏的人都应该保存录音带母带，以供将来的研究者重新播放。甚至会出现一种可能性，即从原始录音带中发现打印稿无法揭示的新真相。"④ 这种争论在美国逐渐得到平息并达成一种共识，正如斯塔尔在 20 世纪 70 年代所指出的，录音带对于某些用途来说更为合适，反之则是抄本更具优势。但是，需要尽可能同时保留录音带和抄本两种资料类型，并由研究者自己选择。⑤

---

① Elizabeth Rumics, "Oral History: Defining the Term", *Wilson Library Bulletin*, Vol. 40, 1966, p. 602; Frank Freidel (ed.), *Harvard Guide to American History*, Cambridge: Belknap Press of Harvard University Press, revised edition, 1974, p. 107; Dale E. Treleven, "Oral History, Audio Technology, and the TAPE System", *International Journal of Oral History*, Vol. 2, No. 1, 1981, p. 29; Stephen Caunce, *Oral History and the Local Historian*, London: Longman, 1994, p. 171; Ronald J. Grele, "Directions for Oral History in the United States", in David K. Dunaway and Willa K. Baum (eds.), *Oral History: An Interdisciplinary Anthology*, Walnut Creek: AltaMira Press, second edition, 1996, p. 80; Tze-chung Li (ed.), *Social Science Reference Sources: A Practical Guide*, Westport: Greenwood Press, 2000, p. 293.

② Louis Starr, "Oral History", *Encyclopedia of Library and Information Sciences* (Vol. 20), New York: Marcel Dekker, 1977, p. 443.

③ Hilda Clarke Gallaghan, *An Introduction to Oral History*, Los Angeles: Oral History Program, UCLA, 1968, p. 22; William W. Moss, *Oral History Program Manual*, New York, Praeger Publishers, 1974, p. 7; Cullom Davis, Kathryn Back and Kay MacLean, *Oral History: From Tape to Type*, Chicago: American Library Association, 1977, p. 34; Willa K. Baum, *Transcribing and Editing Oral History*, Nashville: American Association for State and Local History, 1977, pp. 14-15.

④ Louis Shores, "Directions for Oral History", in Elizabeth I. Dixon and James V. Mink (eds.), *Oral History at Arrowhead: The Proceedings of the First National Colloquium on Oral History*, Los Angeles: Oral History Association, 1967, p. 40.

⑤ Louis Starr, "Oral History", *Encyclopedia of Library and Information Sciences* (Vol. 20), New York: Marcel Dekker, 1977, p. 444. 当时，斯塔尔还预见未来的研究者可能更注重口述历史的声音性。有关口述历史抄本优劣问题的详细分析，请参阅第六章"数字化革命与美国口述史学"。

　　为了扩大口述史学在学术界与社会领域的影响力以及充分发挥口述历史作为原始资料的史料价值，早期美国口述历史学界也相当关注其公开与出版问题。在 1966 年举行的美国第一届全国口述史学会议上，内文斯就曾明确指出："任何管理良好的口述历史计划都应当着眼于出版书籍，并能够及时直接或间接地获得丰富收益。"① 而且这种出版不仅仅局限于那些口述历史计划的具体执行者或发起机构，它更加强调经过转录、整理、编辑和索引的口述历史资料能够为未来的其他研究者所充分利用，正如罗纳德·格里所说，北美口述史学运动的档案实践起源使得口述历史工作者优先考虑如何为将来保存资料，而不是满足直接的研究需求。② 格里进一步解释指出："然而，不像其他田野科学，口述史学总是具有一种公共特征。从其档案实践起源开始，出于利用目的，口述史学总是将其本身和产品（访谈）呈现给更为广泛的公众，其中包括那些受访者或其他历史学家。在这个意义上，因为他（她）从来不会垄断资料来源，口述历史学家试图继续能够就他们所收集的证词的意义与他们的同行或公众进行对话。"③

　　正是如此，许多美国早期口述历史计划或机构都纷纷出版各种各样的年度报告、收藏目录或完整的口述历史访谈抄本（主要以自传或回忆录形式呈

---

① Allan Nevins, "The Uses of Oral History", in Elizabeth I. Dixon and James V. Mink (eds.), *Oral History at Arrowhead: The Proceedings of the First National Colloquium on Oral History*, Los Angeles: Oral History Association, 1967, p. 27.

② Paul Thompson, "Sharing and Reshaping Life Stories: Problems and Potential in Archiving Research Narratives", in Mary Chamberlain and Paul Thompson (eds.), *Narrative and Genre*, London and New York: Routledge, 2002, p. 167.

③ Ronald J. Grele, "History and the Languages of History in the Oral History Interview: Who Answers Whose Questions and Why?" in Eva M. McMahan and Kim Lacy Rogers (eds.), *Interactive Oral History Interviewing*, Hillsdale: L. Erlbaum Associates, 1994, pp. 16-17.

现)。① 以哥大口述历史研究室为例，它们从 1948 年开始不定期出版年度报
告②，1960 年开始出版《哥伦比亚大学口述历史收藏》等收藏目录③，其
间也将多种完整口述历史访谈抄本以回忆录形式出版④。此后，其他口述
历史计划和机构也纷纷出版类似资料以进一步报告工作进度和推广收藏资
源，其中包括"森林历史口述历史计划"⑤、加州大学伯克利分校地区口述
历史办公室⑥、加州大学洛杉矶分校口述历史项目⑦、克莱蒙特研究学
院⑧、密歇根大学—韦恩州立大学劳工与工业关系研究所（Institute of

---

① 这里仅仅介绍 20 世纪 70 年代末之前的相关情况，其他有关美国口述历史收藏目录的详细
内容可参阅 "Oral History Directories and Catalogs"，in Donald A. Ritchie，*Doing Oral History：A Practical Guide*，Oxford and New York：Oxford University Press，second edition，2003，pp. 290-293.

② 这些报告一直出版到 20 世纪 80 年代初，其间报告标题分别有 "The Oral History Project of
Columbia University"，"Oral History at Columbia"，"Oral History in the United States" 和 "Oral History"
等不同称呼。详细访问 https：//clio. columbia. edu/catalog/404736，2015 年 8 月 26 日访问。

③ 上述已经罗列 1970 年以前出版的收藏目录，此外可参阅 Elizabeth B. Mason and Louis
M. Starr（eds.），*The Oral History Collection of Columbia University*，New York：Oral History Research
Office，1973 and 1979；Columbia University，Oral History Research Office，*Oral History in All 50 States*，
New York：Oral History Research Office，1975；Columbia University，Oral History Research Office，*O-
ral History，The First Thirty Years：Project on American Leaders*，*New Catalogue*，*Highlights 1948-78*，
New York：Oral History Research Office，1978.

④ 比如 Guy Stanton Ford and Dean Albertson，*The Reminiscences of Guy Stanton Ford*，New York：
Oral History Research Office，Columbia University，1956；Benjamin H. Reese and Louis Morris Starr，
The Reminiscences of Benjamin H. Reese，New York：Oral History Research Office，Columbia University，
1957；Max Weber and Carol Singer Gruber，*The Reminiscences of Max Weber*，New York：Oral History
Research Office，Columbia University，1958.

⑤ Barbara D. Holman，*Oral History Collection of the Forest History Society：An Annotated Guide*，
Santa Cruz：Forest History Society，1977.

⑥ Suzanne B. Riess and Willa Baum（eds.），*Catalogue I of the Regional Oral History Office*，
1954-1979，Berkeley：Bancroft Library，University of California，Berkeley，1980. 该办公室也曾出版
一系列访谈录，比如 Horace Marden Albright and Amelia R. Fry，*Three Interviews with Horace
M. Albright：And Related Material*，Berkeley：Regional Oral History Office，1959.

⑦ Elizabeth I. Dixon（ed.），*The Oral History Program at UCLA：A Bibliography*，Los Angeles：
University of California Library，1966；Constance S. Bullock and Saundra Taylor（eds.），*The UCLA Oral
History Program：Catalog of the Collection*，Los Angeles：Regents of the University of California，1982.
该口述历史项目也曾出版一系列回忆录，比如 William Jarvis Carr and Doyce Blackman Nunis，Jr.，
The Memoirs of William Jarvis Carr，Los Angeles，Oral History Program，1959.

⑧ Claremont Graduate School，*The Oral History Program of Claremont Graduate School：Annotated
Bibliography*，Claremont：Claremont University Center，1967；Claremont Graduate School，*Claremont
Graduate School Oral History Program：A Bibliography*，Claremont：Claremont University Center，1978.

Labor and Industrial Relations）①、北德克萨斯州立大学（North Texas State University）②、威斯康星大学河瀑分校（University of Wisconsin-River Falls）③、南达科他口述历史计划④、威廉·维纳口述历史图书馆（William E. Wiener Oral History Library）⑤、内华达大学里诺分校口述历史项目（Oral History Program，University of Nevada，Reno）⑥、西北民俗学会（Northeast Folklore Society）⑦、西部高等教育州际委员会（Western Interstate Commission for Higher Education）⑧、埃默里与亨利学院（Emory and Henry College）⑨、阿巴拉契亚口述历史计划（The Appalachian Oral History Project）⑩、圣路易斯奥比斯波口述历史组织（San Luis Obispo Oral History Organization）⑪、美国空军历史办公室（Office of Air Force History）⑫ 与温斯洛普学院（Winthrop College）⑬ 等。

---

①　*Preliminary Index to the United Auto Workers Oral History*，Ann Arbor：Institute of Labor and Industrial Relations，University of Michigan—Wayne State University，1967.

②　*Oral History Collection*，Denton：North Texas State University，1970.

③　*Voices from the St. Croix Valley：An Oral History Collection：a Guide to the Oral History Collection*，River Falls：University of Wisconsin-River Falls，1972.

④　*The South Dakota Experience：An Oral History Collection of Its People*，Pierre and Vermillion：South Dakota Oral History Project，1972.

⑤　Milton Krents，*William E. Wiener Oral History Library Progress Report：1972-1973*，New York：William E. Wiener Oral History Library，1973.

⑥　Lenore M. Kosso，*University of Nevada，Reno，Oral History，1972-73*，Reno：University of Nevada Oral History Program，1973.

⑦　*The Northeast Archives of Folklore and Oral History：A Brief Description and a Catalog of Its Holdings，1958-1972*，Orono：Northeast Folklore Society，1973.

⑧　Ronald Campbell（ed.），*Guide to An Oral History Archive for the City of Santa Clara，California*，Boulder：Western Interstate Commission for Higher Education，1974.

⑨　Laura Stevenson（ed.），*Author Index Appalachian Oral History Collection at Emory and Henry College*，Richardson：Emory and Henry College，1974；*Appalachian Oral History Project：Program Guide and Manual*，Richardson：Emory and Henry College，1978.

⑩　*The Appalachian Oral History Project Union Catalog*，Pippa Passes：Appalachian Oral History Project，1977.

⑪　Betsy Bertrando，*History Comes Alive：Catalog of Oral History Holdings in San Luis Obispo County*，San Luis Obispo：San Luis Obispo Oral History Organization，1980.

⑫　Albert F. Simpson Historical Research Center，*USAF Oral History Catalog*，Washington：Office of Air Force History，1977.

⑬　Ron Chepesiuk（ed.），*A Guide to the Manuscript and Oral History Collections in the Winthrop College Archives and Special Collections*，Rock Hill：Winthrop College，1978.

  而随着1966 年美国第一届全国口述史学会议(此后定期举办年会, 一直延续至今)的召开与1967 年美国口述历史协会的成立,美国口述史学专业化发展取得重大进展。而口述历史协会在统筹全国性口述历史资源与组织全国性口述历史活动方面也扮演日益重要的角色,尤其是通过编辑与出版口述历史参考文献①、口述历史计划或收藏目录②、《口述历史协会通讯》(*Oral History Association Newsletter*, 1967 年创办至今) 与《口述历史评论》(1973 年创办至今) 等资料与刊物积极扩大口述史学的学术知名度与社会影响力。此外, 经过口述历史协会的积极努力, 美国国会图书馆出版的《全国手稿馆藏联合目录》(*National*

---

  ① Donald J. Schippers and Adelaide G. Tusler (eds.), *A Bibliography on Oral History*, Los Angeles: Oral History Association, 1967; Manfred J. Waserman (ed.), *Bibliography on Oral History*, New York: Oral History Association, 1971; Manfred J. Waserman (ed.), *Bibliography on Oral History*, New York: Oral History Association, revised edition, 1975. 其他还可参阅 Ronald J. Grele and Gaile A. Grele (eds.), *Oral History: An Annotated Bibliography*, Washington: National Institute of Education, U. S. Department of Health, Education and Welfare, 1974; Patricia Pate Havlice, *Oral History: A Reference Guide and Annotated Bibliography*, Jefferson: McFarland & Co., 1985; Robert Perks (ed.), *Oral History: An Annotated Bibliography*, London: British Library National Sound Archive, 1990.

  ② Gary L. Shumway (ed.), *Oral History in the United States: A Directory*, New York: Oral History Association, 1971; Alan M. Meckler and Ruth McMullin (eds.), *Oral History Collections*, New York: R. R. Bowker Company, 1975. 此外、还有其他机构出版国际性、全国性或地区性口述历史计划或收藏目录, 详细参阅 Ann Rune (ed.) *Oral History Index: Washington State Oral/Aural History Program, 1974-1977*, Olympia: State of Washington, 1977; Hubert Humphreys (ed.), *Louisiana Oral History Collections: A Directory*, Shreveport: Louisiana State University, Shreveport, 1980; Betty McKeever Key and Larry E. Sullivan (eds.), *Oral History in Maryland: A Directory*, Baltimore: Maryland Historical Society, 1981; Kathryn Wrigley (ed.), *Directory of Illinois Oral History Resources*, Springfield: Oral History Office, Sangamon State University, 1981; Margot H. Knight (ed.), *Directory of Oral History in Washington State*, Pullman: Washington State University, 1981; Madeline Buckendorf and Elizabeth P. Jacox (eds.), *Directory of Oral History Resources in Idaho*, Boise: Idaho Oral History Center, Idaho State Historical Society, 1982; Pasty A. Cook (ed.), *A Directory of Oral History Programs in the United States*, Glen Rock: Microfilming Corporation of America, 1982; Lila Johnson Goff and James E. Fogerty (eds.), *The Oral History Collections of the Minnesota Historical Society*, St. Paul: Minnesota Historical Society, 1984; Bruce M. Stave and John F. Sutherland (eds.), *Talking about Connecticut: Oral History in the Nutmeg State*, Storrs: University of Connecticut, 1985; Patricia Borneman (ed.), *Directory to Montana Oral History Resources*, Helena: Montana Oral History Association, 1985; Cathryn Gallacher (ed.), *Oral History Collections in the Southwest Region: A Directory and Subject Guide*, Los Angeles: Southwest Oral History Association, 1986; Allen Smith, *Directory of Oral History Collections*, Phoenix: Oryx Press, 1988; Ellen S. Wasserman (ed.), *Oral History Index: An International Directory of Oral History Interviews*, Westport: Meckler, 1990; Cary C. Wilkins (ed.), *The Guide to Kentucky Oral History Collections*, Frankfort: Kentucky Oral History Commission, 1991.

Union Catalog of Manuscript Collections）从 1970 年版本开始将口述历史馆藏纳入其中，这也标志着口述历史作为一种手稿资料而被美国图书馆与档案馆学界所真正认可，也极大地促进了口述历史资源的公开与利用。①

不过，《全国手稿馆藏联合目录》只是将口述历史馆藏（包括单个口述历史抄本）的描述性信息罗列出来，而无法获得全文资料，这对于那些未能实地到口述历史收藏机构查询资料的使用者来说将相当不便。基于此，并为了进一步将全美各大口述历史收藏中心的资料真正向读者开放，《纽约时报》于 1970 年启动"纽约时报口述历史项目"（The New York Times Oral History Program）。该计划通过与美国缩微公司的合作，将那些已经开放的口述历史抄本以缩微胶卷（micro film）或缩微胶片（micro fiche）的形式进行出版。② 该计划得到众多美国口述历史机构和计划的支持，③ 其中以哥大口述历史研究室最具代表性，据粗略统计，到 1976 年之前，该研究室总共大约有 400 份口述回忆录以缩微形式出版。④ 而为方便研究者了解口述历史缩微目录，该计划还出版 3 卷《口述历史指南》，以索引方式详细罗列每个口述历史抄本的基本信息。⑤ 毫无疑问，这些于 20 世纪 70—80 年代初出版的口述历史缩微出版物给当时与后来的研究者提供

---

① "Oral History Holdings To Be Included in National Union Catalog of Manuscript Collections", *Oral History Association Newsletter*, Vol. 4, No. 1, January 1970, p. 2; Arline Custer, "NUCMC Issues Special Circular on Reporting Collections of Oral History Transcripts", *Oral History Association Newsletter*, Vol. 5, No. 3, July 1971, p. 2.

② "Oral History File To Be Microfilmed", *New York Times*, November 15, 1970.

③ 其中还包括以色列耶路撒冷希伯来大学当代犹太人口述历史收藏（Hebrew University Contemporary Jewry Oral History Collection）。

④ "The New York Times and Columbia's Oral History Research Office Agree to Micropublication Plan", *Oral History Association Newsletter*, Vol. 5, No. 1, January 1971, p. 3; "Columbia Reports Significant Progress in Its Oral History Micropublication Plan", *Oral History Association Newsletter*, Vol. 5, No. 2, April 1971, p. 4; Laurie Johnston, "Memoirs of 200 Notables Offered in Micro Forms", *New York Times*, July 7, 1972; The New York Times Oral History Program, *Oral History Guide No. 1: A Bibliographic Listing of the Memoirs in the Micropublished Collections*, Glen Rock: Microfilming Corporation of America, 1976, p. 1.

⑤ The New York Times Oral History Program, *Oral History Guide: A Bibliographic Listing of the Memoirs in the Micropublished Collections*, Glen Rock: Microfilming Corporation of America, 1976, 1979 and 1983.

了诸多方便，据笔者查询相关研究成果的注释来看，很多研究者所参考的口述历史抄本大部分都来自这些缩微出版物，而并非它们所在的口述历史收藏机构的原件或副本。①

正是在当时各个口述历史机构和美国口述历史协会的积极推动下，口述历史作为史料的价值也不断得到学术界的认可与赞赏，其中的重要体现是以口述历史资料为重要来源的研究成果不断增加。以哥大口述历史研究室为例，在 1948—1970 年间，以其口述历史收藏为重要资料来源的研究作品大约是 120 本；而在 1971—1977 年间，相关研究作品的数量将近是过去 22 年总数的三倍多。② 另外，上述已经提到的其他美国早期口述历史机构和计划所保存的口述历史资料也被越来越多的学者所利用，研究成果也日益丰富。而更值得一提的是，从 20 世纪 60 年代中后期开始，美国口述史学界开始出现真正的自成一类的"口述史学作品"。它们既不同于以自传或回忆录形式出版的口述历史抄本，也不同于上述提到的以口述历史资料为重要资料来源的研究作品，更不是指有关口述史学理论与方法论的研究著述，而是指以口述历史资料为绝对来源的研究性史学作品。而这方面的代表性作品是美国著名口述历史学家索尔·本尼松（Saul Benison，1920—2006）于 1967 年出版的《托马斯·里弗斯口述历史回忆录：医学与科学生涯的反思》，③ 它是一本有关美国著名细菌学家和病毒学家托马斯·里弗斯（Thomas Milton Rivers，1888—1962）的口述历史回忆录，该书被美国口述历史学界认为是口述历史

---

① 比如 Francis Paul Prucha, *Indian-white Relations in the United States: A Bibliography of Works Published 1975-1980*, Lincoln: University of Nebraska Press, 1982, p. 5; Akim D. Reinhardt（ed.）, *Welcome to the Oglala Nation: A Documentary Reader in Oglala Lakota Political History*, Lincoln: University of Nebraska Press, 2015, p. 249.

② Louis Starr, "Oral History", *Encyclopedia of Library and Information Sciences*（Vol. 20）, New York: Marcel Dekker, 1977, pp. 457-458.

③ 本尼松曾于 1955—1960 年负责哥大口述历史研究室医学史与社会史口述历史项目（History of Medicine and Social History Oral History Programs）。其生平经历可以参阅 John K. Alexander, "In Memoriam: Saul Benison（1920—2006）", *Perspectives on History*, October 2007.

资料组织与运用的典范之作。① 此外，代表性作品还有 T. 哈里·威廉姆斯（T. Harry Williams，1909—1979）的《休伊·朗》、布鲁斯·斯蒂夫（Bruce M. Stave）的《新政与最后的欢呼：匹兹堡机器政治》与维维安·佩里斯（Vivian Perlis）的《查尔斯·艾夫斯回忆：口述历史》等。②

综上所述，在早期发展的 30 年间，基于哥大口述历史研究室所开创的精英口述历史模式，美国口述史学呈现出相当明显的精英主义特征与档案实践导向，并以填补现存文献记录的空白或弥补其不足为主导宗旨。其间，在这场由大学（学院）、图书馆（档案馆、博物馆）、历史学会、专业协会、公司（企业）、媒体、政府机构、军事部门、医疗卫生机构及慈善组织等不同机构和独立研究者发起与参与的口述史学运动中，美国口述史学基本走上专业化与规范化的发展道路，并奠定其一定的学术地位。正如 1974—1975 年度美国口述历史协会主席塞缪尔·普罗克特（Samuel Proctor）所说："作为一种公认的研究手段，口述史学正日益被历史学家、人类学家、社会学家、小说家、政治科学家、新闻记者、科学作家、系谱专家以及许多其他学者所利用。……口述史学确实已经走向成熟。"③ 不过，在这一时期（尤其是从 20 世纪 60 年代中后期开始），随着美国新社会史（new social history）思潮与一系列社会运动的兴起与发展，深具档案实践功能的口述史学也被一部分美国口述历史工作者用于挖掘与呈现那些历史上甚少有文献记录或文献记录有缺陷的普通人物与边缘（弱势）群体的生命经历与历史记忆，这便是下一章要探讨的美国口述史学的"新社会史转向"。

---

① Thomas Milton Rivers and Saul Benison, *Tom Rivers*: *Reflections on a Life in Medicine and Science*: *An Oral History Memoir*, Cambridge: MIT Press, 1967. 有关书评可参阅 Peter D. Olch, "Book Review: *Tom Rivers*", *Oral History Association Newsletter*, Vol. 2, No. 3, July 1968, p. 3; Thomas N. Bonner, "Book Review: *Tom Rivers*", *American Historical Review*, Vol. 74, No. 1, 1968, pp. 324-325; Leonard G. Wilson, "Book Review: *Tom Rivers*", *Isis*, Vol. 59, No. 4, 1968, pp. 455-458; Edwin Clarke, "Book Review: *Tom Rivers*", *British Journal for the History of Science*, Vol. 4, No. 2, 1968, pp. 185-186; John T. Edsall, "Book Review: *Tom Rivers*", *Political Science Quarterly*, Vol. 84, No. 4, 1969, pp. 675-676.

② T. Harry Williams, *Huey Long*, New York: Alfred A. Knopf, 1969; Bruce M. Stave, *The New Deal and the Last Hurrah*: *Pittsburgh Machine Politics*, Pittsburgh: University of Pittsburgh Press, 1970; Vivian Perlis, *Charles Ives Remembered*: *An Oral History*, New Haven: Yale University Press, 1974.

③ Samuel Proctor, "Oral History Comes of Age", *Oral History Review*, Vol. 3, 1975, pp. 2, 4.

第四章 美国口述史学与"新社会史转向"

戴维·杜那威和维拉·鲍姆指出，进入 20 世纪 60 年代中期，美国开始出现第二代口述历史学家。他们不仅将口述历史视为非传统资料的一种重要来源，而且利用口述史学方法来描述与赋权那些没有文字记录和在历史上被剥夺话语权力的人群，进而超越第一代口述史学家所主导的精英访谈模式以扩展口述历史的搜集范围与视野。① 在很大程度上，这种转变受到当时美国新社会史思潮及民权运动、女权运动、学生运动、反主流文化运动、反战运动与同性恋权利运动等一系列社会激进运动的冲击与影响。正是如此，一部分美国历史学家号召彻底摆脱传统史学只注重社会上层人物的精英史观，而要求重视下层平民大众的历史作用，并撰写有关他们的历史。于是，口述史学逐渐被广泛应用于美国少数族裔史（美国印第安人、非裔美国人、墨西哥裔美国人、意大利裔美国人、华裔美国人等）、女性史、劳工史、同性恋史、家庭（家族）史、社区（社群）史与城市史等新社会史领域。而在这种新的史学领域与视野中，深具档案实践功能的口述史学为挖掘与呈现那些没有记录的经历（undocumented experience）提供了重要途径，并因此恢复和拯救了那些边缘人物与弱势群体的"隐藏的历史"

---

① David K. Dunaway and Willa K. Baum, "Preface", in David K. Dunaway and Willa K. Baum (eds.), *Oral History: An Interdisciplinary Anthology*, Nashville: American Association for State and Local History, 1984, p. xiii.

（hidden history）。① 简言之，从 20 世纪 60 年代中后期开始，在“自下而上看历史”的底层史观的影响下，美国口述史学呈现出极其鲜明的“新社会史转向”，并为其获得“草根支持者”（grass-roots constituency）的美名。②

本章将首先分析美国新社会史的兴起与发展，并以斯塔兹·特克尔口述历史系列作品为例来探讨非精英（民间）口述历史在美国逐渐发展的过程。同时，本章将重点介绍与探讨美国口述史学在少数族裔史、女性史、劳工史与同性恋史等新社会史领域的具体应用。

一　美国新社会史的兴起与发展

受到美国各种社会运动及其欧洲史学思想的影响，新社会史于 20 世纪 60 年代在美国逐渐兴起，并于 20 世纪 70 年代发展成为美国史学

---

① Richard M. Dorson, "The Oral Historian and the Folklorist", in Peter D. Olch and Forrest C. Pogue（eds.）, *Selections from the Fifth and Sixth National Colloquia on Oral History*, New York：Oral History Association, 1972, p. 44；Selma Leydesdorff, Luisa Passerini and Paul Thompson, "Introduction", in Selma Leydesdorff, Luisa Passerini, and Paul Thompson（eds.）, *Gender and Memory*, New Brunswick：Transaction Publishers, 2005, p. 4；Alistair Thomson, "Fifty Years On：An International Perspective on Oral History", *Journal of American History*, Vol. 85, No. 2, 1998, p. 584；Vivian Perlis and Libby Van Cleve, *Composers' Voices from Ives to Ellington：An Oral History of American Music*, New Haven：Yale University Press, 2005, p. xviii；Joan Sangster, "Reflections on the Politics and Praxis of Working-Class Oral Histories", in Kristina R. Llewellyn, Alexander Freund and Nolan Reilly（eds.）, *The Canadian Oral History Reader*, Montreal：McGill-Queen's University Press, 2015, p. 122.

② Michael Frisch, "Oral History and *Hard Times*：A Review Essay", *Oral History Review*, Vol. 7, 1979, p. 73；David K. Dunaway and Willa K. Baum, "Preface", in David K. Dunaway and Willa K. Baum（eds.）, *Oral History：An Interdisciplinary Anthology*, Nashville：American Association for State and Local History, 1984, p. xiii；Trevor Lummis, *Listening to History：The Authenticity of Oral Evidence*, London：Hutchinson Education, 1987, p. 17；Staughton Lynd, "Oral History from Below", *Oral History Review*, Vol. 21, No. 1, 1993, pp. 1-8；John M. Glen, "The War on Poverty in Appalachia：Oral History from the 'Top Down' and the 'Bottom Up'", *Oral History Review*, Vol. 22, No. 1, 1995, pp. 67-93；Daniel Kerr, "'We Know What the Problem Is'：Using Oral History to Develop a Collaborative Analysis of Homelessness from the Bottom Up", *Oral History Review*, Vol. 30, No. 1, 2003, pp. 27-45；Richard Elliott and Andrea Davies, "Using Oral History Methods in Consumers Research", in Russell W. Belk（ed.）, *Handbook of Qualitative Research Methods in Marketing*, Cheltenham：Edward Elgar Publishing, 2006, p. 245；Barbara W. Sommer and Mary Kay Quinlan, *The Oral History Manual*, Walnut Creek：AltaMira Press, second edition, 2009, p. 2.

研究的主流，直至今天仍然是相当重要的研究领域。新社会史的兴起与发展改变了美国史学界以传统政治史为主体的研究格局，并以新的理论、观念、方法与资料来研究传统史学所忽视的历史面向（尤其是普通大众与社会边缘及弱势群体的历史），真正开创和奠定美国史学研究百花齐放的新格局，甚至有学者将其比喻为20世纪60—70年代"横扫整个学术领域的决堤洪水"①。

一般而言，西方较为自觉的社会史研究可以追溯到法国启蒙时代的伏尔泰，但是现代意义上的社会史是由法国年鉴学派在20世纪初开创的。年鉴学派提倡结构功能主义与"整体史观"，推动了西方史学在众多研究领域的不断深入，并奠定社会史研究的基本格局，成为新社会史研究的滥觞。英国著名史学家埃里克·霍布斯鲍姆（Eric J. Hobsbawm，1917—2012）在《从社会史到社会的历史》（From Social History to History of Society）一文中曾指出："1958年创刊的《社会与历史比较研究》（Comparative Studies in Society and History）是社会史研究的第一种专业刊物，至此社会史才正式成为一门学术性专业。"②

由于社会史的研究对象与视角相当广泛，而且其所用理论与方法也具有高度跨学科性，因而造成社会史的概念问题一直颇受史学界争论。在西方史学家关于社会史的众多定义和诠释中，较为代表性的观点有以下几种：（1）英国社会史学家屈威廉（George M. Trevelyan，1876—1962）在《英国社会史》（English Social History）一书中提出"抛开政治的人民的历史就是社会史"，即社会史是关于生活方式和一系列社会生活的历史（比如社区史、人口史、家庭史、婚姻史与犯罪史等），其中各种职业群体

---

① 转引自埃里克·方纳等《新美国历史》，齐文颖、林江等译，北京师范大学出版社1998年版，第204页。原文内容参见 Alice Kessler-Harris，"Social History"，in Eric Foner（ed.），*The New American History*，Philadelphia：Temple University Press，revised and expanded edition，1997，p.231.

② 埃里克·霍布斯鲍姆：《史学家：历史神话的终结者》，马俊亚、郭英剑译，上海人民出版社2002年版，第82页。原文可参见 E. J. Hobsbawm，"From Social History to the History of Society"，*Daedalus*，Vol.100，No.1，1971，pp.20-45.

（如农民、手工业者、知识阶层等）的社会活动与生活状况是主要的研究对象；（2）霍布斯鲍姆则在《从社会史到社会的历史》一文中完整地阐述了一种广义的社会史概念，他认为社会史应当是"社会整体的历史"，即国家政治、经济、文化、军事等制度与活动都在社会史的研究范围之内，各种专门史只是社会史的一个方面，而社会史的任务则需要将各种专门史纳入一个统一的框架之中，并且重视其社会结构及其变迁的研究。此外，美国社会史学家查尔斯·蒂利（Charles Tilly，1929—2008）主张将宏观结构的变迁同人们的日常生活结合起来考察，拉斐尔·塞缪尔则认为社会史是社会下层的历史，而英国学者约翰·布雷维里（John Breuilly）认为社会史研究应该从社会结构与个人经历的中间层次着手。[①]

对于"什么是社会史或新社会史"这个问题，尽管西方学者并没有达成一致的看法，不过从具体实践而言，新社会史仍然具有某些共同的特征与内涵。正如有学者所总结的，所谓新社会史"就是以普通民众的日常生活（包括物质生产活动，也包括精神文化活动）的历史作为主要研究对象，并以此作为探讨社会经济、政治和意识形态结构演变的基础和依据，从而更准确地解释和把握社会历史发展的轨迹"[②]。

---

① 上述概念总结自塞缪尔等《什么是社会史》，公羽译，《国外社会科学文摘》1985 年第 12 期，第 14—17 页；J. 布雷维里等《何谓社会史?》，肖朗译，《国外社会科学》1986 年第 5 期，第 30—33 页；庞卓恒主编：《西方新史学述评》，高等教育出版社 1992 年版，第 38—44 页；徐浩、侯建新：《当代西方史学流派》，中国人民大学出版社 1996 年版，第 177—184 页。其他相关研究可参见 Louise A. Tilly, "Social history and Its Critics", *Theory and Society*, Vol. 9, No. 5, 1980, pp. 668-670；Raphael Samuel, Keith Hopkins, John Breuilly, Joyce Youings, David Cannadine, Royden Harrison and J. C. D. Clark, "*What is Social History?*", *History Today*, Vol. 35, No. 3, 1985, pp. 4-44；蔡少卿主编：《再现过去：社会史的理论视野》，浙江人民出版社 1988 年版；俞金尧：《书写人民大众的历史：社会史学的研究传统及其范式转换》，《中国社会科学》2011 年第 3 期，第 199—219 页。

② 徐浩、侯建新：《当代西方史学流派》，中国人民大学出版社 1996 年版，第 184 页。相关研究可参见 Laurence Veysey, "The 'New' Social History in the Context of American Historical Writing", *Reviews in American History*, Vol. 7, No. 1, 1979, pp. 1-12；Charles Tilly, "The Old New Social History and the New Old Social History", *Review*, Vol. 7, No. 3, 1984, pp. 363-406；拉特曼：《美国的新"社会史"》，董进泉译，《国外社会科学文摘》1990 年第 9 期，第 29—32 页。

概括而言，美国社会史的发展大体经历三个阶段：（1）形成阶段：大约在 19 世纪末期 30 年间；（2）进步史学阶段：大致包括 20 世纪前 40 年；（3）新社会史学阶段：开始于 20 世纪 60 年代。在 20 世纪 40—50 年代，"一致论史学"（consensus history）在美国历史学界占据主流地位，这一代的保守史学家们认为美国的发展是超越种族和阶级区别的，拥有被广泛认同的独特的美国价值体系。但是，这种保守思潮并未能够持续太久，在 20 世纪 60 年代，尽管美国社会经济高速发展，但是大量的社会矛盾和问题也不断涌现，民权运动、女权运动、学生运动及反战运动等一系列社会运动强烈冲击着美国社会的"统一价值体系"。社会现实的变化迫使包括史学界在内的美国学术界与思想界不得不重新审视与反思美国的社会、文化与传统，进而促使历史学家研究历史上女性地位的变化、家庭关系的变迁及黑人与同性恋等少数族裔或社会群体的历史等。[①]

作为一种新的史学范式，新社会史的兴起与发展使美国史学在研究观念、研究领域、研究方法及所用研究资料方面都发生深刻变化，具体而言主要表现在以下几个方面。

首先，美国新社会史强调"整体史观"与"底层史观"。在法国年鉴学派整体史观的影响下，美国新社会史学者认为历史不是过去发生的各种事件的堆积，而是作为一个整体的社会的科学。社会史学家乔夫·埃利

---

① Michael Kraus and Davis D. Joyce, *The Writing of American History*, Norman: University of Oklahoma Press, revised edition, 1985, pp. 311-368；满云龙：《美国社会史学的兴起与美国的社会与文化》，中国留美历史学会编《当代欧美史学评析》，人民出版社1990年版，第85页；倪婷：《将老百姓还原于历史：美国社会史学的发展》，《世界历史》2012 年第 2 期，第 96—106 页；Lynn Dumenil, "Preface", in Lynn Dumenil (ed.), *The Oxford Encyclopedia of American Social History*, Oxford and New York: Oxford University Press, 2013, pp. xxv-xxxi. 有关美国"一致论史学"可参见 John Higham, "The Cult of the American Consensus: Homogenizing Our History", *Commentary*, Vol. 27, No. 2, 1959, pp. 93-100; John Higham, "Changing Paradigms: The Collapse of Consensus History", *Journal of American History*, Vol. 76. No. 2, 1989, pp. 460-466; Kenneth L. Kusmer, "Historiography", in Joan Shelley Rubin and Scott E. Casper (eds.), *The Oxford Encyclopedia of American Cultural and Intellectual History*, Oxford and New York: Oxford University Press, 2013, pp. 510-512.

（Geoff Eley）在《社会史新趋势》一文中把新社会史的发展概括为"整体潜力"的增长，而这种"整体潜力"指"人们开始朝着不只是研究组织而且研究结构和社会关系本身的方向发展"①。在这种情况下，新社会史学家不再将社会史当作历史研究中一个以对象划分的专题分支，而是认为社会史囊括了所有历史学的分支，其研究范围也不再局限于传统社会史领域。在以霍布斯鲍姆和爱德华·汤普森（Edward P. Thompson，1924—1993）为代表的英国马克思主义史学的影响下②，越来越多的美国新社会史学家也逐渐意识到，在社会发展中普通民众也有自己的政治观念与政治意识，而且往往成为影响历史发展的重要因素。因此，他们将关注焦点从传统的领袖人物、政治体制与思想史等传统研究视角转移到那些被忽视或遗忘的历史活动主体，并进而撰写"底层的历史"或"自下而上的历史"。当然，"整体史观"与"底层史观"是相互影响和促进的，它们是新社会史同一个发展方向上的两个方面，同时这也是新社会史发展的最基本的特征。

其次，美国新社会史大大拓展了历史研究领域。如上所述，发生于20世纪60年代的一系列反主流文化的社会运动促使社会史学家认识到对历史发展产生作用的因素不是只有所谓的社会精英，事实上其他社会群体的力量也同样重要。因此，以种族（族裔）、性别、家庭与性关系等主题为研究对象，美国社会史学家对不同社会群体进行了广泛研究。比如，以美国

---

① 乔夫·埃利：《社会史新趋势》，伊格尔斯编《历史研究国际手册》，陈海宏等译，华夏出版社1989年版，第68—69页。原文可参见 Geoff Eley，"Some Recent Tendencies in Social History"，in Georg G. Iggers and Harold T. Parker（eds.）*International Handbook of Historical Studies：Contemporary Research and Theory*，Westport：Greenwood Press，1979，pp. 55-70.

② Peter Novick，*That Noble Dream：The "Objectivity Question" and the American Historical Profession*，Cambridge：Cambridge University Press，1988，pp. 440-443；姜芃：《霍布斯鲍姆与新社会史》，陈启能主编《八十年代的西方史学》，中国社会科学出版社1990年版，第256—275页；梁民愫：《英国新社会史思潮的兴起及其整体社会史研究的国际反响》，《史学月刊》2006年第2期，第5—14页；王立端：《新社会史的文化语境——以 E. P. 汤普森的文化史研究为例》，《淮北煤炭师范学院学报》（哲学社会科学版）2006年第2期，第115—118页。

史学家尤金·吉诺维斯（Eugene D. Genovese，1930—2012）为代表的黑人史研究，他在《奔腾吧，约旦河：奴隶创造的世界》一书中以奴隶为主要研究对象，从他们的宗教信仰、伦理道德、生活习俗及婚姻家庭等各个方面论述了他们的文化发展。[1] 而赫伯特·古特曼（Herbert G. Gutman，1928—1985）则代表了美国工人阶级历史的研究，他在《工业化美国的工作、文化、社会》一书中揭示了广大默默无闻的工人阶级的存在与力量。[2] 另外，女性史和家庭史也日益成为美国史学界相当活跃的研究领域，据统计，在20世纪70年代初（1971年6月—1972年3月），全美各种学术刊物每年发表的女性史论文只有5篇，而到20世纪80年代初（1980年6月—1982年3月），该数量已增至112篇，增长幅度达22倍。[3] 同样，家庭史研究的论文数量在1922—1926年间只有6篇，但到1972—1976年间已增至338篇。[4] 此外，人口史、城市史、族裔史、社区史、儿童史以及性史等方面的研究成果也不断增加。[5]

最后，美国新社会史研究不断吸收与利用其他相关社会科学的理论与方法并拓宽所使用的史料类型。在某种意义上，新社会史是在历史学与相关社会科学的交叉与互动研究中逐渐产生的。它从社会学、人类学及相关学科领域吸收与借鉴了诸多概念与分析方法，运用口述历史与计量方法等新的研究手段，并使之成为新社会史研究的重要部分。同时，美国新社会

---

① Eugene D. Genovese, *Roll, Jordan, Roll: The World the Slaves Made*, New York: Pantheon Books, 1974.

② Herbert G. Gutman, *Work, Culture, and Society in Industrializing America*, New York: Knopf, 1976.

③ 参见徐浩、侯建新《当代西方史学流派》，中国人民大学出版社1996年版，第197页。

④ 同上书，第207页。

⑤ 详细内容可参见 James B. Gardner and George Rollie Adams (eds.), *Ordinary People and Everyday Life: Perspectives on the New Social History*, Nashville: American Association for State and Local History, 1983; Olivier Zunz, "The Synthesis of Social Change: Reflections on American Social History", in Olivier Zunz (ed.), *Reliving the Past: The Worlds of Social History*, Chapel Hill: University of North Carolina Press, 1985, pp.53-114; Mary Kupiec Cayton, Elliott J. Gorn and Peter W. Williams (eds.) *Encyclopedia of American Social History*, New York: Charles Scribner's Sons, 1993.

史学家也拓宽了史料的来源与范围，除政府档案与手稿等传统文献资料以外，他们也大量发掘和使用其他类型的史料来源，比如事件当事人或目击者的口述历史、团体集会记录、种植园记录、地方报纸、历史小说、地方教会手册及监狱记录等。

当然，美国新社会史在发展中也存在许多问题并招致诸多批评。有学者曾指出："当代社会史家所做到的只是描述了社会结构在不同历史时期的形态，并没有找到一种能够解释社会从一种结构形态转向另一种形态的理论，因而无力把握多样复杂的社会变化的主脉。"[1] 而美国著名史学家埃里克·方纳（Eric Foner）则批评美国新社会史学家热衷于研究中等层次的课题，其研究与写作没有公认的中心和主线，缺乏对于重大的综合性课题的重视，因而陷入极端分散化的局面。[2] 此外，新社会史还被批评刻意忽略美国历史上某些重要人物、重大历史事件、重要政治体制及政府机构等政治史范畴的研究，同时其研究理论与方法也过度依赖其他社会科学。[3] 尽管如此，美国新社会史所取得的巨大成就与学术意义仍然是不可忽视的，正如有学者所评价的："新社会史学在拓展史学领域和推动史学的革命性发展问题上做出了巨大的贡献，其研究

---

[1]　满云龙：《美国社会史学的兴起与美国的社会与文化》，中国留美历史学会编《当代欧美史学评析》，人民出版社 1990 年版，第 98 页。

[2]　参见凤鸣整理《方纳谈当代美国史学》，《史学理论研究》2000 年第 4 期，第 144 页。

[3]　Geoff Eley and Keith Nield, "Why Does Social History Ignore Politics", *Social History*, Vol. 5, No. 2, 1980, pp. 249-171; Joyce Appleby, Lynn Hunt and Margaret Jacob, *Telling the Truth about History*, New York: W. W. Norton, 1994, pp. 158-159; Alice Kessler-Harris, "Social History", in Eric Foner (ed.), *The New American History*, Philadelphia: Temple University Press, revised and expanded edition, 1997, pp. 248-250; 参见陈其《历史"重塑"中的得与失：美国新社会史评析》，《历史教学》2003 年第 4 期，第 42—46 页; Daniel J. Walkowitz, "The Cultural Turn and a New Social History: Folk Dance and the Renovation Class in Social History", *Journal of Social History*, Vol. 39, No. 3, 2006, pp. 781-802; Robert E. Weir, "New Social History", in Robert E. Weir (ed.), *Class in America: An Encyclopedia*, Westport: Greenwood Press, 2007, pp. 576-577; Lawrence B. Glickman, "The Impact of the Cultural Concept on Social History", in Karen Halttunen (ed.), *A Companion to American Cultural History*, Malden: Blackwell Publishing, 2008, pp. 396-405; Michael Kammen, "New Social History", in Carol Kammen and Amy H. Wilson (eds.), *Encyclopedia of Local History*, Walnut Creek: AltaMira Press, second edition, 2013, pp. 407-408.

成果揭示了美国历史过程中的不同群体美国人的不同历史经验，不同群体用自己特有的方式努力争取政治上的平等和经济上的独立，学会使用美国政治机制和理论作为自己的斗争武器，他们的历史活动极大地丰富了美国历史的内容，也推翻了新保守派'和谐主导美国历史发展'的旧史观。"①

正是随着美国新社会史的逐渐发展，从 20 世纪 60 年代中后期开始，以精英访谈模式为主导的美国口述史学也出现"新社会史转向"，一部分口述历史工作者开始将其记录与研究对象转向美国普通大众与社会边缘（弱势）群体，而典型代表则是被尊称为"美国民间口述历史先驱"的斯塔兹·特克尔。

二 美国民间口述历史先驱：斯塔兹·特克尔

特克尔是美国传奇口述历史学家、知名作家、广播名人与社会评论家，他于 1912 年出生在纽约，在他 8 岁时全家移居到芝加哥，并在此度过生命的大部分时光。从 1926 年到 1936 年，他的父母经营一家家庭公寓（rooming house），而这里同时也是社会各行业人士聚会的场所。特克尔正是从聚集在大厅的租户、访客及那些在精神病院广场（Bughouse Square）附近聚集的人们那里形成了对人性与社会交往（social interaction）的理解。正如有学者所评论的，特克尔有关世界的民粹主义观点（populist view）来自他对那些出入家庭公寓的工人、工会会员与移民的观察。② 特克尔于 1934 年获得芝加哥大学法学院（University of Chicago Law School）法学学位，

---

① 夏学花：《美国新社会史述评》，《史学史研究》2002 年第 1 期，第 76 页。
② Brook Willensky-Lanford, "Studs Terkel (1912—)", in Gary L. Anderson and Kathryn G. Herr (eds.), *Encyclopedia of Activism and Social Justice*, Thousand Oaks: Sage Publications, 2007, p. 1365.

不过他并没有打算从事律师工作，而是希望成为旅馆的看门人，随后又很快加入一个剧团。

此后，作为一名政治自由派人士，特克尔加入美国公共事业振兴署的联邦作家计划，主要从事广播工作。其工作内容包括广播一些肥皂剧、新闻和体育消息，主持一些音乐类节目并撰写广播稿与广告等。在 1945 年前后，特克尔终于在芝加哥一家广播电台拥有自己的广播节目，主要介绍爵士乐并推荐一些当时不为人知的乡村音乐、民谣、歌剧和圣歌，同时还会邀请一些作曲者和演唱者到节目里做访谈。而这段工作经历也为他 1957 年出版第一本书《爵士巨人》奠定基础，该书是一本基于访谈的爵士乐领域的名人传记合集。[①]

当 20 世纪 40 年代末和 50 年代初美国电视行业出现时，特克尔曾短暂主持过一档名为《斯塔兹地盘》（Studs' Place）的非剧本电视剧，在该节目中，特克尔就充分展示了过人的访谈与主持天赋。不过其广播事业生涯的真正转折点在 1952 年，当年他受雇于一家芝加哥刚刚成立的古典与民俗音乐广播电台——WFMT。而在随后的 45 年间，特克尔一直主持知名广播节目——"斯塔兹·特克尔栏目"（The Studs Terkel Program），它是一个从周一到周五播放的、为时 1 小时的评论与访谈节目。在该节目中，特克尔曾经采访过马丁·路德·金（Martin Luther King）、雷昂纳德·伯恩斯坦（Leonard Bernstein）、鲍勃·迪伦（Bob Dylan）、亚历山大·弗雷（Alexander Frey）、田纳西·威廉姆斯（Tennessee Williams）、桃乐丝·帕克尔（Dorothy Parker）和让·谢泼德（Jean Shepherd）

---

① Studs Terkel, *Giants of Jazz*, New York：Thomas Y. Crowell, 1957. 其他版本参见 Studs Terkel, *Giants of Jazz*, New York：Thomas Y. Crowell, revised and updated edition, 1975；New York：The New Press, 2006.

等众多名人。①

　　而特克尔职业生涯经历的另外一个重要转折点，则是他所开创的主要针对美国普通民众的口述历史访谈与一系列口述历史畅销书的出版工作，其口述历史实践模式被认为是对内文斯所开创的精英模式的挑战与超越。特克尔希望通过口述历史来帮助对抗他所谓的美国的全国性阿尔茨海默症（Alzheimer's disease，即老年痴呆症），正是如此，他被尊称为

　　① 上述有关特克尔的生平经历，具体参见 "Studs Terkel: Writer and Radio Interviewer", in Jack Huber and Dean Diggins, *Interviewing the World's Top Interviewers: The Inside Story of Journalism's Most Momentous Revelations*, New York: S. P. I. Books, 1993, pp. 206-213; Richard Stern, "Studs Terkel", *The Antioch Review*, Vol. 53, No. 4, 1995, pp. 454-464; Philip A. Greasley, "(Louis) Studs Terkel", in Philip A. Greasley (ed.), *Dictionary of Midwestern Literature* (Volume One), Bloomington: Indiana University Press, 2001, pp. 488-490; Gina L. Taglieri, "Studs Terkel", in Steven R. Serafin and Alfred Bendixen (eds.), *The Continuum Encyclopedia of American Literature*, New York: The Continuum International Publishing, 2003, pp. 1132-1133; Robert E. Weir, "Studs Terkel", in Robert E. Weir (ed.), *Class in America: An Encyclopedia*, Westport: Greenwood Press, 2007, pp. 856-858; Alan H. Stein, "Studs Terkel", in Andrew R. L. Cayton, Richard Sisson and Chris Zacher (eds.), *The American Midwest: An Interpretive Encyclopedia*, Bloomington: Indiana University Press, 2007, pp. 497-498; Kimberly K. Porter, " 'Curiosity Could Not Kill This Cat' ", *Oral History Review*, Vol. 34, No. 2, 2007, pp. 77-80; Rick Kogan, "Studs Terkel Dies", *The Chicago Tribune*, October 31, 2008; Williamn Gramies, "Studs Terkel, Listener to Americans, Dies at 96", *New York Times*, October 31, 2008; Caryn Rousseau, "Pulitzer Prize-Winning Author Terkel Dies at 96", *The Associated Press*, October 31, 2008; William Grimes, "Studs Terkel, Listener to Americans, Is Dead at 96", *New York Times*, November 1, 2008; "Studs Terkel", *The Daily Telegraph*, November 3, 2008; Ed Vulliamy, "Obituary: Studs Terkel: Broadcaster, Author and Master Chronicler of Everyday Life in 20th-Century America", *The Guardian*, November 3, 2008; "Tribute to Studs Terkel", *Congressional Record-Senate*, Vol. 154, Pt. 18, November 19, 2008, pp. 24173-24174; Ed Vulliamy, "Obituary: Studs Terkel, 1912-2008", *Oral History*, Vol. 37, No. 1, 2009, pp. 29-31; Sarah Gregson, "Oral Historian and Activist, 'Studs' Terkel (1912-2008)", *Labour History*, No. 96, 2009, pp. 233-234; Michael Frisch, "Studs Terkel, Historian", *History Workshop Journal*, No. 69, 2010, pp. 189-198; Tim Pollard, "Louis 'Studs' Terkel (1912-2008)", in Christopher H. Sterling (ed.), *The Biographical Encyclopedia of American Radio*, London and New York: Routledge, 2011, pp. 380-382; Kevin Coval, "Studs Terkel (1912-2008)", in Michele Bollinger and Dao X. Tran (eds.), 101 *Changemakers: Rebels and Radicals Who Changed U. S. History*, Chicago: Haymarket Books, 2012, pp. 85-86; "Studs Terkel", from Wikipedia, https://en. wikipedia. org/wiki/Studs_ Terkel, 2015 年 8 月 26 日访问。有关他的传记、回忆录和读本可参见 James Thomas Baker, *Studs Terkel*, New York: Twayne Publishers, 1992; Studs Terkel, *Touch and Go*, New York: The New Press, 2007; Studs Terkel, *The Studs Terkel Reader: My American Century*, New York: The New Press, 2007.

"美国声音的记录者"（recorder of America's voices）和"自下而上的历史建构者"①。尽管他也遭到部分学院派口述历史学家的批判，不过特克尔对于美国口述史学的贡献是毋庸置疑的。在他 1997 年获得美国国家人文奖（National Humanities Medal）时，时任美国总统克林顿就曾给予他高度评价："没有人能比斯塔兹·特克尔更能丰富那座充满着美国人声音的图书馆。他已经相当明确地定义了口述历史的艺术。"②

除上述提到的 20 世纪 60 年代美国学术新思潮与一系列社会运动的兴起及发展这一大背景之外，特克尔的口述历史实践则直接源于瑞典作家、新闻记者杨·米尔达（Jan Myrdal）的影响。他与他的妻子古恩·科斯勒（Gun Kessle）在 1962 年通过与中国陕西延安柳林村农民的口述历史访谈来研究革命对于中国农村社会的影响。该研究最先于 1963 年在瑞典出版，而由美国潘塞恩图书出版公司（Pantheon Books）于 1965 年出版的英文版《来自中国农村的报道》则取得很好的反响，这促使该出版商希望能够出版一本有关美国的同类书籍。③ 而当时身为潘塞恩图书出版公司编辑和经营者的安德烈·希夫林（André Schiffrin，1935—2013）就建议特克尔撰写一本当时的社会变迁对于美国乡村影响的书，而希夫林最先建议的所谓乡村则是美国大都市芝加哥。听完他的这个建议之后，特克尔的第一句话就是："你疯了吗？你怎么能拿

---

① "Studs Terkel, Oral Historian and Radio Legend, 96", *NPR*, October 31, 2008; "Louis 'Studs' Terkel, Recorder of America's Voices, Died on October 31st, aged 96", *The Economist*, November 6, 2008.

② 转引自 John de Graaf and Alan Harris Stein, "The Guerrilla Journalist as Oral Historian: An Interview with Louis 'Studs' Terkel", *Oral History Review*, Vol. 29, No. 1, 2002, p. 88.

③ Jan Myrdal, *Report from a Chinese Village*, New York: Pantheon Books, 1965. 作者于 1984 年还出版重返该村的研究成果，具体参见 Jan Myrdal, *Return to a Chinese Village*, New York: Pantheon Books, 1984.

中国的一个小农村与芝加哥这个大都市相比呢?"① 不过，最后他还是依照策划做了一次尝试，其成果便是 1967 年出版的首本口述历史作品《断街：美国》。②

正如特克尔所说，芝加哥的确有一条横贯城市东西的主要街道——"Division Street"（狄维逊大街）③，不过该书标题本身具有隐喻意义，主要强调那些造成城市生活中的不同人群被划分与区隔的社会与制度因素。④该书以芝加哥市民为主要访谈对象，大约 70 位具有不同阶级、民族、族裔、肤色、性别、年龄、职业、宗教信仰、经济状况、教育水平与政治立场等身份差异的受访者从其自身经历出发，谈论了他们的过去与现在、家庭与工作，以及困惑与理想，同时也涉及他们对于民权、越南战争、移民、劳工及就业等一系列社会问题的看法。简言之，该书相当细腻且生动地捕捉与呈现了美国普通人对于 20 世纪城市生活的真实声音与历史记忆。正如该书 2006 年新版封底所总结的："《断街》揭示了那些对于我们大多数人来说通常不可见的人们的生活，它是对于处于 20 世纪关键时刻的城市与社会的一种令人着迷的调查。" 该书的出版深受各界好评，

---

① Jeffrey C. Kinkley, "The Cultural Choices of Zhang Xinxin, a Young Writer of the 1980s", in Paul A. Cohen and Merle Goldman (eds.), *Ideas across Cultures*: *Essays on Chinese Thought in Honor of Benjamin I. Schwartz*, Cambridge: Council on East Asian Studies, Harvard University, 1990, p. 153; Thomas Maier, *Newhouse*: *All the Glitter*, *Power & Glory of America's Richest Media Empire & the Secretive Man Behind It*, Boulder: Johnson Books, 1997, p. 201; André Schiffrin, *The Business of Books*: *How International Conglomerates Took Over Publishing and Changed the Way We Read*, New York: Verso, 2000, pp. 55-56; Studs Terkel, *Touch and Go*, New York: The New Press, 2007, p. 170. 特克尔在其回忆录中曾解释，当时的芝加哥有许多阿巴拉契亚山区人、山地人口、穷苦白人及大量的南方黑人，或许是在这个意义上，可以将其理解为一个乡村。

② Studs Terkel, *Division Street*: *America*, New York: Pantheon Books, 1967. 其他版本参见 Studs Terkel, *Division Street*: *America*, New York: The New Press, 1993 and 2006.

③ "Division Street", from Wikipedia, https://en.wikipedia.org/wiki/Division_Street。2015 年 8 月 26 日访问。

④ James Thomas Baker, *Studs Terkel*, New York: Twayne Publishers, 1992, p. 50; Paul M. Hirsch, "Studs Terkel", in Vicki Smith (ed.), *Sociology of Work*: *An Encyclopedia*, Thousand Oaks: Sage Publications, 2013, p. 880.

美国著名作家、新闻记者汤姆·沃尔夫（Tom Wolfe）曾指出："作为斯塔兹·特克尔的首本口述历史作品，《断街》确立了他作为美国最重要的口述历史学家的名誉，同时也让他成为真正愿意走出去并与这个国家的那些难以置信的人们进行交谈的罕见的思想者之一。"① 当然，该作品也获得口述历史学界的高度认可，其中英国著名口述历史学家保罗·汤普森也曾评论道："《断街》充分展示了这座苦苦挣扎的城市的阶级、种族与文化多样性（class，racial，and cultural variety），它无疑是口述历史的杰作之一。"②

继《断街：美国》获得成功之后，希夫林再次建议特克尔撰写一部有关 20 世纪 30 年代的口述历史，因为很多那个时代的经历者仍然可以接受访谈，③ 其成果便是特克尔于 1970 年出版的第二本口述历史作品《艰难时代：经济大萧条口述历史》④。该书是一部超过 150 位美国人生活自我写照（self-portraits）的庞大合集，这些自述内容精选自特克尔所做的数百个有关 20 世纪 30 年代美国人生活与工作经历的口述历史访谈。同《断街：美国》一样，《艰难时代：经济大萧条口述历史》的受访者也相当广泛，从新政官员、著名商人、艺术家和作家到贫困农夫、工人、非法酒吧经营者、诈骗者和罢工者等普通百姓，甚至包括许多年轻受访者，而他们对于大萧条的认识与理解只能从相关阅读或他人转述当中获取。《艰难时代：经济大萧条口述历史》一经出版便引起媒体与学界广泛关注，《新闻周刊》

---

① 上述总结与沃尔夫的评论可参见 Studs Terkel, *Division Street*：*America*, New York：The New Press, 2006, http：//thenewpress. com/books/division-street, 2015 年 8 月 26 日访问。

② Paul Thompson, *The Voice of the Past*：*Oral History*, Oxford and New York：Oxford University Press, third edition, 2000, p. 106.

③ André Schiffrin, *The Business of Books*：*How International Conglomerates Took Over Publishing and Changed the Way We Read*, New York：Verso, 2000, pp. 56-57.

④ Studs Terkel, *Hard Times*：*An Oral History of the Great Depression*, New York：Pantheon Books, 1970. 其他版本参见 Studs Terkel, *Hard Times*：*An Oral History of the Great Depression*, New York：Pantheon Books, 1986；New York：The New Press, 2000 and 2005；Studs Terkel, *Hard Times*：*An Illustrated Oral History of the Great Depression*, New York：The New Press, 2012.

（*Newsweek*）评论指出："在我们所有阅读此书的人当中，它将让你重拾信心。"而《星期六评论》（*Saturday Review*）则称此书为"美国精神的一首宏达赞美诗"①。需要指出的是，该书不仅仅是一个众多鲜为人知的信息金矿，同时也是记忆与事实（memory and fact）的有趣互动。《艰难时代：经济大萧条口述历史》充分展示了经济大萧条如何影响那些亲历者的生活，并经常将那些最痛苦的记忆转变为一种令人惊讶的怀旧。正如特克尔在该书《个人回忆录》开篇所说："这是一本记忆之书，而不是客观事实（hard fact）和准确统计中的任何一种。"② 正是如此，该书也被认为是对口述历史当中的事实与记忆问题进行探讨与反思的重要开始，因而引起众多口述历史学家的积极评论与批判。③

而于 1974 年出版的《工作：人们谈论他们整天在做什么和他们对所做工作的感受》则是特克尔的第三部口述历史作品，该书基于 100 多位来自不同行业的美国人的口述历史访谈，进而呈现他们的工作经历及不同工作对于

---

① Michael Frisch, "Oral History and *Hard Times*: A Review Essay", *Oral History Review*, Vol. 7, 1979, p. 70.

② "A Personal Memoir", in Studs Terkel, *Hard Times*: *An Oral History of the Great Depression*, New York: The New Press, 2000, p. 3.

③ Michael Frisch, "Oral History and *Hard Times*: A Review Essay", *Oral History Review*, Vol. 7, 1979, pp. 70-79; Ronald J. Grele and Studs Terkel, "Riffs and Improvisations: An Interview with Studs Terkel (April 10, 1973)", in Ronald J. Grele (ed.), *Envelopes of Sound*: *The Art of Oral History*, New York: Praeger Publishers, second edition, revised and enlarged, 1991, pp. 10-49（在该访谈中，特克尔详细谈了《断街：美国》和《艰难时代：经济大萧条口述历史》的写作过程）; Alan Wieder, "Trust and Memory: Explorations in Oral History and Biography", in Craig Kridel (ed.), *Writing Educational Biography*: *Explorations in Qualitative Research*, New York: Garland Publishing, 1998, pp. 117-118; Andrea Gustavson, "From 'Observer to Activist': Documentary Memory, Oral History, and Studs Terkel's 'Essence' Narratives", *Journal of American Studies*, Vol. 46, No. 1, 2012, pp. 103-119. 该书其他书评可参见 Arvarh E. Strickland, "Book Review: *Hard Times*: *An Oral History of the Great Depression*", *Journal of the Illinois State Historical Society*, Vol. 63, No. 4, 1970, pp. 440-441; Amelia R. Fry and Willa K. Baum, "Book Review: *Hard Times*: *An Oral History of the Great Depression*", *The Pacific Northwest Quarterly*, Vol. 62, No. 4, 1971, pp. 154-155; Adrian Sinfield, "Book Review: *Hard Times*: *An Oral History of the Great Depression*", *Oral History*, Vol. 1, No. 2, 1972, pp. 28-29.

他们各自的不同意义。① 对于作者来说，他更希望展示不同美国人对于自我工作的不同感受，因而其叙述是在平凡的细节、情感的真实与存在的质疑之间不断流转。正如作者在《前言》所说："这本关于工作的书在本质上也是关于人们身心所遭受的暴力。"② 显然，在众多受访者的口述中，我们既能够看到人们面对某些工作的无奈、焦虑与羞辱，同时也能感受到他们因为工作而获得的满足、幸福与骄傲。正如有评论者指出的，"工作本身与《工作》这本书拥有多个面向，既有很多悲哀，也有很多光彩"③。同之前两部作品一样，该书也获得《新闻周刊》、《洛杉矶时报》（*Los Angeles Times*）、《商业周刊》（*Business Week*）与《旧金山纪事报》（*San Francisco Chronicle*）等美国主流媒体与学界的高度赞誉，《洛杉矶时报》更是称该书为"会话艺术的一本杰作"。更值得一提的是，该书于 1978 年被改编为一部同名百老汇歌舞剧，并于 1982 年在美国公共电视网（Public Broadcasting Service）播出。而就口述历史角度而言，也有学者称该书是"现代口述史学的一个里程碑"④。

特克尔的第四部口述历史作品《美国梦寻》于 1980 年出版，该书也是从数百个口述历史访谈中精选一百多位受访者的口述内容集结而成。⑤ 该书生动而又深刻地呈现了众多美国人的"美国梦"（American Dream），

---

① Studs Terkel, *Working: People Talk about What They Do All Day and How They Feel about What They Do*, New York: Pantheon Books, 1974；其他版本参见 Studs Terkel, *Working: People Talk about What They Do All Day and How They Feel about What They Do*, New York: Ballantine Books, 1985; New York: The New Press, 1997 and 2004. 其他相关资料可参见 Rick Ayers, *Studs Terkel's Working: A Teaching Guide*, New York: The New Press, 2001; Harvey Pekar and Paul Buhle, *Studs Terkel's Working: A Graphic Adaptation*, New York: The New Press, 2009.

② "Introduction", in Studs Terkel, *Working: People Talk about What They Do All Day and How They Feel about What They Do*, New York: Ballantine Books, 1985, p. xiii.

③ Gus Tyler, "Book Review: *Working: People Talk about What They Do All Day and How They Feel about What They Do*", *Industrial and Labor Relations Review*, Vol. 28, No. 2, 1975, p. 325. 其他相关评论可参见 Dorothy Deering, "Egalitarian History in Studs Terkel's Working", *Journal of General Education*, Vol. 28, No. 2, 1976, pp. 103-113.

④ James Ciment (ed.), *Postwar America: An Encyclopedia of Social, Political, Cultural, and Economic History*, Armonk: M. E. Sharpe, 2007, p. 1473.

⑤ Studs Terkel, *American Dreams: Lost and Found*, New York: Pantheon Books, 1980. 其他版本参见 Studs Terkel, *American Dreams: Lost and Found*, New York: The New Press, 1999 and 2005.

尤其是他们在寻求"美国梦"的过程中所经历的喜怒哀乐与所失所得，其中包括美国小姐、雇佣枪手、影星、歌手、政界和媒体人士、老板、流浪者、大学生、罪犯、教徒、三 K 党成员、城里的街坊邻客、贫民区的姑娘、山区的乡下佬，以及移民及其后代等。而这些"美国梦"的时代大背景正是美国在 20 世纪 60—70 年代所经历的一系列社会问题与矛盾冲击，其中包括越南战争、古巴导弹危机（Cuban Missile Crisis）、肯尼迪遇刺、反战运动、民权运动、性解放运动、学生运动以及"水门事件"（Watergate Scandal）等。而特克尔的口述历史访谈正是基于此种背景下的劈头直问："美国梦对你来说意味着什么？你的美国梦是什么？"尽管不同受访者的回答不一，但特克尔在该书中还是试图展现美国人的信心与希望。正如有评论指出："通过我们这位著名口述历史学家的镜头过滤，《美国梦寻》的异口同声突显了那些来到和居住在美国的人们的希望与奋斗。"① 而在特克尔接受的一次国家电视访谈的结语中，美国国家广播公司（National Broadcasting Company）主持人也曾评论说，要知道如此之多的美国人（指《美国梦寻》中的 104 位受访者）仍然在努力创造一个更好的世界，这是多么了不起，"它让人成为一个乐观主义者"②。

　　而特克尔的第五部口述历史作品则是 1984 年出版并于 1985 年获得普利策奖的《"正义的战争"：二战口述历史》，③ 该书以口述历史方式呈现了 120 位美国人（包括步兵、海军上将、国防工人、政府官员、艺人、商人、拒服兵役者等）在"二战"前后与"二战"中的主要经历以及战争对于他们的影响，同时也包含他们对于战争及美国政治与外交问题的自我

① 该评论可参见 Studs Terkel, *American Dreams*: *Lost and Found*, New York: The New Press, 2005, http://thenewpress.com/books/american-dreams, 2015 年 8 月 26 日访问。

② Ronald J. Grele, "Book Review: *American Dreams*: *Lost and Found*", *Oral History Review*, Vol. 9, 1981, p. 135. 有关该书的其他评论可参见 Robert Sherrill, "Looking at America", *New York Times*, September 14, 1980; Dick Krooth, "American Voices", *Economic and Political Weekly*, Vol. 15, No. 51, 1980, pp. 2136-2138; Charles T. Morrissey, "Book Review: *American Dreams*: *Lost and Found*", *International Journal of Oral History*, Vol. 2, No. 1, 1981, pp. 57-60.

③ "Studs Terkel", in Elizabeth A. Brennan and Elizabeth C. Clarage, *Who's Who of Pulitzer Prize Winners*, Phoenix: The Oryx Press, 1999, p. 270.

理解与反思。① 该书出版后也是好评如潮，《人民杂志》（*People*）认为它书写了"一部二战的壮丽史诗"，《纽约时报》则认为其叙述"是相当具有吸引力的，同时还有某种戏剧性与亲密性"，而《波士顿环球报》（*Boston Globe*）则认为该书是"有关美国人二战经历的最为丰富和最具震撼力的单一记录（single document）"②。

　　而作为对"美国梦"的重新思索，特克尔于 1988 年出版他的第六部口述历史作品《大分裂：美国梦的反思》，它以口述历史的形式生动而又深刻地呈现出 20 世纪 80 年代美国社会的多元图景及美国人的梦想与心态。③ 同样是对美国梦的思考与探索，不过与《美国梦寻》不同，特克尔在此书中显示出更多的忧虑，他认为美国人对自己的历史知之甚少，并正在"遭受令人担忧的重度集体性阿尔茨海默症的折磨"。正是如此，该书试图通过一系列口述历史访谈来挽救、恢复与重写被遗忘的美国历史与记忆，而与官方历史不同，特克尔更加关注那些之前不被关注与倾听的普通美国人的非凡梦想。特克尔指出，生活在美国的意义应当通过其公民来揭示，不仅在于他们生活的具体现实（可以衡量的成功和失败），而且在于

---

① Studs Terkel, "*The Good War*": *An Oral History of World War Two*, New York: Pantheon Books, 1984. 其他版本参见 Studs Terkel, "*The Good War*": *An Oral History of World War Two*, New York: The New Press, 1997 and 2004.

② 上述评论来自作品封面和网络介绍，详细参见 Studs Terkel, "*The Good War*": *An Oral History of World War Two*, New York: The New Press, 2004, http://thenewpress.com/books/good-war, 2015 年 8 月 27 日访问；Loudon Wainwright, "'I Can Remember Every Hour'", *New York Times*, October 7, 1984. 其他相关评论可参见 Anatole Broyard, "Book Review: 'The Good War': An Oral History of World War Two", *New York Times*, September 26, 1984; Goddis Smith, "Book Review: 'The Good War': An Oral History of World War Two", *Foreign Affairs*, Vol. 63, No. 2, 1984, p. 419; Lonnie L. Willis, "Book Review: 'The Good War': An Oral History of World War Two", *Rocky Mountain Review of Language and Literature*, Vol. 39, No. 2, 1985, pp. 165-167; Marvin Mudrick, "The Age of Innocents", *The Hudson Review*, Vol. 38, No. 2, 1985, pp. 247-255.

③ Studs Terkel, *The Great Divide*: *Second Thoughts on the American Dream*, New York: Pantheon Books, 1988.

他们的梦想、希望、抱负与渴望。① 基于此，特克尔也坦言他无意追求"客观"和寻找当今美国人生活中的"事实"（facts）与"统计"（statistics），而是力图挖掘某种尚未定型的潜藏于人们记忆中的"真实"（truth）。②

此后，特克尔还陆续出版 7 部分别涉及种族关系、老年化、电影与戏剧创作、信仰与死亡、音乐，以及自我反思等主题的口述历史作品，它们分别是《种族：黑人和白人如何思考与感受美国迷恋》（1992）、《光辉岁月：我们所经历的世纪故事》（1995）、《观众：与那些制作者谈论电影与戏剧》（1999）、《生生不息：关于死亡、重生与信仰渴望的反思》（2001）、《希望永不磨灭：在困难时期保持信心》（2003）、《他们都在歌唱：一个折衷派电台音乐节目主持人的历险经历》（2005）与《附言：一生倾听的深层思考》（2008）。③

除出版上述图书之外，1998 年特克尔与 WFMT 电台将大约 7000 份有关特克尔访谈与广播节目的录音带捐赠给芝加哥历史博物馆（Chicago

---

① Jim Stull, "Book Review: *The Great Divide: Second Thoughts on the American Dream*", *Oral History Review*, Vol. 17, No. 2, 1989, pp. 184-186. 其他相关评论可参见 John Gault, "Book Review: *The Great Divide: Second Thoughts on the American Dream*", *Maclean's*, Vol. 101, November 21, 1988, p. 62; Esmond Wright, "Book Review: *The Great Divide: Second Thoughts on the American Dream*", *Contemporary Review*, Vol. 254, March 1989, p. 162; Carl Ryant, "Book Review: *The Great Divide: Second Thoughts on the American Dream*", *Oral History*, Vol. 18, No. 1, 1990, p. 73; 赵毅：《过去与现在的分裂——读〈大分裂：对美国梦的重新思索〉》,《美国研究》1991 年第 1 期，第 144—153 页；孙毅：《一部使人全面正确认识美国的好"教材"——读斯塔兹·特克尔的〈大分裂：美国梦的反思〉》,《社会科学辑刊》1994 年第 1 期，第 158—159 页。

② Studs Terkel, *The Great Divide: Second Thoughts on the American Dream*, New York: Pantheon Books, 1988, pp. 3-4.

③ Studs Terkel, *Race: What Blacks and Whites Think and Feel about the American Obsession*, New York: The New Press, 1992; Studs Terkel, *Coming of Age: The Story of Our Century by Those Who've Lived It*, New York: The New Press, 1995; Studs Terkel, *The Spectator: Talk about Movies and Plays with Those Who Make Them*, New York: The New Press, 1999; Studs Terkel, *Will the Circle Be Unbroken: Reflections on Death, Rebirth and Hunger for a Faith*, New York: The New Press, 2001; Studs Terkel, *Hope Dies Last: Keeping the Faith in Difficult Times*, New York: The New Press, 2003; Studs Terkel, *And They All Sang: Adventures of an Eclectic Disc Jockey*, New York: The New Press, 2005; Studs Terkel, *P. S.: Further Thoughts from a Lifetime of Listening*, New York: The New Press, 2008.

History Museum)。芝加哥历史博物馆还于 2002 年创建"斯塔兹·特克尔：与美国对话"（Studs Terkel：Conversations with America）网站，并将相关图书信息与录音资料在线上传供读者浏览与下载。① 而为进一步发挥口述历史资料的声音特质与价值，2010 年芝加哥历史博物馆与美国国会图书馆宣布一项多年合作计划。该计划将对所有特克尔的访谈录音进行数字化处理，并上传到两家机构网站供读者浏览与访问。毫无疑问，这些资料的价值是相当重要的，正如国会图书馆所说，"这是有关生活在 20 世纪下半叶的普通人物和重要人物的思想与观点的极其丰富的历史"。而芝加哥历史博物馆主席盖瑞·约翰逊（Gary T. Johnson）也指出："对于斯塔兹而言，所有声音都应该被倾听，所有故事都应该被讲述。他相信每个人都有权利被听到和讲述某些重要的东西。他在那里倾听和记录，并确保他们的故事会被记住。"② 而目前 WFMT 电台、芝加哥历史博物馆斯塔兹·特克尔口述历史中心（Studs Terkel Center for Oral History）与其他合作机构联合创建的"斯塔兹·特克尔广播档案馆"（The Studs Terkel Radio Archive）网站也已经正式上线，该网站将在线上传与保存特克尔的所有访谈资料。③

当然，特克尔的口述历史实践与系列作品也受到部分学者的质疑与批判，在他们看来，他的"游击式新闻"（guerilla journalism）的访谈方法并不符合更为传统的历史学家所理解与倡导的口述历史方法。④ 此外，他们

---

① "Studs Terkel：Conversations with America"，http：//conversations. studsterkel. org/，2015 年 8 月 28 日访问。

② 转引自 "Studs Terkel"，from Wikipedia，https：//en. wikipedia. org/wiki/Studs＿ Terkel，2015 年 8 月 28 日访问。相关资料可参见 "Library Collaborates With Chicago History Museum To Preserve Radio Icon Studs Terkel's Historic Recordings"，May 14，2010，http：//www. loc. gov/today/pr/2010/10-115. html，2015 年 8 月 28 日访问。

③ "The Studs Terkel Radio Archive"，http：//studsterkel. org/，2015 年 8 月 28 日访问。

④ Gina L. Taglieri，"Studs Terkel"，in Steven R. Serafin and Alfred Bendixen（eds.），*The Continuum Encyclopedia of American Literature*，New York：The Continuum International Publishing，2003，p. 1133. 当然，特克尔本人并不喜欢称自己为"口述历史学家"，而更强调自己是一位"游击新闻记者"。详细参见 John de Graaf and Alan Harris Stein，"The Guerrilla Journalist as Oral Historian：An Interview with Louis 'Studs' Terkel"，*Oral History Review*，Vol. 29，No. 1，2002，pp. 87-107。

认为在口述历史作品的编辑过程中，特克尔将自己的观点与意识过多地渗透到受访者的口述内容当中，而且，其呈现与表达方式具有明显的文学甚至小说手法。① 尽管如此，特克尔的口述历史实践、口述历史畅销书以及原始录音资料的当下与未来价值都已经得到媒体、学界与公众的充分认可和高度赞誉。尤其需要强调的是，他所开创的以普通人物为主要访谈对象的非精英口述历史模式极大地促进了美国口述史学的流行与普及，正如美国学者艾伦·钱伯斯（Aaron Chambers）所说："无论如何，特克尔已经确立了自己作为其技艺大师的地位。……在学术与非学术圈中，他都被视为口述历史学家而受到尊重。事实上，口述史学在非学术人群中的流行则要归功于他，同时他也帮助推动了一场草根口述史

---

① 相关评论参见 Edmund J. Farrell，"The Language Game：Oral Histories as Living Literature"，*The English Journal*，Vol. 71，No. 4，1982，pp. 87-92；Charles T. Morrissey，"Oral History and the Boundaries of Fiction"，*The Public Historian*，Vol. 7，No. 2，1985，pp. 41-46；William W. Moss，"Oral History or Literary Impressionism？"*Oral History Review*，Vol. 13，1985，pp. 131-135. 需要指出的是，正是由于这样一种具有文学色彩与手法的编辑与行文特点，在 20 世纪 80 年代，特克尔的口述历史作品被翻译为中文时基本上都是被理解为报告文学、口头文学或口述实录文学作品。而特克尔的作品也深刻地影响了中国作家张辛欣与桑晔，她们采用类似的访谈方法并于 1986 年出版《北京人：一百个普通人的自述》。而更有意思的是，特克尔口述历史作品的出版商美国潘塞恩图书出版公司于 1987 年将《北京人：一百个普通人的自述》翻译为英文时，就将其理解为是一部口述历史作品。详细内容参见斯特兹·特克尔《美国人谈美国》，王槐挺、徐存尧、陶朔玉注释，中国对外翻译出版公司 1982 年版（该书翻译自《工作》）；斯特兹·特克尔：《美国梦寻》，徐复等译，中国对外翻译出版公司 1984 年版；斯塔兹·特克尔：《大分裂：美国梦的反思》，华灿译，外文出版社 1989 年版；张辛欣、桑晔：《北京人：一百个普通人的自述》，上海文艺出版社 1986 年版；Zhang Xinxin and Sang Ye，*Chinese Lives：An Oral History of Contemporary China*，New York：Pantheon Books，1987；Jeffrey C. Kinkley，"The Cultural Choices of Zhang Xinxin, a Young Writer of the 1980s"，in Paul A. Cohen and Merle Goldman（eds.），*Ideas across Cultures：Essays on Chinese Thought in Honor of Benjamin I. Schwartz*，Cambridge：Council on East Asian Studies，Harvard University，1990，pp. 151-159；Geremie Barmé，"History for the Mass"，in Jonathan Unger（ed.），*Using the Past to Serve the Present：Historiography and Politics in Contemporary China*，Armonk：M. E. Sharpe，1993，p. 272；Anthony J. Kane，"The Humanities in Contemporary China Studies：An Uncomfortable Tradition"，in David Shambaugh（ed.），*American Studies of Contemporary China*，Armonk：M. E. Sharpe，1993，p. 76；王晖：《元文化视野中民众生态与心态的书写方式——〈美国梦寻〉与〈北京人〉回眸》，《外国文学研究》，2001 年第 4 期，第 72—78 页；Charles A. Laughlin，*Chinese Reportage：The Aesthetics of Historical Experience*，Durham：Duke University Press，2002，p. 263.

学运动（grass-roots oral history movement）。"① 当然，特克尔也引领与推动了美国口述史学的"新社会史转向"，促使更多学院派口述历史工作者将口述历史方法应用于少数族裔史、女性史、劳工史与同性恋史等新兴史学领域。

三　少数族裔口述历史

从人口种族与族裔构成来说，美国是一个多元化的移民国家。美国官方政府承认六大种族：白人、美国印第安人、阿拉斯加人、亚裔美国人、非裔美国人以及夏威夷与太平洋岛屿原住民。根据 2010 年美国人口普查显示，到 2010 年 4 月 1 日，美国少数族裔人口大约为 1.11 亿，占全国总人口（大约 3.08 亿）的 36.04%。而在少数族裔人口中，其中拉美裔大约占 16.33%，非裔大约占 12.85%，亚裔大约占 4.43%，美国印第安人大约占 0.9%。② 随着社会各界日益认识到少数族裔群体对于美国政治、经济、社会与文化多元化发展的重要性，美国学术界对于它们的研究兴趣与重视度也在不断加强。不过，研究者却很快发现有关它们的资料相当稀缺，而且现有记录也具有明显的歪曲与偏见，正是如此，口述史学迅速成为挖掘与

---

① Aaron Chambers, "History from the Bottom Up: Using Chicago as a Microcosm, Studs Terkel Has Helped Define America, with All Its Divisions and Unions", *Illinois Issues*, December 2001, http://illinoisissues. uis. edu/features/2001dec/terkel. html, 2015 年 8 月 28 日访问。

② 《少数族裔在美国》，《中国社会科学报》2011 年 7 月 14 日；《美国人口》，维基百科，https://zh. wikipedia. org/wiki/美国人口；《美国种族及民族》，维基百科，https://zh. wikipedia. org/wiki/美国种族及民族。上述访问时间为 2015 年 8 月 29 日。

呈现美国少数族裔群体声音与历史的重要手段。①

在有关美国少数族裔群体的众多口述历史计划当中，其中具有相当代表性的是针对美国印第安人（American Indian）的"桃瑞丝·杜克美国印第安人口述历史项目"（Doris Duke American Indian Oral History Program）。② 在 1966—1972 年期间，在美国烟草大王詹姆斯·杜克（James B. Duke，1856—1925）女儿、遗产继承人桃瑞丝·杜克（Doris Duke，1912—1993）的资助下，该项目在美国多所大学各自设立计划来搜集与保存有关印第安人的口述历史资料，这些大学分别是加州大学洛杉矶分校（一年后退出）、亚利桑那大学（University of Arizona）、伊利诺伊大学厄巴纳-香槟分校（University of Illinois at Urbana-Champaign）、新墨西哥大学（University of New Mexico）、俄克拉荷马大学（University of Oklahoma）、南达科他大学、犹他大学（University of Utah）与佛罗里达大学（University of Florida，该校在加州大学洛杉矶分校退出后加入）。③ 该项目的总体目标是通过口述历史方法并从印第安人的视角来搜集有关他们的原始历史资料，并强调其视角并不

① Francis Paul Prucha, *Handbook for Research in American History：A Guide to Bibliographies and Other Reference Works*, Lincoln：University of Nebraska Press, second edition, revised, 1994, p. 97. 另外，《口述历史与有色社群》一书就集中探讨了口述历史在亚裔美国人、美国印第安人、拉丁裔美国人、非裔美国人与穆斯林美国人等五个不同种族与族裔社群研究中的具体应用。具体参见 Teresa Barnett and Chon A. Noriega（eds.），*Oral History and Communities of Color*, Los Angeles：UCLA Chicano Studies Research Center Press, 2013. 其他有关口述历史与族裔问题的研究可参见 Gary Y. Okihiro, "Oral History and the Writing of Ethnic History", *Oral History Review*, Vol. 9, 1981, pp. 27-46；*Canadian Oral History Association Journal*, No. 9, 1989（Special Issue：Oral History and Ethnicity）；*Oral History*, Vol. 21, No. 1, 1993（Special Issue：Ethnicity and Oral History）；Alexander Freund, *Oral History and Ethnic History*（Immigration and Ethnicity in Canada Series 32），Ottawa：Canadian Historical Association, 2014.

② 需要指出的是，"美国印第安人"这个概念包括多元部落与文化，与"印第安人"（Indian）、"民族"（Nationals）、"原住民"（Native）、"土著"（Indigenous）或加拿大的"第一民族"（First Nations）等概念有诸多相似与重合之处。而在 20 世纪 70 年代印第安人权利运动期间，"美国原住民"（Native American）这个术语则使用得更为普遍。详细参见 Charles E. Trimble, Barbara W. Sommer and Mary Kay Quinlan, *The American Indian Oral History Manual：Making Many Voices Heard*, Walnut Creek：Left Coast Press, 2008, p. 10.

③ Polly Grimshaw, *Images of the Other：A Guide to Microfilm Manuscripts on Indian-White Relations*, Urbana：University of Illinois Press, 1991；Bradford Koplowitza, "The Doris Duke Indian Oral History Projects", *Popular Culture in Libraries*, Vol. 1, No. 3, 1993, pp. 23-38.

是单一的和单向的。正如美国口述历史协会前主席（1985—1986 年度）塞缪尔·汉德（Samuel Hand，1931—2012）所说："要在多个大学建立口述历史中心的决定反映了对于美国印第安人内部多样性的日益认可，尤其对于联邦、州和地方机构而言，他们的文化视角与特殊的历史经历都是相当多元的。"① 当然，该项目还有一个同样重要的目标，即将记录的录音带副本返回给相应的印第安人部落，以此作为部落与大学相互合作与交流的互惠协议。②

需要指出的是，该项目是否真正能够实现从印第安人的视角来记录与保存他们的口述历史这一总体目标则很难判断，尽管所有计划都尽量安排一些来自印第安人部落的研究生、教师或研究者参与具体的访谈工作。正如该项目俄克拉荷马大学负责人茱莉娅·乔丹（Julia A. Jordan，1928—）所说："搜集印第安人口述历史并不会水到渠成地让人们更加理解印第安人在美国历史中的地位，也不会创造出新的印第安人历史的书写模式。"但是，她也强调该项目所搜集的大量宝贵史料则是迈向这一目标的重要一步。③ 据不完全统计，该项目总共搜集的录音访谈资料将近达到 5000 份，④ 成为研究美国印第安人历史与文化的重

① Samuel Hand, "Some Words on Oral Histories", in David K. Dunaway and Willa K. Baum (eds.), *Oral History: An Interdisciplinary Anthology*, Nashville: American Association for State and Local History, 1984, p. 53.

② Dianna Repp, "The Doris Duke American Indian Oral History Program: Gathering the 'Raw Material of History'", *Journal of the Southwest*, Vol. 47, No. 1, 2005, p. 11.

③ 转引自 Dianna Louise Repp, "Inscribing the Raw Materials of History: An Analysis of the Doris Duke American Indian Oral History Program", Ph. D. dissertation, Arizona State University, 2009, p. 267.

④ Lee S. Dutton (ed.), *Anthropological Resources: A Guide to Archival, Library, and Museum Collections*, London and New York: Routledge, 1999, p. 339. 而作为对该项目的纪念与反思，美国《西南杂志》(*Journal of the Southwest*) 还于 2005 年出版专刊《回忆口述历史：美国原住民、桃瑞丝·杜克与青年人类学家》(Oral History Remembered: Native Americans, Doris Duke, and the Young Anthropologists, Vol. 47, No. 1)。

要资料来源。[1]

　　而在这些美国印第安人口述历史资料的使用方面，最具开创意义的是由南达科他大学约瑟夫·凯希（Joseph H. Cash）和赫伯特·胡佛（Herbert T. Hoover）于 1971 年编写出版的《身为印第安人：口述历史》。该书可以说是南达科他大学美国印第安人研究计划的直接产物，同时也是杜克项目中第一本完全依赖口述历史资料编写而成的著作。两位作者从搜集的 800 多份录音访谈中精选了 70 多份编辑而成，主题从印第安人的精神生活与民俗文化到他们的保留地（reservations）生活。其受访者大多为印第安苏族人（Sioux），他们向读者讲述了 19 世纪与 20 世纪初被强迫迁移至保留地所遭受的痛苦。同时，还涉及经济大萧条（the Great Depression）、第二次世界大战与美国新政对于他们的影响及保留地的存废问题。正如作者们所指出的，传统的历史学家对于印第安人的过去、未来与精神生活充满想象，并且从不关注他们自己的想法与意见，而本书的宗旨就在于以印第安人自己的视角来恢复与呈现他们的历史与

────────────────

　　[1]　有关每个大学相应计划的资料情况可参见 C. Gregory Crampton，"The Archives of the Duke Projects in American Indian Oral History"，in Jane F. Smith and Robert M. Kvasnicka（eds.），*Indian-White Relations：A Persistent Paradox*，Washington：Howard University Press，1981，pp. 119-128；Kathryn L. Jasper，"The Doris Duke Program in Scope and Sequence"，*Journal of the Southwest*，Vol. 47，No. 1，2005，pp. 153-164. 而在数字化时代，大部分大学已经将相关口述历史收藏的目录或抄本全文资料上传到网络上，具体可访问 "The Duke Collection of American Indian Oral History at University of Oklahoma"，https：//digital. libraries. ou. edu/whc/duke/；"Doris Duke Indian Oral History Program Archives：An Inventory of Its Records at the University of Illinois Archives"，http：//archives. library. illinois. edu/ead/ua/1502032/1502032f. html；"Doris Duke Oral History Project，1966-1972，University of Utah"，http：//archiveswest. orbiscascade. org/ark：/80444/xv34603；"The American Indian Research Project at University of South Dakota"，http：//www. usd. edu/library/sdohc/airp；"American Indian Oral History Recordings，University of New Mexico"，http：//econtent. unm. edu/cdm/landingpage/collection/amerindian；"Native Americans Oral History Collections at University of Florida"，http：//ufdc. ufl. edu/oh4. 此外，亚利桑那大学目前正在对这些口述历史资料进行数字化处理，详细参见 "Preserving the Arizona State Museum Doris Duke American Indian Oral History Collection"，http：//oric. arizona. edu/node/55. 上述访问时间为 2015 年 8 月 29 日。

文化。① 此后，这些口述历史资料也不断为相关领域的研究者所利用，而丰富的研究成果对于改变印第安人的传统刻板形象与探索新的印第安人历史书写视角都具有相当重要的意义。②

随着杜克项目影响的扩大，其他印第安人口述历史计划也相继开展，其中比较有代表性的是美国原住民教育服务学院（Native American Educational Services College）与纽贝里图书馆（Newberry Library）于 1983 年启动的"芝加哥美国印第安人口述历史计划"（Chicago American Indian Oral History Project）。③ 同时，就资料来源与研究视角而言，口述历史对于印第安人历史与文化研究的意义与价值也开始

---

① Joseph H. Cash and Herbert T. Hoover (eds.), *To Be an Indian: An Oral History*, New York: Holt, Rinehart and Winston, 1971. 相关书评可参见 C. Gregory Crampton, "Book Review: *To Be an Indian: An Oral History*", *Western Historical Quarterly*, Vol. 3, No. 4, 1972, pp. 436-437; Lonnie E. Underhill, "Book Review: *To Be an Indian: An Oral History*", *Journal of the Southwest*, Vol. 14, No. 4, 1972, pp. 369-371.

② 代表性成果包括 Peter Nabokov (ed.), *Native American Testimony: An Anthology of Indian and White Relations, First Encounter to Dispossession*, New York: Harper & Row, 1978; Lester George Moses and Raymond Wilson (eds.), *Indian Lives: Essays on Nineteenth- and Twentieth-Century Native American Leaders*, Albuquerque: University of New Mexico Press, 1985; David Rich Lewis, *Neither Wolf Nor Dog: American Indians, Environment, and Agrarian Change*, Oxford and New York: Oxford University Press, 1994; Troy R. Johnson, *The Occupation of Alcatraz Island: Indian Self-determination and the Rise of Indian Activism*, Urbana: University of Illinois Press, 1996; Thomas A. Britten, *American Indians in World War I: At Home and at War*, Albuquerque: University of New Mexico Press, 1997; Kenneth William Townsend, *World War II and the American Indian*, Albuquerque: University of New Mexico Press, 2000; Theodore Rios and Kathleen M. Sands, *Telling a Good One: The Process of a Native American Collaborative Biography*, Lincoln: University of Nebraska Press, 2000; Donald Fixico, *The American Indian Mind in a Linear World: American Indian Studies and Traditional Knowledge*, London and New York: Routledge, 2003; Daniel M. Cobb, *Native Activism in Cold War America: The Struggle for Sovereignty*, Lawrence: University Press of Kansas, 2008; Rose Stremlau, *Sustaining the Cherokee Family: Kinship and the Allotment of an Indigenous Nation*, Chapel Hill: University of North Carolina Press, 2011; Donald L. Fixico, *Call for Change: The Medicine Way of American Indian History, Ethos, and Reality*, Lincoln: University of Nebraska Press, 2015; Tash Smith, *Capture These Indians for the Lord: Indians, Methodists, and Oklahomans, 1844-1939*, Tucson: University of Arizona Press, 2014; Andrew Woolford, *This Benevolent Experiment: Indigenous Boarding Schools, Genocide, and Redress in Canada and the United States*, Lincoln: University of Nebraska Press, 2015.

③ *Chicago American Indian Oral History Pilot Project: Transcript Description and Index*, Chicago: Newberry Library, 1984; Terry Straus, *Indians of the Chicago Area*, Chicago: Native American Educational Services College, 1989, p. 211.

得到更为主流学术界的认可。事实上，早在 1969 年，美国著名人类学家伯纳德·方塔纳（Bernard L. Fontana，1931—）就在美国知名刊物《历史与理论》（*History and Theory*）上发表文章强调口述历史对于理解与研究美国印第安人的重要性。[①] 此后，更多学者表达了类似观点，在 1996 年出版的《剑桥美洲原住民史》一书中，著名美国原住民研究专家彼得·纳博科夫（Peter Nabokov）就强调口述历史对于从原住民视角来书写印第安人历史的重要性。[②] 而 1997 年出版的《重新反思美国印第安人历史》也有多篇文章强调口述历史对于重建印第安人观点与恢复印第安人声音的重要性。[③] 而在面对其他学者批判印第安人口述历史资料的客观性问题时，更多学者强调口述历史资料本身有其自身的真实性与可靠性，[④] 并且主张应该从记忆的角度来深入理解口述历史所呈现的印第安人内心世界与客观现实之间的张力关系。[⑤]

当然，在《身为印第安人：口述历史》于 1971 年出版之后，美国学术界也有众多印第安人口述历史作品相继问世。其中比较有代表性的包括《祖尼人：自我形象》（1972）、《行走的人：美国原住民口述历史》（1993）、《永恒的回声：美国原住民口述历史》（1997）、《城市声音：旧金山湾区美国印第安人社群》（2002）与《口述历史与青年原住民：加强

① Bernard L. Fontana, "American Indian Oral History: An Anthropologist's Note", *History and Theory*, Vol. 8, No. 3, 1969, pp. 366-370.

② Peter Nabokov, "Native Views of History", in Bruce G. Trigger and Wilcomb E. Washburn (eds.), *The Cambridge History of the Native Peoples of the Americas* (Volume I: North America), Cambridge: Cambridge University Press, 1996, pp. 1-60.

③ Donald Lee Fixico (ed.), *Rethinking American Indian History*, Albuquerque: University of New Mexico Press, 1997.

④ Philip J. Deloria, "Historiography", in Philip J. Deloria and Neal Salisbury (eds.), *A Companion to American Indian History*, Malden: Blackwell Publishers, 2002, pp. 15-22.

⑤ William Bauer, " 'Everybody Worked Back Then': Oral History, Memory, and Indian Economies in Northern California", in Jessie L. Embry (ed.), *Oral History, Community, and Work in the American West*, Tucson: University of Arizona Press, 2013, pp. 61-81.

传统美国印第安人教育》（2010）等。①

　　需要特别指出的是，为帮助、指导美国印第安人口述历史计划的具体操作与实施，查尔斯·特林布（Charles E. Trimble，1935—）等人于 2008 出版《美国印第安人口述历史手册》。该手册详细论述了印第安人口述历史的意义、法律与伦理、项目规划、设备与预算、访谈准备与执行、访谈后续处理及口述历史资料的使用等诸多问题，同时还附录口述历史相关表格与法律文书范本、美国口述历史协会《口述历史评估指南》（*Oral History Evaluation Guidelines*）与重要参考文献。毫无疑问，对于那些从事印第安人口述历史实践与研究的工作者来说，该手册是一本绝佳的操作指南。②

　　而从 20 世纪 60 年代中后期开始，口述史学在非裔美国人历史（African American history）研究中的价值与意义也逐渐得到认可，并开始应用于

---

①　The Zuni People, *The Zuni*: *Self Portrayals*, Albuquerque: University of New Mexico Press, 1972; Paula Underwood, *The Walking People*: *A Native American Oral History*, San Anselmo: A Tribe of Two Press, 1993; Joseph Bruchac, *Lasting Echoes*: *An Oral History of Native American People*, San Diego: Silver Whistle, 1997; Susan Lobo（ed.）, *Urban Voices*: *The Bay Area American Indian Community*, Tucson: University of Arizona Press, 2002; Jeanne A. Lacourt, *Oral History and Native Youth*: *Strengthening Traditional American Indian Education*, Verlag: Lambert Academic Publishing, 2010. 其他印第安人口述历史作品还可参见 Pamela J. Dobson（ed.）, *The Tree that Never Dies*: *Oral History of the Michigan Indians*, Grand Rapids: Grand Rapids Public Library, 1978; Theda Perdue, *Nations Remembered*: *An Oral History of the Cherokees, Chickasaws, Choctaws, Creeks, and Seminoles*, Norman: University of Oklahoma Press, 1993; Rita T. Kohn, William Lynwood Montell, and Michelle Mannering（eds.）, *Always a People*: *Oral Histories of Contemporary Woodland Indians*, Bloomington: Indiana University Press, 1997; Sally McBeth, *Native American Oral History and Cultural Interpretation in Rocky Mountain National Park*, Damascus: Penny Hill Press, 2007; Alison Owings, *Indian Voices*: *Listening to Native Americans*, New Brunswick: Rutgers University Press, 2011; Malcolm D. Benally（ed.）, *Bitter Water*: *Diné Oral Histories of the Navajo-Hopi Land Dispute*, Tucson: University of Arizona Press, 2011.

②　Charles E. Trimble, Barbara W. Sommer and Mary Kay Quinlan, *The American Indian Oral History Manual*: *Making Many Voices Heard*, Walnut Creek: Left Coast Press, 2008. 相关书评可参见 Lu Ann Jones, "Book Review: *The American Indian Oral History Manual*", *CRM*: *The Journal of Heritage Stewardship*, Vol. 6, No. 2, 2009, pp. 92-93; Ki-Shan Lara, "Book Review: *The American Indian Oral History Manual*", *American Indian Quarterly*, Vol. 34, No. 2, 2010, pp. 265-267; Linda P. Wood, "Book Review: *The Oral History Manual* and *The American Indian Oral History Manual*", *Oral History Review*, Vol. 37, No. 2, 2010, pp. 335-338. 其他有关美国印第安人口述历史的理论与方法论研究可参见 Debbie Lee, "Listening to the Land: The Selway-Bitterroot Wilderness as Oral History", *Oral History Review*, Vol. 37, No. 2, 2010, pp. 235-248.

具体实践与研究当中。① 正如有学者指出："口述历史在保存非裔美国人历史与文化的过程中扮演着至关重要的作用。它充当一种双重角色，一方面将历史从种族主义、男性至上主义（sexism）与阶级压迫的威胁中恢复出来；而另一方面，通过教育以及回忆与重新解释历史等过程，它可以成为向非裔美国人赋权的一种手段。……通过20世纪中期口述历史的复兴，与少数群体、工人阶级、女性和其他边缘群体成员的访谈已经将他（她）们的经历铭刻在历史记录上，而且呈现了他（她）们对于历史的自我解释。更为特别的是，访谈记录了那些往往容易被其他资料来源所忽视的历史经历，比如个人关系、家务劳动或家庭生活，而且它们与生活经验的个人意义产生共鸣。"② 而美国著名历史学家《马尔科姆·爱克斯：革新的生命》（*Malcolm X：A Life of Reinvention*，该书获2012年普利策奖）作者曼宁·马拉布尔（Manning Marable，1950—2011）更以自己的亲身实践来强调口述历史对于重写非裔美国人历史的重要性，他指出："我采访了许多曾经与马尔科姆·爱克斯一起共事的人，其中一些人提供了有关他在1965年遇刺的目击叙述。……当与爱克斯共事者的口述历史访谈结合起来，这些资料能够对这位仍然被广泛误解的非裔美国人领袖的实际活动做出新的阐述。通过这些技术和历史研究的跨学科方法，就有可能创造'新的历史'，即一种能够从他们自己的观点出发来更为准确地呈现黑人真实故事的历史，正如他们所经历的。"③

同美国印第安人一样，那些早期被贩卖到美洲新大陆的非洲奴隶的历

---

① 美国学术界也会使用"negro history"和"black history"这两个术语来表示"黑人历史"，现在基本习惯于使用"African American history"。比如，于1916年创刊的《黑人历史杂志》（*Journal of Negro History*）从2002年开始更名为《非裔美国人历史杂志》（*Journal of African American History*）。详细内容可参见 Pero Gaglo Dagbovie, *African American History Reconsidered*, Urbana：University of Illinois Press, 2010；Pero Gaglo Dagbovie, *What is African American History*? Malden：Polity Press, 2015.

② Christopher M. Span and Chamara J. Kwakye, "Black Oral History Collection", in Kofi Lomotey (ed.), *Encyclopedia of African American Education* (Volume 1), Thousand Oaks：Sage Publications, 2010, p. 100.

③ Manning Marable, *Living Black History：How Reimagining the African-American Past Can Remake America's Racial Future*, New York：Basic Civitas Books, 2006, p. 33.

史与文化的传递很大程度上依赖于口头传统。因此，在现代口述史学诞生之前，在有关美国奴隶制与早期非裔美国人的历史研究当中，口头传统与基于访谈的调查方式成为相当重要的资料搜集方法。[1] 有学者指出，搜集奴隶叙述（slave narrative）或许是非裔美国人口述历史实践的最早范例，其最早可以追溯到 19 世纪 70 年代美国著名废奴主义者威廉·斯蒂尔（William Still, 1821—1902）所开展的有关逃亡奴隶的访谈工作。而且，该传统一直延续下来，而到 20 世纪 30 年代美国联邦作家计划所开展的奴隶叙述计划时，此项工作的规模与影响达到鼎盛。[2]

在 1948 年美国现代口述史学诞生之后，以精英人物为主要访谈对象的美国早期口述历史计划也记录和保存了少数非裔美国人领袖或精英的口述历史资料。以哥伦比亚大学口述历史研究室为例，由于早期访谈对象主要聚焦于白人精英，因此，最初 20 年间，在 200 位受访者当中也只有 3 位黑人（而且都是知名人物），他们分别是杜波伊斯（W. E. B. Du Bois, 1868—1963）、乔治·斯凯勒（George S. Schuyler, 1895—1977）和罗伊·威尔金斯（Roy Wilkins, 1901—1981）。[3] 不过，20 世纪 50 年代中期兴

---

① Joe R. Feagin and Melvin P. Sikes, *Living with Racism: The Black Middle-Class Experience*, Boston: Beacon Press, 1994, p. 123; Mitchell A. Kachun, "African American History", in Carol Kammen and Norma Prendergast (eds.), *Encyclopedia of Local History*, Walnut Creek: AltaMira Press, 2006, p. 8. 其他相关资料可参见 Robert H. Lowie, "Oral Tradition and History", *American Anthropologist*, Vol. 17, No. 3, 1915, pp. 597-599; Robert H. Lowie, "Oral Tradition and History", *Journal of American Folklore*, Vol. 30, No. 116, 1917, pp. 161-167; Richard M. Dorson, "Oral Tradition and Written History: The Case for the United States", *Journal of the Folklore Institute*, Vol. 1, No. 3, 1964, pp. 220-234; Leslie M. Alexander and Curtis J. Austin, "Africana Studies and Oral History: A Critical Assessment", in Jeanette Ross Davidson (ed.), *African American Studies*, Edinburgh: Edinburgh University Press, 2010, pp. 171-193.

② 有关美国奴隶叙述搜集的历史，可参见 Elinor Des Verney Sinnette, "Oral History", in Evelyn Brooks Higginbotham, Leon F. Litwack, Darlene Clark Hine, and Randall K. Burkett (eds.), *The Harvard Guide to African-American History*, Cambridge: Harvard University Press, 2001, pp. 113-115; Albert S. Broussard, "Race and Oral History", in Donald A. Ritchie (ed.), *The Oxford Handbook of Oral History*, Oxford and New York: Oxford University Press, 2011, pp. 186-190. 此外还可参见 Alan B. Govenar, *African American Frontiers: Slave Narratives and Oral Histories*, Santa Barbara: ABC-CLIO, 2000.

③ Benjamin Quarles, *Black Mosaic: Essays in Afro-American History and Historiography*, Amherst: University of Massachusetts Press, 1988, p. 190.

起并在 60 年代中期达到高潮的美国黑人反对种族歧视和压迫及争取政治经济和社会平等权利的民权运动催生了一大批有关非裔美国人的口述历史计划与研究成果。当然，这其中跟美国著名非裔作家亚历克斯·哈利（Alex Haley, 1921—1992）的引领与示范效应也有很大关系。通过与著名黑人领袖马尔科姆·爱克斯（Malcolm X, 1925—1965）的多次口述历史访谈，哈利于 1965 年出版《马尔科姆·爱克斯自传》，而该书也一定程度上促进了口述史学在美国黑人史研究中的不断应用与流行。[①]

而在有关非裔美国人的口述历史计划当中，发起时间较早且具代表性的是美国霍华德大学莫兰德—斯宾加恩研究中心（Moorland-Spingarn Research Center, Howard University）于 1967 年启动的"民权运动记录计划"（Civil Rights Documentation Project），其目的是记录 20 世纪 50—60 年代美国民权运动参与者的经历与观点。该计划最初由美国著名政治科学家、外交家拉尔夫·本奇（Ralph J. Bunche, 1903—1971）提议，并由其学生、霍华德大学教授文森特·布朗恩（Vincent J. Browne, 1917—1997）担任计划负责人。而在计划实施的 6 年间，它还获得教育促进基金会（Fund for the Advancement of Education）与福特基金会（Ford Foundation）的联合资助。根据统计，该计划总共收集 700 多份口述历史访谈资料，并成为日后

---

① Malcolm X and Alex Haley, *The Autobiography of Malcolm X*, New York: Grove Press, 1965. 该书自 1965 年问世后一直都是畅销书，据《纽约时报》报道，到 1977 年该书总共销售 600 万册。而就口述史学角度而言，它被保罗·汤普森认为是口述历史方法应用于自传写作与黑人史研究的杰出范例。详细参见 Paul Thompson, *The Voice of the Past: Oral History*, Oxford and New York: Oxford University Press, third edition, 2000, p. 116. 需要指出的是，哈利于 1976 年出版并于 1977 年获得普利策奖的长篇家史小说《根》（还被改编成电视连续剧）也极大地促进了美国学术界对于口述历史、黑人史与谱系学关系的探讨与思考。详细参见 Alex Haley, "Black History, Oral History, and Genealogy", *Oral History Review*, Vol. 1, 1973, pp. 1-25; Courtney Brown, "Oral History and the Oral Tradition of Black America: The Kinte Foundation", *Oral History Review*, Vol. 1, 1973, pp. 26-28; Alex Haley, *Roots: The Saga of an American Family*, Garden City: Doubleday, 1976; Thad Sitton, George L. Mehaffy, and O. L. Davis, Jr., *Oral History: A Guide for Teachers (and Others)*, Austin: University of Austin Press, 1983, p. 9.

众多学者研究成果的重要资料来源。① 在本奇于 1971 年去世之后，为纪念他对于该计划的贡献，霍华德大学特意设立"拉尔夫·本奇口述历史馆藏"（Ralph J. Bunche Oral History Collection）来集中保存这些口述历史资料。尤其需要指出的是，莫兰德—斯宾加恩研究中心后来还陆续启动有关霍华德大学校史、投票权法案（*Voting Rights Act*）与黑人军事史相关的口述历史计划，同时还专门设立捐赠口述历史项目（Donor's Oral History Program）负责其他机构有关非裔美国人与民权运动相关的口述历史资料的捐赠与保存事宜。②

　　另外一个重要的口述历史计划是于 1972 年启动的杜克大学口述历史项目（Duke University Oral History Program），在洛克菲勒基金会的资助下，杜克大学著名历史学家劳伦斯·古德温（Lawrence C. Goodwyn，1928—2013）③ 创办了美国首个口述史学博士课程。而该项目的主要目标是希望在培养学生的基础上，通过利用口述历史资料来重新书写传统的美国历史，尤其是有关黑人与其他群体的历史。而为了书写一种平衡的多种族的历史（multiracial history），该项目以新建的民权与种族关系研究中心（Center for the Study of Civil Rights and Race Relations）为依托，通过口述历

① Benjamin Quarles, "The Future of Negro Past", *Negro Digest*, Vol. 17, No. 4, February 1968, p. 38; Vincent J. Browne, "Oral History and the Civil Rights Documentation Project", in Peter D. Olch and Forrest C. Pogue（eds.），*Selections from the Fifth and Sixth National Colloquia on Oral History*, New York: Oral History Association, 1972, pp. 90-95; Vincent J. Browne and Norma O. Leonard（eds.），*Bibliography of Holdings of the Civil Rights Documentation Project*, Washington: Howard University, 1974. 利用这些口述历史资料的代表性研究成果有 Mark V. Tushnet, *Making Civil Rights Law: Thurgood Marshall and the Supreme Court, 1936-1961*, Oxford and New York: Oxford University Press, 1994; Peter B. Levy, *Civil War on Race Street: The Civil Rights Movement in Cambridge, Maryland*, Gainesville: University Press of Florida, 2003; Sekou M. Franklin, *After the Rebellion: Black Youth, Social Movement Activism, and the Post-Civil Rights Generation*, New York: New York University Press, 2014.

② 上述信息可访问 Moorland-Spingarn Research Center, "Oral History Collections", http://www. coas. howard. edu/msrc/manuscripts_ oralhistory. html, 2015 年 8 月 30 日访问。目前该中心网站提供所有收藏中单个口述历史访谈的索引指南信息。

③ William Yardley, "Lawrence Goodwyn, Historian of Populism, Dies at 85", *New York Times*, October 4, 2013.

史访谈来记录与保存非裔美国人参与民权运动的经历与观点。就其意义而言，正如该项目联合主任威廉·雪夫（William H. Chafe）所说："它是学术界第一个系统地对种族关系和民权进行全面研究的计划。"[①] 需要指出的是，在该项目的影响下，杜克大学林德赫斯特纪录片研究中心（Lyndhurst Center for Documentary Studies）于 1990 年启动"面纱背后：记录南方黑人区的非裔美国人生活"（Behind the Veil：Documenting African-American Life in the Jim Crow South）口述历史计划，它主要致力于记录和保存 19 世纪 80 年代至 20 世纪 50 年代美国南方种族隔离合法时期的非裔美国人生活的鲜活记忆。目前，该计划所搜集的口述历史访谈数量将近达到 1700 份，而其中 400 多份访谈录音和抄本资料都已经可以在线访问、浏览或下载。[②]

此外，在 20 世纪 70 年代末之前，包括马丁·路德·金非暴力社会变迁中心（Martin Luther King, Jr. Center for Nonviolent Social Change）、菲斯克大学（Fisk University）[③]、华盛顿州立大学（Washington

① Alphine W. Jefferson, "Echoes from the South：The History and Methodology of the Duke University Oral History Program, 1972-1982", *Oral History Review*, Vol. 12, 1984, p. 46.

② "Guide to the Behind the Veil：Documenting African-American Life in the Jim Crow South Records, 1940-1997 and undated, bulk 1993-1997", http：//library. duke. edu/rubenstein/findingaids/btv/, 2015 年 8 月 30 日访问。有关该计划的相关研究可参见 William H. Chafe, "'The Gods Bring Threads to Webs Begun'：African American Life in the Jim Crow South", *Journal of American History*, Vol. 86, No. 4, 2000, pp. 1531-1551.

③ 菲斯克大学黑人口述历史项目（Black Oral History Program）启动于 1970 年，在美国国家人文科学基金会的资助下，该项目总共搜集 700 多份有关各个领域的非裔美国人的口述历史资料，其中包括著名作家、杜波伊斯遗孀雪莉·杜波伊斯（Shirley Graham Du Bois, 1896—1977）、知名历史学家约翰·霍普·富兰克林（John Hope Franklin, 1915—2009）和亚历克斯·哈利等人。而且，访谈主题也相当广泛，涉及民权运动、哈莱姆文艺复兴（Harlem Renaissance）、黑人宗教信仰与日常生活等。值得一提的是，美国首次和唯一一次有关黑人口述历史为主题的全国性会议也是在菲斯克大学举行（1972）。详细内容可参见 Gladys-Marie Fry, *Night Riders in Black Folk History*, Knoxville：University of Tennessee, 1975, p. 28；Benjamin Houston, *The Nashville Way：Racial Etiquette and the Struggle for Social Justice in a Southern City*, Athens：University of Georgia Press, 2012, p. 297；Fisk University, "Black Oral History Program", http：//www. loc. gov/folklife/civilrights/survey/view_ collection. php? coll_ id =2115, 2015 年 8 月 30 日访问。

State University)①、威斯康星州历史学会、南密西西比大学（University of Southern Mississippi)②、阿拉巴马大学伯明翰分校（University of Alabama at Birmingham)③、拉德克利夫学院（Radcliffe College)④、北卡罗来纳大学教堂山分校（University of North Carolina at Chapel Hill)⑤、美国艺术档案馆、杜兰大学阿米斯塔德研究中心（Amistad Research Center）、查尔斯顿学院非裔美国人历史与文化艾弗里研究中心（Avery Research Center for African American History and Culture，College of Charleston）与南卡罗来纳圣海伦娜岛海岛居民佩恩中心（Penn Center of the Sea Islanders on St. Helena Island）在内的许多大学和相关机构都启动了有

---

① 华盛顿州立大学"黑人口述历史收藏"（Black Oral History Collection）创建于1972年，内容包括华盛顿、俄勒冈、爱达荷和蒙大拿等地的非裔美国人先驱及其后裔的口述历史访谈资料，主题涉及非裔美国人雇佣模式、社会生活、政治与社区机构等。详细内容参见 Christopher M. Span and Chamara J. Kwakye, "Black Oral History Collection", in Kofi Lomotey（ed.），*Encyclopedia of African A-merican Education*（Volume 1），Thousand Oaks: Sage Publications, 2010, pp. 99-100; Washington State University, "Black Oral History Collection", http: //content. libraries. wsu. edu/cdm/landingpage/collec-tion/5985/, 2015 年 8 月 30 日访问。

② 南密西西比大学从20世纪70年代就开始启动有关民权运动的口述历史计划，目前该计划统称为"民权记录计划"（Civil Rights Documentation Project），详细资料访问网站 http: //www. usm. edu/crdp/和 http: //digilib. usm. edu/crmda. php, 2015 年 8 月 30 日访问。

③ 该校口述历史研究室（Oral History Office）与历史系在1975—1984年间搜集了大约180个涉及阿拉巴马州历史与文化的口述历史访谈资料，其中绝大部分都与非裔美国人与民权运动相关。详细内容访问 "Inventory of the University of Alabama at Birmingham: Mervyn H. Sterne Library: Oral History Collection, 1975-1984", http: //digital. mhsl. uab. edu/oralhistory_ html/UAB_ oral_ history_ Findingaids. html#controlaccess, 2015 年 8 月 30 日访问。

④ 拉德克利夫学院黑人女性口述历史计划（Black Women Oral History Project）启动于1976年，到1981年之前，该计划总共采访72位非裔美国女性。详细内容参见 Ruth Edmond Hill（ed.），*Black Women Oral History Project：From the Arthur and Elizabeth Schlesinger Library on the History of Women in America*，*Radcliffe College*，Westport: Meckler Publishing, 1991; "Black Women Oral His-tory Project Interviews, 1976-1981", https: //www. radcliffe. harvard. edu/schlesinger-library/collection/black-women-oral-history-project, 2015 年 8 月 30 日访问。

⑤ 该校于1974年创建的南方口述历史项目（Southern Oral History Program）从一开始就关注美国南方非裔美国人与民权运动的口述历史工作，在其丰富的"美国南方口述历史收藏"中就有众多访谈资料涉及民权运动。详细内容访问 "Oral Histories of American South: The Civil Rights Movement", http: //docsouth. unc. edu/sohp/civil_ rights. html, 2015 年 8 月 30 日访问。

关非裔美国人和民权运动的口述历史计划。[①] 而在新近设立的相关口述历史计划当中，较具代表性的是肯塔基州历史学会（Kentucky Historical Society）肯塔基口述历史委员会（Kentucky Oral History Commission）于 1998 年启动的肯塔基州民权运动口述历史计划（Civil Rights Movement in Kentucky Oral History Project）。该计划目前搜集两百多个口述历史访谈，而且已经将大部分资料进行数字化处理并实现在线访问，还利用这些资料创作了一部颇受关注的获奖纪录片《生活故事：肯塔基民权运动》（*Living the Story: The Civil Rights Movement in Kentucky*）。[②]

另外，需要指出的是，美国国会于 2009 年 5 月通过《2009 年民权历史计划法案》（*The Civil Rights History Project Act of 2009*）之后，随即要求国会图书馆和史密森学会启动有关民权运动口述历史收藏的全国调查，其结果可根据收藏机构、收藏名称与主题分类进行浏览与检索。而且，为更加完善和补充现有口述历史收藏，该法案也要求启动一部分新的针对民权运动的口述历史计划。[③] 显然，这也足以说明口述历史在民权运动史研究中具有特殊意义，正如美国著名口述历史学家金姆·罗杰斯（Kim Lacy Rogers，1951—2014；她曾于 2004—2005 年度担任美国口述历史协会主席）所说："口述历史对于那些试图理解民权运动和其他社会运动的学者来说是一种关键的资料。……口述历史能够

---

① Elinor Des Verney Sinnette, "Oral History", in Evelyn Brooks Higginbotham, Leon F. Litwack, Darlene Clark Hine, and Randall K. Burkett (eds.), *The Harvard Guide to African-American History*, Cambridge: Harvard University Press, 2001, pp. 117-123.

② 具体内容访问 http://205.204.134.47/civil_rights_mvt/ 和 https://www.ket.org/civilrights/，2015 年 8 月 30 日访问。

③ 详细资料参见 Timothy Lloyd, "The Civil Rights Oral History Survey Project", *Oral History Review*, Vol. 40, No. 1, 2013, pp. 50-53; Library of Congress and Smithsonian Institution, "Civil Rights History Project: National Survey of Collection", http://www.loc.gov/folklife/civilrights/index.html, 2015 年 8 月 30 日访问。

产生在当代文献记录中很难获得的证据。……口述历史的最为重要的贡献之一是能够让我们理解社会运动的起源与发展，从个人的角度来记录社会动员，而且经常能够揭示运动参与者的心智变化。……民权运动的口述历史显示社会变迁并不仅仅是伟大人物和立法的事情，而是一个更为复杂的过程，其中普通个体的生活也经历了一种革命性的转变。"①

　　当然，受益于上述口述历史计划所获得的大量宝贵资料，同时也因为部分研究者个人兴趣的提高，过去四十多年来，美国学术界有关非裔美国人与民权运动的口述历史研究成果也不断增加。就研究主题而言，它们包括个人自传与家庭（家族）历史②、民权运动③、

　　① Kim Lacy Rogers, "Oral History and the History of Civil Rights Movement", *Journal of American History*, Vol. 75, No. 2, 1988, pp. 567-576.

　　② Theodore Rosengarten, *All God's Dangers: the Life of Nate Shaw*, New York: Alfred A. Knopf, 1974; John Langston Gwaltney, *Drylongso: A Self-Portrait of Black America*, New York: Random House, 1980; David J. Garrow, *Bearing the Cross: Martin Luther King Jr. and the Southern Christian Leadership Conference*, New York: William Morrow, 1986; David Hilliard and Lewis Cole, *This Side of Glory: The Autobiography of David Hilliard and the Story of the Black Panther Party*, Boston: Little, Brown, 1992; Kay Mills, *This Little Light of Mine: The Life of Fannie Lou Hamer*, New York: E. P. Dutton, 1993; Leon Dash, *Rosa Lee: A Mother and Her Family in Urban America*, New York: Basic Books, 1996; Albert S. Broussard, *African-American Odyssey: The Stewarts, 1853-1963*, Lawrence: University Press of Kansas, 1998; Cynthia Griggs Fleming, *Soon We Will Not Cry: The Liberation of Ruby Doris Smith Robinson*, Lanham: Rowman & Littlefield, 2000; Manning Marable, *Malcolm X: A Life of Reinvention*, New York: Viking Penguin, 2011.

　　③ Robert Hamburger, *Our Portion of Hell: Fayette County, Tennessee: An Oral History of the Struggle for Civil Rights*, New York: Links Books, 1973; Henry Hampton and Steve Fayer, *Voices of Freedom: An Oral History of the Civil Rights Movement from the 1950s through the 1980s*, New York: Bantam Books, 1990; Kim Lacy Rogers, *Righteous Lives: Narratives of the New Orleans Civil Rights Movement*, New York: New York University Press, 1993; Gretchen Cassel Eick, *Dissent in Wichita: The Civil Rights Movement in the Midwest, 1954-72*, Urbana: University of Illinois Press, 2001; Matthew C. Whitaker, *Race Work: The Rise of Civil Rights in the Urban West*, Lincoln: University of Nebraska Press, 2005; Catherine Fosl and Tracy E. K'Meyer, *Freedom on the Border: An Oral History of the Civil Rights Movement in Kentucky*, Lexington: University Press of Kentucky, 2009.

非裔美国人社群①、种族关系②、非裔美国女性③、非裔美国劳

① Paul Bullock (ed.), *Watts: The Aftermath: An Inside View of the Ghetto by the People of Watts*, New York: Grove, 1969; William Lynwood Montell, *The Saga of Coe Ridge: A Study in Oral History*, Knoxville: University of Tennessee Press, 1970; Howell Raines, *My Soul Is Rested: Movement Days in the Deep South Remembered*, New York: Putnam, 1977; George C. Wright, "Oral History and the Search for the Black Past in Kentucky", *Oral History Review*, Vol. 10, 1982, pp. 73-91; Albert S. Broussard, "Oral Recollection and the Historical Reconstruction of Black San Francisco", *Oral History Review*, Vol. 12, 1984, pp. 63-80; Albert S. Broussard, *Black San Francisco: The Struggle for Racial Equality in the West, 1900-1954*, Lawrence: University Press of Kansas, 1993; Elaine Latzman Moon, *Untold Tales, Unsung Heroes: An Oral History of Detroit's African American Community, 1918-1967*, Detroit: Wayne State University Press, 1994; Don Wallis, *All We Had was Each Other: The Black Community of Madison, Indiana: An Oral History of the Black Community of Madison, Indiana*, Bloomington: Indiana University Press, 1998; Ann Morris (ed.), *Lift Every Voice and Sing: St. Louis African-Americans in the Twentieth Century: Narratives Collected by Doris A. Wesley*, Columbia: University of Missouri Press, 1999; Shirley Ann Wilson Moore, *To Place Our Deeds: The African American Community in Richmond, California, 1910-1963*, Berkeley: University of California Press, 2000; William H. Chafe, Raymond Gavins, and Robert Korstad (eds.), *Remembering Jim Crow: African Americans Tell About Life in the Segregated South*, New York: The New Press, 2001; Benjamin D. Brotemarkle, *Crossing Division Street: An Oral History of the African-American Community in Orlando*, Cocoa: Florida Historical Society Press, 2005; Kim Lacy Rogers, *Life and Death in the Delta: African American Narratives of Violence, Resilience, and Social Change*, New York: Palgrave Macmillan, 2006.

② Scott Ellsworth, *Death in a Promised Land: The Tulsa Race Riot of 1921*, Baton Rouge: Louisiana State University Press, 1982; Bob Blauner (ed.), *Black Lives, White Lives: Three Decades of Race Relations in America*, Berkeley: University of California Press, 1989.

③ Darlene Clark Hine, *When the Truth Is Told: A History of Black Women's Culture and Community in Indiana, 1875-1950*, Indianapolis: National Council of Negro Women (Indianapolis Section), 1981; Gwen Etter-Lewis, *My Soul Is My Own: Oral Narratives of African American Women in the Professions*, London and New York: Routledge, 1993; Gretchen Lemke-Santangelo, *Abiding Courage: African American Migrant Women and the East Bay Community*, Chapel Hill: University of North Carolina Press, 1996; Debra Schultz, *Going South: Jewish Women in the Civil Rights Movement*, New York: New York University Press, 2001; Christina Greene, *Our Separate Ways: Women and the Black Freedom Movement in Durham, North Carolina*, Chapel Hill: University of North Carolina Press, 2005; Kimberly Springer, *Living for the Revolution: Black Feminist Organizations, 1968-1980*, Durham: Duke University Press, 2005; Anne Valk and Leslie Brown, *Living with Jim Crow: African American Women and Memories of the Segregated South*, New York: Palgrave Macmillan, 2010; Lisa Krissoff Boehm, *Making a Way out of No Way: African American Women and the Second Great Migration*, Jackson: University Press of Mississippi, 2009.

工①、非裔美国军人②、教育③与运动④等广泛内容。此外，也包括相当多的有关非裔美国人的口述历史资料汇编，这些成果一般以州或地区为单位加以整理编辑。⑤

同样，就美国学术界而言，口述历史对于其他少数族裔群体研究的重要价值与意义也被日益认可，除大小规模不等的口述历史计划之外，也有相当多的口述历史研究成果相继问世，而成果比较集中的族裔群体包

---

① Michael K. Honey, *Southern Labor and Black Civil Rights：Organizing Memphis Workers*, Urbana：University of Illinois Press, 1993; Rick Halpern and Roger Horowitz, *Meatpackers：An Oral History of Black Packinghouse Workers and Their Struggle for Racial and Economic Equality*, New York：Twayne Publishers, 1996; David D. Perata, *Those Pullman Blues：An Oral History of the African American Railroad Attendant*, New York：Twayne Publishers, 1996; William Julius Wilson, *When Work Disappears：The World of the New Urban Poor*, New York：Knopf, 1997; Michael K. Honey, *Black Workers Remember：An Oral History of Segregation, Unionism, and the Freedom Struggle*, Berkeley：University of California Press, 1999; Robert Rodgers Korstad, *Civil Rights Unionism：Tobacco Workers and the Struggle for Democracy in the Mid-twentieth-Century South*, Chapel Hill：University of North Carolina Press, 2003; Sheree Scarborough, *African American Railroad Workers of Roanoke：Oral Histories of the Norfolk & Western*, Charleston：The History Press, 2014.

② Mary Penick Motley, *The Invisible Soldier：The Experience of the Black Soldier in World War II*, Detroit：Wayne State University Press, 1975; Wallace Terry, *Bloods：An Oral History of the Vietnam War by Black Veterans*, New York：Random House, 1984; Paul Stillwell (ed.), *The Golden Thirteen：Recollections of the First Black Naval Officers*, Annapolis：Naval Institute Press, 1993; James E. Westheider, *Fighting on Two Fronts：African Americans and the Vietnam War*, New York：New York University, 1997; J. Todd Moye, *Freedom Flyers：The Tuskegee Airmen of World War II*, Oxford and New York：Oxford University Press, 2010.

③ Gabrielle S. Morris, *Head of the Class：An Oral History of African-American Achievement in Higher Education and Beyond*, New York：Twayne Publishers, 1995; Ron Suskind, *A Hope in the Unseen：An American Odyssey from the Inner City to the Ivy League*, New York：Broadway Books, 1998; Kate Willink, *Bringing Desegregation Home：Memories of the Struggle Toward School Integration in Rural North Carolina*, New York：Palgrave Macmillan, 2009.

④ John Holway, *Voices from the Great Black Baseball Leagues*, New York：Dodd, Mead, 1975; John Christopher Walter and Jennifer L. Dobson (eds.), *The Blacks in Sports Oral History Project*, Seattle：American Ethnic Studies Department, University of Washington, 1995; Reuben A. Buford May, *Living Through the Hoop：High School Basketball, Race, and the American Dream*, New York：New York University Press, 2008.

⑤ Brenda B. Johns and Alonzo Nelson Smith, *Black Oral History in Nebraska*, Lincoln：Black Studies Department, University of Nebraska, 1980; Barbara J. Stevenson (ed.), *An Oral History of African Americans in Grant County*, Charleston：Arcadia Publishing, 2000. 有关英国黑人口述历史研究可参见 *Oral History*, Vol. 8, No. 1, 1980 (Oral History and Black History).

括亚裔①、拉丁裔②、犹太裔③和意大利裔④等。而事实上，上述有关美国少数族裔群体的口述历史研究，很大程度上也是更为广泛的移民口述

---

① John Tateishi (ed.), *And Justice for All: An Oral History of the Japanese American Detention Camps*, New York: Random House, 1984; Michael P. Onorato, *Forgotten Heroes: Japan's Imprisonment of American Civilians in the Philippines, 1942-1945: An Oral History*, Westport: Meckler, 1990; Joann Faung Jean Lee, *Asian American Experiences in the United States: Oral Histories of First to Fourth Generation Americans from China, the Philippines, Japan, India, the Pacific islands, Vietnam, and Cambodia*, Jefferson: McFarland & Co., 1991; Arthur A. Hansen (ed.), *Japanese American World War II Evacuation Oral History Project*, Westport: Meckler, 1991; Judy Yung, *Unbound Feet: A Social History of Chinese Women in San Francisco*, Berkeley: University of California Press, 1995; Judy Yung, *Unbound Voices: A Documentary History of Chinese Women in San Francisco*, Berkeley: University of California Press, 1999; Eric C. Wat, *The Making of A Gay Asian Community: An Oral History of Pre-AIDS Los Angeles*, Lanham: Rowman and Littlefield, 2002; Judy Yung, Gordon H. Chang, and H. Mark Lai (eds.), *Chinese American Voices: From the Gold Rush to the Present*, Berkeley: University of California Press, 2006; Huping Ling, *Voices of the Heart: Asian American Women on Immigration, Work, and Family*, Kirksville: Truman State University Press, 2007; Joann Faung Jean Lee, *Asian Americans in the Twenty-first Century: Oral Histories of First-to Fourth-generation Americans from China, Japan, India, Korea, the Philippines, Vietnam, and Laos*, New York: The New Press, 2008; Miki Ward Crawford, Katie Kaori Hayashi, and Shizuko Suenaga, *Japanese War Brides in America: An Oral History*, Santa Barbara: Praeger, 2010.

② Patricia Preciado Martin, *Images and Conversations: Mexican Americans Recall a Southwestern Past*, Tucson: University of Arizona Press, 1983; Marilyn P. Davis, *Mexican Voices/American Dreams: An Oral History of Mexican Immigration to the United States*, New York: Henry Holt, 1990; Beatrice Rodriguez Owsley, *The Hispanic-American Entrepreneur: An Oral History of the American Dream*, New York: Twayne Publishers, 1992; Patricia Preciado Martin, *Songs My Mother Sang to Me: An Oral History of Mexican American Women*, Tucson: University of Arizona Press, 1992; Patricia Preciado Martin (ed.), *Beloved Land: An Oral History of Mexican Americans in Southern Arizona*, Tucson: University of Arizona Press, 2004; David Carey, Jr. and Robert Atkinson, *Latino Voices in New England*, Albany: State University of New York Press, 2009.

③ Sylvia Rothchild, *A Special Legacy: An Oral History of Soviet Jewish Emigrés in the United States*, New York: Simon & Schuster, 1985; Neil M. Cowan and Ruth Schwartz Cowan, *Our Parents' Lives: The Americanization of Eastern European Jews*, New York: Basic Books, 1989; Myrna Frommer and Harvey Frommer (eds.), *Growing Up Jewish in America: An Oral History*, New York: Harcourt Brace, 1995; Dan Rottenberg, *Middletown Jews: The Tenuous Survival of an American Jewish Community*, Bloomington: Indiana University Press, 1997.

④ Gary Ross Mormino and George E. Pozzetta, *The Immigrant World of Ybor City: Italians and Their Latin Neighbors in Tampa, 1885-1985*, Chicago: University of Illinois Press, 1987; Stephen R. Fox, *The Unknown Internment: An Oral History of the Relocation of Italian-Americans During World War II*, New York: Twayne Publishers, 1990; Adria Bernardi, *Houses with Names: The Italian Immigrants of Highwood, Illinois*, Urbana: University of Illinois Press, 1990; Luisa Del Giudice, *Oral History, Oral Culture, and Italian Americans*, New York: Palgrave Macmillan, 2009.

历史研究的重要组成部分。[1]

四　女性口述历史

　　作为人类历史活动的重要参与者，女性长期以来都是以男性精英为主体的传统历史叙述与书写的"缺席者"或"失语者"，而口述历史正是试图将那些被忽视或遗忘的女性生活、经历与情感融入我们对历史与现实理解与反思的基本手段。正如美国著名女性口述历史学家肖娜·格拉克（Sherna Berger Gluck，1935—）所说："拒绝再被历史上无声地呈现，女性们正在创造一种新的历史——利用我们自己的声音和经历。我们正在挑战传统的历史观念和什么是'历史上重要的'，我们正在确认我们的日常生活（everyday lives）就是历史。利用一种正如人类记忆一样古老的口头传统（oral tradition），我们正在重建我们自己的过去。"[2]而英国著名女性口述历史学者乔安娜·博纳特（Joanna Bornat）和汉娜·戴蒙德（Hanna Diamond）也指出："女性史与口述历史一起兴起与发展，各自致力揭示、颠覆、挑战和抗争那些被社会性别和阶级所塑造

---

①　June Namias, *First Generation: In the Words of Twentieth-century American Immigrants*, Boston: Beacon, 1978; Joan Morrison and Charlotte Fox Zabusky (eds.), *American Mosaic: The Immigrant Experience in the Words of Those Who Lived It*, New York: E. P. Dutton, 1980; Al Santoli, *New Americans: An Oral History: Immigrants and Refugees in the U. S. Today*, New York: Viking, 1988; Rudolph Vecoli (ed.), *Voices from Ellis Island: An Oral History of American Immigration*, Frederick: University Publications of America, 1990; Bruce M. Stave and John F. Sutherland, with Aldo Salerno, *From the Old Country: An Oral History of European Migration to America*, New York: Twayne Publishers, 1994; Timuel D. Black, Jr., *Bridges of Memory: Chicago's First Wave of Black Migration: An Oral History*, Evanston: Northwestern University Press, 2003; Warren Lehrer and Judith Sloan, *Crossing the Blvd.: Strangers, Neighbors, Aliens in a New America*, New York: W. W. Norton, 2003; Emmy E. Werner, *Passages to America: Oral Histories of Child Immigrants from Ellis Island and Angel Island*, Washington: Potomac Books, 2009; Isabel Wilkerson, *The Warmth of Other Suns: The Epic Story of America's Great Migration*, New York: Random House, 2010.

②　Sherna Gluck, "What's So Special About Women? Women's Oral History", *Frontiers: A Journal of Women Studies*, Vol. 2, No. 2 (Women's Oral History), 1977, p. 3.

的主流论述（dominant discourses）。"①

综观当代美国女性口述历史的发展过程，那些来自学术界与公众领域的一代又一代的口述历史实践者通过记录与呈现具有多元认同特征（阶级、种族、族裔、教育、宗教信仰、性取向与文化等）的美国女性的历史活动与生命经历，试图实现其根植于女性运动与新社会史运动的学术追求与赋权目标，即她（他）们倡导女性口述历史不仅仅是有关女性的，而且是由女性开展并与女性共同完成的，其最终目的也是造福于女性的。② 概括而言，过去六十多年来美国女性口述历史发展主要经历以下四个阶段。

（一）早期起源

男性精英口述历史模式下的女性口述历史实践。如上所述，在内文斯开创和斯塔尔继续引领的以男性精英人物为主要访谈对象的口述历史模式下，极少部分美国知名女性也开始成为哥伦比亚大学口述历史访谈计划的重要对象，但其真正关注点并不是女性受访者的个人活动、生命经历与自我感受，而是让女性受访者叙述其个人视角的公共事件。根据口述历史研究室记录显示，早在 1949 年开展的"纽约政治研究计划"（New York Political Studies Project）中，纽约女性政治家简·托德（Jane H. Todd，1890-

---

① Joanna Bornat and Hanna Diamond, "Women's History and Oral History: Developments and Debates", *Women's History Review*, Vol. 16, No. 1, 2007, p. 19.

② Sherna Berger Gluck and Daphne Patai, "Introduction", in Sherna Berger Gluck and Daphne Patai (eds.), *Women's Words: The Feminist Practice of Oral History*, London and New York: Routledge, 1991, p. 2; Michael Roper, "Oral History", in Brian Brivati, Julia Buxton, and Anthony Seldon (eds.), *The Contemporary History Handbook*, Manchester: Manchester University Press, 1996, p. 350; Edith Sizoo, "A Polylogue", in Edith Sizoo (ed.), *Women's Lifeworlds: Women's Narratives on Shaping Their Realities*, London and New York: Routledge, 1997, p. 7; Nan Alamilla Boyd and Horacio N. Roque Ramírez, "Introduction: Close Encounters: The Body and Knowledge in Queer Oral History", in Nan Alamilla Boyd and Horacio N. Roque Ramírez (eds.), *Bodies of Evidence: The Practice of Queer Oral History*, Oxford and New York: Oxford University Press, 2012, pp. 4-7.

1966）便是其口述历史访谈对象。① 而到 20 世纪 60 年代末之前，在哥伦比亚大学口述历史研究室所开展的"每月读书会计划"（Book-of-the-Month Club Project）、"麦格劳希尔集团计划"（McGraw-Hill Project）、"大众艺术计划"（Popular Arts Project）、"航空计划"（Aviation Project）、"哈特·克莱恩计划"（Hart Crane Project）、"社会保障计划"（Social Security Project）、"纽约卡耐基公司口述历史计划"（Carnegie Corporation of New York Oral History Project）与"艾森豪威尔政府计划"（Eisenhower Administration Project）等系列口述历史计划中，众多美国政界、商界与艺术界的女性精英都是重要的访谈对象。②

而这一时期专门以女性为访谈对象的口述历史计划则是加州大学伯克利分校地区口述历史办公室所开展的"妇女参政论者口述历史计划"（Suffragists Oral History Project），该计划于 1959—1977 年期间，对争取女性权利与平等做出重要贡献的 7 位著名妇女参政论者进行了系统的口述历史访谈，其主题涉及妇女投票权、福利与劳工改革、世界和平与《平等权利修正案》（*Equal Rights Amendment*）等重要内容。③

（二）姐妹情谊与女性口述历史运动

恢复与解放女性自己的声音。从 20 世纪 60 年代末和 70 年代初开始，随着第二波女性运动和新社会史运动的兴起与发展，女性史研究焦点逐渐发生转变，从过去的以精英女性的生活和经历为重心，进而转向普通女性（尤其是少数族裔或有色女性）的日常工作与生活。正

---

　　① 具体内容参见 Columbia Center for Oral History, "Reminiscences of Jane H. Todd: Oral History, 1949", https: //clio. columbia. edu/catalog/4074879, 2015 年 9 月 1 日访问。

　　② 有关这些口述历史计划的具体内容，可查询哥伦比亚大学口述历史中心"口述历史在线门户"（Oral History Portal），访问 http: //library. columbia. edu/find/oral-history-portal. html, 2015 年 9 月 1 日访问。

　　③ 目前，这些口述历史访谈抄本都可以全文浏览与下载，详细访问 Regional Oral History Office, "Suffragists Oral History Project", http: //bancroft. berkeley. edu/ROHO/projects/suffragist/, 2015 年 9 月 1 日访问。

是在这种社会与学术背景下，美国女性口述历史运动开始迅速兴起与蓬勃发展。这场运动的主要动力来自一些学院派女性学者与社区积极分子所开展的基层计划，其中比较有代表性的包括 1972 年由肖娜·格拉克主持的"女性主义历史研究计划"（Feminist History Research Project）、1973 年由考基·布什（Corky Bush）主持的"爱达荷州农村女性历史计划"（Idaho Rural Women's History Project）①、1975 年由苏珊·阿米蒂奇（Susan H. Armitage，1937—）主持的"博尔德女性口述历史计划"（Boulder Women's Oral History Project）及 1976 年由拉德克利夫学院开展的"黑人女性口述历史计划"② 等。据统计，到 1977 年全美总共有 18 个州开展或设有大约 30 个集体性女性口述历史计划或收藏，此外，还有众多个体女性口述历史计划。③

20 世纪 70 年代美国女性口述历史主要处于发现被忽略和遗忘的女性生活经历的"恢复与挖掘过程"，其焦点主要集中于普通女性的日常工作、生活经历与特定经验。正如有位从事 20 世纪 70 年代初美国边疆女性口述历史访谈的学者所说："我提问她们……移民的故事与经历以及她们对于新的家园和故地的感受。我也提问她们有关分娩、避孕、堕胎以及育儿的经历。她们告诉我有关男女之间的关系，以及自己对于她们的工作所蕴含的价值的认知，包括那些家庭之外的有偿工作和家庭中的家务。我们还讨论有关卫生保健、技术变化、娱乐和社会生活。"④ 而其实践动力与学术信念则是基于女性之间的姐妹情谊（sisterhood）与"个人的即政治的"

---

① "Rural Women's History Project", http：//www. lib. uidaho. edu/special-collections/Manu-scripts/mg068. htm, 2015 年 9 月 1 日访问。

② Patrice McDermott, *Politics and Scholarship*：*Feminist Academic Journals and the Production of Knowledge*, Urbana：University of Illinois Press, 1994, p. 93；Susan Armitage, "Here's to the Women：Western Women Speak Up", *Journal of American History*, Vol. 83, No. 2, 1996, pp. 551-555.

③ 具体内容参见 "Part IV：Women's Oral History Project and Collections", *Frontiers*：*A Journal of Women Studies*, Vol. 2, No. 2（Women's Oral History）, 1977, pp. 125-128.

④ Eliane Silverman, "In Their Own Words：Mothers and Daughters on the Alberta Frontier, 1890-1929", *Frontiers*：*A Journal of Women Studies*, Vol. 2, No. 2（Women's Oral History）, 1977, p. 38.

（the personal is political）等观念与主张。① 阿米蒂奇就曾强调："20 世纪 60 年代女性解放运动带来的最为强有力的见识之一就是让我们明白'个人的即政治的'，即公共世界的结构和政治与我们对于自己的私人认同之间存在着一种直接的联系。……正如对于女性口述历史兴趣的持续增加已经证明这一点，即口述历史被认为是一种探讨女性生活的私人的、个人的以及那些被忽视的宝贵方法。"②

而作为这一阶段美国女性口述历史实践的学术成果，就是 1977 年《边疆：女性研究杂志》（*Frontiers：A Journal of Women Studies*）出版的"女性口述历史"专刊，该专刊主要集中于分析女性口述历史学家参与具体计划的实际经验，同时还涉及一些女性口述历史方法论的初步思考。③此外，在 20 世纪 70 年代末之前，也有一些女性口述历史研究成果相继问世，其中比较有代表性的包括《乡下女人：南阿巴拉契亚的山区妇女谈她们的挣扎与欢乐》（1973）、《从客厅到监狱》（1976）、《汉娜的女儿：一个美国家庭的六代（1876—1976）》（1976）、《犹太祖母》（1976）和《女人危机：奋斗与希望的生活》（1978）等。④

---

① Robin Morgan （ed.）, *Sisterhood Is Powerful：An Anthology of Writings from the Women's Liberation Movement*, New York：Random House, 1970; Carol Hanisch, "The Personal Is Political", in Shulamith Firestone and Anne Koedt （eds.）, *Notes from the Second Year*, New York：Radical Feminism, 1969, pp. 76-78; Linda J. Nicholson, "'The Personal is Political'：An Analysis in Retrospect", *Social Theory and Practice*, Vol. 7, No. 1, 1981, pp. 85-98.

② Susan Armitage, "Review Essay：Making the Personal Political：Women's History and Oral History", *Oral History Review*, Vol. 17, No. 2, 1989, pp. 107-108.

③ 具体内容参见 *Frontiers：A Journal of Women Studies*, Vol. 2, No. 2 （Women's Oral History）, 1977.

④ Kathy Kahn, *Hillbilly Women：Mountain Women Speak of Struggle and Joy in Southern Appalachia*, Garden City：Doubleday, 1973; Sherna Berger Gluck, *From Parlor to Prison：Five American Suffragists Talk About Their Lives：An Oral History*, New York：Vintage Books, 1976; Dorothy Gallagher, *Hannah's Daughters：Six Generations of an American Family, 1876-1976*, New York：Thomas Cromwell, 1976; Sydelle Kramer and Jenny Masur （eds.）, *Jewish Grandmothers*, Boston：Beacon Press, 1976; Robert Coles and Jane Hallowell Coles, *Women of Crisis：Lives of Struggle and Hope*, New York：Delacorte Press, 1978.

（三）挑战女性概念与范畴

女性口述历史实践与研究的初步反思。1983 年《边疆》杂志出版第二辑"女性口述历史"① 专刊，意味着美国女性口述历史进入格拉克所说的"第二个十年"或阿米蒂奇所谓的"下一步"。② 可以说，这一阶段的美国女性口述历史继续延续了 20 世纪 70 年代女性口述历史实践的基本主旨，即通过发现女性的声音并进而颂扬她们的生活与工作经历。她们甚至借用和提出"女性文化"（women's culture）这个概念，③ 希望口述历史实践者着重记录与呈现那些女性所共享的完全不同于男性的独特的生活与工作经验。④ 正是如此，在这一时期，集体性的女性口述历史计划继续在全美如火如荼地进行。据 1983 年《边疆》杂志统计，当时总共有 27 个州开展和设有大约 50 个涉及女性主题的集体性口述历史计划或收藏。⑤

不过，差不多是在同一时期，对于女性概念与范畴的质疑与批判则直接挑战了有关女性口述历史的某些基本假设，众多学者认为"女性"这个概念并不是一个普同或同质概念，而且并不存在单一性的"女性"范畴。

---

① 具体内容参见 *Frontiers: A Journal of Women Studies*, Vol. 7, No. 1 (Women's Oral History Two), 1983.

② Sherna Berger Gluck, "Women's Oral History, the Second Decade", *Frontiers: A Journal of Women Studies*, Vol. 7, No. 1 (Women's Oral History Two), 1983, pp. 1-2; Susan H. Armitage, "The Next Step", *Frontiers: A Journal of Women Studies*, Vol. 7, No. 1 (Women's Oral History Two), 1983, pp. 3-8.

③ Carol Gilligan, *In a Different Voice*, Cambridge: Harvard University Press, 1982; Mary Field Belenky, Blythe McVicker Clinchy, Nancy Rule Goldberger, and Jill Mattuck Tarule, *Women's Ways of Knowing: The Development of Self, Voice, and Mind*, New York: Basic Books, 1986.

④ U. Kalpagam, "Oral History: Reconstructing Women's Role", *Economic and Political Weekly*, Vol. 21, No. 38/39, 1986, pp. 1683, 1685-1687; Susan N. G. Geiger, "Women's Life Histories: Method and Content", *Signs*, Vol. 11, No. 2, 1986, pp. 334-351; Sue Armitage, "The Stages of Women's Oral History", in Donald A. Ritchie (ed.), *The Oxford Handbook of Oral History*, Oxford and New York: Oxford University Press, 2011, pp. 173-174.

⑤ Nancy D. Mann (ed.), "Directory of Women's Oral History Projects and Collections", *Frontiers: A Journal of Women Studies*, Vol. 7, No. 1 (Women's Oral History Two), 1983, pp. 114-121.

尤其是在黑人女性主义、女同性恋女性主义与第三世界女性主义等多元跨文化女性主义的影响下，越来越多的女性主义者开始强调文化的多元性（种族、族裔、阶级、性取向、宗教信仰等）及女性内部的差异性，并质疑与批判所谓的"姐妹情谊"不过是另外一种形式的跨文化父权体制。正是如此，在20世纪80年代中后期，作为女性运动的主要团结动力——"姐妹情谊是强大的"（sisterhood is powerful）的美好宣言也正处于崩溃的边缘。① 而对于女性口述历史学家来说，她们开始更为严肃地思考与反思其方法论问题，尤其是在受访对象的选择问题上，她们已经关注受访者当中的种族、族裔、阶级与宗教信仰等多元差异。而在具体访谈过程中，为了充分发挥女性口述历史的潜力，女性主义口述史学家主张应该提问更多有关意义、可比性与背景性问题，以呈现女性生活与经历背后的社会、文化与心理因素。② 同时，有关口述历史访谈过程中所涉及的访谈者与受访者之间的主体间性（intersubjectivity）与自反性（reflexivity）问题也开始进入女性口述历史研究者的视野。而到20世纪80年代晚期，后结构主义对于女性口述历史实践的理论与方法论问题也开始产生影响和带来冲击，其核心观点是主张口述历史并不是对于过去经历的透明复制（transparent reproduction），而是一种更为复杂的再现（representation）。简言之，女性口述历史并不一定能够让女性真正发出属于她们自己的真实声音，需

---

① Dolores Janiewski, *Sisterhood Denied: Race, Class and Gender in a New South Community*, Philadelphia: Temple University Press, 1985; Linda K. Kerber, "Separate Spheres, Female Worlds, Woman's Place: The Rhetoric of Women's History", *Journal of American History*, Vol. 75, No. 1, 1988, pp. 9-39; Christine Bolt, *Sisterhood Questioned?: Race, Class and Internationalism in the American and British Women's Movements*, *c. 1880s-1970s*, London and New York: Routledge, 2004.

② Daphne Patai, "U. S. Academics and Third World Women: Is Ethical Research Possible", in Sherna Berger Gluck and Daphne Patai (eds.), *Women's Words: The Feminist Practice of Oral History*, London and New York: Routledge, 1991, pp. 137-154; Karen Olson and Linda Shopes, "Crossing Boundaries, Building Bridges: Doing Oral History among Working-Class Women and Men", in Sherna Berger Gluck and Daphne Patai (eds.), *Women's Words: The Feminist Practice of Oral History*, London and New York: Routledge, 1991, pp. 189-204; Margaretta Jolly, Polly Russell, and Rachel Cohen, "Sisterhood and After: Individualism, Ethics and an Oral History of the Women's Liberation Movement", *Social Movement Studies: Journal of Social, Cultural and Political Protest*, Vol. 11, No. 2, 2012, pp. 211-226.

要对其口述历史叙述进行更为细腻和具体的情境化思考与分析。

而就实践与研究成果而言，这一阶段的代表就是上述谈到的《边疆》杂志于 1983 年出版的第二辑"女性口述历史"专刊。正如该期特别顾问编辑所说，第二辑专刊主要讨论女性口述历史学家在实践与利用口述历史访谈过程中所遇到的更为复杂和具体的方法论与理论问题。[①] 而格拉克也指出，第二辑专刊除继续强调口述历史在挖掘、记录与颂扬女性经历与生活中的重要价值之外，它也更加关注女性口述历史实践与理论研究的新问题与新视野，比如多元身份特征（种族、族裔、宗教信仰、教育水平、经济状况、性取向等）对于女性口述历史实践的影响。[②] 同时，这一时期《边疆》与《口述历史评论》、《加州历史》（*California History*）、《标志：文化与社会中的女性》（*Signs：Journal of Women in Culture and Society*）与《女性主义研究》（*Feminist Studies*）等杂志也发表了一些女性口述历史的文章。[③]

---

① Susan Armitage and Joan Jensen, "To Our Readers", *Frontiers：A Journal of Women Studies*, Vol. 7, No. 1 (Women's Oral History Two), 1983, p. iv.

② Sherna Berger Gluck, "Women's Oral History, the Second Decade", *Frontiers：A Journal of Women Studies*, Vol. 7, No. 1 (Women's Oral History Two), 1983, pp. 1-2.

③ Marge Grevatt, "Oral History as a Resource in Teaching Women's Studies", *The Radical Teacher*, No. 10, 1978, pp. 22-25; Jean M. Humez and Laurie Crumpacker, "Oral History in Teaching Women's Studies", *Oral History Review*, Vol. 7, 1979, pp. 53-69; Margo McBane and Mary Winegarden, "Labor Pains：An Oral History of California's Women Farmworkers", *California History*, Vol. 58, No. 2, 1979, pp. 179-181; Stephen Plummer and Suzanne Julin, "Lucy Swan, Sioux Woman：An Oral History", *Frontiers：A Journal of Women Studies*, Vol. 6, No. 3, 1981, pp. 29-32; Claire Robertson, "In Pursuit of Life Histories：The Problem of Bias", *Frontiers：A Journal of Women Studies*, Vol. 7, No. 2, 1983, pp. 63-69; Sherna Berger Gluck, "Reflections on Linking the Academy and the Community", *Frontiers：A Journal of Women Studies*, Vol. 8, No. 3, 1986, pp. 46-49; Susan N. G. Geiger, "Women's Life Histories：Method and Content", *Signs*, Vol. 11, No. 2, 1986, pp. 334-351; Madeline Davis and Elizabeth Lapovsky Kennedy, "Oral History and the Study of Sexuality in the Lesbian Community：Buffalo, New York, 1940- 1960", *Feminist Studies*, Vol. 12, No. 1, 1986, pp. 7-26; Beverly V. Romberger, "'Aunt Sophie Always Said…'：Oral Histories of the Commonplaces Women Learned About Relating to Men", *American Behavioral Scientist*, Vol. 29, No. 3, 1986, pp. 342-367. 1989 年《口述历史评论》还刊登《口述历史与美国农村女性》（"Oral History and Rural Women in the United States", *Oral History Review*, Vol. 17, No. 2, 1989）专栏，详细参见 Nancy Grey Osterud and Lu Ann Jones, "'If I Must Say So Myself'：Oral Histories of Rural Women", pp. 1-24; Seena B. Kohl, "Memories of Homesteading and The Process of Retrospection", pp. 25-45; Devra Anne Weber, "Raiz Fuerte：Oral History and Mexicana Farmworkers", pp. 47-62; Lu Ann Jones, "'Mama Learned Us to Work'：An Oral History of Virgie St. John Redmond", pp. 63-90.

此外，正如上述有关非裔美国女性口述历史研究的丰富成果所展现的，在 20 世纪 80 年代，美国学术界出版了一大批反映多元美国女性的口述历史研究成果，她们可能居住在不同的地理区域（社群）、来自不同的职业领域与社会层级以及具有不同的种族（族裔）身份或性别取向。其中比较有代表性的包括《女人：来自一个西班牙社区的对话》（1980）、《我们并没有多少，但我们肯定有很多：她们自己口中的农村女性》（1981）、《购物袋女士：无家可归的女性讲述她们的生活》（1981）、《女牛仔：美国西部女性口述历史》（1982）、《为她们自己说话：西部女性》（1984）、《美国移民女性：下东区的生活与文化（1890—1925）》（1985）、《从职业女孩到职业母亲：美国女性劳动力（1820—1980）》（1985）、《时光飞逝：老年女同性恋者的生活》（1986）、《第一代、第二代、战时新娘：从事家政服务的三代日裔美国女性》（1986）、《重访铆工露斯：女性、战争与社会变迁》（1987）、《塑造者：作为社区建设者的蒙大拿女性：口述历史范本与指南》（1987）、《在战区：越战中美国女性的口述历史》（1987）、《南方女性的回忆：种族隔离时期南方的家庭佣工与她们的雇主》（1988）与《女性回忆：口述历史》（1989）等。①

① Nan Elsasser, Kyle Mackenzie, and Yvonne Tixier, *Las Mujeres*：*Conversations from a Hispanic Community*, New York：The Feminist Press, 1980；Sherry Thomas, *We Didn't Have Much*，*But We Sure Had Plenty*：*Rural Women in Their Own Words*, New York：Anchor Books, 1981；Ann Marie Rousseau, *Shopping Bag Ladies*：*Homeless Women Speak About Their Lives*, New York：Pilgrim Press, 1981；Teresa Jordan, *Cowgirls*：*Women of the American West*：*An Oral History*, Garden City：Anchor Press, 1982；Maxine Alexander（ed.）, *Speaking for Ourselves*：*Women of the South*, New York：Pantheon Books, 1984；Elizabeth Ewen, *Immigrant Women in the Land of Dollars*：*Life and Culture on the Lower East Side*, *1890-1925*, New York：Monthly Review Press, 1985；Lynn Y. Weiner, *From Working Girl to Working Mother*：*The Female Labor Force in the United States*, *1820-1980*, Chapel Hill：University of North Carolina Press, 1985；Marcy Adelman（ed.）, *Long Time Passing*：*Lives of Older Lesbians*, Boston：Alyson Publications, 1986；Evelyn Nakano Glenn, *Issei*, *Nisei*, *War Bride*, *Three Generations of Japanese American Women in Domestic Service*, Philadelphia：Temple University Press, 1986；Sherna Berger Gluck, *Rosie the Riveter Revisited*：*Women*, *the War*, *and Social Change*, New York：Twayne Publishers, 1987；Laurie Mercier, Mary Murphy, Linda Peavy, Diane Sands, and Ursula Smith, *Molders and Shapers*：*Montana Women as Community Builders*：*An Oral History Sampler and Guide*, Helena：Montana Historical Society Oral History Office, 1987；Kathryn Marshall, *In the Combat Zone*：*An Oral History of American*

（四）从女性口述历史（women's oral history）到女性主义口述历史（feminist oral history）

口述历史的女性主义实践。从 20 世纪 80 年代末期和 90 年代初期开始，在后结构主义、后现代主义以及人类学、语言学、交际学、民俗学、心理学、叙事学、当代文学理论与女性主义理论等跨学科理论的影响下，[①]美国女性口述历史进入一个全面的理论反思时代，其核心问题是挑战早期女性口述历史实践所宣称的天真和看上去是本质主义的女性主义假设，即女性口述历史实践与研究如何真正体现其女性主义特征、视角与目标。[②]凯瑟瑞·安德森（Kathryn Anderson）、苏珊·阿米蒂奇、丹娜·杰克（Dana Jack）与朱迪斯·维特纳（Judith Wittner）早在 1987 年就指出，为了更好地让女性讲述其真实的生活经历与感受，口述历史学家应该发展一种跨学科的女性主义方法论。[③]而在 1990 年，苏珊·盖格（Susan Geiger）更是提

Women in Vietnam, 1966-1975, Boston：Little, Brown and Company, 1987；Susan Tucker, *Telling Memories among Southern Women*：*Domestic Workers and Their Employers in the Segregated South*, Baton Rouge：Louisiana State University Press, 1988；Anne Smith, *Women Remember*：*An Oral History*, London and New York：Routledge, 1989. 需要指出的是，这一时期美国学者对其他国家和地区的女性口述历史研究及英国女性口述历史的发展都共同促进了美国女性口述历史研究的进一步深化。详细参见 *Oral History*, Vol. 5, No. 2, 1977（Women's History Issue）；Oscar Lewis, Ruth M. Lewis and Susan M. Rigdon, *Four Women*：*Living the Revolution*：*An Oral History of Contemporary Cuba*, Urbana：University of Illinois Press, 1978；*Oral History*, Vol. 10, No. 2, 1982（Women's History）；Elizabeth Roberts, *A Woman's Place*：*An Oral History of Working-Class Women*, 1890-1940, Oxford：Basil Blackwell, 1984；"Articles：Oral History & Puerto Rican Women", *Oral History Review*, Vol. 16, No. 2, 1988, pp. 1-94；Jacqueline Sarsby, *Missuses and Mouldrunners*：*An Oral History of Women Pottery Workers at Work and at Home*, Milton Keynes：Open University Press, 1988；Sherna Berger Gluck, "Review：The Voices of Palestinian Women：Oral History, Testimony, and Biographical Narrative", *Oral History Review*, Vol. 18, No. 2, 1990, pp. 115-123.

① Personal Narratives Group（ed.）, *Interpreting Women's Lives*：*Feminist Theory and Personal Narratives*, Bloomington：Indiana University Press, 1989；Judy Long, *Telling Women's Lives*：*Subject/Narrator/Reader/Text*, New York：New York University Press, 1999；Selma Leydesdorff, Luisa Passerini, and Paul Thompson（eds.）, *Gender and Memory*, New Brunswick：Transaction Publishers, 2005.

② 鲍晓兰：《西方女性主义口述史发展初探》，《浙江学刊》1999 年第 6 期，第 85—90 页。

③ Kathryn Anderson, Susan Armitage, Dana Jack, and Judith Wittner, "Beginning Where We Are：Feminist Methodology in Oral History", *Oral History Review*, Vol. 15, No. 1, 1987, pp. 103-127.

出了衡量女性口述历史是否具有女性主义目标的四个标准：（a）社会性别（gender）是否是一个核心分析概念；（b）女性研究所关注的问题域（problematic）能否从历史上和情境上（historically and situationally）体现和创造特定的经济、社会、文化、民族和种族（族裔）现实；（c）通过确立或促进一种新的理解女性生活和更为广泛的社会世界的性别化因素的知识基础（knowledge base），从而使女性口述历史成为一种挑战有关"什么是'正常的'"（what is "normal"）的男性中心主义观念和假设的矫正物；（d）它们接受女性对于它们的认同、经历与社会世界的自我解释，因为这些解释包含和反映了重要的真实，而不是出于概括目的将它们归类和贬低为仅仅是主观的。①

而在女性主义口述历史研究领域，最具代表性的则是肖娜·格拉克与达芬尼·帕泰（Daphne Patai，1943—）主编并于1991年出版的《女性的话语：口述历史的女性主义实践》。该书试图解构或抛弃早期女性口述历史的核心宣称——女性口述历史是由女性所做的有关于女性的口述历史，其目的也是为了女性（oral history by，about and for women）。基于此，两位主编认为"女性或女性主义口述历史"这一概念应该更为准确地理解为口述历史的女性主义实践（feminist practice of oral history），即强调不管是从访谈者、访谈对象或访谈主题来说，女性并不是女性口述历史的唯一焦点。在该书中，来自不同学科背景的16位学者（共13篇论文，不包括前言和后记）分别从"语言与交际"（Language and Communication，侧重于访谈技巧）、"权威与解释"（Authority and Interpretation，侧重于解释模式）、"困境与矛盾"（Dilemmas and Contradictions，侧重于跨文化因素）与"社区和倡导"（Community and Advocacy，侧重于口述历史的赋权与倡导功能）四个方面深入探讨了女性口述历史记录、解释与应用等全过程所涉及的复杂的问题与解

---

① Susan Geiger，"What's So Feminist About Doing Women's Oral History?" *Journal of Women's History*，Vol. 2，No. 1，1990，p. 170.

决方法。①

简言之，口述历史的女性主义实践要求实践者或研究者能够从社会性别视角出发思考口述历史整个生产过程所涉及的各种问题与关系。概括而言，其研究与反思焦点集中于以下几个方面：（a）口述历史访谈的客观性：经历抑或论述；（b）口述历史访谈过程的复杂性与多元性；（c）如何倾听：记忆、语言、叙述与表演；（d）谁的声音与历史：共享权威（sharing authority）；（e）赋权与倡导：口述历史的民主化和解放性力量何以可能?② 当然，这些问题也是口述历史学界所共同面临的，不过女性口述历史却为这些问题的深化研究做出特殊贡献。同时，这些问题也深刻反映了女性口述历史的多样性及复杂性，此后，它们一直成为美国女性口述历史学界理论研究的关注焦点。正因如此，以关注女性口述历史著称的《边疆》杂志在1998年连续出版两辑"女性口述历史"专刊。③ 而作为对于这一问题持续关注的重要体现，由苏珊·阿米蒂奇、帕特丽夏·哈特（Patricia Hart，1950—）和凯伦·魏特摩恩（Karen Weathermon，1961—）联合主编的《女性口述历史：〈边

---

① Sherna Berger Gluck and Daphne Patai（eds.），*Women's Words: The Feminist Practice of Oral History*，London and New York: Routledge，1991. 该书已经成为女性主义口述历史研究的经典文献，相关书评可参见 Susan Armitage，George Lipsitz，and Gary R. Mormino，"*Women's Words*: A Review Symposium"，*Oral History Review*，Vol. 20，No. 1/2，1992，pp. 105-111；Mary Blewett，"Book Review: *Women's Words: The Feminist Practice of Oral History*"，*Women's Review of Books*，Vol. 9，No. 5，1992，pp. 10-11；Susan Geiger，"Book Review: *Women's Words: The Feminist Practice of Oral History*；*The Hour of the Poor, the Hour of Women: Salvadoran Women Speak*；*I Could Speak until Tomorrow: Oriki, Women and the Past in a Yoruba Town*"，*Signs*，Vol. 19，No. 2，1994，pp. 499-503；Rebecca Maksel，"Book Review: *Women's Words: The Feminist Practice of Oral History*"，*Journal of American Folklore*，Vol. 107，No. 424，1994，pp. 332-335.

② Reinharz Shulamit，"Feminist Oral History"，in Reinharz Shulamit，*Feminist Methods in Social Research*，Oxford and New York: Oxford University Press，1992，pp. 126-144；Joan Sangster，"Telling Our Stories: Feminist Debates and the Use of Oral History"，*Women's History Review*，Vol. 3，No. 1，1994，pp. 5-28；Emily Honig，"Striking Lives: Oral History and the Politics of Memory"，*Journal of Women's History*，Vol. 9，No. 1，1997，pp. 139-157；Penny Summerfield，*Reconstructing Women's Wartime Lives: Discourse and Subjectivity in Oral Histories of the Second World War*，Manchester: Manchester University Press，1998.

③ 具体内容参见 *Frontiers: A Journal of Women Studies*，Vol. 19，No. 2，1998（Varieties of Women's Oral History）；*Frontiers: A Journal of Women Studies*，Vol. 19，No. 3，1998（Problems and Perplexities in Women's Oral History）.

疆〉读本》也于 2002 年出版，该书由《边疆》杂志 1977 年、1983 年和 1998 年四辑"女性口述历史"专刊中的优秀论文集结而成。全书主要分成三个部分，第一部分"基本方法"（Basic Approaches）主要涉及从事女性口述历史的原因与意义及具体实践的方法论思考。而第二部分"口述历史应用"（Oral History Applications）则探讨女性口述历史的具体应用方式，其中包括传记、社区史、生命回顾（life review）、幻灯片与影像呈现，以及历史艺术与博物馆展示等。第三部分"口述历史发现与视角"（Oral History Discoveries and Insights）则主要探讨口述历史如何被用于挖掘与恢复被遗忘的女性历史，比如涉及非法堕胎、洛杉矶学校暴动、非裔美国女性移民、无家可归者与女性避难所等。① 在进入 21 世纪之后，美国女性口述历史学界的研究成果仍然层出不穷，不过其理论研究关注点仍然没有超越上述问题。②

---

① Susan H. Armitage, Patricia Hart, and Karen Weathermon (eds.), *Women's Oral History: The Frontiers Reader*, Lincoln: University of Nebraska Press, 2002. 有关书评可参见 Debbie A. Hanson, "Book Review: *Women's Oral History: The Frontiers Reader*", Western Folklore, Vol. 61, No. 3/4, 2002, pp. 349-351; Kathryn L. Nasstrom, "Book Review: *Women's Oral History: The Frontiers Reader*", Biography, Vol. 26, No. 4, 2003, pp. 725-727; Laura McCreery, "Book Review: *Women's Oral History: The Frontiers Reader*", Oregon Historical Quarterly, Vol. 105, No. 2, 2004, pp. 338-339; Joanna Bornat, "Book Review: *Women's Oral History: The Frontiers Reader*", Oral History, Vol. 34, No. 1, 2006, pp. 108-110.

② Kathryn McPherson, "Oral History", in Lorraine Code (ed.), *Encyclopedia of Feminist Theories*, London and New York: Routledge, 2000, pp. 370-372; Sherna Berger Gluck, "Women's Oral History: Is It So Special?" in Thomas L. Charlton, Lois E. Myers, and Rebecca Sharpless (eds.), *Handbook of Oral History*, Walnut Creek: AltaMira Press, 2006, pp. 357-383; Patricia Lina Leavy, "The Practice of Feminist Oral History and Focus Group Interviews", in Sharlene Nagy Hesse-Biber and Patricia Lina Leavy (eds.), *Feminist Research Practice: A Primer*, Thousand Oaks: Sage Publications, 2007, pp. 149-186; Susan Armitage, "Turner's Ghost: A Personal Retrospective on Western Women's History", in S. Jay Kleinberg, Eileen Boris, and Vicki L. Ruiz (eds.), *The Practice of U. S. Women's History: Narrative, Intersections and Dialogues*, New Brunswick: Rutgers University Press, 2007, pp. 126-145; Carol Frances Cini, "Voices of the Next Generation: Revealing the Impact of Gender, Race, Class, and Feminism", Oral History Review, Vol. 24, No. 2, Winter, 1997, pp. 107-116; Sue Armitage, "The Stages of Women's Oral History", in Donald A. Ritchie (ed.), *The Oxford Handbook of Oral History*, Oxford and New York: Oxford University Press, 2011, pp. 169-185; Sherna Berger Gluck, "Has Feminist Oral History Lost Its Radical/Subversive Edge?" Oral History, Vol. 39, No. 2, 2011, pp. 63-72; Sherna Berger Gluck, "From California to Kufr Nameh and Back: Reflections on 40 Years of Feminist Oral History", in Anna Sheftel and Stacey Zembrzycki (eds.), *Oral History off the Record: Toward an Ethnography of Practice*, New York: Palgrave Macmillan, 2013, pp. 25-42.

　　而进入20世纪90年代以来，美国学术界有关女性口述历史的研究成果也不断问世，其中比较有代表性的包括《祖母、母亲和女儿：三代美国少数族裔女性的口述历史》（1991）、《阁下：美国女大使口述历史》（1995）、《母亲、姐姐和抵抗者：大屠杀女性幸存者口述历史》（1998）、《肥沃大地、狭窄选择：德克萨斯州棉花农场的女性（1900—1940）》（2002）、《美国的法国战时新娘：口述历史》（2008）、《习惯的改变：美国修女口述历史》（2011）和《古巴性革命：激情、政治与记忆》（2012）等。①

---

① Corinne Azen Krause, *Grandmothers, Mothers, and Daughters: Oral Histories of Three Generations of Ethnic American Women*, New York: Twayne Publishers, 1991; Ann Miller Morin, *Her Excellency: An Oral History of American Women Ambassadors*, New York: Twayne Publishers, 1995; Brana Gurewitsch, *Mothers, Sisters, Resisters: Oral Histories of Women Who Survived the Holocaust*, Tuscaloosa: University of Alabama Press, 1998; Rebecca Sharpless, *Fertile Ground, Narrow Choices: Women on Texas Cotton Farms, 1900-1940*, Chapel Hill: University of North Carolina Press, 2002; Hilary Kaiser, *French War Brides in America: An Oral History*, Westport: Praeger, 2008; Carole Garibaldi Rogers, *Habits of Change: An Oral History of American Nuns*, Oxford and New York: Oxford University Press, 2011; Carrie Hamilton, *Sexual Revolutions in Cuba: Passion, Politics, and Memory*, Chapel Hill: University of North Carolina Press, 2012. 其他相关成果还可参见 Julie Jones-Eddy, *Homesteading Women: An Oral History of Colorado, 1890-1950*, New York: Twayne Publishers, 1992; Mary Logan Rothschild and Pamela Claire Hronek, *Doing What the Day Brought: An Oral History of Arizona Women*, Tucson: University of Arizona Press, 1992; Kathleen Casey, *I Answer with My Life: Life Histories of Women Teachers Working for Social Change*, London and New York: Routledge, 1993; Elizabeth Lapovsky Kennedy and Madeline D. Davis, *Boots of Leather, Slippers of Gold: The History of a Lesbian Community*, London and New York: Routledge, 1993; Esther Newton, *Fire Island: Sixty Years in America's First Gay and Lesbian Town*, Boston: Beacon, 1993; Brett Harvey, *The Fifties: A Women's Oral History*, New York: HarperCollins, 1993; Jewell Fenzi and Carl L. Nelson, *Married to the Foreign Service: An Oral History of the American Diplomatic Spouse*, New York: Twayne Publishers, 1994; Marat Moore, *Women in the Mines: Stories of Life and Work*, New York: Twayne Publishers, 1996; Carole Garibaldi Rogers, *Poverty, Chastity, and Change: Lives of Contemporary American Nuns*, New York: Twayne Publishers, 1996; Melissa Walker, *All We Knew Was to Farm: Rural Women in the Upcountry South, 1919-1941*, Baltimore: Johns Hopkins University Press, 2000; Jewell Fenzi and Allida Black, *Democratic Women: An Oral History of the Woman's National Democratic Club*, Washington: WNDC Education Foundation, 2000; Lu Ann Jones, *Mama Learned Us to Work: Farm Women in the New South*, Chapel Hill: University of North Carolina Press, 2002; Melissa Walker, *Country Women Cope with Hard Times: A Collection of Oral Histories*, Columbia: University of South Carolina Press, 2004; Suroopa Mukherjee, *Surviving Bhopal: Dancing Bodies, Written Texts, and Oral Testimonials of Women in the Wake of an Industrial Disaster*, New York: Palgrave Macmillan, 2010; Nan Alamilla Boyd and Horacio N. Roque Ramírez (eds.), *Bodies of Evidence: The Practice of Queer Oral History*, Oxford and New York: Oxford University Press, 2012.

需要指出的是，作为一种兼具学术研究与公众实践特征的研究领域与方法，女性口述历史已经成为丰富与改变美国历史书写内容与视角的重要组成部分，不过，近 20 年来美国女性口述历史发展也呈现出一种过度理论化的趋势。基于此，美国大部分实践者与研究者仍然强调女性口述历史的第一要务在于"恢复、恢复、恢复"（recover，recover，recover）与"收集、收集、收集"（collecting，collecting，collecting），即如何更好地恢复、挖掘、记录与解放女性自己的声音。①

五　其他口述历史

相对于其他新社会史家来说，美国劳工史学家较早地意识到口述史学的价值与意义所在。② 早在 1959—1963 年期间，密歇根大学与韦恩州立大学的劳工与工业关系研究所（Institute of Labor and Industrial Relations）就开展了一项围绕美国联合汽车工会（United Automobile Workers）创建与早期发展的口述历史计划。③ 该计划总共采访 150 多位工会人员，而这些宝

---

① Susan Armitage and Sherna Berger Gluck，"Reflections on Women's Oral History: An Exchange"，*Frontiers: A Journal of Women Studies*，Vol. 19，No. 3（Problems and Perplexities in Women's Oral History），1998，pp. 8，10.

② 需要指出的是，哥伦比亚大学口述历史研究室早期收藏中有相当一部分涉及美国劳工运动领袖及其重要人士的口述历史资料。具体内容参见 D. F. Shaughnessy，"Labor in the Oral History Collection of Columbia University"，*Labor History*，Vol. 1，No. 2，1960，pp. 177-195.

③ Philip P. Mason，"Labor history archives at Wayne State University"，*Labor History*，Vol. 5，No. 1，1964，pp. 67-75；Jack W. Skeels，"Oral History Project on the Development of Unionism in the Automobile Industry"，*Labor History*，Vol. 5，No. 2，1964，pp. 209-212. 此外可参见 *Preliminary Index to the United Auto Workers Oral History*，Ann Arbor: Institute of Labor and Industrial Relations，University of Michigan-Wayne State University，1967；Joyce L. Kornbluh and M. Brady Mikusko（eds.），*Working Womenroots: An Oral History Primer*，Ann Arbor: Institute of Labor and Industrial Relations，University of Michigan-Wayne State University，1979；M. Brady Mikusko，*Soucebook of Oral Histories of Trade Union and Working Women in the United States*，Ann Arbor: Institute of Labor and Industrial Relations，University of Michigan-Wayne State University，1982.

贵资料也成为美国劳工史研究的重要资料来源。①

而随着 20 世纪 70 年代初新劳工史（new labor history）的兴起②，口述史学日益成为一种重要的研究手段，它不仅超越工会制度史的局限扩展了研究视野，而且挖掘了一段原先被忽视的有组织的劳工本身内部的争斗历史。通过让工人积极致力撰写他们自己的历史，口述历史提供了一种与工人阶级社群建立新型关系和赋权于工人阶级的手段。③ 20 世纪 70 年代以来，劳工口述历史研究取得重大进展，概括而言，其主要研究内容集中于工人（阶级）或特定的劳工事件。就工人（阶级）口述历史而言，其代表性研究成果有《普通大众：工人阶级组织者的个人历史》（1973）、《痛苦世界：工人阶级家庭的生活》（1976）、《不工作：职业者口述历史》（1979）、《哈纳哈纳：夏威夷劳动者口述历史文集》（1984）、《用我们的双手：马萨诸塞州的木匠故事》（1986）、《工作生活：罗德岛劳工口述历史》（1987）、《绵长微笑，针扎岁月：普尔曼黑人搬运工的故事》（1989）、《团结与生存：20 世纪爱荷华州劳工口述历史》（1993）、《普尔曼蓝领：非裔美国人铁路服务员口述历史》（1996）、《口述历史：肉类加工厂黑人工人与他们争取种族与经济平等的斗

---

① Sidney Fine, *Sit-Down: The General Motors Strike of 1936-1937*, Ann Arbor: University of Michigan Press, 1969; Martin Halpern, *UAW Politics in the Cold War Era*, Albany: State University of New York Press, 1988; Margaret Weir, *Politics and Jobs: The Boundaries of Employment Policy in the United States*, Princeton: Princeton University Press, 1992; Sol Dollinger and Genora Dollinger, *Not Automatic: Women and the Left in the Forging of the Auto Workers' Union*, New York: Monthly Review Press, 2000; Karen Pastorello, *A Power Among Them: Bessie Abramowitz Hillman and the Making of the Amalgamated Clothing Workers of America*, Urbana: University of Illinois Press, 2008.

② Thomas A. Krueger, "American Labor Historiography, Old and New", *Journal of Social History*, Vol. 4, No. 3, 1971, pp. 277-285; David Brody, "The Old Labor History and the New: In search of an American Working Class", *Labor History*, Vol. 20, No. 1, 1979, pp. 111-126; Lawrence T. McDonnell, " 'You Are Too Sentimental': Problems and Suggestions for a New Labor History", *Journal of Social History*, Vol. 17, No. 4, 1984, pp. 629-654; Leon Fink, "The New Labor History and the Powers of Historical Pessimism: Consensus, Hegemony, and the Case of the Knights of Labor", *Journal of American History*, Vol. 75, No. 1, 1988, pp. 115-136; Mari Jo Buhle and Paul Buhle, "The New Labor History at the Cultural Crossroads", *Journal of American History*, Vol. 75, No. 1, 1988, pp. 151-157; Ava Baron (ed.), *Work Engendered: Toward a New History of American Labor*, Ithaca: Cornell University Press, 1991.

③ Rick Halpern, "Oral History and Labor History: A Historiographic Assessment after Twenty-Five Years", *Journal of American History*, Vol. 85, No. 2, 1998, pp. 596-610; Peter Winn, "Oral History and the Factory Study: New Approaches to Labor History", *Latin American Research Review*, Vol. 14, No. 2, 1979, pp. 130-140.

争》（1996）、《兄弟会中的姐妹：争取平等的纽约职业女性》（2008）与
《我看到它的到来：工厂关闭和失业的工人叙述》（2009）等。①

就特定劳工事件而言，其代表性口述历史研究成果包括《我仍然像今天
一样记得：1934 年汽车工人大罢工》（1988）、《修建胡佛大坝：经济大萧条
口述历史》（1993）与《新南方秩序争议：1914—1915 年亚特兰大富尔顿磨
坊大罢工》（2002）等。② 此外，还有一些研究成果涉及劳工社群、劳工组织
（工会）与劳工领袖等众多议题。③

对于同性恋史（gay and lesbian history）研究来说，口述史学同样具有

①　Alice Lynd and Staughton Lynd（ed.），*Rank and File：Personal Histories by Working-Class Or-ganizers*，Boston：Beacon Press，1973；Lillian B. Rubin，*Worlds of Pain：Life in the Working-Class Fami-ly*，New York：Basic Books，1976；Harry Mauer，*Not Working：An Oral History of the Unemployed*，New York：Holt，Rinehart，and Winston，1979；Michi Kodama-Nishimoto，Warren S. Nishimoto，and Cynthia A. Oshiro，*Hanahana：An Oral History Anthology of Hawaii's Working People*，Honolulu：University of Ha-waii at Manoa，1984；Mark Erlich，*With Our Hands：The Story of Carpenters in Massachusetts*，Philadel-phia Temple University Press，1986；Paul M. Buhle（ed.），*Working Lives：An Oral History of Rhode Island Labor*，Providence：Rhode Island Historical Society，1987；Jack Santino，*Miles of Smiles*，*Years of Strug-gle：Stories of Black Pullman Porters*，Urbana：University of Illinois Press，1989；Shelton Stromquist，*Sol-idarity and Survival：An Oral History of Iowa Labor in the Twentieth Century*，Iowa City：University of Iowa Press，1993；David D. Perata，*Those Pullman Blues：An Oral History of the African American Railroad At-tendant*，New York：Twayne Publishers，1996；Rick Halpern and Roger Horowitz，*Meatpackers：An Oral History of Black Packinghouse Workers and Their Struggle for Racial and Economic Equality*，New York：Twayne Publishers，1996；Jane Latour，*Sisters in the Brotherhoods：Working Women Organizing for Equality in New York City*，New York：Palgrave Macmillan，2008；Tracy E. K'Meyer and Joy L. Hart，*I Saw it Coming：Worker Narratives of Plant Closings and Job Loss*，New York：Palgrave Macmillan，2009.
②　Philip A. Korth and Margaret R. Beegle，*I Remember Like Today：The Auto-Lite Strike of* 1934，East Lansing：Michigan State University Press，1988；Andrew J. Dunar and Dennis McBride，*Building Hoo-ver Dam：An Oral History of the Great Depression*，New York：Twayne Publishers，1993；Clifford M. Kuhn，*Contesting the New South Order：The 1914-1915 Strike at Atlanta's Fulton Mills*，Chapel Hill：University of North Carolina Press，2001.
③　Peter Friedlander，*The Emergence of a UAW Local*，*1936-1939：A Study in Class and Culture*，Pittsburgh：University of Pittsburgh Press，1975；Tamara Hareven and Randolph Langenbach，*Amoskeag：Life and Work in an American Factory-City*，New York：Pantheon Books，1978；Jeremy Brecher，Jerry Lombardi，and Jan Stackhouse，*Brass Valley：The Story of Working People's Lives and Struggles in an Ameri-can Industrial Region*，Philadelphia：Temple University Press，1982；Jacquelyn Dowd Hall，James Lelou-dis，Robert Korstad，Mary Murphy，Lu Ann Jones，and Christopher B. Daly，*Like a Family：The Making of a Southern Cotton Mill World*，Chapel Hill：University of North Carolina Press，1987；Clara H. Friedman，*Between Management and Labor：Oral Histories of Arbitration*，New York：Twayne Publishers，1995；Sandy Polishuk，*Sticking to the Union：An Oral History of the Life and Times of Julia Ruuttila*，New York：Palgrave MacMillan，2003.

非常重要的价值。正如伊丽莎白·肯尼迪（Elizabeth Lapovsky Kennedy，1939—）所说："在 20 世纪 70 年代之前，因为缺乏有关女同性恋的文献记录，口述历史在创建有关 20 世纪女同性恋知识的过程中扮演重要角色。它扩展了女同性恋史的事实基础（factual base），同时也有助于认识与理解女同性恋的意识与主体性。"① 在主流的性别意识与文化主导下，同性恋行为通常被认为是反常的和变态的，因而有关这个群体的现有记录一般都是那些带有明显歧视意味的司法或医疗记录。而仅有的有关同性恋的自我记录也一般都是那些更具开明意识的社会上层人士所留下的日记或回忆录，因而也无法真正反映那些来自不同阶层、种族及族裔群体的男女同性恋者的多样性与复杂性。

20 世纪 60—70 年代兴起的同性恋解放运动（gay and lesbian liberation movement）极大地促进了美国学术界对于该群体历史的研究兴趣，而口述史学则理所当然地成为挖掘与呈现这个特殊群体被隐藏的声音与历史记忆的重要手段。② 在 20 世纪 70 年代末之前，就同性恋口述历史计划而言，

---

① Elizabeth Lapovsky Kennedy, "Oral History", in Bonnie Zimmerman（ed.）, *Lesbian Histories and Cultures: An Encyclopedia*, New York: Garland Publishing, 2000, p. 560;

② Jonathan Katz, *Gay American History: Lesbians and Gay Men in the U. S. A.: A Documentary*, New York: Crowell, 1976, pp. 249-250; Terry Wolverton and Christine Wong, "An Oral Herstory of Lesbianism", *Frontiers: A Journal of Women Studies*, Vol. 4, No. 3, 1979, pp. 52-53; Jeffrey Weeks, *Sexuality*, Chichester: Ellis Horwood, 1986, p. 12; Martin B. Duberman, Martha Vicinus, and George Chauncey, Jr.（eds.）, *Hidden from History: Reclaiming the Gay and Lesbian Past*, New York: New American Library, 1994; Daneel Buring, "Softball and Alcohol: The Limits of Lesbian Community in Memphis from the 1940s through the 1960s", in John Howard（ed.）, *Carryin' on in the Lesbian and Gay South*, New York: New York University Press, 1997, p. 204; Rob B. Ridinger, "Oral Histories", in Timothy Murphy（ed.）, *Reader's Guide to Lesbian and Gay Studies*, London and New York: Routledge, 2000, pp. 425-427; Ann Cvetkovich, "Legacies of Trauma, Legacies of Activism: ACT UP's Lesbians", in David L. Eng and David Kazanjian（eds.）, *Loss: The Politics of Mourning*, Berkeley: University of California Press, 2003, pp. 435-437; Steve Estes, "Ask and Tell: Gay Veterans, Identity, and Oral History on a Civil Rights Frontier", *Oral History Review*, Vol. 32, No. 2, 2005, pp. 21-47; Nan Alamilla Boyd, "Who Is the Subject?: Queer Theory Meets Oral History", *Journal of the History of Sexuality*, Vol. 17, No. 2, 2008, pp. 177-189; Nan Alamilla Boyd, "History as Social Change: Queer Archives and Oral History Projects", in Leila J. Rupp and Susan K. Freeman（eds.）, *Understanding and Teaching U. S. Lesbian, Gay, Bisexual, and Transgender History*, Madison: University of Wisconsin Press, 2014, pp. 311-319.

比较有代表性的包括"布法罗女性口述历史计划"（Buffalo Women's Oral History Project）、"旧金山同性恋历史计划"（San Francisco Lesbian and Gay History Project）和"波士顿地区同性恋历史计划"（Boston Area Gay and Lesbian History Project）等。① 而就口述历史研究成果而言，其主题集中于同性恋发展史、政治激进主义、同性恋社群与日常生活等领域，其代表性作品包括《创造历史：争取同性恋平等权口述历史（1945—1990）》（1992）、《皮革长靴，金色拖鞋：一个女同性恋社区的历史》（1993）、《孤独猎人：同性恋南方生活口述历史（1948—1968）》（1997）、《一个男同性恋社群的形成：前艾滋病时代的洛杉矶口述历史》（2002）与《身体证词：同性恋口述历史实践》（2012）等。②

在上述有关少数族裔、女性、劳工与同性恋的口述历史研究中，其中众多问题都涉及家庭（家族）史、社区（社群）史、地方史与城市史研

---

① 具体参见 Judith Schwarz, "Questionnaire on Issues in Lesbian History", *Frontiers: A Journal of Women Studies*, Vol. 4, No. 3, 1979, pp. 1-12; Esther Newton, "The Mythic Mannish Lesbian: Radclyffe Hall and the New Woman", *Signs*, Vol. 9, No. 4, 1984, pp. 557-575; Madeline Davis and Elizabeth Lapovsky Kennedy, "Oral History and the Study of Sexuality in the Lesbian Community: Buffalo, New York, 1940-1960", *Feminist Studies*, Vol. 12, No. 1, 1986, pp. 7-26; Will Roscoe, "History's Future: Reflections on Lesbian and Gay History in the Community", *Journal of Homosexuality*, Vol. 24, No. 1/2, 1992, pp. 161-179; Elizabeth Lapovsky Kennedy, "Telling Tales: Oral History and the Construction of Pre-Stonewall Lesbian History", *Radical History Review*, No. 62, 1995, pp. 59-79.

② Eric Marcus, *Making History: The Struggle for Gay and Lesbian Equal Rights, 1945-1990: An Oral History*, New York: HarperCollins, 1992; Elizabeth Lapovsky Kennedy and Madeline D. Davis, *Boots of Leather, Slippers of Gold: The History of a Lesbian Community*, London and New York: Routledge, 1993; James T. Sears, *Lonely Hunters: An Oral History of Lesbian and Gay Southern Life, 1948-1968*, Boulder: Westview, 1997; Eric C. Wat, *The Making of A Gay Asian Community: An Oral History of Pre-AIDS Los Angeles*, Lanham: Rowman and Littlefield, 2002; Nan Alamilla Boyd and Horacio N. Roque Ramírez (eds.), *Bodies of Evidence: The Practice of Queer Oral History*, Oxford and New York: Oxford University Press, 2012. 其他还可参见 Marcy Adelman (ed.), *Long Time Passing: Lives of Older Lesbians*, Boston: Alyson Publications, 1986; Allan Bérubé, *Coming Out Under Fire: The History of Gay Men and Women in World War II*, New York: Free Press, 1990; Esther Newton, *Fire Island: Sixty Years in America's First Gay and Lesbian Town*, Boston: Beacon, 1993; Eric Marcus, *Making Gay History: The Half-Century Fight for Lesbian and Gay Equal Rights*, New York: HarperCollins, 2002; Jack Drescher and Joseph P. Merlino (eds.) *American Psychiatry and Homosexuality: An Oral History*, Binghamton: The Haworth Press, 2007; Twin Cities GLBT Oral History Project, *Queer Twin Cities*, Minneapolis: University of Minnesota Press, 2010.

究，而对于这些明显具有草根性质的研究领域来说，口述史学也扮演着相当重要的角色。同样是在新社会史浪潮的影响下，从 20 世纪 60 年代中期以来，口述史学就被相当普遍地应用于有关美国家庭（家族）史、社区（社群）史、地方史与城市史等领域。①除专业史学家之外，为真正发挥口述史学的公众参与性与社区影响力，尤其是鼓励社区历史爱好者、志愿者与学生参与其中，美国州与地方历史协会和口述历史协会等机构，以及一些学者出版了一大批相关的口述历史实践指南，并且发表了一系列有关经验反思的学术论文。其中比较有代表性的实践指南包括《地方史的录音记录》（1966）、《地方历史学会口述历史指南》（1969）、《你的家庭史：如何利用口述历史家庭档案和公共记录来发现你的传统》（1978）、《口述历史：学生导论》（1979）、《利用口述历史开展家庭史计划》（1980）、《从记忆到历史：在地方史研究中利用口述资料》（1981）、《你身边的历史：探索你身边的过去》（1982）、《大家来做地方史》（1986）、《在社区史计划中利用口述历史》（1992）、《口述历史与家庭史学家：基础指南》（2006）与《捕捉故事：口述历史实践指南》（2009）等。②

需要指出的是，在美国主流口述史学界所出版的相关口述历史实践指南与文集当中，口述史学在家庭史、社区史与地方史的应用问题也是一个相当重要的议题。比如，由戴维·杜那威和维拉·鲍姆主编并于 1980 年出版的《口述史学：跨学科论文集》的第三部分就是"口述史学应用：地方

---

① Michael Frisch, "Oral History", in Carol Kammen and Amy H. Wilson（eds.）, *Encyclopedia of Local History*, Walnut Creek: AltaMira Press, 2013, pp. 439-443.

② William G. Tyrrell, *Tape-Recording Local History*, Nashville: American Association for State and Local History, 1966; Willa K. Baum, *Oral History for the Local Historical Society*, Stockton: Conference of California Historical Societies, 1969; Allan J. Lichtman, *Your Family History: How to Use Oral History Family Archives and Public Documents to Discover Your Heritage*, New York: Vintage Books, 1978; James Hoopes, *Oral History: An Introduction for Students*, Chapel Hill: University of North Carolina Press, 1979; Linda Shopes, *Using Oral History for a Family History Project*, Nashville: American Association for State and Local History, 1980; Barbara Allen William Lynwood Montell, *From Memory to History: Using Oral Sources in Local Historical Research*, Nashville: American Association for State and Local History, 1981; David E. Kyvig and Myron A. Marty, *Nearby History: Exploring*

史、族裔史、家庭史与妇女史"（Oral History Applied：Local，Ethnic，Family，and Women's History），其中共有 9 篇文章具体探讨了口述史学在这些领域中的应用问题。①而瓦拉利·姚于 1994 年出版的《记录口述历史：社会科学家实践指南》则专门有两章内容探讨口述史学在社区（社群）研究

the Past around You，Nashville：American Association for State and Local History，1982（Walnut Creek：AltaMira Press，second edition，1996）；Carol Kammen，On Doing Local History，Nashville：American Association for State and Local History，1986（Walnut Creek：AltaMira Press，second edition，2003；Lanham：Rowman and Littlefield，third edition，2014）；Laurie Mercier and Madeline Buckendorf，Using Oral History in Community History Projects，Los Angeles：Oral History Association，1992（Carlisle：Oral History Association，2007）；Linda Barnickel，Oral History for the Family Historian：A Basic Guide，Carlisle：Oral History Association，2006；Donna M. DeBlasio，Charles F. Ganzert，David H. Mould，Stephen H. Paschen and Howard L. Sacks，Catching Stories：A Practical Guide to Oral History，Athens：Ohio University Press，2009. 其他相关指南还可参见 Edward D. Ives，The Tape-Recorded Interview：A Manual for Fieldworkers in Folklore and Oral History，Knoxville：University of Tennessee Press，1980；Margaret Rose Yocom，"Fieldwork in Family Folklore and Oral History：A Study in Methodology"，Ph. D. dissertation，University of Massachusetts，1980；Brad Jolly，Videotaping Local History，Nashville：American Association for State and Local History，1982；Thomas L. Charlton，Oral History for Texans，Austin：Texas Historical Commission，1981 and 1985；Jeremy Brecher，History from Below：How to Uncover and Tell the Story of Your Community，Association，or Union，New Haven：Commonwork Pamphlets/Advocate Press，1986；William P. Fletcher，Recording Your Family History：A Guide to Preserving Oral History with Videotape，Audiotape，Suggested Topics and Questions，Interview Techniques，New York：Dodd，Mead，1986；Carol Kammen，The Pursuit of Local History：Readings on Theory and Practice，Walnut Creek：AltaMira Press，1996；Cynthia Hart and Lisa Samson，The Oral History Workshop：Collect and Celebrate the Life Stories of Your Family and Friends，New York：Workman Publishing Company，2009；Angela Zusman，Story Bridges：A Guide to Conducting Intergenerational Oral History Projects，Walnut Creek：Left Coast Press，2010；Dina C. Carson，Publish Your Family History：A Step by Step Guide to Writing the Stories of Your Ancestors，Niwol：Iron Gate Publishing，2015.

① David K. Dunaway and Willa K. Baum（eds.），Oral History：An Interdisciplinary Anthology，Nashville：American Association for State and Local History，1984（Walnut Creek：AltaMira Press，second edition，1996）. 具体文章信息如下 Lynwood Montell，"Preface to The Saga of Coe Ridge"，pp. 165-176；Larry Danielson，"The Folklorist，the Oral Historian，and Local History"，pp. 177-188；Jacquelyn Dowd Hall，"Documenting Diversity：The Southern Experience"，pp. 189-194；Gary Okihiro，"Oral History and the Writing of Ethnic History"，pp. 195-211；Theodore Rosengarten，"Preface to All God's Dangers"，pp. 212-220；Sherna Gluck，"What's So Special About Women？ Women's Oral History"，pp. 221-237；Linda Shopes，"Using Oral History for a Family History Project"，pp. 238-247；Tamara K. Hareven，"The Search for Generational Memory"，pp. 248-263；Alex Haley，"Black History，Oral History，and Genealogy"，pp. 264-287. 需要指出的是，这些文章在编入该书之前，都已经公开出版或发表。

（community studies）和家庭（家族）研究（family research）中的具体应用方法。① 唐纳德·里奇于 1995 年首次出版的经典口述史学作品《大家来做口述历史》在第八章"口述历史呈现"（Presenting Oral History）中也分别以"社区史"和"家庭访谈"为例来分析口述历史的主要呈现方式，而在随后的 2003 年和 2014 年两个版本中，这两部分内容也有相应更新。② 而近年来反映美国口述历史学界关注社区（社群）口述历史实践的重要体现是南希·麦凯（Nancy Mackay，1945—）、玛丽·昆兰（Mary Kay Quinlan）和芭芭拉·索姆（Barbara W. Sommer）于 2013 年出版的 5 卷本《社区口述历史工具箱》，分别从导论和一项口述历史计划的完整过程来具体论述社区口述历史实践的基本规范。③

　　除上述以实践指南出版为主的方法论探讨之外，美国口述历史学界有关家庭史、社区史与地方史研究等议题的口述史学理论研究成果也相当丰

---

① Valerie Raleigh Yow, *Recording Oral History：A Practical Guide for Social Scientists*, Thousand Oaks：Sage Publications, 1994. 两章内容分别为"Varieties of Oral History Projects：Community Studies", pp. 143-166；"Varieties of Oral History Projects：Family Research", pp. 192-219. 该书第二版和第三版参见 Valerie Raleigh Yow, *Recording Oral History：A Guide for the Humanities and Social Sciences*, Walnut Creek：AltaMira Press, second edition, 2005（Lanham：Rowman and Littlefield, third edition, 2015）.

② Donald A. Ritchie, *Doing Oral History*, New York：Twayne Publishers, 1995. 两章内容分别为"Community History", pp. 186-192；"Family Interviewing", pp. 193-195. 该书第二版和第三版参见 Donald A. Ritchie, *Doing Oral History：A Practical Guide*, Oxford and New York：Oxford University Press, second edition, 2003；Donald A. Ritchie, *Doing Oral History*, Oxford and New York：Oxford University Press, third edition, 2014.

③ Mary Kay Quinlan, Nancy Mackay, and Barbara W. Sommer, *Community Oral History Toolkit*（five volumes）, Walnut Creek：Left Coast Press, 2013. 具体参见 Mary Kay Quinlan, Nancy MacKay, and Barbara W. Sommer, *Introduction to Community Oral History*；Barbara W. Sommer, Nancy MacKay, and Mary Kay Quinlan, *Planning A Community Oral History Project*；Barbara W. Sommer, Nancy MacKay, and Mary Kay Quinlan, *Managing A Community Oral History Project*；Mary Kay Quinlan, Nancy MacKay, and Barbara W. Sommer, *Interviewing in Community Oral History*；Nancy MacKay, Mary Kay Quinlan, and Barbara W. Sommer, *After the Interview in Community Oral History*. 需要指出的是，该出版社从 2015 年开始出版由南希·麦凯担任主编的"口述历史实践"（Practicing Oral History）丛书，目前已经出版两本分别针对移民与历史组织的实践指南。详细参见 Carol McKirdy, *Practicing Oral History with Immigrant Narrators*, Walnut Creek：Left Coast Press, 2015；Barbara W Sommer, *Practicing Oral History in Historical Organizations*, Walnut Creek：Left Coast Press, 2015.

富。①当然，就口述历史计划或收藏而言，有关这些主题的口述历史资源更

---

① Gould P. Colman, "Taped Interviews and Community Studies", *Social Education*, Vol. 29, 1965, pp. 537-538; Margaret Sullivan, "Into Community Classrooms: Another Use for Oral History", *Oral History Review*, Vol. 2, 1974, pp. 53-58; Jacquelyn Dowd Hall, "Documenting Diversity: The Southern Experience", *Oral History Review*, Vol. 4, 1976, pp. 19-28; Tamara K. Hareven, "The Search for Generational Memory: Tribal Rites in Industrial Society", *Daedalus*, Vol. 107, No. 4, 1978, pp. 137-149; Ingrid Winther Scobie, "Family and Community History through Oral History", *The Public Historian*, Vol. 1, No. 4, 1979, pp. 29-39; Larry Danielson, "The Folklorist, the Oral Historian, and Local History", *Oral History Review*, Vol. 8, 1980, pp. 62-72; Linda Shopes, "The Baltimore Neighborhood Heritage Project: Oral History and Community Involvement", *Radical History Review*, No. 25, 1981, pp. 27-44; Linda Shopes, "Oral History and Community Involvement: The Baltimore Neighborhood Heritage Project", in Susan Porter Benson, Stephen Brier, and Roy Rosenzweig (eds.), *Presenting the Past: Essays on History and the Public*, Philadelphia: Temple University Press, 1986, pp. 249-263; Douglas Henry Daniels, "Oral History, Masks, and Protocol in the Jazz Community", *Oral History Review*, Vol. 15, No. 1, 1987, pp. 143-164; Michael Gordon, "Seeing and Fleeing Ourselves: Local Oral Histories of Communities and Institutions", *Oral History Review*, Vol. 17, No. 1, 1989, pp. 117-128; John Bodnar, "Power and Memory in Oral History: Workers and Managers at Studebaker", *Journal of American History*, Vol. 75, No. 4, 1989, pp. 1201-1221; Josiah Heyman, "The Oral History of the Mexican American Community of Douglas, Arizona, 1901-1942", *Journal of the Southwest*, Vol. 35, No. 2, 1993, pp. 186-206; Carrie Nobel Kline, "Giving It Back: Creating Conversations to Interpret Community Oral History", *Oral History Review*, Vol. 23, No. 1, 1996, pp. 19-39; Anna Green, "Returning History to the Community: Oral History in a Museum Setting", *Oral History Review*, Vol. 24, No. 2, 1997, pp. 53-72; Spencie Love, "Chatham County, Community at the Crossroads: A Southern/African American Oral History Seminar", *Journal of American History*, Vol. 87, No. 2, 2000, pp. 614-621; Linda Shopes, "Oral History and the Study of Communities: Problems, Paradoxes, and Possibilities", *Journal of American History*, Vol. 89, No. 2, 2002, pp. 588-598; A. Glenn Crothers, "'Bringing History to Life': Oral History, Community Research, and Multiple Levels of Learning", *Journal of American History*, Vol. 88, No. 4, 2002, pp. 1446-1451; Darlene Richardson, "Reconstructing a Community with Oral History", *Oral History Review*, Vol. 29, No. 2, 2002, pp. 97-102; Rose T. Diaz and Andrew B. Russell, "Oral Historians: Community Oral History and the Cooperative Ideal", in James Gardner and Peter LaPaglia (eds.), *Public History: Essays from the Field*, Malabar: Krieger Publishing, 2004, pp. 203-216; Charles Hardy Ⅲ, "A People's History of Industrial Philadelphia: Reflections on Community Oral History Projects and the Uses of the Past", *Oral History Review*, Vol. 33, No. 1, 2006, pp. 1-32; Paul Thompson, "Community and Individual Memory: An Introduction", *Oral History Review*, Vol. 36, No. 2, 2009, pp. i-v; Sally Alexander, "'Do Grandmas Have Husbands?' Generational Memory and Twentieth-Century Women's Lives", *Oral History Review*, Vol. 36, No. 2, 2009, pp. 159-176; Daniela Koleva, "Daughters' Stories: Family Memory and Generational Amnesia", *Oral History Review*, Vol. 36, No. 2, 2009, pp. 188-206; Stacey Zembrzycki, Erin Jessee, Eleanor Beattie, Audrey Bean, Mireille Landry, and Sandra Baines, "Oral History and Adult Community Education: Notes from the Field", *Oral History Review*, Vol. 38, No. 1, 2011, pp. 120-135; Anne Valk, Amy Atticks, Rachael Binning, Elizabeth Manekin, Aliza Schiff, Reina Shibata, and Meghan Townes, "Engaging Communities and Classrooms: Lessons from the Fox Point Oral History Project", *Oral History Review*, Vol. 38, No. 1, 2011, pp. 136-157; Brooke Bryan, "A Closer Look at Community Partnerships", *Oral History Review*, Vol. 40, No. 1, 2013, pp. 75-82; Katie Kuszmar, "From Boat to Throat: How Oral Histories Immerse Students in Ecoliteracy and Community Building", *Oral History Review*, Vol. 41, No. 2, 2014, pp. 325-340.

是极其丰富。而就具体的口述历史研究作品而言，比较有代表性的包括《汉娜的女儿：一个美国家庭的六代（1876—1976）》（1976）、《口述历史与城市史的形成》（1977）、《乡村声音：一个日裔美国人家庭农场社区的口述历史》（1987）、《活生生的亚特兰大：一部城市口述历史（1914—1948）》（1990）、《没有讲述的故事，未被赞颂的英雄：底特律非裔美国人社区口述历史（1918—1967）》（1994）、《发生在曼哈顿：20世纪中叶城市生活口述历史》（2001）、《跨越断街：奥兰多非裔美国人社区口述历史》（2005）、《南方农户与他们的故事：口述历史中的记忆与意义》（2006）、《小龙虾的底部：恢复一个消失的肯塔基社区》（2011）与《口述历史与美国西部的社区与工作》（2013）等。①

---

① Dorothy Gallagher, *Hannah's Daughters: Six Generations of an American Family, 1876-1976*, New York: Thomas Cromwell, 1976; Bruce M. Stave, *The Making of Urban History: Historiography through Oral History*, Beverly Hills: Sage Publications, 1977; David Mas Masumoto, *Country Voices: The Oral History of a Japanese American Family Farm Community*, Del Rey: Inaka Countryside, 1987; Cliff Kuhn, Harlon E. Joye and E. Bernard West, *Living Atlanta: An Oral History of the City, 1914-1948*, Athens: University of Georgia Press, 1990; Elaine Latzman Moon, *Untold Tales, Unsung Heroes: An Oral History of Detroit's African American Community, 1918-1967*, Detroit: Wayne State University Press, 1994; Myrna Katz Frommer and Harvey Frommer, *It Happened in Manhattan: An Oral History of Life in the City during the Mid-Twentieth Century*, New York: Berkley Books, 2001; Benjamin D. Brotemarkle, *Crossing Division Street: An Oral History of the African-American Community in Orlando*, Cocoa: Florida Historical Society Press, 2005; Melissa Walker, *Southern Farmers and Their Stories: Memory and Meaning in Oral History*, Lexington: University Press of Kentucky, 2006; Douglas A. Boyd, *Crawfish Bottom: Recovering a Lost Kentucky Community*, Lexington: University Press of Kentucky, 2011; Jessie L. Embry (ed.), *Oral History, Community, and Work in the American West*, Tucson: University of Arizona Press, 2013. 其他还可参见 Henry H. Glassie, *Passing the Time in Ballymenone: Culture and History of an Ulster Community*, Philadelphia: University of Pennsylvania Press, 1982; Patsy Moore Ginns, *Snowbird Gravy and Dishpan Pie: Mountain People Recall*, Chapel Hill: University of North Carolina Press, 1982; John Egerton, *Generations: An American Family*, Lexington: University Press of Kentucky, 1983; Jeff Kisseloff, *You Must Remember This: An Oral History of Manhattan from the 1890s to World War II*, New York: Harcourt Brace Jovanovitch, 1989; Ron Strickland (ed.), *Whistlepunks and Geoducks: Oral Histories from the Pacific Northwest*, New York: Paragon House, 1990; Elizabeth Fee, Linda Shopes, and Linda Zeidman, *The Baltimore Book: New Views of Local History*, Philadelphia: Temple University Press, 1991; Linda Shapiro Goldberg (ed.), *Here on This Hill: Conversations with Vermont Neighbors*, Middlebury: Vermont Folklore Center, 1991; Bob Greene and D. G. Fulford, *To Our Children's Children: Preserving Family Histories for Generations to Come*, New York: Doubleday, 1993; Elaine Krasnow Ellison and Elaine Mark Jaffe, *Voices from Marshall Street: Jewish Life in a Philadelphia Neighborhood, 1920-1960*, Philadelphia: Camino Books, 1994; Hugo Slim and Paul Thomson, *Listening for a Change: Oral Testimony and Community Development*, Philadelphia: New Society, 1995; Mildred Beik, *The Miners of*

综上所述，从 20 世纪 60 年代中后期开始，美国口述史学所呈现的上述"新社会史转向"不仅为那些处于非主流社会的边缘人物与弱势群体记录和保存了大量原始资料，而且口述史学所具有的民主动力（democratic impulses）很大程度上也挑战和改变了传统美国史学主要基于精英白人男性的传统书写模式。[①]正如保罗·汤普森所说："相反，口述史学能够进行更为公平的尝试：证据现在也可以来自下层阶级、无特权者和失败者。它可以提供一种对于历史的更为现实和公平的重建，并且挑战既定的叙述。这样做，总体而言，口述史学对于历史的社会启示（social message）则具有激进意义。……通过从底层引入新的证据、转变研究焦点和开辟新的探

Windber: The Struggles of New Immigrants for Unionization, 1890-1930, University Park: Pennsylvania State University Press, 1996; Dan Rottenberg, *Middletown Jews: The Tenuous Survival of an American Jewish Community*, Bloomington: Indiana University Press, 1997; Thad Sitton and Dan Utley, *From Can See to Can't: Texas Cotton Farmers on the Southern Prairies*, Austin: University of Texas Press, 1997; Robert Archibald, *A Place to Remember: Using History to Build Community*, Walnut Creek: AltaMira Press, 1999; Leland Cooper and Mary Lee Cooper, *The People of the New River: Oral Histories from the Ashe, Alleghany, and Watauga Counties of North Carolina*, Jefferson: McFarland & Co., 2001; Allen Meyers and Carl Nathans, *The Jewish Community under the Frankford El*, Charleston: Arcadia Publishing, 2003; Winona L. Fletcher and Sheila Mason Burton (eds.), *Community Memories: A Glimpse of African American Life in Frankfort, Kentucky*, Frankfort: Kentucky Historical Society, 2003; Jacob J. Podber, *The Electronic Front Porch: An Oral History of the Arrival of Modern Media in Rural Appalachia and the Melungeon Community*, Macon: Mercer University Press, 2007; Ellie Wymard, *Talking Steel Towns: The Men and Women of America's Steel Valley*, Pittsburgh: Carnegie Mellon Press, 2007; Shelley Trower (ed.), *Place, Writing, and Voice in Oral History*, New York: Palgrave Macmillan, 2011; Audrey Petty (ed.), *High Rise Stories: Voices from Chicago Public Housing*, San Francisco: Voice of Witness, 2013; Christopher Bell, *East Harlem Remembered: Oral Histories of Community and Diversity*, Jefferson: McFarland & Co., 2013; Stacey Zembrzycki, *According to Baba: A Collaborative Oral History of Sudbury's Ukrainian Community*, Vancouver: University of British Columbia Press, 2014; Ronald E. Marcello, *Small Town America in World War II: War Stories from Wrightsville, Pennsylvania*, Denton: University of North Texas Press, 2014.

① Ronald J. Grele, "History and the Languages of History in the Oral History Interview: Who Answers Whose Questions and Why?" in Eva M. McMahan and Kim Lacy Rogers (eds.), *Interactive Oral History Interviewing*, Hillsdale: L. Erlbaum Associates, 1994, p. 1; Carrie Hamilton, "On Being a 'Good' Interviewer: Empathy, Ethics and the Politics of Oral History", *Oral History*, Vol. 36, No. 2, 2008, p. 35; Donald A. Ritchie, *Doing Oral History*, Oxford and New York: Oxford University Press, third edition, 2014, p. 247.

究领域、挑战历史学家的假设和公断以及重新认识那些被忽视的实质性群体，一个转变的累积过程正在启动。……简而言之，历史变得更加民主。"① 而琳达·肖普斯也指出："口述史学在民主化我们对于过去的集体理解（collective understanding）方面已经扮演着一个重要角色，访谈已经增加了有关之前被排除的或没有记录的群体的新知识，同时也已经将声音和能动性（agency）还原给那些通常被现存记录所客体化的人。"②

---

① Paul Thompson, *The Voice of the Past: Oral History*, Oxford and New York: Oxford University Press, third edition, 2000, pp. 7-9.
② Linda Shopes, "Oral History", in Norman K. Denzin and Yvonna S. Lincoln (eds.), *The Sage Handbook of Qualitative Research*, Thousand Oaks: Sage Publications, fourth edition, 2011, p. 455.

第五章　美国口述史学的理论转向与反思

综观 20 世纪 70 年代末以前美国口述史学的主要发展趋势，不管是"档案实践模式"还是"新社会史转向"都着重强调口述史学的档案功能与史料价值，前者主要为精英人物撰写口述自传提供补充证据，而后者则为恢复边缘人物或弱势群体的"隐藏历史"提供全新资料。在这些实践中，口述历史的生产过程被认为是并不复杂的，作为口述历史学家的访谈者从客观和中立的态度出发来记录受访者关于过去经历的记忆，而为了回应来自实证主义社会科学家和传统文献历史学家的激烈批评，早期口述历史实践者试图通过倡导一种访谈的科学模式来宣称口述历史的真实性与客观性。[1] 正如罗纳德·格里所说："因为对于追求'客观'历史的需要，以及对于历史的实证主义与经验主义观点，档案倾向（archival impulse）一直主导着美国口述史学的发展，因而很少有空间讨论访谈者与被访谈者之间的个人与社会关系，或访

---

① Nathan Wachtel, "Introduction", in Marie-Noëlle Bourguet, Lucette Valensi, and Nathan Wachtel (eds.), *Between Memory and History*, New York: Harwood Academic Publishers, 1990, pp. 2-3; Geoffrey H. Hartman, *The Longest Shadow: In the Aftermath of the Holocaust*, Bloomington: Indiana University Press, 1996, p. 31; Jean-Pierre Wallot and Normand Fortier, "Archival Science and Oral Sources", in Robert Perks and Alistair Thomson (eds.), *The Oral History Reader*, London and New York: Routledge, 1998, p. 365; Alistair Thomson, "Fifty Years On: An International Perspective on Oral History", *Journal of American History*, Vol. 85, No. 2, 1998, pp. 581-582; Guy Beiner, *Remembering the Year of the French: Irish Folk History and Social Memory*, Madison: University of Wisconsin Press, 2007, p. 20.

谈本身的性质。"① 琳达·肖普斯也指出，到 20 世纪 70 年代，尽管口述历史访谈的目的和主题已经发生明显转变，并且实践领域也有所扩展，不过作为一种资料来源，因为深受实证主义传统的影响，口述历史还是被更多地看成"透明的记录"（transparent documents）和"事实的供应者"（purveyors of facts），因而其评价标准也是基于真实或错误。②

正是如此，进入 20 世纪 70 年代末以来，一些更具理论导向的口述历史学家呼吁重新思考口述历史的实践与解释方式。而在这种背景下，一系列深具理论意识与跨学科特征的新问题与新视角脱颖而出，其中有三个问题备受关注：（1）"记忆转向"（memory turn）：如何理解作为口述历史来源的记忆的主观性与真实性问题？（2）"叙事转向"（narrative turn）：受访者的记忆呈现依赖访谈者与受访者之间的互动对话与口头叙述，因而受政治环境、访谈场合、社会性别、族裔与教育等社会文化因素所影响的叙事形式与叙事策略如何影响口述历史内容的呈现与诠释？（3）作为共享口述历史著作权的访谈者与受访者，其各自的主体性意识及相互关系如何影响口述历史的访谈过程与解释结果？③

---

① Ronald J. Grele，"Directions for Oral History in the United States"，in David K. Dunaway and Willa K. Baum（eds.），*Oral History：An Interdisciplinary Anthology*，Walnut Creek：AltaMira Press，second edition，1996，p. 67. 罗纳德·格里被美国口述历史学界认为是理论研究的主要推动者，详细参见 Richard Cándida Smith，"Ronald Grele on the Role of Theory in Oral History"，*Oral History Review*，Vol. 21，No. 2，1993，pp. 99-104. 此外，有关他对当代口述史学理论研究的最新反思，可参见 Ronald J. Grele，"Oral History Theory"，*Oral History Review*，Vol. 38，No. 2，2011，pp. 354-359；Ronald J. Grele，"Postscript"，in Kristina R. Llewellyn，Alexander Freund and Nolan Reilly（eds.），*The Canadian Oral History Reader*，Montreal：McGill-Queen's University Press，2015，pp. 347-360.

② Linda Shopes，"Oral History"，in Norman K. Denzin and Yvonna S. Lincoln（eds.），*The Sage Handbook of Qualitative Research*，Thousand Oaks：Sage Publications，fourth edition，2011，p. 457.

③ 简单而言，琳达·肖普斯认为口述史学理论转向的一个重要体现是对于口述历史访谈概念理解的转变，即从"作为记录的访谈"（interview as a document）向"作为文本的访谈"（interview as a text）的转变。详细参见 Linda Shopes，"'Insights and Oversights'：Reflections on the Documentary Tradition and the Theoretical Turn in Oral History"，*Oral History Review*，Vol. 41，No. 2，2014，pp. 257-268.

　　需要指出的是，美国口述史学在 20 世纪 70 年代所出现的理论转向（theoretical turn）是内外因素共同作用的结果。从内部而言，越来越多的人以个人学术研究为主要目标的学院派口述历史学家开始超越单纯的资料搜集导向，并转而关注口述历史的生产过程与诠释问题。而外部因素则主要涉及两个方面，一方面是当时不断兴起与发展的跨学科理论与思潮的冲击，其中包括文学研究、文化研究、人类学、民俗学、心理学、语言学、叙事学、交际研究，以及后结构主义与后现代主义等；另一方面则是以英国和意大利为代表的国际口述史学理论研究成果的影响，同时，以国际会议和学术杂志为主要平台的国际口述史学交流也极大地促进了美国口述史学发展的理论转向。①

　　而根据上述提出的三个问题，本章将从"记忆转向"、"叙事转向"与"'共享（的）权威'：口述历史关系反思"三个角度来分析和论述美国口述史学的理论转向与反思。

---

　　①　Ronald J. Grele, "Directions for Oral History in the United States", in David K. Dunaway and Willa K. Baum (eds.), *Oral History: An Interdisciplinary Anthology*, Walnut Creek: AltaMira Press, second edition, 1996, pp. 68-69. 至于国际口述历史大会的相关情况，上述已有所交代。而当时国际交流的另外一个重要平台则是 1980 年创刊并由罗纳德·格里和查尔斯·莫里斯先后担任主编的《国际口述历史杂志》（*International Journal of Oral History*），它在 1989 年停刊之后并于 1990 年更名为《国际口述历史年刊》（*International Annual of Oral History*）。不过，该刊只于 1992 年出版一期主题为《口述历史中的主体性与多元文化主义》的专刊，随后于同年更名为《国际口述历史与生活故事年鉴》（*International Yearbook of Oral History and Life Stories*），在 1992—1996 年期间，该年鉴总共出版四卷。而国际口述历史协会官方刊物《话语与沉默》（*Words and Silences*）于 1997 年创刊之后，年鉴也随即停刊。上述年刊参见 Ronald J. Grele (ed.), *International Annual of Oral History*, 1990: *Subjectivity and Multiculturalism in Oral History*, Westport: Greenwood Press, 1992. 四卷年鉴分别参见 Luisa Passerini (ed.), *Memory and Totalitarianism*, Oxford and New York: Oxford University Press, 1992; Daniel Bertaux and Paul Thompson (eds.), *Between Generations: Family Models, Myths, and Memories*, Oxford and New York: Oxford University Press, 1993; Rina Benmayor and Andor Skotnes (eds.), *Migration and Identity*, Oxford and New York: Oxford University Press, 1994; Selma Leydesdorff, Luisa Passerini, and Paul Thompson (eds.), *Gender and Memory*, Oxford and New York: Oxford University Press, 1996. 除第三卷外，其余三卷于 2005 年由 Transaction Publishers 再版。有关《话语与沉默》杂志，可访问 http://wordsandsilences.org/，2015 年 9 月 1 日访问。

一 "记忆转向"

首先，需要指出的是，20 世纪 70 年代出现的口述史学研究的"记忆转向"并不是美国所特有的，而且它也是更为广泛的西方史学"记忆转向"及不同学科领域对于记忆研究兴趣不断增加的一个重要组成部分。对于西方史学界的记忆转向，有学者观察指出："我们曾经论及的民间历史或大众历史或口述历史或公共历史或者甚至于神话，现在我们则用作为一种元史学范畴（metahistorical category）的记忆将所有这些不同的术语涵盖进来。⋯⋯记忆正在取代诸如自然、文化和语言等旧爱而成为与历史最常匹配的术语，而这种转变正在重塑历史想象。"①当然，在某种意义上，现代口述史学的诞生早于记忆研究的兴盛，因此也有学者

---

① Kerwin Lee Klein, "On the Emergence of Memory in Historical Discourse", *Representations*, No. 69（Special Issue: Grounds for Remembering）, Winter, 2000, p. 128. 有关历史与记忆研究的代表性成果可参见 Jacques Le Goff, *History and Memory*, New York: Columbia University Press, 1992; Patrick H. Hutton, *History as an Art of Memory*, Hanover: University Press of New England, 1993; Raphael Samuel, *Theatres of Memory: Past and Present in Contemporary Culture*, London: Verso, 1994; Pierre Nora and Lawrence D. Kritzman（eds.）, *Realms of Memory: Rethinking the French Past*（Vol. 1: Conflicts and Divisions）, New York: Columbia University Press, 1996; Pierre Nora and Lawrence D. Kritzman（eds.）, *Realms of Memory: The Construction of the French Past*（Vol. 2: Traditions）, New York: Columbia University Press, 1997; Pierre Nora and Lawrence D. Kritzman（eds.）, *Realms of Memory: The Construction of the French Past*（Vol. 3: Symbols）, New York: Columbia University Press, 1998; Dominick LaCapra, *History and Memory After Auschwitz*, Ithaca: Cornell University Press, 1998; Endel Tulving and Fergus I. M. Craik（eds.）, *The Oxford Handbook of Memory*, Oxford and New York: Oxford University Press, 2000; Paul Ricoeur, *Memory, History, Forgetting*, Chicago: University of Chicago Press, 2004; Katharine Hodgkin and Susannah Radstone（eds.）, *Memory, History, Nation: Contested Pasts*, New Brunswick: Transaction Publishers, 2006; Geoffrey Cubitt, *History and Memory*, Manchester: Manchester University Press, 2007; Susannah Radstone and Bill Schwarz（eds.）, *Memory: Histories, Theories, Debates*, New York: Fordham University Press, 2010; Michael S. Roth, *Memory, Trauma, and History: Essays on Living with the Past*, New York: Columbia University Press, 2012; Joan Tumblety（ed.）, *Memory and History: Understanding Memory as Source and Subject*, London and New York: Routledge, 2013; Stefan Berger and Bill Niven（eds.）, *Writing the History of Memory*, London: Bloomsbury Academic, 2014; 彭刚:《历史记忆与历史书写——史学理论视野下的"记忆的转向"》,《史学史研究》2014 年第 2 期, 第 1—12 页。

指出："口述史研究为史家从事记忆研究提供了前提。如果史家仍然像19世纪的兰克那样，坚持认为史学研究必须基于'硬邦邦'的一手史料（最好是政府档案），那么口述史就无从兴起，当今的记忆研究也无法进入史学的殿堂。"①

口述历史对于记忆研究的重要性主要是因为记忆是口述历史的唯一来源与核心问题，不同于其他历史研究，口述历史主要是基于活生生的受访者的口述回忆。正是如此，甚至有学者指出，除精神分析学家和心理学家之外，口述历史学家比任何其他专业人员都更感兴趣于人类记忆和与之进行接触。不过，在早期美国口述史学"档案实践"取向的主导下，很少有口述历史学家真正将记忆作为合适的研究主题，他们主要着眼通过口述历史访谈来收集和保存记忆，而不是试图研究记忆本身。② 此外，主要来自心理学家和其他社会科学家有关记忆问题的大量而复杂的研究成果足以导致当时主要来自历史学、档案学和图书馆学领域的口述历史工作者很少有兴趣从事这些研究。正如美国著名心理学家罗伯特·门宁格（Robert Menninger, 1922—2015）在一次全国口述史学会议上所说："记忆是很难定义和研究的。"③

尽管如此，从20世纪70年代初开始，依托记忆与回忆的口述历史不断遭到那些奉行客观主义与实证主义的传统文献历史学家的质疑与批判，其矛头直指记忆的主观性与不可靠性。他们认为受访者在回忆时，无论其记忆如何清晰、鲜明和生动，都不可避免地受到各种内外因素的影响，比如受访者的记忆力、岁月流逝、价值立场、怀旧情绪、生命经历、感情因

---

① 王晴佳：《历史学的"记忆转向"》，《中国社会科学报》2010年3月2日第3版。王晴佳有关该问题的详细论述可参见王晴佳《记忆、历史和记忆史学》，王晴佳《新史学讲演录》，中国人民大学出版社2010年版，第84—95页。

② John A. Neuenschwander, "Remembrance of Things Past: Oral Historians and Long-Term Memory", *Oral History Review*, Vol. 6, 1978, pp. 45-46.

③ Robert Menninger, "Some Psychological Factors Involved in Oral History Interviewing", *Oral History Review*, Vol. 3, 1975, p. 68.

素及健康原因等。① 而这些因素极有可能导致受访者在口述时出现遗忘（forgetting）、错记（misremembering）、说谎乃至虚构等诸多情况。② 更为重要的是，作为访谈者、受访者与所处社会环境共同互动的过程与结果，口述历史也受到访谈者的提问与倾听方式以及访谈时间和访谈环境等综合因素的影响。因此，口述历史所呈现的记忆具有高度的流动性与易变性，而很大程度上，文献资料所承载的历史记忆则具有相对的稳定性与固定性，尽管其解读也因研究者不同而有所差异。

当然，当时对于记忆主观性与不可靠性的质疑与批判则是一种共同的国际现象，而在众多批评者当中，以澳大利亚历史学家帕特里克·弗雷尔（Patrick O'Farrell，1933—2003）的观点最为尖锐。在《口述历史：事实与虚构》一文中，他严正指出："关于过去的口述证词的基本问题在于其真实性（truth）主要不是关于发生了什么或如何发生，而是关于过去是如何被回忆的。……关于口述历史的准确性、直接性与真实性的所有宣称都遭受到最为严重的质疑，我们正在进入想象、选择性记忆、事后虚饰和完全主观的世界。……它将把我们引向何处？那不是进入我们的历史，而是神话。"③ 而为回应这些实证主义历史学家的抨击，早期口述历史实践者予以坚决反驳，并发展了一套评估口述历史记忆真实性与可靠性的实践指南。从社会心理学和人类学的角度，他们展示了如何确定记忆的偏见与虚构；从社会学的角度，他们采用抽样方法以确保访谈对象的代表性与普遍性；而且，他们也从文献历史学家那里吸收了检验原始资料可靠性与内在一致性的

---

① William W. Cutler Ⅲ, "Accuracy in Oral History Interviewing", *Historical Methods Newsletter*, Vol. 3, No. 3, 1970, pp. 1-7; Barbara Tuchman, "Distinguishing the Significant from the Insignificant", *Radcliffe Quarterly*, Vol. 56, No. 4, 1972, pp. 9-10.

② Sandy Polishuk, "Secrets, Lies, and Misremembering: The Perils of Oral History Interviewing", *Frontiers: A Journal of Women Studies*, Vol. 19, No. 3, 1998, pp. 14-23; Paula Hamilton, "The Oral Historian as Memorist", *Oral History Review*, Vol. 32, No. 1, 2005, pp. 11-18.

③ Patrick O'Farrell, "Oral History: Facts and Fiction", *Oral History Association of Australia Journal*, No. 5, 1982/1983, pp. 4, 9. 该文原载 *Quadrant*, Vol. 23, No. 11, 1979, pp. 4-8.

原则与方法，并强调文献资料也具有选择性和偏见色彩。① 而在阿利斯泰尔·汤姆森看来，采取上述应对策略的代表性口述历史学家是保罗·汤普森，他在 1978 年首次出版的《过去的声音：口述历史》一书中就利用上述方法来证明口述历史作为历史证据的可靠性与合理性。当然，他也强调信件、日记、报告和议会文件等文献资料同口述历史资料一样都是社会建构（social construction）的产物，而不应该单独苛求口述历史的完全客观性。②

同样，为合理化和提升口述史学在历史学当中的专业地位，美国早期口述历史学界也习惯以实证主义史学的客观性与真实性标准来看待记忆的可靠性问题，尤其强调通过与其他史料来源的相互印证来核对或确认口述历史资料的真实性与可靠性。约瑟夫·凯希和赫伯特·胡佛在 1971 年编辑出版的《身为印第安人：口述历史》一书中就指出："尽管它具有很大价值，不过严肃的学者已经注意到口述历史也有其局限性。人的记忆的准确性可能会随着时间的流逝而降低。……因为这些原因，如果学者们要合适地利用口述历史，他们必须利用他们所有的判断能力。他们也必须利用其他类型的资料来平衡口述证词。"③ 而维维安·佩里斯在 1974 年出版的《查尔斯·艾夫斯回忆：口述历史》一书中也指出："口述历史的主要危险之一就是记忆的不可靠性（fallibility），因此必须通过修改以纠正事实性

---

① Michael Rope, "Oral History", in Brian Brivati, Julia Buxton, and Anthony Seldon (eds.), *The Contemporary History Handbook*, Manchester: Manchester University Press, 1996, p. 347; Alistair Thomson, "Unreliable Memories? The Use and Abuse of Oral History", in William Lamont (ed.), *Historical Controversies and Historians*, London: University College London Press, 1998, pp. 26-27; Alistair Thomson, "Memory and Remembering in Oral History", in Donald A. Ritchie (ed.), *The Oxford Handbook of Oral History*, Oxford and New York: Oxford University Press, 2011, pp. 79-80.

② Paul Thompson, *The Voice of the Past: Oral History*, Oxford and New York: Oxford University Press, 1978, pp. 101-149. 相关书评可参见 Louis M. Starr, "Book Review: *The Voice of The Past: Oral History*", *Oral History Review*, Vol. 6, 1978, pp. 67-68; Bill Williams, "Book Review: *The Voice of The Past: Oral History*", *Oral History*, Vol. 7, No. 1, 1979, pp. 63-65; Willa Baum and Amelia Fry, "Book Review: *The Voice of The Past: Oral History*", *American Historical Review*, Vol. 84, No. 3, 1979, p. 711; William W. Moss, "Book Review: *The Voice of The Past: Oral History*", *The American Archivist*, Vol. 43, No. 1, 1980, pp. 84-85; Thomas L. Charlton, "Book Review: *The Voice of The Past: Oral History*", *The History Teacher*, Vol. 14, No. 1, 1980, pp. 148-149.

③ Joseph H. Cash and Herbert T. Hoover (eds.), *To Be an Indian: An Oral History*, New York: Holt, Rinehart and Winston, 1971, p. xxii.

错误（factual errors）。"① 直到 20 世纪 70 年代末 80 年代初，这种观念与做法仍然主导美国口述历史学界，其根本目的是为了确保与提升口述历史的证据价值（evidentiary value）。在 1977 年举行的第十二届全国口述史学会议上，几位学者围绕"追忆逝水年华：记忆的可靠性"（Remembrance of Things Past：Reliability of Memory）议题展开激烈讨论，尽管众多学者也强调记忆的重建性和不准确性，但是讨论焦点仍然聚焦于口述历史资料本身的正确性与可靠性，尤其是要采取尽可能的措施来改善口述历史资料中的事实性信息（factual information）。② 而当时出版的大部分美国口述史学实践手册与指南也奉行这种主流观念，其中以《从记忆到历史：在地方史研究中利用口述资料》最具代表性，其中第四章"检验口述资料的历史真实性"（Testing Oral Sources for Historical Validity）就专门从"内证"（internal tests）和"外证"（external tests）两个方面来分析口述资料历史真实性与准确性的基本程序与方法。③

当然，当时也有美国口述历史学家强调记忆的不可靠性并不是口述历史所独有的，因而不能苛求口述历史的完全客观性与真实性。正如 1977—1978 年度美国口述历史协会主席瓦迪·摩尔（Waddy M. Moore）在 1978 年所说："作为毫无根据批评的第一种观点是认为由于人类记忆很可能是

---

① Vivian Perlis, *Charles Ives Remembered：An Oral History*, New Haven：Yale University Press, 1974, p. xx. 其他类似观点还可参见 David F. Musto and Saul Benison, "Studies on the Accuracy of Oral Interviews", in Gould P. Colman（ed.）, *The Fourth National Colloquium on Oral History*, New York：Oral History Association, 1970, pp. 167-181；Alice Hoffman, "Reliability and Validity in Oral History", *Today's Speech*, Vol. 22, No. 1, 1974, pp. 23-27；William Moss, "Oral History：An Appreciation", *American Archivist*, Vol. 40, No. 4, 1977, pp. 429-443.

② "Proceedings of the Twelfth Annual Colloquium", *Oral History Review*, Vol. 6, 1978, p. 62.

③ Barbara Allen William Lynwood Montell, *From Memory to History：Using Oral Sources in Local Historical Research*, Nashville：American Association for State and Local History, 1981. 相关书评可参见 Charles T. Morrissey, "Book Review：*From Memory to History：Using Oral Sources in Local Historical Research*", *The Public Historian*, Vol. 4, No. 3, 1982, pp. 103-105；Joel Gardner, "Book Review：*From Memory to History：Using Oral Sources in Local Historical Research*", *Oral History Review*, Vol. 10, 1982, pp. 153-154；Francis A. de Caro, "Book Review：*From Memory to History：Using Oral Sources in Local Historical Research*", *Western Folklore*, Vol. 41, No. 2, 1982, pp. 148-150；Eric L. Pumroy, "Book Review：*From Memory to History：Using Oral Sources in Local Historical Research*", *The Library Quarterly*, Vol. 52, No. 3, 1982, pp. 283-284.

有错误的,因而口述历史是有缺陷的。……当然记忆是有错误的。它也是变化不定的、短暂的、混淆的,甚至通常是完全错误的。但是这仅仅发生在口述历史回忆录中吗?日记作者、写信者和传记作者的记忆也不是有缺陷的吗?相对于那些写作或出版回忆录的人来说,为什么口述历史受访者的记忆就这样不能被认可和接受呢?事实上,口述历史访谈可能更加接近真实,因为访谈者会帮助澄清模糊之处,刺激那些模糊的记忆,挑战自我服务和有选择性的记忆,甚至能够相互对质。"[1]

不过,当时也有少数学者比较早地改变对于实证主义历史学家批评的态度与回应策略,并提出应该以一种新的观点与视角来看待口述历史当中的记忆问题,即口述史学开始出现所谓的"记忆转向"。从后实证主义(post-positivism)立场出发,他们主张"记忆的不可靠性"(unreliability of memory)正是口述历史的优势与资源所在,而并非是缺点和问题。而且,他们认为记忆的主观性不仅能够了解历史经历的意义,同时也能够为理解过去与现在、记忆与个人认同以及个体记忆与集体记忆之间的关系提供线索和启示。[2]就美国而言,其代表人物是迈克尔·弗里斯科,他于1972年在关于斯塔兹·特克尔的《艰难时代》的书评中指出:"记忆问题,不管是个人的和历史的,还是个体的和代际的,它应该成为焦点。记忆是口述历史的对象,而不仅仅是方法。随后出现的值得思考的问题则主要聚焦于过程和变化:在经历成为记忆的过程中发生了什么?在经历成为历史的过程中又发生了什么?当一个具有强烈的集体经历(collective experience)的时代成为过去时,记忆与历史概括(historical generalization)之间又有什么关系?这些问题对于思考文

---

① Waddy M. Moore, "Critical Perspectives", *Oral History Review*, Vol. 6, 1978, p. 1.

② Alistair Thomson, Michael Frisch, and Paula Hamilton, "The Memory and History Debates: Some International Perspectives", *Oral History*, Vol. 22, No. 2, 1994, p. 33; Alistair Thomson, "Writing about Learning: Using Mass-Observation Educational Life-Histories to Explore Learning through Life", in Julia Swindells (eds.), *The Uses of Autobiography*, London: Taylor and Francis, 1995, pp. 163-165; Robert Perks and Alistair Thomson, "Critical Developments: Introduction", in Robert Perks and Alistair Thomson (eds.), *The Oral History Reader*, London and New York: Routledge, second edition, 2006, p. 3; Alistair Thomson, "Four Paradigm Transformations in Oral History", *Oral History Review*, Vol. 34, No. 1, 2007, p. 54.

化和个性（individuality）如何随着时间的变化而相互作用都是非常基本的，而诸如此类的问题却是特别适合或者唯一只能通过口述历史才能洞悉。"①

随后，在 1973 年 4 月于芝加哥举行的美国历史学家组织（Organization of American Historians）年会上，罗纳德·格里与斯塔兹·特克尔、简·范西纳（Jan Vansina）、丹尼斯·特德洛克（Dennis Tedlock）、索尔·本尼松和爱丽丝·科斯勒·哈里斯（Alice Kessler Harris）等人围绕口述历史的深层次理论、方法与跨学科问题展开激烈讨论。而其中的一个重要议题便是记忆问题，他们基本主张要超越关于记忆真实与错误的简单争论，正如斯塔兹·特克尔所强调的，他的《艰难时代》不是历史而是记忆，他所要寻找的不是事实（fact），而是事实背后的真实（truth）。② 在 1975 年首次发表的《没有目标的运动：口述史学的方法论与理论问题》一文中，罗纳德·格里也强调口述历史学界必须从新的视角来回应实证主义历史学家对于记忆可靠性问题的质疑，并提出需要借鉴跨学科概念与理论来理解记忆的主观性与可变性。③ 同在 1975 年，美国著名口

---

① Michael Frisch, "Oral History and *Hard Times*: A Review Essay", *Oral History Review*, Vol. 7, 1979, p. 75. 该文最初发表于 *Red Buffalo: A Journal of American Studies*, Vol. 1, No. 2/3, 1972, pp. 217-231, 而后又刊登于 Michael Frisch, *A Shared Authority: Essays on the Craft and Meaning of Oral History and Public History*, Albany: State University of New York Press, 1990, pp. 5-13.

② Ronald J. Grele and Studs Terkel, "Riffs and Improvisations: An Interview with Studs Terkel (April 10, 1973)", in Ronald J. Grele (ed.), *Envelopes of Sound: The Art of Oral History*, New York: Praeger Publishers, second edition, revised and enlarged, 1991, pp. 10-49.

③ Ronald J. Grele, "Movement Without Aim: Methodological and Theoretical Problems in Oral History", in Ronald J. Grele (ed.), *Envelopes of Sound: The Art of Oral History*, New York: Praeger Publishers, second edition, revised and enlarged, 1991, pp. 126-154. 需要说明的是，上述 1973 年会议上有关口述历史问题的讨论内容最终于 1975 年成书出版，详细参见 Ronald J. Grele (ed.), *Envelopes of Sound: Six Practitioners Discuss the Method, Theory and Practice of Oral History and Oral Testimony*, Chicago: Precedent Publishing, 1975. 在该书中，除《没有目标的运动：口述史学的方法论与理论问题》之外，还包括 "Riffs and Improvisations: An Interview with Studs Terkel"（Ronald J. Grele and Studs Terkel）、"It's Not the Song, It's the Singing: Panel Discussion on Oral History"（Studs Terkel, Jan Vansina, Alice Kessler Harris, Dennis Tedlock, Saul Benison, and Ronald J. Grele）和 "Oral History as Poetry"（Dennis Tedlock）三篇文章。该书于 1985 年再版时，罗纳德·格里又增加他于 1975—1985 年间撰写的四篇论文（构成 1985 年版本的第五至第八章），而且书名有所更改，详细参见 Ronald J. Grele (ed.), *Envelopes of Sound: The Art of Oral History*, Chicago: Precedent Publishing, second edition, revised and enlarged, 1985. 而为满足读者需求，该书又于 1991 年由 Praeger Publishers 原样再版，而本书所有引用均来自 1991 年版本。

述历史学家彼得·弗里德兰登（Peter Friedlander）在其口述历史作品前言《理论、方法与口述历史》中也强调记忆并不是挖掘事实的静态资源，而回忆本身就是一个历史解释过程。[1] 他指出："记忆并不能为我们提供文献记录中可以发现的那种高度精确性。……然而，如果记忆的内容仅仅是上述讨论的'事实'（facts），那么我们跟那些处理更为正统的资料来源也没有太大区别。……而记忆本身就是一种印象和感受的巨大混合，同时也是一种更具结构性和理性的构图（schemata）。"[2] 随后，罗纳德·格里又于 1978 年指出，口述历史学家应当关注历史记忆及对话的语言与认知结构，尤其需要熟悉记忆、记忆形成、记忆维持，以及记忆在人类生活中的地位等心理学相关的理论与方法。[3] 此外，当时还有一些美国学者专门从长时段记忆理论等心理学视角重点探讨了口述历史当中的记忆问题与由此引发的有关口述证词有效性与可靠性的争论。[4]

而在 20 世纪 70 年代末，对于推动和促进美国乃至国际口述史学研究的"记忆转向"做出重要贡献的是两位意大利著名口述历史学家：路易莎·帕萨里尼（Luisa Passerini，1941—）和阿利桑乔·波特利（Alessandro Portelli，1942—）。在 1979 年发表的《意大利法西斯主义下的工作意识形态与共识》一文中，帕萨里尼认为除了加强口述资料（oral sources）的事实性应用（factual use）之外，还需要充分挖掘口述

---

① Robert Perks and Alistair Thomson, "Interpreting Memories: Introduction", in Robert Perks and Alistair Thomson（eds.）, *The Oral History Reader*, London and New York: Routledge, 1998, p. 270.

② Peter Friedlander, "Introduction: Theory, Method, and Oral History", in Peter Friedlander, *The Emergence of a UAW Local, 1936-1939: A Study in Class and Culture*, Pittsburgh: University of Pittsburgh Press, 1975, pp. xxvi-xxvii.

③ Ronald Grele, "Can Anyone over Thirty Be Trusted: A Friendly Critique of Oral History", *Oral History Review*, Vol. 6, 1978, p. 43. 该文重刊于 Ronald J. Grele（ed.）, *Envelopes of Sound: The Art of Oral History*, New York: Praeger Publishers, second edition, revised and enlarged, 1991, pp. 196-210.

④ Robert Menninger, "Some Psychological Factors Involved in Oral History Interviewing", *Oral History Review*, Vol. 3, 1975, pp. 68-75; John A. Neuenschwander, "Remembrance of Things Past: Oral Historians and Long-Term Memory", *Oral History Review*, Vol. 6, 1978, pp. 45-53.

资料的独特性。在她看来，口述历史原始资料（raw material）不仅包含事实性陈述（factual statements），而且在很大程度上还是文化的表达与再现，因此，除字面叙述（literal narrations）之外，还包含记忆、意识形态与潜意识欲望（subconscious desires）等维度。① 此外，她注意到在与意大利工人的口述历史访谈中总是听到无关的或前后矛盾的回答，甚至有些人对于法西斯主义时代的经历及其影响总是保持沉默或刻意"遗忘"。基于此，帕萨里尼提醒口述历史学家要更为广泛地注意记忆的变化无常，更要关注社会文化、道德价值与意识形态对于个体记忆的影响。②

而在 1979 年首次发表的《什么令口述历史与众不同》一文中，阿利桑乔·波特利就明确挑战众多批评者对于记忆可靠性问题的质疑，进而提出口述性（orality）、叙事形式、主体性和记忆的"与众不同的可信性"等口述历史特质以及访谈者与受访者之间的关系应当被视为口述历史的优势，而不是缺点。至于这种"与众不同的可信性"，波特利指出："口述证词的重要性可能不在于它紧贴事实，而在于与事实的背离，正如所呈现的想象、象征与欲望。因此，并不存在'错误的'（false）口述资料。……口述历史的多样性由这样一个事实构成，即'错误的'（wrong）叙述在心理上仍然是'真实的'（true），而这种真实可能与事实上可靠的叙述（factually reliable accounts）同等重要。"而对于记忆问题，他强调指出："真正重要的是，记忆不是事实的一个消极的储藏室（passive depository of facts），而是一个意义创造的积极过程（active process of creation of meanings）。因此，对于历史学家来说，口述资料的特殊价值更多的不在于它们

① Luisa Passerini, "Work Ideology and Consensus under Italian Fascism", *History Workshop*, No. 8, 1979, p. 84.

② Ibid., pp. 82-108.

保存历史的作用，而在于记忆所能产生的显著变化。"①

需要指出的是，20 世纪 80 年代以来，相关学科记忆理论研究的发展也为口述历史学界探讨记忆问题提供了重要概念与理论来源。② 而与此同时，国际口述史学界也开始逐步形成共识，即对于历史解释和重建来说，"不可靠的记忆"可能是一种财富，而不是一个问题。③ 以罗纳德·格里、路易莎·帕萨里尼、约翰·博德纳（John Bodnar, 1944—）、迈克尔·弗里斯科与阿利桑乔·波特利为代表的口述历史学家在他们的具体个案研究中都强调口述历史有助于理解特定环境中的个体记忆、主体性、社会认同，以及它们与更为广泛的社会背景与公共记忆之间的互动关系。在她们看来，口述历史学家应该超越传统的局限于回忆或访谈内容的片面关注，而更应该思考受访者为什么回忆（遗忘）、如何回忆，以及回忆的意义等更为深层次的问题。

如上所述，在 1985 年再版的《声音外壳：口述历史的艺术》一书中，罗纳德·格里对于记忆问题的思考也更加重视和深入。尤其是在《私人记

---

① Alessandro Portelli, "What Makes Oral History Different", in Alessandro Portelli, *The Death of Luigi Trastulli and Other Stories：Form and Meaning of Oral History*, Albany：State University of New York Press, 1991, pp. 51 and 52. 需要指出的是，该文最先于 1979 年以意大利语发表，随后于 1981 年在英国《历史工作坊》（*History Workshop*）再次发表，而 1991 年收入该书时，题目和内容都有所修改。具体参见 Alessandro Portelli, "Sulla specificità della storia orale", *Primo Maggio*, Vol. 13, 1979, pp. 54-60；Alessandro Portelli, "On the Peculiarities of Oral History", *History Workshop*, No. 12, 1981, pp. 96-107.

② 根据笔者查询，以下是口述历史学界较为常见引用的出版于 20 世纪 80 年代的研究成果。详细参见 Ulrich Neisser（ed.）, *Memory Observed：Remembering in Natural Contexts*, San Francisco：W. H. Freeman, 1982；Popular Memory Group, "Popular Memory：Theory, Politics, Method", in Richard Johnson, Gregor McLennan, Bill Schwarz, David Sutton（eds.）, *Making Histories：Studies in History-Writing and Politics*, London：Hutchinson, 1982, pp. 205-252；David C. Rubin（ed.）, *Autobiographical Memory*, Cambridge：Cambridge University Press, 1986；David S. Gorfein and Robert R. Hoffman（eds.）, *Memory and Learning：The Ebbinghaus Centennial Conference*, Hillsdale：Lawrence Erlbaum and Associates, 1987；Judith Greene, Memory, *Thinking and Language：Topics in Cognitive Psychology*, London：Methuen, 1987；Edmund Blair Bolles, *Remembering and Forgetting：Inquires Into the Nature of Memory*, New York：Walker and Company, 1988；Thomas Butler, *Memory：History, Culture and the Mind*, London：Basil Blackwell, 1989；Paul Connerton, *How Societies Remember*, Cambridge：Cambridge University Press, 1989.

③ Alistair Thomson, "Fifty Years On：An International Perspective on Oral History", *Journal of American History*, Vol. 85, No. 2, 1998, p. 584.

忆与公共呈现：口述历史的艺术》一文中，作者更是详细分析了保存于受访者头脑中的私人记忆如何经由口述历史访谈得以向公众呈现，正如格里所说："它们（口述历史）告诉我们发生了什么事情，同时也告诉我们人们以为发生了什么事情，以及它们如何内化和解释所发生的事情。它们告诉我们个体特征（individual personalities）与社会因素（social forces）如何重建记忆以促进或阻碍那些理解过去的特定方式的发展。"① 而在 1987 年出版的《大众记忆中的法西斯主义：都灵工人阶级的文化经历》一书中，路易莎·帕萨里尼进一步强调了历史行动者的主体性在历史进程中的作用，并且展示了公共文化与意识形态对于个体记忆和主体性的影响，以及它们如何在个人证词的沉默、矛盾与独特风格（idiosyncrasies）中得以揭示。② 而在 1989 年发表的有关印第安纳州南本德（South Bend）斯图特贝克工厂（Studebaker Plant）汽车工人的口述历史研究中，约翰·博德纳发现受访者的个体记忆会受到公共领域所呈现的相关解释的强烈影响，即个体记忆与社会记忆、公共记忆之间的互动关系。③

继 1972 年那篇较早讨论口述历史与记忆问题的经典论文之后，迈克尔·弗里斯科在 20 世纪 70—80 年代撰写的 13 篇有关口述历史与公

---

① Ronald J. Grele, "Private Memories and Public Presentation: The Art of Oral History", in Ronald J. Grele (ed.), *Envelopes of Sound: The Art of Oral History*, New York: Praeger Publishers, second edition, revised and enlarged, 1991, p. 245.

② Luisa Passerini, *Fascism in Popular Memory: The Cultural Experience of the Turin Working Class*, Cambridge: Cambridge University Press, 1987. 帕萨里尼的相关研究还可参见 Luisa Passerini, "Mythbiography in Oral History", in Raphael Samuel and Paul Thompson (eds.), *The Myths We Live By*, London and New York: Routledge, 1990, pp. 49-60; Luisa Passerini, *Autobiography of a Generation: Italy, 1968*, Hanover: Wesleyan University Press, 1996.

③ John Bodnar, "Power and Memory in Oral History: Workers and Managers at Studebaker", *Journal of American History*, Vol. 75, No. 4, 1989, pp. 1201-1221. 在该杂志同期中，还有一篇美国著名历史学家戴维·西伦（David Thelen）有关美国记忆与历史的文章，详细参见 David Thelen, "Memory and American History", *Journal of American History*, Vol. 75, No. 4, 1989, pp. 1117-1129. 博德纳的相关记忆研究还可参见 John Bodnar, *Remaking America: Public Memory, Commemoration and Patriotism in the Twentieth Century*, Princeton: Princeton University Press, 1992; John Bodnar, "Saving Private Ryan and Postwar Memory in America", *American Historical Review*, Vol. 106, No. 3, 2001, pp. 805-817; John Bodnar, *The "Good War" in American Memory*, Baltimore: Johns Hopkins University Press, 2010.

共历史的文章于 1990 年结集出版。① 在这本极富影响力的著作——《一种共享的权威：口述历史与公共历史的技艺与意义》中，作者以大量个案研究来证明口述历史对于历史记忆研究的重要意义。正如他所说："口述历史是一种用来发现、探索和评估历史记忆过程（process of historical memory）性质的强有力工具——人们如何理解他们的过去，他们如何将个人经历与社会背景联系起来，过去如何成为现在的一部分，以及人们如何利用它来解释他们的生活与他们周围的世界。……让有关记忆的明智反思成为口述历史规划的焦点，因为它是方法论本身的核心。"②

同样，继 1979 年那篇广受学者引用的经典论文之后，阿利桑乔·波特利有关口述历史研究的代表性成果《卢奇·特拉斯图利之死与其他故事：口述历史的形式与意义》于 1991 年出版，该书主要以意大利特尔尼（Terni）和美国哈兰郡（Harlan）两个工业化城市的口述历史研究为例来探讨一系列相关的理论与方法论问题。而在其中有关一位 21 岁的特尔尼钢铁工人卢奇·特拉斯图利（Luigi Trastulli）死亡日期的研究中，波特利集中阐释了他对于口述历史当中所呈现的记忆主观性与流动性的观点。据相关文献记录显示，特拉斯图利死于 1949 年 3 月 17 日，当时钢铁厂工人为了反对意大利政府签署《北大西洋公约》（North Atlantic Treaty）而举行集会，他正是在与警察的冲突当中无辜遇难。不过，在大约 30 年后的口述历史访谈中，波特利发现众多普通工人的口述证词都认为特拉斯图利死于 1953 年的一场因工厂大量解雇工人而引发的罢工与街斗当中。波特利指出，对于这种死亡日期的错误回忆不能简单地归结为个体记忆的错误或说明口述资料的不可靠。相反，波特利认为叙述者将象征挫败和羞辱的无辜遇害事件改变为能够为工人挽回某些自尊的工会罢工事件则是为了突显特拉斯图利之死对

---

① 这些文章的具体出处，请参见 Michael Frisch，"Acknowledgements"，in Michael Frisch，*A Shared Authority：Essays on the Craft and Meaning of Oral and Public History*，Albany：State University of New York Press，1990，pp. xii-xiii.

② Michael Frisch，"Quality in History Program：From Celebration to Exploration of Values"，in Michael Frisch，*A Shared Authority：Essays on the Craft and Meaning of Oral and Public History*，Albany：State University of New York Press，1990，pp. 188-189.

于意大利工人阶级的政治意义与象征价值。[1] 正如波特利指出："……错误、虚构和神话引领我们穿过并超越事实进而获得它们的意义。……事实与记忆之间的矛盾最终提高了口述资料作为历史证据的价值。它不是由错误的回忆所造成的，而是由记忆和想象所积极和创新性地生产的，目的是为了让关键的事件和一般的历史富有意义。"[2]

概括而言，上述口述历史学家都认为记忆有助于我们理解过去经历与现实生活之间的互动关系，而且它"远远不仅仅是一种消极的容器或储存系统，也不仅仅是一个有关过去的图像库（image bank），而是一种积极的塑造力量；即它是动态的——它试图象征性遗忘的同它所记住的是同样重要的"[3]。正是如此，越来越多的口述历史学家都意识到口述历史不仅要尽量客观地描述过去发生的真实经历，而且更要发挥记忆的主观性特质，即从历史当事人或者目击者的口述访谈中更为深刻地认识与理解过去。那就是在历史的背后：人们如何看待他们的过去？人们想从他们的过去经历中

---

[1] Alessandro Portelli, "The Death of Luigi Trastulli: Memory and the Event", in Alessandro Portelli, *The Death of Luigi Trastulli and Other Stories: Form and Meaning of Oral History*, Albany: State University of New York Press, 1991, pp. 1-26.

[2] Alessandro Portelli, "The Death of Luigi Trastulli: Memory and the Event", in Alessandro Portelli, *The Death of Luigi Trastulli and Other Stories: Form and Meaning of Oral History*, Albany: State University of New York Press, 1991, pp. 2 and 26. 在后续研究中，波特利继续强调记忆有助于我们理解与揭示物质事实（material facts）、个人主观性（personal subjectivity）与社会背景（social contexts）之间的复杂关系。相关研究可参见 Alessandro Portelli, *The Battle of Valle Giulia: Oral History and The Art of Dialogue*, Madison: University of Wisconsin Press, 1997; Alessandro Portelli, *The Order Has Been Carried Out: History, Memory, and Meaning of a Nazi Massacre in Rome*, New York: Palgrave Macmillan, 2003; Alessandro Portelli, *They Say in Harlan County: An Oral History*, Oxford and New York: Oxford University Press, 2011. 围绕上述 1997 年和 2003 年出版的两本书，《口述历史评论》还刊登《阿利桑乔·波特利作品中的历史与记忆》（"History and Memory in the Work of Alessandro Portelli", *Oral History Review*, Vol. 32, No. 1, 2005, pp. 1-33）专题文章，详细参见 Jacquelyn Dowd Hall, "Introduction to the Session", pp. 1-3; David W. Blight, "Fossilized Lies: A Reflection on Alessandro Portelli's *The Order Has Been Carried Out*", pp. 5-9; Paula Hamilton, "The Oral Historian as Memorist", pp. 11-18; Edward T. Linenthal, "Stories and Bodies: A Personal Reflection on Alessandro Portelli's *The Order Has Been Carried Out*", pp. 19-26; Alessandro Portelli, "Response to Commentaries", pp. 27-33. 有关波特利的口述历史研究经历，可参见 Betsy Brinson, "Crossing Cultures: An Interview with Alessandro Portelli", *Oral History Review*, Vol. 28, No. 1, 2001, pp. 87-113.

[3] Raphael Samuel, "Preface: Memory Work", in Raphael Samuel, *Theatres of Memory: Past and Present in Contemporary Culture*, London: Verso, 2012, p. xxiii.

得到些什么？人们又怎样用过去解释他们现在的生活和周围世界？而现在的生活与处境又如何影响他们对于过去的回忆与解释？人们又如何有意识或无意识地记住、遗忘或虚构某些经历？或许，这在一定程度上能够诠释意大利著名史学家贝内德托·克罗齐（Benedetto Croce，1866—1952）于1917 年所提出的"一切真历史都是当代史"（Every True History is Contemporary History）这句史学名言。①简单而言，口述历史能够让人们从当下生活与现实需要出发来叙述或解释过去的某些经历，并赋予经历以某种合理性与意义。

进入 20 世纪 90 年代以来，在上述口述历史学家与相关学科记忆研究学者的影响下②，以美国为主的国际口述历史学界出版了一大批以口

---

① Benedetto Croce, *History: Its Theory and Practice*, New York: Russell & Russell, 1960, p. 12.

② 在口述历史学界较为常见引用的出版于 20 世纪 90 年代以来的记忆研究成果中，比较有代表性的包括 Maurice Halbwachs, *On Collective Memory*, Chicago: University of Chicago Press, 1992; James Fentress and Chris Wickham, *Social Memory*, Oxford: Blackwell Publishers, 1992; Iwona Irwin-Zarecka, *Frames of Remembrance: The Dynamics of Collective Memory*, New Brunswick: Transaction Publishers, 1994; Frederic C. Bartlett, *Remembering: A Study in Experimental and Social Psychology*, Cambridge: Cambridge University Press, 1932 and 1995; Ulric Neisser and Robyn Fivush (eds.), *The Remembering Self: Construction and Accuracy in the Self-Narrative*, Cambridge: Cambridge University Press, 1994; David C. Rubin (ed.), *Remembering Our Past: Studies in Autobiographical Memory*, Cambridge: Cambridge University Press, 1995; Daniel L. Schacter (ed.), *Memory Distortion: How Minds, Brains, and Societies Reconstruct the Past*, Cambridge: Harvard University Press, 1995; Daniel Schacter, *Searching for Memory: The Brain, the Mind, and the Past*, New York: Basic Books, 1996; Charles P. Thompson, Douglas J. Herrmann, Darryl Bruce, J. Don Read, David G. Payne and Michael P. Toglia (eds.), *Autobiographical Memory: Theoretical and Applied Perspectives*, Mahwah: Lawrence Erlbaum, 1998; Susannah Radstone (ed.), *Memory and Methodology*, London: Berg, 2000; Daniel L. Schacter, *The Seven Sins of Memory: How the Mind Forgets and Remembers*, Boston: Houghton Mifflin, 2001; Jacob J. Climo and Maria G. Cattell (eds.), *Social Memory and History: Anthropological Perspectives*, Walnut Creek: AltaMira Press, 2002; Barbara A. Mistral, *Theories of Social Remembering*, Buckingham: Open University Press, 2003; Susannah Radstone and Katharine Hodgkin (eds.), *Memory Cultures: Memory, Subjectivity, and Recognition*, New Brunswick: Transaction Publishers, 2006; Geoffrey Cubitt, *History and Memory*, Manchester: Manchester University Press, 2007; Michael Rossington and Anne Whitehead (eds.), *Theories of Memory: A Reader*, Edinburgh: University of Edinburgh Press, 2007; Harriet Harvey Wood and A. S. Byatt (eds.), *Memory: An Anthology*, London: Vintage Books, 2009; Emily Keightley and Michael Pickering (eds.), *Research Methods for Memory Studies*, Edinburgh: University of Edinburgh Press, 2013; David Dean, Yana Meerzon and Kathryn Prince (eds.), *History, Memory, Performance*, New York: Palgrave Macmillan, 2015.

述历史与记忆问题的研究成果，其内容涉及个体/私人记忆（individual/private memory）、自传记忆（autobiographical memory）、社会记忆（social memory）、集体记忆（collective memory）、官方记忆（official memory）、公共记忆（public memory）、大众记忆（popular memory）、创伤记忆（traumatic memory）、档案记忆（archival memory），以及记忆与神话（memory and myth）、记忆与社会性别（memory and gender）、记忆与遗忘（memory and forgetting）、记忆与沉默（memory and reticence）、记忆与老年化（memory and ageing）、记忆与表演（memory and performance）等广泛主题。其中较具代表性和影响的口述历史作品包括《我们赖以生存的神话》（1990）、《记忆档案：一个士兵的二战回忆》（1990）、《记忆与极权主义》（1992）、《世代之间：家庭模式、神话与记忆》（1993）、《记忆与历史：经历的回忆与解释》（1994）、《澳新军团士兵的记忆：与传奇共生》（1994）、《社会性别与记忆》（1996）、《关于倾听大屠杀幸存者：叙述与生活史》（1998）、《创伤与生活故事：国际视野》（1999）、《多娜·玛丽亚的故事：生活史、记忆与政治认同》（2000）、《口述历史的力量：记忆、治疗与发展》（2002）、《回忆：口述历史书写》（2004）、《回忆：口述历史表演》（2005）、《南方农户与他们的故事：口述历史中的记忆与意义》（2006）、《回忆剧场：从记忆中创作戏剧》（2007）、《口述历史与公共记忆》（2008）、《口述历史与老年化》（2010）、《记忆、战争与创伤》（2010）、《古巴性革命：激情、政治与记忆》（2012）、《口述历史、社区与离散：想象后种族隔离时代的南非记忆》（2012）、《东南亚的口述历史：记忆与碎片》（2013）、《边缘之声：危机后的口述历史》（2014）与《超越证词与创伤：大规模暴力之后的口述历史》

（2015）等。①

　　美国口述史学界对于记忆问题感兴趣的另外一个重要体现是在多本有关口述史学方法与理论读本或指南的权威著作中，都将口述历史当中的记忆问题作为重要专题来讨论。总体而言，在 20 世纪 90 年代中期以前出版的绝大部分读本或指南中，除历史证据视角的可靠性与真

---

① Raphael Samuel and Paul Thompson （eds.）, *The Myths We Live By*, London and New York： Routledge, 1990; Alice M. Hoffman and Howard S. Hoffman, *Archives of Memory： A Soldier Recalls World War II*, Lexington： University Press of Kentucky, 1990; Luisa Passerini （ed.）, *Memory and Totalitarianism*, Oxford and New York： Oxford University Press, 1992; Daniel Bertaux and Paul Thompson （eds.）, *Between Generations： Family Models, Myths, and Memories*, Oxford and New York： Oxford University Press, 1993; Jaclyn Jeffrey and Glenace E. Edwall （eds.）, *Memory and History： Essays on Recalling and Interpreting Experience*, Lanham： University Press of America, 1994; Alistair Thomson, *Anzac Memories： Living with the Legend*, Oxford and New York： Oxford University Press, 1994 （Clayton： Monash University Press, 2013）; Selma Leydesdorff, Luisa Passerini, and Paul Thompson （eds.）, *Gender and Memory*, Oxford and New York： Oxford University Press, 1996; Henry Greenspan, *On Listening to Holocaust Survivors： Recounting and Life History*, Westport： Praeger Publishers, 1998; Kim Lacy Rogers, Selma Leydesdorff, and Graham Dawson （eds.）, *Trauma and Life Stories： International Perspectives*, London and New York： Routledge, 1999; Daniel James, *Doña María's Story： Life History, Memory, and Political Identity*, Durham： Duke University Press, 2000; Philippe Denis and James Worthington（eds.）, *The Power of Oral History： Memory, Healing and Development*, Pietmaritzburg： University of Natal, 2002; Anna Green and Megan Hutching（eds.）, *Remembering： Writing Oral History*, Auckland： Auckland University Press, 2004; Della Pollock （ed.）, *Remembering： Oral History Performance*, New York： Palgrave Macmillan, 2005; Melissa Walker, *Southern Farmers and Their Stories： Memory and Meaning in Oral History*, Lexington： University Press of Kentucky, 2006; Pam Schweitzer, *Reminiscence Theatre： Making Theatre From Memories*, London： Jessica Kingsley Publishers, 2007; Paula Hamilton and Linda Shopes （eds.）, *Oral History and Public Memories*, Philadelphia： Temple University Press, 2008; Joanna Bornat and Josie Tetley （eds.）, *Oral History and Ageing*, London： Centre for Policy on Ageing, 2010; Nigel C. Hunt, *Memory, War, and Trauma*, Cambridge： Cambridge University Press, 2010; Carrie Hamilton, *Sexual Revolutions in Cuba： Passion, Politics, and Memory*, Chapel Hill： University of North Carolina Press, 2012; Sean Field, *Oral History, Community and Displacement： Imagining Memories in Post-Apartheid South Africa*, New York： Palgrave Macmillan, 2012; Kah Seng Loh, Ernest Koh, and Stephen Dobbs （eds.）, *Oral History in Southeast Asia： Memories and Fragments*, New York： Palgrave Macmillan, 2013; Mark Cave and Stephen M. Sloan （eds.）, *Listening on the Edge： Oral History in the Aftermath of Crisis*, Oxford and New York： Oxford University Press, 2014; Steven High （ed.）, *Beyond Testimony and Trauma： Oral History in the Aftermath of Mass Violence*, Vancouver： University of British Columbia Press, 2015.

实性问题之外，它们都较少系统和全面地讨论记忆问题的复杂性与深度性。而这方面的代表作则是唐纳德·里奇于 1995 年首次出版的经典作品《大家来做口述历史》，除第一章列出"记忆与口述历史"（Memory and Oral History）专节之外，全书众多地方都讨论了记忆问题的复杂性。而在随后的 2003 年和 2014 年两个版本中，作者对该问题的探讨又进一步深化，并吸收与借鉴了学术界的最新研究成果。① 而由英国著名口述历史学家罗伯特·佩克斯（Robert Perks）和澳大利亚著名口述历史学家阿利斯泰尔·汤姆森（1983—2007 年长期在英国大学任教，2007 年返回澳大利亚 Monash University 工作）主编并由众多美国学者参与撰稿的《口述史学读本》（1998）也相当重视记忆问题，该书第三部分"解释记忆"（Interpreting Memories）共有 7 篇文章从跨学科角度分析了记忆问题对于口述史学研究的重要意义，并且强调记忆研究要超越传统的客观性视角，进而关注其主观性特征。该书于 2006 年和 2015 年再版时，该专题主题保持不变，不过部分文章有所增删。② 另外一本是美国著名口述历史学家瓦拉利·姚于 2005 年再版的《记录口述历史：人文与社会科学指南》，其中第二章"口述历史与记忆"（Oral History and Memory）在吸收和借鉴众多相关学科记忆研究理论的基础上，相当全面和深入分析了口述历史当中的记忆问题，而在 2015 年修订再版时又有所

---

① Donald A. Ritchie, *Doing Oral History*, New York: Twayne Publishers, 1995, pp. 11-17; Donald A. Ritchie, *Doing Oral History: A Practical Guide*, Oxford and New York: Oxford University Press, second edition, 2003, pp. 30-41; Donald A. Ritchie, *Doing Oral History*, Oxford and New York: Oxford University Press, third edition, 2014, pp. 14-28. 此外，该书有关记忆问题的其他论述，可参见该书索引（index）中有关"memory"关键词的页码分布。

② Robert Perks and Alistair Thomson (eds.), *The Oral History Reader*, London and New York: Routledge, 1998, pp. 269-355; Robert Perks and Alistair Thomson (eds.), *The Oral History Reader*, London and New York: Routledge, second edition, 2006, pp. 211-331; Robert Perks and Alistair Thomson (eds.), *The Oral History Reader*, London and New York: Routledge, third edition, 2015, pp. 297-444.

更新。① 不过，该书于 1994 年首次出版时，仅仅只有 4 页篇幅涉及该问题，足见记忆问题在 20 世纪 90 年代中期以后不断受到美国口述史学界的关注与重视。②而由托马斯·查尔顿（Thomas L. Charlton）、洛伊斯·迈尔斯（Lois E. Meyers，1946—）和瑞贝卡·夏普莱斯（Rebecca Sharpless）三位美国著名口述历史学家主编并于 2006 年出版的《口述史学手册》一书中，除罗纳德·格里与爱丽丝·霍夫曼（Alice M. Hoffman）和霍华德·霍夫曼（Howard S. Hoffman）专门或专题讨论记忆问题之外，其余 14 篇文章也都相当重视该问题。③ 2011 年出版并由唐纳德·里奇担任主编的《牛津口述史学手册》同样突显了记忆问题在口述史学研究中的核心地位，该书第二部分"记忆与历史"（Memory and History）共有 6 篇文章分别探讨了口述历史中的记忆与回忆过程以及记忆的政治性、个体性、集体性与公共性等问题，并以两个实例研究考察了口述历史对于记录、反思和治疗创伤记忆的重要意义。④ 此外，值得一提的是两位英国学者保罗·汤普森与林恩·阿布拉姆斯（Lynn Abrams）对于记忆问题研究的重要贡献，在其经典作品《过去的声音：口述历史》的第二版和第三版中，汤普森新增专章"记忆与自我"（Memory and the Self）讨论记忆与主

---

① Valerie Raleigh Yow, *Recording Oral History: A Guide for the Humanities and Social Sciences*, Walnut Creek: AltaMira Press, second edition, 2005, pp. 35-67; Valerie Raleigh Yow, *Recording Oral History: A Guide for the Humanities and Social Sciences*, Lanham: Rowman and Littlefield, third edition, 2015, pp. 41-76.

② Valerie Raleigh Yow, *Recording Oral History: A Practical Guide for Social Scientists*, Thousand Oaks: Sage Publications, 1994, pp. 19-22.

③ Ronald J. Grele, "Oral History as Evidence", in Thomas L. Charlton, Lois E. Myers, and Rebecca Sharpless (eds.), *Handbook of Oral History*, Walnut Creek: AltaMira Press, 2006, pp. 43-101; Alice M. Hoffman and Howard S. Hoffman, "Memory Theory: Personal and Social", in Thomas L. Charlton, Lois E. Myers, and Rebecca Sharpless (eds.), *Handbook of Oral History*, Walnut Creek: AltaMira Press, 2006, pp. 275-296. 该书有关记忆问题的其他论述，可参见该书索引中有关记忆问题（第 612 页）的页码分布。

④ Donald A. Ritchie (ed.), *The Oxford Handbook of Oral History*, Oxford and New York: Oxford University Press, 2011, pp. 75-165. 该书有关记忆问题的其他论述，可参见该书索引中有关记忆问题（第 530 页）的页码分布。

体性、精神分析和怀旧疗法等问题。①而阿布拉姆斯于 2010 年出版的《口述史学理论》一书中也有专章"记忆"（Memory）讨论口述历史相关的记忆问题，并且从记忆理论最新进展、自传记忆、记忆与老年化、记忆与社会性别、记忆与创伤以及集体记忆等方面具体分析口述历史学界对于记忆问题的思考与应用。②

而作为美国口述史学界发表理论研究成果的重要平台，《口述历史评论》从 20 世纪 80 年代末以来就相当关注记忆问题，其探讨内容也涉及上述论及的广泛主题。③

如上所述，当代美国口述史学理论研究具有高度的跨学科性与国际性，因而作为核心的记忆问题也引起《美国历史评论》（*American*

---

① Paul Thompson, *The Voice of the Past: Oral History*, Oxford and New York: Oxford University Press, second edition, 1988, pp. 150-165; Paul Thompson, *The Voice of the Past: Oral History*, Oxford and New York: Oxford University Press, third edition, 2000, pp. 173-189. 据汤普森向笔者透露，该书第四版即将于 2017 年春季出版，感谢作者将新版前言、第三章和第五章内容提前发给笔者阅读。

② Lynn Abrams, *Oral History Theory*, London and New York: Routledge, 2010, pp. 78-105. 其相关研究可参见 Lynn Abrams, "Memory as Both Source and Subject of Study: The Transformations of Oral History", in Stefan Berger and Bill Niven (eds.), *Writing the History of Memory*, London: Bloomsbury Academic, 2014, pp. 89-134.

③ Kim Lacy Rogers, "Memory, Struggle, and Power: On Interviewing Political Activists", *Oral History Review*, Vol. 15, No. 1, 1987, pp. 165-184; William S. Schneider, "Memories of Daily Life in Reconstructing the Cultural History of Inupiat Eskimo", *Oral History Review*, Vol. 15, No. 2, 1987, pp. 64-76; Seena B. Kohl, "Memories of Homesteading and The Process of Retrospection", *Oral History Review*, Vol. 17, No. 2, 1989, pp. 25-45; Shaun S. Nethercott and Neil O. Leighton, "Memory, Process, and Performance", *Oral History Review*, Vol. 18, No. 2, 1990, pp. 37-60; Alistair Thomson, "Memory as a Battlefield: Personal and Political Investments in the National Military Past", *Oral History Review*, Vol. 22, No. 2, 1995, pp. 55-73; Michael Berenbaum, "Review Essays: When Memory Triumphs", *Oral History Review*, Vol. 22, No. 2, 1995, pp. 91-95; Valerie Grim, "History Shared Through Memory: The Establishment and Implementation of Education in the Brooks Farm Community, 1920-1957", *Oral History Review*, Vol. 23, No. 1, 1996, pp. 1-18; Tracy E. K'Meyer, "'What Koinonia was All About': The Role of Memory in a Changing Community", *Oral History Review*, Vol. 24, No. 1, 1997, pp. 1-22; Naomi Norquay, "Identity and Forgetting", *Oral History Review*, Vol. 26, No. 1, 1999, pp. 1-21; Joseph F. Spillane, "Review Essay: Myth, Memory, and the American Outlaw", *Oral History Review*, Vol. 26, No. 1, 1999, pp. 113-117; Max Paul Friedman, "Private Memory, Public Records, and Contested Terrain: Weighing Oral Testimony in the Deportation of Germans from Latin America during World War II", *Oral History Review*, Vol. 27, No. 1, 2000, pp. 1-15; Yong Chen, "Remembering Ah Quin: A Century of Social Memory in a Chinese American Family", *Oral History*

Historical Review）、《美国历史杂志》、《国际口述历史杂志》、《口述历史》
（英国）、《历史工作坊》、《记忆研究》（*Memory Studies*）与《老年化与社会》

Review, Vol. 27, No. 1, 2000, pp. 57-80; Charles T. Morrissey, "Oral History, Memory, and the Hallways of Academe: Tenure Decisions and Other Job Skirmishes", *Oral History Review*, Vol. 27, No. 1, 2000, pp. 99-116; Donna Krolik Hollenberg, "At the Western Development Museum: Ethnic Identity and the Memory of the Holocaust in the Jewish Community of Saskatoon, Saskatchewan", *Oral History Review*, Vol. 27, No. 2, 2000, pp. 85-127; Jonathan Friedman, "Togetherness and Isolation: Holocaust Survivor Memories of Intimacy and Sexuality in the Ghettos", *Oral History Review*, Vol. 28, No. 1, 2001, pp. 1-16; Kayoko Yoshida, "From Atomic Fragments to Memories of the Trinity Bomb: A Bridge of Oral History over the Pacific", *Oral History Review*, Vol. 30, No. 2, 2003, pp. 59-75; Janet A. McDonnell, "Documenting Cultural and Historical Memory: Oral History in the National Park Service", *Oral History Review*, Vol. 30, No. 2, 2003, pp. 99-109; Neal R. Norrick, "Talking about Remembering and Forgetfulness in Oral History Interviews", *Oral History Review*, Vol. 32, No. 2, 2005, pp. 1-20; Katharina Hering, " 'That Food of the Memory which Gives the Clue to Profitable Research': Oral History as A Source for Local, Regional, and Family History in the Nineteenth and Early Twentieth Century", *Oral History Review*, Vol. 34, No. 2, 2007, pp. 27-48; Keith A. Erekson, "Method and Memory in the Midwestern 'Lincoln Inquiry': Oral Testimony and Abraham Lincoln Studies, 1865-1938", *Oral History Review*, Vol. 34, No. 2, 2007, pp. 49-72; Stephen Sloan, "Oral History and Hurricane Katrina: Reflections on Shouts and Silences", *Oral History Review*, Vol. 35, No. 2, 2008, pp. 176-186; Loh Kah Seng, "History, Memory, and Identity in Modern Singapore: Testimonies from the Urban Margins", *Oral History Review*, Vol. 36, No. 1, 2009, pp. 1-24; Robert F. Jefferson, "Whose War Is It Anyway? Ken Burns' The War and American Popular Memory", *Oral History Review*, Vol. 36, No. 1, 2009, pp. 71-81; Paul Thompson, "Community and Individual Memory: An Introduction", *Oral History Review*, Vol. 36, No. 2, 2009, pp. i-v; Sally Alexander, " 'Do Grandmas Have Husbands?' Generational Memory and Twentieth-Century Women's Lives", *Oral History Review*, Vol. 36, No. 2, 2009, pp. 159-176; Mary Chamberlain, "Diasporic Memories: Community, Individuality, and Creativity-A Life Stories Perspective", *Oral History Review*, Vol. 36, No. 2, 2009, pp. 177-187; Daniela Koleva, "Daughters' Stories: Family Memory and Generational Amnesia", *Oral History Review*, Vol. 36, No. 2, 2009, pp. 188-206; Kevin Blackburn, "Recalling War Trauma of the Pacific War and the Japanese Occupation in the Oral History of Malaysia and Singapore", *Oral History Review*, Vol. 36, No. 2, 2009, pp. 231-252; Rodney Earl Walton, "Memories from the Edge of the Abyss: Evaluating the Oral Accounts of World War II Veterans", *Oral History Review*, Vol. 37, No. 1, 2010, pp. 18-34; Rina Benmayor, "Contested Memories of Place: Representations of Salinas' Chinatown", *Oral History Review*, Vol. 37, No. 2, 2010, pp. 225-234; Rina Benmayor, "Tracking Holocaust Memory: 1946-2010", *Oral History Review*, Vol. 39, No. 1, 2012, pp. 92-99; Tracy E K' Meyer, "Remembering the Past and Contesting the Future of School Desegregation in Louisville, Kentucky, 1975-2012", *Oral History Review*, Vol. 39, No. 2, 2012, pp. 230-257; Miguel Cardina, "To Talk or Not to Talk: Silence, Torture, and Politics in the Portuguese Dictatorship of Estado Novo", *Oral History Review*, Vol. 40, No. 2, 2013, pp. 251-270; Anika Walke, "Memories of an Unfulfilled Promise: Internationalism and Patriotism in Post-Soviet Oral Histories of Jewish Survivors of the Nazi Genocide", *Oral History Review*, Vol. 40, No. 2, 2013, pp. 271-298; Alistair Thomson, "Anzac Memories Revisited: Trauma, Memory and Oral History", *Oral History Review*, Vol. 42, No. 1, 2015, pp. 1-29; Bethan Coupland, "Remembering Blaenavon: What Can Group Interviews Tell Us about 'Collective Memory'?" *Oral History Review*, Vol. 42, No. 2, 2015, pp. 277-299.

（*Ageing and Society*）等众多学术杂志的关注。[①]

当然，经由口述历史访谈过程的记忆呈现终归需要通过口述、文字抄本、录音或录影等媒介形式加以表达，而对于口述历史访谈过程的叙事关注则促使美国口述史学发生同"记忆转向"紧密联系且同样重要的"叙事转向"。

二 "叙事转向"

有学者指出，20 世纪 60—70 年代以来，西方历史哲学（philosophy of history）领域发生了从分析的历史哲学向叙事主义的历史哲学的重大转型，

---

① 其中英国《口述历史》杂志对记忆问题尤其关注，众多专题涉及该问题。详细参见 *Oral History*, Vol. 17, No. 2, 1989 (Special Issue: Reminiscence); Vol. 18, No. 1, 1990 (Special Issue: Popular Memory); Vol. 19, No. 2, 1991 (Special Issue: Remembering); Vol. 23, No. 1, 1995 (Special Issue: Working with Memories); Vol. 26, No. 2, 1998 (Special Issue: Memory, Trauma and Ethics); Vol. 27, No. 2, 1999 (Special Issue: Contexts of Remembering); Vol. 28, No. 1, 2000 (Special Issue: Landscapes of Memory); Vol. 28, No. 2, 2000 (Special Issue: Memory and Place); Vol. 32, No. 2, 2004 (Special Issue: Memory and Society); Vol. 33, No. 2, 2005 (Special Issue: Memory Work); Vol. 34, No. 2, 2006 (Special Issue: War Memory)。其他代表性成果可参见 Alistair Thomson, "Anzac Memories: Putting Popular Memory Theory into Practice in Australia", *Oral History*, Vol. 18, No. 1, 1994, pp. 25-31; Alistair Thomson, Michael Frisch, and Paula Hamilton, "The Memory and History Debates: Some International Perspectives", *Oral History*, Vol. 22, No. 2, 1994, pp. 33-43; Daniel James, "Meatpackers, Peronists, and Collective Memory: A View from the South", *American Historical Review*, Vol. 102, No. 5, 1997, pp. 1404-1412; Susan A. Crane, "Writing the Individual Back into Collective Memory", *American Historical Review*, Vol. 102, No. 5, 1997, pp. 1372-1385; Alistair Thomson, "Making the Most of Memories: The Empirical and Subjective Value of Oral History", *Transactions of the Royal Historical Society*, Vol. 9, 1999, pp. 291-301; Joanna Bornat, "Reminiscence and Oral History: Parallel Universes or Shared Endeavour?" *Ageing and Society*, Vol. 21, No. 2, 2001, pp. 219-241; Mary Marshall Clark, "The September 11, 2001, Oral History Narrative and Memory Project: A First Report", *Journal of American History*, Vol. 89, No. 2, 2002, pp. 569-579; Mary Marshall Clark, "Holocaust Video Testimony, Oral History and Narrative Medicine: The Struggle Against Indifference", *Literature and Medicine*, Vol. 24, No. 2, 2005, pp. 266-282; Robert N. Kraft, "Archival Memory: Representations of the Holocaust in Oral Testimony", *Poetics Today*, Vol. 27, No. 2, 2006, pp. 311-330; *Memory Studies*, Vol. 6, No. 1, 2013 (Special Issue: Challenging Dominant Discourses of the Past: 1968 and the Value of Oral History)。

而这一转型通常被称为"叙事的转向"，因为学科背景的差异，又有学者称为"修辞的转向"（rhetoric turn）或"语言学的转向"（linguistic turn）。① 而随着叙事主义的不断发展与应用，西方学术界也逐渐发展出具有高度跨学科性与交叉性的叙事理论（narrative theory）与叙事学（narratology）。② 而在当代西方史学"叙事转向"及叙事理论和叙事学的冲击与影响下，美国口述史学界也日益意识到应该利用相关理论与方法来研究口述历史本身所具有的两种基本特质——"口述性"与"叙事性"。③ 简单而言，口述史学的"叙事转向"促使研究者超越对于口述内容的片面关注，继而关注口述历史访谈中访谈者与受访者的叙事形式、叙事策略和叙事风格如何影响口述历史内容的呈现与诠释，进而深入理解叙事背后所体现的社会文化与意识形态等因素。

---

① 参见彭刚《叙事的转向：当代西方史学理论的考察》，北京大学出版社 2009 年版，第 2 页。彭刚认为美国著名历史哲学家海登·怀特（Hayden White，1928—）是促成"叙事转向"的最关键人物，其主要理论可以参见 Hayden White, *Metahistory*: *The Historical Imagination in Nineteenth-Century Europe*, Baltimore：Johns Hopkins University Press, 1973. 其他相关研究可参见 Elizabeth A. Clark, *History*, *Theory*, *Text*: *Historians and the Linguistic Turn*, Cambridge：Harvard University Press, 2004；Geoffrey Roberts（ed.），*The History and Narrative Reader*, London and New York：Routledge, 2001.

② 国内也有学者称为"叙述学"，有关"叙事"与"叙述"两个概念之间的区别，参见申丹《也谈"叙事"还是"叙述"?》，《外国文学评论》2009 年第 3 期，第 219—229 页。有关叙事理论与叙事学的相关研究可参见 Gerald Prince, *Narratology*: *The Form and Functioning of Narrative*, Berlin：Mouton, 1982；H. Porter Abbott, *The Cambridge Introduction to Narrative*, Cambridge：Cambridge University Press, 2002；Barbara Czarniawska, *Narratives in Social Science Research*, Thousand Oaks：Sage Publications, 2004；David Herman, Manfred Jahn, and Marie-Laure Ryan（eds.），*Routledge Encyclopedia of Narrative Theory*, London and New York：Routledge, 2005；Luc Herman and Bart Vervaeck, *Handbook of Narrative Analysis*, Lincoln：University of Nebraska Press, 2005；David Herman（ed.），*The Cambridge Companion to Narrative*, Cambridge：Cambridge University Press, 2007；Monika Fludernik, *An Introduction to Narratology*, Hoboken：Taylor and Francis, 2009；Mieke Bal, *Narratology*: *Introduction to the Theory of Narrative*, Toronto：University of Toronto Press, third edition, 2009；申丹、王丽亚：《西方叙事学：经典与后经典》，北京大学出版社 2010 年版；Ivor F. Goodson, *Developing Narrative Theory*: *Life Histories and Personal Representation*, London and New York：Routledge, 2013；Peter Hühn, Jan Christoph Meister, John Pier, and Wolf Schmid（eds.），*Handbook of Narratology*, Berlin：Walter De Gruyter, second edition, 2014.

③ Alessandro Portelli, "On the Peculiarities of Oral History", *History Workshop*, No. 12, 1981, pp. 97-99.

总体而言，以档案实践与史料功能为主要导向的早期美国口述史学界倾向于将口述历史理解为以文字抄本（written transcript）为主要呈现形式的历史记录，而忽视了口述历史的原生形态——录音或录影记录（audio or video recordings）。显然，口述历史音视频记录向文字抄本的转换已经伴随众多信息与意义的丢失与变化。正如阿利桑乔·波特利所说："抄本将听觉对象（aural objects）转变为视觉对象，这不可避免地意味着改编和篡改。……更为重要的是这样一个事实，即期待抄本能够出于科学研究目的而取代录音带则相当于用复制品来从事艺术批评或用译文来从事文学批评。"① 更为重要的是，这种导向也往往过于强调作为结果与内容的口述历史，而严重限制了对于口述历史作为一个叙事、对话与解释等互动过程的思考与分析，但这个过程才真正有助于了解口述历史访谈乃至历史生产过程中所涉及的访谈者、受访者与社会环境等多元因素之间的互动关系。

在某种程度上，"叙事转向"的核心是发现了"语言"在"社会现实"（social reality）与"有关那种现实的论述"（discourse about that reality）之间的桥梁作用，即我们对于过去经历的认识与理解是依赖一定的呈现形式与表达手段。② 而作为口述历史核心的访谈者与受访者之

---

① Alessandro Portelli, "On the Peculiarities of Oral History", *History Workshop*, No. 12, 1981, p. 97. 这里波特利所谓的"视觉对象"，是指便于阅读和浏览的口述历史抄本，而不是现在意义上的口述历史录影记录，因为在 20 世纪七八十年代，口述历史访谈主要是利用录音手段。

② Ronald J. Grele, "Directions for Oral History in the United States", in David K. Dunaway and Willa K. Baum（eds.）, *Oral History: An Interdisciplinary Anthology*, Walnut Creek: AltaMira Press, second edition, 1996, p. 78. 有关访谈背景的叙事分析研究，可以参见 Elliot G. Mishler, *Research Interviewing: Context and Narrative*, Cambridge: Harvard University Press, 1986; Susan E. Chase, "Taking Narrative Seriously: Consequences for Method and Theory in Interview Studies", in Ruthellen Josselson and Amia Lieblich（eds.）, *Interpreting Experience: The Narrative Study of Lives*, Thousand Oaks: Sage Publications, 1995, pp. 1-26; Molly Andrews, Shelley Day Sclater, Corinne Squire, and Amal Treacher（eds.）, *The Uses of Narrative: Explorations in Sociology, Psychology, and Cultural Studies*, New Brunswick: Transaction Publishers, 2004; Mary Jo Maynes, Jennifer L. Pierce, and Barbara Laslett, *Telling Stories: The Use of Personal Narratives in the Social Sciences and History*, Ithaca: Cornell University Press, 2008.

间的主要基于口头语言交流的叙事与对话则直接影响受访者对于过去经历的呈现与表达，其中双方的叙事（提问）模式、叙事（提问）策略与叙事（提问）风格及互动关系都是至关重要的因素。正因如此，有学者指出，在20世纪70年代"叙事转向"和"语言转向"的影响下，口述历史学家开始关注叙事本身的多样性，而这一转向的结果之一是不仅关注讲述的故事和传达的信息，同时也关注叙述模式（mode of telling）。① 甚至，有学者认为口述历史本身就是"语言学转向"的一个有机组成部分。②

　　而在美国口述史学界，该领域的开拓者是罗纳德·格里，他于1975年就提出应该将口述历史访谈作为一种"会话叙事"（conversational narrative）来理解。格里指出，他试图以法国著名哲学家、结构主义马克思主义（structural Marxism）奠基人路易·阿尔都塞（Louis Althusser, 1918—1990）的理论为基础，通过对口述历史访谈结构的分析来理解历史文本（historical text）的语言、社会与意识形态结构，而这些结构的分析则有赖于从"会话叙事"的视角来理解口述历史访谈。③ 在他看来，"考虑到历史学家/访谈者的积极参与，即使这种参与由一系列姿势或咕哝组成，同时考虑到所有言语交际（verbal communication）所强加的逻辑形式，访谈只能被描述为一种会话叙事：因为访谈者与受访者之间的关系，我们称其为会话；而之所以称为叙事则是因为阐释（exposition，即故事讲述）形式。……不管叙事建构是什么，我们创建的结果是一种会话叙事，而它也只能通过理解包含在这种结构中的各种关系来理

---

①　Lynn Abrams, *Oral History Theory*, London and New York：Routledge, 2010, p. 109.

②　Richard Cándida Smith, "Storytelling as Experience", *Oral History Review*, Vol. 22, No. 2, 1995, p. 90.

③　Ronald J. Grele, "Oral History as Evidence", in Thomas L. Charlton, Lois E. Myers, and Rebecca Sharpless（eds.）, *Handbook of Oral History*, Walnut Creek：AltaMira Press, 2006, p. 60.

解"①。而格里认为口述历史访谈中包含三种或三组相互关联的关系结构：（1）访谈本身的语言、语法和文学结构；（2）受访者与访谈者之间的互动关系；（3）受访者与更为广泛的社会之间的关系。② 事实上，格里于1975年在英国《口述历史》杂志上发表的论文《倾听他们的声音：口述历史访谈解释中的两个个案研究》就已经实践了他的上述理念。对于他来说，感兴趣的并不是口述历史访谈的具体内容，而是不同的叙事方式所传递的受访者对于他们个人经历理解背后的社会文化与意识形态基础。③

显然，对于口述历史访谈深层次关系与结构的分析有助于理解与解释作为访谈结果的历史叙事的生产过程及其意义建构。而在罗纳德·格里的"会话叙事"理论及相关学科有关交际研究（communication studies）理论的影响下，从20世纪70年代末以来，E. 卡尔佩珀·克拉克（E. Culpepper Clark，1943—）、迈克尔·海德（Michael J. Hyde，1950—）与伊娃·麦克马汉（Eva M. McMahan）就不断提出和强调应该从交际研究理论出发来理解口述历史。他们主张将口述历史的会话叙事看成一种"诠释行为"（hermeneutic act），而诠释学才是连接交际研究理论家与历史学家的重要纽带。基于此，他们指

---

① Ronald J. Grele, "Movement Without Aim: Methodological and Theoretical Problems in Oral History", in Ronald J. Grele (ed.), *Envelopes of Sound: The Art of Oral History*, New York: Praeger Publishers, second edition, revised and enlarged, 1991, pp. 135-136.

② Ronald J. Grele, "Movement Without Aim: Methodological and Theoretical Problems in Oral History", in Ronald J. Grele (ed.), *Envelopes of Sound: The Art of Oral History*, New York: Praeger Publishers, second edition, revised and enlarged, 1991, pp. 136-143. 格里对于"会话叙事"概念的反思，可以参见 Ronald J. Grele, "Reflections on the Practice of Oral History: Retrieving What We Can from an Earlier Critique", *Suomen Antropologi: Journal of the Finnish Anthropological Society*, Vol. 32, No. 4, 2007, pp. 11-23.

③ Ronald J. Grele, "Listen to Their Voices: Two Case Studies in the Interpretation of Oral History Interviews", *Oral History*, Vol. 7, No. 1, 1975, pp. 33-42. 该文又载 Ronald J. Grele (ed.), *Envelopes of Sound: The Art of Oral History*, New York: Praeger Publishers, second edition, revised and enlarged, 1991, pp. 212-241.

出："口述历史可能因此被定义为是一个过程，其中历史学家试图通过与那些生活经历值得记忆的人们的会话来创建历史证据。而这个过程则涉及对于过去事件的理解与解释，通过这种方式能够将其意义沉淀在某一给定的时刻。……只有通过理解交际的性质以及交际变量因素对于所收集的资料的影响，历史学家才能够合适地评估他所获得的证据。诠释学范式有助于为这样的理解提供基础。"① 在他们看来，口述历史访谈的意义呈现及访谈者与受访者之间的共时关系如何影响未来的理解都将取决于双方如何能够实现"诠释性会话"（hermeneutical conversation）。而在这种会话过程中，研究者需要更深层次地理解与分析四种互相依赖的关系：（1）访谈者与受访者之间的关系；（2）访谈者与历史事件之间的关系；（3）受访者与历史事件之间的关系；（4）访谈者、受访者与历史事件三者之间的相互关系。② 需要指出的是，美国著名历史学家、人类学家查尔斯·乔伊纳（Charles W. Joyner）也早在 1979 年就提出将口述历史作为交际事件（communicative event）来理解，他则从民俗学视角建议口述历史学家应该关注访谈场景中的表演与社会语言学因素。③

随后，在 1985 年再版的《声音外壳：口述历史的艺术》一书中，罗纳德·格里进一步阐释了"叙事会话"概念，并指出它有助于我们更好地

---

① E. Culpepper Clark, Michael J. Hyde, and Eva M. McMahan, "Communication in the Oral History Interview: Investigating Problems of Interpreting Oral Data", *International Journal of Oral History*, Vol. 1. No. 1, 1980, p. 30. 该文最先于 1978 年 11 月举行的言语交际协会（Speech Communication Association）年会上宣读。

② E. Culpepper Clark, Michael J. Hyde, and Eva M. McMahan, "Communication in the Oral History Interview: Investigating Problems of Interpreting Oral Data", *International Journal of Oral History*, Vol. 1. No. 1, 1980, pp. 30-38. 他们的相关研究还可参见 E. Culpepper Clark, Michael J. Hyde, and Eva M. McMahan, "Developing Instruction in Oral History: A New Avenue for Speech Communication", *Communication Education*, Vol. 30, No. 3, 1981, pp. 238-244.

③ Charles W. Joyner, "Oral History as Communicative Event: A Folkloristic Perspective", *Oral History Review*, Vol. 7, 1979, pp. 47-52. 该文又载 Charles Joyner, "Oral History as Communicative Event", in David K. Dunaway and Willa K. Baum (eds.), *Oral History: An Interdisciplinary Anthology*, Nashville: American Association for State and Local History, 1984, pp. 300-305.

理解由访谈者与受访者共同构成的历史事件的认识、解释与意义。① 而在 1990 年首次发表的《口述历史访谈中的历史与历史语言：谁回答谁的问题和为什么？》一文中，格里更进一步探讨了作为"会话叙事"的口述历史访谈所潜藏的权力关系与政治意识形态因素。② 在其上述团队合作研究的基础上，伊娃·麦克马汉进一步将哲学、诠释学（philosophical hermeneutics）应用于口述历史访谈分析，并且提出将访谈作为一种"言语行为"（speech act）来理解，进而试图探讨这些"言语行为"所具有的特定规则与准则及背后所潜藏的社会文化与意识形态因素。③ 后来，在其主编的《互动性口述历史访谈》和撰写的《口述历史访谈的一种会话分析方法》等研究成果中，麦克马汉对上述概念与理论继续有所发展，并提出一种"会话分析框架"（conversational analytic framework），该概念主要用来理解与分析意义在口述历史访谈中被协调的具体方式。④

此外，对于美国口述史学"叙事转向"具有重要推动作用的还有迈克尔·弗里斯科，他在 1990 年出版的《一种共享的权威：口述历史与公共历史的技艺与意义》一书中就提出应该将口述历史访谈视为"互动性对话"（interactive dialogue）。⑤ 尽管他没有对该概念进行详细阐述，不过他

① Ronald J. Grele, "Private Memories and Public Presentation: The Art of Oral History", in Ronald J. Grele (ed.), *Envelopes of Sound: The Art of Oral History*, New York: Praeger Publishers, second edition, revised and enlarged, 1991, pp. 257-272.

② Ronald J. Grele, "History and the Languages of History in the Oral History Interview: Who Answers Whose Questions and Why?" Presented at the Workshop on "Structure and Experience in the Making of Apartheid", Johannesburg: University of the Witwatersrand, February 6-10, 1990. 该文后载 Eva M. McMahan and Kim Lacy Rogers (eds.), *Interactive Oral History Interviewing*, Hillsdale: L. Erlbaum Associates, 1994, pp. 1-18.

③ Eva M. McMahan, "Speech and Counterspeech: Language-in-Use in Oral History Fieldwork", *Oral History Review*, Vol. 15, No. 1, 1987, pp. 185-207; Eva M. McMahan, *Elite Oral History Discourse: A Study of Cooperation and Coherence*, Tuscaloosa: University of Alabama Press, 1989.

④ Eva M. McMahan and Kim Lacy Rogers (eds.), *Interactive Oral History Interviewing*, Hillsdale: L. Erlbaum Associates, 1994; Eva M. McMahan, "A Conversation Analytic Approach to Oral History Interviewing", in Thomas L. Charlton, Lois E. Myers, and Rebecca Sharpless (eds.), *Handbook of Oral History*, Walnut Creek: AltaMira Press, 2006, pp. 336-356.

⑤ Michael Frisch, "Introduction", in Michael Frisch, *A Shared Authority: Essays on the Craft and Meaning of Oral and Public History*, Albany: State University of New York Press, 1990, p. xix.

所强调的访谈双方的互动关系还是为众多学者所认可。[1] 而肖娜·格拉克和达芬尼·帕泰于 1991 年主编出版的《女性的话语：口述历史的女性主义实践》一书则相当强调女性独特的话语模式与语言风格对于女性口述历史访谈实践与意义诠释的重要影响，其中第一个部分就是"语言与交际"专题。[2]

需要指出的是，20 世纪 80 年代末以来，对于促进口述史学"记忆转向"起到重要作用的意大利口述历史学家路易莎·帕萨里尼和阿利桑乔·波特利也同样是"叙事转向"的重要推动者。帕萨里尼强调要从口述历史与生活故事叙事的沉默、遗忘与矛盾中理解其背后的社会心理与文化意义，而不是片面地将其解读为受访者的不善言辞。在其名著《大众记忆中的法西斯主义：都灵工人阶级的文化经历》中，她发现很多来自都灵工人阶级的受访者在口述中经常没有提及法西斯主义对于他们日常生活与工作的影响，甚至在叙事过程中直接绕过或避开整个法西斯主义统治时代。而在帕萨里尼看来，沉默可能是他们遭受深度创伤的表现或应对机制，同时也可能意味着即使在极权统治时期普通人们的专注点仍然在工作、婚姻和孩子等日常生活方面，而对法西斯主义漠不关心。[3] 而在另外一项研究中，她认为法国政府在镇压

① Sucheng Chan (ed.), *Not Just Victims: Conversations with Cambodian Community Leaders in the United States*, Urbana: University of Illinois Press, 2003, p. xv; Peter Jackson and Polly Russell, "Life History Interviewing", in Dydia DeLyser, Steve Herbert, Stuart Aitken, Mike Crang, and Linda McDowell (eds.), *The SAGE Handbook of Qualitative Geography*, Thousand Oaks: Sage Publications, 2010, p. 180.

② Sherna Berger Gluck and Daphne Patai (eds.), *Women's Words: The Feminist Practice of Oral History*, London and New York: Routledge, 1991. 关于女性语言对于访谈等质性研究的影响，其理论主要来自美国著名女性主义者、心理学家卡罗尔·吉利根 (Carol Gilligan, 1936—)和个人叙事研究团体 (Personal Narratives Group)。详细参见 Carol Gilligan, *In a Different Voice: Psychological Theory and Women's Development*, Cambridge: Harvard University Press, 1982; Personal Narratives Group (ed.), *Interpreting Women's Lives: Feminist Theory and Personal Narratives*, Bloomington: Indiana University Press, 1989.

③ Luisa Passerini, "Italian Working Class Culture Between the Wars: Consensus to Fascism and Work Ideology", *International Journal of Oral History*, Vol. 1. No. 1, 1980, pp. 4-27; Luisa Passerini, *Fascism in Popular Memory: The Cultural Experience of the Turin Working Class*, Cambridge: Cambridge University Press, 1987.

1961 年反对阿尔及利亚战争（Algerian War, 1954—1962）游行示威问题上的沉默及所刻意施加的"记忆缺失"（amnesia）也让众多目击者在该问题上保持沉默。① 同样，基于口述历史的"口述性"与"叙事性"特质，波特利也强调应该利用叙事理论来分析口述历史访谈，并将故事讲述视为一种文化实践（cultural practice）。他曾指出："我利用文学、民俗学和语言学来发展一种研究主体性的方法，主要是聚焦于叙事者所使用的言语策略（verbal strategies）的意义。……大部分口述叙事者、民间故事讲述者和工人阶级史学家都有一种在叙事形式中埋伏他们的观念的习惯，因此他们的话语充斥着不可言说、象征意义、暗示与模糊不清等可能性。"② 他继续指出："因此，口述历史资料的分析必须利用文学与民俗学中的叙事理论所发展起来的一些普遍范畴（general categories）。"③ 事实上，波特利对于叙事分析的强调与重视从《卢奇·特拉斯图利之死与其他故事：口述历史的形式与意义》一书的标题中就可以看出。简单而言，该书试图通过对口述证词中所包含的叙事形式的详细分析，进而理解人们如何表述他们的历史以及不同表述背后所反映的大众意识与社会心理。而在 1997 年出版的《瓦莱·朱利亚冲突：口述历史与对话艺术》一书中，作者更是极其关注口述历史访谈的对话性质、叙事形式与主体性等问题。④

① Luisa Passerini, "Memories between Silence and Oblivion", in Katharine Hodgkin and Susannah Radstone (eds.), *Memory, History, Nation: Contested Pasts*, New Brunswick: Transaction Publishers, 2006, pp. 238-254.

② Alessandro Portelli, "Introduction", in Alessandro Portelli, *The Death of Luigi Trastulli and Other Stories: Form and Meaning of Oral History*, Albany: State University of New York Press, 1991, p. xii.

③ Alessandro Portelli, "The Death of Luigi Trastulli: Memory and the Event", in Alessandro Portelli, *The Death of Luigi Trastulli and Other Stories: Form and Meaning of Oral History*, Albany: State University of New York Press, 1991, p. 48.

④ Alessandro Portelli, *The Battle of Valle Giulia: Oral History and The Art of Dialogue*, Madison: University of Wisconsin Press, 1997. 在该书中，波特利认为口述历史是一种对话话语（dialogic discourse），详见第 3 页。

除上述两位意大利口述历史学家之外，就国际学术界而言，在 20 世纪 90 年代，对于美国口述史学"叙述转向"产生重要影响的是伊丽莎白·托金（Elizabeth Tonkin）、玛丽·张伯伦（Mary Chamberlain, 1947—）、保罗·汤普森和林恩·阿布拉姆斯四位英国学者。在 1992 年出版的《叙述我们的过去：口述历史的社会建构》一书中，托金分析了口述历史访谈中的叙事结构、叙事时间以及叙事与社会环境之间的相互关系等问题，并强调口述叙事既是社会建构也是个体表演。① 而在由张伯伦与汤普森主编并于 1998 年首次出版的《叙事与类型》一书中，众多学者探讨了口述历史、生活故事、自传与家庭寓言中所呈现的叙事形式、叙事结构以及影响叙事结果的语言、社会与意识形态因素。② 作为当代西方口述史学理论较新研究的代表性作品，阿布拉姆斯于 2010 年出版的《口述史学理论》一书就有专章《叙事》（Narrative）讨论口述历史的叙事问题，其中包括基本的叙事概念、叙事结构分析以及影响叙事的社会性别、族裔与创伤等因素。③

相对于"记忆转向"而言，美国口述史学界并没有太多有关叙事问题的专著出版，④ 当然上述有关口述历史记忆问题的研究专著也已经相当多地涉及叙事问题。尽管如此，从 20 世纪 80 年代以来，美国《口述历史评论》对于该问题还是相当重视，在众多具体个案研究中，它们重点讨论了跨学科的叙事理论、叙事与认同建构、创伤叙事以及影响口述历史叙事的

---

① Elizabeth Tonkin, *Narrating Our Pasts: The Social Construction of Oral History*, Cambridge: Cambridge University Press, 1992.

② Mary Chamberlain and Paul Thompson (eds.), *Narrative and Genre: Contexts and Types of Communication*, London and New York: Routledge, 1998; New Brunswick: Transaction Publishers, 2004. 张伯伦有关口述历史与叙事理论问题的研究，还可参见 Mary Chamberlain, "Narrative Theory", in Thomas L. Charlton, Lois E. Myers, and Rebecca Sharpless (eds.), *Handbook of Oral History*, Walnut Creek: AltaMira Press, 2006, pp. 384-407.

③ Lynn Abrams, *Oral History Theory*, London and New York: Routledge, 2010, pp. 106-129.

④ Paul Atkinson and Sara Delamont (eds.), *Narrative Methods: Oral History and Testimony*, Thousand Oaks: Sage Publications, 2006.

社会性别、族裔与文化因素等广泛主题。①

三 "共享（的）权威"：口述历史关系反思

就口述历史关系而言，上述口述史学的"记忆转向"与"叙事转向"更多的是突显与强调受访者的主体性意识与特征。正是如此，越来越多的美国口述历史学家并不赞同和喜欢"受访者"（interviewee）或

① Michael Angrosino, "Personal Narratives and Cultural Complexity: An Oral Anthropology of Aruba, Netherlands Antilles", *Oral History Review*, Vol. 10, No. 1, 1982, pp. 93-118; Kim Lacy Rogers, "Organizational Experience and Personal Narrative: Stories of New Orleans's Civil Rights Leadership", *Oral History Review*, Vol. 13, No. 1, 1985, pp. 23-54; Alessandro Portelli, "The Best Trash-Can Wiper in Town: The Life and Times of Valtéro Peppoloni, Worker", *Oral History Review*, Vol. 16, No. 1, 1988, pp. 69-90; W. Edward Orser, "Toward a New Local History: The Possibilities and Pitfalls of Personal Narrative", *Oral History Review*, Vol. 16, No. 1, 1988, pp. 111-118; Sherna Berger Gluck, "The Voices of Palestinian Women: Oral History, Testimony, and Biographical Narrative", *Oral History Review*, Vol. 18, No. 2, 1990, pp. 115-124; Gwendolyn Etter-Lewis, "Hard Times and Strong Women: African-American Women's Oral Narratives", *Oral History Review*, Vol. 19, No. 1, 1991, pp. 89-97; Robert S. Newman, "Objectivity and Subjectivities: Oral Narratives from Cambodia, Laos, and Vietnam", *Oral History Review*, Vol. 21, No. 2, 1993, pp. 89-98; Ralph Mavis, "'Go Tell Americans...': Soldiers' Narratives and Recent Histories of the Vietnam War", *Oral History Review*, Vol. 22, No. 2, 1995, pp. 105-114; Molly Andrews, "Against Good Advice: Reflections on Conducting Research in a Country Where You Don't Speak the Language", *Oral History Review*, Vol. 22, No. 2, 1995, pp. 75-86; Alexander Freund and Laura Quilici, "Exploring Myths in Women's Narratives: Italian and German Immigrant Women in Vancouver, 1947-1961", *Oral History Review*, Vol. 23, No. 2, 1996, pp. 19-43; Roger Horowitz and Rick Halpern, "Work, Race, and Identity: Self-Representation in the Narratives of Black Packinghouse Workers", *Oral History Review*, Vol. 26, No. 1, 1999, pp. 23-43; Warren D. Anderson, "Oral History and Migrant Wage Labor: Sources of Narrative Distortion", *Oral History Review*, Vol. 28, No. 2, 2001, pp. 1-20; Marta Crivos, "Narrative and Experience: Illness in the Context of an Ethnographic Interview", *Oral History Review*, Vol. 29, No. 2, 2002, pp. 13-15; Rebecca Jones, "Blended Voices: Crafting a Narrative from Oral History Interviews", *Oral History Review*, Vol. 31, No. 1, 2004, pp. 23-42; Gloria Holguín Cuádraz, "Myths and the 'Politics of Exceptionality': Interpreting Chicana/o Narratives of Achievement", *Oral History Review*, Vol. 33, No. 1, 2006, pp. 83-105; Carolyn Lunsford Mears, "A Columbine Study: Giving Voice, Hearing Meaning", *Oral History Review*, Vol. 35, No. 2, 2008, pp. 159-175; Stephen Sloan, "Oral History and Hurricane Katrina: Reflections on Shouts and Silences", *Oral History Review*, Vol. 35, No. 2, 2008, pp. 176-186; Anna Hirsch and Claire Dixon, "Katrina Narratives: What Creative Writers Can Teach Us about Oral History", *Oral History Review*, Vol. 35, No. 2, 2008, pp. 187-195; Jelena vorovi, "Serbian Gypsy Narrative: BetweenPreferred and True Identity", *Oral History Review*, Vol. 36, No. 1, 2009, pp. 45-70; Lenore

"回应者"（respondent）等称呼，因为他们认为这些称呼本身就具有消极和被动意味，因此主张使用诸如"信息提供者"（informant）、"口述作者"（oral author）或"叙述者"（narrator）等更加具有主动性的术语。[1]

　　而另一方面，伴随着"叙事转向"所引发的对于口述历史生产过程中访谈者与受访者之间互动关系的重视与反思，访谈者的主体性与主观性也日益得到认可和正视，尤其是20世纪80年代以来女性主义理论家、后现代人类学家与质性社会学家开始不断质疑访谈者（研究者）所宣称的客观和中立角色。同样是为了记录和保存尽量客观的历史资料，在美国口述史学发展初期，众多实践者都强调访谈者应该极力保持客观与中立地位。阿兰·内文斯就是这种观点的积极倡导者，正是如此，哥伦比亚大学口述历史研究室的早期口述历史抄本将访谈者的提问删除，而当时许多自称口述历史作品的书籍也同样看不到访谈者的任何提问或信息。[2]这种对于访谈者角色的无视或忽视显然并没有理解访谈者是构成口述历史访谈必不可少的重要元素，正如唐纳德·里奇所说："口述历史访谈通常是指一位准备充分的访谈者向受访

Layman, "Reticence in Oral History Interviews", *Oral History Review*, Vol. 36, No. 2, 2009, pp. 207-230; Emilye Crosby, "White Privilege, Black Burden: Lost Opportunities and Deceptive Narratives in School Desegregation in Claiborne County, Mississippi", *Oral History Review*, Vol. 39, No. 2, 2012, pp. 258-285; Alexander Freund, "'Confessing Animals': Toward a Longue Durée History of the Oral History Interview", *Oral History Review*, Vol. 41, No. 1, 2014, pp. 1-26; Henry Greenspan, "The Unsaid, the Incommunicable, the Unbearable, and the Irretrievable", *Oral History Review*, Vol. 41, No. 2, 2014, pp. 229-243; Paul Ortiz, "Tearing Up the Master's Narrative: Stetson Kennedy and Oral History", *Oral History Review*, Vol. 41, No. 2, 2014, pp. 279-289; Jeff Friedman, "Oral History, Hermeneutics, and Embodiment", *Oral History Review*, Vol. 41, No. 2, 2014, pp. 290-300; Kim Lacy Rogers, "Being Peace and Practicing Peace: New Mexico Buddhists and the Peace Within", *Oral History Review*, Vol. 41, No. 2, 2014, pp. 301-313; Jennifer Helgren, "A 'Very Innocent Time': Oral History Narratives, Nostalgia and Girls' Safety in the 1950s and 1960s", *Oral History Review*, Vol. 42, No. 1, 2015, pp. 50-69.

[1] Valerie Raleigh Yow, *Recording Oral History: A Guide for the Humanities and Social Sciences*, Walnut Creek: AltaMira Press, second edition, 2005, p. 157; Mary Kay Quinlan, "The Dynamics of Interviewing", in Donald A. Ritchie (ed.), *The Oxford Handbook of Oral History*, Oxford and New York: Oxford University Press, 2011, pp. 26.

[3] Donald A. Ritchie, *Doing Oral History: A Practical Guide*, Oxford and New York: Oxford University Press, second edition, 2003, p. 28.

者提出问题，并且以录音或录影的形式记录下他们之间的交流。……口述历史不包括随意的录音……也不是指演讲录音、窃听、个人日记录音或其他不是经由访谈者与受访者对话而产生的声音记录（sound recordings）。"①

此外，也有学者强调访谈者的介入是区别口述历史访谈与自传的重要特征之一②，尽管很多口述历史访谈以自传形式加以呈现或出版。而且，具体访谈实践也足以证明访谈者在口述历史生产过程中的至关重要性，因为访谈者的提问（回应）内容、方式与能力直接影响乃至决定受访者的口述结果，而且在后续的转录、编辑、整理、解释、出版与利用方面，一般兼具研究者角色的访谈者更加具有主动权。

当然，对于作为访谈者与研究者的口述史学家主体性意识的强调并不意味着盲目肯定和发挥，在上述所说的后实证主义的冲击与抨击下，美国口述史学家也开始反思自己的性别、阶级、族裔、宗教信仰、职业身份与教育水平等一系列身份和文化因素如何影响口述历史的生产过程与结果及对于它们的解释与分析。其中，美国著名独立口述史学家瓦拉利·姚就倡导一种相对于我们自己主体性的客观关系，并且提出一些相当实用的问题来帮助实践者发展一种能够改善访谈和解释的自我反思意识。这些问题包括：（1）我如何看待叙述者？（2）渗透在人与人之间的关系中的相似性与差异性？（3）我自己的意识形态如何影响访谈过程？在这个过程之外，我认同什么群体？（4）为什么我首先做这个计划？（5）在选择主题和问题时，我还可能采取其他什么方法？而我为什么又没有选择呢？（6）是不是存在其他可能性？为什么我拒绝它们？（7）当我从事这项研究时，对我造成什么影响？而我的反应又如何渗透到研究中？③

---

① Donald A. Ritchie, *Doing Oral History*：*A Practical Guide*, Oxford and New York：Oxford University Press, second edition, 2003, p. 19.

② Lynn Abrams, *Oral History Theory*, London and New York：Routledge, 2010, pp. 26-27.

③ Valerie Yow, " 'Do I Like Them Too Much?' Effects of the Oral History Interview on the Interviewer and Vice-Versa", *Oral History Review*, Vol. 24, No. 1, 1997, p. 79；Alistair Thomson, "Four Paradigm Transformations in Oral History", *Oral History Review*, Vol. 34, No. 1, 2007, pp. 61-62. 在其最新版的口述历史实践指南中，瓦拉利·姚详细分析了访谈中的人际关系（interpersonal relations）。详细参见 Valerie Raleigh Yow, *Recording Oral History*：*A Guide for the Humanities and Social Sciences*, Lanham：Rowman and Littlefield, third edition, 2015, pp. 185-214.

需要指出的是，上述受访者与访谈者主体性意识与特征的呈现与发挥并不是毫无限制的，它们受制于双方所共存的互动关系及所处的时代背景与社会环境。20 世纪 70 年代以来，在抛弃纯粹的实证主义与完全的客观主义之后，美国口述史学界基本上认可和赞同口述历史是访谈双方互动对话、意义诠释乃至相互妥协的竞争性合作结果。而为了理解与分析该结果的产生过程及影响因素，在上述叙事分析理论的基础上，迈克尔·弗里斯科所发明和阐述的"共享的权威"（shared authority）这个概念广受学界认可与引用。按照弗里斯科的设想，最佳的口述历史访谈是一种动态的和对话的关系，它鼓励访谈双方在相互平等且又认同差异的基础之上进行更为积极的会话叙事与意义诠释，即充分呈现与展示各自所拥有的叙述与解释权威。① 当然，正如有些学者所指出的，在实践过程中不仅很难维持一种"共享的权威"，而且弗里斯科也没有具体阐明如何在访谈过程中真正实现共享。②

不过，这个概念却成为美国众多口述历史学家的重要分析手段，并且其意义也逐渐演变为更具过程导向的"共享权威"（sharing authority），即通过考察与分析那些影响口述历史访谈过程与造成历史解释差异的特定因

① Michael Frisch, *A Shared Authority*: *Essays on the Craft and Meaning of Oral History and Public History*, Albany: State University of New York Press, 1990.

② Alistair Thomson, "Fifty Years On: An International Perspective on Oral History", *Journal of American History*, Vol. 85, No. 2, 1998, p. 591; Ronald J. Grele, "Oral History as Evidence", in Thomas L. Charlton, Lois E. Myers, and Rebecca Sharpless (eds.), *Handbook of Oral History*, Walnut Creek: AltaMira Press, 2006, p. 75. 《口述历史评论》曾刊登《特辑：共享的权威》（"Special Feature: Shared Authority", *Oral History Review*, Vol. 30, No. 1, 2003, pp. 23-114）讨论该概念及其演变。详细参见 Alistair Thomson, "Introduction: Sharing Authority: Oral History and the Collaborative Process", pp. 23-26; Daniel Kerr, "'We Know What the Problem Is': Using Oral History to Develop a Collaborative Analysis of Homelessness from the Bottom Up", pp. 27-46; Wendy Rickard, "Collaborating With Sex Workers in Oral History", pp. 47-60; Alicia J. Rouverol, "Collaborative Oral History in a Correctional Setting: Promise and Pitfalls", pp. 61-86; Lorraine Sitzia, "A Shared Authority: An Impossible Goal?" pp. 87-102; Linda Shopes, "Commentary: Sharing Authority", pp. 103-110; Michael Frisch, "Commentary: Sharing Authority: Oral History and the Collaborative Process", pp. 111-114. 此外还可参见 Michael Frisch, "From *A Shared Authority* to the Digital Kitchen, and Back", in Bill Adair, Benjamin Filene, and Laura Koloski (eds.), *Letting Go*?: *Sharing Historical Authority in a User-Generated World*, Walnut Creek: Left Coast Press, 2011, pp. 126-137.

素，进而争取各自在口述历史生产过程中的话语权与解释权。这个概念主要被用来发现、分析，以及合理化口述历史过程中经常出现的两个问题：受访者的表演性（performance）与访谈双方的解释冲突（interpretive conflict）。受访者的表演特征一方面反映在叙事风格与特征（包括语言与非语言信息）上，而更为重要的是体现在受访者叙事内容的高度预演性，而这些有意或无意的表演都是其生活经历与身份认同的重要表征。[①] 而所谓的解释冲突是指受访者与访谈者对于口述内容的解释分歧，在实际过程中，因为受访者处于相对劣势（包括信息不平等）的位置，作为访谈者的研究者通常更加容易控制与决定最终的解释权。正如美国女性口述历史研究者凯瑟琳·博兰德（Katherine Borland）在其经典论文《"那不是我说的"：口述叙事研究中的解释冲突》中所指出的，如果她没有将其著作送给她的祖母或询问她的看法的话，她可能已经忽视了自己对于文本的过分介入问题。而其感叹是源于她对其祖母口述历史的当代女性主义解读并没有得到祖母的认可，正因如此，祖母说这已经不再是她的故事，而已经完全变成

---

① 《口述历史评论》曾刊登《口述历史剧场与表演》（"Oral History Theatre and Performance"，*Oral History Review*，Vol. 18，No. 2，1990，pp. 1-108）专题文章，详细参见 Della Pollock，"Telling the Told：Performing Like a Family"，pp. 1-36；Shaun S. Nethercott and Neil O. Leighton，"Memory，Process，and Performance"，pp. 37-60；Chris Howard Bailey，"Precious Blood：Encountering Inter-Ethnic Issues in Oral History Research，Reconstruction，and Representation"，pp. 61-108. 其他相关研究可参见 Della Pollock（ed.），*Remembering：Oral History Performance*，New York：Palgrave Macmillan，2005；Jeff Friedman，"Fractious Action：Oral History-Based Performance"，in Thomas L. Charlton，Lois E. Myers，and Rebecca Sharpless（eds.），*Handbook of Oral History*，Walnut Creek：AltaMira Press，2006，pp. 465-509；Della Pollock，"Oral History"，in Shannon Rose Riley and Lynette Hunter（eds.），*Mapping Landscapes for Performance as Research：Scholarly Acts and Creative Cartographies*，New York：Palgrave Macmillan，2009，pp. 145-148；Lara D. Nielsen，"Oral History Project：Practice-Based Research in Theatre and Performance"，in Shannon Rose Riley and Lynette Hunter（eds.），*Mapping Landscapes for Performance as Research：Scholarly Acts and Creative Cartographies*，New York：Palgrave Macmillan，2009，pp. 164-170；Lynn Abrams，"Performance"，in Lynn Abrams，*Oral History Theory*，London and New York：Routledge，2010，pp. 130-152；Steven High，Edward Little，and Thi Ry Duong（eds.），*Remembering Mass Violence：Oral History*，*New Media and Performance*，Toronto：University of Toronto Press，2014；Jeff Friedman，"Minding the Gap：The Choreographer as Hyper-Historian in Oral History-Based Performance"，in David Dean，Yana Meerzon，and Kathryn Prince（eds.），*History*，*Memory*，*Performance*，New York：Palgrave Macmillan，2015，pp. 53-67.

你自己的故事。[1]

概括而言，以"共享的权威"或"共享权威"等概念为代表的对于口述历史关系的探讨不仅有助于发现与挖掘访谈者与受访者的创新性角色与主体性意识，同时也有助于反思那些影响访谈关系与造成解释冲突的更为深层次的自我、社会、政治与文化等多元因素。事实上，上述以"记忆转向"与"叙事转向"为主要表现形式的美国口述史学的理论转向与研究很大程度上也是基于对口述历史生产过程的深度描述与全面反思。[2]

毫无疑问，对于口述历史中的记忆、叙事与关系等问题的深度理论研究不仅有助于理解作为独特类型的口述历史的生成过程与影响机制，而且从现实角度而言，也有助于提升实践者与研究者学术专业水平的认可度。不过，也有一些口述历史学家提出要警惕口述史学研究中的理论过度（surfeit of theory）问题，这与早期美国口述史学发展的理论稀缺状况形成

---

[1]　Katherine Borland, "'That's Not What I Said': Interpretive Conflict in Oral Narrative Research", in Sherna Berger Gluck and Daphne Patai (eds.), *Women's Words: The Feminist Practice of Oral History*, London and New York: Routledge, 1991, pp. 63-75. 相关研究还可参见 Joanna Bornat, "Two Oral Histories: Valuing Our Differences", *Oral History Review*, Vol. 21, No. 1, 1993, pp. 73-95; Tracy E. K'Meyer and A. Glenn Crothers, "'If I See Some of This in Writing, I'm Going to Shoot You': Reluctant Narrators, Taboo Topics, and the Ethical Dilemmas of the Oral Historian", *Oral History Review*, Vol. 34, No. 1, 2007, pp. 71-93; Anna Sheftel and Stacey Zembrzycki, "Only Human: A Reflection on the Ethical and Methodological Challenges of Working with 'Difficult' Stories", *Oral History Review*, Vol. 37, No. 2, 2010, pp. 191-214.

[2]　当然，对于口述历史（访谈）关系的反思也是美国口述史学界的重要研究内容。代表性成果可参见 Charles T. Morrissey, "The Two-Sentence Format as an Interviewing Technique in Oral History Fieldwork", *Oral History Review*, Vol. 15, No. 1, 1987, pp. 43-53; Michael Kenny, "The Patron-Client Relationship in Interviewing: An Anthropological View", *Oral History Review*, Vol. 15, No. 1, 1987, pp. 71-79; Valerie Yow, "Ethics and Interpersonal Relationships in Oral History Research", *Oral History Review*, Vol. 22, No. 1, 1995, pp. 51-66; Kathleen M. Ryan, "'I Didn't Do Anything Important': A Pragmatist Analysis of the Oral History Interview", *Oral History Review*, Vol. 36, No. 1, 2009, pp. 25-44; Erin McCarthy, "'Is Oral History Good for You?' Taking Oral History beyond Documentation and into a Clinical Setting: First Steps", *Oral History Review*, Vol. 37, No. 2, 2010, pp. 159-169; William Schneider, "Interviewing in Cross-Cultural Settings", in Donald A. Ritchie (ed.), *The Oxford Handbook of Oral History*, Oxford and New York: Oxford University Press, 2011, pp. 51-64; Christine Reiser Robbins and Mark W. Robbins, "Spatial Relations in Oral History: The Robstown Migrant Labor Camp beyond the Federal Period", *Oral History Review*, Vol. 42, No. 2, 2015, pp. 255-276.

鲜明对比。[1] 在对路易莎·帕萨里尼的《大众记忆中的法西斯主义：都灵工人阶级的文化经历》一书的评论中，美国口述历史协会前主席（1996—1997 年度）理查德·史密斯（Richard Cándida Smith）就曾指出，在将口述历史访谈视为一种融合主体性（主观性）与叙事模式的文化形式（cultural form）之外，更需要思考口述历史如何作为证据（evidence）来体现与诠释文化与政治行动之间的交互作用。[2] 而迈克尔·弗里斯科也认为有关主体性（主观性）和叙事的理论争论有时候已经代替"真实文化与生活"的联系，并且警告用理论（theory）侵吞经历（experience）的危险，而是应该利用理论来理解经历与促进变革。[3] 简而言之，大部分口述历史工作者还是相当强调证据价值（evidentiary value）仍然是口述史学发展的首要目标，而数字化革命则进一步推动和促进了美国口述历史的数字化记录、后续管理与开发利用。

---

[1] Linda Shopes, " 'Insights and Oversights': Reflections on the Documentary Tradition and the Theoretical Turn in Oral History", *Oral History Review*, Vol. 41, No. 2, 2014, p. 264.

[2] Richard Cándida Smith, "Popular Memory and Oral Narratives: Luisa Passerini's Reading of Oral History Interviews", *Oral History Review*, Vol. 16, No. 2, 1988, p. 106; Ronald J. Grele, "Oral History as Evidence", in Thomas L. Charlton, Lois E. Myers, and Rebecca Sharpless (eds.), *Handbook of Oral History*, Walnut Creek: AltaMira Press, 2006, p. 65. 史密斯还于 2001—2012 年期间担任加州大学伯克利分校地区口述历史办公室主任，他的口述历史研究成果包括 Richard Cándida Smith, "Exquisite Corpse: The Sense of the Past in Oral Histories with California Artists", *Oral History Review*, Vol. 17, No. 1, 1989, pp. 1-38; Richard Cándida Smith, "Modern Art and Oral History in the United States: A Revolution Remembered", *Journal of American History*, Vol. 78, No. 2, 1991, pp. 598-606; Richard Cándida Smith, "Analytic Strategies for Oral History Interviews", in Jaber F. Gubrium and James A. Holstein (eds.), *Handbook of Interview Research*, Thousand Oaks: Sage Publications, 2001, pp. 711-732; Richard Cándida Smith, "Publishing Oral History: Oral Exchange and Print Culture", in Thomas L. Charlton, Lois E. Myers, and Rebecca Sharpless (eds.), *Handbook of Oral History*, Walnut Creek: AltaMira Press, 2006, pp. 411-424; Richard Cándida Smith, "Case Study: What Is It That University-Based Oral History Can Do? The Berkeley Experience", in Donald A. Ritchie (ed.), *The Oxford Handbook of Oral History*, Oxford and New York: Oxford University Press, 2011, pp. 417-428.

[3] 转引自 Alistair Thomson, "Fifty Years On: An International Perspective on Oral History", *Journal of American History*, Vol. 85, No. 2, 1998, p. 587.

第六章　数字化革命与美国口述史学

作为一种实践性和操作性很强的研究领域与方法，美国口述史学的兴起与发展与现代技术的发明、创新与应用有着非常深远和紧密的联系。阿兰·内文斯直言美国口述史学诞生于现代发明与技术（modern invention and technology），[①] 在 20 世纪 50 年代初，他就曾指出，电话、汽车和飞机等现代通讯与交通技术的发展使得人们之间的相互接触变得更加容易，它们将逐渐取代旧有的秘密信件来往，而可能使将来的历史学家失去不可估量的宝贵原始资料。正是如此，内文斯认为，随着手写记录（holographic document）的进一步衰退，口述历史在弥补传统文献资料的不足方面将大有可为。[②]

另一方面，美国口述史学的发展很大程度上又得益于现代技术手段的革新与应用，录音机、录像机（摄影机、摄像机）、记录介质（recording media）、转录器（transcriber）、文字处理机（word processor）、计算机、互联网以及相关的信息管理技术（信息存储、编目、索引、检索与访问）的发明与普及性应用都极大地提升了口述历史学家的工作效率与社会影响

[①]　Allan Nevins, "Oral History: How and Why It Was Born", *Wilson Library Bulletin*, Vol. 40, 1966, p. 600.

[②]　Louis Starr, "Oral History", *Encyclopedia of Library and Information Sciences* (Vol. 20), New York: Marcel Dekker, 1977, pp. 441-442; Herbert H. Hoover, "Oral History in the United States", in Michael Kammen (ed.), *The Past Before Us: Contemporary Historical Writing in the United States*, Ithaca: Cornell University Press, 1980, p. 392.

力。① 在 20 世纪 70 年代，路易斯·斯塔尔就曾强调，口述历史运动可以被看成一种利用技术（不仅仅包括录音机，而且也包括缩微、计算机及这个时代的其他技术手段）的有意识的努力，进而抗衡内文斯所哀叹的技术侵袭。② 而 20 世纪 90 年代以来以个人电脑、智能手机与互联网（包括电子邮件、网站、网络视频会议系统、网络摄像机、网络社交媒体与网络应用程序等）等计算机、网络通信、信息管理及多媒体技术为代表的数字化革命（digital revolution）则给美国口述史学发展带来前所未有的机遇与挑战。③

---

① 有关数字化时代的历史写作、研究与教学，可参阅 Dennis A. Trinkle and Scott A. Merriman (eds.), *The History Highway：A Guide to Internet Resources*, Armonk：M. E. Sharpe, 1997；Dennis A. Trinkle and Scott A. Merriman (eds.), *The History Highway 2000：A Guide to Internet Resources*, Armonk：M. E. Sharpe, 2000；Dennis A. Trinkle and Scott A. Merriman(eds.), *The History Highway 3.0：A Guide to Internet Resources*, Armonk：M. E. Sharpe, 2002；D. Antonio Cantu and Wilson J. Warren, *Teaching History in the Digital Classroom*, Armonk：M. E. Sharpe, 2003；Dennis A. Trinkle and Scott A. Merriman (eds.), *The History Highway：A 21st Century Guide to Internet Resources*, Armonk：M. E. Sharpe, 2006；Daniel J. Cohen and Roy Rosenzweig, *Digital History：A Guide to Gathering, Preserving and Presenting the Past on the Web*, Philadelphia：University of Pennsylvania Press, 2006；Michael J. Galgano, J. Chris Arndt, and Raymond M. Hyser, *Doing History：Research and Writing in the Digital Age*, Boston：Thomson Wadsworth, 2008 and 2013；Roy Rosenzweig, *Clio Wired：The Future of the Past in the Digital Age*, New York：Columbia University Press, 2011；项洁编《数位人文在历史学研究的应用》，台湾大学出版中心 2011 年版；Toni Weller(ed.), *History in the Digital Age*, London and New York：Routledge, 2013；T. Mills Kelly, *Teaching History in the Digital Age*, Ann Arbor：The University of Michigan Press, 2013；Jack Dougherty and Kristen Nawrotzki(eds.), *Writing History in the Digital Age*, Ann Arbor：The University of Michigan Press, 2013；Terry Haydn(ed.), *Using New Technologies to Enhance Teaching and Learning in History*, London and New York：Routledge, 2013.

② Louis Starr, "Oral History", *Encyclopedia of Library and Information Sciences* (Vol. 20), New York：Marcel Dekker, 1977, p. 442.

③ 所谓"数字化"（digital）是指借助计算机技术将语言、文字、声音、图像、影像和动画等转换为数字形式进行信息交流的过程。它是一种以二进制代码"0"和"1"为载体，以网络技术为基础，通过计算机的自动符号处理来实现信息交流的方式。而数字化革命则是指 20 世纪 50 年代后期开始的在计算和通信技术领域所发生的从传统的模拟、机械和电子式技术（analog, mechanical and electronic technology）向数字化技术（digital technology）的转变过程及由此带来的深刻变革。这些概念界定参考自闵大洪《数字化时代与数字化传媒》，《新闻实践》2011 年第 11 期，第 37 页；郑保卫、樊亚平、王静、张薇薇、郭平《数字化技术与传媒的数字化革命》，《国际新闻界》2007 年第 11 期，第 5 页；"Digital Revolution", from Wikipedia, http：//en. wikipedia. org/wiki/Digital_ Revolution, 2014 年 4 月 28 日访问。而近年来，随着"大数据"（big data）概念的兴起及实际应用的扩展，又有人惊呼"大数据时代"（the age of big data）的到来。相关研究可参阅 Viktor Mayer-Schönberger and Kenneth Cukier, *Big Data：A Revolution that Will Transform How We live, Work, and Think*, Boston：Houghton Mifflin Harcourt, 2013；涂子沛《大数据：数据革命如何改变政府、商业与我们的生活》，香港中和出版有限公司 2013 年版。

在 21 世纪到来之际，美国《口述历史评论》就组织了一场有关新世纪口述史学发展趋势的圆桌讨论，其中一个最主要的问题就是数字化技术对于口述史学未来发展的影响。①

对于数字化革命给口述史学发展所带来的直接好处与潜在希望，大部分口述史学家都兴奋不已。布雷特·艾农（Bret Eynon）在上述圆桌讨论中就指出，我们日益提高的对信息进行数字化处理、控制及传播的能力将会影响新世纪口述史学发展的许多方面，其中包括改善口述历史馆藏的可访问性（accessibility）、可用性（usability）和透明性（transparency）；转变口述历史在教学与学习过程中的应用方式；促使我们回到口述性（orality）及回到包括讲述和倾听（speaking and listening）在内的作为过程的口述历史的基本核心问题。② 而阿利斯泰尔·汤姆森则进一步强调："数字化技术正在改变我们作为口述历史学家的工作的许多面向，包括人们回忆与叙述他们生活的方式，而且随着时间的变迁，它们将改变我们思考记忆与个人叙述、讲述与搜集生活故事、共享记忆与创作历史的方式。……口述史学的将来以及口述历史学家的角色从来都没有如此兴奋，或者如此不确定。"③

但是，对于口述历史学家来说，新技术并不是万能药，许多与技术本身直接相关的挑战仍然存在，而且许多新问题也将不断涌现。艾农继续指出，不管技术如何发展，人的因素（human element）对于我们这个领域的未来来说仍然是至关重要的。技术的影响及口述史学在 21 世纪的活力与方向将取决于我们。① 甚至有学者质疑是不是存在一种由技术所定义的口述史学发展模式，罗纳德·格里认为，"恐怕不是技术定义我们的实践，而是

---

① Sherna Berger Gluck, Donald A. Ritchie, and Bret Eynon, "Reflections on Oral History in the New Millennium: Roundtable Comments", *Oral History Review*, Vol. 26, No. 2, 1999, pp. 1-27.

② Sherna Berger Gluck, Donald A. Ritchie, and Bret Eynon, "Reflections on Oral History in the New Millennium: Roundtable Comments", *Oral History Review*, Vol. 26, No. 2, 1999, p. 17. 迈克尔·弗里斯科也持有类似看法，详细内容参阅 Michael Frisch, "Oral History and the Digital Revolution: Toward a Post-Documentary Sensibility", in Robert Perks and Alistair Thomson (eds.), *The Oral History Reader*, London and New York: Routledge, second edition, 2006, pp. 102-114.

③ Alistair Thomson, "Four Paradigm Transformations in Oral History", *Oral History Review*, Vol. 34, No. 1, 2007, p. 70.

历史编纂学（historiography）。如果我们的确正在进入一种新的转变，那它也应该是一个由全球化问题所定义的转变……数字化世界开始了许多新的可能性，但是真正的问题仍然是历史中的人的问题"[2]。

数字化技术不管存在或带来哪些问题与挑战，可是它已经成为过去20年来美国口述历史学界实践与理论思考的一个热点问题，众多口述历史学家都宣称我们正在快速步入新的数字化时代（new digital era）或飞跃进入新的数字化信息技术世界（new world of digital information technology）。[3]而除了相对零散地探讨该主题的单篇论文或著作中的某些篇章及学术研讨会之外，[4]

---

① Sherna Berger Gluck, Donald A. Ritchie, and Bret Eynon, "Reflections on Oral History in the New Millennium: Roundtable Comments", *Oral History Review*, Vol. 26, No. 2, 1999, p. 25.

② Ronald J. Grele, "Commentary on Alistair Thomson's Essay, 'Four Paradigms Transformations in Oral History'", *Oral History Review*, Vol. 34, No. 2, 2007, p. 123.

③ Donald A. Ritchie, *Doing Oral History: A Practical Guide*, Oxford and New York: Oxford University Press, second edition, 2003, p. 11; Donald A. Ritchie, "At the Crossroads: Oral History in the 21st Century", *Oral History Association Newsletter*, Vol. 35, No. 1, Winter 2001, p. 3.

④ 相关研究可参阅 David H. Mould, "Digital Archive Storage for Oral History", *International Journal of Oral History*, Vol. 10, No. 1, 1989, pp. 59-63; Marjorie L. McLellan, "Oral History in the Classroom and on the World Wide Web", *Oral History Association Newsletter*, Vol. 31, No. 3, Fall 1997, p. 9; Sherna Berger Gluck, "Opportunity or Burden? Oral History, the Digital Revolution and Cyberspace", *Oral History Association Newsletter*, Vol. 32, No. 1, Winter 1998, p. 12; Mary Larson, "Beyond the Page: Nonprint Oral History Resources for Educators", *Oral History Review*, Vol. 25, No. 1-2, 1998, pp. 129-135; Mary A. Larson, "Potential, Potential, Potential: The Marriage of Oral History and the World Wide Web", *Journal of American History*, Vol. 88, No. 2, 2001, pp. 596-603; T. Fogg, "Using New Computer Technologies for Oral History Interviews and Archival Research", *American Educational History Journal*, Vol. 28, 2001, pp. 135-141; Donald A. Ritchie, *Doing Oral History: A Practical Guide*, Oxford and New York: Oxford University Press, second edition, 2003, pp. 79-84, 171-179 and 245-251; Ellen D. Swain, "Oral History in the Archives: Its Documentary Role in the Twenty-First Century", *American Archivist*, Vol. 66, No. 1, 2003, pp. 139-158; Michael Frisch, "Oral History and the Digital Revolution: Toward a Post-Documentary Sensibility", in Robert Perks and Alistair Thomson (eds.), *The Oral History Reader*, London and New York: Routledge, second edition, 2006, pp. 102-114; Howard Levin, "Authentic Doing: Student-Produced Web-Based Digital Video Oral Histories", *Oral History Review*, Vol. 38, No. 1, 2011, pp. 6-33; Ken Woodard, "The Digital Revolution and Pre-Collegiate Oral History: Meditations on the Challenge of Teaching Oral History in the Digital Age", *Oral History Review*, Vol. 40, No. 2, 2013, pp. 325-331. 值得一提的是，唐纳德·里奇主编的《牛津口述史学手册》的第四部分"技术影响"与第六部分"口述历史的呈现"都侧重于讨论数字化技术对于口述史学的影响，足见该主题在当代口述史学界的重要性。详细内容（具体章节信息不再罗列）参阅 Donald A. Ritchie (ed.), *The Oxford Handbook of Oral History*, Oxford and New York: Oxford University Press, 2011, pp. 6-11, 266-348, 427-516. 另外，2008 年美国口述历史协会年会主题就是"数字化时代的口述历史"（Oral History in the Digital Age），会议议程可访问 http://www.oralhistory.org/wp-content/uploads/2008/11/2008final program. pdf, 2014 年 4 月 28 日访问。

最能体现美国口述历史学界在该领域所做的努力就是 2010 年启动并于 2012 年上线的"数字化时代的口述历史"（Oral History in the Digital Age，简称"OHDA"）网站及 2013 年出版的美国《口述历史评论》特刊《数字化时代的口述历史》（Oral History in the Digital Age）和 2014 年出版的口述历史专著《口述历史与数字人文科学》。[①]

概括而言，数字化革命对于口述史学的影响是全方位的，[②] 它不仅极大地促进了更为广泛而深入的国际交流，更为重要的是，它也改变着记录、保存、编目、索引、检索、解释、分享与呈现口述历史的方式与内容，这些都将严重挑战以书写抄本（written transcript）为基础的美国口述史学的传统模式。本章将从数字化记录、数字化管理及数字化传播与交流等三个方面来分别阐述数字化革命与美国口述史学之间的紧密关系。

---

① 该网站网址为 http：//ohda. matrix. msu. edu/，2014 年 4 月 28 日访问。《数字化时代的口述历史》特刊请参阅 *Oral History Review*，Vol. 40，No. 1，2013. 有关《口述历史与数字人文科学》的详细内容可参阅 Douglas A. Boyd and Mary A. Larson（eds.），*Oral History and Digital Humanities*：*Voice*，*Access*，*and Engagement*，New York：Palgrave Macmillan，2014.

② Sarah McLennan，"How Digital Technology Has Changed Oral History"，March 21，2013，具体内容访问 http：//at. blogs. wm. edu/how – digital – technology – has – changed – oral – history/，2014 年 4 月 28 日访问；Clifford Kuhn，"The Digitization and Democratization of Oral History"，*Perspectives on History*，November 2013；Michael Frisch，"Oral History in the Digital Age"，Keynote Address at the Conference of Australian Generations：Researching 20th Century Lives and Memories（Melbourne：State Library of Victoria，October 30，2014）；Caitlin Haynes，"A Whole New World：Oral Histories in the Digital Age"，April 6，2015，具体内容访问 http：//www. dighist. org/2015/04/a – whole – new – world – oral – histories – in – the – digital – age/，2015 年 4 月 21 日访问。甚至有学者认为，在数字化时代，有关口述历史收集、管理与应用的几乎每个传统假设都在崩塌。详细内容参阅 Michael Frisch and Douglas Lambert，"Mapping Approaches to Oral History Content Management in the Digital Age"，in Doug Boyd，Steve Cohen，Brad Rakerd，and Dean Rehberger（eds.），*Oral History in the Digital Age*，Washington：Institute of Museum and Library Services，2012，http：//ohda. matrix. msu. edu/2012/07/mapping/，2014 年 4 月 28 日访问；John A. Neuenschwander，*A Guide to Oral History and the Law*，Oxford and New York：Oxford University Press，second edition，2014，p. 91.

一 数字化记录

作为口述历史计划完整过程的一个最为重要的核心环节，口述历史访谈过程的适当记录是保证和实现口述历史资料后续处理及有效性应用的重要因素。正是如此，在过去60多年间，美国口述历史工作者总是紧随记录技术（recording technology）的发展潮流，进而选择那些便利且经济实用的高质量记录设备和技术手段。唐纳德·里奇强调指出："记录设备的进步使得所有这些发展成为可能。……那些未能跟上技术发展的（口述历史）计划将很快过时，而且限制了它们的收藏的有用性。而其他计划则能与时俱进，它们善于抓住新的机遇以不久前还无法想象的方式来执行和传播访谈。"[①]

从1857年法国发明家斯科特（Édouard-Léon Scott de Martinville）发明声波记振仪（phonautograph）开始，记录（录音与录影）技术取得重大进展，而从20世纪70年代开始日益发展的模拟记录（analog recording）向数字记录（digital recording）的转变更被认为是人类记录技术史上的数字化革命。[②] 所谓模拟记录是指用来记录模拟信号（analog signals）的技术，这些信号包括用于后来回放（later playback）的音频（audio frequency）、模拟音频（analog audio）及模拟视频信息。模拟记录技术是将信号作为一种连续波（continual wave）储存在一定介质上，这种连续波可以作为一种物理结构（physical texture）储存在留声机唱片

---

① Donald A. Ritchie, "Introduction: The Evolution of Oral History", in Donald A. Ritchie (ed.), *The Oxford Handbook of Oral History*, Oxford and New York: Oxford University Press, 2011, p. 6.

② "History of Sound Recording", from Wikipedia, http://en. wikipedia. org/wiki/History_ of _ sound_ recording, 2014 年 4 月 28 日访问。

（phonograph record）上，或者作为一种波动（fluctuation）储存在磁记录（magnetic recording）的磁场强度中。而在数字记录中，数字音频（digital audio）和数字视频（digital video）是作为一连串离散数字（discrete numbers）被直接记录在存储设备上，并且用气压（气流声）变化来代表音频，而用随着时间变化的色度和亮度值（chroma and luminance value）来代表视频，因此为原始的声音或动态影像生成一个抽象模板（abstract template）。[1] 这种记录技术的数字化革命对于口述历史访谈记录手段的应用带来了相当重要的影响，它为口述历史学家的录音与录影访谈提供了日益优良、便利、经济与高效的多元化选择。正如唐纳德·里奇所说："自从第一套记录设备问世以来，由蜡筒式留声机（wax cylinder recorder）发展到钢丝录音机（wire recorder）、盘式磁带录音机（reel-to-reel recorder）、盒式磁带录音机（cassette recorder）、盒式磁带录像机（videocassette recorder）、数字磁带录音机（digital audio tape recorder）和迷你光盘录音机（mini-disk recorder），访谈者们已经采访了政治家和抗议者、原住民和移民、艺术家和工匠、士兵和平民、神职人员和世俗大众。……口述历史学家通过记录他（她）们的声音以建构一个更加多元和准确的历史图景。"[2] 而如今又可以为这个设备名单添加许多口述历史工作者日益普遍使用的记录手段，比如数码录音笔（digital audio/voice recorder）、数码摄像机（digital video camera, digital camcorder）及苹果公司系列产品 iPod、iPad 和 iPhone 等。

就录音技术发展历史而言，它大致经历了三个发展阶段：机械（声

---

[1] Cram101 Textbook Reviews, *e-Study Guide for Mass Media in a Changing World*, *Textbook by George Rodman*, Cram101 Publishing, fourth edition, 2014. 上述模拟记录和数字记录定义来自该书第七章"记录技术与音乐产业"（Recordings and the Music Industry），由于是通过 Google Books 阅读而无法获得具体页码。

[2] Donald A. Ritchie, *Doing Oral History：A Practical Guide*, Oxford and New York：Oxford University Press, second edition, 2003, pp. 13-14.

学）录音、电声录音和数字（数码）录音。① 留声机作为声音记录的第一种技术形式，经过19世纪70—80年代的开发与改良，到19世纪90年代之前，留声机已经较为普遍地进入商业市场。② 对于这些录音技术的发明与应用，从事田野记录（field recording）的工作者总是能够保持高度的敏锐度。而从19世纪80年代末期开始，包括历史学、民俗学、人类学、民族学、民族音乐学（ethnomusicology）、语言学、社会学，以及其他相关学科的田野工作者开始利用录音技术来记录他们所需的资料。据记载，首位从事田野录音工作的可能是美国民俗学家、人类学家、民族学者杰西·菲克斯（Jesse Walter Fewkes），他于1889年（还有一个说法是1890年）开始用蜡筒式留声机（wax cylinder phonograph）在缅因州（Maine）记录巴萨马瓜迪族印第安人（Passamaquoddy Indians）的歌曲、祈祷文和传说故事，后来又继续在亚利桑那州（Arizona）记录祖尼族（Zuni）和霍皮族

---

① 也有学者将第一个阶段再细分为圆筒留声机录音和声学录音两个阶段。有关录音技术发展历史可以参阅李学明编《数字影视技术概论》，高等教育出版社2012年版，第109-113页；杨健、黄莺《从圆筒留声机到早期声学录音——古典音乐录音技术发展简史》（上），《音响技术》2009年第4期，第69—72页；杨健、黄莺《从模拟录音到数码时代——古典音乐录音技术发展简史》（下），《音响技术》2009年第5期，第70-72页；Andre Millard, *America on Record：A History of Recorded Sound*, Cambridge and New York：Cambridge University Press, 1995 and 2005；David Morton, *Off the Record：The Technology and Culture of Sound Recording in America*, New Brunswick：Rutgers University Press, 2000；"Recording Technology History, revised July 6, 2005, by Steven Schoenherr", http：//web. archive. org/web/20070730075306/http：//history. sandiego. edu/gen/recording/notes. html；"History of Sound Recording", from Wikipedia, http：//en. wikipedia. org/wiki/History_ of_ sound_ recording；"Recording History：The History of Recording Technology", http：//www. recording – history. org. 上述访问时间为2014年4月28日。

② 留声机主要有三种类型，即托马斯·爱迪生（Thomas A. Edison, 1847—1931）于1877年发表的锡筒式留声机（tinfoil cylinder phonograph）、奇切斯特·贝尔（Chichester A. Bell, 1848—1924）和查尔斯·泰恩特（Charles S. Tainter, 1854—1940）于1885年发明的蜡筒式留声机（wax cylinder phonograph，英文专称为"graphophone"）及爱米尔·贝利纳（Emile Berliner, 1851-1929）于1887年发明的唱片式留声机（disc phonograph，英文专称为"gramophone"），随后留声机技术又有所发展和改进，在19世纪80年代—20世纪40年代，它成为当时主导的录音技术。详细参阅Alexander Boyden Magoun, "Shaping the Sound of Music：The Evolution the Phonograph Record, 1877-1950", Doctor of Philosophy, University of the Maryland, 2000；"Phonograph Record Technologies from Their Invention to the Death of 78-rpm Records", http：//www. recording – history. org/HTML/phono_ technology1. php, 2014年4月28日访问。

（Hopi）普韦布洛印第安人（Pueblo Indians）的有关生活方式和仪式的资料。① 菲克斯声称："原住民民俗（aboriginal folk-lore）研究无法达到它的最高科学价值，除非能够采用某些方法，只有这样，有关故事的准确记录（accurate record）才能获得和保存。"② 正是如此，在 19 世纪末和 20 世纪初，在菲克斯的引领下，③ 一些人类学家、民俗学家和民族音乐学家开始较为广泛地利用留声机来记录那些以前只能费劲地抄写在纸上的回忆、音乐、语言、民俗与传说故事。④ 其中比较有代表性的是美国印第安人民族学者弗朗西斯·弗莱斯彻（Francis La Flesche）和美国人类学家爱丽丝·弗莱彻（Alice C. Fletcher），她们在 1895—1897 年也同样利用蜡筒式留声机记录美国奥马哈族印第安人（Omaha Indians）的歌曲。⑤

　　而从 19 世纪末期开始，随着唱片技术和驱动技术的发展，尤其是 20 世纪 20 年代电驱动唱片式留声机（electrically-driven gramophones）的问

---

① Timothy Day, *A Century of Recorded Music: Listening to Musical History*, New Haven: Yale University Press, 2000; Elmar Schenkel and Stefan Welz (eds.), *Magical Objects: Things and Beyond*, Berlin: Galda, 2007, p. 114; Daniel Makagon and Mark Neumann, *Recording Culture: Audio Documentary and the Ethnographic Experience*, Thousand Oaks: Sage Publications, 2009, pp. 3-4; J. Walter Fewkes, "On the Use of the Phonograph in the Study of the Languages of American Indians", *Science*, Vol. 15, No. 378, May 1890, pp. 267-269; J. Walter Fewkes, "On the Use of the Phonograph Among the Zuni Indians", *American Naturalist*, Vol. 24, July 1890, pp. 687-691; J. Walter Fewkes, "Additional Studies of Zuni Songs and Rituals with the Phonograph", *American Naturalist*, Vol. 24, November 1890, pp. 1094-1098.

② J. Walter Fewkes, "A Contribution to Passamaquoddy Folk-Lore", *Journal of American Folklore*, Vol. 3, No. 11, 1890, p. 257, 全文页码为第 257—280 页。

③ 菲克斯于 1895 年加入美国史密森学会（Smithsonian Institution）下属的美国民族学局（Bureau of American Ethnology），并于 1918 年担任该局局长，他一直倡导和致力于通过录音技术来记录美国印第安人的历史文化与社会生活。详细内容参阅 Walter Hough, "Jesse Walter Fewkes", *American Anthropologist*, Vol. 33, No. 10, 1931, pp. 92-97; Walter Hough, *Biographical Memoir of Jesse Walter Fewkes, 1850-1930*, Washington: The National Academy of Sciences, 1932.

④ Donald A. Ritchie, "Oral History in the Federal Government", *Journal of American History*, Vol. 74, No. 2, 1987, pp. 587-588; Trevor Lummis, "Oral History", in Richard Bauman (ed.), *Folklore, Cultural Performances, and Popular Entertainments: A Communications-centered Handbook*, Oxford and New York: Oxford University Press, 1992, p. 93.

⑤ Andie Diane Palmer, "Life History", in Albert J. Mills, Gabrielle Durepos, and Elden Wiebe (eds.), *Encyclopedia of Case Study Research* (Volume 2), Thousand Oaks: Sage Publications, 2010, p. 529.

世，在田野记录中，不断改进的唱片式留声机开始逐渐代替旧的蜡筒式留声机。美国民俗学家罗伯特·格登（Robert W. Gordon）是最早的引领者之一，他于1932年在西弗吉尼亚州（West Virginia）、肯塔基州（Kentucky）和弗吉尼亚州（Virginia）的田野考察中就利用了这种电驱动唱片式留声机。① 而另外一位知名学者则是美国音乐学者、民俗学家约翰·洛马克斯（John A. Lomax），他与他的18岁儿子从1933年7月开始利用他的首台电驱动唱片式留声机在美国南部广泛地记录当地人的蓝调音乐、民歌与劳动歌曲。② 尽管留声机技术取得了重大进展，可是对于田野工作来说总体上还是不切实际的，尤其是携带便利性问题。根据相关记录显示，洛马克斯1933年使用的唱片式留声机重量就达到315磅（加上电池等其他设备，更是达到500磅左右），即使到20世纪30年代末，一些手提式唱片留声机的重量还在80—100磅左右，因此，当时的田野记录工作都必须借用汽车来运输这些设备。③ 正是如此，作为20世纪30年代美国最大规模的口述资料搜集计划，联邦作家计划所开展的针对美国昔日奴隶的访谈工作绝大部分都是基于访谈者的速记法（stenography）。④

在1948年美国现代口述史学正式诞生之后，美国口述历史工作者最先应用的记录手段则是继留声机技术之后的磁性记录（magnetic recording）

---

① Debora Kodish, *Good Friends and Bad Enemies: Robert Winslow Gordon and the Study of American Folksong*, Urbana: University of Illinois Press, 1986, pp. 185-186. 有关格登的美国民歌收藏可参阅 "Folk-Songs of America: The Robert Winslow Gordon Collection, 1922-1932", http://www. loc. gov/folklife/Gordon/, 2014年5月1日访问。

② John A. Lomax, "Field Experiences with Recording Machines", *Southern Folklore Quarterly*, Vol. 1, No. 2, 1937, pp. 57-60; David King Dunaway and Molly Beer, *Singing Out: An Oral History of America's Folk Music Revivals*, Oxford and New York: Oxford University Press, 2010, p. 24. 有关洛马克斯在美国南方收集民歌的内容可参阅 "Southern Mosaic: The John and Ruby Lomax 1939 Southern States Recording Trip", http://memory. loc. gov/ammem/lohtml/lohome. html, 2014年5月1日访问。

③ Erika Brady, *A Spiral Way: How the Phonograph Changed Ethnography*, Jackson: University of Mississippi Press, 1999. p. 26; Guy Bailey, Natalie Maynor, and Patricia Cukor-Avila (eds.), *The Emergence of Black English: Text and Commentary*, Amsterdam and Philadelphia: John Benjamins Publishing, 1991, p. 161.

④ Leonard Rapport, "How Valid Are the Federal Writers' Project Life Stories: An Iconoclast among the True Believers", *Oral History Review*, Vol. 7, 1979, p. 12.

技术的初代产品——钢丝录音机（wire recorder）。① 磁性记录技术最早源于美国工程师奥柏林·史密斯（Oberlin Smith）于 1888 年 9 月 8 日在《电子世界》上发表的一篇文章，他提出了以磁性钢丝来记录声音的设想。② 1898 年丹麦工程师瓦尔德马尔·普尔森（Valdemar Poulsen）发明了实际可用的磁性钢丝录音机（magnetic wire recorder）。钢丝录音机的出现解决了传统留声机无法复制拷贝的问题，因而具有极好的商业前景。③ 不过，直到 20 世纪 40 年代，钢丝录音机在美国才真正登上历史舞台，其中很大程度上是源于 1939 年美国伊利诺伊理工学院（Illinois Institute of Technology）的一位 22 岁研究生马文·卡姆拉斯（Marvin Camras）所发明的新式钢丝录音机。它与传统的钢丝录音机相比，在携带便利性、录音时长、重复录音及钢丝质量等方面都有重大改进。在第二次世界大战中，钢丝录音机被美军广泛地应用于各种军事用途和历史资料保存。比如，在诺曼底登陆战役中，它被用来释放假声（decoy sounds）迷惑敌军。此外，在战斗结束后，美军还会利用钢丝录音机将士兵的战场叙述记录下来，随后将录音经过编辑以宣传册的形式在战争大后方进行分发，当然同时也有助于保存战争史料。第二次世界大战后，钢丝录音机的市场销售规模不断扩大，并被主要应用于商业（主要用于记录口

---

① 甚至有学者认为美国现代口述史学的诞生和迅速发展很大程度上是源于磁性钢丝录音机的发明。具体内容参阅 Barbara W. Sommer and Mary Kay Quinlan, *The Oral History Manual*, Walnut Creek：AltaMira Press, second edition, 2009, p. 31；Robert Kuttner and Sharland Trotter, *Family Re-union：Reconnecting Parents and Children in Adulthood*, New York：Simon and Schuster, 2002, p. 208.

② Oberlin Smith, "Some Possible Forms of Phonograph", *Electrical World*, Vol. 12, No. 10, September 8, 1888, pp. 116-117.

③ 普尔森的这款钢丝录音机被称为"录音电话机"（telegraphone）。Valdemar Poulsen, "The Telegraphone：A Magnetic Speech Recorder", *The Electrician*, Vol. 46, November 30, 1900, pp. 208-210；Robert M. Yoder, "Young Man with a Wire", *The Rotarian*, February 1944, pp. 14-16；Ric Viers, *The Sound Effects Bible：How to Create and Record Hollywood Style Sound Effects*, Studio City：Michael Wiese Productions, 2011, p. 49.

授)、课堂（通常是语言类课程）及学术领域。[1]

  而在学术应用领域中，最具代表性的例子则是哥伦比亚大学口述历史研究室，它在创建之后不久的 1949 年 1 月 21 日的一次与勒恩德·汉德（Learned Hand）法官的口述历史访谈中首次使用钢丝录音机。[2] 需要指出的是，由于没有录音设备，1948 年 5 月 18 日，阿兰·内文斯所做的哥大口述历史研究室的第一个口述历史访谈就是由其研究生助理迪恩·艾伯森（Dean Albertson）以速记的方式来记录，访谈结束之后就立即回去凭借笔录和记忆将访谈内容用打字机打印出来。艾伯森估计以这样的方式来记录将会有 20% 的访谈内容会丢失，而内文斯认为，这样只能收集到受访者全部叙述内容的 60% 左右。正是如此，为了能够捕捉口述历史访谈中的每一句话，艾伯森很快向内文斯推荐了钢丝录音机，尽管内文斯对于钢丝录音机的使用有诸多不满和失望，可是在他购买第一台磁带录音机（tape recorder）之前，他在口述历史访谈中还是相当倚重钢丝录音机，使用达几年之久。[3] 从这里也可以看出钢丝录音机相对于传统速记方法的优势所在，它使口述历史成为真正的"有声音的历史"（aural history）。而且，它不仅使口述历史访谈的逐字抄本（verbatim transcripts）成为可能，甚至有学者认为它改变了一切，为整个口述史学领域提供了便利性、即时性和全新的可能性。[4]

---

① Alan Rosen, *The Wonder of Their Voices: The 1946 Holocaust Interviews of David Boder*, Oxford and New York: Oxford University Press, 2010, p. 153; Mark H. Clark, "Steel Tape and Wire Recorders", in Eric D. Daniel, C. Denis Mee, and Mark H. Clark (eds.), *Magnetic Recording: The First 100 Years*, Hoboken: John Wiley & Sons, 1999, pp. 41-43.

② "History Recorded by Wire and Film: Current 'History in the Making' Documented at Columbia", *New York Times*, January 13, 1950; "History on a Sound Track", *New York Times*, January 14, 1950; Louis Starr, "Oral History", p. 445; Richard Wolkomir, "Plug It In, Switch It On: Instant History", *The Rotarian*, May 1973, p. 37.

③ Dean Albertson, "History in the Deep-Freeze: The Story of Columbia's Oral History Project", *Columbia Library Columns*, Vol. 2, No. 2, 1953, p. 2; Willa K. Baum, "Oral History in the United States", *Oral History*, Vol. 1, No. 3, 1972, p. 17.

④ David E. Kyvig and Myron A. Marty, *Nearby History: Exploring the Past around You*, Walnut Creek: AltaMira Press, 2010, p. 114; Cynthia Hart, *The Oral History Workshop: Collect and Celebrate the Life Stories of Your Family and Friends*, New York: Workman Publishing Company, 2009, p. 24.

　　尽管钢丝录音机也不再那么昂贵，而且在市场上也很容易购得，可是其缺点也相当明显，由于其体积庞大而限制了室外使用。此外，由于钢丝录音机使用钢琴丝（piano wire）进行记录，这些钢琴丝尽管能保存很长时间，可是总是很容易弄乱和损坏，也很难编辑。艾伯森在回想哥大购置的首批钢丝录音机时就说："它们用的不是一卷磁带，它们有一个一卷细线穿过的磁性录音头。从来没有一台机器会比它更让人痛苦的。其原因远不是因为它重达40磅左右，而是散落在地板上的一大堆东缠西绕的和令人眼花缭乱的钢丝。"① 当然，导致钢丝录音机逐渐被淘汰的根本原因在于磁带录音机（magnetic tape recorder）的发明。② 在20世纪30年代中期，德国通用电气公司（Allgemeine Elektrizitts Gesellschaft，简称"AEG"）发明了首台磁带录音机——磁音机（Magnetophon 或 Magnetophone）。第二次世界大战后，美国对德国磁带录音机技术进行重大改良，美国安培（Ampex）公司于1948年4月首次推出2台商业磁带录音机。③ 显然，磁带录音机在哥大口述历史研究室进行首次口述历史访谈之前就已经存在，而且它的首次录音访谈也还只是利用钢丝录音机。不过，从20世纪50年代初开始，以哥大为代表的口述历史计划纷纷开始转向利用容易操作且相对便宜的磁带录音机，④ 进而逐渐代替那些在操作上经常打击历史学家热情的钢丝录

---

① Dean Albertson, "Remembering Oral History's Beginning", *The Annual of the New England Association*, Vol. 1, 1987/1988, p. 3. 转引自 Donald A. Ritchie, *Doing Oral History: A Practical Guide*, Oxford and New York: Oxford University Press, second edition, 2003, p. 57.

② Donald A. Ritchie, "Introduction: The Evolution of Oral History", in Donald A. Ritchie (ed.), *The Oxford Handbook of Oral History*, Oxford and New York: Oxford University Press, 2011, p. 7.

③ John T. Mullin, "Creating the Craft of Tape Recording", *High Fidelity Magazine*, April 1976, pp. 62-67; Beverley R. Gooch, "Building on the Magnetophon", in Eric D. Daniel, C. Denis Mee and Mark H. Clark (eds.), *Magnetic Recording: The First 100 Years*, Hoboken: John Wiley & Sons, 1999, pp. 72-91.

④ 据记录，哥大口述历史研究室在1951年已经利用磁带录音机进行口述历史访谈，详细内容参阅 Martin Lichterman, "History, Straight: A Columbia Project Is Recording the Verbal Reports of Many Actors in Current Events", *New York Times*, May 13, 1951.

音机。① 正如有学者指出的，"多年来，口述历史依赖于访谈者的记忆或访谈期间所做的粗略笔记。钢丝录音机乃至最终磁带录音机的引入极大地改变了口述历史程序。在今天，几乎所有的口述历史计划都利用磁带录音机来收集访谈资料"②。

在口述历史访谈中，根据所用磁带格式的不同，一般可以将磁带录音机分为盘式磁带录音机（reel-to-reel tape recorder）和盒式磁带录音机（cassette tape recorder）。③ 1948 年 4 月，美国安培公司推出的首批商业磁带录音机就是盘式磁带录音机，而对口述历史访谈录音技术产生划时代影响的另外一个里程碑事件则是荷兰飞利浦公司（Philips Electronics）于 1962 年发明了盒式磁带（compact cassette），它们分别于 1963 年和 1964 年进入欧洲和美国市场，而盒式磁带录音机也随之问世。④ 相对于盘式磁带录音机来说，盒式磁带录音机在携带便利性、操作容易性和价格经济性方面具有更多优势，因而逐渐受到越来越多的经费来源并不充足的个体口述历史工作者的偏爱。⑤ 不过，需要指出的是，在录音质量和磁带长期保存

① Willa Klug Baum, "Oral History: A Revived Tradition at the Bancroft Library", *Pacific Northwest Quarterly*, Vol. 58, No. 2, 1967, p. 58; Charles Hardy Ⅲ and Pamela Dean, "Oral History in Sound and Moving Image Documentaries", in Thomas L. Charlton, Lois E. Myers, and Rebecca Sharpless (eds.), *Handbook of Oral History*, Walnut Creek: AltaMira Press, 2006, p. 519; Linda Shopes, "Oral History", in Norman K. Denzin and Yvonna S. Lincoln (eds.), *The Sage Handbook of Qualitative Research*, Thousand Oaks: Sage Publications, fourth edition, 2011, p. 462.

② Thad Sitton, George L. Mehaffy, and O. L. Davis, Jr., *Oral History: A Guide for Teachers (and Others)*, Austin: University of Austin Press, 1983, p. 69.

③ Elizabeth B. Merrill, *Oral History Guide: A Handbook for Amateurs, Students, Teachers and Institutions*, Salem: Sheffield Publishing Company, 1985, p. 35. 盘式磁带录音机又称"开盘式磁带录音机"或"开卷式磁带录音机"，英文名称还可以表述为"reel-to-reel (audio) tape recorder"或"open-reel (tape) recorder"。盒式磁带录音机又称"卡式磁带录音机"，英文还可以表述为"audiocassette recorder"或"compact cassette recorder"。有关这两种录音机设备和录音技术的发展历程可参阅 Mark H. Clark, "Product Diversification", in Eric D. Daniel, C. Denis Mee and Mark H. Clark (eds.), *Magnetic Recording: The First 100 Years*, Hoboken: John Wiley & Sons, 1999, pp. 92-109.

④ "Compact Cassette", from Wikipedia, http://en. wikipedia. org/wiki/Compact _ Cassette, 2014 年 5 月 3 日访问; David John Cole, Eve Browning, Fred E. H. Schroeder, *Encyclopedia of Modern Everyday Inventions*, Westport: Greenwood Publishing Group, 2003, p. 28.

⑤ Valerie Raleigh Yow, *Recording Oral History: A Guide for the Humanities and Social Sciences*, Walnut Creek: AltaMira Press, second edition, 2005, p. 3; Gaynor Kavanagh, *Dream Spaces: Memory and the Museum*, London: Leicester University Press, 2000, p. 54.

方面，盘式磁带录音机和盘式磁带则更具优势。① 正因如此，在20世纪50年代至20世纪70年代初，美国许多口述历史计划（尤其是那些经费充裕的口述历史机构）还是偏向于利用盘式磁带录音机，甚至一些计划和保存机构要求将记录口述历史访谈的盒式磁带转换为盘式磁带。② 但是随着盘式磁带录音机市场销售的不断萎缩，如果继续利用盘式磁带进行访谈录音，这些盘式磁带的未来利用空间将会不断减少；而如果要将盘式磁带转换为盒式磁带，则又需要巨大的人力、物力与财力投入。③ 基于此，从20世纪60年代中期开始，盒式磁带录音机日益成为美国口述历史工作者的主要记录手段，而进入80年代之后，盘式磁带录音机已经基本为口述历史工作者所遗忘。维拉·鲍姆在1987年曾指出，使用盘式磁带录音机或盒式磁带录音机的争论已经被市场解决了，现在几乎没有可以获得的盘式磁带录音机，因此磁带录音机就是意味着盒式磁带录音机。④ 更加重要的是，随着便携式盒式磁带录音机的日益流行与普及，同时，在"自下而上看历史"（history from the bottom up）的新社会史运动的影响下，美国口述史学被广泛地应用于美国少数族裔史（土著美国人、非裔美国人、墨西哥裔美国人、华裔美国人等）、妇女史、劳工史、社区史、家庭史，以及性史等

---

① 有学者指出，在合适的温度和湿度环境下，一盘高质量的盘式磁带通常可以保存达125年或更长时间，而一盒同样质量的盒式磁带的保存时限可能不会超过25年。详细内容参阅 Thad Sitton, George L. Mehaffy, and O. L. Davis, Jr. , *Oral History: A Guide for Teachers (and Others)*, Austin: University of Austin Press, 1983, p. 69; Edward D. Ives, *The Tape-Recorded Interview: A Manual for Field Workers in Folklore and Oral History*, Knoxville: University of Tennessee Press, second edition, 1995, p. 2.

② Sherna Gluck, "What's So Special About Women? Women's Oral History", *Frontiers: A Journal of Women Studies*, Vol. 2, No. 2, 1977, p. 14; Stacy Erickson, *A Field Notebook for Oral History*, Boise: Idaho Center for Oral History, second edition, 1993, p. 43.

③ Donald A. Ritchie, "Introduction: The Evolution of Oral History", in Donald A. Ritchie (ed.), *The Oxford Handbook of Oral History*, Oxford and New York: Oxford University Press, 2011, p. 8.

④ Willa K. Baum, "Preface to the 1987 edition", in Willa K. Baum, *Oral History for the Local Historical Society*, Walnut Creek: AltaMira Press, third edition, revised, 1995, p. xi.

新兴史学领域。①

从 1889 年菲克斯利用蜡筒式留声机进行首次田野录音到 20 世纪 80 年代盒式磁带录音机在田野录音中的主导地位的确立，在这一百年间，无论是录音质量，还是录音设备的携带便利性、操作容易性及价格经济性都得到了很大程度的提高与改善，它们为包括口述历史实践者在内的美国田野工作者提供了重要的技术支持，并深刻地影响了他们对于所记录的资料与信息的研究与利用方式。不过，对美国口述史学产生更具革命性影响的则是始于 20 世纪 80 年代的数字化录音技术的兴起与发展及相应的记录介质的不断开发与应用，正如唐纳德·里奇所说，"在 20 世纪 80 年代，数字化电子技术（digital electronics）就像浪潮一样席卷模拟记录世界"②。

在 20 世纪 70 年代，荷兰飞利浦公司和日本索尼公司（Sony）在数字音频技术上的努力不断取得进展，1980 年两家公司联合发布了一项在光学盘片（optical disc）上进行录音（audio recording）的数字音乐光盘（Compact Disc Digital Audio，简称"CDDA"或"CD-DA"）标准。③ 该标准首次引入数字信号技术，音频信号采集采用 44.1Hz 的取样频率和 16bit 的量化精度，后以线性脉冲编码调制（Linear Pulse Code Modulation，LPCM）方式编码成数字信号，在一张标准的直径为 12 厘米的盘片中可存储 74 分钟

---

① Sara Leuchter, "Oral History with Holocaust Survivors", in David M. Szonyi (ed.), *The Holocaust: An Annotated Bibliography and Resource Guide*, New York: KTAV Publishing House, 1985, p. 371; Frederick J. Stielow, *The Management of Oral History Sound Archives*, Westport: Greenwood Press, 1986, pp. 2 and 20-21; Mary Patrice Erdmans, "The Problems of Articulating Beingness in Women's Oral Histories", in Marta Kurkowska-Budzan and Krzysztof Zamorski (eds.), *Oral History: The Challenges of Dialogue*, Amsterdam and Philadelphia: John Benjamins Publishing, 2009, pp. 87-88；杨祥银《当代美国口述史学的主流趋势》,《社会科学战线》2011 年第 2 期，第 71—72 页；Michael Frisch, "Oral History", in Carol Kammen and Amy H. Wilson (eds.), *Encyclopedia of Local History*, Walnut Creek: AltaMira Press, second edition, 2012, p. 440.

② Donald A. Ritchie, "Introduction: The Evolution of Oral History", in Donald A. Ritchie (ed.), *The Oxford Handbook of Oral History*, Oxford and New York: Oxford University Press, 2011, p. 9.

③ Norman Clark, "CD-R, CD-ROM, and DVD", Steve Jones (ed.), *Encyclopedia of New Media: An Essential Reference to Communication and Technology*, Thousand Oaks: Sage Publications, 2003, p. 63.

高保真音频信号。[1] 而 1982 年首批光盘（Compact Disc，简称"CD"）及光盘播放机（Compact Disc Player，简称"CD 播放机"）在日本、欧洲和美国的相继面世则正式标志着数字化录音（音频）技术的开始。[2] 光盘作为记录和存储声音信号的介质，它采用数字编码技术进行高密度记录和重放，其优点充分体现在高保真、记录密度高、寿命长、功能多及体积小等方面，因此问世不久就成为发达国家和地区音频技术发展与音乐销售市场的新宠。[3]

尽管光盘最初的设计目的是为了储存高品质的数字音乐，但由于它采用了数字技术来储存音频信息，因此使光盘逐渐发展成为一种适用于计算机使用的储存数字资料（digital data）的大容量存储介质，即只读光盘（Compact Disc Read-Only Memory，简称"CD-ROM"）。1985 年飞利浦与索尼联合推出适用于计算机数据存储的 CD-ROM 标准，CD-ROM 盘片在外观上与 CD 光盘完全相同，数据存取方法也十分相似，因此 CD-ROM 又被称为增强型 CD，它不仅能够存储音乐，有可以存储计算机数据。作为一种在计算机上使用的光盘，CD-ROM 只能写入数据一次，信息将永久保存在光盘上，而使用时则要通过光盘驱动器（CD-ROM Drive）读出信息。当然，存储音乐的 CD-ROM 则可以直接用 CD 播放机来播放。相对于标准的 1.44MB 和 1.2MB 的软盘（floppy disc）容量来说，CD-ROM 超过 600MB 的容量极大地满足了计算机操作系统、软件开发及相关业务的大数据存储需求。[4]

---

① 张永旭：《数字光盘 30 年发展史回顾》，《记录媒体技术》2009 年第 6 期，第 8 页。

② Ken C. Pohlmann, *The Compact Disc Handbook*, Oxford and New York：Oxford University Press, 1992, p. 12；Pekka Gronow and Ilpo Saunio, *An International History of the Recording Industry*, London：Cassell, 1998, pp. 190-196；David Morton, *Sound Recording：The Life Story of a Technology*, Baltimore：Johns Hopkins University Press, 2004, pp. 170-172. "光盘"中文名又称为"激光唱片（唱盘）"、"镭射唱片"或"光碟"；而"光盘播放机"中文名又可以称为"激光唱机"、"光碟播放机"或"光盘（光碟）播放器"。在行文中，这些称谓将根据中文习惯而做出相应调整。

③ 黄锦章：《CD 唱机发展近况纵览》，《电声技术》1986 年第 6 期，第 42 页；马效先、王铁林编著：《影碟机原理与维修》，电子工业出版社 1999 年版，第 3 页。

④ "CD-ROM", from Wikipedia, http：//en. wikipedia. org/wiki/CD-ROM, 2014 年 5 月 5 日访问；Chris Sherman（ed.）, *The CD-ROM Handbook*, New York：Intertext Publications, 1994.

不过，传统的 CD 和 CD-ROM 均是采用母盘灌制的方式，即在盘片压制过程中就将数据存储于盘片中，因此用户只能被动接收并通过相应播放机或驱动器来播放或读取存在于光盘上的信息，而用户则无法将已有的数据自行写入光盘中。随后，经过多年发展，飞利浦和索尼等公司分别于 1990 年和 1996 年推出可录光盘（Compact Disc-Recordable，简称"CD-R"；更准确而言，它是一种"一次写，多次读"光盘）和可重复录写光盘（Compact Disc-ReWritable，简称"CD-RW"）标准。而随着 CD-DA 中数字技术在视频领域中的开发与应用，一系列数字多功能影音光盘（Digital Versatile Disc，Digital Video Disk，简称"DVD"）随之诞生。DVD 光盘与高密度只读光盘（Digital Video Disk-Read Only Memory，简称 DVD-ROM）分别于 1995 年和 1996 年推出之后，同 CD 光盘一样，DVD 刻录光盘（只能写入一次）的两个产品系列 DVD-R 光盘与 DVD + R 光盘分别于 1997 年和 2002 年推出；而可重复录写 DVD 光盘的三个产品系列 DVD-RW 光盘、DVD + RW 光盘和 DVD-RAM 光盘（DVD – Random Access Memory）则分别于 1999 年、1997 年和 1996 年推出。① 进入 21 世纪之后，光盘技术市场上还出现了另外两种竞争激烈的产品——蓝光光盘（Blu-ray Disc，简称"BD"）和高清 DVD 光盘（High Definition/Density Digital Versatile Disc，简称"HD DVD"）。在 2002 年 BD 光盘推出之后，随后也出现了一系列可录 BD 光盘，包括 BD-R（Blu-ray Disc Recordable）、BD-RE（Blu-ray Disc Recordable Erasable）、BD-R LTH（BD-R Low To High）、BD5、BD9、BDXL（High Capacity Recordable and Rewritable Disc）及 IH-BD（Intra-Hybrid Blu-ray）等。而 HD DVD 光盘于 2003 年推出之后，也随即出现一系列可录 HD DVD 光盘，其中包括 HD DVD-R、HD DVD-RW、HD DVD-RAM、DVD/HD DVD Hybrid Disc、HD

---

① 这里需要指出的是，在 DVD 光盘推出之前，视频高密光盘（Video Compact Disc，简称"VCD"）于 1993 年推出。此外，当时跟 VDV 光盘相互竞争的还有 1994 年和 1995 年相继推出的多媒体光盘（Multi Media Compact Disc，简称"MMCD"）与超密度光盘（Super Density Compact Disc，简称"SD"）。

DVD/Blu-ray Disc Hybrid Disc、3DVD、HD REC 及 CBHD（China Blue High-definition Disc）等。显然，上述光盘（尤其是可录光盘）技术的发展以及产品的不断开发为数字化录音与录影设备的研发提供了必要的技术支持。[①]

　　尽管 20 世纪 80 年代以来的光盘技术发展对音乐行业与数据存储业务产生了巨大影响，可是标志着数字化录音时代到来的光盘技术并没有引领光盘类数字录音机（digital recorder）市场的开发。因此，为了满足市场对于数字录音机的需求，一些以传统的磁带为介质的数字录音机开始面世。1982 年，索尼公司率先推出第一代数字磁带录音机——固定磁头盘式数字磁带录音机（Digital Audio Stationary Head Recorder，简称"DASH"），它是一款通过固定磁头将数字信号记录在盘式磁带上的多轨高质量录音设备。[②] 而另外一种数字磁带录音机被称为"盒式数字磁带录音机"（Digital Audio Tape Recorder，简称"DAT"），它与 DASH 录音机的一个重要区别在于记录介质是盒式磁带而不是盘式磁带，不过它的磁带盒尺寸大约为 73mm × 54mm × 10.5mm，比模拟盒式磁带盒尺寸 102mm × 64mm × 12mm 要小得多。DAT 技术起源于 20 世纪 80 年代初，经过多年发展，1987 年索尼公司推出第一代 DAT 录音机。DAT 录音机是可以记录和重放脉冲编码调制（Pulse Code Modulation，"PCM"）信号的数字磁带录音机，它根据磁头及其伺服系统工作原理的不同，又分为

　　[①]　需要强调的是，上述有关不同光盘的推出时间有可能是该光盘标准的制定时间或光盘的上市时间。有关上述 CD、DVD、BD 及 HD DVD 光盘技术的发展历史可以参阅 Wikipedia 上相关词条的详细解释，此外还可参阅张永旭《数字光盘 30 年发展史回顾》，《记录媒体技术》2009 年第 6 期，第 7—19 页；Jan Maes and Marc Vercammen（eds.），*Digital Audio Technology*：*A Guide to CD*，*MiniDisc*，*SACD*，*DVD*（*A*），*MP3 and DAT*，Burlington and Oxford：Focal Press, fifth edition, 2013；Scott Mueller, *Upgrading and Repairing PCs*, Indianapolis：Pearson Education, 21st edition, 2013, pp. 525-609.

　　[②]　郑利民：《开盘数字磁带录音机》，《广播与电视技术》1996 年第 10 期，第 27—35 页；李学明编：《数字影视技术概论》，高等教育出版社 2012 年版，第 131 页；"Digital Audio Stationary Head"，from Wikipedia，http：//en. wikipedia. org/wiki/Digital_ Audio_ Stationary_ Head，2014 年 5 月 5 日访问；Luc Baert, *Digital Audio and Compact Disc Technology*, Burlington and Oxford：Focal Press, third edition, 1995, p. 14.

旋转磁头数字磁带录音机（Rotary Head DAT Recorder，简称"R-DAT"）和固定磁头数字磁带录音机（Stationary Head DAT Recorder，简称"S-DAT"）。① 第三种以磁带为记录介质的数字录音机是普通盒式磁带数字录音机（Digital Compact Cassette Recorder，简称"DCC"），1992年飞利浦公司和松下公司（Matsushita）研发的第一代 DCC 录音机正式面世。DCC 录音机也采用固定磁头型技术，并使用和普通盒式磁带相同的带盒，可兼容普通的模拟盒式磁带放音。而且，从技术指标上看，DCC 录音机已经达到 CD 的音质，而且还可以记录一些相关的文本信息。②

在这三类磁带类数字录音机中，DAT（尤其是 1989 年首款便携式 DAT 录音机的面世）成为 20 世纪 80 年代末和 90 年代初美国一部分口述历史工作者的选择。尽管 DAT 录制的音频质量很高，可是由于它所使用的记录介质与模拟磁带类似，如不妥善保存会造成品质下降，因此并不适合长久保存。1992 年索尼推出的第一代磁光盘（Magneto-Optical Disc，简称"MO"）类数字录音机——迷你光盘录音机（Minidisc/Mini-Disc/Mini Disc

---

① 需要强调的是我们平常所说的"数字磁带录音机"一般是指 R-DAT 录音机，有时候直接称为 DAT 录音机。"Digital Audio Tape"，from Wikipedia，http：//en. wikipedia. org/wiki/Digital_ Audio_ Tape，2014 年 5 月 5 日访问；Paul Trynka and Tony Bacon（eds. ），*Rock Hardware*，London：Balafon Books，1996，p. 135；Elizabeth Walters，Bob Pymm and Matthew Davies，"Sound Materials"，in Ross Harvey and *Martha R. Mahard*（eds. ），*The Preservation Management Handbook*：*A 21st-Century Guide for Libraries*，*Archives*，*and Museums*，Lanham：Rowman & Littlefield，p. 225；钟晓流、吴庚生、曾亚、黄远智《多媒体视听技术与应用环境》，清华大学出版社 2007 年版，第 57—59 页；陈华编著《音频技术及应用》，西南交通大学出版社 2007 年版，第 80—85 页。

② 李学明编《数字影视技术概论》，高等教育出版社 2012 年版，第 130 页；陈华编著《音频技术及应用》，西南交通大学出版社 2007 年版，第 85—86 页；"Digital Compact Cassette"，from Wikipedia，http：//en. wikipedia. org/wiki/Digital_ Compact_ Cassette，2014 年 5 月 5 日访问；Thom Holmes，"Digital Compact Cassette（DCC）"，in Frank Hoffmann（ed. ），*Encyclopedia of Recorded Sound*（Volume 1），London and New York：Routledge，second edition，2004，p. 557；Thom Holmes（ed. ），*The Routledge Guide to Music Technology*，London and New York：Routledge，2006，p. 76.

Recorder，简称"MD"）又开始取代 DAT 成为美国口述历史者的又一新选择。[1] 迷你光盘既具有 CD 音质和长期保存的特点，又具有磁带功效，且尺寸只有 CD 唱片的一半左右，能够储存 74 分钟的录音内容。迷你光盘录音机推出以后，以易于携带、价格适中、CD 音质和录制方便等优点而颇受田野记录工作者欢迎。[2]

如上所述，20 世纪 80 年代发展起来的光盘技术并没有迅速催生以光盘为介质的录音技术的发展。1988 年雅马哈（Yamaha）推出首款以 CD-ROM 光盘为记录介质的录音设备——PDS 录音机（Programmable Disc Subsystem Audio Recorder），随后几年，包括雅马哈、索尼、飞利浦和胜利在内的几家公司都相继推出各自的以 CD-ROM 和 CD-R 光盘为介质的录音设备，可是这些录音设备除了价格昂贵之外，还有一个很重要的缺点是它们大部分都是专业录音系统的一个组成部分，并不能独立运行，因此，这些录音设备的功能更像是具有刻录功能的光盘驱动器。[3] 直到 1998 年和 2002

---

① Charles Hardy Ⅲ and Pamela Dean，"Oral History in Sound and Moving Image Documentaries"，in Thomas L. Charlton，Lois E. Myers，and Rebecca Sharpless（eds.），*Handbook of Oral History*，Walnut Creek：AltaMira Press，2006，p. 537. 磁光盘在 20 世纪 80 年代初开始研制，1985 年（又一说法为 1988 年）开始面世，它是传统磁盘技术与现代光学技术结合的产物，通过磁光盘驱动器可以实现数据的重复写入。在外观上，磁光盘盘片大小类似于 3 寸软盘，可是其容量要远远大于软盘，一般从几十 MB 到 9GB 左右不等。详细内容参阅 Terry W. McDaniel and Randall Victory（eds.），*Handbook of Magneto-Optical Data Recording：Materials，Subsystems，Techniques*，Westwood：Noyes Publications，1997；David C. Jiles，*Introduction to the Electronic Properties of Materials*，Boca Raton：CRC Press，second edition，2001，p. 313.

② 李学明编：《数字影视技术概论》，高等教育出版社 2012 年版，第 131-133 页；Jeffrey D. Harman，"Digital Recording"，in Christopher H. Sterling（ed.），*Encyclopedia of Radio*，London and New York：Routledge，2003，pp. 746-747；David Miles Huber and Robert E. Runstein，*Modern Recording Technique*，Burlington and Oxford：Focal Press，eighth edition，2013，p. 228；"MiniDisc"，from Wikipedia，http：//en. wikipedia. org/wiki/MiniDisc，2014 年 5 月 5 日访问。有关口述历史工作者对于迷你光盘与盒式磁带使用的优劣评价，可参阅 Alan Ward，Rob Perks and Peter Copeland，"Minidisc versus Cassette"，*Oral History*，Vol. 27，No. 2，1999，pp. 90-92.

③ Paul Worthington and Nico Krohn，"Sony Products Will Let PC Users Master CD ROM Disc"，*InfoWorld*，March 5，1990，p. 8；Paul Verna，"CD-R Enjoys Massive Growth in a Wide Range of Markets"，*Billboard*，April 3，1999，p. 52；Dana Parker and Bob Starrett，*CD-ROM Professional's CD-Recordable Handbook：The Complete Guide to Practical Desktop CD*，Pemberton Press，1996，pp. 39-40；"Can you afford a writeable CD-ROM?" http：//archive. today/FZlto#selection-219. 0-219. 35，2014 年 5 月 8 日访问。

年前后，市场上才首次出现单体光盘录音机（standalone CD Recorder）和便携式光盘录音机（Portable CD Recorder），它们分别是 Philips CDR-870 和 Marantz CDR-300。① 因此，作为一种能够为田野工作者所使用的录音设备，光盘录音机直到 21 世纪初才逐渐普遍起来。不过，这种录音机在录音过程中必须保持水平和远离任何震源，任何移动都会影响数据写入。② 因此，尽管光盘录音机所使用的光盘也较为廉价，但是由于这些缺点而未能被包括美国口述历史工作者在内的田野记录者所广泛采用。

　　而造成光盘录音机未能普及的一个更为重要的原因是硬盘类录音机和存储卡（memory card）录音机的日益流行。所谓硬盘类录音机就是直接将音频信息存储在录音机硬盘上，相对于 DAT、MD 和光盘类录音机来说，它的最大优势是存储容量大。可是，它的明显缺点是硬盘（是一种可写性磁性媒介）易受震动和强磁场干扰以及容易出现故障。而在数字化录音时代，真正为美国口述历史工作者带来革命性影响的是 21 世纪初以存储卡为存储介质的便携式（手持式）数码录音笔（digital audio/voice recorder）的广泛流行。③ 数码录音笔通过对模拟信号的采样和编码将模拟信号转化为数字信号，并进行一定程度的压缩后存储在可插播的

---

① 苏隆坡：《CD 录音与 CD-R、CD-RW》，《多媒体视听》2001 年第 5 期，第 36 页；"Marantz CDR300 CD Recorder"，http：//www. ebay. ca/ctg/Marantz－CDR300－CD－Recorder－/92441980，2014 年 5 月 8 日访问。

② Oral History Centre, National Archives of Singapore（ed. ），*Memories and Reflections：The Singapore Experience：Documenting A Nation's History Through Oral History*，Singapore：Oral History Centre，National Archives of Singapore，2007，p. 71.

③ 存储卡主要有：紧凑式闪存卡（compact flash memory card）、安全数字记忆卡（secure digital memory card，简称"SD"）和安全数字高容量记忆卡（secure digital high capacity，简称"SDHC"）。据相关记录显示，世界上首款数码录音笔由朗讯（Lucent）于 1995 年推出，而首款为消费者广泛应用的数码录音笔则由奥林巴斯（Olympus）于 2001 年推出。具体参阅"The Benefits of Using Digital Voice Recorders"，http：//www. ebay. com/gds/The－Benefits－of－Using－Digital－Voice－Recorders－/10000000177630749/g. html，2014 年 5 月 8 日访问；Steve Traiman， "Lucent Technologies，Bell Labs Innovations：A Century of Audio Innovation"，*Billboard*，January 29，2000，pp. L-7.

闪存卡上。相对于以往的模拟盒式磁带录音机及 DAT、MD 和光盘类数字录音机来说，它有众多无可比拟的优点，主要体现在：（1）设备外形灵活轻便、设计时尚并且易于操作；（2）连续录音时间长且录制过程中噪音少；（3）与计算机连接方便，可以实现即插即用；（4）录音笔价格实惠（价位选择多）并且使用寿命长；（5）记录的电子文件的后期处理相当便利。① 正因如此，目前，各种便携式（手持式）数码录音笔已经成为美国口述历史工作者最为主流的录音手段。与此相适应的是，美国也出现越来越多的介绍适用于口述历史访谈的各种数码录音设备的网站和博客平台。②

当然，近 10 年来，一些具有录音功能的更为多功能的音频、视频播放器及智能手机也开始为一部分美国口述历史工作者（尤其是学生实践者）所利用，当然为了提高录音效果，可以配备一个高质量的麦克风。比如，从 2001 年苹果公司（Apple）推出 iPod 开始，iPod（ipod classic/nano/touch 等系列）、ipad（ipad classic/mini/air 等系列）及 iPhone（iphone4/4s/5/5s/6 等系列）等产品都具有录音或录影功能（部分产品需要配件支持），这些设备除了自带录音或录影软件（如 iPhone 的语音备忘录和相机）之外，用户还可以在苹果商店（App Store）下载各种免费（或付费）录音与录影软件，甚至有些录音软件（如 Recordium 和 Smart Recorder）具有强调、标记（文字和图片）、注解、分割、剪辑及上

---

① 陈华编著：《音频技术及应用》，西南交通大学出版社 2007 年版，第 100—101 页；Valerie J. Janesick, *Oral History for the Qualitative Researcher*：*Choreographing the Story*, New York：Guilford Press, 2010, p. 48；Valerie J. Janesick, "Oral History Interviewing：Issues and Possibilities", in Patricia Leavy（ed.）, *The Oxford Handbook of Qualitative Research*, Oxford and New York：Oxford University Press, 2014, pp. 301-302.

② Doug Boyd, "Digital Omnium：Oral History, Archives and Digital Technology", http：//digitalomnium. com/；MATRIX（Center for Digital Humanities & Social Sciences, Michigan State University）, "Oral History in the Digital Age", http：//ohda. matrix. msu. edu/askdoug/；Vermont Folklife Center, "Digital Audio Field Recording Equipment Guide", http：//www. vermontfolklifecenter. org/archive/res_ audioequip. htm. 上述网站访问时间为 2014 年 5 月 8 日。

传云端存储平台等有利于录音文件后续处理与管理的功能。而且，这些产品的内存和储存容量都在不断增加，完全可以满足较长时间的口述历史录音和录影访谈。正是如此，近年来，美国许多以学生和社区志愿者为主导的校园、家庭（家族）与社区口述历史计划都在不断地探讨与尝试如何将这些新式的数字化手段更好地应用于口述历史访谈当中。① 当然，对于这些设备是否适合于口述历史访谈也存有诸多争议和质疑，比如那些以口述历史资料保存为目的的档案型口述历史计划是否适合采用这些设备。②

当然，同录音技术一样，录影技术也经历了从模拟技术向数字技术的革命性转变。1956 年首台实用性磁带录像机（video tape recorder，简称"VTR"）由美国安培公司（Ampex Corporation）推出，随后东芝（Toshiba）、飞利浦及索尼公司相继推出各种类型的磁带录像机，其中索尼于 1965 年推出首款家用磁带录像机。不过，这些早期磁带录像机的记录介质都是盘式磁带（reel-to-reel tape），直到 1971 年索尼才推出首款商用盒式磁带录像机（videocassette recorder，简称"VCR"）。③ 而从 20 世纪 80 年代初开始，数字化技术不断地影响录像和摄像技术的发展。1986 年索尼推出首款商用数字盒式磁带录像机（digital videocassette recorder），

① "Family Oral History Using Digital Tools", http：//familyoralhistory. us/news/C6；Joe Hoover, "Using your iPhone/iPad to Record Oral History", March 12, 2012, http：//discussions. mnhs. org/mn-localhistory/blog/2012/03/12/using – your – iphoneipad – to – record – oral – history；Wesley Fryer, "Recommended Smartphone Apps & Digital Recorders for Storychasing Oral History", January 25, 2013, http：//storychasers. org/2013/01/25/recommended – smartphone – apps – digital – recorders – for – sto-rychasing – oral – history；"iPodigital Storytelling Oral History Project", https：//www. youtube. com/watch? v = OC – 7ks_ 2Soc；Wesley Fryer, "Creating Oral History Interview Videos on an iPod Touch", November 13, 2011, http：//www. speedofcreativity. org/2011/11/13/creating – oral – history – interview – videos – on – an – ipod – touch/。上述访问时间为 2014 年 5 月 8 日。

② Doug Boyd, "Iphone and Oral History?" http：//digitalomnium. com/low – cost – digital – video – and – oral – history/，2014 年 5 月 8 日访问。

③ "Video tape recorder", from Wikipedia, http：//en. wikipedia. org/wiki/Video_ tape_ record-er；"Videocassette recorder", from Wikipedia, http：//en. wikipedia. org/wiki/Videocassette_ recorder. 访问时间为 2014 年 5 月 10 日。

随后包括索尼在内的多家公司相继推出以盒式磁带、光盘、硬盘及储存卡为介质的数字磁带录像机（digital video recorder，简称"DVR"）。① 而索尼于 1995 年推出的以磁带为记录介质的首款数码摄像机（digital video camera）则标志着民用摄像机也开始步入数字化时代，随后各家公司相继推出以 DVD 光盘、硬盘及存储卡为介质的便携式数码摄像机（英文习惯称为"digital camcorder"）。②

　　同口述历史录音访谈一样，数字化技术也为口述历史录影访谈的进一步发展提供了切实可行的物质基础与技术支持。正如美国口述历史学家道格拉斯·博伊德（Douglas A. Boyd，英文名经常简称为"Doug Boyd"）所说，数字录影（digital video recording）正受到消费者的广泛欢迎。而且，新兴技术使得以下发展成为可能：利用价格实惠的摄像机来捕捉高质量的数字信号、在家庭电脑上编辑视频、创建和分发DVD 光盘或者再次从家庭电脑中将压缩文件上传到 YouTube 上。③ 同录音技术一样，美国口述历史工作者也相当关注录影技术在口述历史访谈中的应用。早在盘式和盒式磁带录音机占据主导地位的 20 世纪 60年代中期，一些美国口述历史学家就提出在集中关注口述历史录音与抄本资料的同时，也需要记录口述历史的视觉信息。其中最具代表性的是时任佛罗里达州立大学图书馆学院（Library School, Florida State University）院长路易斯·肖尔斯（Louis Shores），他在 1966 年 9月 25—28 日于加州阿罗黑德湖举行的第一届美国口述历史年会上就建议利用 16 毫米电影胶片（16 mm motion picture film）来记录访谈的那

---

　　① "Digital video", from Wikipedia, http：//en. wikipedia. org/wiki/Digital_ video, 2014 年 5月 10 日访问。

　　② "Video camera", from Wikipedia, http：//en. wikipedia. org/wiki/Video_ camera；"DV", from Wikipedia, http：//en. wikipedia. org/wiki/DV；"Camcorder", from Wikipedia, http：//en. wikipedia. org/wiki/Camcorder. 访问时间为 2014 年 5 月 10 日。

　　③ Doug Boyd, "Achieving the Promise of Oral History in a Digital Age", in Donald A. Ritchie (ed.), *The Oxford Handbook of Oral History*, Oxford and New York：Oxford University Press, 2011, p. 290.

些第一手的无形的东西（intangibles），他认为视觉胶片（visual film）能够刺激受访者更为有意义地叙述。同时，他还呼吁图书管理员应当协助口述历史学家更为系统地处理这些现成的有关访谈的音像记录。①

在20世纪70年代初，随着价格更为低廉及携带和操作更为便利的商用盒式磁带录像机的问世及流行，美国口述历史工作者利用视频媒介（video medium）进行口述历史计划的数量呈对数增加趋势。② 不过总体而言，即使到20世纪80年代，大部分美国口述历史工作者对于口述历史录影还是持观望或迟疑态度，甚至在1984年出版的美国口述历史学界最具代表性的著作《口述史学：跨学科文集》中根本没有提及口述历史录影这个概念（该书索引也没有任何"video"或"visual"等术语）。③

而且，当时美国口述历史学界关于口述历史录影利弊的争论也相当激烈。总结而言，其弊端主要体现在：（1）相对于口述历史录音来说，其费用（设备与人员）更加昂贵，而且其操作过程与后续处理（转录与保存）也更为复杂，对于那些预算相对紧张的口述历史计划来说则是难以负担

① Louis Shores, "Directions for Oral History", in Elizabeth I. Dixon and James V. Mink (eds.), *Oral History at Arrowhead: The Proceedings of the First National Colloquium on Oral History*, Los Angeles: Oral History Association, 1967, pp. 38-46; "Louis Shores", from Wikipedia, http://en. wikipedia. org/wiki/Louis_ Shores, 2014年5月10日访问。

② William W. Moss, "The Future of Oral History", *Oral History Review*, Vol. 3, 1975, pp. 10-11; Joel Gardner, "Oral History and Video in Theory and Practice", *Oral History Review*, Vol. 12, 1984, p. 105.

③ David K. Dunaway and Willa Baum (eds.), *Oral History: An Interdisciplinary Anthology*, Nashville: American Association for State and Local History, 1984. 正是如此，当时很少有口述历史工作者探讨如何口述历史录影的技术性操作问题，而更多实践指南或手册都来自其他相关学科。详细内容参阅 Edith Ann Verrall, "The Use of Videotaping in Folklore Fieldwork, Some Problems in the Transcription of a Children's Game", M. A. Thesis, Memorial University of Newfoundland, 1975; Karl Heider, *Ethnographic Film*, Austin: University of Texas Press, 1976; Peter Bartis, *Folklife and Field-work: A Layman's Introduction to Field Techniques*, Washington: American Folklife Center, 1979; Brad Jolly, *Videotaping Local History*, Nashville: American Association for State and Local History, 1982; Richard Blaustein, "Using Video in the Field", in Richard M. Dorson (ed.), *Handbook of American Folklore*, Bloomington: Indiana University Press, 1983, pp. 397-401; Peter Lazendorf, *The Video Ta-ping Handbook*, New York: Harmony Press, 1983; 而比较例外的是美国民俗学家爱德华·艾维斯（Edward D. Ives, 1925-2009）于1980年出版的著作，详细内容参阅 Edward D. Ives, *The Tape-Recor-ded Interview: A Manual for Field Workers in Folklore and Oral History*, Knoxville: University of Tennessee Press, 1980.

的；（2）口述历史录影因为需要更多的工作人员和设备器材，这些容易给受访者带来冒犯性感觉，因而比较难以让受访者感觉轻松自在而影响和睦访谈关系的建立，同时也因为访谈者所谓的"科技恐惧症"（technopho-bia）而宁愿采用较易操作的录音设备；（3）而对于那些熟悉和适应录影的受访者来说，口述历史录影可能会成为受访者的表演活动，进而影响对于真正有价值的历史信息的挖掘；（4）口述历史录影涉及受访者影像形象的呈现及针对影像资料的恶意或无意的编辑和修改，它比口述历史抄本和声音资料来说存在更多潜在的法律与伦理问题。而口述历史录影的积极倡导者则认为它具有口述历史录音和抄本资料无法比拟的优势所在，具体而言包括：（1）它不仅允许"阅读"和"倾听"口述历史，而且能够"观看"口述历史，即它能够为口述历史增加更为丰富的视觉维度（visual di-mensions），其中包括口述历史访谈的自然环境、摄像机视域所捕捉的非言语信息（面部表情、肢体语言）、受访者与访谈者的个性特征及他们之间的互动关系；（2）口述历史录影也扩展了口述历史资料在博物馆展览、纪录片制作、网站发布及其他形式的公共呈现中的潜在用途。①

　　正是如此，随着研究者与更为广泛的受众对于口述历史视觉信息价

---

① 上述有关口述历史录影利弊的讨论，可参阅 W. Richard Whitaker, "Why Not Try Videotaping Oral History?" *Oral History Review*, Vol. 9, 1981, pp. 115-124；Joel Gardner, "Oral History and Video in Theory and Practice", *Oral History Review*, Vol. 12, 1984, pp. 105-111；Dale E. Treleven, "Oral Historians: Masters of or Slaves to Technology?" *Oral History Review*, Vol. 12, 1984, pp. 101-104；Thomas Charlton, "Videotaping Oral Histories: Problems and Prospects", *American Archivist*, Vol. 47, No. 3, 1984, pp. 228-236；David King Dunaway, "Field Recording Oral History", *Oral History Review*, Vol. 15, No. 1, 1987, pp. 21-42；Dan Snipe, "The Future of Oral History and Moving Images", *Oral History Review*, Vol. 19, 1991, No. 1/2, pp. 75-87；Donald A. Ritchie, *Doing Oral History: A Practical Guide*, Oxford and New York: Oxford University Press, second edition, 2003, pp. 134-154（Chapter 5: Videotaping Oral History）；James E. Fogerty, "Oral History and Archives: Documenting Context", in Thomas L. Charlton, Lois E. Myers, and Rebecca Sharpless（eds.）, *Handbook of Oral History*, Walnut Creek: AltaMira Press, 2006, pp. 221-226. 此外，有关更为广泛的历史录影的研究可参阅 Ron Chepesiuk and Ann Y. Evans, "Videotaping History: The Winthrop College Archives' Experience", *American Archivist*, Vol. 48, No. 1, 1985, pp. 65-68；Pamela M. Henson and Terri A. Schorzman, "Videohistory: Focusing on the American Past", *Journal of American History*, Vol. 78, No. 2, 1991, pp. 618-627；Terri A. Schorzman（ed.）, *A Practical Introduction to Videohistory: The Smithsonian Institution and the Alfred P. Sloan Foundation Experiment*, Malabar: Krieger Publishing Company, 1993.

值的逐渐认可及 20 世纪 90 年代以来便携式数码摄像机的日渐流行，在美国口述历史学界开始出现一些主要以口述历史录影为记录手段的视频口述历史计划。其中最具代表性的是美国著名导演史蒂文·斯皮尔伯格（Steven Spielberg）与南加州大学（University of Southern California，简称"USC"）于 1994 年共同合作启动的南加州大学大浩劫幸存者影像历史基金会（USC Survivors of the Shoah Visual History Foundation），作为一个非营利机构，它致力于以视频的形式来记录犹太人大屠杀（the Holocaust）幸存者与其他目击者的证词。在 1994—1999 年，该基金会对来自 56 个国家（访谈语言达到 32 种）的将近 5.2 万受访者进行了录影访谈，录影时长总共多达 10.7 万小时，目前该基金会下属的影像历史档案馆（Visual Historical Archive）是全世界有关对犹太人进行大屠杀的最大的视频口述历史资料库。近年来，该基金会还成立南加州大学大浩劫基金会影像历史与教育研究所（USC Shoah Foundation-The Institute for Visual History and Education），其宗旨和目的也有所发展，尤其是它的记录对象扩展至其他大屠杀事件的幸存者和目击者，同时还强调这些口述历史影像资料的教育与行动价值。[1] 而如今，如果需要了解美国口述历史学界所开展的类似的视频口述历史计划，则可以通过 Google 或 You Tube 等搜索引擎或视频网站检索"visual oral history"或"video oral history"等关键词来查询更多项目信息。

而与此同时，美国口述历史学界在出版的学术刊物与理论方法著述及网站中对于口述历史录影问题的探讨也日渐增多，除了具体的实践操作方

---

[1] 有关该基金会和研究所的资料可以访问 http：//sfi. usc. edu/，2014 年 5 月 12 日访问；其他资料还可以参阅"Shoah Foundation"，from Wikipedia，http：//en. wikipedia. org/wiki/Shoah_Foundation，2014 年 5 月 12 日访问。这里需要提及的是，在 2014 年 2 月，12 位南京大屠杀幸存者的音像访谈资料也纳入该影像历史档案馆。详细内容可参阅张楠、王琦《南京大屠杀纪念馆与南加州大学合作，保留幸存者证言》，2013 年 12 月 13 日，http：//www. chinanews. com/cul/2013/12 - 13/5617998. shtml；"Nanjing Massacre Collection Integrated into Visual History Archive"，February 28，2014，http：//sfi. usc. edu/news/2014/02/Nanjing - massacre - collection - integrated - visual - history - archive。上述访问时间为 2014 年 5 月 12 日。

法之外,① 还提出了视频（影像）口述历史对于理解和诠释口述历史多元价值与意义的理论性思考。② 甚至有学者提出今天的口述历史实践与研究正处于一个日益被数字视频（digital video）所主导的文化与技术背景（cultural and technical context）当中。基于此，这位学者认为口述历史应当相当自然地成为视频历史（video history），而口述历史学家至少可能需要考虑配置视频技术，其目的不仅仅是为了满足屏幕和视频时代（screen and

---

① Stacy Erickson, *A Field Notebook for Oral History*, Boise: Idaho Center for Oral History, second edition, 1993, pp. 40-42; Donald A. Ritchie, *Doing Oral History*, New York: Twayne Publishers, 1995, pp. 109-130 (Chapter 5: Videotaping Oral History); Nancy MacKay, *Curating Oral Histories: From Interview to Archive*, Walnut Creek: Left Coast Press, 2007, pp. 41-48; Barbara W. Sommer and Mary Kay Quinlan, *The Oral History Manual*, Walnut Creek: AltaMira Press, second edition, 2009, pp. 31-43; Mary Kay Quinlan, Nancy MacKay, and Barbara W. Sommer, *Introduction to Community Oral History*, Walnut Creek: Left Coast Press, 2013, pp. 39-43 (Chapter 4: Community Oral History Tools and Technology); Barbara W. Sommer, Nancy MacKay, and Mary Kay Quinlan, *Planning A Community Oral History Project*, Walnut Creek: Left Coast Press, 2013, pp. 77-85 (Chapter 5: Equipment Planning). 以下文章来自"数字化时代的口述历史"网站, 具体包括 Scott Pennington and Dean Rehberger, "Video Equipment: Guide to Selecting and Use", in Doug Boyd, Steve Cohen, Brad Rakerd and Dean Rehberger (eds.), *Oral History in the Digital Age*, Washington: Institute of Museum and Library Services, 2012, http://ohda. matrix. msu. edu/2012/06/video – equipment/; Doug Boyd, "The Art of Lighting for Recording Video Oral History Interviews", http://ohda. matrix. msu. edu/2012/06/the – art – of – lighting – for – recording – video/; Joanna Hay, "Case Study: Using Video in Oral History: Learning from One Woman's Experiences", http://ohda. matrix. msu. edu/2012/06/using – video – in – oral – history/; Scott Pennington and Dean Rehberger, "Quick Tips for Better Interview Video", http://ohda. matrix. msu. edu/2012/08/quick – tips – for – better – interview – video/; Doug Boyd, "Audio or Video for Recording Oral History: Questions, Decisions", http://ohda. matrix. msu. edu/2012/06/audio – or – video – for – recording – oral – history/. 上述访问时间为 2014 年 5 月 12 日。

② Mary Marshall Clark, "Holocaust Video Testimony, Oral History, and Narrative Medicine: The Struggle against Indifference", *Literature and Medicine*, Vol. 24, No. 2, 2005, pp. 266-282; Michael Frisch, "Oral History and the Digital Revolution: Toward a Post-Documentary Sensibility", in Robert Perks and Alistair Thomson (eds.), *The Oral History Reader*, London and New York: Routledge, second edition, 2006, pp. 102-114; Charles Hardy III and Pamela Dean, "Oral History in Sound and Moving Image Documentaries", in Thomas L. Charlton, Lois E. Myers, and Rebecca Sharpless (eds.), *Handbook of Oral History*, Walnut Creek: AltaMira Press, 2006, pp. 510-561; Brien R. Williams, "Doing Video Oral History", in Donald A. Ritchie (ed.), *The Oxford Handbook of Oral History*, Oxford and New York: Oxford University Press, 2011, pp. 267-276; Michael Frisch, "Three Dimensions and More: Oral History Beyond the Paradoxes of Method", in Sharlene Nagy Hesse-Biber and Patricia Leavy (eds.), *Handbook of Emergent Methods*, New York: Guildford Press, 2008, pp. 221-238; Alexander Freund and Alistair Thomson (eds.), *Oral History and Photography*, New York: Palgrave Macmillan, 2011.

video age）的关注需求，同时也是为后代记录尽可能多维度的人类（受访者）经历。①

当然，需要指出的是，随着网络通信技术的发展，目前在日常生活与工作环境中以网络摄像机、个人电脑与智能手机为技术支撑的各种通讯（聊天）软件和远程网络视频会议系统日益成为人们之间的语音与视频交流的重要媒介。如果这种交流方式为口述历史工作者所采纳，那么这种跨越地理障碍的"跨空间访谈"将严重挑战传统的"面对面访谈"（face-to-face interview）模式，这对口述历史最基本的定义、方法与理论问题都势必产生重大冲击，而口述历史学家唯一能做的则是如何积极地应对与利用这些可能出现的挑战与机遇。

综上所述，记录技术从模拟时代向数字时代的转变为美国口述历史工作者提供了携带便利、操作容易、价格实惠及品质优良的数字记录设备的多样选择，它们不仅为研究者与未来的潜在用户提供了更高质量和更具多元信息（文字、声音与影像）的口述历史记录，同时也吸引越来越多的不同实践者参与到这场"大家来做口述历史"的学术与社会运动当中。在某种程度上，数字化记录技术为实现口述历史的民主化（democratization）提供了坚实的物质基础与技术条件，也部分实现了美国历史学家卡尔·贝克（Carl L. Becker）在20世纪30年代所倡导的"人人都是他自己的历史学家"这一崇高目标。② 当然，从技术角度而言，口述历史数字化记录的最大优势在于它们为后续的数字化管理与数字化传播（应用）提供了诸多便利。

---

① Peter B. Kaufman, "Oral History in the Video Age", *Oral History Review*, Vol. 40, No. 1, 2013, pp. 1-7.

② Carl L. Becker, "Everyman His Own Historian", *American Historical Review*, Vol. 37, No. 2, 1932, pp. 221-236. 此外，还可参阅卡尔·贝克尔《人人都是他自己的历史学家：论历史与政治》，马万利译，北京大学出版社 2013 年版。

二　数字化管理

美国口述史学界习惯于用管理（curation）这个术语来指代所收集的口述历史资料的后续处理、维护与保管工作。在南希·麦凯（Nancy MacKay）看来，管理是指历史记录（historical documents）的长期维护与管理（care and management），目的是确保对它们在当前和未来的最大程度的访问（maximum access）。[①] 而在数字化时代，信息管理者（curator）的任务与职责会变得更加复杂和多元。简言之，所谓数字化管理（digital curation）就是指数字资产（digital assets）的选择、保存、维护、收集与保管。[②] 而英国数字化管理中心（Digital Curation Centre）将这个概念进行进一步阐释，将其定义为"为了当前和未来的使用而对可信的数字化研究资料库（a trusted body of digital research data）进行维护和增值；它包含在整个研究生命周期（research lifecycle）其间对资料的积极管理。"[③] 该中心还指出，数字化管理生命周期包括以下几个基本步骤：概

[①] Nancy MacKay, *Curating Oral Histories: From Interview to Archive*, Walnut Creek: Left Coast Press, 2007, p. 19; Nancy MacKay, "Oral Historians and Curators: Friends, Foes or Strangers?" *Oral History Association Newsletter*, Vol. 39, No. 1, Sping 2005, pp. 1, 6-8.

[②] "Digital Curation", from Wikipedia, http://en. wikipedia. org/wiki/Digital_ curation, 2014 年 5 月 13 日访问。有关数字化管理的相关研究，还可参阅 Neil Beagrie, "Digital Curation for Science, Digital Libraries, and Individuals", *International Journal of Digital Curation*, Vol. 1, No. 1, 2006, pp. 3-16; Elizabeth Yakel, "Digital curation", *OCLC Systems & Services: International Digital Library Perspectives*, Vol. 23, No. 4, 2007, pp. 335-340; Adrian Cunningham, "Digital Curation/Digital Archiving: A View from the National Archives of Australia", *American Archivist*, Vol. 71, No. 2, 2008, pp. 530-543; Douglas Ross Harvey, *Digital Curation: A How-To-Do-It Manual*, New York: Neal-Schuman Publishers, 2010; Sarah Higgins, "Digital Curation: The Emergence of a New Discipline", *International Journal of Digital Curation*, Vol. 6, No. 2, 2011, pp. 78-88; Christopher A. Lee and Helen Tibbo, "Where's the Archivist in Digital Curation? Exploring the Possibilities through a Matrix of Knowledge and Skills", *Archiviaria*, Vol. 72, 2011, pp. 123-168; Arjun Sabharwal, *Digital Curation in the Digital Humanities: Preserving and Promoting Archival and Special Collections*, Oxford: Chandos Publishing, 2015.

[③] "What is digital curation?" http://www. dcc. ac. uk/about – us/dcc – charter/dcc – charter – and – statement – principles, 2014 年 5 月 13 日访问。

念化（conceptualise）、创建（create）、访问和使用（access and use）、评估和选择（appraise and select）、处置（dispose）、摄取（ingest）、保存行动（preservation act）、重新评估（reappraise）、储存（store）、访问和重新使用（access and reuse）及转换（transform）。① 那么，上述概念及其衍生内涵对于数字化时代的口述历史管理意味着什么呢？它们又可以提供哪些借鉴意义呢？不管怎样，它们至少强调了口述历史管理在口述历史整个环节当中的重要性，尤其对于充分发挥口述历史资料的未来应用价值更是如此。

综观美国口述史学的发展历程，可以发现一个非常明显的特征，就是美国口述历史工作者对于口述历史记录的兴趣与热情远远超过口述历史资料管理工作。而反映到口述历史方法论研究上，美国口述历史学界有关口述历史管理问题的探讨则明显滞后于口述历史记录（收集）问题。② 尤其是对于那些为了特定研究课题而从事口述历史访谈工作的个体研究者而言，他们的主要目的可能是从中寻找某些用以论证特定问题的证词而已，而在利用完之后则很少对收集到的口述历史资料进行较为系统的转录、编目、索引与保存，甚至有些口述历史资料被随意处置或丢弃。而事实上，即使对于那些以保管为目的部分档案馆、图书馆或历史学会来说，它们所收集的口述历史资料也未能得到很好的管理，尤其是它们的保存与开放利用问题。如在 2005—2006 年，美国口述历史协会与"学院中的民俗学、民族音乐学与口述历史"

---

① "The digital curation lifecycle"，http：//www.dcc.ac.uk/digital – curation/what – digital – curation，2014 年 5 月 13 日访问。

② Nancy MacKay，*Curating Oral Histories：From Interview to Archive*，Walnut Creek：Left Coast Press，2007，p.19；Michael Frisch，"Three Dimensions and More：Oral History Beyond the Paradoxes of Method"，in Sharlene Nagy Hesse – Biber and Patricia Leavy（eds.），*Handbook of Emergent Methods*，New York：Guildford Press，2008，p.222. 尽管维拉·鲍姆在 1978 年就呼吁应该重视口述历史的管理工作，她认为图书馆口述历史工作者应该肩负四个职责：创建（creating）、管理（curating）、利用（consuming）与咨询（counseling）。不过，这种主张并没有引起大部分美国口述历史工作者的足够重视。详细内容请参阅 Willa Baum，"The Expanding Role of the Librarian in Oral History"，in David K. Dunaway and Willa K. Baum（eds.），*Oral History：An Interdisciplinary Anthology*，Walnut Creek：AltaMira Press，second edition，1996，p.321.

梅隆基金会计划（Andrew W. Mellon Foundation Project on Folklore, Eth-nomusicology and Oral History in the Academy）共同发起的问卷调查中就发现很多回应者都反映口述历史访谈记录的保存与访问问题已经成为他们面临的最为紧迫的专业问题。回应者回复指出，成千上万的访谈仍然没有被转录、编目和索引，甚至没有公开，因而造成访问与利用的困难。[①]

究其原因，一个很重要的因素就是传统的以人工处理为主的口述历史管理模式给大部分人力、物力与财力不足的口述历史计划带来了诸多困难，而且无法更好地满足不同使用者对于以多元形态存在的口述历史资源的充分利用与开发。以转录（transcription）为例，作为口述历史访谈的一种文字呈现形式，从美国现代口述史学诞生开始，它就被认为是口述历史实践的一个不可缺少的组成部分。[②] 而在最初阶段，口述历史抄本甚至被看成一个口述历史访谈能够幸存下来并被存档、保存和研究的唯一记录。根据一些美国实践者回忆，除了保留一小段为展示访谈主体的声音与风格的原始访谈记录之外，访谈磁带通常会被擦除，因为书写抄本被认为能够提供足够

[①]　Linda Shopes，"Oral History and the Academy: An Assessment for the Mellon Foundation"，具体内容访问 https://web. archive. org/web/20130702211909/http: //www. oralhistory. org/wiki/index. php/Oral_ History_ and_ the_ Academy: _ An_ Assessment_ for_ the_ Mellon_ Foundation，2014 年 5 月14 日访问。

[②]　简单而言，所谓转录就是将口述历史访谈的录音或录影记录转换为具有一定可读性与逻辑性的书写抄本（transcript），而为保持口述历史访谈的互动性特征，口述历史抄本通常是以访谈者与受访者会话的形式进行整理与编辑。琳达·肖普斯认为，最理想的口述历史转录应该包括以下几个步骤：（1）对访谈中的言语和非言语话语（non-verbal utterances）进行逐字呈现，其原则是保持最低限度的编辑干预；（2）将随后产生的文件交由访谈者进行必要的准确性校正与核查；（3）交由叙述者进行必要的准确性校正、编辑及补充，有时候也可以对某些资料进行重新编辑或设限；（4）根据叙述者的修改进行重新修订；（5）根据意义和上下文等内容进行编辑和注释；（6）索引；（7）编目。详细内容参阅 Linda Shopes，"Transcribing Oral History in the Digital Age"，in Doug Boyd，Steve Cohen，Brad Rakerd and Dean Rehberger（eds.），*Oral History in the Digital Age*，http: //ohda. matrix. msu. edu/2012/06/transcribing – oral – history – in – the – digital – age/，2014 年 5 月 15 日访问。

的信息。① 当然,由于研究者对以音频、视频与文本信息多元呈现的口述历史访谈资料的不同需求,使得口述历史访谈是否与如何转录这个问题一直成为美国口述历史学界的争论焦点,而这个问题也直接引发了音视频记录与抄本二者何为真正的口述历史原始资料的激烈争论。实质上,这些争论主要是基于不同研究者对于口述历史访谈原始记录与抄本的利弊权衡。

综合美国口述历史学界的观点,口述历史转录(抄本)的优势主要体现在:(1)有助于提高口述历史资料使用的便利性。相对于录音或录影记录来说,研究者更加偏好或习惯于利用纸质抄本,而且更加容易浏览或查找抄本中的某一相关内容,同时也无须依赖于特定的播放设备。(2)可以在抄本上通过使用脚注、手写注释或删除线来编辑和记录修改过程,同时也能核对受访者口述的错误与片面之处,提高口述历史记录的完整性与准确性。(3)通过转录过程可以提高访谈者(研究者)对于访谈内容的理解程度,尤其有助于澄清访谈记录中的难以理解的内容。(4)由于抄本更像是一种传统的文献资料,因而更加容易成为不同使用者的一种固定的引用形式。(5)相对于模拟和数字媒介来说,纸质资料具有更长的寿命周期,因而抄本仍然是一种实现长期保存的最为稳定的媒介类型。(6)抄本可以作为口述历史录音或录影记录的一种索引,从而提高原始记录的使用效率。② 因此,大部分

① Elinor A. Mazé, "The Uneasy Page: Transcribing and Editing Oral History", in Thomas L. Charlton, Lois E. Myers, and Rebecca Sharpless (eds.), *Handbook of Oral History*, Walnut Creek: AltaMira Press, 2006, p. 237. 详细内容参阅 Alice Kessler Harris, "Introduction", Ronald J. Grele (ed.), *Envelopes of Sound: The Art of Oral History*, New York: Praeger, second edition, Revised and Enlarged, 1991, pp. 1-2.

② Louis Starr, "Oral History", *Encyclopedia of Library and Information Sciences* (Vol. 20), New York: Marcel Dekker, 1977, pp. 443-444; Thad Sitton, George L. Mehaffy, and O. L. Davis, Jr., *Oral History: A Guide for Teachers (and Others)*, Austin: University of Austin Press, 1983, pp. 17-18, 80-82; Tracy E. K'Meyer, "An Interview with Willa K. Baum: A Career at the Regional Oral History Office", *Oral History Review*, Vol. 24, No. 1, 1997, p. 101; Carl Wilmsen, "For the Record: Editing and the Production of Meaning in Oral History", *Oral History Review*, Vol. 28, No. 1, 2001, pp. 69-70; Elinor A. Mazé, "The Uneasy Page: Transcribing and Editing Oral History", in Thomas L. Charlton, Lois E. Myers, and Rebecca Sharpless (eds.), *Handbook of Oral History*, Walnut Creek: AltaMira Press, 2006, pp. 239-241; Nancy MacKay, *Curating Oral Histories: From Interview to Archive*, Walnut Creek: Left Coast Press, 2007, pp. 49-50.

美国口述历史实践指南或手册都提倡在条件许可的情况下应该尽可能地对口述历史访谈资料进行转录。①

　　当然，口述历史转录（抄本）的局限与弊端也日益显现，正如一些学者所指出的，口述历史转录会造成许多内在意义的扁平化（flattening），尤

① Mary Jo Deering and Barbara Pomeroy, *Transcribing without Tears: A Guide to Transcribing and Editing Oral History*, Washington: Oral History Program, George Washington University Library, 1976; David Kay Strate, *The Process of Oral History*, Dodge City: Cultural Heritage and Arts Center, 1976, pp. 45-48; Cullom Davis, Kathryn Back, and Kay MacLean, *Oral History: From Tape to Type*, Chicago: American Library Association, 1977, pp. 34-76; Willa K. Baum, *Transcribing and Editing Oral History*, Nashville: American Association for State and Local History, 1977 and 1991; James Hoopes, *Oral History: An Introduction for Students*, Chapel Hill: University of North Carolina Press, 1979, pp. 110-122; Frederick J. Stielow, *The Management of Oral History Sound Archives*, New York: Greenwood Press, 1986, pp. 17-26, 79-81, 89-91; Willa K. Baum, *Transcribing and Editing Oral History*, Walnut Creek: AltaMira Press, 1995; Willa K. Baum, *Oral History for the Local Historical Society*, Walnut Creek: Alta-Mira Press, third edition, revised, 1995, pp. 39-43; Edward D. Ives, *The Tape-Recorded Interview: A Manual for Field Workers in Folklore and Oral History*, Knoxville: University of Tennessee Press, second edition, 1995, pp. 75-85; Donald A. Ritchie, *Doing Oral History: A Practical Guide*, Oxford and New York: Oxford University Press, second edition, 2003, pp. 64-75; Glenn Whitman, *Dialogue with the Past: Engaging Students & Meeting Standards Through Oral History*, Walnut Creek: AltaMira Press, 2004, pp. 133-134; Valerie Raleigh Yow, *Recording Oral History: A Guide for the Humanities and Social Sciences*, Walnut Creek: AltaMira Press, second edition, 2005, pp. 315-324; Nancy MacKay, *Curating Oral Histories: From Interview to Archive*, Walnut Creek: Left Coast Press, 2007, pp. 49-56; Barbara W. Sommer and Mary Kay Quinlan, *The Oral History Manual*, Walnut Creek: AltaMira Press, second edition, 2009, pp. 67-78; Donna M. DeBlasio, "Transcribing Oral History", in Donna M. DeBlasio, Charles F. Ganzert, David H. Mould, Stephen H. Paschen, and Howard L. Sacks, *Catching Stories: A Practical Guide to Oral History*, Athens: Ohio University Press, 2009, pp. 115-135; Nancy MacKay, Mary Kay Quinlan, and Barbara W. Sommer, *After the Interview in Community Oral History*, Walnut Creek: Left Coast Press, 2013, pp. 55-70; 还可以参考其他国家的口述历史实践指南或手册，比如 David Lance, *An Archive Approach to Oral History*, London: Imperial War Museum and International Association of Sound Archives, 1978; David Henige, *Oral Historiography*, London and New York: Longman, 1982, pp. 63-64; Ken Howarth, *Oral History: A Handbook*, Stroud: Sutton Publishing LTD, 1998, pp. 153-157; Paul Thompson, *The Voice of the Past: Oral History*, Oxford and New York: Oxford University Press, third edition, 2000, pp. 257-264; Beth M. Robertson, *Oral History Handbook*, Adelaide: Oral History Association of Australia (South Australia Branch), fourth edition, 2000; Oral History Centre, National Archives of Singapore (ed.), *Memories and Reflections: The Singapore Experience: Documenting A Nation's History Through Oral History*, Singapore: Oral History Centre, National Archives of Singapore, 2007, pp. 79-88; Patricia Leavy, *Oral History: Understanding Qualitative Research: Understanding Qualitative Research*, Oxford and New York: Oxford University Press, 2011, pp. 49-66; Anna Bryson and Seán McConville, *The Routledge Guide to Interviewing: Oral History, Social Enquiry and Investigation*, London and New York: Routledge, 2014, pp. 35-51.

其是散失了口述历史自身所具有的口述性与视觉性特征。① 迈克尔·弗里斯科指出："口述历史的令人费解的秘密是没有人花费很多时间倾听或观看记录和收集的访谈记录。……每个人都承认口述历史的核心的音频与视频维度（audio-video dimension）并没有得到充分利用。一个更为浅显的道理是：在话语之外还存在意义世界（worlds of meaning），在任何真正意义上，没有人可以假设抄本相对于声音本身来说是一种对于访谈的更好再现（representation）。意义是依赖于背景和环境、姿态、语调、身体语言、停顿、表演技巧与运动的，并且需要通过它们表现出来。如果我们被局限于文本和转录的某种程度中，我们将永远找不到诸如此类的瞬间和意义，我们也将更少有机会研究、反思、学习和分享它们。"② 此外，就实际操作而言，口述历史转录是一项需要专业技巧、人力、物力与财力投入的复杂工作。③ 事实上，即使对于一些大型口述历史机构来说，高昂的费

---

① 琳达·肖普斯就认为转录将"口述"从口述历史中剥离出来，英文原文为"transcribing strips oral history of oral"。详细内容参阅 Linda Shopes, "Transcribing Oral History in the Digital Age", in Doug Boyd, Steve Cohen, Brad Rakerd, and Dean Rehberger (eds.), *Oral History in the Digital Age*, http://ohda. matrix. msu. edu/2012/06/transcribing – oral – history – in – the – digital – age/, 2014 年 5 月 15 日访问。

② Michael Frisch, "Three Dimensions and More: Oral History Beyond the Paradoxes of Method", in Sharlene Nagy Hesse-Biber and Patricia Leavy (eds.), *Handbook of Emergent Methods*, New York: Guildford Press, 2008, p. 223. 有关口述历史转录（抄本）弊端的讨论，还可参阅 Raphael Samuel, "Perils of the Transcript", *Oral History*, Vol. 1, No. 2, 1972, pp. 19-22; Susan Emily Allen, "Resisting the Editorial Ego: Editing Oral History", *Oral History Review*, Vol. 10, 1982, pp. 33-45; David K. Dunaway, "Transcription: Shadow or Reality", *Oral History Review*, Vol. 12, 1984, pp. 113-117; Graham Hitchcock and David Hughes, *Research and the Teacher: A Qualitative Introduction to School-Based Research*, London and New York: Routledge, 1995, pp. 222-223, 264-265; Donald A. Ritchie, "Oral History: From Sound to Print and Back Again", *OAH Magazine of History*, Vol. 11, No. 3, 1997, pp. 6-8; Conor McGrath, "Oral History and Political Elites: Interviewing (and Transcribing) Lobbyists", in Marta Kurkowska-Budzan and Krzysztof Zamorski (eds.), *Oral History: The Challenges of Dialogue*, Amsterdam and Philadelphia: John Benjamins Publishing, 2009, pp. 47-62; Marjorie L. McLellan, "Beyond the Transcript: Oral History as Pedagogy", in Douglas A. Boyd and Mary A. Larson (eds.), *Oral History and Digital Humanities: Voice, Access, and Engagement*, New York: Palgrave Macmillan, 2014, pp. 99-118.

③ Donald A. Ritchie, *Doing Oral History: A Practical Guide*, Oxford and New York: Oxford University Press, second edition, 2003, p. 65; Robert B. Perks, "Messiah with a Microphone? Oral Historians, Technology and Sound Archives", in Donald A. Ritchie (ed.), *The Oxford Handbook of Oral History*, Oxford and New York: Oxford University Press, 2011, p. 327.

用支出也让他们无法转录所有的口述历史访谈资料。以肯塔基大学图书馆（University of Kentucky Libraries）的路易·纳恩口述历史中心（Louie B. Nunn Center for Oral History）为例，目前该中心口述历史馆藏达到 9130 份访谈（截至 2015 年 1 月 7 日），而且有时候一年的新增访谈数量就达到 700 份。[①] 据该中心主任道格拉斯·博伊德坦言，即使能够获得适当的经费资助，也永远不可能转录所有的口述历史访谈资料。据他估计，该中心还有数以千计的访谈资料尚未转录，如果要对它们进行转录和整理则至少需要数百万美元，而这种可能性是非常小的。更为重要的是很多口述历史机构已经转录的抄本并没有很好的质量控制，其中许多抄本仅仅是"初稿"而已，这也直接影响了它们的使用价值。[②]

　　同口述历史转录一样，传统的编目（cataloging）与索引（indexing）方法不仅主要依赖于人工操作，[③] 而且其实际效果也并不尽如人意。就编

---

　　① 作为美国口述历史收藏和保存领域的领导者与创新者，路易·纳恩口述历史中心创建于 1973 年，其口述历史收集范围主要涉及 20 世纪与 21 世纪的肯塔基历史，主题侧重点包括政治史、农业史、体育史和老兵史等。该中心详细内容可以参阅 "Louie B. Nunn Center for Oral History", from Wikipedia, http：//en. wikipedia. org/wiki/Louie_ B. _ Nunn_ Center_ for_ Oral_ History；"The University of Kentucky College of Education Alumni Hall of Fame", http：//www. uky. edu/Education/ho-famers/Birdwhistell. html. 此外还可以访问其官方网站和博客 http：//libraries. uky. edu/nunncenter, http：//nunncenter. org/和 http：//www. kentuckyoralhisto ry. org/。上述访问时间为 2014 年 5 月 20 日。

　　② Doug Boyd, "OHMS：Enhancing Access to Oral History for Free", *Oral History Review*, Vol. 40, No. 1, 2013, p. 99.

　　③ 有关口述历史编目问题可参阅 James Fogerty, "Minnesota Receives Grant to Develop Oral History Cataloguing Guidelines", *Oral History Association Newsletter*, Vol. 27, No. 1, Winter 1993, p. 3；Marion Matters, *Oral History Cataloging Manual*, Chicago：Society of American Archivists, 1995；Nancy MacKay, *Curating Oral Histories：From Interview to Archive*, Walnut Creek：Left Coast Press, 2007, pp. 57-63；Beth M. Robertson, "The Archival Imperative：Can Oral History Survive the Funding Crisis in Archival Institutions", in Donald A. Ritchie（ed.）, *The Oxford Handbook of Oral History*, Oxford and New York：Oxford University Press, 2011, pp. 398-400；Nancy MacKay, Mary Kay Quinlan, and Barbara W. Sommer, *After the Interview in Community Oral History*, Walnut Creek：Left Coast Press, 2013, pp. 71-90.

目而言，在 20 世纪 90 年代末以前，美国大部分口述历史机构对于口述历史资料的编目处理主要是基于口述历史收藏（oral history collection）层次的信息描述，即使那些针对个别口述历史访谈（individual oral history interview）层次的信息描述也过于简单，除了提供基本的受访者、访谈者、访谈时间、访谈时长、访谈地点、访谈主题、访谈设限条件及保存与访问方式等简略信息之外，很难让使用者真正了解口述历史访谈中所包含的具体内容。而索引信息的制作也主要是基于访谈中所涉及的重要人物、地点、机构、事件与主题等基本信息，而且索引的制作很大程度上依赖于口述历史抄本，也就是说很少对口述历史访谈的音视频记录进行有效的索引编制。正是如此，对于一些使用者来说，如果缺乏耐心和时间的话，他们可能会倾向于阅读抄本资料和选择聆听或观看与抄本相应的音视频资料，而不会选择聆听或观看全部的音视频资料。① 而上述编目与索引方法的局限也直接影响了使用者对于口述历史资料的深度与有效检索（searching），进而直接影响了口述历史资源的使用价值。

正因如此，美国口述历史学界一直在寻找和探索改善口述历史管理水平和提高口述历史资料访问率和使用率的替代性选择。比如，在改善转录技术方面，除了利用转录器、文字处理机、电脑及文字处理软件等辅助工具之外，美国口述历史工作者最为期待的选择是利用自动语音识别技术（automatic speech/voice recognition）与转录软件来代

---

① Doug Boyd, "Achieving the Promise of Oral History in a Digital Age", in Donald A. Ritchie (ed.), *The Oxford Handbook of Oral History*, Oxford and New York: Oxford University Press, 2011, p. 292.

替人工转录。① 不过，真正产生影响的则是以数字化馆藏（内容）管理系统（digital collection/content management system）、元数据（metadata）、数字化编目与索引（digital cataloging and indexing）及数字化检索与保存（digital searching and preservation）为代表的数字化技术的开发与应用，它们在很大程度上改变了口述历史资料的转录、编目、索引、检索、访问与保存方式，进而最大限度地发挥它们的应用价值。需要强调的是，数字化时代的口述历史管理的主要对象是以数字化形态存在的口述历史文本、音频、视频、图像资料及有关它们的元数据信息，其主要特征是能够依托数字化管理系统实现

---

① 美国口述历史学界比较普遍使用的具有自动语音识别技术的转录软件包括 Express Scribe Transcription、Start-Stop Universal Digital Transcription、Dragon Naturally Speaking、HyperTranscribe、MacSpeech Dictate 及 Transana 等，有关它们及相关软件（输入检索词：automatic speech/voice recognition）的详细信息可以通过网络进行查询。此外，还可以在口述历史论坛 H-Oralhist（https：//networks. h－net. org/h－oralhist）上检索"transcribing"、"transcription"或"transcribing equipment/machine"等关键词来了解相关讨论。其他相关内容还可参阅 Julie Park，"An Evaluation of Voice Recognition Software for Use in Interview-Based Research：A Research Note"，*Qualitative Research*，Vol. 5，No. 2，2005，pp. 245-251；Jennifer L. Matheson，"The Voice Transcription Technique：Use of Voice Recognition Software to Transcribe Digital Interview Data in Qualitative Research"，*Qualitative Report*，Vol. 12，No. 4，2007，pp. 547-560；Kirstin Duffin，"Voice Recognition Software：A Brief Case Study"，*Oral History Association Newsletter*，Vol. 42，No. 2，Fall 2008，pp. 3-4；Brian Edward Johnson，"The Speed and Accuracy of Voice Recognition Software-assisted Transcription Versus the Listen-and-Type Method：A Research Note"，*Qualitative Research*，Vol. 11，No. 1，2011，pp. 91-97. 当然，实践证明这种较为适应商业办公业务的技术并不能很好地满足口述历史转录工作，尤其是遇到那些口述历史访谈中出现多种声音、口音、方言、嘟哝声及其他需要人工转录克服的障碍时，该系统就会出现大量识别错误。显然，对于口述历史转录工作来说，这种技术还远未成熟，正如马里兰大学帕克分校（University of Maryland-College Park）信息学专家道格拉斯·奥德（Douglas W. Oard，习惯简写为"Doug Oard"）教授所说："我们的最具挑战的内容的容易阅读的全自动转录（fully automatic transcription）功能还没有实现，甚至在将来也很难预见"。详细参阅 Paul Thompson，*The Voice of the Past：Oral History*，Oxford and New York：Oxford University Press，third edition，2000，pp. 257-258；Donald A. Ritchie，*Doing Oral History：A Practical Guide*，Oxford and New York：Oxford University Press，second edition，2003，p. 65；Cynthia Hart and Lisa Samson，*The Oral History Workshop：Collect and Celebrate the Life Stories of Your Family and Friend*，New York：Workman Publishing，2009，pp. 134-135；Bonnie S. Brennen，*Qualitative Research Methods for Media Studies*，London and New York：Routledge，2013，pp. 132-133；Doug Oard，"Can Automatic Speech Recognition Replace Manual Transcription?" in Doug Boyd，Steve Cohen，Brad Rakerd，and Dean Rehberger（eds.），*Oral History in the Digital Age*，http：//ohda. matrix. msu. edu/2012/06/automatic－speech－recognition/，2014 年 5 月 15 日访问。

这些不同形态的口述历史资料的一体化编目、索引、检索与访问。以下将以近年来广受美国口述历史学界关注的口述历史元数据同步系统（Oral History Metadata Synchronizer，简称"OHMS"）为例来重点介绍数字化管理系统对于改善口述历史管理水平与访问和利用效果的重要影响。

口述历史元数据同步系统于 2008 年由美国肯塔基大学图书馆路易·纳恩口述历史中心设计和开发，是为了使口述历史的在线管理、访问、检索与利用变得更为有效、流畅和经济，并以此提升口述历史资料使用者的用户体验（user experience）。作为一个以网络为基础的免费的开源（open source）应用程序，该系统能够为用户提供字词检索功能（word-level search capability）和标有时间码（time code）的口述历史访谈抄本或索引，并且将文本检索词（textual search term）与在线口述历史访谈（online oral history interviews）的音视频记录的相应时刻（corresponding moment）连接起来。[①]

口述历史元数据同步系统主要由 OHMS 应用程序（OHMS Application）和 OHMS 浏览器（OHMS Viewer）两个组件构成。前者是该系统的工作后台（back-end），通过它可以完成口述历史访谈记录（interview record）的导入和元数据的创建、口述历史抄本的编码与同步、口述历史音视频记录的编码索引（time-coded index）及包含访谈记录的 XML 文件或 CSV 文件的导出。而 OHMS 浏览器则是该系统的用户界面（user interface），当导出的 XML 文件被放置在网络服务器（web server）上的时候，可以通过 OHMS 浏览器实现该文件与在线口述历史访谈所依托的内容管理系统的相互连接，而最终呈现在用户面前的 OHMS 浏

---

① Doug Boyd，"OHMS: Enhancing Access to Oral History for Free"，*Oral History Review*，Vol. 40，No. 1，2013，p. 95；关于口述历史元数据同步系统的详细内容，可访问官方网站 http://www.oralhistoryonline.org/ohms/，2014 年 5 月 20 日访问。

览器则是包含播放器（可以播放音频或视频）①、编码抄本或索引及检索三个板块于一体的整合界面（见图1）。② 在浏览器页面下方的两个板块中，有些口述历史访谈记录可能会同时提供抄本和索引信息，而有些只提供其中一种信息。

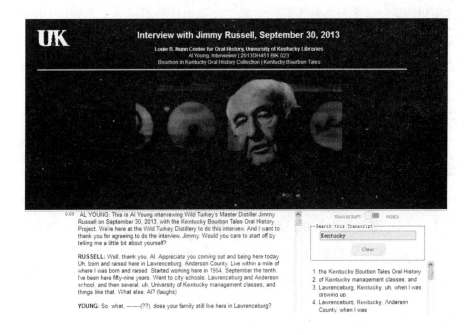

图1　OHMS 浏览器页面截图

图片来源：路易·纳恩口述历史中心网站（http://www.nunncenter.org/OHMS - Viewer/viewer.php? cachefile = 2013oh451_ bik023_ russell_ ohm.xml），2014 年 5 月 20 日访问。

---

① 口述历史元数据同步系统当前所使用的播放器是 jPlayer，它是一个用 JavaScript 写的完全免费和开源的媒体库（media library）。作为 jQuery 插件的一员，使用 jPlayer 可以在你的网页上轻松加入跨平台的音频和视频。具体内容可访问官方网站 http：//jplayer.org/，2014 年 5 月 20 日访问。

② "Oral History Metadata Synchronizer（OHMS）", from Wikipedia, http：//en.wikipedia.org/wiki/Oral_ History_ Metadata_ Synchronizer_ （OHMS）；"OHMS（Oral History Metadata Synchronizer）Getting Started Guide（V.2.1.19）", Last Updated：August 11, 2014, p.1. 该指南具体内容访问 http：//www.oralhistoryonline.org/wp - content/uploads/2013/06/OHMS_ Getting_ Started_ v2 - 1 - 19.pdf. 上述访问时间为 2014 年 5 月 20 日。

作为口述历史元数据同步系统的核心组件，OHMS 应用程序是需要用户验证的，因而个人用户必须拥有他们自己的账号(用户名和密码)。目前，路易·纳恩口述历史中心提供账号免费申请服务，同时还提供 OHMS 浏览器最新版本的免费下载。[①] 当使用账号登录 OHMS 应用程序之后，就可以开始对口述历史访谈记录进行各种不同的管理工作。而这些不同的工作则由 OHMS 应用程序的不同组件构成，它们主要包括访谈管理（Interview Manager）、元数据管理（Metadata Manager）[②]、索引模块（Indexing Module）、抄本同步模块（Transcript Synchronization Module）、叙词表管理（Thesaurus Manager）、访谈导入（Interview Import）和用户管理（User Management）等。当然，这些组件也会随着口述历史元数据同步系统版本的不断更新而有所调整。而在这些组件中，访谈管理则是 OHMS 应用程序的主枢纽（main hub），口述历史访谈记录的管理工作基本由它完成，其功能主要包括（见图 2）：(A) 创建新的访谈记录；(B) 预览完成的访谈；(C) 更新或编辑个别访谈层次的元数据（interview-level metadata）；(D) 启动索引模块；(E) 上传抄本；(F) 启动抄本同步模块；(G) 对访谈进行注释标记；

---

① 具体内容可访问 http：//www. oralhistoryonline. org/start – using – ohms/，2014 年 5 月 20 日访问。

② 对于在线口述历史资源的有效发现很大程度上取决于元数据的描述与获得，正是如此，有些口述历史工作者甚至提出要建立诸如"口述历史核心"（Oral History Core）等适用于口述历史的特定的元数据描述系统。相关内容可以参阅 Elinor A. Mazé，"Metadata：Best Practices for Oral History Access and Preservation"，in Doug Boyd，Steve Cohen，Brad Rakerd，and Dean Rehberger（eds.），*Oral History in the Digital Age*，http：//ohda. matrix. msu. edu/2012/06/metadata/，2014 年 5 月 20 日访问；Nancy MacKay，"'Oral History Core'：An Idea for a Metadata Scheme"，in Doug Boyd，Steve Cohen，Brad Rakerd，and Dean Rehberger（eds.），*Oral History in the Digital Age*，http：//ohda. matrix. msu. edu/2012/06/oral – history – core/，2014 年 5 月 20 日访问；Lindsey Barnes and Kim Guise，"World War Words：The Creation of a World War II-Specific Vocabulary for the Oral History Collection at The National WWII Museum"，*Oral History Review*，Vol. 40，No. 1，2013，pp. 126-134；Elinor Mazé，"Deconstruction Without Destruction：Creating Metadata for Oral History in a Digital World"，in Douglas A. Boyd and Mary A. Larson（eds.），*Oral History and Digital Humanities：Voice，Access，and Engagement*，New York：Palgrave Macmillan，2014，pp. 145-156. 有关元数据的相关研究可以参阅 Murtha Baca（ed.），*Introduction to Metadata：Pathways to Digital Information*，Los Angeles：Getty Publications，second edition，2008；Steven J. Miller，*Metadata for Digital Collections：A How – To – Do – It Manual*，London：Facet Publishing，2011.

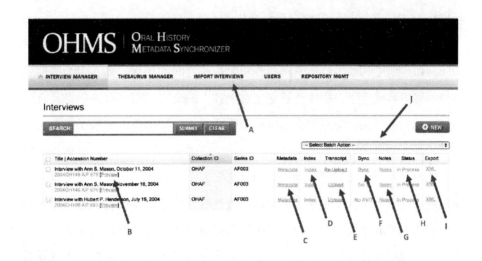

图 2　OHMS 应用程序截图

　　图片来源："OHMS（Oral History Metadata Synchronizer）Getting Started Guide（V. 2. 1. 19）"，Last Updated：August 11，2014，pp. 2-3.

（H）工作流程管理；（I）导出有关一个访谈的最后的 XML 文件或 CSV 文件；（J）批量导出或删除访谈。①

　　上文简单介绍了口述历史元数据同步系统的基本构成与操作方法，下文将侧重分析该系统的发展过程、功能演变与重要价值。正如一些学者所指出的，尽管以数字化网络平台和电子数据库为代表的数字化技术已经改变了口述历史资源的管理、呈现与访问方式，但是它们仍然是将以不同形态存在的口述历史资源（包括抄本、音频、视频、索引和元数据等）以独立的方式进行管理和呈现。通过这些网络平台或数据库，用户可以获得不同形态的口述历史资源，甚至能够实现文本检索（除了站内检索之外，还可以通过 Google 进行检索）。但是，这些不同形态的资源却很少被纳入一

　　①　"OHMS（Oral History Metadata Synchronizer）Getting Started Guide（V. 2. 1. 19）"，Last Updated：August 11，2014，pp. 2-3. 限于篇幅，有关口述历史元数据同步系统的基本构成和操作方法，请参考该入门指南。同时还可以访问其官方网站获得最新更新信息及在 YouTube 上检索"Oral History Metadata Synchronizer"关键词获得相关视频资料。

种能够促进访问与利用的整合系统当中。[1]

而于 2008 年设计和开发的第一版口述历史元数据同步系统就是为了实现同一口述历史访谈的抄本资料与音视频记录之间的相互联系，因为即使大部分网络平台或电子数据库能够实现对于抄本的全文检索，可是如果要查找与抄本相关的音视频记录则仍然依赖于手动查询。简单而言，该系统首先对已经转录好的口述历史抄本与音视频记录中的时间码进行同步，根据系统设计，抄本时间码设置以每分钟为间隔，这项工作由上述提到的抄本同步模块来完成。尽管它主要依赖于人工完成，可是其效率还是不错的，据路易·纳恩口述历史中心主任、该系统主要设计者道格拉斯·博伊德博士估算，一个小时的口述历史抄本可以在几分钟之内完成同步和上传，甚至在聆听或观看访谈的同时还可以完成索引工作。[2] 图 3 呈现了 OHMS 浏览器的一个页面和用户体验的初步感受，如图所示，在吉米·拉塞尔（Jimmy Russell）口述历史访谈抄本中检索 "Kentucky" 这个关键词，在浏览器页面下方的右边板块中就显示出抄本的上下文检索结果（contextual search results）。当点击任一检索结果就可以将用户带到浏览器页面下方左边板块所显示的抄本中的相应位置；而当用户点击相应的时间码标识时，则能够直接听到或看到口述历史音视频记录中的相应时刻。依此类推，用户就可以相当便利和有效地查找口述历史音视频记录中所有出现 "Kentucky" 这一关键词的相关内容，从而实现不同形态资源的互动。

可以说，口述历史元数据同步系统的最初版本相当有效和经济地完成了口述历史抄本的编码过程，并很好地实现了口述历史抄本与音视频记录

---

[1] Doug Boyd, "Achieving the Promise of Oral History in a Digital Age", in Donald A. Ritchie (ed.), *The Oxford Handbook of Oral History*, Oxford and New York: Oxford University Press, 2011, pp. 291-296.

[2] Doug Boyd, "OHMS: Enhancing Access to Oral History for Free", *Oral History Review*, Vol. 40, No. 1, 2013, p. 98. 需要指出的是，随着转录软件在口述历史抄本制作过程中的不断应用，大部分口述历史抄本在生成时都已经标有时间码，因此可省略同步这个过程。相关内容可以参阅 Michael Sesling, "Case Study: Transcripts, Time-Coding and You", in Doug Boyd, Steve Cohen, Brad Rakerd, and Dean Rehberger (eds.), *Oral History in the Digital Age*, http: //ohda. matrix. msu. edu/2012/06/transcripts – time – coding – and – you/, 2014 年 5 月 20 日访问。

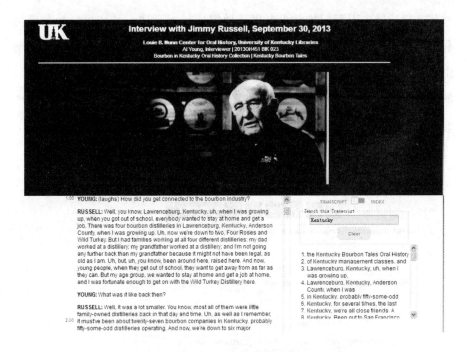

图 3　OHMS 浏览器（抄本）页面和用户体验截图

图片来源：路易·纳恩口述历史中心网站（http：//www. nunncenter. org/OHM S – Viewer/viewer. php？cachefile = 2013oh451_ bik023_ russell_ ohm. xml），2014 年 5 月 20 日访问。

之间的同步检索。不过，这个版本也存在两个非常明显的缺陷，道格拉斯·博伊德博士将其归结为两点：（1）主要针对那些已经完成转录工作的口述历史访谈；（2）其范围只适用于肯塔基州数字图书馆（Kentucky Digital Library）的口述历史收藏。[1] 基于上述缺陷，路易·纳恩口述历史中心对该系统进行了进一步开发，2011 年该中心将开发工作外包给阿特菲克斯技术咨询公司（Artifex Technology Consulting），新系统则新增索引模块并支持口述历史视频记录的处理功能。[2] 如上所述，因为财力与人力问题，

---

[1]　Doug Boyd，"OHMS：Enhancing Access to Oral History for Free"，*Oral History Review*，Vol. 40，No. 1，2013，pp. 95-96.

[2]　"Oral History Metadata Synchronizer（OHMS）"，from Wikipedia，http：//en. wikipedia. org/wiki/Oral_ History_ Metadata_ Synchronizer_ （OHMS），2014 年 5 月 20 日访问。

大部分口述历史保存机构并没有很好地完成转录工作，如何更好地处理与利用那些未经转录的口述历史资料则成为它们的当务之急。而新版口述历史元数据同步系统的索引功能则解决了这个问题，其操作既简单又高效。如图 2 所示，当登陆 OHMS 应用程序之后，用户只需点击访谈管理模块中的"索引"按钮，随后并会出现一个包含播放器和"现在标记"（Tag Now）

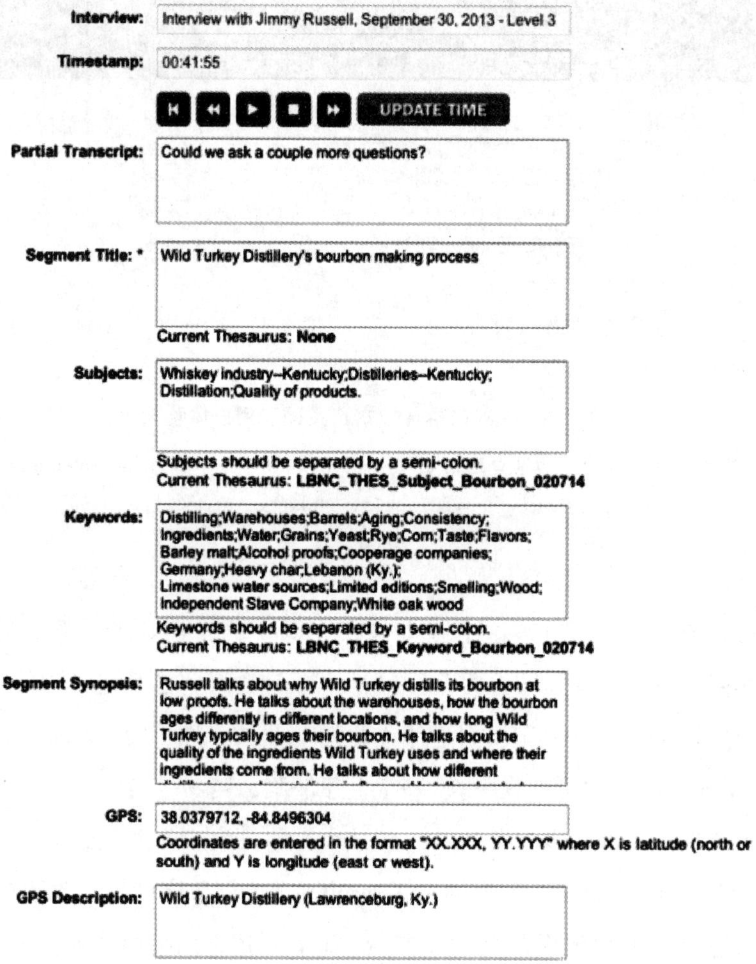

图 4　OHMS 应用程序索引模块截图

图片来源：来自视频教程（OHMS Indexing Levels：Level 3）截图，具体内容访问网址 http：//youtu. be/yImE3m1zSf8，2014 年 5 月 20 日访问。因屏幕所限，"超链接"（Hyperlink）和"链接描述"（Link Description）两个字段没有显示出来。

按钮的界面。在聆听或观看口述历史访谈的同时，索引编制者选择他们希望描述的片段（segment）。按下"现在标记"（Tag Now）按钮之后，系统会自动打开一个索引编制模块（见图4），其中包括以下几个字段：时间标识（Time Stamp）、部分抄本（Partial Transcript）、片段标题（Segment Title）、主题（Subjects）、关键词（Keywords）、片段概要（Segment Synopsis）、GPS 坐标（GPS Coordinates）、GPS 描述（GPS Description）、"超链接"（Hyperlink）和"链接描述"（Link Description）。等索引编制者完成这些字段的描述之后，点击"保存"（Save）按钮和关闭片段窗口，进而继续下一个片段的编制工作。[①]

需要指出的是，索引编制是一个非常主观的过程，在广度和深度上可能会有很大差异。在上述几个字段中，必须填写的是"片段标题"，而其他字段则依赖于用户对于口述历史访谈内容了解程度的不同需求。同时，如何对一个访谈进行较为合理的片段分割也依赖于用户的不同需求，路易·纳恩口述历史中心在参考教程中提供了三种不同层次的索引编制方法，以一个小时的口述历史访谈为例，第一层次的索引编制大概分割为5—10 个片段（描述字段包括片段标题和关键词）；第二层次的索引编制则大概分割为 10—15 个片段（描述字段包括片段标题、部分抄本、关键词、主题和片段概要）；而第三层次的索引编制则大概分割为 10—20 个片段（描述内容则包括上述全部字段）。[②]

当完成口述历史访谈的索引编制之后，通过 OHMS 浏览器就可以实现索引中的某一片段与口述历史访谈音视频记录相应时刻的同步检索。

---

① 详细内容可参阅 "OHMS（Oral History Metadata Synchronizer）Getting Started Guide（V. 2. 1. 19）"，Last Updated：August 11，2014，pp. 9-14；"Indexing Interviews in OHMS：An Overview"，Last Updated：May 15，2014，pp. 1-14，该指南具体内容访问 http：//www. oralhistoryonline. org/wp － content/uploads/2013/06/OHMS－Indexing －guide－5－15－14. pdf，2014 年 5 月 20日访问。

② "Indexing Interviews in OHMS：An Overview"，Last Updated：May 15，2014，pp. 1-2. 关于口述历史元数据同步系统的索引编制教程，可访问 http：//www. oralhistoryonline. org/documentation/，2014 年 5 月 20日访问。同时也可以在 YouTube 上检索 "OHMS Indexing"关键词获得相关视频资料。

如图 5 所示，在吉米·拉塞尔（Jimmy Russell）口述历史访谈索引中检索"Kentucky"这个关键词，在浏览器页面下方的右边板块中就显示出不同索引片段的检索结果。当点击任一检索结果就可以将用户带到浏览器页面下方左边板块所显示的索引片段的相应位置，而在点击该片段之后，将会显示所有的索引字段内容。同时，当点击"播放片段"（Play Segment）这个按钮时，用户还可以直接聆听或观看口述历史音视频记录的相应片段。以此类推，用户就可以相当便利和有效地查找索引字段中所有出现"Kentucky"这一关键词的片段，并访问相应的音视频记录。

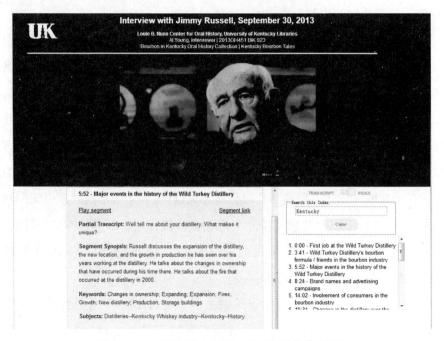

图 5　OHMS 浏览器（索引）页面和用户体验截图

图片来源：路易·纳恩口述历史中心网站（http：//www. nunncenter. org/OHMS – Viewer/viewer. php? cachefile = 2013oh451_ bik023_ russell_ ohm. xml），2014 年 5 月 20 日访问。

口述历史元数据同步系统索引功能的开发被认为是相当有效的，道格拉斯·博伊德博士认为它很好地解决了口述历史转录工作所需的财力与人力负担。相比较而言，完成一个小时的口述历史访谈的转录工作可能需要

6—8 小时，而利用该系统进行索引编制则只需 2—3 个小时，其成本也相应降低。以路易·纳恩口述历史中心为例，它们聘请研究生进行转录工作的费用是每小时 180—200 美元，而完成同时长访谈的索引编制的费用则低于 30 美元。① 此外，该系统索引功能还有助于实现对于口述历史访谈内容信息的准确检索与深度挖掘。② 如上所述，索引编制可以通过对于不同字段的多元描述，进而呈现口述历史访谈所包含的丰富内容，这相对于逐字抄本来说更具优势。特别是在检索过程中，以口述历史逐字稿抄本为基础的关键词检索是有局限性的，即用户检索时所用的关键词未必出现在抄本中，这样可能检索不到任何内容；而在索引编制时，用户会通过对于访谈内容主题的多元描述，尤其会用不同的关键词或国会图书馆标题表（Library of Congress Subject Headings）和其他叙词表（thesaurus）来描述同一个主题，这时所用检索关键词尽管并非受访者原词，也能保证检索到相关主题的内容。③ 正是如此，越来越多的美国口述历史工作者倡导将索引（以及交叉引用和标注）而不是转录作为创建口述历史资源描述性访问点（descriptive access points）的一种方式。④

---

① Doug Boyd, "OHMS: Enhancing Access to Oral History for Free", *Oral History Review*, Vol. 40, No. 1, 2013, pp. 99, 102-103.

② Brad Wolverton, "New Tool Could Help Researchers Make Better Use of Oral Histories", *The Chronicle of Higher Education*, July 7, 2011.

③ "Indexing Interviews in OHMS: An Overview", Last Updated: May 15, 2014, pp. 15-16. 近年来，美国一些口述历史计划制定了适用于特定主题的口述历史收藏的词汇表系统，比如南加州大学大浩劫基金会影像历史在线档案馆（USC Shoah Foundation Visual History Archive Online）就开发了一套大屠杀主题的口述历史索引词汇（Indexing term）系统。具体内容访问 http://vhaonline.usc.edu/keywordsearch/keywordSearch.aspx, 2014 年 7 月 4 日访问。

④ Michael Frisch, "Oral History and the Digital Revolution: Toward a Post-Documentary Sensibility", in Robert Perks and Alistair Thomson (eds.), *The Oral History Reader*, London and New York: Routledge, second edition, 2006, p. 105; Michael Frisch and Douglas Lambert, "Case Study: Between the Raw and the Cooked in Oral History: Notes from the Kitchen", in Donald A. Ritchie (ed.), *The Oxford Handbook of Oral History*, Oxford and New York: Oxford University Press, 2011, pp. 333-348; Douglas Lambert and Michael Frisch, "Meaningful Access to Audio and Video Passages: A Two-tiered Approach for Annotation, Navigation, and Cross-referencing within and across Oral History Interviews", in Doug Boyd, Steve Cohen, Brad Rakerd, and Dean Rehberger (eds.), *Oral History in the Digital Age*, Washington: Institute of Museum and Library Services, 2012, http://ohda.matrix.msu.edu/2012/06/meaningful – access – to – audio – and – video – passages – 2/, 2014 年 7 月 4 日访问。

　　而第二个关于兼容问题的解决则有赖于美国政府经费的大力支持，2011 年美国博物馆和图书馆服务研究院（Institute of Museum and Library Services）向路易·纳恩口述历史中心提供一项金额达 195853 美元的国家领袖基金（National Leadership Grant），资助该中心继续开发口述历史元数据同步系统。该基金主要是为了将口述历史元数据同步系统发展成为开源应用程序，使该系统能够作为一种插件与诸如 Omeka、Drupal、WordPress 和 Kora 等开源内容管理系统和 CONTENDdm 等大型商业内容管理系统实现兼容。① 而作为整个计划的一部分，肯塔基大学图书馆和路易·纳恩口述历史中心将与那些利用不同内容管理系统的各种机构进行直接合作，其目的是为了能够测试口述历史元数据同步系统与其他系统之间的兼容性问题。这些机构包括贝勒大学口述历史研究所（Baylor University's Institute for Oral History）、俄克拉荷马州立大学俄克拉荷马口述历史研究项目（Oklahoma State University's Oklahoma Oral History Research Program）、密歇根州立大学数字人文与社会科学中心（Matrix, the Center for Digital Humanities and Social Sciences, Michigan State University）和克利夫兰州立大学公共历史与数字人文科学中心（Center for Public History + Digital Humanities, Cleveland

---

　　① 在数字化时代，内容管理系统是在线发布和管理口述历史馆藏（包括文字、抄本、图像和音视频）的好方法。相关研究参阅 Eric Weig, Kopana Terry and Kathryn Lybarger, "Large Scale Digitization of Oral History: A Case Study", *D-Lib Magazine*, Vol. 13, No. 5/6, 2007; Kimberly Weatherford Stevens and Bethany Latham, "Giving Voice to the Past: Digitizing *Oral History*", OCLC*Systems & Services: International Digital Library Perspectives*, Vol. 25, No. 3, 2009, pp. 212-220; Sara Price, "Collection Management Systems: Tools for Managing Oral History Collections", in Doug Boyd, Steve Cohen, Brad Rakerd, and Dean Rehberger (eds.), *Oral History in the Digital Age*, Washington: Institute of Museum and Library Services, 2012, http: //ohda. matrix. msu. edu/2012/06/collection – management – systems/, 2014 年 7 月 4 日访问; Dean Rehberger, "Getting Oral History Online: Collections Management Applications", *Oral History Review*, Vol. 40, No. 1, 2013, pp. 83-94; Douglas Lambert and Michael Frisch, "Digital Curation through Information Cartography: A Commentary on Oral History in the Digital Age from a Content Management Point of View", *Oral History Review*, Vol. 40, No. 1, 2013, pp. 135-153.

State University)。① 当然，该系统也会与那些希望提升口述历史数字化管理水平与在线访问和传播率的小型机构乃至个别口述历史计划进行直接合作，而最终目标是能够满足用户的不同需求。正如道格拉斯·博伊德博士在 2013 年的一篇文章中所指出的，"口述历史元数据同步系统的任务已经从提高对于路易·纳恩口述历史中心口述历史馆藏的访问而转向支持其他大大小小的机构，为它们大批量地处理口述历史资源提供一个有效的、以用户为中心的发现平台（discovery interface），同时又能保证较低成本"②。

经过几年测试和完善，目前口述历史元数据同步系统已经成为其他口述历史机构管理和利用其馆藏的重要手段。据了解，贝勒大学口述历史研究所、佐治亚大学理查德·拉塞尔政治研究图书馆（Richard B. Russell Library for Political Research and Studies，University of Georgia）口述历史与媒体组（Oral History and Media Unit）、布鲁克林历史学会（Brooklyn Historical Society）和北卡罗来纳格林斯博罗分校（University of North Carolina at Greensboro）特殊馆藏与大学档案馆（Special Collections and University Archives）等机构就已经利用该系统对它们的口述历史资料进行处理和实现在线访问与利用。③ 图 6 和图 7 呈现了贝勒大学口述历史研究所和佐治亚大学理查德·拉塞尔政治研究图书馆利用口述历史元数据同步系统的浏览器页面和用户体验截图。

----

① 详细内容参阅 "New Web Search Technology to Aid Researchers Using Oral Histories"，*Newswise*，November 1，2011，http：//www. newswise. com/articles/new – web – search – technology – to – aid – researchers – using – oral – histories，2014 年 5 月 20 日访问。

② Doug Boyd，"OHMS：Enhancing Access to Oral History for Free"，*Oral History Review*，Vol. 40，No. 1，2013，p. 106.

③ 具体内容访问 http：//www. baylor. edu/oralhistory/index. php？id = 859918，http：//russell-doc. galib. uga. edu/russell/view？docId = ead/RBRL345GEOH – ead. xml；query = ；brand = default，http：//mnylc. org/metrocon15/schedule/project – briefing – session – 3/和 http：//uncgsp-ecial. blogspot. com/2014/10/enhancing – access – to – oral – history. html。上述访问时间为 2015 年 1 月 20 日。

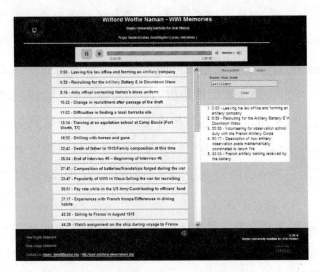

图6　贝勒大学口述历史研究所 OHMS 浏览器页面和用户体验截图

图片来源：贝勒大学口述历史研究所网站（http：//buelr. net/ohms – viewer/viewer. php？cachefile = Naman WWI. xml），2015 年 1 月 15 日访问。

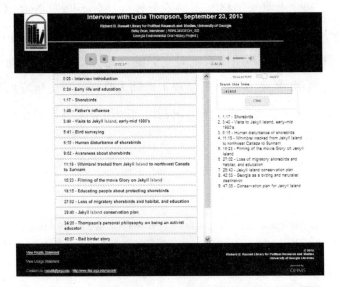

图7　佐治亚大学图书馆 OHMS 浏览器页面和用户体验截图

图片来源：佐治亚大学图书馆网站（http：//ohms. libs. uga. edu/viewer. php？cachefile = russell/RBRL345GEOH _ 002. xml），2015 年 1 月 15 日访问。

同时，该系统的价值也不断得到各种保存机构管理者与口述历史工作者的高度认可，它不仅能够让各种各样的机构提升数字化口述历史馆藏的使用，并且能够为那些具有丰富经验或缺乏经验的研究者节省大量时间。① 美国国会图书馆美国民俗生活中心（American Folklife Center）主任佩吉·巴尔杰（Peggy A. Bulger）就曾给予高度评价："在实现口述历史访谈的音视频记录与它们的抄本之间的同步方面，口述历史元数据同步系统是一项独创性的发明。……在某种程度上，它保存了口述历史的完整性。……在最近的时期内，在口述历史转录领域，我相信不会出现一个像口述历史元数据同步系统那么重要的发展。"② 此外，美国口述历史协会执行主任克利福德·库恩（Clifford Kuhn）也高度赞扬博道格拉斯·博伊德引领开发的这个系统具有相当的开创性，它真正将口述历史访谈当中丰富的字词（word）内容呈现出来。而道格拉斯·博伊德自己也坦言该系统具有潜在的革命性。③ 随着该系统应

_____

① Denise Harrison and Cindy Skalsky, "U Kentucky Goes Digital with Thousands of Oral Histo-ries", *Campus Technology*, September 9, 2009, http: //campustechnology. com/articles/2009/09/09/u‒kentucky‒goes‒digital‒with‒thousands‒of‒oral‒histories. aspx。在 2014 年 10 月 8—12 日于威斯康星麦迪逊（Madison, Wisconsin）召开的美国口述历史协会年会上，就有专门议题讨论口述历史元数据同步系统，其主题为《口述历史元数据同步系统的操作问题：多机构视角》（Imple-menting OHMS: Multi‒Institutional Perspectives），得到与会者高度认可。具体内容访问 http: //www. oralhistorycentre. ca/reports‒annual‒meeting‒oral‒history‒association‒implementing‒ohms‒multi‒institutional‒perspectives. 上述访问时间为 2014 年 5 月 20 日。

② "New Web Search Technology to Aid Researchers Using Oral Histories", *Newswise*, November 1, 2011, http: //www. newswise. com/articles/new‒web‒search‒technology‒to‒aid‒researchers‒u-sing‒oral‒histories, 2014 年 5 月 20 日访问。

③ Taylor Harrison, "University of Kentucky's Oral History Program 'Potentially Revolutionary'", June 30, 2013, http: //www. kentucky. com/2013/06/30/2699101/university‒of‒kentuckys‒oral‒history. html. 道格拉斯·博伊德在美国被认为是推动与促进口述历史数字化的开拓性人物，相关内容参阅 Mike Ashenfelder, "Doug Boyd and the Power of Digital Oral History in the 21st Century", Januar-y 4, 2013, http: //blogs. loc. gov/digitalpreservation/2013/01/doug‒boyd‒and‒the‒power‒of‒digital‒oral‒history‒in‒the‒21st‒century/; Doug Boyd, "Search, Explore, Connect: Enhancing Access to Oral History", Workshop in Columbia Center for Oral History, New York City, February 14, 2013, https: //www. youtube. com/watch? v = FF8o5SJgEWg; Doug Boyd, "Curating Voices: Oral History Archives in the Digital Age", Lectured in the International Conference on "Accounts of the Con-flict: Digitally Archiving Stories for Peacebuilding", Belfast, November 17-18, 2014, https: //www. youtube. com/watch? v = OGHlSZSoUAA. 上述访问时间为 2014 年 5 月 20 日。

用价值的不断推广，美国一些机构（比如布鲁克林历史学会）在招聘口述历史管理的档案工作人员时甚至要求应聘者能够了解和熟悉诸如口述历史元数据同步系统等相关技术与应用程序，这也从另外一个方面体现了该系统的重要性。[①]

除了口述历史元数据同步系统之外，近十多年来，美国口述历史学界还不断开发与应用各种类型的数字化管理系统，其中较具代表性的是美国著名口述历史学家迈克尔·弗里斯科所创建的兰德福斯联合有限责任公司（Randforce Associates LLC）为满足口述历史工作者需求而改进和定制的应用软件"InterClipper"，它于2002年首次发布。[②] 该软件被称为"实时音视频管理器"（realtime audio/video organizer），它能够对口述历史视频记录进行数字化、标注和索引，使其可以检索和使用。因为该软件允许每段口述历史视频记录都可以被标注、编码和复制到一个互动性数据库（interactive database）当中，从而能够实现

[①] 具体内容访问 https：//archivesgig. wordpress. com/2014/05/13/new – york – ny – oral – history – processing – archivist – brooklyn – historical – society/，2014 年 5 月 21 日访问。另外，布鲁克林历史学会于2005年3月宣布将利用口述历史元数据同步系统来促进对其"跨越边界、连接代际口述历史馆藏"（Crossing Borders，Bridging Generations Oral History Collection）的管理与利用。具体内容访问 http：//www. brooklynhistory. org/blog/2015/03/23/accessing – the – crossing – borders – bridging – generations – oral – history – collection – through – the – digital – humanities/，2015 年 3 月 25 日访问。

[②] Patricia Donovan，"Marketing Software Puts the 'Oral' Back in Oral History"，UB Reporter，May 1，2002，http：//www. buffalo. edu/ubreporter/campus/campus – host – page. host. html/content/shared/university/news/news – center – releases/2002/05/5676. detail. html. 有关兰德福斯公司的详细内容，可访问官方网站 http：//www. randforce. com/. 上述访问时间为2014年7月5日。

对于口述历史访谈内容的更深层次的分析。①

---

①　有关该软件的使用方法及价值可参阅 David Sworn，"InterClipper Report One（first version）"，November 13，2007，http：//storytelling. concordia. ca/storiesmatter/wp – content/ uploads/2008/10/interclipper – report – david – sworn – 2007. pdf；Steve High and David Sworn，"After the Interview：The Interpretive Challenges of Oral History Video Indexing"，*Digital Studies/ Le champ numérique*，Vol. 1，No. 2，2009，http：//www. digitalstudies. org/ojs/index. php/dig-ital_ studies/article/viewArticle/173/215；Douglas Lambert and Michael Frisch，"Meaningful Access to Audio and Video Passages：A Two – tiered Approach for Annotation，Navigation，and Cross – referencing within and across Oral History Interviews"，in Doug Boyd Steve Cohen，Brad Rakerd，and Dean Rehberger（eds. ），*Oral History in the Digital Age*，Washington：Institute of Museum and Library Services，2012，http：//ohda. matrix. msu. edu/2012/06/meaningful – ac-cess – to – audio – and – video – passages – 2/；Robert E. Warren，Michael P. Maniscalco，Eric K. Schroeder，James S. Oliver，Sue Huitt，Douglas Lambert and Michael Frisch，"Restoring the Human Voice to Oral History：The Audio – Video Barn Website"，*Oral History Review*，Vol. 40，No. 1，2013，pp. 115-118；Steven High，*Oral History at the Crossroads：Sharing Life Stories of Survival and Displacement*，Vancouver：University of British Columbia Press，2014，pp. 198-203；Michael Frisch，"Where is Oral History Heading? Trends in Oral History Indexing"，A Sem-inar presented by Oral History NSW in collaboration with the State Library of NSW（Sydney，15 No-vember 2014）此外，近年来还较受美国口述历史学界关注的口述历史数字化管理系统是卡耐基梅隆大学（Carnegie Mellon University）开发的"Informedia"技术，它可以实现可检索的口述历史抄本与视频记录之间的同步，该技术已经被用于"The HistoryMakers"数字档案馆计划（该计划包含350多份非裔美国人口述历史视频访谈）。相关资料访问 http：//www. idvl. org/，http：//www. informedia. cs. cmu. edu/和 http：//www. idvl. org/thehistorymak-ers/. 上述网站访问时间为 2014 年 7 月 5 日。详细内容还可以参阅 Michael G. Christel，Julieanna Richardson and Howard D. Wactlar，"Facilitating Access to Large Digital Oral History Ar-chives through Informedia Technologies"，Proceedings of the ACM/IEEE – CS Joint Conference on Digital Libraries（Chapel Hill，2006）；Michael G. Christel and Michael Frisch，"Evaluating the Contributions of Video Representation for a Life Oral History Collection"，Proceedings of the ACM/ IEEE – CS Joint Conference on Digital Libraries（Pittsburgh，2008）；Michael G. Christel，Rob-ert V. Baron，Geoff Froh，Dan Benson and Julieanna Richardson，"Accessing the Densho and His-toryMakers Oral History Collections via Informedia Technologies"，Proceedings of the ACM/IEEE – CS Joint Conference on Digital Libraries（Austin，TX，2009）；Michael G. Christel，Scott M. Stevens，Bryan S. Maher and Julianna Richardson，"Enhanced Exploration of Oral History Ar-chives through Processed Video and Synchronized Text Transcripts"，Proceedings of the 2010 Inter-national Conference on Multimedia（Florence，Italy：International Conference on Multimedia，2010）；Michael G. Christel，Bryan S. Maher and Julieanna Richardson，"An Interactive Flash Website for Oral Histories"，Proceedings of the ACM/IEEE – CS Joint Conference on Digital Librar-ies（Ottawa，2011）.

而与美国口述历史学界有着密切交流的加拿大口述历史工作者在该领域也做了相当有益的探索，其中最具代表性的是康考迪亚大学口述历史与数字故事中心（Concordia University Centre for Oral History and Digital Storytelling）于 2009 年所开发的口述历史数据库系统"Stories Matter"。它被称为由口述历史学家为口述历史学家开发的免费开源软件，因而具有非常明确的定制性，近年来也开始受到美国口述历史学界的不断关注。[①]

需要指出的是，诸如口述历史元数据同步系统这样的数字化管理系统并不是一个数字化保存机构（digital repository），[②] 因而它们仍然

---

① 限于篇幅，这里将不再详细介绍，具体内容可访问其官方网站 http：//storytelling. concordia. ca/storiesmatter/（2014 年 7 月 5 日访问）。有关该系统的使用方法与价值，可以参阅 Erin Jessee, Stacey Zembrzycki and Steven High, "Stories Matter：Conceptual Challenges in the Development of Oral History Database Building Software", *Forum：Qualitative Sozialforschung/Forum：Qualitative Social Research*, Vol. 12, No. 1, 2011, 具体内容访问 http：//www. qualitative – research. net/index. php/fqs/article/view/1465/3077, 2014 年 7 月 5 日访问；Steven High, "Telling Stories：A Reflection on Oral History and New Media", *Oral History*, Vol. 38, No. 1, 2010, pp. 101-112. 需要指出的是，康考迪亚大学口述历史与数字故事中心近年来积极致力于探讨口述历史（公共历史）与新媒体之间的关系，并于 2010 年发表了一份研究报告。该报告还罗列了 93 种口述（公共）历史学家可能感兴趣的数字化工具，这些工具包括索引和数据库、在线内容管理与网络发布系统、移动应用程序、音视频编辑和社交媒体等 12 种类型。具体内容可参阅 Steven High, Jessica J. Mills and Stacey Zembrzycki, "Telling Our Stories/Animating Our Past：A Status Report on Oral History and New Media", December 1, 2010, 具体内容访问 http：//storytelling. concordia. ca/sites/default/files/Knowledge Synthesis Report_ 0. pdf, 2014 年 7 月 5 日访问。

② 有关数字化保存的相关研究可参阅 Douglas Ross Harvey, *Preserving Digital Materials*, München：De Gruyter Saur, 2005；Douglas Ross Harvey, *Preserving Digital Materials*, Berlin：De Gruyter Saur, second edition, 2012；Adrian Brown, *Practical Digital Preservation：A How-To Guide for Organizations of Any Size*, London：Facet Publishing, 2013；Edward M. Corrado and Heather Lea Moulaison, *Digital Preservation for Libraries, Archives, and Museums*, Lanham：Rowman & Littlefield, 2014.

无法解决数字化时代的口述历史资源的保存问题。① 概括而言，目前大部分美国口述历史保存机构面临的主要挑战是原有记录介质和格式的日益退化和由此带来的资料保存的安全问题以及数字化音视频记录的大容量存储和存储的不稳定性问题。就前者而言，主要是那些以模拟记录格式记录的口述历史音视频资料开始面临快速的退化（obsolescence）危机，② 而针对这个问题，美国口述历史学界的普遍做法是将模拟记录转换成数字化格式，当然这项费用成本也是相当高的。③ 当

---

① 有关口述历史保存问题可参阅 Donald A. Ritchie, *Doing Oral History: A Practical Guide*, Oxford and New York: Oxford University Press, second edition, 2003, pp. 155-187; Nancy MacKay, *Curating Oral Histories: From Interview to Archive*, Walnut Creek: Left Coast Press, 2007, pp. 65-72; Doug Boyd, "The Digital Mortgage: Digital Preservation of Oral History", in Doug Boyd, Steve Cohen, Brad Rakerd, and Dean Rehberger (eds.), *Oral History in the Digital Age*, Washington: Institute of Museum and Library Services, 2012, http://ohda. matrix. msu. edu/2012/06/digital – video – preservation – and – oral – history/, 2014 年 7 月 5 日访问; Nancy MacKay, Mary Kay Quinlan, and Barbara W. Sommer, *After the Interview in Community Oral History*, Walnut Creek: Left Coast Press, 2013, pp. 91-102; Donald A. Ritchie, *Doing Oral History*, Oxford and New York: Oxford University Press, third edition, 2014, pp. 161-192.

② 南希·麦凯罗列了不同记录介质的生命周期与相关的保存问题，详细内容参阅 Nancy MacKay, *Curating Oral Histories: From Interview to Archive*, Walnut Creek: Left Coast Press, 2007, p. 68.

③ Doug Boyd, "Achieving the Promise of Oral History in a Digital Age", in Donald A. Ritchie (ed.), *The Oxford Handbook of Oral History*, Oxford and New York: Oxford University Press, 2011, p. 299; Sarah Cunningham, "The Preservation of Analog Oral History Collections through Digitization", in Doug Boyd, Steve Cohen, Brad Rakerd and, Dean Rehberger (eds.), *Oral History in the Digital Age*, Washington: Institute of Museum and Library Services, 2012, http://ohda. matrix. msu. edu/2012/06/preservation – of – analog – collections – through – digitization/; Scott Pennington and Dean Rehberger, "The Preservation of Analog Video through Digitization", in Doug Boyd, Steve Cohen, Brad Rakerd, and Dean Rehberger (eds.), *Oral History in the Digital Age*, Washington: Institute of Museum and Library Services, 2012, http://ohda. matrix. msu. edu/2012/06/preservation – of – analog – video – through – digitization/; Kara Van Malssen, "Digital Video Preservation and Oral History", in Doug Boyd, Steve Cohen, Brad Rakerd and, Dean Rehberger (eds.), *Oral History in the Digital Age*, Washington: Institute of Museum and Library Services, 2012, http://ohda. matrix. msu. edu/2012/06/digital – video – preservation – and – oral – history/. 上述访问时间为 2014 年 7 月 5 日。

然，那些最初就以数字化方式记录的口述历史资料也会因为格式问题（比如 cd，wav，mpeg，midi，mp3，mp4，ogg，wma，ra，ape，avi，wmv 和 rmvb 等）而存在播放困难，基于此，美国很多口述历史保存机构会规定一些口述历史音视频的标准记录和保存格式。不过，随着音视频播放技术的发展，大量兼容性播放软件技术的开发也一定程度上解决了这些难题。

尽管光盘（硬盘）技术的发展为大规模保存口述历史音视频资料提供了可能，不过光盘（硬盘）本身的生命周期问题及音视频保存的超大容量问题，也促使美国口述历史保存机构将口述历史资料保存在离线或在线（网络）服务器上面。而在数字化时代，为促进口述历史资源更为广泛的传播与利用，从 20 世纪 90 年代末以来，网络服务器更是日益成为美国大部分口述历史保存机构的重要选择。而网络服务器存储本身也存在一个相当致命的保存稳定性问题，数字化文件会因为病毒等原因而导致破坏或丢失。而为解决这个问题，近年来美国一些保存机构开始致力于发展数字化保存网络技术。其中最具代表性的是美国亚拉巴马州六所大学（Auburn University，Spring Hill College，Troy University，University of Alabama，University of Alabama at Birmingham 和 University of North Alabama）和亚拉巴马州档案历史局（Alabama Department of Archives & History）于 2006 年共同参与开发的亚拉巴马州数字化保存网络（Alabama Digital Preservation Network，简称"ADP-Net"），该项目也同样获得美国博物馆和图书馆服务研究院国家领袖基金的资助。该网络以服务器为基础，并利用斯坦福大学一个团队开发的多备份资源保存（Lots of Copies Keeps Stuff Safe，简称"LOCKSS"）软件作为技术支撑，从而实现同一数字资源的多节点保存与互补。简单而言，上述每个大学的数字资源的副本都可以保存在另外五个大学；如果其中一个文件出现损坏情况，另外五个文件将会用一个新的副本来代替或更新它。① 尽管这项网络技术并不是针对口述历史资料的数字化保存，可是其应用原理是完全相同的，尤其能够通过不同机构之间的合作伙伴关系来解决小型口述历史机构（因经费或人力所限）所面临的日益严重的超负荷保存问题。②

综上所述，以数字化馆藏（内容）管理系统、元数据、数字化编目与索引及数字化检索与保存为代表的数字化技术的开发与应用不仅改变了口述历史资料的转录、编目、索引、检索、访问与保存方式；更为重要的是，通过数字化管理能够更大限度地开发与挖掘口述历史资源中所潜藏的多元的和深层次的历史与文化信息，而这也将为口述历史的数字化传播与应用提供内容来源与技术支持。

三　数字化传播与交流

一般而言，开展一项口述历史计划的最终目的是为了让访谈资料能够为研究者乃至更为广泛的普通公众所了解与应用，这就直接涉及

---

① Aaron Trehub, "The Alabama Digital Preservation Network（ADPNet）", *Against the Grain*, Vol. 21, No. 1, 2009, pp. 46-47; Katherine Skinner and Matt Schultz（eds.）, *A Guide to Distributed Digital Preservation*, Atlanta: Educopia Institute, 2010, pp. 33-34; 42-45 and 113-114; Doug Boyd, "Achieving the Promise of Oral History in a Digital Age", in Donald A. Ritchie（ed.）, *The Oxford Handbook of Oral History*, Oxford and New York: Oxford University Press, 2011, p. 301; Donald A. Ritchie, *Doing Oral History*, Oxford and New York: Oxford University Press, third edition, 2014, p. 176. 有关阿拉巴马州数字化保存网络的详细内容可以访问 http://www.adpn.org, 2014 年 7 月 5 日访问。而有关 LOCKSS 的研究可参阅 Michael Seadle, "A Social Model for Archiving Digital Serials: LOCKSS", *Serials Review*, Vol. 32, No. 2, 2006, pp. 73-77; 吴振新、李春旺、郭家义《LOCKSS 数字资源长期保存策略》，《现代图书情报技术》2006 年第 2 期，第 35—39 页；王若琳《LOCKSS——实现网络电子资源的持久保存》，《图书馆杂志》2007 年第 2 期，第 58—60 页；吴晓骏《LOCKSS 数字资源长期保存策略及其应用初探》，《图书馆学研究》，2007 年第 3 期，第 25—27 页；黄田青、陈清文、陈心蓉《LOCKSS：图书馆数字资源长期保存的新机制》，《图书馆学研究》2007 年第 5 期，第 29—31 页；Vicky Reich and David S. H. Rosenthal, "LOCKSS（Lots of Copies Keeps Stuff Safe）", *New Review of Academic Librarianship*, Vol. 6, No. 1, 2000, pp. 155-161. 更多信息还可访问官方网站 http://www.lockss.org/, 2014 年 7 月 5 日访问。

② 当然，除 LOCKSS 之外，还有诸如 EPrints 和 DSpace 等数字化保存管理软件，详细内容参阅 Marion Prudlo, "E-Archiving: An Overview of Some Repository Management Software Tools", *Ariadne*, No. 43, April 2005, 具体内容访问 http://www.ariadne.ac.uk/issue43/prudlo, 2014 年 7 月 5 日访问。

口述历史资源的公共传播与应用问题。正如道格拉斯·博伊德所说：
"我们之所以努力采访叙述者、记录社群和保存口述历史，是因为我们
希望最终能够将个人故事连接到历史记录当中，并有助于形成一种更
为全面的社会、文化与人类理解。并不是所有的计划都是为了实现即
时和广泛传播，其中有些甚至是终身设限保存。然而，我们的希望是
那些记录的口述历史访谈最终能够与未来的研究者产生共鸣并有所联
系。"① 而在 21 世纪到来之际，美国伊利诺伊大学厄巴纳—香槟分校
（University of Illinois at Urbana-Champaign）图书馆与信息科学研究院
（Graduate School of Library and Information Science）伊丽莎白·菲加（E-
lizabeth Gremore Figa）通过调查总结了兼具传统与创新特征的口述历史
资源的主要传播形式与成果类型，其中包括：（1）书籍（历史、传记、
诗歌、出版的抄本）；（2）讲故事盒式录音带、口述历史录音带、有声
读物（audio books）和光碟；（3）各种形式的电影；（4）培训视频与书
籍；（5）博物馆与多媒体展览、艺术设施（art installations）；（6）文化
保护和遗产计划；（7）流动/语音导览（driving/audio tours）；（8）广播
节目；（9）为孩子与老师提供的教育资料；（10）戏剧作品（表演、歌
剧、戏剧和喜剧）；（11）舞蹈设计；（12）万维网网站；（13）法律诉
状（legal briefs）和其他法律相关文件。② 尽管如此，在很多口述历史学
家看来，口述历史资料（尤其是它的音视频记录）仍然是一种尚未得到
充分利用的历史与文化信息资源，部分原因在于研究者和普通公众在访

---

① Douglas A. Boyd, "Search, Explore, Connect: Disseminating Oral History in the Digital Age", in Douglas A. Boyd, Steve Cohen, Brad Rakerd, and Dean Rehberger (eds.), *Oral History in the Digital Age*, Washington: Institute of Museum and Library Services, 2012, http://ohda.matrix.msu.edu/2012/06/search–explore–connect/, 2014 年 7 月 5 日访问。

② Elizabeth Gremore Figa, "Products of Oral History Work", H-Oralhist, June 22, 2000. 具体内容访问 http://h–net.msu.edu/cgi–bin/logbrowse.pl? trx = vx&list = h – oralhist&month = 0006&w = d&msg = xymGV0IVnjCtA8VDMsJobQ&user = &pw = , 2014 年 7 月 5 日访问。

问与利用口述历史收藏方面存在困难或不便。①

而 20 世纪 90 年代以来，以计算机和互联网为代表的数字化革命则大大提升了口述历史资料进行全球传播与共享的机会与可能性；② 道格拉

---

① Bruce H. Bruemmer, "Access to Oral History: A National Agenda", *American Archivist*, Vol. 54, No. 4, 1991, pp. 494-501; Michael Frisch, "Three Dimensions and More: Oral History Beyond the Paradoxes of Method", in Sharlene Nagy Hesse-Biber and Patricia Leavy (eds.), *Handbook of Emergent Methods*, New York: Guildford Press, 2008, pp. 223; Richard Cándida Smith, "Case Study: What Is It That University-Based Oral History Can Do? The Berkeley Experience", in Donald A. Ritchie (ed.), *The Oxford Handbook of Oral History*, Oxford and New York: Oxford University Press, 2011, p. 422; Doug Boyd, "OHMS: Enhancing Access to Oral History for Free", *Oral History Review*, Vol. 40, No. 1, 2013, p. 95.

② 严格来说，美国口述历史学界利用互联网访问和传播口述历史信息主要开始于 20 世纪 90 年代末和 21 世纪初，阿拉斯加大学费尔班克斯分校口述历史项目（Oral History Program, University of Alaska Fairbanks）研究助理凯伦·布鲁斯特（Karen Brewster）在 2000 年 10 月撰写的有关在线口述历史计划的调查（从 1999 年 11 月开始）报告中就曾指出："五年前，网络访问口述历史是无法想象的。而今天，技术已经有所进步，网络日益成为信息分享与检索的主流方法。"而唐纳德·里奇的经典之作《大家来做口述历史》三个版本的出版时间及对于数字化与口述历史关系的分析也能说明这一点。在第一版于 1995 年出版时，作者甚至没有提到互联网与数字化等术语，只是在第八章"展现口述历史"（Presenting Oral History）最后一节中以"计算机与互动视频"（Computers and Interactive Video）为题来说明计算机技术对于呈现口述历史资料的重要意义。在第二版于 2003 年出版时，作者则重点强调了数字化革命对于口述历史的全方位影响，而第八章"展现口述历史"最后一节的题目也修改为"光盘与互联网"（CD-ROM and the Internet）。而在 2014 年出版的第三版中，作者更是将第八章"展现口述历史"第一节安排为"口述历史网站"（Oral History Websites），足见以互联网为基础的数字化技术对于口述历史资料传播与呈现的重要意义。具体内容请参阅 Karen Brewster, "Internet Access to Oral Recordings: Finding the Issues", October 25, 2000, 具体内容访问 http://library. uaf. edu/aprc/brewster1/, 2014 年 7 月 5 日访问; Donald A. Ritchie, *Doing Oral History*, New York: Twayne Publishers, 1995, pp. 205-206; Donald A. Ritchie, *Doing Oral History: A Practical Guide*, Oxford and New York: Oxford University Press, second edition, 2003, pp. 80-83, 245-251; Donald A. Ritchie, *Doing Oral History*, Oxford and New York: Oxford University Press, third edition, 2014, pp. 70-72, 235-242. 另外, 笔者查询 1997 年的美国口述历史协会网站时发现它所提供的其他网站链接中，美国大概只有 21 个口述历史机构或计划设有网站。具体内容访问 https://web. archive. org/web/19970616065251/http://www. baylor. edu/~OHA/, 2014 年 7 月 5 日访问。据笔者查询相关网站推测，美国最早设立官方网站的口述历史机构可能是加州州立大学长滩分校口述历史项目（Oral History Program, California State University at Long Beach）, 该网站创建于 1995 年。具体内容访问 https://web. archive. org/web/19970516113201/http://www. csulb. edu/~agunns/relprm/oral01. html, 2014 年 7 月 5 日访问。随后加州大学伯克利分校地区口述历史办公室、犹他州立大学口述历史项目（Utah State University Oral History Program）和康涅狄格大学斯托尔斯分校口述历史中心（Center for Oral History, University of Connecticut at Storrs）等官方网站于 1996 年创建。而美国口述历史协会官方网站（当时网址是 http://www. baylor. edu/~OHA/）则是创建于 1997 年, 详细内容参阅 Rebecca Sharpless, "Executive Secretary's Report", *Oral History Association Newsletter*, Vol. 31, No. 1, Winter 1997, p. 2.

斯·博伊德就曾指出，从口述历史角度而言，数字化革命的最具革命性的影响是以新的、创造性的和创新性的方式为口述历史的访问、出版与最终传播提供各种各样的可能性。这些可能性包括：在数字化资源库（digital repository）中保存、归档或访问口述历史资料；设计互动性社群网站；制作播客系列（podcast series）；制作音频或视频纪录片；创建电子出版物；设计移动应用程序；策划实体或数字展览；在数字化背景中设计口述历史计划；在数字化领域（digital domain）中传播口述历史计划。① 当然，以互联网技术为核心的数字化发布与传播形式之所以日益受到重视和欢迎，其根本原因在于互联网本身的诸多优势都相当符合口述历史学家的工作性质。南希·麦凯将这些优势归纳为以下几个方面：（1）实现全球访问；（2）提供精确检索；（3）提供多媒体展示；（4）提供超链接；（5）设置在线访问权限。② 而对于互联网为口述历史学家所带来的好处，唐纳德·里奇在其最新版《大家来做口述历史》一书中更是称赞不已，"互联网为分享和推广口述历史访谈开启了世界范围内的可能性（worldwide possibilities），不管是以抄本还是以音视频记录形式存在。不需要长途跋涉到遥远的档案馆，研究者就能够从他们自己所在的位置访问访谈资料，并且可以实现主题或关键词检索及链接到相关的收藏。家庭与社区都能查看它们自己的口述历史。学生们可以通过考察其他访谈来学习访谈技巧。档案馆可以通过淘汰那些过时的目录和其他

---

① Douglas A. Boyd, "Search, Explore, Connect: Disseminating Oral History in the Digital Age", in Douglas A. Boyd, Steve Cohen, Brad Rakerd, and Dean Rehberger (eds.), *Oral History in the Digital Age*, Washington: Institute of Museum and Library Services, 2012, http://ohda.matrix.msu.edu/2012/06/search-explore-connect/, 2014 年 7 月 5 日访问。

② Nancy MacKay, *Curating Oral Histories: From Interview to Archive*, Walnut Creek: Left Coast Press, 2007, p. 73. 克利福德·库恩还指出，互联网的直接性（immediacy）、可访问性（accessibility）、动态性（dynamism）、民主性（democratic quality）、互动性（interactivity），以及结合交流与信息的多元形式的能力为超越传统的空间和时间界限与促进口述历史的巨大衍生提供了众多可能性。详细参阅 Clifford M. Kuhn, "Oral History: Media, Message, and Meaning", in Donald A. Ritchie (ed.), *The Oxford Handbook of Oral History*, Oxford and New York: Oxford University Press, 2011, p. 307.

印刷的检索工具（printed finding aids）来节省成本。"① 下文将从数字化
传播的内容与形式两个方面并结合一些典型口述历史机构或计划的具体
实践来分析美国口述历史学界在促进与推动口述历史数字化传播与应用
领域的探索与努力。②

　　就传播内容而言，网络传播和呈现口述历史资料的主要形态包括以数
字化形式存在的口述历史目录、口述历史计划（收藏）或个别口述历史访
谈的元数据信息、完整抄本、音视频摘录和完整音视频记录。在互联网时
代到来之前，美国一些口述历史机构或保存口述历史资料的专业机构（图
书馆、档案馆、博物馆和历史学会等）从 20 世纪 50 年代开始就以纸质或
缩微形式出版口述历史馆藏指南或目录来介绍和宣传其馆藏资源。比如拉
德克利夫学院施莱辛格图书馆（Radcliffe College Schlesinger Library）、哥伦
比亚大学口述历史研究室、普林斯顿大学图书馆（Princeton University
Library）、森林历史学会、加州大学伯克利分校地区口述历史办公室、加州

---

　　① Donald A. Ritchie, *Doing Oral History*, Oxford and New York：Oxford University Press, third e-
dition, 2014, p. 235.

　　② 尽管具有上述优势，可是口述历史学家最初接触互联网时还是有些忧虑并保持谨慎态度，
其原因包括技术、行政管理、法律与伦理等诸多问题。因此，在 21 世纪最初几年间，美国口述历
史学界推动口述历史资源在线化传播与呈现的步伐还是比较缓慢的。2000 年凯伦·布鲁斯特的调
查显示，在 64 个在线口述历史计划中，不足一半的计划将口述历史访谈内容上传到网络上（大部
分都只上传口述历史摘录，而不是完整的访谈资料，其中只有一个计划上传了完整的音频记录），
而剩下的计划只提供口述历史访谈资料的清单、检索工具或有关口述历史计划的描述。而 2004 年
南希·麦凯有关口述历史管理的调查也反映了类似特征，在 62 个接受问卷调查的口述历史机构或
计划中，其中有 20 个没有上网，而有机构或计划网站的超过半数（不过无法在线访问它们的口述
历史收藏）。在剩下的机构或计划当中，其中有 27 个回复指它们在线提供有关口述历史资料的摘
要、检索工具或某种形式的摘录（文本或音频），只有 1 个回复指它们提供完整的视频和抄本数字
化档案资料，并向登记访客开放。具体内容参阅 Karen Brewster, "Internet Access to Oral Recordings：
Finding the Issues", October 25, 2000, 具体内容访问 http：//library. uaf. edu/aprc/brewster1/, 2014
年 7 月 5 日访问；Nancy MacKay, "Curating Oral Histories：Survey Results", 2004, 具体内容访问
https：//web. archive. org/web/20081121014308/http：//www. nancymackay. net/curating/final　Survey
Results. htm, 2014 年 7 月 5 日访问；Nancy MacKay, *Curating Oral Histories：From Interview to Archive*, Walnut Creek：Left Coast Press, 2007, pp. 73-74.

大学洛杉矶分校口述历史项目、美国参议院历史办公室、明尼苏达州历史学会 (Minnesota Historical Society)、贝勒大学口述历史研究所、美国国家航空航天博物馆 (National Air and Space Museum)、哈佛大学中东研究中心 (Center for Middle Eastern Studies, Harvard University) 和杜鲁门总统图书馆等。除此之外,一些机构和个人还编辑出版了全国性或地区性的口述历史收藏指南或目录,在一定程度上,它们也有助于了解美国口述史学发展的整体情况与地区特征。

　　而对于那些希望在线呈现和传播其口述历史馆藏信息的早期实践者而言,[①] 将这些已经编辑和整理好的口述历史指南或目录上传到网络上则成为首选。除了以网页或在网页上提供 Word 或 PDF 等格式的下载链接形式之外,[②] 有些口述历史机构还开发了专门用于检索和访问其口述历史目录

---

　　① 据相关报告显示,美国口述历史协会出版物委员会 (Publications Committee) 于 1997 年开始讨论在互联网上传播口述历史资料这一问题上所存在的分歧,从这里也可以看出当时一些人对于在线传播口述历史资料也是持保留和谨慎态度的。详细内容参阅 Rebecca Sharpless, "Executive Secretary's Report", *Oral History Association Newsletter*, Vol. 31, No. 2, Spring 1997, p. 2.

　　② 比如,惠顿学院葛培理中心档案馆 (Wheaton College Billy Graham Center Archives) 从 1997 年开始就将其口述历史馆藏指南上传到中心档案馆网站上。目前该网站还新增包括完整抄本、音频记录和以口述历史资料为基础的相关成果。具体内容访问 https://web. archive. org/web/19970416064413/http://www. wheaton. edu/bgc/archives/oralhist. html 和 http://www2. wheaton. edu/bgc/archives/oralhist. html。而加州大学伯克利分校地区口述历史办公室从 1998 年开始就将它们出版的纸质印刷目录全部上传到官方网站上。具体内容访问 https://web. archive. org/web/19980209172750/http://www. lib. berkeley. edu/BANC/ROHO/。此外,更多信息可通过 Google 检索 "oral history catalogue/catalog/index/guide" 等关键词来查询,便可以发现各种主题的口述历史目录,比如美国国家航空和宇宙航行局口述历史馆藏 (NASA Oral History Collection, http://history. nasa. gov/hqinventory. pdf)、普林斯顿大学图书馆杜勒斯口述历史目录 (John Foster Dulles Oral History Catalog, http://www. princeton. edu/~mudd/finding_ aids/jfdoral. html)、北密歇根大学意大利裔美国移民口述史目录 (Northern Michigan University Italian – American Immigrant Oral History Catalog, http://www. nmu. edu/archives/node/103)、加州州立大学富尔顿分校口述历史与公共历史中心 (Center for Oral and Public History, California State University, Fullerton) 口述历史馆藏目录 (http://coph. fullerton. edu/collections. asp)、美国空军历史研究部口述历史目录 (Air Force Historical Research Agency Oral History Catalogue, http://www. afhra. af. mil/documents/oralhist-orycatal-ogue. asp) 和美国海军学会口述历史项目在线目录 (U. S. Naval Institute Oral History Program Online Catalog, http://www. usni. org/heritage/oral – history) 等。上述访问时间为 2014 年 7 月 5 日。

以及相关元数据信息的在线查询系统，其中目前最具代表性的是哥伦比亚大学口述历史中心与哥大图书馆数字保存团队联合设计的"口述历史在线门户"（Oral History Portal）及肯塔基大学图书馆路易·纳恩口述历史中心开发的在线口述历史目录查询系统——"SPOKE"。这两个系统都能够实现针对口述历史馆藏、口述历史计划及个别口述历史访谈的关键词检索，相对来说，"SPOKE"的功能则更为强大，它同时具有浏览功能（按照主题），而且可以根据目录检索结果直接链接到那些能够在线阅读或观看的口述历史抄本或音视频记录。① 当然，那些没有专门口述历史目录查询系统的口述历史机构或计划会将相关编目信息纳入它们所在的图书馆或档案馆的馆藏目录系统以及诸如研究图书馆信息网络（Research Libraries Information Network，简称 RLIN）或联机计算机图书馆中心（Online Computer Library Center，简称 OCLC）等在线联合目录系统当中，以实现口述历史目录的全球在线检索与访问。②

与此同时，随着计算机编目系统（尤其是元数据描述系统）的发展及在口述历史编目过程中的不断应用，传统的较为简单地呈现口述历史基本信息（可能只包括访谈者、受访者、访谈时间、访谈时长、访谈主题等）的人工编目方法已经不再适应数字化时代对于检索与访问目录深度内容的

---

① 具体内容访问 http：//oralhistoryportal. cul. columbia. edu/和 http：//www. kentuckyoralhistory. org/。就具体口述历史计划而言，有些机构也会专门设立数据库提供检索和浏览功能，比如哈佛大学伊朗人口述历史计划（Iranian Oral History Project）和肯塔基州历史学会（Kentucky Historical Society）肯塔基州民权运动口述历史计划（Civil Rights Movement in Kentucky Oral History Project），具体内容访问 http：//ted. lib. harvard. edu/ted/deliver/advancedsearch？collection = iohp 和 http：//205. 204. 134. 47/civil_ rights_ mvt/。上述访问日期为 2014 年 7 月 8 日。需要指出的，在 20 世纪 80 年代末期，美国西南口述历史协会（Southwest Oral History Association）就开始创建口述历史馆藏目录在线数据库。详细内容参阅 Cathryn A. Gallacher and Dale E. Treleven，"Developing An Online Database and Printed Directory and Subject Guide to Oral History Collections"，*Oral History Review*，Vol. 16，No. 1，1988，pp. 33-68.

② RLIN 于 2006 年并入 OCLC，目前 OCLC 拥有全球最大的图书馆在线联合目录系统——"WorldCat"（https：//www. worldcat. org/），而且 WorldCat 的编目记录还可以通过 Google 等搜索引擎进行直接检索。笔者在 WorldCat 上以标题"oral history"进行检索，查询到的相关记录达 12 万多条（2015 年 3 月 18 日检索）。

需求。① 如上所述，一些诸如 OHMS 等口述历史内容管理系统为深度描述口述历史计划（收藏）或个别口述历史访谈的元数据信息提供了可能，而有些机构或计划也会利用 OCLC 提供的数字化馆藏管理系统——"CONT-ENTdm"来描述和上传口述历史内容（有些还提供全文抄本、音视频摘录或完整音视频记录）。②

尽管以元数据信息为基础的不断发展和日益完善的编目系统为发现和检索在线口述历史资源提供了重要手段，可是，数字化革命已经极大地改变了用户对于互联网所能提供的服务内容的期望，他们已经不再局限于在线访问和检索有关口述历史资源的编目记录，而是希望能够在家里、办公室、机场或任何能够上网的地方在线浏览甚至免费下载完整抄本、音视频摘录或完整音视频记录。在这些数字化探索与努力当中，一些口述历史资料保存机构开始以网页或在网页上提供 Word 或 PDF 等格式的下载链接形式来上传完整抄本，这使得口述历史资料能够被更为广泛的用户所访问和获取。根据笔者查询，肯塔基大学口述历史项目（O-ral History Program，即路易·纳恩口述历史中心前身）从 1997 年开始就

① 比如，1997 年新墨西哥大学档案馆口述历史馆藏（University of New Mexico Archives Oral History Collection）和印第安纳大学口述历史研究中心（Indiana University Oral History Research Center）网页就显示，它们所提供的每个口述历史访谈的编目记录信息都是比较简单的。具体内容访问 https：//web. archive. org/web/19970529013742/http：//www. unm. edu/ ~ unmarchv/oralhist. html 和 https：//web. archive. org/web/19970418080 714/http：//www. indiana. edu/ ~ ohrc/collect. htm。上述访问时间为 2014 年 7 月 8 日。

② 贝勒大学口述历史研究所就是利用 CONTENTdm 来发布与呈现其口述历史馆藏，以其中的 "Ernestine Garrett Anderson" 口述历史访谈为例，有关该访谈的元数据信息包括受访者、访谈者、标题、访谈详情、访谈次数、访谈日期、资源类型、格式、类型、语言、抄本描述、音频记录描述、馆藏类型、计划名称、摘要、主办机构、主办机构所在地及权限等信息。此外，还可能包括国会图书馆标题表、关键词、GPS 坐标及超链接等元数据信息。具体内容访问 http：//digitalcollec-tions. baylor. edu/cdm/compoundobject/collection/buioh/id/7289/rec/1。而有些并不具备元数据信息检索功能的机构会在线提供主题索引（subject index）、受访者索引（interviewee index）和馆藏/档案索引（collection/archive index）等信息，从而促进用户对于访谈内容的深度了解。比如，在 20 世纪 90 年代末，南密西西比大学民权记录计划（University of South Mississippi Civil Rights Documen-tation Project）就已经提供这些功能，具体内容访问 http：//www. usm. edu/crdp/index. html。上述访问时间为 2014 年 7 月 9 日。

将部分口述历史完整抄本以网页形式发布在其官方网站上。① 为了方便读者阅读与下载，还有些机构会在网站提供 Word 或 PDF 下载链接，而加州大学伯克利分校地区口述历史办公室网站从 2000 年开始就以 PDF 形式提供完整抄本下载服务。② 当然，在 2000 年前后，当时提供完整抄本下载服务的网站基本都不具备抄本全文检索功能，③ 这对于那些希望了解与查询特定访谈中特定内容的用户来说是相当不便的。基于此，目前越来越多的网站开始提供抄本全文检索功能，比如约翰逊总统图书馆（Lyndon Baines Johnson Presidential Library）口述历史馆藏不仅提供目录浏览与抄本 PDF 下载功能，而且还可以对在线抄本进行全文检索。④ 为提升检索的深度与广度，除抄本全文检索之外，有些机构还会提供访谈标题、访谈日期、访谈摘要、访谈主题、访谈计划、受访者与访谈者等多字段检索功能。⑤

而为超越传统的口述历史抄本所呈现的印刷文字（printed words）的限制，并充分地挖掘真正体现口述历史访谈核心特征的音视频维度，一些保存机构也开始将音视频记录的摘录或完整资料上传到网络上。这个方面的开拓者则是一项学生口述历史计划——"全世界在注视：1968 年口述历史"（The Whole World Was Watching：An Oral History of 1968），该计划由南金斯顿中学（South Kingstown High School）和布朗大学学术技术组（Brown University Scholarly Technology Group）共同主持。该计划始于 1998

---

① 具体访问 https：//web. archive. org/web/19970406114701/http：//www. uky. edu/Libraries/Special/oral_ history/，2014 年 7 月 9 日访问。

② 具体访问 https：//web. archive. org/web/20000817010848/http：//www. lib. berkeley. edu/BANC/ROHO/ohonline/，2014 年 7 月 9 日访问。

③ 到目前为止，加州大学伯克利分校地区口述历史办公室网站仍然没有提供抄本全文检索功能（只有浏览和 PDF 下载功能），不过曾经通过加州在线档案馆（Online Archive of California）来实现对其抄本的全文检索。具体内容访问 http：//bancroft. berkeley. edu/ROHO/，2014 年 7 月 9 日访问。

④ 具体内容访问 http：//www. lbjlibrary. net/collections/oral－histories/，2014 年 7 月 9 日访问。

⑤ 比如，罗格斯大学口述历史档案馆（Rutgers Oral History Archive，http：//oralhistory. rutgers. edu/）、加州大学洛杉矶分校口述历史研究中心（Center for Oral History Research，University of California，Los Angeles，http：//oralhistory. library. ucla. edu/advSearch. do）和夏威夷大学马诺亚分校口述历史中心（Center for Oral History，University of Hawaii at Manoa，http：//manoa. hawaii. edu/hawaiiancollection/coh/index. html）。上述访问时间为 2014 年 7 月 9 日。

年春季，旨在记录罗德岛居民对于 20 世纪 60 年代尤其是 1968 年的历史记忆，而为改变口述历史资源的传统呈现方式与扩展受众范围，该计划将搜集到的口述历史访谈的完整抄本和音频记录全部上传到网络上。此外，为提升其教育与研究价值，该网站还提供了有关该口述历史计划所涉及的重要历史主题的专业术语、大事年表与参考文献及学生访谈体会等重要资料。① 当然，除了要充分展现口述历史资源的音视频特征之外，有些机构之所以选择在线上传完整音视频记录，部分原因可能是因为它们未能提供完整的抄本资料。比如，到 2002 年 7 月，加州州立大学长滩分校虚拟口述/声音历史档案馆（CSULB Virtual Oral/Aural History Archive，简称 VOA-HA）已经将该校保存的有关妇女史、劳工史和长滩地区史的长达 300 小时的完整的口述历史音频记录上传到网络上。为满足不同用户需求，该网站同时提供浏览与检索功能，而且每个访谈都被分割成若干标有时间码的片段（每个片段还提供内容摘要），用户不仅可以聆听整个音频记录，也可以根据检索结果来聆听特定片段。② 经过 10 多年运行，该虚拟档案馆在馆

① 具体内容访问 https：//web. archive. org/web/19990221032811/http：//www. stg. brown. edu/projects/1968/；目前该网站地址为 http：//cds. library. brown. edu/projects/1968/。上述访问时间为 2014 年 7 月 9 日。有关该计划的评论可以参阅 Sherna Berger Gluck，Donald A. Ritchie，and Bret Eynon，"Reflections on Oral History in the New Millennium：Roundtable Comments"，*Oral History Review*，Vol. 26，No. 2，1999，pp. 22-23；Glenn Whitman，"Teaching Students How to Be Historians：An Oral History Project for the Secondary School Classroom"，*The History Teacher*，Vol. 33，No. 4，2000，pp. 474-475.

② 具体内容访问 https：//web. archive. org/web/20020805153539/http：//back. acs. csulb. edu：8080/oralhistory/index. html，2014 年 7 月 10 日访问。相关内容还可参阅："Oral History Recordings Online：The CSULB Virtual Oral/Aural History Archive"，H-Net Announcement，9 October 2002；Sherna Berger Gluck，"Pitch，Pace，Performance-and Even Poetry：The CSULB Virtual Oral/Aural History Project"，*Oral History Association Newsletter*，Vol. 36，No. 1，Spring 2002，pp. 4-5；Sherna Berger Gluck，"Brief Note on CSULB Project Methodology and Procedures"，*Oral History Association Newsletter*，Vol. 36，No. 1，Spring 2002，p. 6；Sherna Berger Gluck，"Pitch，Pace，Performance-and Even Poetry：Returning to Orality：The CSULB Virtual Oral/Aural History Archive Model"，paper presented to the XIIIth International Oral History Conference（Rome，Italy，23-26 June 2004）；Linda Shopes，"Electronic Media Reviews：*VOAHA*：*The Virtual Oral/Aural History Archive*"，*The Public Historian*，Vol. 29，No. 1，2007，pp. 111-113；Sherna Berger Gluck，"Why Do We Call It Oral History? Refocusing on Orality/Aurality in the Digital Age"，in Douglas A. Boyd and Mary A. Larson（eds.），*Oral History and Digital Humanities*：*Voice*，*Access*，*and Engagement*，New York：Palgrave Macmillan，2014，pp. 35-52.

藏内容、元数据描述与技术设施方面都有很大改善，目前在线音频记录达到 1000 多个小时（包括 350 多位来自不同领域的受访者）。因此，该虚拟档案馆也进入所谓的第二阶段（VOAHA II），以区别于之前的第一阶段（VOAHA I），而网站地址也有所变更。① 而近年来较受美国口述历史学界关注的一个在线完整呈现口述历史视频记录的网站是伊利诺伊州博物馆（Illinois State Museum）主办的伊利诺伊州农业口述历史计划（Oral History of Illinois Agriculture，简称 OHIA）——"音视频谷仓"（Audio-Video Barn）。该计划启动于 2007 年并获得美国博物馆和图书馆服务研究院国家领袖基金资助，致力于在线呈现有关伊利诺伊州农业与农村生活的口述历史音视频记录，并努力实现它所宣称的多种功能，包括"聆听"（hear）、"观看"（see）、"定位"（locate）、"查找"（find）、"阅览"（look）、"学习"（learn）、"教学"（teach）、"前瞻"（peek）、"导航"（navigate）与"求助"（need help）等。同样，该网站所上传的访谈记录都没有完整抄本，为帮助用户更为准确地查询相关内容，每个访谈也被分割成若干标有时间码的片段并提供每个片段的内容摘要。② 此外，为考虑某些口述历史主题对于视频呈现的特殊需求，有些计划则会选择在线上传口述历史完整视频。比如，创建于 1997 年的美国电视学院基金会美国电视档案馆（Archive of American Television，Television Academy Foundation）目前已经将其大部分口述历史视频（馆藏总时长超过 4000 多个小时）上传到网络上，其受访者是见证美国电视行业发展的各个领域的专业人士。③

① 该网站属于该校图书馆数字化资源库的一部分，具体内容访问 http：//symposia. library. csulb. edu/iii/cpro/CommunityViewPage. external? lang = eng&sp = 1000026&suite = def，2014 年 7 月 10 日访问。笔者经过测试，直接输入网址（http：//www. csulb. edu/voaha）也可自动链接至上述网址。

② 具体内容访问 http：//avbarn. museum. state. il. us/，2015 年 3 月 24 日访问。相关研究参阅 Robert E. Warren，Michael P. Maniscalco，Erich K. Schroeder，James S. Oliver，Sue Huitt，Douglas Lambert，and Michael Frisch，"Restoring the Human Voice to Oral History：The Audio-Video Barn Website"，*Oral History Review*，Vol. 40，No. 1，2013，pp. 107-125.

③ 具体内容访问 http：//www. emmytvlegends. org/，2015 年 3 月 24 日访问。

　　不过，越来越多的机构也开始将完整抄本或音视频记录同时在线上传，为那些希望阅读抄本或聆听和观看音视频资料的用户提供多元选择，同时还提供了更为详细的有关口述历史访谈计划的描述性资料、索引信息及与访谈相关的其他资料（包括照片、地图与报纸等相关资料）。而就整体网站设计及抄本、音频、视频与其他元素的融合与互动程度来说，其中相当具有代表性的网站是启动于 1996 年的"伝承：日裔美国人遗产计划"（Densho：The Japanese American Legacy Project）。该计划旨在以影像口述历史方式记录"二战"期间日裔美国人的拘禁经历，目前该计划数字档案馆总共包含 700 多位受访者的 800 多份访谈资料，视频长达 1600 多小时，并同时在线收录多达 12000 多份照片、文件和报纸等资料。该数字档案馆（需要简单注册）除了提供浏览与检索功能之外，每个访谈还同时提供完整抄本与音视频记录（音视频可互换聆听或观看，每个音视频记录也被分割成若干标有时间码的片段）及元数据信息。① 此外，在这个方面做得比较成功的口述历史网站还包括哥大口述历史研究室于 2006 年创建并上线的"纽约名人"（Notable New Yorkers）网站与卡内基基金会口述历史计划（Carnegie Corporation Oral History Project）网站，② 以及近年来越来越多的

---

① 具体内容访问 http：//www. densho. org/densho. asp，2015 年 3 月 24 日访问。有关该网站的评论可参阅 Allan W. Austin，"Review：*Denshō：The Japanese American Legacy Project*；*A More Perfect Union：Japanese Americans & the U. S. Constitution*；*Life Interrupted：The Japanese American Experience in WWII Arkansas*"，*Journal of American History*，Vol. 92，No. 1，2005，pp. 326-328；Michael Ellis，"Densho：The Japanese American Legacy Project"，*Reference Reviews*，Vol. 28，Vol. 3，2014，pp. 51-53；Tom Ikeda，"Densho：The Japanese American Legacy Project"，in Douglas A. Boyd and Mary A. Larson（eds.），*Oral History and Digital Humanities：Voice，Access，and Engagement*，New York：Palgrave Macmillan，2014，pp. 133-144. 跟该计划类似的是美国最大的非裔美国人影像口述历史馆藏——"The HistoryMakers"，目前该数字档案馆包含长达 2000 多小时的影像片段，不过需要支付每月 30 美元的费用才能完全访问。具体内容访问 http：//www. thehistorymakers. com/，2015 年 3 月 24 日访问。相关评论还可以参阅 Juliana Nykolaiszyn，"The HistoryMakers"，*Reference Reviews*，Vol. 26，Vol. 6，2012，pp. 59-60。

② 前者除提供完整抄本与音频记录之外，还能实现特定抄本内容与相应音频片段的手动同步及抄本全文检索等功能。具体内容访问 http：//www. columbia. edu/cu/lweb/digital/collections/nny/index. html. 后者则同时提供完整抄本、音频与视频记录。具体内容访问 http：//www. columbia. edu/cu/lweb/digital/collections/oral_ hist/carnegie/。上述访问时间为 2015 年 3 月 24 日。

利用 CONTENTdm 与数字共享空间（Digital Commons）等内容管理系统来管理与呈现口述历史资源（一般同时提供完整抄本与音视频记录）的数字资源库。①

　　当然，考虑到口述历史完整音视频记录在线上传的技术支持与内容控制等问题，美国大部分口述历史机构或计划在提供完整抄本的同时一般只选择上传音视频摘录。② 在某种程度上，这些片段主要是起到介绍与推广的作用，如果需要聆听或观看完整音视频记录，则需要到实体保存机构申请借阅或在线购买。而随着 YouTube 与 SoundCloud 等社交媒体的不断应用，也有机构或计划会通过这些平台来推介其口述历史音视频摘录，比如

---

① 比如，贝勒大学口述历史研究所（http：//digitalcollections. baylor. edu/cdm/landingpage/collection/buioh）、北卡罗来纳大学教堂山分校南方口述历史项目（Southern Oral History Program, University of North Carolina at Chapel Hill）访谈数据库（http：//www2. lib. unc. edu/dc/sohp/）、爱达荷州历史学会口述历史馆藏（Idaho State Historical Society Oral History Collection, http：//idaho-history. cdmhost. com/cdm/search/collection/p15073coll1）、犹他大学埃弗雷特·库利口述历史计划（University of Utah Everett L. Cooley Oral History Project, http：//content. lib. utah. edu/cdm/landing-page/collection/uu - elc）、帕诺拉学院帕诺拉口述历史馆藏（Panola College Panola Oral Histories Collection, http：//cdm16076. contentdm. oclc. org/cdm/landingpage/collection/p15279coll1）、华盛顿州立大学民权口述历史馆藏（Washington State University Civil Rights Oral History Collection, http：//content. libraries. wsu. edu/cdm/landingpage/collection/cvoralhis）、南密西西比大学口述历史与文化遗产中心（Center for Oral History and Cultural Heritage, University of Southern Mississippi）口述历史数字馆藏（Oral History Collection, http：//digilib. usm. edu/cdm/landingpage/collection/coh）、德克萨斯大学埃尔帕索分校口述历史研究所（Institute of Oral History, University of Texas at El Paso, ht-tp：//digitalcommons. utep. edu/oral_ history/）、霍普学院口述历史馆藏（Hope College Oral History Collection, http：//digitalcommons. hope. edu/oral_ histories/）和温斯洛普大学口述历史项目（Winthrop University Oral History Program, http：//digitalcommons. winthrop. edu/oralhistoryprogram/）等。上述访问时间为 2015 年 3 月 24 日。另外有关 CONTENTdm 与数字共享空间等内容管理系统在口述历史当中的应用，请参阅 Betty S. Leberman, "Oral History with CONTENTdm: A Public Library – University Partnership", paper presented to the Fifth Midwest CONTENTdm Users Group Annual Meeting (Iowa City, Iowa, 8-9 April 2010); Jack Dougherty and Candace Simpson, "Who Owns Oral History? A Creative Commons Solution", in Doug Boyd, Steve Cohen, Brad Rakerd, and Dean Rehberger (eds.), *Oral History in the Digital Age*, Washington: Institute of Museum and Library Services, 2012, http：//ohda. matrix. msu. edu/2012/06/a – creative – commons – solution/, 2014 年 3 月 24 日访问。

② 比如，肯塔基州民权运动口述历史计划（http：//205. 204. 134. 47/civil_ rights_ mvt/）、加州大学伯克利分校地区口述历史办公室（http：//bancroft. berkeley. edu/ROHO/collections/av_ online. html）、美国参议院历史办公室口述历史计划（Oral History Project, United States Senate Historical Office, ht-tps：//www. senate. gov/pagelayout/history/e_ one_ section_ no_ teasers/OralHistoryList. htm）与现代艺术博物馆口述历史项目（Oral History Program, Museum of Modern Art, http：//www. moma. org/learn/re-sources/archives/oralhistory#iohp）等网站。上述访问时间为 2015 年 3 月 24 日。

加州大学伯克利分校地区口述历史办公室在 YouTube 和 SoundCloud 上都设有专门频道。①

　　上述以具体网站为例呈现了过去 20 年来美国口述历史在线传播的主要内容、形式与基本特征，尽管大部分网站都能够实现口述历史目录（指南、索引）、元数据信息、完整抄本、音视频摘录与完整音视频记录等不同类型资源的浏览与检索功能。可是，相对来说，这些网站都很难实现作为口述历史资源核心的索引、抄本与音视频记录之间的互动与同步功能。而路易·纳恩口述历史中心于 2008 年设计和开发的口述历史元数据同步系统则弥补了这种不足，如前文所述，作为一个以网络为基础的免费开源应用程序，该系统不仅能够为用户提供索引编制与字词检索功能，而且能够通过字词检索进而实现标有时间码的口述历史访谈抄本或索引与相应的口述历史访谈音视频记录的同步功能。因此，该系统目前被认为是改善与提高口述历史资源在线管理、访问、检索与利用效果的最具开拓性的尝试，而且已经被越来越多的口述历史机构或计划所采用。②

　　当然，考虑到用户对于涉及相关主题的不同类型资料的需求，也有机构或计划将口述历史资料与诸如书籍、文件、日记、报纸、杂志、信件（包括电子邮件）、手稿、照片、明信片、剪贴本、地图与影片等不同类型的资料共同上传到网络数据库或数字资源库当中，并提供浏览与检索功能。这方面的代表性网站包括美国国会图书馆美国民俗生活中心老兵历史计划（Veterans History Project）、美国大屠杀纪念博物馆（United States Holocaust Memori-

---

　　①　具体内容访问 https：//www. youtube. com/user/ROHOucb 和 https：//soundcloud. com/rohoucb，2015 年 3 月 24 日。如果要了解更多信息，可以在这两个平台上查询关键词"oral history"。

　　②　Ty Pierce and Phil Sager，"Oral History Interactives：Going Beyond the Interview to Create Multimedia Experiences"，*MW*2015：*Museums and the Web* 2015，February 1，2015，http：//mw2015. museumsandtheweb. com/paper/oral – history – interactives – going – beyond – the – interview – to – create – multimedia – experiences/。为促进该系统的推广与使用，美国口述历史协会还于 2015 年 5 月 20 日在佐治亚州立大学（Georgia State University）图书馆举办"口述历史元数据同步系统"工作坊。具体内容访问 http：//www. cvent. com/events/ohms – enhancing – access – to – oral – history – online/event – summary – b63f5472672145d189de6205b33b6214. aspx。上述访问时间为 2015 年 3 月 25 日。

al Museum）与肯塔基州数字图书馆，① 以及那些利用 CONTENTdm 等内容管理系统来呈现其馆藏（其中包含口述历史资源）的各种类型的数字资源库。②

需要强调的是，面对个别口述历史机构与计划在数字化呈现与传播口述历史资源方面的相对迟缓，口述历史商业数据库也应运而生。其中最具代表性的就是美国亚历山大出版社（Alexander Street Press）开发的《口述历史在线》（Oral History Online）数据库，它提供全球超过 2700 个主要英文口述历史收藏的文本、音频和视频的阅读（聆听、观看）、浏览（按照保存机构、收藏名称、访谈名称、访谈日期、地域、历史事件与主题词进行分类）、检索、下载与延伸链接等服务。该数据库目前（以 2015 年 4 月 8 日使用该数据库为准）收录的文本资料达到 33 万页左右、而音频和视频文件及编目记录也分别达到 4200 多份和 2 万余条，而且通过定期（每季）更新以实现逐年增加。其目标是对网络上可以获得的大部分英文口述历史收藏进行深度索引，并为其提供尽可能详细和完整的编目记录。③

上述口述历史资源的数字化传播主要是依托于静态或动态网站及具有浏览与检索功能的网络数据库或数字资源库，而且从其传播内容

---

① 具体内容访问 http：//lcweb2. loc. gov/diglib/vhp/html/search/search. html，http：//collections. ushmm. org/search/和 http：//kdl. kyvl. org/。当然，美国越来越多的各种数字图书馆也开始提供这种功能，比如美国数字公共图书馆（Digital Public Library of America，http：//dp. la/）、HathiTrust 数字图书馆（HathiTrust Digital Library，http：//www. hathitrust. org/）与互联网档案馆（Internet Archive，https：//archive. org/）等。上述访问时间为 2015 年 3 月 25 日。

② 比如，鲍尔州立大学图书馆数字媒体资源库（Digital Media Repository，Ball State University Libraries，http：//libx. bsu. edu/cdm/）、阿拉巴马大学伯明翰分校数字馆藏（Digital Collections，University of Alabama at Birmingham，http：//www. mhsl. uab. edu/dc/）、华盛顿大学图书馆数字馆藏（Digital Collections，University of Washington Libraries，http：//digitalcollections. lib. washington. edu/cdm/specialcollections）、路易斯维尔大学图书馆数字馆藏（Digital Collections，University of Louisville Libraries，http：//digital. library. louisville. edu/）、中田纳西州立大学"发现在线美国妇女史"数据库（Discovering American Women's History Online，Middle Tennessee State University，http：//digital. mtsu. edu/cdm/landingpage/collection/women）与新墨西哥大学图书馆新墨西哥州数字馆藏（New Mexico Digital Collections，University of New Mexico Libraries，http：//econtent. unm. edu/）等。上述访问时间为 2015 年 3 月 25 日。

③ 具体内容访问 http：//alexanderstreet. com/products/oral – history – online，2015 年 4 月 8 日访问。需要指出的是，该数据库必须购买才能使用，当然它提供的某些口述历史机构或计划的在线链接则可以完整访问相关资料。

来看，主要是以原始资料形式存在的口述历史抄本与音视频记录。① 相对而言，这些资料对于研究者、教育者或各种类型的节目制作人来说是具有吸引力的。可是，对于普通公众来说，如果要提高他们对于口述历史资源的兴趣与关注度，则需要考虑对以原始形态存在的口述历史资料进行更为多元的利用与开发。而在数字化时代，除了将传统的口述历史光盘电子书（CD-ROM electronic books）、广播、实体展览（physical exhibits）与音视频纪录片等成果实现在线传播与呈现之外，②在线（数字）展览

---

① Irene Reti, "Oral History on the Web", *Oral History Review*, Vol. 26, No. 2, 1999, pp. 147-149.

② 从 20 世纪 80 年代开始，口述历史资料在这些媒体当中得到不断应用与呈现，具体成果可以参阅美国《口述历史评论》的"媒体评论"（Medial Reviews）栏目。相关研究请参阅 David K. Dunaway, "Radio and the Public Use of Oral History", *The Public Historian*, Vol. 6, No. 2, 1984, pp. 77-90; Dan Sipe, "The Future of Oral History and Moving Images", *Oral History Review*, Vol. 19, No. 1/2, 1991, pp. 75-87; Donald A. Ritchie, *Doing Oral History*, New York: Twayne Publishers, 1995, pp. 199-206; Anna Green, "Returning History to the Community: Oral History in a Museum Setting", *Oral History Review*, Vol. 24, No. 2, 1997, pp. 53-72; Jerry Lembcke, "From Oral History to Movie Script: The Vietnam Veteran Interviews for Coming Home", *Oral History Review*, Vol. 26, No. 2, 1999, pp. 65-86; Ron Chew, "Collected Stories: The Rise of Oral History in Museum Exhibitions", *Museum News*, November/December, 2002; Donald A. Ritchie, *Doing Oral History: A Practical Guide*, Oxford and New York: Oxford University Press, second edition, 2003, pp. 237-251; Charles Hardy III and Pamela Dean, "Oral History in Sound and Moving Image Documentaries", in Thomas L. Charlton, Lois E. Myers, and Rebecca Sharpless (eds.), *Handbook of Oral History*, Walnut Creek: AltaMira Press, 2006, pp. 510-561; Charles Hardy III, "Authoring in Sound: Aural History, Radio and the Digital Revolution", in Robert Perks and Alistair Thomson (eds.), *The Oral History Reader*, London and New York: Routledge, second edition, 2006, pp. 393-405; Anna Green, "The Exhibition that Speaks for Itself: Oral History and Museum", in Robert Perks and Alistair Thomson (eds.), *The Oral History Reader*, London and New York: Routledge, second edition, 2006, pp. 416-424; Selma Thomas, "Private Memory in a Public Space: Oral History and Museums", in Paula Hamilton and Linda Shopes (eds.), *Oral History and Public Memories*, Philadelphia: Temple University Press, 2008, pp. 87-100; Ieuan Franklin, "Folkways and Airwaves: Oral History, Community & Vernacular Radio", (Ph. D. dissertation, Bournemouth: Bournemouth University, 2009); Elif Ekin Akşit, "Women's Oral History and Documentary Film", in Fatma Türe and Birsen Talay Keşolu (eds.), *Women's Memory: The Problem of Sources*, Newcastle upon Tyne: Cambridge Scholars Publishing, 2011, pp. 141-152; Siobhán McHugh, "The Affective Power of Sound: Oral History on Radio", *Oral History Review*, Vol. 39, No. 2, 2012, pp. 187-206; "Oral History in Museums", January 28, 2013, 具体内容访问 http://historianforhire. blogspot. com/2013/01/oral – history – in – museums. html, 2015 年 3 月 25 日访问; Donald A. Ritchie, *Doing Oral History*, Oxford and New York: Oxford University Press, third edition, 2014, pp. 258-267; "Lost Neighbourhoods: Can Oral History be the Center of an Exhibit?" May 30, 2014, 具体内容访问 http://uncatalogedmuseum. blogspot. com/2014/05/lost – neighbourhoods – can – oral – history – be. html, 2015 年 3 月 25 日访问; Megan Webster and Noelia Gravotta, "Co-Creating Our Story: Making a Documentary Film", in Steven High, Edward Little, and Thi Ry Duong (eds.), *Remembering Mass Violence: Oral History, New Media and Performance*, Toronto: University of Toronto Press, 2014, pp. 152-170. 此外，口述历史在其他媒体当中的应用，还可以参阅美国《公共历史学家》（*The Public Historian*）和英国《口述历史》（*Oral History*）等刊物当中的相关文章。

（online/digital exhibits）、语音导览（audio tours/audio guides）①、播客系列（podcast series）与移动应用程序（mobile applications）等新媒体也成为近年来美国口述历史学界促进口述历史资源数字化传播与呈现的重要方式。②

在口述历史在线展览方面，不管是从展现方式还是从展现内容来说，相当具有开拓性的是阿拉斯加大学费尔班克斯分校口述历史项目的"自动点唱机计划"（Project Jukebox）。该计划启动于 1988 年，最初是基于数字化保存的考虑，即对该校所保存的口述历史录音磁带进行数字化处理，然后保存在光盘上。1990 年在苹果公司苹果未来图书馆（Apple Library of Tomorrow）项目的资助下，该计划发展成为一个集口述历史录音、抄本以及与访谈相关的历史照片、地图与背景性信息等资料于一体的互动性多媒体计算机系统（interactive, multimedia computer system），而且每个"自动点唱机计划"都围绕特定的区域、社区或主题来设计。就当时而言，该计划是一项令人兴奋且独特的解决口述历史记录的保护、储存、检索与访问等老问题的方法。简而言之，该计划允许用户查找合适的访谈，并且能够聆听访谈，浏览与访谈相关的历史照片，在地图上定位与访谈相关的地点及阅读访谈抄本。而为进一步扩展其访问受众，1992 年该系统发展成为一个由苹果计算机、光驱和打印机等设备组成的可以安置在合适位置的自动点唱机工作台（Jukebox Workstation）。同年，该工作台受到美国国家公园管理局（National Park Services）的关注，它们希望在它们所属的两个阿拉斯加国家公园设置独立的工作台，并以此向访客、居民与工作人员展示与特定主题相关的口述历史资料、历史图片与地图等信息。1992 年夏天，育空—查理河国家保护区（Yukon- Charley Rivers National

---

① 语音导览还可以称为"徒步导览"（walking tours）、"流动导览"（driving tours）或"语音漫步"（audio walks）。

② Aaron Hayworth, "Oral History and New Media Methods of Presentation", April 7, 2014，具体内容访问 http：//sohp. org/2014/04/07/oral－history－and－new－media－methods－of－presentation/，2015 年 3 月 25 日访问。

Preserve）的自动点唱机工作台正式进入测试与运行阶段。从严格意义上而言，真正实现该计划在线展示的功能则依赖于互联网的逐渐普及与应用。① 2000 年首个"自动点唱机计划"正式上线；截至目前，阿拉斯加大学费尔班克斯分校口述历史项目通过对其口述历史馆藏资源与其他相关资料的数字化处理，并按照特定主题进行在线展示，计划总数超过 35 个。②

　　相对于实体展览而言，在线展览能够更加方便与生动地展示口述历史的音视频记录（通常只提供片段），并且实现它们与其他相关资料的互动与补充。正因如此，在线展览日益成为美国众多机构或计划介绍、推广与展示其口述历史资源的重要手段。在 Google 中检索关键词"oral history online（digital）exhibits（exhibitions）"，就能够发现大量的主题性口述历史在线展览计划。其中，比较有代表性的包括路易斯安那州立大学 T. 哈里·威廉姆斯口述历史中心（T. Harry Williams Center for Oral History, Louisiana State University）主办的涉及多个主题的在线展览与展示计划③、大底特律都市区（Metropolitan Detroit）大屠杀幸存者与家庭计划（Program for Holocaust Survivors and Families）主办的互动性在线展览"荣誉肖像：密歇根大屠杀幸存者"（Portraits of Honor: Our Michigan Holocaust

---

① 上述详细内容参阅 Gretchen L. Lake, "Project Jukebox: An Innovative Way to Access and Preserve Oral History Records", *Provenance, Journal of the Society of Georgia Archivists*, Vol. 9, No. 1-2, 1991, pp. 24-41; William Schneider and Daniel Grahek, *Project Jukebox: Where Oral History and Technology Come Together*, Anchorage: Center for Information Technology, University of Alaska Anchorage, 1992; William Schneider, *So They Understand: Cultural Issues in Oral History*, Logan: Utah State University Press, 2002, pp. 27-28; Donald A. Ritchie, *Doing Oral History*, Oxford and New York: Oxford University Press, third edition, 2014, p. 236; William Schneider, "Oral History in the Age of Digital Possibilities", in Douglas A. Boyd and Mary A. Larson (eds.), *Oral History and Digital Humanities: Voice, Access, and Engagement*, New York: Palgrave Macmillan, 2014, pp. 19-34.

② "自动点唱机计划"属于阿拉斯加大学费尔班克斯分校口述历史项目的数字化部门（digital branch），该计划通常被认为是美国首个对口述历史资料进行数字化保存与访问的大型计划。具体内容访问 http://jukebox. uaf. edu/, 2015 年 3 月 26 日访问。

③ 具体内容访问 http://oralhistory. blogs. lib. lsu. edu/exhibits – and – presentations/, 2015 年 3 月 26 日访问。

Survivors)①、南卡罗来纳大学口述历史办公室（Office of Oral History, University of South Carolina）主办的"南卡罗来纳罗森瓦尔德学校：口述历史展览"（Rosenwald Schools of South Carolina：An Oral History Exhibit)②、南犹他大学（Southern Utah University）主办的在线展览"科罗拉多高原之声"（Voices of the Colorado Plateau)③、哈福德社区学院（Harford Community College）历史学生发起的口述历史在线展览"哈福德声音"（Harford Voices)④、耶鲁大学纽黑文口述历史计划（New Haven Oral History Project）主办的在线展览"模范城市的生活：纽黑文城市重建故事"（Life in the Model City：Stories of Urban Renewal in New Haven)⑤、美国国家历史博物馆（National Museum of American History）主办的在线展览"9.11：为历史见证"（September 11：Bearing Witness to History)⑥、亚利桑那大学（University of Arizona）主办的在线展览"通过我们父母的眼睛：亚利桑那南部的历史与文化"（Through Our Parents' Eyes：History & Culture of Southern Arizona)⑦，以及美国国会图书馆、史密森学会与美国大屠杀纪念博物馆等机构举办的各种以口述历史馆藏为主要内容的在线展览。⑧

而随着移动互联网、智能手机、媒体播放器、平板电脑、应用程序、全球定位系统（Global Position System）与二维码等硬件与软件技术的不

---

① 具体内容访问 http：//www. portraitsofhonor. org/，2015 年 3 月 26 日访问。有关该展览的评论请参阅 Mark Stryker，"Online Exhibit Tells Mich. Holocaust Survivors' Stories"，*Detroit Free Press*，January 7，2013.

② 具体内容访问 http：//library. sc. edu/digital/collections/scrosenwald/，2015 年 3 月 26 日访问。

③ 具体内容访问 http：//archive. li. suu. edu/voices/，2015 年 3 月 26 日访问。

④ 具体内容访问 http：//harfordvoices. org/。有关该展览的评论请参阅"Harford Voices – A Digital Oral History Exhibit Created by Harford Community College Students"，具体内容访问 http：//www. oralhistory. org/2013/07/29/blog – harford – voices – a – digital – oral – history – exhibit – created – by – harford – community – college – students/。上述访问时间为 2015 年 3 月 26 日。

⑤ 具体内容访问 http：//www. yale. edu/nhohp/modelcity/index. html，2015 年 3 月 26 日访问。

⑥ 具体内容访问 http：//amhistory. si. edu/september11/，2015 年 3 月 26 日访问。

⑦ 具体内容访问 http：//parentseyes. arizona. edu/，2015 年 3 月 26 日访问。

⑧ 具体内容访问 http：//www. loc. gov/exhibits/，http：//siarchives. si. edu/history/exhibits 和 http：//www. ushmm. org/information/exhibitions/online – features/online – exhibitions。上述访问时间为 2015 年 3 月 26 日。

断发展，作为在线展览的变体，语音导览日益成为呈现与展示口述历史资源的重要媒介。在涉及博物馆、历史街区、历史遗迹、消逝社群与特定历史文化路线等记忆景观（memoryscape）的虚拟展示中，与导览（游览）主题相关的口述历史音视频记录成为设计语音导览的重要选材。诸多学者认为语音导览使历史处于流动当中，它不仅让游客离开美术馆、图书馆和博物馆大厅而进入街道当中，而且通过聆听或观看那些历史当事人或见证者的口述历史音视频记录而帮助游客理解现在与过去之间的联系，从而以新的方式来体验（游览）地点并因此再次唤醒与该地方相关的诗意和情感联系（poetic and emotional connections）。① 2013 年，布朗大学公共人文学科课程《口述历史与社区记忆》（Oral History and Community Memory）的学生们制作了一个手机语音导览计划——"玛莎保格的街坊邻里：来自池塘之外的声音"（Mashapaug's Neighbors：Voices from Beyond the Pond），其主要资料来源于他们收集的有关美国罗德岛普罗维登斯（Providence）玛莎保格池塘（Mashapaug Pond）及其附近居民的口述历史

---

① Toby Butler, "Memoryscape: How Audio Walks Can Deepen Our Sense of Place by Integrating Art, Oral History and Cultural Geography", *Geography Compass*, Vol. 1, No. 3, 2007, pp. 360-372; Toby Butler, "Teaching and Learning Guide for: Memoryscape: How Audio Walks Can Deepen Our Sense of Place by Integrating Art, Oral History and Cultural Geography", *Geography Compass*, Vol. 2, No. 5, 2008, pp. 1750-1754; Charles Hardy III, "Painting in Sound: Aural History and Audio Art", in Marta Kurkowska-Budzan and Krzysztof Zamorski (eds.), *Oral History: The Challenges of Dialogue*, Amsterdam and Philadelphia: John Benjamins Publishing, 2009, pp. 147-168; Toby Butler, "The Historical Hearing Aid: Located Oral History from the Listener's Perspectives", in Shelley Trower (ed.), *Place, Writing, and Voice in Oral History*, New York: Palgrave Macmillan, 2011, pp. 193-216; Steven High, "Mapping Memories of Displacement: Oral History, Memoryscapes, and Mobile Methodologies", in Shelley Trower (ed.), *Place, Writing, and Voice in Oral History*, New York: Palgrave Macmillan, 2011, pp. 217-232; Simon Bradley, "History to Go: Oral History, Audiowalks and Mobile Media", *Oral History*, Vol. 40, No. 1, 2012, pp. 99-110; Steven High, "Embodied Ways of Listening: Oral History, Genocide and the Audio Tour", *Anthropologica*, Vol. 55, No. 1, 2013, pp. 73-85; Donald A. Ritchie, *Doing Oral History*, Oxford and New York: Oxford University Press, third edition, 2014, p. 263; Steven High, *Oral History at the Crossroads: Sharing Life Stories of Survival and Displacement*, Vancouver: University of British Columbia Press, 2014, pp. 223-240.

访谈。① 该语音导览旨在通过聆听那些关注池塘环境、社会与经济发展历史的人们所讲述的故事来了解池塘及其周边社区，以提升池塘环境保护的公众意识。② 另外一个比较有代表性的口述历史流动导览计划是巴尔的摩大学（University of Baltimore）开发的"巴尔的摩 68：暴乱与重生"（Baltimore '68：Riots and Rebirth），该计划旨在通过流动导览所展示的口述历史资料让游客能够更为深刻地理解 1968 年巴尔的摩暴乱所造成的影响范围与真实后果。③ 正如该计划负责人所解释的，"该导览之所以如此有价值是因为它将那些硬信息（hard information）呈现在熟悉的和想当然的破坏场景（scenes of devastation）前面，包括火到底是在哪里和何时起的，石头在哪里和何时扔的，窗户在哪里和何时被打破的"④。

为提高青年一代对于自然或人文景观展示内容的吸引力，越来越多的美国博物馆、历史学会与图书馆都努力尝试开发各种类型的以口述历史音

---

① 该口述历史计划启动于 2011 年，由布朗大学约翰·布朗公共人文学科与文化遗产中心（John Nicholas Brown Center for Public Humanities and Cultural Heritage）与城市池塘行动队（Urban Pond Procession）联合主持。该计划尤其强调如何以数字化手段（数字档案馆、多媒体与在线展览、语音导览）实现社区艺术与口述历史的创新性诠释与信息分享，进而促进口述历史计划的社区参与度与倡导能力（提升环保意识）。具体内容访问 http://www.brown.edu/academics/public-humanities/initiatives/mashapaug-pond，2015 年 3 月 28 日访问。此外，相关研究还可参阅 Anne Valk and Holly Ewald，"Bringing a Hidden Pond to Public Attention：Increasing Impact through Digital Tools"，*Oral History Review*，Vol. 40，No. 1，2013，pp. 8-24.

② 有关该语音导览的具体内容，请访问 http://storiesfrombeyondthepond.com/，2015 年 3 月 28 日访问。

③ 有关该流动导览的具体内容，请访问 http://archives.ubalt.edu/bsr/index.html，2015 年 3 月 28 日访问。

④ Jessica I. Elfenbein，"Bringing to Life Baltimore '68：Riots and Rebirth - A How-to Guide"，*The Public Historian*，Vol. 31，No. 4，2009，p. 19. 需要指出的是，流动导览只是"巴尔的摩 68：暴乱与重生"研究计划的一个组成部分，有关该研究计划的相关研究还可以参阅《公共历史学家》对于它的专题探讨（*The Public Historian*，Vol. 31，No. 4，2009，pp. 11-67）。

视频资料为主要来源的语音导览项目。① 而对于那些属于数字原住民（digital native）一代的青年学生来说，他们也习惯于将语音导览作为呈现与推广其口述历史计划的重要手段。②

　　同样，伴随着新媒体与 Web 2.0 应用程序的发展，播客也日益成为美国口述历史实践者推广与利用口述历史资源的重要技术革新。简单而言，播客（音频或视频）是一个压缩的数字媒体文件的网络广播节目，它以网站、播客或 iTunes 为平台并允许制作者与用户通过 RSS 订阅来发布或接收文件。同时，播客是专门为下载或在电脑、平板电脑、智能手机和 MP3 等数字媒体播放器上播放而设计的，而且通常是定期更新，因此用户可以在任何方便时间下载或聆听观看。由于播客制作简单且经济有效，而且其节目也容易为公众所获取，因此口述历史播客节目成为美国一些口述历史机构吸引受众、展示馆藏内容、增加机构知名度、扩展公共推广计划、改善口述历史教育效果与提升公

---

　　① Faye Sayer, *Public History: A Practical Guide*, New York: Bloomsbury Academic, 2015, pp. 59-60. 比如，路易斯安那州立博物馆（Louisiana State Museum）的在线展览与手机语音导览计划——"阿查法拉亚之声"（Voices of Atchafalaya, http://www.atchafalayavoices.com/）、布鲁克林历史学会的"格林堡和克林顿山丘居民区语音导览"（Fort Greene/Clinton Hill Audio Tour, http://www.brooklynhistory.org/blog/2011/01/13/fort－greene－clinton－hill－audio－tour/）和下东区房屋博物馆（Lower East Side Tenement Museum）的徒步导览计划——"店面故事"（Storefront Stories, http://www.tenement.org/blog/museums－oral－history－and－social－change－hearing－voices－on－the－lower－east－side/）等。另外，国际上有关口述历史语音导览的代表性计划，可以访问 http://www.soundwalk.com, http://www.memoryscape.org.uk/, http://storytelling.concordia.ca/research－creation/audio－walks, http://murmurtoronto.ca/, http://www.portsofcall.org.uk/和 http://www.towerhamlets.gov.uk/lgsl/451－500/461_parks/victoria_park/memoryscape.aspx 等。上述访问时间为 2015 年 3 月 28 日。

　　② 比如，加州州立大学蒙特利海湾分校（California State University, Monterey Bay）与亚洲文化节（Asian Cultural Experience）共同参与的有关唐人街历史的学生口述历史计划就设计了一项语音导览项目——"想象萨林纳斯唐人街：口述历史流动导览"（Imagine Salinas Chinatown: An Oral History Walking Tour, http://salinasace.org/walkingtour）。此外还包括非裔美国人谱系研究中心（Centre for African American Genealogical Research, Inc）主持的"桑科法计划"（The Sankofa Project, http://sankofatheproject.tumblr.com/）和布朗大学约翰·布朗公共人文学科与文化遗产中心主持的手机徒步导览计划——"谈起威肯登：来自福克斯博恩特口述历史档案馆的声音"（Speaking of Wickenden: Voices from the Fox Point Oral History Archive, http://www.shanaweinberg.com/#!speaking－of－wickendon/ctom）等。上述访问时间为 2015 年 3 月 28 日。

众参与度的重要选择。①

美国口述历史学界利用播客技术制作音视频节目（以音频为主）开始于 2005 年前后，② 在这个领域具有开创性尝试的则是北卡罗来纳大学教堂山分校的"美国南方口述历史"（Oral Histories of the American South）播客系列。"美国南方口述历史"收藏来源于该校南方口述历史项目所收集的口述历史资料，并从中选择 500 份相关访谈进行数字化处理并实现在线访问。而该播客系列则是其中精选的访谈摘录（音频），并辅以介绍性说明和评论，从而制作成一个个单集播客节目。简而言之，该收藏之所以希望通过播客系列来发布这些访谈摘录，其目的就是希望向更为广泛的受众推广与呈现它们的内容。在选择访谈摘录时，主要是基于以下两点标准：（1）选择的访谈摘录对于专业研究者与普通用户来说都是感兴趣的；（2）考虑到音质（audio quality）的重要性，所选择的访谈音频摘录必须足以准确和独立地传递访谈的丰富内容，而无须相应文本的支持。③ 据北卡罗来纳大学教堂山分校威尔逊图书馆特藏部（Special Collections，Louis Round Wilson Library）工作人员蒂姆·霍奇登（Tim Hodgdon）所述，该播

---

① 具体内容可参阅 "Podcast"，from Wikipedia，http：//en. wikipedia. org/wiki/Podcast；Linda W. Braun，*Listen Up*！：*Podcasting for Schools and Libraries*，Medford：Information Today，2007，p. 42；Kelly Schrum，Sheila Brennan，James Halabuk，Sharon M. Leon and Tom Scheinfeldt，"Oral History in the Digital Age"，in Donald A. Ritchie（ed.），*The Oxford Handbook of Oral History*，Oxford and New York：Oxford University Press，2011，pp. 505-506；Peter Gutierrez，*The Power of Scriptwriting*！：*Teaching Essential Writing Skills through Podcasts*，*Graphic Novels*，*Movies*，*and More*，New York：Teachers College Press，2013，pp. 128-129；Jennifer Abraham Cramer and Erin M. Hess，"What Endures：Producing and Publishing an Oral History Podcast"，in Doug Boyd，Steve Cohen，Brad Rakerd，and Dean Rehberger（eds.），*Oral History in the Digital Age*，Washington：Institute of Museum and Library Services，2012，http：//ohda. matrix. msu. edu/2012/06/what-endures/；Anna Bryson and Seán McConville，*The Routledge Guide to Interviewing*：*Oral History*，*Social Enquiry and Investigation*，London and New York：Routledge，2014，p. 97. 上述网站访问时间为 2015 年 3 月 28 日。

② 一般认为，播客技术诞生于 2004 年，详细内容参阅 Kathleen P. King，"Podcasting as Mobile Learning"，in Patricia L. Rogers，Gary A. Berg，Judith Boettcher，Caroline Howard，Lorraine Justice，and Karen D. Schenk（eds.），*Encyclopedia of Distance Learning*，Hershey：Information Science Reference，second edition，2009，pp. 1644-1650.

③ 具体内容访问 https：//web. archive. org/web/20080908111352/http：//docsouth. unc. edu/cgi-bin/feed/sohp_ daily _ excerpt/和 http：//docsouth. unc. edu/sohp/about/podcast. html。上述访问时间为 2015 年 4 月 1 日。

客系列于 2005 年 11 月制作首个音频节目（时长一般为 3—5 分钟），随后定期发布。① 近年来，作为该系列馆藏来源的南方口述历史项目陆续将其更为丰富的口述历史资料制作成播客节目，并通过 SoundCloud 发布，目前节目总量达到 330 个左右。②

随后，美国一些著名的口述历史机构也纷纷将播客节目作为它们推广口述历史馆藏资源的重要手段。比如，路易斯安那州立大学 T. 哈里·威廉姆斯口述历史中心在经过多年筹划之后（想法最初开始于 2005 年）于 2009 年 10 月正式发布口述历史播客系列"持之以恒"（*What Endures*）的第一集（时长为 15—20 分钟），并在随后的 4 年间，该系列总共定期发布了 20 集。目前，该系列所有节目可以通过中心博客、iTunes 和 SoundCloud 在线收听和下载。③ 同年，佛罗里达大学塞缪尔·普罗克特口述历史项目（Samuel Proctor Oral History Program，University of Florida）在其雇员、本科生与研究生及社区志愿者的努力下也开始利用其馆藏资料制作播客节目，并通过该大学数字馆藏和 iTunes 进行发布，其目的就是为了能够让学生、教师与普通公众更为便利地获取地方史资源。目前，它们总共发布播客节目 82 集，每集时长都在 15 分钟以下或者更短。④ 当然，也有一些机构为了让用户能够更好地了解播客节目的详细内容，甚至会提供与播放内

---

① 详细内容参阅蒂姆·霍奇登先生于 2015 年 4 月 7 日给笔者的电邮回信。

② 具体内容访问 http：//sohp. org/oral‐history‐interviews/podcasts/和 https：//soundcloud. com/sohp。上述访问时间为 2015 年 4 月 1 日。需要指出的是，目前该项目没有将播客节目上传到 iTunes 上。

③ 具体内容访问 http：//oralhistory. blogs. lib. lsu. edu/podcast‐library/，https：//itunes. apple. com/us/podcast/what‐endures…/id491489896？mt＝2 和 https：//soundcloud. com/lsu‐oralhistory。关于该系列的相关信息可参阅 Jennifer Abraham Cramer and Erin M. Hess，"What Endures：Producing and Publishing an Oral History Podcast"，in Doug Boyd，Steve Cohen，Brad Rakerd，and Dean Rehberger（eds. ），*Oral History in the Digital Age*，Washington：Institute of Museum and Library Services，2012，http：//ohda. matrix. msu. edu/2012/06/what‐endures/；"LSU Williams Center for Oral History Launches Podcast 'What Endures'"，H‐Oralhist，October 7，2009. 具体内容访问 https：//www. h‐net. org/announce/show. cgi？ID＝171141。上述访问时间为 2015 年 4 月 3 日。

④ 具体内容访问 http：//oral. history. ufl. edu/collection/podcasts/，http：//ufdc. ufl. edu/oral/contains/？t＝%22 Podcast% 22&f＝TO 和 https：//itunes. apple. com/us/podcast/samuel‐proctor‐oral‐history/id783697696？mt＝2。上述访问时间为 2015 年 4 月 3 日。

容相关的完整的抄本或音频记录。比如，上述提到的"美国南方口述历史"（Oral Histories of the American South）播客系列与美国艺术档案馆（Archives of American Art）口述历史馆藏播客系列，后者所有内容均可以通过其网站和 iTunes 在线聆听或下载。①

当然，也有一些机构会将它们已经制作好的口述历史广播节目以播客形式进行呈现与传播。比如，始创于 2003 年的美国故事团（StoryCorps）将其广泛收集的有关美国人日常生活与故事的口述历史访谈资料制作成 3—10 分钟不等的广播节目在美国国家公共电台（National Public Radio）播出（2013 年 12 月 10 日首播）。而从 2007 年 3 月 30 日开始，国家公共电台将其广播节目以播客形式在网站、iTunes 与 Sound Cloud 等平台进行发布，并同时提供在线聆听与下载功能。根据国家公共电台故事团播客网页显示，目前（截至 2015 年 4 月 8 日）该播客系列节目总量达到 422 个。②同样，南密西西比大学口述历史与文化遗产中心、密西西比州人文学科理事会（Mississippi Humanities Council）与密西西比公共广播电视台（Mississippi Public Broadcasting）于 2006 年开始合作，将口述历史与文化遗产中心所保存的口述历史资料制作成每周广播节目（时长为 4.5 分钟左右）——"密西西比时分"（Mississippi Moments）在电台播放。为进一步扩大其影响力，从 2009 年 3 月开始，该广播节目以播客形式通过网站、iTunes 与应用程序等方式进行发布，提供在线聆听与下载功能。根据 iTunes 显示，目前（截至 2015 年 3 月 30 日）播客节目总量达到 298 个。③

---

①　具体内容访问 http：//www. aaa. si. edu/podcasts 和 https：//itunes. apple. com/us/podcast/oral‐history‐collection‐from/id414926839？mt＝2。上述访问时间为 2015 年 4 月 3 日。

②　具体内容访问 http：//storycorps. org/podcast/，http：//www. npr. org/podcasts/510200/storycorps，http：//www. npr. org/series/4516989/storycorps，https：//soundcloud. com/storycorps。上述访问时间为 2015 年 4 月 8 日。

③　具体内容访问 http：//mississippimoments. org/和 https：//itunes. apple. com/us/podcast/mississippi‐moments‐podcast/id312847589？mt＝2。相关信息参阅 "Mississippi Moments Brings History Alive With Expanded Broadcast Schedule"，*Southern Miss Now*，February 3，2015；具体内容访问 http：//www. usm. edu/news/article/mississippi‐moments‐brings‐history‐alive‐expanded‐broadcast‐schedule。上述访问时间为 2015 年 4 月 3 日。

除此之外，对于那些规模较小的个体性口述历史计划来说，播客节目也成为它们推广计划、传播历史内容与提升公众参与的重要手段。这方面的代表性计划包括纽约州立大学石溪分校口述历史计划（Oral History Project，Stony Brook University）、新墨西哥州洛斯阿拉莫斯历史学会（Los Alamos Historical Society）播客系列、摩斯拉数字记忆库（Mozilla Digital Memory Bank）播客系列、飓风数字记忆库（Hurricane Digital Memory Bank）播客系列、缅因州故事库（Story Bank Maine）播客系列、威斯康星大学麦迪逊分校（University of Wisconsin-Madison）1970 年英镑厅爆炸案（Sterling Hall Bombing of 1970）口述历史计划播客系列、纽约大学爱尔兰裔美国人口述历史计划（Oral History of Irish America Project，New York University）播客系列、布鲁克林历史学会播客系列、博尔德公共图书馆玛丽亚·罗杰斯口述历史项目（Maria Rogers Oral History Program，Boulder Public Library）播客系列"听听这个"（Listen to This）、堪萨斯大学罗伯特·多尔政治研究所（Robert J. Dole Institute of Politics，University of Kansas）口述历史计划播客系列以及涉及性议题的口述历史播客系列（The Oral History Podcast）等。[1]

而近年来，随着移动技术革命（mobile technology revolution）与 WordPress、Omeka 和 Drupal 等内容管理系统的不断发展，移动应用程序也成为呈现与传播口述历史信息的重要手段，真正实现在掌上聆听与观看口述历史。在这方面具有开创性意义的是克利夫兰州立大学公共历史与数字人文科学中心（Center for Public History + Digital Humanities，Cleveland State Uni-

---

[1] 具体内容分别访问网址 https://web.archive.org/web/20131002144734/https://podcast.ic.sunysb.edu/weblog/oralhistory/, http://www.losalamoshistory.org/podcasts.htm, http://mozillamemory.org/blog/category/podcast/, http://hurricanearchive.org/items/browse/tag/podcast, http://storybankmaine.org/category/oral-history-podcast/, http://archives.library.wisc.edu/oral-history/sterlinghallwebpage.html, http://irelandhouse.as.nyu.edu/page/ohp.podcasts, http://www.brooklynhistory.org/podcast/BHSpodcast/Brooklyn_Historical_Society.xml, https://boulder oralhistory.wordpress.com/, http://dolearchives.ku.edu/oralhistory 和 http://theoralhistorypodcast.com/。上述访问时间为 2015 年 4 月 4 日。其中部分播客内容还可以在 iTunes 聆听或下载。

versity）于 2010—2011 年开发的免费移动应用程序 "Cleveland Historical"
（该程序可以在 App Store 和 Android App Market 免费下载）。该程序可以让
克利夫兰州的历史触手可及，即通过分层的、以地图定位为基础的多媒体
信息（包括文字、图像与口述历史为主的音视频记录）展示，让用户能够
探索与浏览塑造该城市历史的人们、地方与重要历史瞬间的精彩故事。简
单而言，用户可以在手机等移动设备上下载该免费程序，通过点击地图上
相应的 "地方" 并可以呈现与该地方相关的各种历史信息。目前，"Cleve-
land Historical" 提供了大约 500 多个故事（stories）和 30 余条历史旅游路
线（tours），其中文字 30 万字、图片 4000 幅、音频文件 1000 个与视频文
件 100 个左右。[1] 正如该程序主要设计者马克·特博（Mark Tebeau）所说，
基于口述历史与数字人文学科理论与实践的交叉应用，该程序提出了一种
强调动态的、分层的和背景化的讲故事活动的管理模式（model of cura-
tion），其中尤其强调口述历史的音视频元素对于数字（移动）历史解释计
划的重要性。而随后的管理过程将景观（landscape）转换为一个活生生的
博物馆，在其中，社区可以积极地参与空间和社区认同（place and community identity）理解的重新构造。[2]

为改善与提升该程序的影响力与利用率，该中心还设计了一个同名网
站（http：//clevelandhistorical. org/）与该程序开发的核心技术平台——
"Curatescape"，该平台是一个利用 Omeka 内容管理系统来发表基于位置的
人文科学内容（location-based humanities content）的低成本开源移动框架

---

① 具体内容访问 http：//clevelandhistorical. org/，http：//csudigitalhumanities. org/，http：//
curatescape. org/和 https：//itunes . apple. com/us/app/id401222855。上述访问时间为 2015 年 4 月 4
日。有关该程序与网站的评论请参阅 Daniel Kerr, "Media Review：Cleveland Historical：A Free Mo-
bile App that Puts Cleveland History at Your Fingertips", *Oral History Review*, Vol. 39, No. 2, 2012,
pp. 314-317.

② Mark Tebeau, "Listening to the City：Oral History and Place in the Digital Era", *Oral History
Review*, Vol. 40, No. 1, 2013, p. 25. 相关研究还可参阅 Paul McCoy, "Case Study：StoryMapper -
A Case Study in Map-based Oral History", in Doug Boyd, Steve Cohen, Brad Rakerd, and Dean Reh-
berger（eds. ）, *Oral History in the Digital Age*, Washington：Institute of Museum and Library Services,
2012, http：//ohda. matrix. msu. edu/2012/06/storymapper/, 2015 年 4 月 4 日访问。

（open-source mobile framework）。正是如此，目前该平台为全世界 30 多个机构与组织所采用，它们纷纷开发了与"Cleveland Historical"几乎完全相同的以口述历史资源为核心元素的免费应用程序与同名网站。其中包括"New Orleans Historical"，"Explore Kentucky History"，"Rhode Tour"，"Discover Medina History"，"Native Voices"，"Salt River Stories"，"Connecticut Communities"，"Adelaide City Explorer"，"TribeTrek"，"Stories of the Reach"，"NWPaHeritage"与"Virginia African American Historic Sites Database"等。①

其实，移动应用程序不仅仅是简单地呈现与传播已经事先收集和整理好的口述历史资源，其最新发展技术甚至可以实现口述历史数字化记录、管理与传播的一体化功能。而目前最具前沿性的探索则是美国故事团于2015 年 3 月 18 日发布的免费移动应用程序"StoryCorps"，同时它也设有同名网站（https：//storycorps. me/），其宗旨是希望它们能够成为聆听、连接与分享人类经历故事的全球平台，进而打造人类智慧档案馆。到目前为止，故事团计划通过流动录音棚已经记录了大约 5 万多份访谈（受访者达到 10 万人左右），而该免费移动应用程序则试图实现"自己动手做口述历史"（DIY Oral History）。简单而言，用户在手机等移动设备上下载该免费程序之后，并可以分步实现口述历史访谈的前期准备（问题设置与受访者选择）、正式访谈记录、访谈初步整理与编辑及保存、在线发布与分享访谈等完整程序。尤其需要强调的是，在访谈问题设置环节，除提供20 多个最佳问题之外；该程序还按照主题提供了大量访谈问题范例（总数达到100 多个），这些主题包括家族传统、祖父母、成长经历与学校生活、爱情与关系、父母、宗教信仰与精神生活、对于爱人的回忆、严重疾病经历、战争经历及工作经历等。显然，这些问题对于访谈者来说是非常具有参考与借鉴意义的，当然也可以自行准备与设置访谈问题。而为真正实现其打造人类智慧档案馆的目的，在该程序运行至少一年之后，故事团准备将所

---

① 有关这些免费应用程序可以访问 https：//itunes. apple. com/us/artist/dxy – solutions – llc/id385508000，2015 年 4 月 4 日访问。另外还可以通过 Google 检索这些程序找到它们的官方网站。

有访谈资料保存在美国国会图书馆的美国民俗生活中心。① 尽管美国口述历史学界对于故事团开展的访谈活动是否可以称为真正意义上的口述历史存在诸多争论，不过无法忽视的是，它已经成为广泛记录普通美国人日常生活经历的重要手段。而"StoryCorps"移动应用程序的开发则更加直接方便了每个人自己动手做口述历史及传播与分享口述历史。据相关统计，在发布 20 天左右，该程序下载量达到 16.5 万次左右，上传访谈数量达到 1000 多份（经笔者查询，2015 年 4 月 7 日共上传访谈 50 份）。②

需要指出的是，数字化革命不仅为口述历史原始资料（抄本与音视频记录）及后续开发产品（如播客、在线展览、语音导览与纪录片等）的在线呈现与传播提供了巨大潜能，而且互联网本身就是一个资源异常丰富的口述历史在线指南库。许多口述历史网站与博客为各种层次的口述历史实践者（尤其是学生、教师与志愿者）提供了各种各样的操作指南，其内容涉及口述历史实践的方方面面。只要在 Google 上检索"oral history guides（techniques，primers）"或"tips（steps，introductions）for oral history"等关键词，便可以发现众多相关的口述历史指南类网络资源。③

作为美国口述历史学界的全国性组织，口述历史协会有关口述历史实践的原则、标准与评估指南自然成为绝大部分美国口述历史工作者的重要操作规范。④ 在 1997 年美国口述历史协会官方网站创建时，于 1989 年修

---

① 具体内容访问 https：//storycorps. me/和 https：//itunes. apple. com/us/app/storycorps/id359071069？mt = 8，2015 年 4 月 8 日访问。有关该移动应用程序的相关资料还可参阅 Anne Quito，"StoryCorps，the beloved US Oral History Project，Is Now Going Global"，*Quartz*，March 18，2015；Christoph Hitz，"Collecting Human Voices With a StoryCorps App"，*New York Times*，March 27，2015；Patt Morrison，"Dave Isay on StoryCorps' DIY Oral History Project"，*Los Angeles Times*，April 7，2015.

② Patt Morrison，"Dave Isay on StoryCorps' DIY Oral History Project"，*Los Angeles Times*，April 7，2015. 另外，目前已经上传的访谈资料可以访问 https：//storycorps. me/interviews/，2015 年 4 月 8 日访问。

③ 比较集中的口述历史指南类网络资源可参阅 Linda Shopes（ed.），Web Guides to Doing Oral History，具体内容访问 http：//www. oralhistory. org/web – guides – to – doing – oral – history/和 http：//ohda. matrix. msu. edu/featured – resources/shopes – web – guides/，2015 年 4 月 9 日访问。

④ 美国口述历史协会的原则、标准与评估指南分别于 1968 年、1979 年、1989 年、2000 年和 2009 年进行多次拟定与修改，每次修改都充分反映了口述历史实践的最新变革与发展趋势。

订的《口述历史评估指南》（*Oral History Evaluation Guidelines*）就直接上传到该网站上，该指南包括《美国口述历史协会原则与标准》（*Principles and Standards of the Oral History Association*）和《口述历史评估指南》（*Oral History Evaluation Guidelines*）两部分。前者还从《对于受访者的责任》（Responsibility to Interviewees）、《对于公众与专业的责任》（Responsibility to the Public and to the Profession）和《赞助机构与档案机构的责任》（Responsibility for Sponsoring and Archival Institutions）等三方面为厘清口述历史实践过程中的不同关系体的权责关系制定了一些基本原则与标准；而《口述历史评估指南》则分别从《项目/计划指南》（Program/Project Guidelines）、《伦理/法律指南》（Ethical/Legal Guidelines）、《录音/抄本处理指南》（Tape/Transcript Processing Guidelines）、《访谈内容指南》（Interview Content Guidelines）、《访谈行为指南》（Interview Conduct Guidelines）、《独立/非附属研究者指南》（Independent/Unaffiliated Researcher Guidelines）与《教师/学生指南》（Educator and Student Guidelines）等方面制定了相当完整和详细的评估规范。[1] 目前，美国口述历史协会网站提供的最新原则、标准与评估指南是于 2009 年修订的，即《口述历史原则与最佳实务》（*Principles for Oral History and Best Practices for Oral History*），它包括《口述历史一般原则》（*General Principles for Oral History*）和《口述历史最佳实务》（*Best Practices for Oral History*）两部分，后者则从"访谈前"、"访谈"与"访谈后"三个阶段分别提出实现口述历史最佳操作的实务指南。[2]

此外，一些口述历史机构或计划也会根据它们的具体情况提供有关口述历史实践完整过程的在线指南。这方面做得比较好的是贝勒大学口述历史研究所网站所提供的"工作坊与资源"（Workshops & Resources）页面，

---

① 具体内容访问 https：//web. archive. org/web/19970616135829/http：//www. baylor. edu/~OHA/EvaluationGuidelines. html，2015 年 4 月 12 日访问。

② 具体内容访问 http：//www. oralhistory. org/about/principles – and – practices/。该页面还提供了于 2000 年修订的《口述历史评估指南》，具体内容访问 http：//www. oralhistory. org/about/principles – and – practices/oral – history – evaluation – guidelines – revised – in – 2000/。上述访问时间为 2015 年 4 月 12 日。

其内容包括既丰富又实用的《口述历史导论》（Introduction to Oral History）、《口述历史入门指南（在线工作坊）》（Getting Started with Oral History）、《转录格式指南》（Transcribing Style Guide）、《口述历史的核心：如何访谈》（The Heart of Oral History：How to Interview）、《组织口述历史计划》（Organizing Oral History Projects），以及关于口述历史应用的经典论文集《过去遇到现在》（*The Past Meets The Present*）等。① 而另外一个相当值得参考的口述历史在线指南是美国著名口述历史学家琳达·肖普斯撰写的《理解口述历史》（Making Sense of Oral History，http：//historymatters. gmu. edu/mse/oral/），该指南由纽约市立大学（City University of New York）美国社会史计划（American Social History Project）、媒体与学习中心（Center for Media and Learning）与乔治梅森大学（George Mason University）罗伊·罗森茨维格历史与新媒体中心（Roy Rosenzweig Center for History and New Media）联合创建的美国概况网络课程（U. S. Survey Course on the Web）——《历史很重要》（History Matters）于 2002 年正式推出。同样，北卡罗来纳大学教堂山分校南方口述历史项目和佛罗里达大学塞缪尔·普罗克特口述历史项目也分别在其官方网站"资源（Resources）"与"学习指南"（Tutorials）页面提供了各种口述历史实践指南，其中前者包括《10个访谈者贴士》（10 Tips for Interviewers）、《学生访谈者指南》（Student Interviewer Guidelines）与《口述历史实践指南》（A Practical Guide to Oral History）；② 而后者则包括《口述历史八步法》（8 Steps to Doing Oral History）、《口述历史工作坊》（Oral History Workshop）与《口述历史转录与编辑指南》（Guidelines for Transcribing and Editing Oral History）。③ 而创建于 1991 年的美国世纪口述历史计划（American Century Oral History Pro-

---

① 具体内容访问 http：//www. baylor. edu/oralhistory/index. php？ id＝23560，2015 年 4 月 12 日访问。

② 具体内容访问 http：//sohp. org/resources－2/，2015 年 4 月 12 日访问。

③ 具体内容访问 http：//oral. history. ufl. edu/files/march－2014－8－steps. pdf，http：//oral. history. ufl. edu/files/2014－Oral－History－Workshop. pdf 和 http：//ufdc. ufl. edu/IR00002513/00001，2015 年 4 月 12 日访问。

ject）网站则为学生与教师提供了丰富的口述历史资源，其内容包括《转录工作坊》（Transcription Workshop）、《作为教育方法论的口述历史》（Oral History as an Educational Methodology）、《口述历史培训工作坊》（Oral History Training Workshops）、《大学预科历史计划》（Pre-Collegiate History Projects）和《美国世纪口述历史计划资源指南》（OHP Resource Guide）等。①

此外，比较有参考价值的口述历史在线指南还包括国会图书馆美国民俗生活中心的《民俗生活与田野：田野技巧指南》（Folklife and Fieldwork：An Introduction to Field Techniques，http：//www. loc. gov/folklife/fieldwork/index. html）及老兵历史计划的《计划参与入门指南》（Getting Started for Participating in the Project，http：//www. loc. gov/vets/questions. html）、美国陆军军事史中心（Center of Military History，United States Army）的《美国陆军口述历史指南》（U. S. Army Guide to Oral History，http：//www. history. army. mil/books/oral. html）、美国国家二战博物馆（The National WWII Museum）的《口述历史指南》（Oral History Guidelines，http：//www. nationalww2museum. org/learn/education/for – students/oral – history – guidelines. html）、美国联邦第九巡回上诉法院历史学会（The Ninth Judicial Circuit Historical Society）的《为明天保存昨天和今天：法官和律师口述历史指南》（Saving Yesterday Today for Tomorrow：A Guide to Oral History for the Bench and Bar，http：//www. njchs. org/GOH. pdf）、哈佛大学电影研究中心（Film Study Center）"做历史"（DoHistory）网站的《口述历史分步指南》（Step – by – Step Guide to Oral History，http：//dohistory. org/on_ your_ own/toolkit/oralHistory. html）、加州大学圣克鲁兹分校区域史计划（Regional History Project，University of California，Santa Cruz）的《口述历史初级读本》（Oral History Primer，http：//library. ucsc. edu/reg – hist/oral –

---

① 具体内容访问 http：//www. americancenturyproject. org/styled/index. html，2015 年 4 月 12 日访问。

history‐primer）、加州州立大学长滩分校口述历史项目（Oral History Program，California State University，Long Beach）的《口述历史初级读本》（An Oral History Primer，http：//www. cla. csulb. edu/departments/history/oral‐history‐program/an‐oral‐history‐primer/）、明尼苏达州历史学会口述历史办公室（Oral History Office）的《口述历史计划指南》（Oral History Project Guidelines，http：//www. mnhs. org/collections/oralhistory/ohguidelines. pdf）、南达科他州历史学会（South Dakota State Historical Society）的《口述历史初学者指南》（A Beginner's Guide to Oral History，http://history. sd. gov/archives/forms/SHRAB/oralbook1. pdf）、内布拉斯加州历史学会（Nebraska Historical Society）的《捕捉活生生的过去：口述历史初级读本》（Capturing the Living Past：An Oral History Primer，http：//www. nebraskahistory. org/lib‐arch/research/audiovis/oral_history/index. htm）、蒙大拿历史学会口述历史项目（Oral History Program，Montana Historical Society）的《口述历史初级读本》（An Oral History Primer，http：//montanawomenshistory. org/wp‐content/uploads/2013/05/Speaking‐of‐Montana‐OH‐Primer‐Pam‐1. pdf）与《课堂上的口述历史》（Oral History in the Classroom，http：//mhs. mt. gov/Portals/11/education/docs/OH%20training%20pamph let%20for%20teachers. pdf）、塞西尔郡历史学会（Historical Society of Cecil County）与塞西尔郡公立学校（Cecil County Public Schools）的《口述历史：记录与研究方法》（Oral History：Methods for Documentation and Research，http：//www. cecilhistory. org/aids/oralhistory. pdf）、弗吉尼亚人文科学基金会弗吉尼亚民俗生活项目（Virginia Folklife Program，Virginia Foundation for the Humanities）的《口述历史基本指南：概念、技巧与策略》（A Basic Guide to the Concepts，Techniques and Strategies of Oral History，https：//web. archive. org/web/20070808010338/http：//www. virginiafolklife. org/program_history. php）、美国兽医医学史学会（American Veterinary Medical History Society）的

《兽医口述历史访谈：访谈者指南》（Conducting Veterinary Oral History Interviews：A Guide to Interviewers，http：//avmhs. org/oralhist/Veterinary% 20Oral% 20 Histories% 20GUIDE% 202013 - Mar - 1. pdf）、犹太女性档案馆（Jewish Women's Archive）的《口述历史工具箱》（Oral History Tools，http：//jwa. org/stories/how - to/guide）、美国大学女性协会（American Association of University Women）的《如何执行你自己的口述历史计划》（How to Conduct Your Own Oral History Project，http：//www. aauw. org/resource/oral - history - project/）、德克萨斯历史委员会（Texas Historical Commission）的《口述历史基础》（Fundamentals of Oral History，http：// www. thc. state. tx. us/public/upload/publications/OralHistory. pdf）、北卡罗来纳大学教堂山分校写作中心（The Writing Center）的《口述历史讲义》（Handouts for Oral History，http：//writingcenter. unc. edu/handouts/oral - history/）、高德灵—沃尔登伯格南方犹太人生活研究所（Goldring-Woldenberg Institute of Southern Jewish Life）的《自己动手做口述历史》（Oral History：Do It Yourself! http：//www. isjl. org/oral - history - guide. html）、路易斯堡学院人类学系（Anthropology Department，Fort Lewis College）的《口述历史指南》（Oral History Guide，https：//www. fortlewis. edu/anthropology/OralHistoryGuide. aspx）、福音派基督教圣约教会（Evangelical Covenant Church）的《为地方圣约教会收集口述历史指南》（A Guide to Collecting Oral History for Local Covenant Churches，http：//www. covchurch. org/wp - content/uploads/sites/2/2013/02/Oral - History - booklet - for - web. pdf）、"FamilySearch"网站的《创建口述历史》（Creating Oral Histories，https：//familysearch. org/learn/wiki/en/Creating_ Oral_ Histories）、皮尔森教育公司（Pearson Education，Inc. ）的《口述历史应用指南》（A Guide to Using Oral History，http：//www. phschool. com/eteach/social_ studies/2003_ 04/essay. html）、美国国家破产法院法官会议档案馆与历史委员会（Archives and History Committee，National Conference of Bankruptcy Judges）的

《破产法院法官口述历史收集指南》（Guide to Taking Oral History of Bankruptcy Judges，http：//c. ymcdn. com/sites/www. ncbj. org/resource/resmgr/
Projects/Projects_ Oral_ History_ Guide. pdf）、杜肯大学（Duquesne Uni-
versity）图书馆的《口述历史实务指南》（Oral History：A How – To Guide，
http：//guides. library. duq. edu/oralhistory）及耶稣基督后期圣徒教会（The
Church of Jesus Christ of Latter-day Saints）的《教会历史指南：口述历史》
（Church History Guides：Oral Histories，https：//www. lds. org/callings/
church – history – adviser/training/oral – histories – guide？ lang = eng）等。①

　　当然，某些在线指南也可能只涉及口述历史实践的某一个方面，比
如，作为口述历史实践的核心部分，许多网站都提供了有关口述历史访谈
操作的最佳实务建议。早在 20 世纪 90 年代中后期，印第安纳大学口述历
史研究中心就在其官方网站发布由该中心口述历史学家芭芭拉·特鲁斯德
尔（Barbara Truesdell）撰写的口述历史访谈指南《口述历史技巧：如何组
织与执行口述历史访谈》（Oral History Techniques：How to Organize and
Conduct Oral History Interviews）。② 而在差不多同一时期，加州大学伯克利
分校地区口述历史办公室也在其官方网站提供访谈指南《口述历史操作贴
士》（Tips for Conducting an Oral History）与《口述历史一分钟指南》（The
One-Minute Guide to Oral History）。③ 此外，较有代表性的口述历史访谈在
线指南还包括美国大屠杀纪念博物馆的《口述历史访谈指南》（Oral Histo-
ry Interview Guidelines，http：//www. ushmm. org/m/pdfs/20121003 – oral –

---

　　① 上述网址访问日期为 2015 年 4 月 12 日。
　　② 该中心于 2002 年更名为历史与记忆研究中心（Center for the Study of History and Memory），
而该指南也几经修改，不过它一直是该网站的重要内容。具体内容访问 https：//web. archive. org/
web/19961227104135/http：//www. indiana. edu/ ~ ohrc/pamph1. htm 和 http：//www. indiana. edu/ ~
cshm/oral_ history_ techniques. pdf. 上述访问时间为 2015 年 4 月 9 日。
　　③ 《口述历史操作贴士》编辑自 Willa K. Baum，*Oral History for the Local Historical Society*，
Walnut Creek：AltaMira Press，third edition，revised，1995. 目前这些指南综合修订为《访谈者贴
士》（Tips for Interviewers），具体内容访问 https：//web. archive. org/web/19970607091720/ht-
tp：//www. lib. berkeley. edu/BANC/ROHO/和 http：//bancroft. berkeley. edu/ROHO/resources/ro-
hotips. html，2015 年 4 月 9 日访问。

history – interview – guide. pdf）、美国史密森学会的《史密森学会民俗学与口述历史访谈指南》（The Smithsonian Folklore and Oral History Interviewing Guide, http：//www. folklife. si. edu/resources/pdf/InterviewingGuide. pdf）、国会图书馆美国民俗生活中心的《口述历史访谈》（Oral History Interviews, http：//www. loc. gov/folklife/familyfolklife/oralhistory. html）、加州大学洛杉矶分校口述历史研究中心的《访谈指南》（Interviewing Guidelines, http：//oralhistory. library. ucla. edu/interviewGuidelines. html）、历史频道（The History Channel）的《口述历史访谈指南》（Guidelines for Oral History Interviews, http：//www. history. com/images/media/interactives/oralhistguidelines. pdf）、肯塔基口述历史委员会（Kentucky Oral History Commission）的《执行口述历史访谈》（Conducting an Oral History Interviewing, http：//history. ky. gov/portfolio/the – oral – history – collection – resources/）、美国海军历史基金会海军历史中心（Naval Historical Center, Naval Historical Foundation）的《口述历史：海军历史访谈指南》（Oral History：A Guide for Conducting Naval Historical Interviews, http：//www. navyhistory. org/wp – content/uploads/2011/04/OralHistoryGuide. pdf）、密西西比大学威廉·温特种族和解研究所（William Winter Institute for Racial Reconciliation, University of Mississippi）的《口述历史指南》（Oral History Guidelines, http：//winterinstitute. org/community – relations/community – resources/oral – history – guide/）、美国国家盲人联盟（National Federation of the Blind）的《口述历史访谈指南》（A Guide to Oral History Interviewing, https：//nfb. org/images/nfb/publications/articles/aguidetooralhistoryinterviewing. html）、伟谷州立大学（Grand Valley State University）的《口述历史收集指南》（Guide to Collecting Oral Histories, http：//www. gvsu. edu/speaking/guide – to – collecting – oral – histories – 7. htm）及美国南方饮食联盟（Southern Foodways Alliance）的《SFA 口述历史计划：访谈问题与贴士》（SFA Oral History Initiative：Interview Questions and Tips, http：//www. southernfoodways. org/oh – interview – questions – and

-tips／）等。①

　　还有一些在线指南则是有关口述历史转录与编辑等后续处理环节，其中比较值得参考的有弗吉尼亚大学米勒公共事务中心（Miller Center of Public Affairs, University of Virginia）的《口述历史抄本编辑指南》（Oral History Transcript Editing Guidelines, http：//millercenter. org/oralhistory/styleguide）、林肯总统图书馆口述历史项目（Oral History Program, Abraham Lincoln Presidential Library）的《转录与编辑格式指南》（Transcribing & Editing Style Guide, http：//www. illinois. gov/alplm/library/collections/oralhistory/Documents/resources/transcription%20editing%20style%20guide. pdf）、明尼苏达州历史学会口述历史办公室的《转录、编辑与处理指南》（Transcribing, Editing and Processing Guidelines, http：//www. mnhs. org/collections/oralhistory/ohtranscribing. pdf）、俄勒冈交通署研究部（Oregon Department of Transportation Research Section）的《口述历史转录与摘要指南》（Guide to Transcribing and Summarizing Oral Histories, http：//www. oregon. gov/odot/td/tp_ res/docs/otherpublications/guide_ to_ transcribing_ and _ summarizing_ oral_ histories. pdf）及迈阿密大学图书馆（University of Miami Libraries）的《口述历史转录指南》（Transcription Guidelines for Oral Histories, http：//library. miami. edu/wp – content/uploads/2014/01/Transcription_ Guidelines_ 2012 – 08. docx）等。②

　　而对于那些学生实践者来说，有关"课堂上的口述历史"的在线指南则是很好的学习资源。其中较有代表性的包括美国口述历史协会与历史频道（The History Channel）联合推出的《口述历史教育：原则与最佳实务》（Principles and Best Practices for Oral History Education, http：//www. oralhistory. org/oral – history – classroom – guide/）、哥大口述历史中心的《讲述生活口述历史课程指南》（The Telling Lives Oral History Curriculum

---

① 上述网址访问日期为 2015 年 4 月 12 日。

② 上述网址访问日期为 2015 年 4 月 12 日。

Guide，http：//incite. columbia. edu/storage/Telling _ Lives _ Curriculum _ Guide. pdf)、"HistoryLink" 网站推出的《课堂上的口述历史》（Oral Histo-ries in the Classroom，http：//www. historylink. org/_ content/education/downloads/Oral%20History%20Curriculum. pdf)、北卡罗来纳大学教堂山分校教育学院（School of Education）主办项目——"LEARN NC" 的《课堂上的口述历史》（Oral History in the Classroom，http：//www. learnnc. org/lp/editions/oralhistory2002/cover)、美国当代犹太人博物馆（Contemporary Jewish Museum）的《幸存故事：在课堂上创建与探索口述历史》（Stories of Survival：Creating and Exploring Oral Histories in the Classroom，http：//www. thecjm. org/storage/documents/education/2013/Oral_ History_ Cur-riculum_ Resource – FINAL. pdf)、中康涅狄格州立大学老兵历史计划（Veterans History Project，Central Connecticut State University）的《课堂上的口述历史》（Oral History in the Classroom，http：//web. ccsu. edu/vethisto-ryproject/educators/files/CCSUVHP_ Oral_ History_ in_ Classroom. pdf)、德克萨斯文化研究所（Institute of Texan Cultures）的《课堂上的口述历史》（Oral History in the Classroom，http：//www. texancultures. com/assets/1/15/ITC_ Oral_ History_ Analysis_ 2013. pdf）及 "课堂上的二战声音"（WWII Voices in the Classroom）计划的《如何做视频口述历史》（How to do Oral History on Video，http：//www. wwiihistoryclass. com/projects/oral. html）等。①

　　而随着数字化革命对于口述历史影响的不断加深，许多网站也专门针对相关主题发布在线指南。其中影响最大的就是美国博物馆和图书馆服务研究院国家领袖基金计划——"数字化时代的口述历史" 网站，该网站致力于传播和发布与口述历史实践各个阶段相关的数字化技术的最新信息与资源。该网站是一个多方参与的跨学科合作计划，除美国博物馆和图书馆服务研究院之外，合作方还包括密歇根州立大学数字人文与社会科学中

---

① 　上述网址访问日期为 2015 年 4 月 12 日。

心、美国国会图书馆美国民俗生活中心、史密森民俗生活和文化遗产中心（Smithsonian Center for Folklife and Cultural Heritage）、美国民俗学会（American Folklore Society）、肯塔基大学图书馆路易·纳恩口述历史中心及美国口述历史协会。该网站核心内容包括"入门指南"（其中包括档案学与音视频资料相关的术语简介）、"论文"（涉及口述历史数字化收集、管理与传播三个方面的大量优秀论文）、"向道格拉斯·博伊德提问"（可以就记录设备、麦克风等问题向博伊德博士提问）、"头脑风暴"（包括众多美国著名口述历史学家有关口述历史与数字化技术的视频演讲）及"维基资源"（包括口述历史最佳实务与网络资源等众多维基条目）等。简单而言，该网站不管是从内容还是从形式来说，对于那些正处于数字化时代的口述历史工作者来说，它已经成为不可或缺的必备指南，同时也深受美国乃至国际口述历史学界的广泛关注与好评。①

此外，值得参考的有关口述历史与数字化技术问题的在线指南还包括佛蒙特州民俗生活中心（Vermont Folklife Center）推出的适用于口述历史的系列数字记录与编辑指南，其中包括《数字音频田野记录设备指南》（Digital Audio Field Recording Equipment Guide, http://www.vermontfolklifecenter.org/archive/res_ audioequip.htm）、《数字化时代的田野记录》（Field Recording in the Digital Age, http://www.vermontfolklifecenter.org/archive/res_ digital-age.html）与《田野录音的数字化编辑》（Digital Editing of Field Audio, http://www.vermontfolklifecenter.org/archive/res_ digitalediting.htm）。另外，还可以参考"佛罗里达之声"（Florida Voices）计划的《口述历史指南与数字化最佳实务》（Oral History How-To Guide and Digital Best Practices, http://www.fcla.edu/FloridaVoices/guidelines.shtml）、威廉与玛丽学院（College of

---

① 有关该网站的具体内容请访问 http://ohda.matrix.msu.edu/，2015 年 4 月 12 日访问。有关该网站的评论请参阅"Keeping Oral History Alive in a Digital World"，具体内容访问 http://www.imls.gov/keeping_ oral_ history_ alive_ in_ a_ digital_ world.aspx；Stephen M. Sloan, Donald A. Ritchie, Sarah-Jane M. Poindexter, Michael Pasquier and Kelly Sellers Wittie, "Media Review: Oral History in the Digital Age", *Oral History Review*, Vol. 40, No. 2, 2013, pp. 371-377.

William & Mary）博客——"学术技术"（Academic Technology）的《口述历史策划基础技术简短指南》（A Brief Guide to Basic Technology Planning for Oral History Projects，http：//at. blogs. wm. edu/a－brief－guide－to－basic－technology－planning－for－oral－history－projects/）、路易斯安那州立大学 T. 哈里·威廉姆斯口述历史中心的《网络上的口述历史：初级读本》（Oral History on the Web：A Primer，https：//web. archive. org/web/20020826134323/http：//www. lib. lsu. edu/special/williams/webprimer/index. html）、马里兰大学巴尔的摩郡分校（University of Maryland，Baltimore County）的"数字化讲故事资源"（Resources for Digital Storytelling，http：//stories. umbc. edu/resources. php）、"利用数字化工具记录家庭口述历史"（Family Oral History Using Digital Tools，http：//familyoralhistory. us/）网站及道格拉斯·博伊德的个人博客（http：//dougboyd. org/和 http：//digitalomnium. com/）等。①

　　上述从传播形式与内容等方面并结合美国口述历史学界的具体实践详细分析了数字化革命对于口述历史资源呈现与传播的巨大影响与深远意义。而另一方面，作为数字化革命的重要组成部分，以电子邮件、简单信息聚合订阅（RSS feed）、博客（微博，比如 WordPress、Blogger 和 Tumblr 等）、社交网络（比如 Facebook、Twitter、MySpace、LinkedIn 和 Google Plus 等）、内容社区（如 YouTube、Vimeo、Flickr、Picasa、Instagram 和 Sound Cloud 等）、维基（Wiki）、播客、网络论坛与即时通信（如 MSN、Skype 等）为代表的社交媒体（social media）的发展与不断应用则极大地促进了美国口述历史学界的国内外交流。②

---

① 上述网址访问日期为 2015 年 4 月 12 日。

② 有关社交媒体与社交网络的具体信息可以访问 "Social Media"，from Wikipedia，http：//en. wikipedia. org/wiki/Social_ media；"Social Network"，from Wikipedia，http：//en. wikipedia. org/wiki/Social_ network. 上述访问时间为 2015 年 4 月 18 日。相关研究还可参阅 Todd Kelsey，*Social Networking Spaces：From Facebook to Twitter and Everything In Between A Step-by-Step Introduction to Social Networks for Beginners and Everyone Else*，Berkeley：Apress，2010；George A. Barnett（ed.），*Encyclopedia of Social Networks*，Thousand Oaks：Sage Publications，2011；Michael Mandiberg（ed.），*The Social Media Reader*，New York：New York University Press，2012；Christian Fuchs，*Social Media：A Critical Introduction*，Thousand Oaks：Sage Publications，2013.

　　与较为迟缓地将口述历史资料上传到网络相比，美国口述历史学界还是比较积极地利用电子邮件、邮件列表与网站等网络技术作为促进交流与合作的重要手段。根据笔者查询《美国口述历史协会通讯》显示，美国口述历史工作者最早大概从 1992 年开始就利用因时网（BITNET）服务器来获取或订阅邮件列表，当时路易斯维尔大学（University of Louisville）历史系卡尔·赖恩特（Carl Ryant）教授在该通讯上发布有关 1993 年美国文化协会（American Culture Association）年会分议题"口述历史与美国文化"（Oral History and American Culture）征文时就提供了他的因时网电子邮件地址——"CGRYAN01 @ UL-KYVM"。① 而在 1993 年该通讯发布的同一征文消息中，卡尔·赖恩特教授除提供上述因时网电子邮件地址之外，还同时提供了互联网电子邮件地址——"cgryan01@ ulkyvm. louisvil-le. edu"，这也是该通讯最早出现互联网电子邮件的记录。② 正是如此，从 20 世纪 90 年代初开始，电子邮件也逐渐成为美国口述历史工作者的重要交流方式。而为进一步加强同行之间的交流与深化对于某些口述历史问题的讨论，以电子邮件为基础，美国口述历史协会从 1993 年开始提供邮件用户清单服务，即口述历史协会讨论组（Oral History Association Discussion List）——"OHA-L"，由时任肯塔基大学口述历史项目主任特里·伯德惠斯勒（Terry Birdwhistell）负责。通过该网络论坛，任何订阅者都可以提出问题或发布口述历史计划、出版与会议等消息。③ 而从 1996 年开始，该讨论组发展成为以网站为基础的在线论坛——"口述历史论坛"（H-OralHist），其功能基本不变，即通过电子邮件与网站平台向任何在论坛登记的用户提供

---

①　*Oral History Association Newsletter*, Vol. 26, No. 1, Spring 1992, p. 4.
②　*Oral History Association Newsletter*, Vol. 27, No. 2, Fall 1993, p. 6.
③　Terry Birdwhistell, "OHA Electronic List Now Available", *Oral History Association Newsletter*, Vol. 27, No. 2, Fall 1993, p. 3.

信息交流与提问服务。① 登记用户可以向论坛发表有关口述历史计划的信息和研究成果，同时也可以提出任何相关的问题以及获得有关这些问题的各种回复信息。到目前为止，该论坛已经发展成为美国乃至国际口述历史学界最具规模和权威的交流平台。② 此外，上述提到的在 1995 年和 1996年前后出现的美国最早一批口述历史网站的基本功能也主要是出于交流目的，其内容主要是介绍口述历史机构或计划的基本信息。③

而就数字化交流而言，真正对美国口述历史学界产生深刻影响的则是上述提到的以 Web2.0 技术为核心的社交媒体的兴起与发展。作为人们彼此之间用来发表见解、观点与分享经验、体会的工具与平台，它以参与性、共享性、交流性、社区性、互动性与连通性等基本特征而广受用户欢迎。正如有学者指出："诸如 Facebook、Twitter 和 YouTube 等社交网站为包括口述历史学家在内的任何人开启了大门，有助于人们在一种虚拟的合作性环境中分享内容、创建关系和进行对话。"④ 正是如此，这些社交媒

---

① 该论坛网站于 1996 年 4 月 2 日发布首条帖子。详细内容访问 http://h - net. msu. edu/cgi - bin/logbrowse. pl? trx = lx&list = H - Oralhist&user = &pw = &month = 9604，2015 年 4 月 18 日访问。有关该论坛的发展历史还可参阅 Jeff Charnley，"OHA Links with H - Net to Create H - Oralhist"，*Oral History Association Newsletter*，Vol. 32，No. 1，Winter 1998，pp. 1，3。

② 目前，该论坛网址为 https://networks. h - net. org/h - oralhist，2015 年 4 月 18 日访问。笔者从 1999 年开始从事口述史学研究时就是通过该论坛与世界各地的 100 多位口述史学家建立了学术联系，笔者在该论坛提交的问题与来自其他学者的答复及发布的相关信息都可以在该论坛上找到，可以说是笔者学习和研究口述史学的最好交流平台。

③ 美国口述历史协会官方网站于 1997 年创建时，其页面内容主要包括奖项、会员利益、委员会组织、年会信息、评估指南、出版物、基本信息、其他网站链接及联系方式。具体内容访问 https://web. archive. org/web/19970616065251/http://www. baylor. edu/ ~ OHA/，2015 年 4 月 18日访问。

④ Juliana Nykolaiszyn，"Oral History and Social Networks: From Promotion to Relationship Building"，in Douglas A. Boyd，Steve Cohen，Brad Rakerd，and Dean Rehberger（eds.），*Oral History in the Digital Age*，Washington: Institute of Museum and Library Services，2012，http://ohda. matrix. msu. edu/2012/06/oral - history - and - social - networks/，2015 年 4 月 18 日访问。此外还可参阅 Peter B. Kaufman，"Oral History in the Video Age"，*Oral History Review*，Vol. 40，No. 1，2013，p. 5；Donald A. Ritchie，*Doing Oral History*，Oxford and New York: Oxford University Press，third edition，2014，pp. 159-160，189；Reisa Levin，"Oral History in the Age of Social Media Networks: Life Stories on CitizenShift and Parole Citoyenne"，in Steven High，Edward Little，and Thi Ry Duong（eds.），*Remembering Mass Violence: Oral History，New Media and Performance*，Toronto: University of Toronto Press，2014，pp. 131-151.

体深受美国众多口述历史机构或计划的欢迎，它们一般都会在这些社交媒体上创建自己的主页，并结合各种社交媒体的主要特征定期发布各种各样的信息，其信息类型包括文本、图像、音频与视频等多元形式。只要在 Facebook 或 Twitter 上检索关键词"oral history"，就可以找到众多机构或计划的主页，比如美国口述历史协会、西南口述历史协会、西北口述历史协会、密歇根口述历史协会、德克萨斯口述历史协会、中大西洋地区口述历史组织、哥伦比亚大学口述历史中心、加州大学伯克利分校地区口述历史办公室、贝勒大学口述历史研究所、肯塔基大学路易·纳恩口述历史中心、北卡罗来纳大学教堂山分校南方口述历史项目、精神分裂症口述历史计划（The Schizophrenia Oral History Project）与口述历史暑期学校（Oral History Summer School）等。而且，它们还会利用多种社交媒体同步或交替发布类似信息，以美国《口述历史评论》为例，除官方网站（http：//ohr. oxfordjournals. org/）之外，它还通过 Twitter、Facebook、Google Plus、Tumblr、SoundCloud 与博客帖子（Blog Posts，通过电子邮件和简单信息聚合订阅）等社交媒体实现预览、学习、连接、发现与研究口述历史的目的。[①]

此外，就口述历史工作者之间的交流而言，在 Facebook 和 Twitter 等社交媒体上，很多美国口述历史工作者都有自己的主页，而且他们之间互为好友，并且经常发布有关口述历史的最新信息或思考。而为促进对某一问题的深入讨论与交流，一些口述历史组织或个人也会通过社交媒体创建相关讨论群组。比如，Facebook 上就有一个讨论组"数字化时代的口述历史"（Oral History in the Digital Age），目前其成员达到 284 位（笔者也在其中）。在该讨论组中，任何成员都可以围绕该主题发表见解或提出问题，而相关问题也会引起群组成员间的相互讨论与交流。[②]

---

① 具体内容查阅该网址（http：//blog. oup. com/2015/03/linda－shopes－oral－history－curation/）页面右边有关《口述历史评论》的简介信息。上述访问时间为 2015 年 4 月 18 日。

② 具体内容访问 https：//www. facebook. com/groups/246603815398919/，2015 年 4 月 18 日访问。

尽管将口述历史纳入社交媒体当中需要相当的人力与物力资源，但是其积极作用也是不言而喻的，它不仅有助于推广与分享来自档案馆或图书馆等实体空间的口述历史资源，同时还能够以新的方式实现口述历史工作者与公众乃至他们之间的相互联系与交流。简言之，以互联网为核心的数字化革命超越了地理空间界限而将美国乃至全世界的口述历史实践者联系起来，他们相互交流与分享信息，紧随当代口述史学发展的最新趋势。

第七章 美国口述历史教育的兴起与发展

口述历史作为一种教育手段，它在美国兴起于 20 世纪 60 年代，现在已经发展成为当代美国历史学和相关学科教育的重要教学方法之一。它不仅适用于中小学、大学与研究生教育，同时也广泛应用于社区和继续教育；同时，在应用专业领域，它已经超越历史学而成为英文、新闻学、文学、社会学、民俗学、人类学和戏剧学等众多学科的重要教育手段。在一系列口述历史教学计划的推动下，口述历史教育在美国已经颇具规模和影响，其积极作用也得到实践者的充分肯定，正如美国口述历史教育家联盟（Consortium of Oral History Educators）前主席巴里·兰曼（Barry A. Lanman）所说："口述历史教育被证明能够以一种富有意义的和深刻的方式来解决我们这个时代的教育要求。"①

综观美国口述历史教育的现有研究成果，它们主要涉及口述历史教育实践的方法论问题，而很少对口述历史教育本身的发展历史进行较为系统的梳理与分析。② 本章将在考察其兴起与发展过程的基础上，对当代（尤其是 20 世纪 90 年代以来）美国口述历史教育发展的基本特征做一概括性总结与评价。

---

① "Introduction", in Barry A. Lanman and Laura M. Wendling (eds.), *Preparing the Next Generation of Oral Historians: An Anthology of Oral History Education*, Lanham: AltaMira Press, 2006, p. xvii.

② 相关研究可参阅 John Neuenschwander, Johnye Mathews, and Thomas Charlton, "The Use of Oral History in Teaching: A Report on the 1974 Survey", *Oral History Review*, Vol. 3, 1975, pp. 59-67; Barry Lanman, "The Use of Oral History in the Classroom: A Comparative Analysis of the 1974 and 1987 Oral History Association Surveys", *Oral History Review*, Vol. 17, No. 1, 1989, pp. 215-226; "Introduction", in Barry A. Lanman and Laura M. Wendling (eds.), *Preparing the Next Generation of Oral Historians: An Anthology of Oral History Education*, Lanham: AltaMira Press, 2006, pp. xix-xxiv.

一 何谓口述历史教育

正如很难给"口述历史"下一个明确的定义一样，什么是"口述历史教育"也会因为教育者不同的教育理念、教育层次及专业深度而得出不同的回答。不过，大多数教育者都同意口述历史教育是指将口述历史作为一种教学方法应用于教育过程当中，即出于教育目的而收集、整理、应用和分析口述历史访谈资料。[①]

根据口述历史教育内容和形式的差异，一般来说，可以将口述历史教育分为两个层次。第一个层次是指类似于《口述历史概论》等课程的纯理论式教学，它的主要目的是让学生能够了解口述史学的发展过程、基本理论与方法以及它的具体应用。当然，随着近年来口述史学理论与方法的不断提高与发展，有关这些问题的高级研讨班和暑期学院（Summer Institute）也日渐增多。在美国、英国和澳大利亚，更有著名大学设立有关口述历史的文科硕士课程（Master of Arts），其中以美国哥伦比亚大学、英国苏塞克斯大学（University of Sussex）和澳大利亚莫纳西大学（Monash University）最具代表性。

第二个层次是指将口述历史作为一种原始资料或教学方法应用于具体的课程教学实践中。根据课程对于口述历史应用深度的不同，又有学者将其分为"消极的口述历史教育"和"积极的口述历史教育"。[②] 所谓"消极的口述历史教育"是指将现有的以文字、音频和视频等各种媒介形式呈现的口述历史资料纳入具体的课程教学中，以补充现有教学资料的缺乏与

---

① "Introduction", in Barry A. Lanman and Laura M. Wendling（eds.），*Preparing the Next Generation of Oral Historians: An Anthology of Oral History Education*，Lanham: AltaMira Press, 2006, p. xviii.

② "Introduction", in Barry A. Lanman and Laura M. Wendling（eds.），*Preparing the Next Generation of Oral Historians: An Anthology of Oral History Education*，Lanham: AltaMira Press, 2006, p. xix.

不足。它侧重于对现有口述历史文本的阅读与分析，而不需要学生亲自参与口述历史访谈。目前，美国大部分口述历史计划都通过网站提供了口述历史资料文字、音频和视频内容的免费阅读与下载功能，这些将有助于学生从教科书之外获得有关课程教学的更为丰富和全面的原始资料。①

"积极的口述历史教育"是指依托于一项具体的口述历史计划，结合口述史学的理论与方法，在教师的指导下，由学生全程参与整个口述历史过程，包括计划的选题、背景资料的搜集与分析、口述历史访谈的准备与执行、口述历史资料的整理与编辑、口述历史资料的应用与评估，甚至还涉及口述历史的道德和法律问题。这种积极的口述历史教育方法一反传统的以教师传授为主的教学模式，充分调动学生的学习主动性、操作性、合作性与创造性。研究和调查都显示通过准备充分的口述历史教学计划能够实现四种主要教育目标：提高课程满意度、传授研究方法、培养主体鉴赏能力及培养综合技能。②

二 "狐火计划"与美国口述历史教育的兴起

巴里·兰曼认为在 19 世纪末和 20 世纪初就已经有教育者开始尝试以口述历史为教育手段，在当时，马里兰州（Maryland）和怀俄明州（Wyoming）的一些教师要求他们的学生去采访当地居民，以记录学校所在地区的历史与文化传统。不幸的是，由于缺乏便携式录音设备，他们的大部分

---

① 美国亚历山大出版社（Alexander Street Press）开发了一个《口述历史在线》（Oral History Online）数据库，提供全球主要口述历史计划的文本、音频和视频资料的阅读与下载服务。有关该数据库的详细内容，可访问官方网站 http://alexanderstreet.com/products/orhi.htm，2015 年 4 月 20 日访问。

② Barry Lanman，"The Use of Oral History in the Classroom：A Comparative Analysis of the 1974 and 1987 Oral History Association Surveys"，*Oral History Review*，Vol. 17，No. 1，1989，p. 215.

工作都未能保存下来。①

不过，在 20 世纪 60 年代之前，有两个口述历史教育计划特别值得一提。第一个计划是 1916 年来自西维吉尼亚州马里恩郡（Marion County, West Virginia）费尔蒙特高中（Fairmont High School）的沃森班级（James Otis Watson Class）的同学在其历史教师多拉·纽曼（Dora Lee Newman）的指导下，通过与当地居民的口述访谈来记录他们的历史文化与民俗传统，访谈主题涉及服饰、风俗习惯、家庭生活、民间医疗与迷信活动及民谣传说等。这些访谈资料最后于 1917 年整理出版，厚达 362 页。② 第二个计划则要回溯到美国现代口述史学兴起之后的 20 世纪 50 年代，在 1953 年秋和 1954 年年初，位于加利福尼亚州马林郡蒂伯龙（Tiburon, Marin County）的里德学校（Reed School）一个八年级班的全体学生在其教师乔伊斯·威尔逊（Joyce Wilson）的指导下，通过口述历史访谈来学习和研究他们社区的历史。最后，学生在结合新闻剪报、书籍与小册子的基础上，以口述历史访谈为主要内容加以整理出版。该书于 1954 年首印出版 2300 册，后来又相继在 1955 年、1958 年和 1970 年多次再版，其影响力可见一斑。③

当然，当时类似上述的口述历史教育计划还是比较零星的，直到 20 世纪 60 年代，随着便携式盒式磁带录音机的普及与美国口述史学发展的"新社会史转向"，口述历史作为一种教育手段才开始得到不断推广与应用，其中以"狐火计划"（Foxfire Project）最具代表性。正是由于该计划的广泛而又深远的影响，美国口述历史教育界一般都将其视为口述历史教

---

① "Introduction", in Barry A. Lanman and Laura M. Wendling (eds.), *Preparing the Next Generation of Oral Historians: An Anthology of Oral History Education*, Lanham: AltaMira Press, 2006, p. xx.

② James Otis Watson Class of Fairmont High School, *Marion County in the Making*, Marion County: Fairmont High School, 1917.

③ Cynthia Stokes Brown, *Like It Was: A Complete Guide to Writing Oral History*, New York: Teachers and Writers Collaborative, 1988, p. 117.

育真正兴起的标志。① 这项结合口述历史、民俗学、地方史与英文写作等多种元素为一体的中学教学计划，由佐治亚州（Georgia）雷本郡盖普－娜库奇中学（Rabun Gap-Nacoochee School）英语教师埃利奥特·威金顿（Eliot Wigginton，1942—）于 1966 年倡导创建。② 他于 1966 年从康奈尔大学毕业之后（获英语文科学士学位和教育学文科硕士学位）便回到位于阿巴拉契亚南部地区的盖普－娜库奇中学任教，负责 9 年级和 10 年级的英语与地理的教学任务。可是，在工作大约 6 个星期之后，他发现他的授课非但没有引起学生的兴趣，学生们还表现出强烈的厌学情绪与敌对倾向。为了激发学生的学习积极性，威金顿试图改变他的教学方法，于是他建议创办一份杂志，让学生通过口述历史访谈来搜集当地社区的历史变迁及其居民的民俗与生活故事，这便是"狐火计划"的开始。③

据埃利奥特·威金顿回忆，杂志名称由学生投票决定，最后命名为《狐火杂志》（*Foxfire Magazine*）。④ 由于学校没有提供任何财政支持，这意味着学生必须自行筹措经费。于是，他们在放学后走遍大街小巷，向街坊邻里劝捐，作为答谢，任何捐赠人的姓名都会刊登在即将出版的杂志上，最后总共募集到 450 美元。第 1 期杂志于 1967 年 3 月顺利出版，并随即取得成功，首次印刷的 600 份杂志在一个星期内全部售完，随后又陆续加印。⑤ 有学者认为该杂志第 1 期的成功销售很大程度上是因为一篇以学生与当地治安官的口述历史访谈为主要内容的文章，它描述了一起发生于

---

① Cliff Kuhn and Marjorie L. McLellan，"From the Editor：Oral History"，*Magazine of History*，Vol. 11，No. 3，1997，p. 4.

② 相关记录显示，美国加州州立学院富勒顿分校（California State College at Fullerton，即现在的加州州立大学富勒顿分校）于同年也让学生带着录音机深入当地社区进行口述历史访谈。转引自 Betty E. Mitson，"Book Review：*Foxfire 2*"，*Journal of Forest History*，Vol. 19，No. 2，1975，p. 98.

③ Eliot Wigginton（ed.），*The Foxfire Book*，Garden City：Doubleday，1972，pp. 9-10.

④ "狐火"是一种某些真菌产生的磷光，在阿巴拉契亚山区茂密的林间地带随处可见。

⑤ Eliot Wigginton（ed.），*The Foxfire Book*，Garden City：Doubleday，1972，p. 12.

1936 年的银行劫案与该治安官逮捕罪犯的故事,① 这也足见口述历史在受众中的魅力。

在狐火基金会（Foxfire Fund）、埃利奥特·威金顿和历届学生的共同努力下，经过 40 多年的发展，"狐火计划"已经发展成为一项集杂志、书籍、电台、电视、电影、戏剧和网络等多媒介应用与"狐火教学与学习方法"（Foxfire Approach to Teaching and Learning）培训为一体的口述历史教学计划，在众多领域都取得了重大进展。概括而言，其成果与影响主要表现在以下几个方面。

（1）杂志出版：从 1967 年第 1 期开始，到 2010 年年底已出版 44 卷。到 20 世纪 70 年代，这份学生杂志已经广受关注，其订阅用户遍及美国 50 个州和全球十几个国家；而且得到了包括《星期六评论》（Saturday Review）、《新共和》（New Republic）和《国家地理校刊》（National Geographic School Bulletin）等美国主流媒体的介绍与评价。1977 年埃利奥特·威金顿将将"狐火计划"从盖普 – 娜库奇中学转移到新创建的雷本郡高中（Rabun County High School），《狐火杂志》也随即搬迁。目前，该杂志每年出版两期，参与杂志编辑工作的所有学生的写作、交流、合作、时间分配、决策和解决问题等综合能力与素质都得到培养。通过他们的不懈努力，《狐火杂志》不仅有助于保存阿巴拉契亚南部地区即将消逝的文化传统，同时也满足了学校的课程要求；参与其中的学生也获得了对自己的能力、特长与自尊的充分自信。②

（2）书籍出版：为满足读者对《狐火杂志》的阅读需求，1972 年"狐火计划"将该杂志中的部分文章结集出版，并命名为《狐火书》（Foxfire Book）。此后又陆续出版了 11 卷，并分别以《狐火 2》（Foxfire 2）至

---

① Adrien Mendonca, "Foxfire", New Georgia Encyclopedia, Athens：University of Georgia Press, 2005. 具体内容访问 http：//www. georgiaencyclopedia. org/nge/Article. jsp? id = h-2424&hl = y，2015 年 4 月 20 日访问。

② 有关《狐火杂志》的具体信息可访问 http：//www. foxfire. org/thefoxfiremagazine. aspx，2015 年 4 月 20 日访问。

《狐火 12》（*Foxfire 12*）依次命名。到目前为止，该系列 12 卷已销售将近
900 万册，可以说取得了销售上的巨大成功，当然版税收入也是支持"狐
火计划"延续至今的重要经费来源。此外，该计划还出版了 7 本以《狐火
杂志》内容为基础的专业性书籍及 3 本有关"狐火计划"阶段性反思的理
论著作。①

（3）电台、电视、电影、戏剧和网络的跨媒介传播：除杂志和书籍之
外，从 20 世纪 70 年代开始，《狐火杂志》的部分内容就被改编成系列节
目在当地电台和电视频道滚动播出。1982 年以《狐火书》系列资料为基础
的同名戏剧《狐火》在百老汇首演，该剧由著名演员休谟·克罗宁
（Hume Cronyn，1911—2003）和剧作家苏珊·库珀（Susan Cooper，
1935—）创作。该剧后来又被改编为一部电视电影，由克罗宁和他的妻子
杰西卡·坦迪（Jessica Tandy，1909—1994）出演。为扩大计划的影响力
和传播"狐火"教育理念，在互联网技术兴起之后不久，"狐火"基金会
和雷本郡高中也相应创建了各种相关网站。

（4）提供"狐火教学与学习方法"培训：为那些希望了解和学习"狐
火计划"教学方法与理念的教师和学生提供学习机会，该计划设立了"狐
火体验"（Taste of Foxfire）和"狐火教师课程"（Foxfire Courses for Teach-
ers）两个培训课程。前者是一个让教师和学校管理者熟悉"狐火计划"和
确定他们学校是否适合效仿"狐火计划"的短期课程；后者根据教师层次
（K-12 和大学教师）的不同而有所区别，该课程与附近的皮埃蒙特学院
（Piedmont College）合作开设并提供继续教育学分，课程时间一般为一个
学期。②

---

① 有关《狐火书》系列的具体信息可访问 http：//www. foxfire. org/thefoxfirebooks. aspx，2015
年 4 月 20 日访问。三本理论著作可参阅 Eliot Wiggington，*Moments：The Foxfire Experience*，Washing-
ton：IDEAS，1975；Eliot Wigginton，*Sometimes a Shining Moment：The Foxfire Experience*，Garden Cit-
y：Doubleday，1985；Eliot Wigginton and His Students（eds.），*Foxfire：25 Years*，New York：Anchor
Books，1991.

② 有关该计划相关课程的具体信息可访问 https：//www. foxfire. org/teaching. html，2015 年 4
月 20 日访问。

（5）维持良好的财务状况：上述项目的正常运行都依赖于稳定的经费来源，从计划的创建开始，埃利奥特·威金顿就相当重视这个问题。在他的领导下，该计划建立了一套面向个人、专业组织、私人基金会和政府基金会筹措经费的有效渠道，这一点从《狐火书》12 卷中的"致谢"部分所罗列的个人、组织和基金会名单就可以看得很清楚，其中包括美国著名政治与商业领袖约翰·戴森（John Dyson）、美国民俗学会（American Folklore Society）、福特基金会（Ford Foundation）、爱德华·罗伯逊基金会（Edward H. Robertson Foundation）和国家人文科学基金会（National Endowment for the Humanities）等等。同时，该计划更注重自力更生，每年都有不菲的版税和狐火基金会的固定收入。据相关资料显示，在 20 世纪 80 年代中期，"狐火计划"每年就有 15 万—20 万美元的版税收入。因此，在将近半个世纪的风风雨雨之后，[1] 它依然能够稳步前进并焕发出更加旺盛的生命力。[2]

从一开始作为提高学生英文写作能力和激发学生学习兴趣的偶然尝试，到发展成为一种积极的教育手段并风靡美国乃至全世界，这或许连当初的创始人及早期参与者都没有预见到。那么，"狐火计划"为什么会引起那么大反响？这种教育方法之所以成功的真正原因是什么？众多实践者都认为它所倡导的让学生走出课堂深入当地社区的口述历史方法是关键所在。正如一位学者在《狐火 2》的书评中所指出的："通过赋予他们调查课堂之外的世界的机会，口述历史成为与那些曾经对教育产生厌烦的年轻

---

[1] 正当"狐火计划"蓬勃发展时，1992 年埃利奥特·威金顿因为骚扰男童案而被控有罪，最后被判入狱 1 年，缓刑 19 年。作为刑罚判决的一部分，他必须辞去教职。他出狱之后便离开雷本郡，从此与该计划没有任何关联。相关内容参阅 Ronald Smothers，"'Foxfire Book' Teacher Admits Child Molestation"，*New York Times*，November 13，1992；"Eliot Wigginton"，from Wikipedia，https：//en. wikipedia. org/wiki/Eliot_ Wigginton，2015 年 4 月 20 日访问。

[2] 上述资料来自狐火基金会官方网站（http：//www. foxfire. org）和以下资料 Eliot Wigginton（ed.），*The Foxfire Book*，Garden City：Doubleday，1972，pp. 9-14；Barry A. Lanman and George L. Mehaffy，*Oral History in the Secondary School Classroom*，Los Angeles：Oral History Association，1988，pp. 4-5.

人相互沟通的一种手段。"① 而在这种沟通过程中，能够促使教师与学生成为工作伙伴，明确各自在教育活动中所扮演的准确角色。

同时，口述历史教学也改变了以往静态的教学模式，成为充满活力、内容丰富的动态活动，极大地提高了学生的学习积极性、主动性与创造性。巴里·兰曼和乔治·麦哈菲（George L. Mehaffy）坦言："口述历史让学生在学习过程中成为积极的参与者，而不是消极的接受者。它倡导提问、激发讨论，并将抽象的概念转换为具体的现实。"② 同时，由于口述历史本质上是跨学科性的，它有助于培养学生的综合能力——组织能力、交际能力、调查能力、语言能力和技术能力，等等。③ 显然，上述优势都是传统的以授课为主的教学模式所无法提供的。

需要指出的是，在"狐火计划"兴起与迅速发展的 20 世纪 60 年代，已经有学者从理论与实践角度倡导在课堂中发展口述历史教育的重要性，其中以康奈尔大学（Cornell University）的古尔德·科尔曼（Gould P. Colman）和佛蒙特州历史学会（Vermont Historical Society）的查尔斯·莫里斯最具代表性④，他们都是美国当时非常著名的口述历史学家。

---

① Betty E. Mitson, "Book Review: *Foxfire 2*", *Journal of Forest History*, Vol. 19, No. 2, 1975, p. 98.

② Barry A. Lanman and George L. Mehaffy, *Oral History in the Secondary School Classroom*, Los Angeles: Oral History Association, 1988, p. i.

③ 关于这几种能力的培养可参阅 Paul Thompson, *The Voice of the Past: Oral History*, Oxford and New York: Oxford University Press, second edition, 1988, pp. 167-168.

④ Gould P. Colman, "Taped Interviews and Community Studies", *Social Education*, Vol. 29, 1965, pp. 537-538; Charles T. Morrissey, "Oral History as a Classroom Tool", *Social Education*, Vol. 32, 1968, pp. 546-549. 莫里斯在文章中主要介绍了于 1967 年 12 月 4 日在佛蒙特州首府蒙彼利埃（Montpelier）召开的一场题为"作为课堂工具的口述历史"的研讨会。此次研讨会由美国历史协会教师服务中心（American Historical Association Service Center for Teachers）、佛蒙特州社会研究理事会（Vermont Council for Social Studies）、佛蒙特州历史学会和佛蒙特州教育署（Vermont Department of Education）联合主办，会议邀请马萨诸塞州大学（University of Massachusetts）历史系教授迪恩·艾伯森（Dean Albertson）担任主讲嘉宾。有关莫里斯的口述历史生涯可参阅 Tracy E. K'Meyer, "An Interview With Charles T. Morrissey: Part I- 'Getting Started: Beginning an Oral History Career'", *Oral History Review*, Vol. 24, No. 2, 1997, pp. 73-94; Tracy E. K'Meyer, "An Interview with Charles T. Morrissey: Part II- 'Living Independently: The Oral History Career of Charles T. Morrissey'", *Oral History Review*, Vol. 26, No. 1, 1999, pp. 85-104.

三 "狐火效应"与美国口述历史教育的发展

通过杂志、书籍、电视、电影、戏剧与网络等各种媒介及相关的演讲与培训课程,"狐火计划"的理念与方法很快在美国乃至全世界传播。众多中小学都创办了类似的口述历史计划,而且都以杂志和书籍的形式在地方或全国发行。[1] 到 20 世纪 80 年代末,其影响甚至扩展到日本、澳大利亚、英国、哥斯达黎加、关岛、海地和多米尼加共和国等国家和地区。正因如此,有学者将这种"狐火"概念的传播与仿效称为"狐火效应"或"狐火运动"[2],在很大程度上它也推动了美国口述历史教育的迅速发展。

"狐火"概念的传播最早开始于 1970 年,源于埃利奥特·威金顿与机构发展与经济事务服务局(Institutional Development and Economic Affairs Service)主任布莱恩·本恩(Brian Beun)之间的一次偶然会面。[3] 当时威金顿正在华盛顿特区聘请"狐火计划"顾问委员会的志愿者,他因此拜访史密森学会人类研究中心(Center for the Study of Man, Smithsonian Institute)的萨姆·斯坦利(Sam Stanley)。同一天,本恩与另外一位同事安妮·维科(Anne Vick)也正好拜访斯坦利,他们看到威金顿留下的《狐火杂志》,便认为"狐火"是一种值得传播的概念。就这样,埃利奥特·威金顿很快与布莱恩·本恩取得联系并达成合作关系。一方面,埃利奥特·威金顿成为机构发展与经济事务服务局合伙人,协助推广"狐火"模式;另

---

① Thad Sitton, George L. Mehaffy, and O. L. Davis, Jr., *Oral History: A Guide for Teachers* (*and Others*), Austin: University of Austin Press, 1983, p. 119.

② Thad Sitton, "The Foxfire-Concept Publications: A First Appraisal", Ph. D. dissertation, Austin: The University of Texas at Austin, 1978; Thad Sitton, "The Descendant of Foxfire", *Oral History Review*, Vol. 6, 1978, pp. 20-35; George L. Mehaffy, "Foxfire Comes of Age", *Oral History Review*, Vol. 13, 1985, pp. 145-149.

③ 机构发展与经济事务服务局是一个位于华盛顿特区的致力于推动经济与教育发展的非营利咨询机构,目标之一就是通过找到创新性计划,并将它们的概念进一步传播与推广。

一方面，威金顿将不再负责盖普 - 娜库奇中学其他班级的教学任务——除了与"狐火计划"有关的课程之外，作为回报，该局将补偿他的薪水损失。①

在协议合作的第一年，机构发展与经济事务服务局成功从福特基金会获得一笔 19.6 万美元的资助，用于推广具有"狐火"概念的计划。同时，威金顿、本恩与其他工作人员开发了一系列将具有"狐火"概念的出版物推广到其他地区和学校的程序。这些程序包括：计划推广学校的选择；对选择的学校提供包括技术、设备和资金在内的支持以及为来自其他学校的教师和学生提供到雷本郡学习的旅费补助。②

第一个在机构发展与经济事务服务局赞助下创办的具有"狐火"概念的杂志是《霍伊基亚》（Hoyekiya，意为"倾诉衷肠"），它由南达科他州松树脊保留地（Pine Ridge Reservation, South Dakota）的苏族印第安人学生于 1971 年创办和出版。此后，具有"狐火"概念的杂志如雨后春笋般快速发展，比如德克萨斯州盖瑞高中（Gary High School, Texas）的《泥沼》（Loblolly，1972 年创办）、缅因州肯纳邦克高中（Kennebunk High School, Maine）的《盐》（Salt，1973 年创办）和密苏里州黎巴嫩高中（Lebanon High School, Missouri）的《甘苦》（Bittersweet，1973 年创办）。③据统计，在美国，这种类型的杂志到 1973 年达到 12 个；到 1976 年达到 43 个；到 1977 年达到 88 个；到 1979 年夏天至少有 160 个。④ 就影响力而言，在这些杂志中最为成功的是《盐》和《甘苦》，⑤ 它们也是最早效仿《狐火书》系列而将杂志的内容以文集的形式出版的，而且发行范围与数量也

---

① Eliot Wiggington, *Moments：The Foxfire Experience*, Washington：IDEAS, 1975, pp. 101-102.

② Thad Sitton, "The Descendant of Foxfire", *Oral History Review*, Vol. 6, 1978, p. 23.

③ Jan Harold Brunvand（ed.）, *American Folklore：An Encyclopedia*, London：Taylor & Francis, 1998, p. 303.

④ Thad Sitton, "The Rise of Cultural Journalism", *Journal of Popular Culture*, Vol. 17, No. 2, 1983, p. 93.

⑤ 甚至有学者认为它们在某种程度上超过"狐火"的技术标准。详细内容参阅 Thad Sitton, "Book Review：*The Salt Book* and *Bittersweet Country*", *Oral History Review*, Vol. 7, 1979, p. 89.

相当可观。①

这些计划虽然超越了"狐火计划"所在的阿巴拉契亚南部地区的地理界限，可是同"狐火计划"一样，它们的核心关注点都是计划所在地的独特的地区历史与文化传统，而且大部分都是类似阿巴拉契亚南部地区这样的偏僻和经济落后的小镇或乡村地区。研究显示，到 1977 年秋季，位于小镇或者乡村地区的类似的计划达到所有计划的 83% 左右，布莱恩·本恩将其定义为"乡村偏爱"（rual bias）。② 尽管这些计划各具特色与风格，不过其核心特征还是基本相同的。概括而言，它们同"狐火计划"一样，即将田野工作、口述历史、文化人类学、民族学和民俗学等方法结合起来，在教师的指导下，通过学生的团队合作以记录他们所在地区的历史与文化，并通过杂志、书籍和其他各种媒介加以传播。

随着"狐火"概念的推广以及类似计划的不断发展，到 20 世纪 70 年代中期，口述历史在美国已经成为一种最重要的新式教育方法之一。③ 口述历史作为一种教育手段的快速发展也引起美国口述历史协会的关注，该协会于 1974 年进行了一次全国性的口述历史教育调查。由于从成立开始，美国口述历史协会的成员主要是一些以研究和档案管理为主的学者和档案工作者，因此在他们的视野中，口述历史作为一种教育方法通常处于次要位置，这从历届口述历史协会年会议程和《口述历史评论》刊登的文章就可以看出。在这种背景下，口述历史协会执行委员会授权由约翰·纽恩斯科范德尔（John Neuenschwander）、约奈·马修斯（Johnye Mathews）和托马斯·查尔顿（Thomas Charlton）组成调查委员会。调查结果显示当时口述历史教育主要集中在大学本科和研究生阶段，应用的课程也主要在历史学专业中，同时还包括英语、民俗学、文学、新闻学、地理学和社会学等

---

① Pamela Wood （ed.）, *The Salt Book*, Garden City：Doubleday, 1977；Ellen Gray Massey （ed.）, *Bittersweet Country*, Garden City：Doubleday, 1978.

② Thad Sitton, "The Descendant of Foxfire", *Oral History Review*, Vol. 6, 1978, p. 24. 在这篇文章中，作者罗列了截止到 1977 年年末所有具有"狐火"概念的计划信息，具体见第 30—35 页。

③ John A. Neuenschwander, *Oral History as a Teaching Approach*, Washington：National Education Association, 1976, p. 7.

学科。在这个阶段，除了将口述历史方法应用于传统的课程教学之外，口述历史也开始成为部分美国大学研究生教育的组成部分，以杜克大学和哥伦比亚大学最具代表性。同时，调查也显示口述历史在高中课程教学中也相当受欢迎，它有助于让学生重新理解历史、培养人际交往能力，以及学习资料搜集和评价等多种研究方法。需要指出的是，此次调查并没有发现小学和初中的老师在课堂教学中使用口述历史方法，这可能跟问卷调查不够全面有关。① 不容否认的是在 20 世纪 70 年代，口述历史的确是一种不断走向成功的教育试验。②

在美国口述历史协会组织的两次口述历史教育调查（第二次是在 1987 年）之间的十几年间，除了口述历史教育实践的不断发展之外，有关这一领域的理论与方法论探讨也日渐成熟。以埃利奥特·威金顿、约翰·纽恩斯科范德尔、乔治·麦哈菲和萨德·席登（Thad Sitton）为代表的实践者出版了一系列具有重要影响的关于口述历史教育理论思考与实践指南的专著。③ 同时，包括《口述历史评论》、《国际口述历史杂志》、《社会教育》（*Social Education*）、《哈佛教育评论》（*Harvard Educational Review*）、《历史教师》（*History Teacher*）及《历史杂志》（*Magazine of History*）等主流学术刊

---

① 调查委员会承认由于人力和物力等各种因素制约，此次调查结果并不具有普遍代表性。这次调查于 1974 年 3 月向所有协会成员和另外 100 名非成员发出 1200 份 4 页的开放式问卷；截止到 1974 年 8 月 1 日，共收到 110 份回复，除去不合格的，有 98 份问卷真正有效。在这些问调查对象中，有相当一部分人与教学没有任何关系，而且即使来自教育机构，也很少是来自高中阶段以下的教育从业者。

② 有关此次调查报告可参阅 John Neuenschwander, Johnye Mathews, and Thomas Charlton, "The Use of Oral History in Teaching: A Report on the 1974 Survey", *Oral History Review*, Vol. 3, 1975, pp. 59-67.

③ 除上述提到的之外，还包括 Pamela Wood, *You and Aunt Arie: A Guide to Cultural Journalism Based on "Foxfire" and Its Descendants*, Washington: IDEAS, 1975; John A. Neuenschwander, *Oral History as a Teaching Approach*, Washington: National Education Association, 1976; George L. Mehaffy, Thad Sitton, and O. L. Davis, *Oral History in the Classroom*, Washington: National Council for the Social Studies, 1979; James Hoopes, *Oral History: An Introduction for Students*, Chapel Hill: University of North Carolina Press, 1979.

物也发表了很多有关这方面的学术论文。① 值得注意的是，在这一时期，口述历史也逐渐成为众多硕士、博士学位论文的研究主题，在这些作者当中，有相当一部分后来都成为美国口述历史教育发展的重要推动者。②

这一时期的另外一项重要进展是 1985 年美国口述历史协会教学委员会（Committee on Teaching）的成立，这足以显示该协会对口述历史教育价值的不断认可与兴趣的日益增加。在时任口述历史协会主席（1984—1985 年度）玛莎·罗斯（Martha Ross，1923—2013）的指导下，教学委员会致力于推动、组织和专业化口述历史在课堂中的应用。为实现这个目标，巴里·兰曼博士被任命为该委员会的负责人；在其努力下，委员会发展了一系列短期和长期目标。在委员会运作的最初两年，它主要致力于实现以下几个短期目标：在教育与口述历史相关的会议上举办工作坊或发表论文；任命地区性顾问以协助对教育者实行一对一指导；出版口述历史教育课程资料。③

为了更加明确教学委员会的长期目标和弥补第一次调查的不足，口述历史协会于 1987 年授权委员会进行第二次有关口述历史教育的全国性调查。此次调查按照口述历史在 K-12（幼儿园到高中阶段）和大学及以上（包括社区学院、大学本科、研究生、工作坊和成人教育）两个教育层次

---

① 代表性成果可参阅 William Cutler，"Oral History as a Teaching Tool"，*Oral History Review*，Vol. 1，1973，pp. 29-30；Eliot Wigginton，"Oral History as a Teaching Tool"，*Oral History Review*，Vol. 1，1973，pp. 30-35；Stan Echols，"Oral History as a Teaching Tool"，*Oral History Review*，Vol. 1，1973，pp. 35-36；Barbara Gallant，"Oral History as a Teaching Tool"，*Oral History Review*，Vol. 1，1973，pp. 36-43；Edward Ives，"Oral History as a Teaching Tool"，*Oral History Review*，Vol. 1，1973，pp. 43-47；Jean M. Humez and Laurie Cnimpacker，"Oral History In Teaching Women's Studies"，Oral History Review，Vol. 7，1979，pp. 53-69；Richard P. Onderdonk，"Piaget and Oral History：Cognitive Development in the Secondary Social Studies Class"，*Oral History Review*，Vol. 11，1983，pp. 75-87.

② 代表性成果包括 Frank John Fonsino，"Oral History as a Research and Teaching Tool"，D. A. dissertation，Illinois State University，1979；Barry A. Lanman，"An Analysis of Traditional and O-ral History Teaching Methods in a High School Immigration and Black History Curriculum"，E-d. D. dissertation，Philadelphia：Temple University，1984；John Lawrence Puckett，"Foxfire Reconsid-ered：A Critical Ethnohistory of A Twenty-Year Experiment in Progressive Education"，Ph. D. dissertation，Chapel Hill：University Of North Carolina，1986.

③ "Introduction"，in Barry A. Lanman and Laura M. Wendling（eds.），*Preparing the Next Gener-ation of Oral Historians：An Anthology of Oral History Education*，Lanham：AltaMira Press，2006，pp. xxi-xxii.

中的应用进行分类，以非常清晰的表格总结了调查结果，内容涉及口述历史教育计划的数量、区域分布、教育层次、应用学科、主要目标、教学效果、时间分配及面临的主要问题等 14 大类。① 比较两次调查之后得出的最为明显的结论是口述历史作为一种教学手段在初中和小学教育中的不断扩张和流行。

另外，此次调查还提出一系列推动口述历史教育发展的改进措施，并强调口述历史协会、其他口述历史组织、教育机构、民间公司和个人都应该发挥各自作用。这些措施共有 13 条，概括而言主要涉及六个方面：（1）通过举办口述历史研讨班和工作坊为初学者提供各种层次的培训课程；（2）出版高质量的有关不同教育层次的口述历史教育的课程大纲与阅读资料；（3）为学生和教师各自设计一套有关口述历史计划基本程序的高质量视频资料；（4）促进口述历史在一些尚未充分挖掘的教育领域中得到发展，尤其是如何实现口述历史教育的跨学科、跨院系、跨教育层次和跨区域的深入合作；（5）出版一本有关口述历史作为一种教育方法论的实践指南或手册；（6）在各种学术杂志上推介口述历史教育和口述历史专业组织，让更多有志于投身这一领域的教育者了解相关信息。②

在 20 世纪 80 年代末，上述部分措施相继得到落实。以口述历史协会为代表的专业组织在其中扮演了主导性作用，不仅在其年会上举办有关口述历史教育的专场研讨会、制订有关口述历史教育的道德和法律指南（Ethical and Legal Guidelines），而且还出版了第一本官方口述历史教育指南《中学课堂中的口述历史》。③ 此外，这一时期，众多历史和教育类杂志对这个主题的兴趣也日渐增加，发表了大量结合口述历史教育实践与经验反思的学术论文。

---

① Barry Lanman, "The Use of Oral History in the Classroom: A Comparative Analysis of the 1974 and 1987 Oral History Association Surveys", *Oral History Review*, Vol. 17, No. 1, 1989, pp. 215-224.

② Barry Lanman, "The Use of Oral History in the Classroom: A Comparative Analysis of the 1974 and 1987 Oral History Association Surveys", *Oral History Review*, Vol. 17, No. 1, 1989, pp. 224-225.

③ Barry A. Lanman and George L. Mehaffy, *Oral History in the Secondary School Classroom*, Los Angeles: Oral History Association, 1988.

四　当代美国口述历史教育的基本特征

正如巴里·兰曼博士所说，经过四分之一个世纪的试验与创新，口述历史教育在美国已经得到了稳步发展。越来越多的教育者相信口述历史能够提供一种结合课堂、社区、现代技术与学生的课程策略，以形成相互关联的和激励的学术环境。① 进入 20 世纪 90 年代以来，口述历史教育在美国的发展可谓一场运动，它的影响范围并不局限在教育和学术领域，而是广泛地深入到社会的各个层面。概括而言，它在当代的发展呈现以下几个鲜明特征。

第一，口述历史教育的应用范围不断扩大。一方面，从教育对象层次来看，从中小学到大专院校，从地方历史学会到博物馆和档案馆，从社区教育辅助计划到继续教育，都有各种各样的口述历史课程。在这些课程中，有的是为期一天、几天或一周的短期培训课程；有些则是长达几个星期的夏季研讨班或暑期学院。这些课程基本上是由口述历史专业组织和研究中心、地方历史学会、博物馆与档案馆及个人主办，最具代表性的是哥伦比亚大学口述历史研究室和加州大学伯克利分校地区口述历史办公室的口述历史暑期学院及著名口述历史学家查尔斯·莫里斯主持的口述历史工作坊（Oral History Workshop）。② 在正规的小学到研究生教育阶段中，口述历史课程基本上是以选修课或必修课的形式出现，时间一般为一个学期或一个学年，其形式包括单纯的口述历史理论与方法的讲授、以具体口述历史计划为主导的实践课程，或二者兼顾。作为口述历史教育的最高阶段，口述历史开始纳入研究生学位教育的一部分。近年来，美国一些大学也开始设立有关口述历史的硕士学位，其中最具影响力的是哥伦比亚大学口述

---

① Barry Lanman, "The Use of Oral History in the Classroom: A Comparative Analysis of the 1974 and 1987 Oral History Association Surveys", *Oral History Review*, Vol. 17, No. 1, 1989, pp. 225-226.

② 具体信息访问网站 https://networks. h-net. org/h-oralhist, 2015 年 4 月 20 日访问。

历史研究室与该校社会与经济研究和政策研究所（Institute for Social and E-conomic Research and Policy）于 2008 年合作设立的口述历史文科硕士学位（Oral History Master of Arts），它是一个结合历史学、社会学、文学、人类学、心理学和公共卫生学的跨学科课程。①

另一方面，从教育对象的专业来看，尽管在字面上，口述史学是属于历史学的分支学科，但这并不妨碍它在其他专业教育中的流行和受欢迎程度。除主要用于历史学之外，口述历史作为一种教育和研究手段还广泛应用于英语、社会学、民俗学、人类学、种族学、戏剧学、新闻学及医学等人文社会和自然科学，体现出极其鲜明的跨学科特征，② 这一点从上述哥伦比亚大学口述历史文科硕士的课程定位就可以看得很清楚。

第二，口述历史教育的发展不断走向正规。如上所述，从 1985 年设立教学委员会开始，口述历史协会一直致力于美国口述历史教育的正规化发展，尤其是制订了影响深远的口述历史教育的《道德与法律指南》。同时，为进一步扩大口述历史教育的概念，该会又将教学委员会更名为教育委员会（Education Committee）。而且，在几届前任协会主席的支持与帮助下，口述历史协会还于 1993 年专门设立两个教学奖以鼓励口述历史教育的发展，它们分别是"玛莎·罗斯大学前教学奖"（Martha Ross Pre-Collegiate Teaching Award）和"中学后教学奖"（Postsecondary Teaching Award），获奖者可以获得荣誉证书、奖金、一年协会成员资格和当年年会的免费注册资格。③

更为重要的是，为了进一步促进教育理念的转变和解决口述历史教育者的需求，一个全国性的口述历史教育组织——口述历史教育家协会（Association of Oral History Educators）于 1999 年创建，巴里·兰曼出任首

---

① 具体信息访问网站 http：//oralhistory. columbia. edu/，2015 年 4 月 20 日访问。

② Timothy P. Fong and Ava F. Kahn， "An Educational Exchange：Teaching Oral History on the Post-Secondary Level"， *Oral History Review*， Vol. 25， No. 1/2， 1998， p. 9.

③ 具体信息访问网站 http：//www. oralhistory. org/education/，2015 年 4 月 20 日访问。

任主席。因组织扩展需要，该会于 2004 年更名为口述历史教育家联盟，其宗旨包括推动学生口述历史研究的专业标准与道德准则的发展、提升口述历史作为一种教育方法的研究水平以及奖励优秀口述历史教育工作者等等，其最终目标是为培养下一代口述历史学家做准备。同时，它还有官方刊物——《口述历史教育家》（*Oral History Educator*）——作为交流口述历史教育信息和推动其发展的重要平台。[1] 正如巴里·兰曼所说，为了更好地满足口述历史教育者的当下需求并确定口述历史教育的未来发展方向，口述历史教育家联盟正与口述历史协会教育委员会和其他相关组织一起努力以实现这些有价值的目标。[2]

第三，口述历史教育不断应用新的技术手段。如上所述，口述史学的发展得益于技术的革新与进步，录音机、转录器、摄影机和计算机的出现与应用都是至关重要的。20 世纪 90 年代以来以互联网、电子邮件、网络摄影机、博客、播客和微博等技术为代表的信息革命给口述史学发展带来前所未有的挑战与机遇。同样，对于教师和学生来说，这些技术手段为口述历史教育的进行提供了许多新的机会。他们不再依赖于传统的录音设备，可以更为方便地利用最新的录音、录影和编辑技术来处理整个口述历史过程。随着计算机的普及与网络技术的发展，口述历史教学成果的传播载体也不再局限于传统的杂志和书籍，更多地依赖于互联网，通过创建口述历史计划的官方网站来实现真正的全球性交流与互动。这些网站不仅介绍计划的相关信息，而且大部分都能够提供口述历史文本、音频和视频的下载。当然，通过访问相关网站，教师和学生不仅能够实现口述历史的在线培训，而且通过它们提供的在线下载功能可以实现对现有口述历史资料

---

[1]　具体信息访问口述历史教育家联盟官方网站 http：// www. coheonline. org/，2015 年 4 月 20 日访问。

[2]　"Introduction"，in Barry A. Lanman and Laura M. Wendling（eds.），*Preparing the Next Generation of Oral Historians：An Anthology of Oral History Education*，Lanham：AltaMira Press，2006，p. xxiv.

的直接利用。①

　　此外，在这 20 多年间，有关口述历史教育理论与方法的研究也在不断深化，② 尤其是《口述历史评论》所刊登的相关文章的数量急剧增加，在 1998 年它更是将《实践与教学：课堂中的口述历史》作为专题刊发。③ 另

---

① 有关数字化技术对于口述历史教学的影响，可参阅 Elly Shodell, "Teaching Oral History: Videos, Educators, and Students", *Oral History Review*, Vol. 27, No. 1, 2000, pp. 148-152; Howard Levin, "Authentic Doing: Student-Produced Web-Based Digital Video Oral Histories", *Oral History Review*, Vol. 38, No. 1, 2011, pp. 6-33; Ken Woodward, "The Digital Revolution and Pre-Collegiate Oral History: Meditations on the Challenge of Teaching Oral History in the Digital Age", *Oral History Review*, Vol. 40, No. 2, 2013, pp. 325-331; Jill Goodman Gould and Gail Gradowski, "Using Online Video Oral Histories to Engage Students in Authentic Research", *Oral History Review*, Vol. 41, No. 2, 2014, pp. 341-350; Aishwarya A. Gautam, Janet H. Morford, and Sarah Joy Yockey, "On the Air: The Pedagogy of Student-Produced Radio Documentaries", *Oral History Review*, Vol. 42, No. 2, 2015, pp. 311-351; Douglas A. Boyd, Janice W. Fernheimer, and Rachel Dixon, "Indexing as Engaging Oral History Research: Using OHMS to 'Compose History' in the Writing Classroom", *Oral History Review*, Vol. 42, No. 2, 2015, pp. 352-367.

② 唐纳德·里奇的经典著作《大家来做口述历史》一直将《口述历史教学》(Teaching Oral History) 作为重要内容，详细参阅 Donald A. Ritchie, *Doing Oral History*, New York: Twayne Publishers, 1995, pp. 159-184; Donald A. Ritchie, *Doing Oral History: A Practical Guide*, Oxford and New York: Oxford University Press, second edition, 2003, pp. 188-221; Donald A. Ritchie, *Doing Oral History*, Oxford and New York: Oxford University Press, third edition, 2014, pp. 193-233. 此外还可参阅 Pamela Dean, Toby Daspit, and Petra Munro, *Talking Gumbo: A Teacher's Guide to Using Oral History in the Classroom*, Baton Rouge: T. Harry Williams Center for Oral History, Louisiana State University, 1998; Glenn Whitman, *Dialogue with the Past: Engaging Students & Meeting Standards through Oral History*, Walnut Creek: AltaMira Press, 2004; Evelyn S. Taylor, *Conducting Oral Histories: A Student's Guide to A Successful Interviewing Experience*, Bloomington: AuthorHouse, 2011.

③ "Special Issue: Practice and Pedagogy: Oral History in the Classroom", *Oral History Review*, Vol. 25, No. 1/2, 1998. 具体文章参阅 Charles R. Lee and Kathryn L. Nasstrom, "Introduction: Practice and Pedagogy: Oral History in the Classroom", pp. 1-8; Timothy P. Fong and Ava F. Kahn, "An Educational Exchange: Teaching Oral History on the Post-Secondary Level", pp. 9-34; Tracy E. K'Meyer, "'It's Not Just Common Sense': A Blueprint for Teaching Oral History", pp. 35-56; Ronald J. Grele, "Values and Methods in the Classroom Transformation of Oral History", pp. 57-70; Vicki L. Ruiz, "Situating Stories: The Surprising Consequences of Oral History", pp. 71-80; Marjorie L. McLellan, "Case Studies in Oral History and Community Learning", pp. 81-112; Sharon O'Brien, "A Short Reflection on Teaching Memoir and Oral History", pp. 113-118. 其他相关论文可参阅 Renate W. Prescott, "The Vietnam War and the Teaching and Writing of Oral History: The Reliability of the Narrator", *Oral History Review*, Vol. 26, No. 2, 1999, pp. 47-64; Lynne Hamer, "Oralized History: History Teachers as Oral History Tellers", *Oral History Review*, Vol. 27, No. 2, 2000, pp. 19-39; Luther Zeigler, "The Grace in Listening to Another's Story: A Theological Reflection on Oral History in the Classroom", *Oral History Review*, Vol. 38, No. 1, 2011, pp. 1-5; Martha Fortunes, "Teaching to Listen: Listening Exercises and

外，需要特别指出的是，作为当前最全面和权威的集理论、方法与实践为一体的口述历史教育手册《培养下一代口述历史学家：口述历史教育文集》于 2006 年出版。毫无疑问，该文集已经成为口述历史教育实践者的必读书目。[①]

当然，口述历史教育在美国的发展并不是一帆风顺的，"狐火计划"的曲折经历及类似计划的过早夭折都表明口述历史教育面临着一定的阻碍与挑战。作为一种新的学习与教育方法，它要求学生和教师重新调整和改变各自的学习与教学方法，并对各自的综合能力与素质提出了更为严格的要求。而作为口述历史教育的实践场所，学校的政策和态度也是重要的影响因素。除此之外，口述历史教育实践者都普遍认为资金缺乏与时间不足是他们遇到的最主要困难。尽管如此，经过将近半个世纪的发展与探索，口述历史教育在美国已经步入一个良性的发展轨道。它或许不是摆脱现代教育困境的灵丹妙药，可对于那些实践者来说，口述历史教育确实是一种值得尝试和努力探索的改革方向。

Self-Reflexive Journals", *Oral History Review*, Vol. 38, No. 1, 2011, pp. 63-108; Stacey Zembrzycki, Erin Jessee, Eleanor Beattie, Audrey Bean, Mireille Landry, and Sandra Baines, "Oral History and Adult Community Education: Notes from the Field", *Oral History Review*, Vol. 38, No. 1, 2011, pp. 120-135; Anne Valk, Amy Atticks, Rachael Binning, Elizabeth Manekin, Aliza Schiff, Reina Shibata, and Meghan Townes, "Engaging Communities and Classrooms: Lessons from the Fox Point Oral History Project", *Oral History Review*, Vol. 38, No. 1, 2011, pp. 136-157; Gregory R. Zieren, "Negotiating between Generations: A Decade of Experience Teaching Oral History", *Oral History Review*, Vol. 38, No. 1, 2011, pp. 158-174; Ruth Stewart Busby, "Learning through Doing: Preservice Teacher Training in Historical Inquiry through Oral History Projects", *Oral History Review*, Vol. 38, No. 1, 2011, pp. 175-184; Mara Waldhorn, "A Storyteller's Story: One Student's Journey", *Oral History Review*, Vol. 38, No. 1, 2011, pp. 185-188; Stephen Sloan, "On the Other Foot: Oral History Students as Narrators", *Oral History Review*, Vol. 39, No. 2, 2012, pp. 298-311; Elizabeth Stone, "Teaching Oral History in a College-Level 'New Wave Immigrant Literature' Course", *Oral History Review*, Vol. 40, No. 2, 2013, pp. 332-363; Amy Starecheski, "Squatting History: The Power of Oral History as a History-Making Practice", *Oral History Review*, Vol. 41, No. 2, 2014, pp. 187-216; Katie Kuszmar, "From Boat to Throat: How Oral Histories Immerse Students in Ecoliteracy and Community Building", *Oral History Review*, Vol. 41, No. 2, 2014, pp. 325-340.

① Barry A. Lanman and Laura M. Wendling (eds.), *Preparing the Next Generation of Oral Historians: An Anthology of Oral History Education*, Lanham: AltaMira Press, 2006.

第八章　美国口述史学的法律与伦理问题

自 1948 年美国现代口述史学诞生以来，经过几代口述历史学家的共同努力，其发展呈现出旺盛的生命力，它已经成为一种记录、保存、传播与解释过去美国政治、经济、社会、文化乃至日常生活等领域的不同参与者的声音与历史记忆的重要方法与研究领域。作为全国性口述历史组织，创建于 1967 年的美国口述历史协会一直致力于规范口述历史实践的原则、标准与评估指南，其核心目标是尽可能预防法律风险与维持更高的专业伦理。① 在过去 60 多年间，尽管美国口述史学呈现迅速发展的趋势，口述历史丰富历史记录的公众意识也在不断提升，但仍然只有少数法院案例涉及口述历史实践的法律与伦理问题。② 可是，随着美国口述史学日益关注和重视战争与冲突、自然灾难、犯罪问题（如毒品贸易与非法移民）、特殊疾病（比如艾滋病）及多元性取

---

① 美国口述历史协会的《原则与标准》（*Principles and Standards*）和《评估指南》（*Evaluation Guidelines*）分别于 1968 年、1979 年、1989 年、2000 年和 2009 年进行多次拟定与修改，每次修改都充分反映口述历史实践的最新变革与发展趋势对其专业标准与伦理规范的影响。详细内容访问 http：//www. oralhistory. org/about/principles-and-practices/，2015 年 4 月 28 日访问。

② John A. Neuenschwander，*A Guide to Oral History and the Law*，Oxford and New York：Oxford University Press，2009，p. xiii. 该书是美国有关口述史学法律问题的最为经典的著作，它的第一、二和三版分别于 1985 年、1993 年和 2002 年由美国口述历史协会出版，这三版的书名都为《口述历史与法律》（*Oral History and the Law*）。如无特别说明，本书引用以 2009 年版为准。另外，该书牛津版第二版于 2014 年出版。

向（LGBTQ）等具有当代性、敏感性与隐私性的议题，同时也因为数字化技术的发展使得口述历史资料的网络传播与应用变得更为容易与便捷，这些因素导致口述历史工作面临的法律与伦理风险进一步加剧。

需要指出的是，口述史学的法律与伦理问题是相辅相成和紧密联系的，对于口述历史实践中潜在的法律问题的预先考虑与规避本身就反映了良好的专业伦理规范，良好的专业伦理规范也能较为有效地预防并规避一定的法律风险。一般而言，口述史学的法律问题主要包括著作权（copyright）、诽谤（libel）、隐私权侵犯（invasion of privacy）、法律授权协议书（Legal Release Agreements）、对于口述历史资料设限的法律挑战、伦理审查委员会（Institutional Review Boards）审查机制（同时也是伦理问题）、口述历史资料网络传播与使用的法律风险与口述历史资料能否作为法院审理相关案件的合法证据。① 口述史学的伦理问题主要指口述历史访谈与记录、整理与编辑、保存与传播以及解释与应用等过程中不同关系体之间的一系列

---

① John A. Neuenschwander, "The Legal Ramifications of Oral History", in Donald A. Ritchie (ed.), *The Oxford Handbook of Oral History*, Oxford and New York: Oxford University Press, 2011, p. 351. 有关口述史学法律问题的其他研究可参阅 E. Douglas Hamilton, "Oral History and the Law of Libel", in Louis M. Starr (ed.), *The Second National Colloquium on Oral History*, New York: Oral History Association, 1968, pp. 41-56; Mason Welch, "A Lawyer Looks at Oral History", in Gould P. Colman (ed.), *The Fourth National Colloquium on Oral History*, New York: Oral History Association, 1970, pp. 182-195; Joseph Romney, "Legal Considerations in Oral History", *Oral History Review*, Vol. 1, 1973, pp. 66-76; Truman W. Eustis III, "Get It in Writing: Oral History and the Law", *Oral History Review*, Vol. 4, 1976, pp. 6-14, 16-18; Joseph Romney, "Oral History, Law and Libraries", *Drexel Library Quarterly*, Vol. 15, No. 4, 1979, pp. 39-49; Valerie Raleigh Yow, *Recording Oral History: A Guide for the Humanities and Social Sciences*, Walnut Creek: AltaMira Press, second edition, 2005, pp. 121-156 (Chapter Five: Legalities and Ethics); Linda Shopes, "Legal and Ethical Issues in Oral History", in Thomas L. Charlton, Lois E. Myers and Rebecca Sharpless (eds.), *Handbook of Oral History*, Walnut Creek: AltaMira Press, 2006, pp. 135-169.

权利与责任。① 具体而言，它主要包括：（1）研究者（访谈者）与主办（赞助、保存）机构对受访者（叙述者）的责任；（2）研究者（访谈者）与主办（赞助、保存）机构之间的相互责任；（3）研究者（访谈者）与主办（赞助、保存）机构对专业本身的责任；（4）研究者（访谈者）与主办（赞助、保存）机构对公众的责任。② 有学者将这些责任进一步具体化为一系列伦理议题，比如知情同意（informed consent）、匿名与保密承诺、对关系与名誉的可能性伤害、不平等的权力关系、对叙述者与其他人的有害信息的公布、对研究成果的诚实呈现以及在委托服务中对访谈者的

---

① 有关口述史学伦理问题的研究可参阅 Amelia R. Fry，"Reflections on Ethics"，*Oral History Review*，Vol. 3，1975，pp. 17-28；Oral History Association，"Oral History Evaluation Guidelines：The Wingspread Conference"，*Oral History Review*，Vol. 8，1980，pp. 6-19；Daphne Patai，"Ethical Problems of Personal Narratives，or，Who Should Eat the Last Piece of Cake"，*International Journal of Oral History*，Vol. 8，No. 1，1987，pp. 5-27；Kathleen M Blee，"Evidence，Empathy，and Ethics：Lessons from Oral Histories of the Klan"，*Journal of American History*，Vol. 80，No. 2，1993，pp. 596-606；Valerie Raleigh Yow，"Ethics and Interpersonal Relationships in Oral History Research"，*Oral History Review*，Vol. 22，No. 1，1995，pp. 51-66；Alessandro Portelli，"Tryin' to Gather a Little Knowledge：Some Thoughts on the Ethics of Oral History"，in Alessandro Portelli，*The Battle of Valle Giulia：Oral History and the Art of Dialogue*，Madison：University of Wisconsin Press，1997，pp. 55-71；Rachel Vagts，"Clashing Discipline：Oral History and the Institutional Review Board"，*Archival Issues*，Vol. 26，No. 2，2002，pp. 145-152；Tracy E. K'Meyer and A. Glenn Crothers，"'If I See Some of This in Writing，I'm Going to Shoot You'：Reluctant Narrators，Taboo Topics，and the Ethical Dilemmas of the Oral Historian"，*Oral History Review*，Vol. 34，No. 1，2007，pp. 71-93；Brigitte Halbmayr，"The Ethics of Oral History：Expectations，Responsibilities and Dissociations"，in Marta Kurkowska-Budzan and Krzysztof Zamorski（eds.），*Oral History：The Challenges of Dialogue*，Amsterdam：John Benjamins Publishing Company，2009，pp. 195-204；Erin Jessee，"The Limits of Oral History：Ethics and Methodology Amid Highly Politicized Research Settings"，*Oral History Review*，Vol. 38，No. 2，2011，pp. 287-307；Martin Meeker，"The Berkeley Compromise：Oral History，Human Subjects，and the Meaning of 'Research'"，in Claire Bond Potter and Renee C. Romano（eds.），*Doing Recent History：On Privacy，Copyright，Video Games，Institutional Review Boards，Activist Scholarship and History that Talks Back*，Athens：University of Georgia Press，2012，pp. 115-138；Mary Larson，"Steering Clear of the Rocks：A Look at the Current State of Oral History Ethics in the Digital Age"，*Oral History Review*，Vol. 40，No. 1，2013，pp. 36-49；Donald A. Ritchie，*Doing Oral History*，Oxford and New York：Oxford University Press，third edition，2014，pp. 227-233.

② 1989 年采纳并于 2000 年重新修订的美国口述历史协会《口述历史评估指南》（*Oral History Evaluation Guidelines*）将法律与伦理原则界定为处理口述历史实践中的各种关系的一系列权利与责任，其中还制定"伦理/法律指南"（Ethical/Legal Guidelines）。详细内容访问网址 http：//www. oralhistory. org/about/principles-and-practices/oral-history-evaluation-guidelines-revised-in-2000/，2015 年 4 月 28 日访问。

保护，等等。①

本章将以分别发生于 1986 年和 2011 年的两个涉及法律与伦理纠纷的美国口述历史案件为例来分析著作权、诽谤与隐私权侵犯、法律挑战与"学者特权"、口述历史伦理审查机制以及口述历史参与者之间基于专业伦理的权责关系等问题。②

一 两个口述历史案例

第一个案例是发生于 1986 年的里加犹太人聚居区幸存者学会（Society of Survivors of Riga Ghetto, Inc.）与纽约城市大学（City University of New York）的亨利·哈特恩巴赫（Henry R. Huttenbach）教授围绕口述历史著作权问题而引发的诉讼案。③ 该案件起始于 20 世纪 70 年代晚期，当时该学会聘请著名的大屠杀研究专家哈特恩巴赫教授搜集和撰写里加犹太人聚居区的历史，他采访了 100 多位大屠杀幸存者并且搜集了部分文字材料和纪念品。1982 年双方就第一部研究作品《里加的大屠杀：里加犹太人聚居区历史》（The Holocaust in Riga: A History of the Riga Ghetto）签署了第一份书面协议，该协议除规定哈特恩巴赫教授获得金钱报酬之外，他还被列为作者并且拥有所有档案材料的唯一使用权，直到所有手稿完成。另外，协议也明确规定将访谈和手稿的著作权划归学会。1985 年年初，学会负责人对哈特恩巴赫教授试图对幸存者之间的不同叙述进行协调的做法表示不满。学会负责人还对哈特恩巴赫教授发表在《奥斯威辛声音》（The Voice

① Valerie Raleigh Yow, *Recording Oral History: A Guide for the Humanities and Social Sciences*, Walnut Creek: AltaMira Press, second edition, 2005, pp. 129-148.

② 本章将重点考察第二个案例并在此基础上重点分析法律挑战与"学者特权"以及口述历史伦理审查机制两个问题，因为这两个问题在美国口述史学界争议最大。

③ 里加犹太人聚居区是纳粹于 1941—1943 年间在拉脱维亚（Latvia）首都里加建立的。详细内容可参阅"Riga Ghetto", from Wikipedia, https://en.wikipedia.org/wiki/Riga_ Ghetto, 2015 年 5 月 1 日访问。

of Auschwitz) 杂志上的评论文章提出反对意见。哈特恩巴赫教授认为这篇文章仅仅是即将出版的著作的宣传，但是学会负责人认为它是未经授权的出版物。随着双方关系的恶化，学会试图将哈特恩巴赫的名字从整个手稿中除去。最终，学会以哈特恩巴赫教授违背协议为由于 1986 年向法院提起诉讼。学会坚持收回哈特恩巴赫教授对所有录音带与纪念品的所有权并要求其赔偿 10 万美元损失费。同样，哈特恩巴赫教授也以学会破坏协议为由发起反诉并且申请金钱赔偿。

在纽约郡最高法院（Supreme Court，New York County）做出审判之前，法院声称最初协议中关于著作权的分配是合法的。学会作为著作权所有者没有权利对手稿做出大规模修改，而且必须仍然以哈特恩巴赫教授的名义出版。最后，双方暂时达成妥协，在没有对方书面许可的前提下，双方都可以出版或使用由哈特恩巴赫教授所搜集的访谈资料或手稿的任何部分。此外，双方可以保存各自所拥有的资料，学会则被要求根据最初协议的规定向哈特恩巴赫教授支付相应报酬。①

发生于 2011 年并持续两年多的波士顿学院口述历史传票案（Boston College Oral History Subpoena Case）是美国现代口述史学有史以来有关法律与伦理问题的影响最为深远的诉讼事件，它不仅成为美国乃至国际口述史学界关注与争论的焦点，而且由于问题的敏感性和复杂性，该案更牵涉政治、外交、法律及新闻言论与学术自由等尖锐问题。

该传票案发生于 2011 年 5 月，英国有关当局依据英美司法互助协议（Mutual Legal Assistance Treaty）通过美国司法部向波士顿学院发出传票②，要求交出保存在该校伯恩斯图书馆（John J. Burns Library）的两位爱尔兰

---

① 该案详情可参阅 Society of Survivors of Riga Ghetto v. Henry R. Huttenbach, Supreme Court of New York, New York County, October 27, 1988, http://www.concernedhistorians.org/content_files/file/LE/211.pdf, 2015 年 5 月 1 日访问；John A. Neuenschwander, *A Guide to Oral History and the Law*, Oxford and New York: Oxford University Press, 2009, pp. 1-2.

② 后来了解到发出传票的英国机构是北爱尔兰警察局（Police Service of Northern Ireland），详细情况可参阅 Catherine Shannon, "This Case Merits Close Inspection", *Special to the Boston Irish Reporter*, June 8, 2011.

共和军（Irish Republican Army）前成员布兰登·休斯（Brendan Hughes，1948—2008）和多勒丝·普莱斯（Dolours Price，1951—2013）的口述历史访谈资料。① 这两位爱尔兰共和军前成员的口述历史资料是完成于 2001 年至 2006 年的波士顿学院"贝尔法斯特计划"（Belfast Project）的一部分，该计划由波士顿学院赞助和发起，旨在通过口述历史访谈来记录和保存那些参与 30 多年（20 世纪 60 年代末期至 90 年代末期）的北爱冲突（The Troubles）双方前军事成员的故事与经历，冲突双方是包括临时爱尔兰共和军（Provisional Irish Republican Army）、爱尔兰临时新芬党（Provisional Sinn Fein）、乌尔斯特志愿军组织（Ulster Volunteer Force）和其他准军事和政治组织在内的代表共和派（统一派）与保皇派（忠诚派）的不同利益派别。②

在某种意义上，"贝尔法斯特计划"缘于 1998 年《美好星期五协议》（*Good Friday Agreement*）的签署，该协议的正式签署标志着北爱和平进程的开始。作为和平进程的一部分，如何从过去 30 多年的内战冲突中吸取经验教训并为未来史学家保存宝贵的历史记录也日益成为众多学者的共识。1999—2000 年，时任伯恩斯图书馆馆长罗伯特·奥尼尔（Robert K. O'Neill）博士向当时正在波士顿学院担任访问学者的贝尔法斯特女王大学（Queen's University Belfast）政治学教授保罗·比尤（Paul Bew）就是否有可能启动一项记录北爱冲突历史的研究计划征求意见。比尤返回爱尔兰之后，随即同爱尔兰新闻记者埃德·莫洛尼（Ed Moloney）讨论此事，二人达成的共识就是创建一个以参与北爱冲突双方前军事成员的故事为基础的口述历史档案馆（oral history archive）。最后，通过与奥尼尔博士和波士顿学院爱尔兰计划中心（Center for Irish Programs）执行主任托马斯·哈奇（Thomas E. Hachey）教授的多次讨论并签订各种协议，"贝尔法斯特计划"

---

① 传票内容显示，这些资料包括所有与口述历史访谈相关的原始录音、访谈抄本、手写笔记与电脑记录等资料。

② Motion of the Trustees of Boston College to Quash Subpoenas, M. B. D. No. 11-MC-91078, United States District Court District of Massachusetts, June 7, 2011, pp. 1-5.

于 2001 年正式启动。根据相关协议，该计划聘请莫洛尼担任计划主任，同时考虑到受访者的特殊经历，还另外聘请爱尔兰共和军前成员安东尼·麦金太尔（Anthony McIntyre）和乌尔斯特志愿军前成员威尔逊·麦克阿瑟（Wilson McArthur）担任首席研究者与访谈者，由他们两位负责各自军事组织成员的访谈工作。①

北爱尔兰警察局之所以要求获得休斯和普莱斯的口述历史访谈资料，是因为它们涉及发生于北爱冲突期间的一些谋杀和绑架活动，并希望利用这些资料调查和审理某些相关案件。② 根据相关保密和捐赠协议，由于休斯已于 2008 年去世，在收到传票之后不久（即 2011 年 5 月 26 日），波士顿学院随即交出他的相关资料。③ 然而，由于普莱斯仍然健在，波士顿学院和相关研究者（包括计划主任和访谈者）仍然有义务维持其访谈资料的保密性。可是，在第一张传票尚未失效之际，2011 年 8 月波士顿学院又收到第二张传票，要求交出所有涉及 1972 年一位名叫珍·麦高伟（Jean Mc-Conville）的北爱尔兰妇女的绑架与谋杀案件的口述历史访谈资料。④

针对上述两张传票，波士顿学院分别于 2011 年 6 月 7 日和 8 月 17 日提出撤销传票的动议，希望法院在裁决时在两个重要的利益之间保持合适的平衡：即一方面是英国有关当局对发生在几十年前的北爱冲突中的暴力活动进行刑事调查时对相关资料的需求；另一方面则是需要保护和促进有关北爱冲突的学术研究，这些研究极其依赖于记录与收集参与者的故事，

---

① Affidavit of Thomas E. Hachey, Affidavit of Ed Moloney, Affidavit of Robert K. O'Neill, Affidavit of Anthony McIntyre, M. B. D. No. 11-MC-91078, United States District Court District of Massachusetts, June 7, 2011; Ed Moloney, *Voices from the Grave: Two Men's War in Ireland*, London: Faber and Faber, 2010, pp. 6-7.

② Jim Dwyer, "Secret Archive of Ulster Troubles Faces Subpoena", *The New York Times*, May 13, 2011.

③ Motion of the Trustees of Boston College to Quash Subpoenas, M. B. D. No. 11-MC-91078, United States District Court District of Massachusetts, June 7, 2011, p. 3.

④ 传票内容显示，这些资料涉及所有与麦高伟绑架与谋杀案相关的访谈资料，包括原始录音和录影、访谈抄本、访谈总结与索引以及描写访谈资料保存和监管的记录等资料。详细内容参阅 Motion of the Trustees of Boston College to Quash New Subpoenas, M. B. D. No. 11-MC-91078, United States District Court District of Massachusetts, August 17, 2011, p. 2.

而只有在获得保密承诺（promise of confidentiality）的条件下，这些参与者才会讲述他们的经历。针对第二个利益，波士顿学院进一步阐述了披露口述历史访谈资料可能造成的三个消极影响：侵犯受访者对于保密性的期望；使计划参与者遭受严重伤害的危险；阻止其他人参与未来的口述历史计划。① 针对波士顿学院要求撤销传票的动议，美国政府也分别于 2011 年 7 月 1 日和 8 月 25 日提出反对撤销传票的动议，其核心理由是适用的英美司法互助协议严格限制了法院在同意撤销传票动议问题上的自由裁量权，并且该协议也迫使法院执行传票要求。同时，美国政府还强调在面对有关刑事调查的传票时，并不存在能够保护资料免受公开的"学者特权"（academic privilege）；而且美国政府也并不认同波士顿学院指出的披露保密性资料所造成的一系列消极影响。②

作为"贝尔法斯特计划"的重要参与者，莫洛尼与麦金太尔认为波士顿学院无法完全代表他们及口述历史计划其他参与者的利益，同时也因为他们对波士顿学院在传票问题上的做法感到失望，因而于 2011 年 8 月 31 日向马萨诸塞州地区法院提起诉讼，要求介入此案。莫洛尼与麦金太尔不仅认为他们在该案中的利益没有被提出，而且特别提醒要注意传票所涉及的政治动机，他们还认为美国总检察长（United States Attorney General）未能做到与英国当局相互协商的责任，以确保其要求符合司法互助协议的制

---

① Motion of the Trustees of Boston College to Quash Subpoenas, M. B. D. No. 11-MC-91078, United States District Court District of Massachusetts, June 7, 2011, pp. 1, 9-15. 为进一步阐述其撤销传票的理由，波士顿学院于 2011 年 7 月 15 日提出了回应美国政府反对撤销传票动议的备忘录，认为"贝尔法斯特计划"访谈资料包含任何诸如此类的谋杀证据纯属猜测。详细内容参阅 Memorandum of Trustees of Boston College in Reply to Government's Opposition to Motion to Quash Subpoenas and in Opposition to Government's Motion to Compel, M. B. D. No. 11-MC-91078, United States District Court District of Massachusetts, July 15, 2011.

② Government's Opposition to Motion to Quash and Motion for an Order to Compel, M. B. D. No. 11-MC-91078-RGS, United States District Court District of Massachusetts, July 1, 2011, pp. 1-2; Government's Opposition to Motion to Quash New Subpoenas and Motion to Compel, M. B. D. No. 11-MC-91078-JLT, United States District Court District of Massachusetts, August 25, 2011.

定目的。① 作为回应，美国政府宣布反对莫洛尼与麦金太尔介入此案的请求，认为两位研究者针对总检察长的指控在法律上是毫无根据的，也无法成为要求介入此案的依据。同时，美国政府还认为两位研究者提出的传票侵犯美国宪法第一修正案和第五修正案的主张也是有缺陷的。②

2011 年 12 月 16 日，马萨诸塞州地区法院作出判决，法院认为必须平衡各方的重要利益：一方面美国政府对于司法互助协议的义务及对于合法的刑事诉讼的公众利益的保护是毋庸置疑的；另一方面，法院也认可波士顿学院和伯恩斯图书馆试图确保"贝尔法斯特计划"的长期保密性的努力以及对于撤销传票动议的简单否决给学术研究所带来的潜在的寒蝉效应。基于此，法院作出两项裁决：（1）法院否决了波士顿学院董事会要求撤销两张传票的动议，并且同意波士顿学院提出的将相关资料交由法院进行秘密审查的请求。法院命令波士顿学院在 2011 年 12 月 21 日中午之前将所有相关资料的复印件交由法院秘密审查，因此留出时间给波士顿学院向上诉法院提出暂缓执行的请求。如果不需要暂缓，法院将会及时对资料进行秘密审查，并根据法官要求发出进一步命令。（2）法院否决了莫洛尼与麦金泰尔要求介入此案的动议，法官认为波士顿学院能够充分代表他们的利益。③

经过多次听证会，地区法院进一步要求波士顿学院在 2011 年 12 月 21 日之前将普莱斯口述历史资料交由法官秘密审查，④ 同时还要求波士顿学院在 2011 年 12 月 27 日之前将另外 24 位北爱尔兰共和军前成员的口述历

①　ECF Motion for Leave to Intervene, M. B. D. No. 11-MC-91078 (JLT), United States District Court District of Massachusetts, August 31, 2011.

②　Government's Opposition to Motion for Leave to Intervene, M. B. D. No. 11-MC-91078-JLT, United States District Court District of Massachusetts, September 21, 2011.

③　United States of America v. Trustees of Boston College, No. 11-91078-WGY, United States District Court District of Massachusetts, December 16, 2011, p. 48; Jennifer Howard, "Boston College Must Release Oral-History Records, but Court Will Review Them First", *The Chronicle of Higher Education*, December 19, 2011.

④　The Letter from Jeffrey Swope to Elizabeth F. Smith (Courtroom Clerk), December 21, 2011.

史资料交由法官秘密审查。① 2011 年 12 月 27 日，马萨诸塞州地区法院裁定普莱斯口述历史资料必须在 2011 年 12 月 30 日中午之前移交给联邦检察官。② 在对波士顿学院提交的另外 24 位受访者的口述历史资料进行秘密审查之后，2012 年 1 月 20 日，马萨诸塞州地区法院作出判决，要求波士顿学院将另外 7 位受访者的口述历史资料移交给联邦检察官。③

上述几项判决引发了两起独立的上诉。第一起上诉由莫洛尼和麦金太尔提出，他们主要是针对地区法院要求交出普莱斯口述历史资料的裁决意见。④ 2011 年 12 月 29 日，他们向美国总检察长艾瑞克·霍尔德（Eric H. Holder）提起诉讼并要求马萨诸塞州地区法院进行司法复核，⑤ 同时向上诉法院提出延缓执行裁决意见的请求。⑥ 12 月 30 日，美国联邦第一巡回上诉法院发布命令，要求暂停将普莱斯口述历史资料交给英国有关当局。⑦ 2012 年 1 月 5 日，霍尔德提出撤销案件的动议，⑧ 在经过 1 月 24 日的听证会之后，地区法院同意政府撤销案件的动议请求，其理由是两位研究者并

① The Letter from Jeffrey Swope to Matthew Payne (Docket Clerk), December 27, 2011.

② United States of America v. Trustees of Boston College, No. 11-91078-WGY, United States District Court District of Massachusetts, December 27, 2011.

③ United States of America v. Trustees of Boston College, No. 11-91078-WGY, United States District Court District of Massachusetts, January 20, 2012. Henry McDonald, "Boston Researchers Fight against Seizure of IRA Interviews", *The Guardian*, January 23, 2012.

④ 莫洛尼与麦金太尔之所以特意针对普莱斯口述历史资料的裁决意见提出上诉，很大程度上是因为波士顿学院放弃了对于地区法院关于普莱斯口述历史资料裁决意见的上诉努力，其理由是学院认为普莱斯在之前的媒体上已经公开了有关她自己参与"贝尔法斯特计划"的相关信息，因而已经违背了保密协议。这个问题将在下文做进一步分析。

⑤ Ed Moloney and Anthony McIntyre vs. Eric H. Holder, Jr., Attorney General of the United States and John T. McNeil, Commissioner, Case 1: 11-CV-12331-WGY, United States District Court District of Massachusetts, December 29, 2011.

⑥ United States of America v. Trustees of Boston College, Case 1: 11-MC-91078-WGY, United States District Court District of Massachusetts, December 29, 2011; Kevin Cullen, "US College Agrees to Give Interviews with Dolours Price to Prosecutors", *The Irish Times*, December 30, 2011.

⑦ United States of America v. Trustees of Boston College, No. 11-2511, United States Court of Appeals for the First Circuit, December 30, 2011; Milton J. Valencia, "Appeals Court Steps into BC Case", *The Boston Globe*, December 31, 2011.

⑧ Ed Moloney and Anthony McIntyre vs. Eric H. Holder, Jr., Attorney General of the United States and John T. McNeil, Commissioner, Case 1: 11-CV-12331-WGY, United States District Court District of Massachusetts, January 5, 2012.

不具备诉讼资格。① 莫洛尼和麦金太尔在地区法院的上诉努力失败后，他们于 2012 年 2 月 17 日正式向美国联邦第一巡回上诉法院提出上诉请求，其理由主要包括：（1）司法互助协议允许私人利益干预，以防止证据被公开；（2）地区法院滥用其自由裁量权；（3）传票侵犯第一修正案赋予研究者的宪法权利。② 美国政府也于 3 月 12 日做出回应，反对莫洛尼和麦金太尔的上诉请求，并一一否决他们的上诉理由。③ 在经过 4 月 4 日的听证会之后，④ 美国联邦第一巡回上诉法院于 7 月 6 日做出正式裁决，支持马萨诸塞州地区法院的判决结果。在一份长达 46 页的判决书中，一个由三位法官组成的审判小组否决了两位研究者提出的三个理由。其中最为重要的否决就是针对两位研究者提出的宪法第一修正案所赋予的言论自由权利，他们主张拥有一种类似 "新闻记者特权"（reporter's privilege）的 "学者特权"。针对此种主张，第一巡回上诉法院援引 1972 年美国最高法院在 "布莱兹伯格案"（Branzburg v. Hayes）中所确立的判决先例而裁定："调查犯罪活动的选择属于政府，而不受制于学术研究者的否决。" 法院还强调帮助其他国家协助刑事犯罪调查的协议义务使得政府在该案中的利益要更大于 "布莱兹伯格案" 中的政府利益。⑤ 针对此项裁决，莫洛尼和麦金太尔向第一巡回上诉法院提出全体法官重新听证和延缓执行裁决意见等多项请

①　Denise Lavoie, "Judge Tosses Lawsuit Seeking to Block Subpoenas for Handover of Secret IRA Tapes", *The Washington Post*, January 24, 2012.

②　Ed Moloney; Anthony McIntyre vs. Eric H. Holder, Jr., Attorney General; John T. McNeil, Commissioner, No. 12-1159, United States Court of Appeals for the First Circuit, February 17, 2012.

③　Ed Moloney; Anthony McIntyre vs. Eric H. Holder, Jr., Attorney General; John T. McNeil, Commissioner, No. 12-1159, United States Court of Appeals for the First Circuit, March 12, 2012.

④　Martine Powers, "Federal Appeals Court Hears Arguments in Case of BC Oral History Project on 'Troubles' in Northern Ireland", *The Boston Globe*, April 4, 2012.

⑤　Ed Moloney; Anthony McIntyre vs. Eric H. Holder, Jr., Attorney General; Jack W. Pirozzolo, Commissioner, No. 12-1159, United States Court of Appeals for the First Circuit, July 6, 2012; Jay Lindsay, "Court: Interview with IRA Car Bomber for Boston College Oral History Project Can Be Released", *The Associated Press*, July 6, 2012; Derek J. Anderson, "Boston College Can't Keep IRA Materials Confidential", *The Boston Globe*, July 7, 2012.

求，不过都被一一否决。① 9 月 28 日他们向美国最高法院提出延缓执行第一巡回上诉法院裁决意见的请求，10 月 1 日美国最高法院大法官斯蒂芬·布雷耶（Stephen G. Breyer）发出一项暂缓命令。② 该案也由此进入新的阶段，莫洛尼和麦金太尔于 11 月 16 日正式向美国最高法院提出调案复审令的请求。③ 对于两位研究者来说，如果最高法院不受理此案，他们就没有其他法律措施能够阻止普莱斯口述历史资料被移交给英国有关当局。遗憾的是，此次诉讼的关键人物普莱斯于 2013 年 1 月 23 日去世，该案也随之发生重要转变。④ 根据捐赠协议，普莱斯去世意味着其口述历史资料可以公开，可是这些资料仍然受到美国最高法院延缓令的保护。不过，对于两位研究者来说，此次诉讼最终没有发生有利于他们的转机，2013 年 4 月 15 日，美国最高法院正式否决了莫洛尼和麦金太尔申请调案复审令的请求，这也意味着波士顿学院最终必须交出普莱斯的口述历史资料。⑤

第二起上诉由波士顿学院提出。对于 2011 年 12 月 16 日马萨诸塞州地区法院的判决结果，波士顿学院并没有提起上诉，⑥ 其解释之一是法院认可波士顿学院提出的理由，即政府对于保密性研究资料的传票需要严格审

---

① David Cote, "Belfast Project Case May Go To Supreme Court", *The Heights*, September 5, 2012; Henry McDonald, "Appeal Launched against IRA Tapes Being Handed Over to Police", *The Guardian*, September 7, 2012.

② Ed Moloney and Anthony McIntyre vs. United States, Et Al., No. 12A310, Supreme Court of the United States, October 1, 2012; "Supreme Court Blocks BC Tape Handover", *Irish American News*, October 1, 2012.

③ Ed Moloney; Anthony McIntyre vs. Eric H. Holder, Jr., Attorney General; Jack W. Pirozzolo, Commissioner, *On Petition for a Writ of Certiorari to the United States Court of Appeals for the First Circuit*, Supreme Court of the United States, November 16, 2012.

④ Paul Vitello, "Dolours Price, Defiant I. R. A. Bomber, Dies at 61", *The New York Times*, January 25, 2013.

⑤ Lawrence Hurley, "Supreme Court Declines Northern Ireland Subpoena Dispute", *The Reuters*, April 15, 2013; Eleanor Hildebrandt, "Supreme Court Rejects Belfast Project Appeal", *The Heights*, April 18, 2013.

⑥ 尽管法院在判决当中同意波士顿学院向上诉法院提出暂缓请求，不过学院并没有这么做，并表示会全面配合法院对其他口述历史资料进行秘密审查，详细内容参阅 Scott Jaschik, "Limited Right to Confidentiality", *The Inside Higher Education*, December 19, 2011.

查并且同意对资料进行秘密审查以帮助保护其中涉及的重要利益;① 另外一个没有提起上诉的原因是为了更好地保护其他受访者的利益,波士顿学院担心如果提出上诉可能会导致被迫交出其他所有有关爱尔兰共和军前成员的口述历史资料。② 波士顿学院的上诉主要是针对 2012 年 1 月 20 日马萨诸塞州地区法院要求交出另外 7 位受访者口述历史资料的裁决结果,不过需要指出的是,学院的上诉努力也是相当迟缓的。③ 直到 2012 年 2 月 21 日,波士顿学院才正式向美国联邦第一巡回上诉法院提出上诉请求,学院认为上级法院需要考虑口述历史资料对于北爱尔兰刑事调查的价值是否超过对于保密性学术研究的保护,而且学院还认为地区法院法官在审查口述历史资料与刑事案件的关联性时错误地使用了他自己的评估标准。④ 5 月 3 日,波士顿学院在其上诉书中更为详细地提出了三个理由:(1)第一巡回上诉法院的判例要求平衡保护信息自由流通的需要,同时对那些试图获取保密性学术研究资料的传票应该保护高度敏感;(2)当面对试图获取保密性学术研究资料的传票时,地区法院在应用第一巡回上诉法院所要求的利益平衡原则时犯了严重错误;(3)地区法院的裁决导致发出一项要求提交相关信息的命令,而根据第一巡回上诉法院的高度敏感标准,这些相关信息是不应该提交的。⑤ 作为回应,美国政府于 7 月 18 日提出反对意见,一一否决波士顿学院提出的三个理由。⑥ 9 月 7 日,第一巡回上诉法院举行听证会,波士顿学院代表律师认为任何需要提交的访谈资料必须与传票主题

---

①　"Statement from Boston College Regarding Today's Appeal of the Belfast Project Subpoena", February 21, 2012.

②　Thomas E. Hachey and Robert K. O'Neill, "College Has Fought to Deny Access to Interview Materials", *The Irish Times*, January 19, 2012.

③　Travis Anderson, "Judge to BC: Turn Over More Materials", *The Boston Globe*, January 23, 2012.

④　*Notice of Appeal*, M. B. D. No. 11-MC-91078, United States District Court District of Massachusetts, February 21, 2012; "Boston College to Fight Federal Court Order to Disclose Secret IRA Interview Tapes", *Washington Post*, February 22, 2012.

⑤　United States of America vs. Trustee of Boston College, *Brief of Appellant Trustees of Boston College*, No. 12-1236, United States Court of Appeals for the First Circuit, May 3, 2012.

⑥　United States of America vs. Trustee of Boston College, *Brief of the United States*, No. 12-1236, United States Court of Appeals for the First Circuit, July 18, 2012.

"直接相关" (directly related)；而美国联邦助理检察官则认为传票所涉范围是非常广泛的，他还认可地区法院法官的资料审查标准，即与传票主题有"一般性关联" (ordinary relevance) 的访谈资料都必须提交。对于双方的各执一词，第一巡回上诉法院并没有当庭做出判决。①

在普莱斯去世之后，波士顿学院在2013年1月28日发表的声明中请求第一巡回上诉法院撤销地方法院的判决结果，并认为围绕"贝尔法斯特计划"的法律争论应当结束。② 2月11日，美国政府提出反对意见，认为波士顿学院并没有提出任何进一步论据来证明为什么普莱斯去世就意味着该案要终结。③ 同莫洛尼与麦金太尔相比，波士顿学院的上诉努力取得部分胜利，2013年5月31日，美国联邦第一巡回上诉法院做出判决。首先，第一巡回上诉法院强烈谴责联邦政府试图将司法制度贬低为一种"橡皮图章" (rubber stamp)，政府认为在司法互助协议下法院没有权利评估传票所要求的资料的关联性问题，而法院坚持认为传票执行本质上是一种司法功能。其次，第一巡回上诉法院批评地区法院滥用自由裁量权，在经过对所有相关资料的详细审查之后，法院认为需要提交的7位受访者的口述历史资料数量从原先的85份减少到11份。在波士顿学院看来，此项判决代表了它在保护这些口述历史资料上的重大胜利。莫洛尼与麦金太尔也发表声明表示支持，他们认为此项判决至少是对整个（诉讼）过程的部分控诉。④

---

① United States of America vs. Trustee of Boston College, *Oral Arguments*, No. 12-1236, United States Court of Appeals for the First Circuit, September 7, 2012; Denise Lavoie, "Boston College: IRA Interviews Should Stay Sealed", *The Associated Press*, September 7, 2012.

② United States of America vs. Trustee of Boston College, *Notice of Boston College of Suggestion of Death*, No. 12-1236, United States Court of Appeals for the First Circuit, January 28, 2013; David Cote, "University Files To Close Belfast Project Case", *The Heights*, January 29, 2013.

③ United States of America vs. Trustee of Boston College, *Government's Opposition to Boston College's Motion to Dismiss Its Appeal as Moot*, No. 12-1236, United States Court of Appeals for the First Circuit, February 11, 2013; Travis Andersen, "Officials Still Seek BC Tapes on IRA", *The Boston Globe*, February 12, 2013.

④ United States of America vs. Trustee of Boston College, No. 12-1236, United States Court of Appeals for the First Circuit, May 31, 2013; Jennifer Howard, "Boston College Wins a Victory in Legal Fight Over Oral-History Records", *The Chronicle of Higher Education*, June 2, 2013.

针对上述判决，美国联邦检察官于 8 月 2 日提出小组复审请求①，不过，第一巡回上诉法院予以否决（9 月 5 日），并且于 2013 年 9 月 13 日正式授权执行 5 月 31 日的裁决结果。②

概括而言，第一个案例主要涉及口述历史的著作权问题；第二个案例除涉及可能的诽谤与隐私权侵犯之外，该案争论焦点还集中于三个问题：（1）对于口述历史资料设限的法律挑战以及是否存在"学者特权"？（2）是否应该通过伦理审查委员会加强对口述历史工作潜在的法律与伦理问题的审查与监管？（3）如何处理和平衡口述历史工作中不同关系体之间基于专业伦理的权责关系？

二 著作权

著作权（又称"版权"）是文学、艺术和科学作品的作者因文学、艺术和科学创作而依法享有的对自己的作品占有、使用和处分的专有民事权利。③ 口述历史作为一种历史事件的当事人或目击者的回忆而保存的口述证词，它产生于访谈者与受访者之间的互动中，其中凝结了双方的原创性创作。因为口述历史不是一般的访谈，它是经过双方精心准备的关于某一特定历史的原创性记录。从上述纽约郡最高法院对里加犹太人聚居区幸存者学会与哈特恩巴赫案件的审判结果来看，显然是以认可口述历史的著作权资格为基础的。

口述历史著作权问题主要包括著作权的所有权、著作权许可使用与转

---

① United States of America vs. Trustee of Boston College, *Government's Request for Modification of the Court's Opinion*, No. 12-1236, United States Court of Appeals for the First Circuit, August 2, 2013.

② "Legal Timeline of Boston College Belfast Project Subpoenas", http://bostoncollegesubpoena. wordpress. com/, 2015 年 5 月 5 日访问。

③ 现行的美国著作权法（Copyright Act）于 1976 年制订，相关法案也有不同程度的修订。详细内容可访问美国版权局（United States Copyright Office）官方网站相关信息 "Copyright Law of the United States", http://copyright. gov/title17/, 2015 年 5 月 5 日访问。

让及著作权侵犯行为与法律责任等。这两个案件的另外一个重要启示是，通过法院对双方所签署的书面协议的有效性认可，足以显示口述历史过程中访谈者、受访者与赞助和保存机构之间签署各种法律协议的必要性。正因如此，美国口述历史工作者在口述历史实践中必须履行一项不可或缺的程序，那就是法律授权协议书的起草、签署与执行问题。它之所以重要，是因为现行的美国著作权法没有关于"口述历史"著作权的明确规定，而且口述历史又以文字、录音、视频乃至展览或舞台表演等多元形式存在，因而使著作权问题更加复杂。法律授权协议书作为著作权当事人之间设立、变更、终止著作权关系的正式声明，显然有助于明确和保护当事人之间的权利与义务关系，进而避免和预防一些不必要的法律纠纷与诉讼。按照一般口述历史项目的设计，与著作权相关的协议书包括著作权许可使用协议、转让协议与赠与协议等。

就理论而言，访谈者与受访者共享著作权，不过实际关注的是受访者签署法律授权协议书的问题。在正式访谈之前，项目负责人或访谈者应当告知受访者在访谈结束后要签署相关法律协议书。在正式访谈结束或录音资料转录、整理和编辑完成之后，再将相关协议书送给受访者，并向对方详细解释内容、目的及如何填写。受访者在协议书中可能要求设定限制条件或长期保留对口述历史的著作权，甚至在他去世之前都不能公开。如果受访者坚持这样做，访谈者也必须尊重其意愿，即使这样会造成口述历史资料无法公开和使用。对于这些问题，在口述历史协会的积极协调与组织下，美国口述史学界已经形成一套相当完善的基本程序与相应的法律授权协议书范本。①

---

① 关于口述历史的著作权与法律授权协议书问题，可参阅 Valerie Raleigh Yow, *Recording Oral History: A Guide for the Humanities and Social Sciences*, Walnut Creek: AltaMira Press, second edition, 2005, pp. 121-125; John A. Neuenschwander, *A Guide to Oral History and the Law*, Oxford and New York: Oxford University Press, 2009, pp. 3-18, 61-86. 协议书范本可分别参阅这两本书的第364—371 页和第 115—130 页。

三　诽谤与隐私权侵犯

　　口述历史虽然是访谈者与受访者之间的互动交际过程，但它必然涉及第三者，尤其是对第三者的诽谤性言论或评价，一旦公开可能会遭到第三者本人或其后代子孙的抗议，严重时甚至会引起法律诉讼。目前，美国口述史学界对于这些涉及个人的敏感评价采取的一般原则是"如果没有确实根据，而且那些评价言论不是很重要，那就在争取受访者同意的基础上尽量予以删除"。如果那些评价确实很重要，而且受访者执意不能删除，一般可以采取匿名等隐蔽受访者个人身份的方式进行处理。当然，如果涉及重要的政治问题或个人人身安全等问题时，则有必要专门签署一份关于限制或封存访谈的书面协议，直到条件允许才可公开。这么做的目的是保护受访者的个人利益，同时也为访谈者或项目负责人规避法律诉讼纠纷。

　　虽然目前美国口述史学界涉及诽谤的案例并不是很多，但口述历史却是产生诽谤行为的沃土。因为口述历史除叙述一般的历史事件和人物经历之外，更多的是涉及主观评价，主观评价往往掺杂着极强的个人好恶，可能出于性别、党派、信仰、政见、种族等因素的差异而造成故意或过失性诽谤。在某些个别口述历史（尤其是政治性议题）访谈中，口述历史也极其容易成为一种政治工具，它不断地被用来攻击政敌与宣扬个人政绩。基于此，作为访谈者与项目负责人一定要注意受访者叙述时的语气与涉及的诽谤性内容，美国著名诽谤法专家布鲁斯·桑福德（Bruce Sanford）教授就总结了一系列"危险信号词语"，意在说明不适当地使用这些语言很有可能导致诽谤行为。而这些"危险信号词语"也成为美国口述历史工作者判断与提醒受访者口述语气与评价内容的重要参考标准。①

---

　　① 有关口述历史诽谤问题，可参阅 John A. Neuenschwander, *A Guide to Oral History and the Law*, Oxford and New York：Oxford University Press，2009，pp. 31-48.

表 8 - 1 　　　　　　　　　桑福德危险信号词语①

addict 沉溺、上瘾	fawning sycophant 奉承者	perjurer 伪证者
adulteration of products 掺假货	fraud 欺骗，骗子	plagiarist 剽窃者
adultery 通奸	gambling den 赌屋	pockets public funds 私吞公共基金
alcoholic 酗酒者	gangster 歹徒	profiteering 牟取暴利的
altered records 被篡改的记录	gay 同性恋者	prostitute 妓女
atheist 无神论者	graft 渎职，贪污	scam 诡计、阴谋
bad moral character 质量败坏	groveling office seeker 卑躬屈节的谋求官职者	scandalmonger 专事诽谤的人
bankrupt 破产	herpes 疱疹	scoundrel 无赖、恶棍
bigamist 重婚者	hit-man 职业杀手	seducer 骗子
blacklisted 列于黑名单	hypocrite 伪君子	sharp dealing 不正当交易
blackmail 勒索	illicit relation 不正当关系	shyster 奸诈之徒
booze-hound 暴饮者	incompetent 无能力者	slacker 懒鬼
bribery 行贿，受贿	infidelity 不忠	smooth and tricky 圆滑
brothel 妓院	informer 密告者	smuggler 走私犯
buys votes 贿选，购买选票	inside trading 私下交易	sneaky 卑鄙的
cheats 欺骗	intemperate 放纵的	sold influence 卖弄权势
child abuse 虐待儿童	intimate 亲密的，私通的	sold out 背叛

---

① John A. Neuenschwander, *Oral History and the Law*, Albuquerque：Oral History Association, Revised Edition, 1993, p. 13. 在该书 2009 年版本中，该表中的很多词已经被删除，具体参阅 John A. Neuenschwander, *A Guide to Oral History and the Law*, Oxford and New York：Oxford University Press, 2009, p. 44.

续　表

collusion 勾结	intolerance 缺乏耐性、不容异说	spy 间谍
con artist 骗子艺术家	Jekyll-Hyde personality 双重人格	stool pigeon 密探、眼线
confidence man 骗子	kept woman 靠男人养活的姘妇	stuffed the ballot box 投入大量假选票
corruption 腐败,贪污	Ku Klux Klan 三 K 党	suicide 自杀
coward 懦弱的人	Mafia 黑手党	swindle 诈骗
crook 骗子	mental illness 精神病	thief 小偷
deadbeat 游手好闲者	mobster 歹徒	unethical 不道德的
defaulter 不履行者	moral delinquency 道德不良	unmarried mother 单身母亲
divorced 离婚的	mouthpiece 喉舌	unprofessional 外行的
double-crosser 叛变者	Nazi 纳粹党人	unsound mind 思想不健全
drug abuser 吸毒成瘾者	paramour 情妇	unworthy of credit 不值得信赖
drunkard 酒鬼	peeping Tom 好偷窥者	vice den 罪恶源泉
ex-convict 从前曾被判刑的人		villain 恶棍

　　所谓隐私，是指个人的与社会公共生活无关而不愿被他人所知或干涉的私人事项。其内容包括三个方面：个人信息的保密、个人生活的不受干扰与个人私事决定的自由。[①] 隐私权没有统一的定义。一般来说，隐私权是指公民个人和死者所享有的个人信息不被非法获悉和公开、个人生活不受外界非法侵扰、个人私事的决定不受非法干涉的一种独立的人格权。[②]

---

　　① 王利明、杨立新（主编）：《人格权与新闻侵权》，中国方正出版社 1995 年版，第 415—421 页。

　　② 同上书，第 412 页。

《美国法律整编侵权行为法》列出四种侵犯隐私权的情形：（1）不合理地侵入他人之隐秘；（2）他人之姓名或肖像之窃用；（3）不合理地公开他人之私生活；（4）使他人有不实形象之公开。① 具体到口述历史中，第三种情况是经常发生的隐私权侵犯行为。因为口述历史访谈中的受访者一般都是某些事件的亲历者与目击者，一般来说比较了解与这些事件相关的个人的资料，尤其是他人不愿被人了解的私生活，所以极有可能造成对第三者隐私权的侵犯。另外一种情况是访谈者或项目负责人在公开口述历史资料时透露了受访者的个人隐私，随着口述历史日益涉及某些敏感主题，如何预防或避免不合理地公开他人私生活变得相当重要。口述历史中发生隐私权侵犯的另外一种情况是未经受访者同意而暗中录音，在美国，自水门事件以后，人们对这类问题更加警惕，口述历史工作者一般不会这么做。②

四　法律挑战与"学者特权"

作为口述历史访谈的主要信息提供者，受访者的开诚布公对于一项口述历史计划的成功来说是至关重要的，如何消除受访者的后顾之忧及更好地保护受访者和他人的利益也成为口述历史工作者的法律义务与职业伦理。为了实现这个目的，许多口述历史计划和访谈者都通过知情同意书（Informed Consent Form）、合约协议（Contractual Agreement）和赠与契约（Deed of Gift）等法律授权协议书为受访者提供各种设限权利，其中包括封存整个或部分访谈内容（设置开放期限）与使用匿名等保密承诺，以及

---

① 台湾"司法院"、"国立"政治大学法律研究所（合译）：《美国法律整编·侵权行为法》，（台北）司法周刊杂志社 1986 年版，第 543 页。

② 有关口述历史隐私权侵犯问题，可参阅 John A. Neuenschwander, *A Guide to Oral History and the Law*, Oxford and New York：Oxford University Press，2009，pp. 49-60.

设置访谈编辑、访问与使用等附加条件。比如，在 1998 年被地方检察官传唤的美国三 K 党（Ku Klux Klan）前党魁塞缪尔·鲍尔斯（Samuel H. Bowers，1924—2006）的口述历史访谈资料就做了类似设限要求，根据鲍尔斯的要求，这项由密西西比州档案与历史局（Mississippi Department of Archives and History）完成于 1983—1984 年的口述历史访谈资料必须封存，直到他去世之后才可以公开。而且，公布的访谈资料显示，其录音记录和抄本都不是访谈的完整版本，录音中没有的某些内容出现在抄本中，而部分录音片段内容也会从抄本中删除，甚至鲍尔斯对抄本中的部分用词也做了修改与调整。尽管密西西比州档案与历史局提出撤销传票的动议，不过，最终法院还是判决该局必须交出鲍尔斯口述历史访谈资料。①

　　同样，对于涉及相当敏感和争议主题的"贝尔法斯特计划"来说，提供保密承诺等诸如此类的设限条件是该计划得以成功的一个必要条件。②正因如此，计划主任莫洛尼在《来自坟墓的声音》一书的序言中就强调，"该计划的一个关键性规则是没有资料能够被使用，除非受访者同意或去世"③。波士顿学院在 2011 年 6 月 7 日提出的撤销传票的动议中也强调保密的重要性，动议指出："从一开始就认识到'贝尔法斯特计划'的成功将完全取决于许多参与者的自愿，即他们能够同意并且坦诚地与访谈者交

---

　　①　不过，在判决中并没有将鲍尔斯口述历史资料作为证据来使用。在该案中，鲍尔斯被指控组织与策划 1966 年的一项暗杀活动，最后并被判处终身监禁。详细内容请参阅 Jay Hughes，"DA Want More Files for Investigation into 1966 Slaying"，*The Associated Press*，March 25，1998；Paul Hendrickson，"From the Fires of Hate，An Ember of Hope；In 1966，the Klan Killed a Man. Now，Finally，His Family May See Justice Rise from the Ashes"，*The Washington Post*，July 22，1998.

　　②　Motion of the Trustees of Boston College to Quash Subpoenas，M. B. D. No. 11-MC-91078，United States District Court District of Massachusetts，June 7，2011，p. 13.

　　③　Ed Moloney，*Voices from the Grave*：*Two Men's War in Ireland*，London：Faber and Faber，2010，p. 7. 该书主要根据属于"贝尔法斯特"计划的爱尔兰共和军前成员休斯和乌尔斯特志愿军前成员大卫·尔文（David Ervine，1953—2007）的口述历史访谈资料撰写而成，由于二人都已去世，根据捐赠协议，他们的访谈资料可以对外公开。2010 年 10 月，爱尔兰电视电台（RTÉ）还根据该书发行了一部 83 分钟的同名纪录片。

谈。同样明显的是，受访者之所以愿意参加这个计划也取决于他们获得保证，即他们的身份和他们在访谈中所说的内容都将严格保密。"波士顿学院进一步解释指出，那些受访者坚持保密不仅仅是为了不连累他们自己或他们的同僚，以普莱斯为例，同样或更为重要的是因为可能受到其他前爱尔兰共和军成员的报复；爱尔兰共和军实施类似于黑手党"拒绝作证"（omerta）原则的"缄默法则"（code of silence），那些被认为违反法则的人将会遭受死亡惩罚，因此，如果没有获得保密承诺，那些与爱尔兰共和军有关联的访谈者和受访者自然不愿意参与"贝尔法斯特计划"①。访谈者麦金太尔在其宣誓书中也直言："当时我的确信理解是我之所以同意进行访谈是它们将得到彻底的和绝对的保护，在我看来，这绝对意味着访谈将不受任何要求披露它们的法律诉讼程序的影响。……否则我将不会参与这样一项充满风险的危险工作。"② 对于受访者来说，他们都被明确告知这个条件，而且签署一份将其访谈资料捐赠给波士顿学院伯恩斯图书馆的《捐赠协议》（*Agreement for Donation*），其中明确表明：任何访谈资料都不能公开，除非受访者去世或同意提前公开。③ 这种保密承诺不仅明确写在《捐赠协议》当中，④ 而且受访者在正式访谈时也被访谈者口头告知这个条件。在已经公布的休斯的访谈录音中，休斯明确表示如果没有这样的保密承诺，他是不会坐下来对着麦克风讲话的。⑤ 波士顿学院在日常管理和保存工作中也相当谨慎和严格地遵守赋予受访者的上述保密期望，据哈奇和奥尼尔透露，访谈资料保存在伯恩斯图书馆的珍稀书籍与特藏室（Rare Books and Special Collections），该特

---

① Motion of the Trustees of Boston College to Quash Subpoenas, M. B. D. No. 11-MC-91078, United States District Court District of Massachusetts, June 7, 2011, pp. 5-7.

② Affidavit of Anthony McIntyre, June 2, 2011, pp. 2-3.

③ Affidavit of Anthony McIntyre, June 2, 2011, p. 3; Affidavit of Ed Moloney, June 2, 2011, p. 10.

④ 详细内容参阅休斯的《捐赠协议》：Brendan Hughes, "Agreement for Donation", John J. Burns Library, Boston College, December 12, 2002.

⑤ Jim Dwyer, "Secret Archive of Ulster Troubles Faces Subpoena", *The New York Times*, May 13, 2011.

藏室由摄像头监控，并且需要配合钥匙锁和安全密码才能进入。而且，图书馆规定只有少数直接参与该计划的访谈者和学者被允许阅读或聆听那些还没有去世的受访者的访谈资料。[①]

可是在实践中，口述历史计划中研究者（访谈者）、受访者与主办（赞助、保存）机构之间所做的各种设限承诺以及为此所签署的各种法律授权协议书受到越来越多的法律挑战。正如美国著名口述历史法律问题专家约翰·纽恩斯科范德尔教授所说："尤其考虑到每年口述历史访谈数量的令人难以置信的增长以及实践者对于更为当代的主题和问题的日益重视，向口述历史档案馆发出更多传票的可能性已经变得不那么遥远。"[②] 纽恩斯科范德尔总结了美国司法体系中两种主要针对设限资料（信息）进行挑战的法律手段：信息自由请求（freedom of information requests）和传票。他进一步指出，通过信息自由法案或公开记录请求（open records requests）的形式，由联邦或州政府机构实施的口述历史项目会面临被要求公开任何封存或设限访谈资料的挑战，其唯一目的就是让公众能够广泛获得政府记录，而任何能够豁免信息自由请求的记录都必须满足法定的豁免类型。[③]

波士顿学院遭遇的传票案就是纽恩斯科范德尔所说的另外一种更为常见的挑战手段。面对传票，接收方要么必须遵守，要么提出撤销或修改传票等方式提出反对意见。在反对传票的辩护理由中，特权主张是一种较为常见的选择，如果这种特权主张获得法院认可，那些被

---

① Affidavit of Thomas E. Hachey, June 2, 2011, p. 3；Affidavit of Robert K. O'Neill, June 2, 2011, pp. 3-4.

② John A. Neuenschwander, *A Guide to Oral History and the Law*, Oxford and New York：Oxford University Press, 2009, p. 29.

③ 据纽恩斯科范德尔了解，目前美国只有肯塔基和德克萨斯两个州已经颁布特定法律豁免信息自由法案对于封存或设限访谈资料的请求。详细内容参阅 John A. Neuenschwander, *A Guide to Oral History and the Law*, Oxford and New York：Oxford University Press, 2009, pp. 27-29. 另外，一位《纽约时报》记者曾于 2002 年依据信息自由法向纽约市消防局（New York City Fire Department）提出信息公开请求，要求公开该局所做的有关"9·11"的口述历史资料。2005 年纽约州上诉法院（New York State Court of Appeals）判决该局交出大部分资料。详细内容参阅 Jim Dwyer, "City to Release Thousands of Oral Histories of 9/11 Today", *The New York Times*, August 12, 2005.

传唤的资料就无须交出，或者被传唤要求作证的人也可以拒绝出庭。在美国的司法体系中，法院要求所有知道相关事实或者消息的人在诉讼中提供证据，正义才能得到最好的实现，除非在既有法律和法院的命令中规定其享有特权。目前在美国普通法体系中，只有律师和当事人、医生和病人、牧师与悔罪者以及夫妻之间享有拒绝提供证据或作证的特权。[1] 此外，还包括那些保护敏感军事和外交信息的"国家机密特权"[2]（state secrets privilege）以及美国宪法第五修正案赋予的"禁止自证其罪"特权。[3]

尽管经常因为了解或拥有某些跟案件调查相关的信息而遭受传票的新闻记者和学者并没有获得上述法定特权，他们一直在努力争取，并希望获得特权来保护他们的信息及其信息来源免受传票威胁。波士顿学院遭遇的"贝尔法斯特计划"传票案中，波士顿学院要求撤销传票的动议与莫洛尼和麦金太尔向地区法院和第一巡回上诉法院提出上诉的主要辩护依据都是坚持保密承诺受到美国宪法第一修正案的保护，并且学院和研究者都援引众多各级法院判例来证明他们拥有一种类似于"新闻记者特权"的"学者特权"，因而通过保密渠道获取的口述历史资料可以拒绝公开。尽管马萨诸塞州地区法院 2011 年 12 月 16 日的裁决意见否决了波士顿学院要求撤销传票和两位研究者要求介入此案的动议，但事实上，地区法院在一定程度上还是认可学院和研究者提出的要求保护保密性学术研究资料的主张，因而法院认为必须平衡两个相互冲突的重要利益：一方面是公众对于信息自由流动的需求和研究者保护学术自由的利益；另一方面则是法院和诉讼当

---

① 唐纳德·M. 吉尔摩等：《美国大众传播法：判例评析》（第六版），梁宁等译，清华大学出版社 2002 年版，第 305 页。

② John Denvir, *Freeing Speech：The Constitutional War over National Security*, New York：New York University Press, 2010, p. 93.

③ Susan Ellis Wild（ed.）, *Webster's New World Law Dictionary*, Hoboken：Wiley, 2006, p. 235.

事人完整了解证据和其他相关信息的利益。①

针对莫洛尼和麦金太尔提出的宪法第一修正案赋予他们拥有类似于"新闻记者特权"的学术研究特权主张，第一巡回上诉法院在 2012 年 7 月 6 日的判决中援引 1972 年美国最高法院在"布莱兹伯格案"中确立的判决先例而予以否决。当时，美国最高法院以 5∶4 的投票结果判决，新闻记者在向大陪审团作证时，没有拒绝透露秘密消息来源或其他消息的宪法第一修正案特权。以拜伦·怀特（Byron White）为首的 4 名大法官在判决意见书中指出："我们面对的唯一一个问题是，是否应该像对待其他人一样强制记者应答大陪审团的传唤并回答与调查犯罪相关的问题。……第一修正案或者其他宪法性的规定都不会允许一般的公民在大陪审团面前隐瞒他秘密得到的消息。……在普通法中，法院一直拒绝承认存在任何特权，可以让新闻从业人员拒绝向大陪审团披露秘密的消息。……大陪审团对犯罪的调查实现着一个基本的政府职能，即保护公民的人身和财产安全。"② 在该案中，由第一巡回上诉法院审判长（Chief Judge）桑德拉·林奇（Sandra L. Lynch）组成的审判小组明确表示该案的判决受制于"布莱兹伯格案"

---

① United States of America v. Trustees of Boston College, No. 11-91078-WGY, United States District Court District of Massachusetts, December 16, 2011.

② 由于发生在 1969—1971 年间的三个案子（"布莱兹伯格案"、"保罗·帕波斯案"和"合众国诉考德威尔案"）都涉及"新闻记者特权"这个共同问题，1972 年美国最高法院因此予以合并审理。需要指出的是，在该案判决中，投出关键的第五张赞成票的刘易斯·鲍威尔（Lewis Powell）大法官尽管拒绝在该案中给予记者宪法特权，但他的简短的协同意见似乎又是支持相反观点，鲍威尔指出："法庭并不认为那些接到大陪审团传唤的新闻记者没有采集新闻的自由权利或者保守他们新闻来源秘密的权利。……特权主张是否正当，应当通过考察新闻自由与所有公民对于刑事犯罪的作证义务之间的适当平衡来判定。"其他提出反对意见的四位大法官也有分歧，其中威廉·道格拉斯（William O. Douglas）单独提出反对意见，他认为第一修正案直接产生了绝对的特权，以对抗强制性的披露新闻来源或信息。而波特·斯图尔特（Potter Stewart）、威廉·布伦南（William Brennan）和瑟古德·马歇尔（Thurgood Marshall）三位大法官则主张有条件的而非绝对的特权。他们认为当记者被要求在大陪审团面前出庭并披露秘密时，政府必须能够证明以下三点：（1）说明存在着可能的理由相信新闻记者掌握着与具体的违法行为有明显关联的消息；（2）证明其所寻求的信息不能通过其他对第一修正案损害较小的渠道获得；（3）证明该信息中包含着令人非信不可的和压倒一切的利益。上述引文来自：唐纳德·M. 吉尔摩等：《美国大众传播法：判例评析》（第六版），梁宁等译，清华大学出版社 2002 年版，第 306—318 页。另外，关于该案的详细判决结果可参阅 Branzburg vs. Hayes, 408 U. S. 665, United States Supreme Court, June 29, 1972.

的判决意见，即在刑事诉讼中通过传票强制披露资料将会导致打破记者的保密承诺这一事实本身并不是一种法律认可的第一修正案或普通法问题。而且判决意见指出，在"布莱兹伯格案"之后，第一巡回上诉法院在三个案件的审理中都确认了这个基本原则。因此，判决意见认为："如果新闻记者在'布莱兹伯格案'中的利益是不充分的，那么在该案中，学者的利益必然也是不充分的。……调查犯罪活动的选择属于政府，而不受制于学术研究者的否决。……很显然，莫洛尼与麦金太尔没有挑战传票的第一修正案依据。"需要指出的是，尽管第一巡回上诉法院否决了两位研究者提出的"学者特权"主张，不过同"布莱兹伯格案"一样，其中一位法官胡安·多鲁拉（Juan R. Torruella）在其发表的协同意见中表示："我勉强同意该案的判决，这样做只是因为我不得不同意最高法院关于'布莱兹伯格案'的判决意见。……在我看来，上诉人不能成功并不是因为他们缺乏第一修正案所认可的利益，而是因为诸如此类的利益经过最高法院的权衡之后，发现并不足以压倒政府在该案中的至关重要的利益。"而且，多鲁拉法官认为两位研究者应该具有独立介入此案的权利，因为他怀疑波士顿学院是否能够充分代表两位研究者的利益。① 或许正是基于这些理由，最高法院大法官布雷耶同意发出一项延缓执行第一巡回上诉法院裁决意见的命令，并等待莫洛尼和麦金太尔向美国最高法院提出调案复审令的请求。不过遗憾的是，普莱斯的突然去世令该案没有最终诉及美国最高法院，否则，该案有可能成为有关"学者特权"案件的经典审理判例。

综观该案和历史上美国各级法院有关"新闻记者特权"和"学者特权"② 的判例，可以发现法院并不认可新闻记者和学者拥有像律师和当事

---

① Ed Moloney; Anthony McIntyre vs. Eric H. Holder, Jr., Attorney General; Jack W. Pirozzolo, Commissioner, No. 12-1159, United States Court of Appeals for the First Circuit, July 6, 2012.

② 有关"新闻记者特权"的研究可参阅 Jason M. Shepard, *Privileging the Press: Confidential Sources, Journalism Ethics and the First Amendment*, El Paso: LFB Scholarly Publishing, 2011. 关于学术研究遭遇法院传票的相关研究可以参阅《法律与当代问题》（*Law and Contemporary Problems*）杂志刊登的专辑（"Court-Ordered Disclosure of Academic Research: A Clash of Values of Science and Law", Vol. 59, No. 3, 1996）。

人、医生和病人、牧师与悔罪者以及夫妻之间的拒绝提供证据或做证的绝对特权。因而在实践中，口述历史工作者也承认保密承诺等设限条件很难应对诸如信息自由请求和传票等法律挑战，哥伦比亚大学口述历史中心主任玛丽·克拉克（Mary Marshall Clark）教授就波士顿学院口述历史传票案接受《纽约时报》采访时就说，"这是我们面临的最糟糕的情况。"而且，她表示哥大口述历史计划的访谈者都会向受访者说明，即他们所说的任何东西在面对诸如传票这样的法院命令时都会被公布，因此要求他们签署知情同意书。① 不过，需要强调的是，美国各级法院的诸多判决都认可有条件的或有限的特权，那些已做出的否定特权存在的判决也都相当谨慎地权衡了双方对于不同利益的需求。在该案中，波士顿学院和两位研究者之所以败诉，很大程度上是因为法院认为政府在刑事诉讼中对于相关资料的需求超过研究机构（学者）对于保密性学术研究资料的保护需求。因此，有学者呼吁包括口述历史工作者在内的研究者应该努力争取获得保护学术研究保密性等设限权利的"学者特权"，否则，强制披露某些设限资料将会对未来的研究造成严重的"寒蝉效应"。②

五 口述历史伦理审查机制

在波士顿学院口述历史传票案中，作为口述历史计划的发起者、赞助者与保存者，波士顿学院被指在计划启动阶段缺乏必要的伦理审查与

---

① Jim Dwyer, "Secret Archive of Ulster Troubles Faces Subpoena", *The New York Times*, May 13, 2011. 当然也有学者认为一些口述历史计划之所以做出这样的声明是为了保护自己免受法律责任，一些口述历史学家质疑完全让受访者权衡或承担法律诉讼风险是否符合专业伦理？详细内容请参阅 David H. Mould, "Legal Issues", in Donna M. DeBlasio, Charles F. Ganzert, David H. Mould, Stephen H. Paschen and Howard L. Sacks, *Catching Stories: A Practical Guide to Oral History*, Athens: Ohio University Press, 2009, pp. 71-72.

② 时任美国口述历史协会第一副主席玛丽·拉尔森（Mary Larson）在评价波士顿学院口述历史传票案时就指出："我们口述历史学界所有人所担心的是这将会对我们所做的事情产生一种不可估量的寒蝉效应。"详细内容参阅 "Oral Historians Express Concern about Boston College Subpoena", *Oral History Association Newsletter*, Vol. 45, No. 2, Summer 2011, pp. 9, 11.

监管。这种审查与监管缺失主要体现在波士顿学院、计划主任、访谈者与受访者之间签署的相关协议中对于保密承诺条款的不同规定以及由此引发的不同理解，这也造成了波士顿学院与莫洛尼和麦金太尔之间在诉讼问题上的直接分歧与冲突。从相关协议可以发现，波士顿学院与莫洛尼签署的协议中明确规定赋予受访者的保密承诺只在美国法律允许的范围内受到保护。而莫洛尼与麦金太尔签署的协议以及波士顿学院与受访者签署的《捐赠协议》则没有明确指出这种保密承诺的有限性。① 因此，第一巡回上诉法院在 2012 年 7 月 6 日的判决意见中指出，如果波士顿学院与莫洛尼和麦金泰尔在保密承诺有限性的问题上达成共识的话，此次诉讼显然是可以避免的。同时，相关协议对于资料保密期限的规定也过于简单，而且考虑到这些相当敏感的口述历史资料的公开对于计划参与者与北爱和平进程的消极影响，波士顿学院被指在计划初始阶段没有征求必要的法律建议并实施尽职的伦理监管。具体而言就是"贝尔法斯特计划"在正式启动之前有没有接受波士顿学院伦理审查委员会的审查与批准？这个问题也反映了近十几年来美国口述史学界的一个争论焦点，即是否应该通过伦理审查委员会加强对口述历史工作潜在的法律与伦理问题的审查与监管？

随着"二战"期间的德国纳粹人体实验与持续 40 年的美国塔斯基吉梅毒试验（Tuskegee Syphilis Experiment）等人体试验丑闻事件的不断曝光，同时也因为 1947 年《纽伦堡公约》（*The Nuremberg Code*）与 1964 年

---

① 除上述提到的休斯的《捐赠协议》之外，已公开的还有该计划的另外两个协议，详细内容参阅 "Agreement between the Trustees of Boston College and Edward Moloney, Project Director, to Interview Members of Irish Republican Paramilitary Organizations and Provisional Sinn Fein Regarding their Role in the 'Trouble'", John J. Burns Library, Boston College, January 31, 2001; "Agreement between Ed Moloney, Director of Boston College/Burns Library Project to Interview Members of Irish Republican Paramilitary and Political Organizations Regarding their Role in the 'Trouble' and Anthony McIntyre, Lead Project Researcher", John J. Burns Library, Boston College, February 26, 2001. 需要强调的是，尽管第二个协议已明确指出它受第一个协议制约，可是如上所述，不管是访谈者还是受访者，他们认为保密承诺是绝对的，不然的话，他们根本不会参与这项计划。

《赫尔辛基宣言》（*The Declaration of Helsinki*）等重要文件的影响，美国学术界、公众与政府日益关注与重视生物医学研究的伦理问题。[①] 因此，在"以人为对象的研究"（human subjects research）中，为确保人类受试者（human subjects）的权利与福祉不受影响和侵害，从 20 世纪 50 年代以来，美国联邦政府就开始制定并颁布一系列政策文件和法规来规范研究过程中所涉及的伦理问题，并形成一套集监管法规、监管机构、监管程序和监管内容于一体的较为完善的伦理审查与监管体制。[②]

美国健康与人类服务部（Department of Health and Human Services）官方网站资料显示，目前，美国大部分"以人为对象的研究"的监管法律是由美国健康与人类服务部下属的人类研究保护办公室（Office for Human Research Protections，OHRP）负责监督与实施的《美国联邦法规》（Code of Federal Regulations）第 45 章第 46 部分（以下简称 45 CFR 46）。[③] 45 CFR 46 最早由美国健康、教育与福利部（Department of Health, Education and Welfare）于 1974 年颁布，目前生效并实施的法规修改于 2009 年，该

---

① George J. Annas and Michael A. Grodin（eds.），*The Nazi Doctors and the Nuremberg Code：Human Rights in Human Experimentation*，Oxford and New York：Oxford University Press，1992；James H. Jones，*Bad Blood：The Tuskegee Syphilis Experiment*，New York：The Free Press，new and expanded edition，1993；Susan K. Grove，Nancy Burns and Jennifer R. Gray，*The Practice of Nursing Research：Appraisal，Synthesis，and Generation of Evidence*，St. Louis：Saunders/Elsevier，2013，pp. 159-163.

② 有关美国"以人为对象的研究"的伦理审查与监管的历史，可参阅 Dennis M. Maloney，*Protection of Human Research Subjects：A Practical Guide to Federal Laws and Regulations*，New York：Plenum Press，1984；Bruce Gordon and Ernest Prentice，"Protection of Human Subjects in the United States：A Short History"，*Journal of Public Health Management and Practice*，Vol. 6，No. 6，2000，pp. 1-8；Todd W. Rice，"The Historical，Ethical and Legal Background of Human-Subjects Research"，*Respiratory Care*，Vol. 53，No. 10，2008，pp. 1325-1329；Zachary M. Schrag，"How Talking Became Human Subjects Research：The Federal Regulation of the Social Sciences，1965-1991"，*Journal of Policy History*，Vol. 21，No. 1，2009，pp. 3-37.

③ 此外还包括美国食品药品管理局（Food and Drug Administration）负责监督与实施的《美国联邦法规》第 21 章第 50、56、312 和 812 部分，主要针对药品、生物制剂与医疗器材的安全性与有效性管理。详细内容可以访问 http：//www. fda. gov/ScienceResearch/SpecialTopics/RunningClinicalTrials/ucm155713. htm（2015 年 7 月 28 日访问）。人类研究保护办公室创建于 2000 年，其前身是成立于 1974 年的研究风险保护办公室（Office for Protection from Research Risks），当时归属美国国家卫生研究院（National Institute of Health）。

法规包括5部分，其中 Subpart A 部分被称为"人类受试者保护联邦政策"（Federal Policy for the Protection of Human Subjects），同时从1991年开始该部分也被习称为"共同规则"（Common Rule）。另外，Subpart B-D 规定了对孕妇、胎儿、新生儿、囚犯和儿童等特殊弱势受试者的附加保护措施，Subpart E 规定了有关伦理审查委员会的登记问题。①

目前，"共同规则"被包括美国健康与人类服务部、国防部（Department of Defense）、教育部（Department of Education）、国家科学基金会（National Science Foundation）和中央情报局（Central Intelligence Agency）在内的18个联邦政府部门和机构所采纳。② 简言之，所有由联邦政府部门或机构执行或受其经费资助的"以人为对象的研究"都必须遵守此项规定，具体工作则由各机构（主要是大学与科研机构）所属的伦理审查委员会负责实施，由其决定是否批准研究或要求修改研究方案或拒绝批准研究。当然，"共同规则"明确强调伦理审查委员会在实质审查之前，首先需要认定该计划是否符合法律上的"研究"定义——所谓"研究"是指"旨在发展或有助于获得普遍性知识（generalizable knowledge）而进行的一种系统性调查（systematic investigation），包括研究发展、测试和评估"。"人类受试者"是指"研究者所研究的具有生命的个体（living individual）"，"研究者（无论是专业人士还是学生）通过对其进行干预或与之互动而获得资料或可识别的私人信息"③。

需要指出的，在实践过程中，美国的大部分研究机构（尤其是大学）为避免伦理危机或法律风险，都会要求该机构内那些并未获得联邦资助的

---

① 有关"45 CFR 46（2009）"的具体内容可访问 http：//www. hhs. gov/ohrp/humansubjects/guidance/45cfr46. html，2015年7月28日访问。

② 具体内容可访问 http：//www. hhs. gov/ohrp/humansubjects/commonrule/index. html，2015年7月28日访问。有关"共同规则"的发展历史，可参阅 Erin D. Williams, *Federal Protection for Human Research Subjects: An Analysis of the Common Rule and Its Interactions with FDA Regulations and the HIPAA Privacy Rule*, Washington: Congressional Research Service, Library of Congress, 2005.

③ 详细内容参阅"45 CFR 46. 102（2009）"，具体访问 http：//www. hhs. gov/ohrp/humansubjects/guidance/45cfr46. html#46. 102，2015年7月28日访问。

研究计划接受伦理审查委员会的审查与监管。①同时，这项主要适用于生物医学和行为研究伦理规范的联邦法规也不断向人文社会科学领域扩张，这些领域的研究者（包括学生）在从事"以人为对象的研究"时都必须合乎伦理审查委员会的规范要求，当然也随之引起众多学者的质疑与批评。

概括而言，对于美国伦理审查委员会制度运作弊端的批评与争议主要体现在基本原则与技术层面两个方面。就前者而言，诸多组织和学者质疑有关伦理审查委员会的联邦法规违反美国宪法第一修正案赋予研究者的言论与出版自由以及思想与研究（学术）自由。②其中以美国大学教授协会

---

① Richard A. Shweder, "Protecting Human Subjects and Preserving Academic Freedom: Prospects at the University of Chicago", *American Ethnologist*, Vol. 33, No. 4, 2006, pp. 507-508. 美国乔治梅森大学（George Mason University）历史学副教授扎克利·施拉格（Zachary M. Schrag）博士认为我们现在理解的美国伦理审查委员会制度创建于1966年2月美国健康、教育与福利部下属的公共卫生署（Public Health Service）署长（Surgeon General）威廉·斯图尔特（William Stewart）发布的有关人类受试者研究的政策声明，该政策声明则起源于全国健康咨询委员会（National Advisory Health Council）于1965年12月发布的有关人类受试者研究的政策决议。上述信息来自施拉格博士于2014年1月24日给笔者的电子邮件回信。其他相关研究可参阅 "Surgeon General's Directives on Human Experimentation", *The American Psychologist*, Vol. 22, No. 5, 1967, pp. 350-355; Max Sherman and John D. Van Vleet, "The History of Institutional Review Boards", *Regulatory Affairs Journal*, Vol. 3, 1991, pp. 615-627; Charles R. MacKay, "The Evolution of the Institutional Review Board: A Brief Overview of its History", *Clinical Research and Regulatory Affairs*, Vol. 12, No. 2, 1995, pp. 65-94; Hazel Glenn Beh, "The Role of Institutional Review Boards in Protecting Human Subjects: Are We Really Ready to Fix a Broken System?" *Law & Psychology Review*, Vol. 26, No. 1, 2002, pp. 1-47; Paul A. Buelow, "The Institutional Review Board: A Brief History of Attempts to Protect Human Subjects in Research", *Clinical Nurse Specialist*, Vol. 25, No. 6, 2011, pp. 277-280; Laura Stark, *Behind Closed Doors: IRBs and the Making of Ethical Research*, Chicago: University of Chicago Press, 2012. 另据《纽约时报》报道，到2011年全美伦理审查委员会总数超过5875个。详细内容参阅 Patricia Cohen, "Questioning Privacy Protections in Research", *New York Times*, 24 October 2011.

② Philip Hamburger, "The New Censorship: Institutional Review Boards", *The Supreme Court Review*, Vol. 2004, 2004, pp. 271-354; Robert L. Kerr, "Unconstitutional Review Board? Considering a First Amendment Challenge to IRB Regulation of Journalistic Research Methods", *Communication Law and Policy*, Vol. 11, No. 3, 2006, pp. 393-447; James Weinstein, "Institutional Review Boards and the Constitution", *Northwestern University Law Review*, Vol. 101, No. 2, 2007, pp. 493-562; Elmer D. Abbo, "Promoting Free Speech in Clinical Quality Improvement Research", *Northwestern University Law Review*, Vol. 101, No. 2, 2007, pp. 575-591; Renée Lettow Lerner, "Unconstitutional Conditions, Germaneness, and Institutional Review Boards", *Northwestern University Law Review*, Vol. 101, No. 2, 2007, pp. 775-789; Jonathan Moss, "If Institutional Review Boards Were Declared Unconstitutional, They Would Have to be Reinvented", *Northwestern University Law Review*, Vol. 101, No. 2, 2007, pp. 801-807; William G. Tierney and Zoë Blumberg Corwin, "The Tensions between Academic Freedom and Institutional Review Boards", *Qualitative Inquiry*, Vol. 13, No. 3, 2007, pp. 388-398; Philip Hamburger, "IRB Licensing", in Akeel Bilgrami and Jonathan R. Cole (eds.), *Who's Afraid of Academic Freedom*? New York: Columbia University Press, 2015, pp. 153-189.

(American Association of University Professors) 最具代表性，该组织从 20 世纪 80 年代起就发布系列报告批评伦理审查委员会对于学术自由的影响与侵犯，并极力主张改革或豁免某些研究类型的伦理审查与监管。① 针对技术层面的批评则主要包括以下几个方面：（1）由于需要遵守特定的审查程序，因而比较容易出现扼杀研究创新性的可能性；（2）由于联邦法规所规定的"研究"定义很难明确界定，因而经常引发伦理审查委员会与研究者在判定提议的研究计划是否属于联邦法规所定义的"研究"范畴这个问题上产生冲突与争执；（3）当出现违反相关法规的情况时，到底应该履行怎样的程序和负担怎样的法律责任以及最终的法律责任归属（是研究者还是研究者所在的机构）等问题都不尽清楚；（4）由于审查规范趋于严格以及审查延宕，因而极容易影响研究成果的产出效率；（5）大部分伦理审查委员会成员由临床与生物医学研究领域的专家组成，他们经常对人文社会科学研究计划的审查施加诸多不合理与无关要求。②

---

① American Association of University Professors, "Regulations Governing Research on Human Subjects: Academic Freedom and the Institutional Review Board", *Academe*, Vol. 67, No. 6, 1981, pp. 358-370; American Association of University Professors, "Protecting Human Beings: Institutional Review Boards and Social Science Research", *Academe*, Vol. 87, No. 3, 2001, pp. 55-67; Jonathan T. Church, Linda Shopes and Margaret A. Blanchard, "Should All Disciplines Be Subject to the Common Rule? Human Subjects of Social Science Research", *Academe*, Vol. 88, No. 3, 2002, pp. 62-69; Judith Jarvis Thomson, Catherine Elgin, David A. Hyman, Philip E. Rubin and Jonathan Knight, "Research on Human Subjects: Academic Freedom and the Institutional Review Board", *Academe*, Vol. 92, No. 5, 2006, pp. 95-100; Judith Jarvis Thomson, Catherine Elgin, David A. Hyman, Zachary Schrag and Jonathan Knight, "Regulation of Research on Human Subjects: Academic Freedom and the Institutional Review Board", *Academe*, Vol. 99, No. 4, 2013, pp. 101-117.

② C. Kristina Gunsalus, "Human Subject Protections: Some Thoughts on Costs and Benefits in the Humanistic Disciplines", Illinois Public Law Research Paper No. 03-02, March 2003; Caroline H. Bledsoe, Bruce Sherin, Adam G. Galinsky, Nathalia M. Headley, Carol A. Heimer, Erik Kjedgaard, James Lindgren, John D. Miller, Michael E. Roloff and David H. Uttal, "Regulating Creativity: Research and Survival in the IRB Iron Cage", *Northwestern University Law Review*, Vol. 101, No. 2, 2007, pp. 593-641; Robert Charrow, "Protection of Human Subjects: Is Expansive Regulation Counter-Productive?" *Northwestern University Law Review*, Vol. 101, No. 2, 2007, pp. 702-721; David A. Hyman, "The Pathologies of Institutional Review Boards", *Regulation*, Vol. 30, No. 2, 2007, pp. 42-49.

上述联邦法规适用范围的过度扩张以及由此引发的各种弊端,使得美国伦理审查委员会制度成为备受质疑与批评的主要目标,甚至有研究机构和学者将这种伦理规范的过度审查与监管称为"任务蠕变"(mission creep)和"伦理帝国主义"(ethical imperialism),[1] 伦理审查委员会也被贬为"学术官僚机构"(academic bureaucracies)和"审查之手"(censor's hand)。[2]

同其他大部分人文社会科学一样,口述史学作为一种主要基于活生生的事件当事人与目击者口述回忆的互动性访谈方法与研究领域,它自然也逐渐成为伦理审查委员会的审查对象。现有资料显示,美国口述历史学界有关口述历史伦理审查问题讨论的最早记录可能是在1988年,当时有一位大学教授询问时任美国口述历史协会执行秘书(Executive Secretary)理查德·史密斯如何评论他所在大学所发布的有关口述历史研究计划需要接受伦理审查的监管指南,该教授担心访谈需要事先接受伦理审查与批准可能会对访谈者产生一种寒蝉效应。不过,理查德·史密斯拒绝直接评论伦理审查问题本身,他更关注的是诸如此类的审查标准是否符合最佳的专业实务原则,并因此能够根据美国口述历史协会于1979年颁布并即将于1989年修订的《口述历史评估指南》进行调整。理查德·史密斯继续指出,除了事先向受访者提供访谈问题副本这一要求之外,他认为该校伦理审查的大部分条例都符合口述历史运动的目标,尤其强调研究对象能够很好地了解研究者的目的。当然,他认为这项主要

---

[1] University of Illinois Center for Advanced Study, *Improving the System for Protecting Subjects: Counteracting IRB Mission Creep*, University of Illinois Law & Economics Research Paper No. LE06-016, 2005; Ronald F. White, "Institutional Review Board Mission Creep: The Common Rule, Social Science, and the Nanny State", *The Independent Review*, Vol. 11, No. 3, 2007, pp. 547-564; Zachary M. Schrag, *Ethical Imperialism: Institutional Review Boards and the Social Sciences, 1965-2009*, Baltimore: Johns Hopkins University Press, 2010.

[2] Todd J. Zywicki, "Institutional Review Boards as Academic Bureaucracies: An Economic and Experiential Analysis", *Northwestern University Law Review*, Vol. 101, No. 2, 2007, pp. 861-896; Carl E. Schneider, *The Censor's Hand: The Misregulation of Human-Subject Research*, Cambridge: The MIT Press, 2015.

适用于科学研究的监管条例也存在许多重要疏忽，其中最重要的是缺乏那些厘定著作权归属与访谈设限条件等问题的法律协议。最后，理查德·史密斯指出，大学对于口述历史计划实施伦理审查可能仅仅是一种侥幸，但也可能是这个领域未来发展的一种迹象。因为机构为了使自己免受法律诉讼风险，它们会采取那些主要适用于科学领域的伦理审查政策和程序，而不会考虑诸如此类的监管是否可能促进或阻碍人文科学研究。①

　　当然，总体而言，在 20 世纪 90 年代初之前，美国伦理审查委员会制度对于口述历史研究计划的审查与监管还不是那么普遍与严格，甚至大部分口述历史工作者都没有意识到伦理审查委员会的存在。② 不过，发生于 1995 年的一件针对口述历史访谈伦理审查问题的事件令美国口述史学界真正意识到了伦理审查委员会对于他们的影响。当时特拉华大学（University of Delaware）拒绝接受该校历史系一位研究生所提交的已经通过答辩的博士论文，因为该研究生在博士学位论文中所使用的部分口述历史访谈资料并未事先经过该校伦理审查委员会的审查与批准。尽管该研究生最终获得了审查委员会追加的豁免证明和博士学位，不过该事件却引发了美国口述史学界对于伦理审查制度的激烈争论与深刻反思。③

① Richard Cándida Smith, "From the Executive Secretary", *Oral History Association Newsletter*, Vol. 22, No. 4, Winter 1988, p. 5. 需要指出的是，该期《口述历史协会通讯》将出版日期错写为 1989 年。

② 据施拉格教授回忆，1998 年他参加哥伦比亚大学口述历史研究室主任罗纳德·格里教授主持的口述历史研究生研习班时，尽管花了很多时间讨论方法和伦理问题，可是从来没有任何人谈及伦理审查委员会。他自己也是直到 2000 年获得国家科学基金会博士论文资助进行一项有关华盛顿地铁发展历史的研究时（该研究需要进行口述历史访谈）才首次了解到需要从所在大学的伦理审查委员会获得批准。详细内容参阅 Zachary M. Schrag, *Ethical Imperialism: Institutional Review Boards and the Social Sciences, 1965-2009*, Baltimore: Johns Hopkins University Press, 2010, pp. ix and 145; Robert B. Townsend, "Ethical Imperialism: A Conversation with Zachary Schrag", *Perspectives on History*, April 2011.

③ Donald A. Ritchie, *Doing Oral History*, Oxford and New York: Oxford University Press, third edition, 2014, p. 228.

　　同时，随着美国伦理审查制度向人文社会科学领域的急剧扩张，该制度的弊端与争议给口述历史工作者带来越来越多的挑战与困难。具体而言，主要包括在正式进行任何口述历史计划之前，研究者被要求向他们所在机构的伦理审查委员会提交该计划的研究方案，其中包括详细的访谈提纲；而且还要求研究者参加有关伦理规范的烦琐培训并填写大量无关表格。同时，伦理审查委员会还提出一系列限制条件，比如要求受访者保持匿名（即使受访者同意公开身份）；在访谈过程中尽量不要提问那些可能令受访者或他人尴尬、遭遇法律责任和心理伤害乃至人身危险的问题；在访谈过程中不能提问那些在预先提交的访谈提纲中没有列出的问题；以及在研究计划结束之后要求销毁录音（录影）资料和抄本。[1] 这些要求与限制条件显然与口述历史实践的基本原则及研究方法背道而驰，尤其对于涉及政治（社会）运动、内战、绑架和谋杀等敏感主题的口述历史计划来说将会带来相当严重的消极影响。因此，口述历史学家也日益关注和担心伦理审查委员会的过度审查与监管会对口述历史产生"寒蝉效应"，甚至侵犯他们的学术自由。[2]

　　如上所述，发生于 1995 年的特拉华大学博士学位论文事件引发了美国口述史学界对于伦理审查问题的激烈争论和担忧。在 1996 年秋冬之际，研究风险保护办公室和美国口述历史协会提议修改美国历史协会于

---

① American Association of University Professors, "Protecting Human Beings: Institutional Review Boards and Social Science Research", p. 57; Linda Shopes, "Oral History", in Norman K. Denzin and Yvonna S. Lincoln (eds.), *The Sage Handbook of Qualitative Research*, Thousand Oaks: Sage Publications, fourth edition, 2011, p. 462; Linda Shopes, "Human Subjects and IRB Review", in Doug Boyd, Steve Cohen, Brad Rakerd, and Dean Rehberger (eds.), *Oral History in the Digital Age*, Washington: Institute of Museum and Library Services, 2012, http://ohda.matrix.msu.edu/2012/08/human-subjects-and-irb-review/, 2015 年 7 月 28 日访问。

② Linda Shopes, "Institutional Review Boards Have a Chilling Effect on Oral History", *Perspectives on History*, September 2000; Cary Nelson, "Can E. T. Phone Home? The Brave New World of University Surveillance", *Academe*, Vol. 89, No. 5, 2003, pp. 30-35; Jennifer Howard, "Oral History Under Review", *The Chronicle of Higher Education*, November 10, 2006.

1989 年 5 月采纳的《为历史记录所做访谈的声明》(Statement on Interviewing for Historical Documentation),[1] 新增内容旨在警告历史学家,如果在他们的研究中涉及以人为对象的访谈方法,他们必须遵守相关的联邦法规。这些修改意见分别于 1997 年 3 月和 6 月被美国历史协会专业部 (Professional Division) 和理事会 (AHA Council) 所采纳,《为历史记录所做访谈的声明》于 1998 年 1 月正式修订并生效。[2] 基于此,美国历史协会和口述历史协会建议历史学家应当了解和遵守所有适用于他们的研究活动的法律、条例和机构政策,甚至有口述历史学家建议同联邦官员沟通以确定自愿遵守口述历史协会的《评估指南》是否可以被看成研究者保护受试者的一种合理的和充分的努力。[3] 不过,大部分历史学家(尤其是口述历史学家)仍然认为基于生物医学与行为科学研究的伦理审查制度并不适用于他们的研究工作,美国历史协会和口述历史协会也断断续续收到其会员对于大学伦理审查委员会审查与监管政策的抱怨。

由此,从 20 世纪 90 年代后期开始,美国历史协会和口述历史协会等历史学组织与一些著名口述历史学家就积极与联邦政府主管人类受试者保护的机构进行磋商和斡旋,希望推动口述历史伦理审查制度的改革,它(他)们主张应该将口述历史直接排除在审查范围之外。这种最初努

---

[1] "AHA Adopts Statement on Interviewing for Historical Documentation", *Oral History Association Newsletter*, Vol. 23, No. 3, Fall 1989, p. 3.

[2] Michael A. Gordon, "Historians and Review Boards", *Perspectives on History*, September 1997. 《为历史记录所做访谈的声明》全文请访问 http://harvey. binghamton. edu/ ~ hist266/oral/statement. htm, 2015 年 7 月 29 日访问。该声明是美国历史协会《职业行为规范声明》(Statement on Standards of Professional Conduct) 的一部分,后者请访问 http://www. historians. org/about-aha-and-membership/governance/policies-and-documents/statement -on-standards-of-professional-conduct, 2015 年 7 月 29 日访问。

[3] 转引自 Zachary M. Schrag, *Ethical Imperialism: Institutional Review Boards and the Social Sciences, 1965-2009*, Baltimore: Johns Hopkins University Press, 2010, p. 146; Richard Candida Smith, "Council Considers Proposed Human Subjects Guidelines", *Oral History Association Newsletter*, Vol. 31, No. 2, Spring 1997, p. 12.

力始于 1997 年，当年 9 月三位著名口述历史学家理查德·史密斯（时任口述历史协会主席）、琳达·肖普斯（时任口述历史协会副主席、候任主席）和霍华德·格林（Howard Green，时任口述历史协会第一副主席）与时任研究风险保护办公室主任加里·埃利斯（Gary B. Ellis）以及托马斯·帕古里斯（Thomas Puglisi）和米歇尔·拉塞尔-艾因霍恩（Michele Russell-Einhorn）两位官员举行会晤。此次会晤一方面是要让历史学界更多地了解有关人类受试者研究监管的联邦法规和伦理审查委员会的运作机制；另一方面也希望研究风险保护办公室了解历史研究（尤其是口述历史）的专业规范。在这次被琳达·肖普斯称为"友善的和非正式的"会晤中，托马斯·帕古里斯认为口述历史协会的《评估指南》与监管人类受试者研究的联邦法规并非不相容。不过，联邦官员进一步建议在开始可能包括口述历史访谈的任何研究之前，历史学家应当联系他们所在大学的伦理审查委员会，以了解和咨询有关人类受试者研究所涉及的政策和条例。简言之，尽管研究风险保护办公室官员支持和认可口述历史协会等专业学术组织的专业规范和伦理指南，但仍然强调它们并不能代替大学伦理审查委员会的审查与监管。对于这些建议，历史学界尽管心存忧虑，但最终还是接受并将相关内容增加到 1998 年 1 月正式修订并生效的《为历史记录所做访谈的声明》中。同时，在 1997—1998 年间，口述历史协会将它们自己和美国历史协会的专业规范与伦理指南副本发给全国各大学历史学与美国研究专业的研究生部主任，并通知他们：历史学家在进行口述历史研究之前需要事先联系他们所在大学的伦理审查委员会。① 在此次会晤的最后，加里·埃利斯向三位口述历史学家透露说他们的办公室正准备修改符合"快速审查"的那些属于最低风险的研

---

① Linda Shopes，"Institutional Review Boards Have a Chilling Effect on Oral History"，*Perspectives on History*，September 2000.

究类型目录，他还建议他们推荐口述历史纳入这个目录中。①

随后，美国健康与人类服务部决定修改有关人类受试者研究的监管条例。1997 年 11 月，研究风险保护办公室就扩展符合"快速审查"的研究类型的提议向社会广泛征求意见。② 在意见征求的截止日期 1998 年 3 月，办公室总共收到 108 份书面意见，其中绝大部分涉及医学或药物研究，跟口述历史相关的书面意见有 6 份。在这 6 份书面意见中，其中一份由美国口述历史协会起草并获得美国历史协会、美国历史学家组织和美国研究协会（American Studies Association）的赞同，意见起草负责人琳达·肖普斯认为新条例正确地假设大部分口述历史计划对于受访者来说只是包含最低风险，因此可能有助于确保伦理审查委员会无须根据主要针对医学和行为科学研究的标准来审查口述历史计划。显然，在医学和行为科学研究中，受试者所面临的风险的确会更大。她继续指出，如果要符合"快速审查"的条件，口述历史计划必须提供知情同意书和由受访者签名的法律授权

---

① 就审查类型而言，各个伦理审查委员会以目前实施的 45 CFR 46（2009）为依据并根据研究活动所涉及的风险程度高低将其分为"豁免审查"（exempt review）、"快速审查"（expedited review）和"一般审查"（又名全体委员会审查，full-board or full-committee review）。"豁免审查"的研究计划一般是属于风险程度极低或零风险，45 CFR 46.101（b）（2009）规定 6 种情况可以列为"豁免审查"，尽管列为"豁免审查"类型，不过它们仍然需要接受伦理审查委员会的审查并进行登记。而那些风险程度低于最低风险（minimal risk）的研究计划或已经获得 IRB 批准并且研究方案仅有微小变化的研究计划则适用于"快速审查"，而且 45 CFR 46.110（a）（2009）还罗列了 9 种研究范畴可以列为"快速审查"。上述两种审查类型可以由伦理审查委员会主席单独审查或由主席指定一名或多名富有经验的委员进行审查。那些不符合豁免和快速审查类型或风险程度高于最低风险的研究计划则需要进行一般审查，即由伦理审查委员会召集法定到会人数对研究计划进行审查，45 CFR 46.108（b）（2009）要求与会者必须占全体委员的大多数，并且其中一名必须来自非科学领域。而至于"豁免审查"与"排除审查"（excluded review）之间的区别，美国历史协会（American Historical Association）曾经做出说明，即如果一个口述历史计划符合联邦法规所定义的"研究"类型，该计划可能会被豁免审查，不过必须向伦理审查委员会提出申请并由其根据"共同规则"所规定的豁免类型来决定是否豁免。"排除审查"是指如果研究者认为一个口述历史计划不符合联邦法规所定义的"研究"类型，他们可以无须咨询伦理审查委员会而直接启动计划。详细参阅 American Historical Association，"Questions Regarding the Policy Statement"，10 November，2003，http://web.archive.org/web/20050306090426/http://www.historians.org/press/2003-11-10IRB.htm，2015 年 7 月 28 日访问。

② Department of Health and Human Services，"Protection of Human Subjects：Suggested Revisions to the Institutional Review Board（IRB）Expedited Review List"，*Federal Register*，Vol. 62，No. 217，November 10，1997，pp. 60607-60611.

书。1998 年 11 月，新规则正式将口述历史纳入"快速审查"的研究类型，这项政策被认为是联邦政府有关口述历史伦理审查与监管的第一次明确阐述。它的颁布也引起历史学界的积极回应，威斯康星大学密尔沃基分校（University of Wisconsin-Milwaukee）历史系的迈克尔·格登（Michael A. Gordon）认为新联邦规则是明智的，并且会让事情变得更加容易，尤其对于那些即将从事口述历史计划和已经做了许多访谈的人来说。不过，他也强调没有伦理审查委员会的严密监管，并不意味着我们没有责任维持更高的伦理标准。美国口述历史协会前主席唐纳德·里奇也强调维持高伦理标准的重要性，他进一步指出，任何遵循口述历史协会《评估指南》的口述历史学家应该不会太难满足研究风险保护办公室或他们所在大学伦理审查委员会的要求。同时，他也认为将口述历史列入"快速审查"范围将有助于历史学界的其他人更加意识到访谈需要适当的伦理标准。[1] 当然，也有历史学家表示反对，佛罗里达州立大学（Florida State University）历史学教授尼尔·朱蒙维拉（Neil Jumonville）就认为美国历史协会等组织在有关历史研究伦理审查问题上的顺从态度（包括同意将口述历史列入"快速审查"研究类型）是相当令人不安的，（过分监管）所造成的最糟糕影响可能会像麦卡锡主义（McCarthyism）那样。[2]

需要指出的是，到 20 世纪 90 年代末期，美国社会科学界对于伦理审

---

[1]　详细内容参阅 Rebecca Sharpless, Sandria Freitag, and Arnita Jones, "Memo on Review of O-ral History Based Research Projects", March 1998；Department of Health and Human Services, "Protec-tion of Human Subjects: Categories of Research That May Be Reviewed by the Institutional Review Board (IRB) Through an Expedited Review Procedure", *Federal Register*, Vol. 63, No. 216, November 9, 1998, pp. 60364-60367；"OHA Involved in New Rules Affecting Academic Oral Historians", *Oral History Association Newsletter*, Vol. 33, No. 1, Winter 1999, p. 3.

[2]　Christopher Shea, "Don't Talk to the Humans: The Crackdown on Social Science Research", *Lingua Franca: The Review of Academic Life*, Vol. 10, No. 6, September 2000, p. 27. 1999 年 6 月 23 日，朱蒙维拉在"口述历史论坛"上发帖指出，佛罗里达州立大学伦理审查委员会已经将其审查与监管对象扩展到那些并不受联邦经费资助或支持的口述历史访谈计划。他担心伦理审查委员会向那些从来没有试图涵盖的领域的扩展会对学术自由产生影响。1998 年 10 月，因为他的研究生所开展的一项涉及访谈的研究计划需要接受审查，导致他与该校伦理审查委员会之间的关系相当紧张。详细内容访问 http://h-net. msu. edu/cgi-bin/logbrowse. pl? trx = vx&list = h-oralhist&month = 9906&week = d&msg = fV4vEHvA2BkfNJxZDFYCyQ&user = &pw = , 2015 年 7 月 29 日访问。

查委员会运作机制的批评也日益增多。在 1999 年 11 月—2000 年 5 月之间，美国大学教授协会召集来自美国人类学协会（American Anthropological Association）、美国历史协会、美国政治科学协会（American Political Science Association）、美国社会学协会（American Sociological Association）、美国口述历史协会和美国历史学家组织的代表举行多次会议，主要分享和讨论这些学术组织的成员在从事有关人类受试者研究过程中所遭遇的伦理审查与监管经历。其中，琳达·肖普斯和唐纳德·里奇分别代表美国历史协会和美国口述历史协会，他们通过相关学术组织的通信进行调查并展示其成员对于伦理审查制度的看法与意见。总体而言，历史学界的回应显示了他们对于大学伦理审查委员会运作机制的失望与不满，认为审查制度严重违反历史研究原则且破坏学术研究自由。同历史学界一样，其他社会科学界的反应也相近。可是，根据这些会议议题并由美国大学教授协会于 2001 年发布的研究报告也仅仅是提倡适度修改伦理审查委员会针对社会科学研究的审查与监管方式，甚至援引 1998 年联邦规则作为暗示，强调伦理审查委员会正在努力使自身适应不断变化的环境，以满足社会科学家的特殊需求，同时又能完成它们保护人类受试者的要求。①

尽管 1998 年的联邦规则将口述历史纳入"快速审查"的研究类型，但这并未缓和史学界对于口述历史伦理审查制度的不满与激烈抨击。② 作为口述历史伦理审查制度改革的主要推动者，琳达·肖普斯也一改之前的较为渐进的改革主张。在 2000 年 4 月举行的国家生物伦理顾问委员会

---

① American Association of University Professors, "Protecting Human Beings: Institutional Review Boards and Social Science Research", pp. 55-67; "Oral Historians Asked About Institutional Review Boards", *Oral History Association Newsletter*, Vol. 34, No. 1, Winter 2000, p. 3; Donald Ritchie, "Institutional Review Boards and Oral History", *Oral History Association Newsletter*, Vol. 35, No. 3, Fall 2001, p. 4; Linda Shopes, "Historians and Institutional Review Boards: An Update", *Perspectives on History*, October 2001.

② "Panelists Defend, Criticize Campus IRB Process", *Oral History Association Newsletter*, Vol. 35, No. 4, Winter 2001, pp. 6-7.

（National Bioethics Advisory Commission）会议上，①·她对于保护人类受试者的联邦法规提出尖锐批评，认为基于生物医学与行为科学研究的伦理审查与监管模式并不适用于口述历史研究，因为口述历史研究有其自身的原则与规范；而且还会严重威胁和破坏学术自由原则。她甚至暗示要进行一种更为激进的改革，即口述历史不应当受制于伦理委员会的审查，对口述历史研究计划的审查应该由院系同行根据口述历史协会的《原则与标准》和《评估指南》以及美国历史协会的《为历史记录所做访谈的声明》等专业规范来进行。在她看来，这种做法有助于防止对人类受试者的不道德对待，同时又不侵犯历史学家的专业实践或危害自由研究。② 琳达·肖普斯的批评与改革建议得到一部分历史学家的积极回应，伊利诺伊州立大学（Illinois State University）历史系 15 位成员高度赞扬她的努力，并且主张通过新的立法来完全豁免口述历史的伦理审查；他们还建议在与联邦官员和国会工作人员的讨论中，美国历史协会与社会科学和人文科学的其他合作机构应当强调学术自由乃至审查扩张所造成的宪法关切。③

　　由此，历史学界开始通过与相关组织和个人的合作转而寻求如何将口述历史排除在伦理委员会的审查范围之外。2000 年 8 月，琳达·肖普斯与另外一位历史学家同国会议员戴安娜·德格特（Diana DeGette）会面，当时德格特正在起草一份旨在修改保护人类受试者的联邦法规的议案，他们的目标就是尽可能明确地将口述历史排除在审查范围之外。同年 11 月，时任美国社会学协会执行主任菲利斯·莱文（Felice Levine）也倾向于这种

---

　　① 国家生物伦理顾问委员会于 1996 年由克林顿总统任命成立，并于 2001 年期满解散。2001年 11 月，小布什总统任命成立总统生物伦理委员会（The President's Council on Bioethics）；2009年 11 月，奥巴马（Barack Hussein Obama, 1961—）总统任命成立生物伦理问题研究总统委员会（Presidential Commission for the Study of Bioethical Issues），总统生物伦理委员会也随之解散。前者是一个负责向白宫和其他政府机构建议和推荐有关人类受试者研究所产生的生物伦理问题的总统委员会，后两者的职能是就生物医学科学和技术发展所造成的生物伦理问题向总统提出建议。

　　② Linda Shopes, "Institutional Review Boards Have a Chilling Effect on Oral History", *Perspectives on History*, September 2000.

　　③ Members of the Illinois State University History Department, "IRBs and History Research", *Perspectives on History*, January 2001.

做法，并且暗示诸如历史学和新闻学等人文学科相对于社会科学来说应该更少接受伦理委员会的审查与监管。① 国家生物伦理顾问委员会于 2011 年 8 月发布的报告也表达了类似观点，该报告指出："许多科学探索领域都是'研究'，而且许多研究也涉及人类参与者，但只有一些需要联邦监管，而其他研究通过专业伦理、社会习俗或其他州和联邦法律可能会得到更好的监管。比如，某些类型的调查和访谈被认为是研究，但是它们无须联邦监管就可以很好地避免伤害，因为这些风险是很小的，而且参与者也能很好地自行决定他们是否参与研究。"最后，报告也建议联邦政策应当明确地确认哪些类型的研究需要接受审查以及哪些类型的研究参与者需要获得保护。②

简而言之，这种排除审查策略的核心思路就是希望主管机构能够相信包括口述历史在内的历史研究并不是联邦法规所定义的"研究"类型。1999 年美国国家科学技术委员会人类受试者研究小组委员会（Human Subjects Research Subcommittee，National Science and Technology Council）的一个工作组就曾主张受制于"共同规则"监管的研究类型通常不包括新闻学、历史学、传记、哲学、"实情调查"研究（"fact-finding" inquiries）和简单的资料收集（data collection），等等。③ 2000 年 12 月，与罗格斯大学（Rutgers University）伦理审查委员会有过纠葛的历史学家迈克尔·卡哈特（Michael Carhart）也主张历史学不是现有的联邦法规所定义的"研究"类型，因为它根本不是一门科学。他进一步指出："我相信伦理审查委员会条例是针对所有那些能够创造普遍性知识的研究，而历史学的全部意义在于我们的结论并不是普遍性的。历史学家们并不会像社会科学或自然科学那样去预测将来，我们研究的整个前提是描述那些集合在一种独特环境

---

① Zachary M. Schrag, *Ethical Imperialism: Institutional Review Boards and the Social Sciences, 1965-2009*, Baltimore: Johns Hopkins University Press, 2010, p. 154.

② National Bioethics Advisory Commission, *Ethical and Policy Issues in Research Involving Human Participants*, Summary Report (Summary), Bethesda, Maryland, August 2001, p. 7.

③ James D. Shelton, "How to Interpret the Federal Policy for the Protection of Human Subjects or 'Common Rule' (Part A)", *IRB: Ethics and Human Research*, Vol. 21, No. 6, 1999, p. 6.

配置下的事件。"其实，对于像琳达·肖普斯这样的要求将口述历史排除在审查范围之外的倡导者而言，她们最初对于这种策略也有些许担忧，因为这意味着口述历史研究将不是联邦法规所认可的研究类型，因而担心资助机构可能不会对这些计划提供经费资助。不过，在 2001 年 9 月，时任美国国家卫生研究院人类受试者研究保护主管艾伦·桑德勒（Alan L. Sandler）就承认他们所开展的口述历史项目就没有接受伦理审查委员会的审查，其理由是口述历史并不是为了获得普遍性知识。① 这种主张成为琳达·肖普斯等历史学家坚持采纳排除审查策略的重要动力，于是，在 2002 年 1 月 29 日召开的美国健康与人类服务部国家人类研究保护顾问委员会（National Human Research Protections Advisory Committee）会议上，她严正指出："历史学家并不追求普遍性知识，而这个术语看上去正是 45 CFR 46 所使用的。"②

在接下来的一年多时间里，经过美国历史协会与口述历史协会的内部交流以及与相关联邦部门的积极沟通，口述历史伦理审查问题终于取得重大进展。2003 年 8 月 26 日，琳达·肖普斯和唐纳德·里奇起草了一份政策声明，声明的主旨是大多数口述历史访谈计划可以排除在伦理审查委员会的审查范围之外。令人意想不到的是，在 2003 年 9 月 22 日给琳达·肖普斯和唐纳德·里奇的信件中，时任人类研究保护办公室监管事务副主任（Associate Director for Regulatory Affairs）迈克尔·卡罗姆表示原则上同意她们的提议，不过部分表述需要修改。修改后的政策声明指出："大多数口述历史访谈计划不受制于 45 CFR part 46 subpart A 中所规定的健康与人类服务部的人类受试者保护条例的要求，可以排除在伦理审查委员会监管之外，因为它们并不包含健康与人类服务部条例所定义的'研究'。……

---

① Zachary M. Schrag, *Ethical Imperialism*: *Institutional Review Boards and the Social Sciences*, *1965-2009*, Baltimore: Johns Hopkins University Press, 2010, pp. 154-155. 有关国家卫生研究院的口述历史项目，请访问 http://history. nih. gov/archives/oral_ histories. html, 2015 年 7 月 29 日访问。

② Department of Health and Human Services, *Meeting of the National Human Research Protections Advisory Committee*, Bethesda, Maryland, 29 January 2002.

其主要理由是口述历史访谈一般而言（in general）不是为了有助于获得'普遍性知识'，它们不受制于 45 CFR part 46 中所规定的健康与人类服务部条例的要求，因而能够被伦理委员会排除在审查之外。……尽管历史学家追求超越他们的特定研究对象的意义，不过不像生物医学和行为科学的研究者，他们不是追求历史或社会发展的普遍性原则，他们也不是追求具有预见价值和能够被应用于其他条件（目的是为了控制结果）的根本原则或自然法则。历史学家解释一种特定的过去；他们不是为了得出有关发生在过去的全部内容的普遍解释，他们也不是预测未来。"① 对于这项政策声明，在 2003 年 10 月举行的美国口述历史协会年会上，人类研究保护办公室教育与发展部（Division of Education and Development）的乔治·波斯皮斯尔（George Pospisil）再次予以重申。尽管上述政策声明所增加的"一般而言"这个定语为后续的政策解释与执行带来了诸多不确定性因素，而且迈克尔·卡罗姆还强调人类研究保护办公室的赞同只是代表健康与人类服务部而不能代表同样采纳"共同规则"的其他联邦机构；但是对于美国历史协会与口述历史协会来说，这项政策声明显然是它们多年努力所取得的重大胜利，它们在其各自官方通讯上都打出相同标题——《口述历史排除在伦理委员会审查之外》。②

对于这项政策声明，包括口述历史学家在内的美国史学界的最初反应还是相当正面的，有文章指出："历史学家为这项决定欢呼喝彩。"琳达·肖普斯也指出："联邦办公室已经听到我们的想法并做出适当回应。"③ 当

---

① "Application of the Department of Health and Human Services Regulations for the Protection of Human Subjects at 45 CFR Part 46, Subpart A to Oral History Interviewing", *Oral History Association Newsletter*, Vol. 37, No. 3, Winter 2003, p. 3. 有关上述信件、2003 年 8 月 26 日起草的政策声明及 9 月 22 日修改后的政策声明的详细内容，请访问 http：//research. unl. edu/orr/docs/OHRPResponse-toOralHistories. pdf，2015 年 7 月 29 日访问。

② Donald A. Ritchie and Linda Shopes, "Oral History Excluded from IRB Review", *Oral History Association Newsletter*, Vol. 37, No. 3, Winter 2003, p. 1; Bruce Craig, "Oral History Excluded from IRB Review", *Perspectives on History*, December 2003.

③ Jeffrey Brainard, "Federal Agency Says Oral-History Research Is Not Covered by Human-Subject Rules", *The Chronicle of Higher Education*, October 31, 2003.

然，在口述历史学家中也有不同的声音，甚至提出尖锐的批评与质疑，其中的代表人物是北伊利诺伊大学（Northern Illinois University）历史系的 E. 泰勒·阿特金斯（E. Taylor Atkins），他在给《历史视野》（*Perspectives on History*）编辑的信中指出：“在过去的二年半里，我作为历史专业的代表在北伊利诺伊大学伦理审查委员会中任职，因此熟悉什么构成‘研究’和‘风险’，我被最近的将口述历史计划排除在伦理审查之外的联邦决定感到震惊。我更加震惊的是美国历史协会与口述历史协会的观点，即口述历史不是联邦法规所定义的‘研究’。在我看来，美国历史协会与口述历史协会已经曲解了口述历史学家的工作，仅仅是为了避免提交审查方案所造成的不便。”①

　　不过，对于这项政策的具体实施来说，其真正阻力来自各个机构的伦理审查委员会。2013 年 10 月 30 日，加州大学洛杉矶分校的研究受试者保护办公室（Office for Protection of Research Subjects）发布了一项有关口述历史、定性访谈（qualitative interviews）与人类受试者研究的备忘录，其内容是与迈克尔·卡罗姆的讨论。该备忘录首先确认：“由口述历史代表向人类研究保护办公室描述的口述历史活动一般而言是为了创建一种特定历史事件的记录，就其本身而言，它们不是为了有助于获得普遍性知识。”但是，该备忘录继续通过三个假设性口述历史计划来解释与评估口述历史活动是否需要接受伦理审查的三个一般原则。第一个原则指出：“只记录一个特定的历史事件或个人经历而不是为了得出结论（draw conclusions）或总结发现结果（generalize findings）的口述历史活动（诸如开放式访谈）将不构成 45 CFR 46 所定义的‘研究’。”所举的例子是一个与大屠杀幸存者进行访谈的口述历史录像，其用途是供大屠杀博物馆展览。该录影带的

① E. Taylor Atkins, "Letters to the Editor: Research and Risk", *Perspectives on History*, December 2003. 针对 E. 泰勒·阿特金斯的来信，琳达·肖普斯和唐纳德·里奇回应指出：“将口述历史排除在伦理审查委员会审查之外并不降低历史访谈的伦理要求，但是能够转移利用和讲授口述历史方法论的阿特金斯教授和其他人的压力，而且让伦理审查委员会将精力集中于它们要做的工作。”详细内容参阅 Linda Shopes and Donald Ritchie, "Letters to the Editor: Institutional Review Boards", *Perspectives on History*, December 2003.

·399·

创建不是为了得出结论、为决策提供信息（inform policy）或总结发现结果，其唯一目的是创建与大屠杀相关的特定的个人事件与经历的历史记录，并且为大屠杀幸存者提供讲述他们故事的渠道。第二个原则强调包括开放式访谈在内的旨在发展或有助于获得普遍性知识的系统性调查将构成 45 CFR 46 所定义的"研究"，所举例子是一个海湾战争幸存老兵的开放式访谈，其目的是记录他们的经历并得出有关他们经历的结论、为决策提供信息或总结结果。第三个原则指出："为了给其他研究者提供资源，口述历史学家和定性调查者可能会创建档案馆。由于档案馆的目的是为从事 45 CFR 46 所定义的'研究'的其他研究者创建信息库（repository of information），那么诸如此类的档案馆的创建将构成 45 CFR 46 所定义的'研究'。"针对该原则所提供的例子是一个有关黑人棒球联盟（Negro League Baseball）健在球员的系列开放式访谈的研究计划，该计划的目的是为未来的研究创建档案馆。诸如此类的档案馆的创建将构成 45 CFR 46 所定义的'研究'，因为其目的是为未来的研究收集资料。最后，该备忘录还指出附在迈克尔·卡罗姆 2003 年 9 月 22 日信件中的 2003 年 8 月 26 日的政策声明并非由人类研究保护办公室起草，因而并不能成为它的政策指南。备忘录还强调政策声明中第三段关于口述历史活动特征的描述无法提供足够的理由让人类研究保护办公室决定口述历史活动一般而言不包含 45 CFR 46 所定义的"研究"。[①]

尽管上述内容用具体例子阐释了其评估原则，可是在实践中还是很难判断一项口述历史计划的具体目的，即到底是为了记录一个特定的历史事件（个人经历）还是为了得出结论、为决策提供信息或总结发现结果，而且口述历史资料所发挥的作用很大程度上还取决于潜在使用者的具体利用方式。更为重要的是，通过结合第一个和第三个原则，可以发现仅用"创

---

① Office for Protection of Research Subjects, University of California, Los Angels, "Memorandum: Outline of October 30, 2002 Discussion with Dr. Michael Carome, Associate Directors, HHS-OHRP, Regarding Oral History, Qualitative Interviews, and Human Subjects Research", http://cphs.berkeley.edu/oral-history-031209.pdf, 2015 年 7 月 30 日访问。

建一个特定的历史记录"（无须审查）与"创建一个档案馆或信息库"
（需要审查）作为衡量一项口述历史计划是否属于联邦法规所定义的"研
究"是相当没有说服力的，而且从根本上说，大部分口述历史工作的一个
重要目的就是希望保存在档案馆中为未来研究者提供资料来源。

就这样，美国历史协会与口述历史协会努力多年并经人类研究保护办
公室确认的大多数口述历史访谈计划排除审查的政策声明又被迈克尔·卡
罗姆所否认，而且他在 2003 年 12 月 1 日给北伊利诺伊大学研究合规办公
室（Office of Research Compliance）的萝莉·布罗斯（Lori Bross）解释有
关口述历史伦理审查问题的电子邮件中还附上上述备忘录，并且明确表示
这份备忘录是与人类研究保护办公室共同讨论的。[①] 更为糟糕的是，在
2003 年 12 月召开的一个来自全美伦理审查委员会管理者的会议上，这份
备忘录被广泛分发。[②] 显然，上述做法已经对 2003 年 9 月 22 日的政策声明
造成严重影响，导致越来越多的伦理审查委员会开始质疑政策声明的合法
性与有效性。

基于此，2004 年 1 月 7 日，琳达·肖普斯和唐纳德·里奇参加了人类
研究保护办公室召集的电话会议，迈克尔·卡罗姆重申了他所在的机构继
续赞同 2003 年 9 月 22 日的政策声明。而在 2004 年 1 月 8 日给琳达·肖普
斯和唐纳德·里奇的电子邮件中，他还表示："人类研究保护办公室一贯
设法确认这个赞同意见，无论何时它收到来自伦理审查委员会的代表或其
他机构官员有关这个问题的询问。"[③] 在 2004 年春季出版的《口述历史协
会通讯》上，琳达·肖普斯和唐纳德·里奇强调造成上述政策声明解读困
惑的主要原因是对"研究"和"普遍性知识"两个概念的理解差异，他们

---

① Michael Carome's E-mail to Lori Bross, December 1, 2003, http: //www. nyu. edu/research/
resources-and-support-offices/getting-started-withyourresearch/human-subjects-research/forms-guidance/
clarification-on-oral-history/michael-caromes-email. html, 2015 年 7 月 30 日访问。

② Zachary M. Schrag, *Ethical Imperialism*: *Institutional Review Boards and the Social Sciences*,
1965-2009, Baltimore: Johns Hopkins University Press, 2010, p. 157.

③ Linda Shopes and Donald Ritchie, "Exclusion of Oral History from IRB Reviews: An Update",
Perspectives on History, March 2004.

指出："尽管口述历史明显包含有助于概括（generalizations）的历史研究与访谈，但是口述历史学家的标准操作程序并不符合联邦法规所定义的'研究'类型。……获得叙述者知情同意并量身定制的访谈并不符合这种'研究'定义；它们也并不有助于获得'普遍性知识'，即使受访者是那些来自一个共同群体或经历共同主题或事件的人，不管访谈者或其他研究者是否可能从众多访谈中得出某些历史概括。"当然，他们也赞同符合联邦定义的访谈计划应当接受伦理委员会的审查，而其中的访谈必须是为了生产科学意义上的普遍性知识而特别设计的。① 随后，在 2004 年 6 月 5 日的会议上，美国历史协会理事会再次重申其支持 2003 年 9 月 22 日的政策声明，并指出："我们强烈要求这项政策被所有伦理审查委员会所采纳，以确保执行全国一致的政策，这将使历史学家能够追求这项重要的研究方法，而没有不必要的限制。"②

然而，口述历史伦理审查政策的解读与具体实施仍然相当混乱，正如 2004 年 12 月出版的《历史视野》中的一篇文章所指出的，尽管部分大学已经采纳了人类研究保护办公室的立场，一般而言已经将口述历史访谈排除在伦理委员会审查之外。③ 形成鲜明对比的是，许多机构却倾向于支持

---

① Donald A. Ritchie and Linda Shopes, "An Update: Excluding Oral History from IRB Review", *Oral History Association Newsletter*, Vol. 38, No. 1, Spring 2004, p. 1.

② AHA Staff, "AHA Council Reaffirms Position on Oral History and Institutional Review Boards", *Perspectives on History*, September 2004. 事实上，美国历史协会在 2013 年 11 月 10 日还发布了一个有关这项政策声明的问题解答。详细内容参阅 American Historical Association, "Questions Regarding the Policy Statement", 10 November, 2003.

③ 2004 年 5 月德克萨斯大学奥斯汀分校（University of Texas at Austin）率先采纳该项政策声明，目前支持该声明的还包括阿默斯特学院（Amherst College）、哥伦比亚大学（Columbia University）、密歇根大学安娜堡分校（University of Michigan-Ann Arbor）、内布拉斯加大学林肯分校（University of Nebraska-Lincoln）、密苏里大学堪萨斯城分校（University of Missouri-Kansas City）、杨百翰大学（Brigham Young University）、普林斯顿大学（Princeton University）、史密森学会（Smithsonian Institution）、霍普学院（Hope College）、南加州大学（University of Southern California）和加州大学圣迭戈分校（University of California, San Diego）等大学和机构。这些信息来自 Office of Research Support and Compliance, University of Texas at Austin, "Oral History Policy Update", May 18, 2004, https://web.archive.org/web/20040525191237/http://www.utexas.edu/research/rsc/humanresearch/special-topics/oral-history.php; Zachary M. Schrag (ed.), *Institutional Review Blog* (http://www.institutionalreviewblog.com/), 2006-2014。上述访问时间为 2015 年 7 月 30 日。

加州大学落砂机分校备忘录所建议的更为保守的政策；当然也仍然有其他机构对于该问题保持沉默，因而进一步加剧了政策的总体模糊性。因此，时任美国历史协会副主席（负责研究部）的罗伊·罗森茨维格（Roy Rosenzweig，1950—2007）指出："我们对于某些伦理审查委员会没有遵守美国历史协会与人类研究保护办公室的协议感到相当困惑。但是我们觉得有必要让我们的会员意识到某些大学仍然坚持对口述历史进行伦理委员会审查。"① 而 2005 年一项由美国历史协会所做的调查进一步显示 2003 年 9 月 22 日的政策声明并没有产生太大的积极影响，大部分伦理审查委员会并不认可其法律效力。为了评估该政策声明在全美不同大学（学院）的实施情况，美国历史协会 5 位工作人员通过调查 252 所大学（其中 152 所是拥有历史学博士课程的研究性大学，剩下的 100 所是随机选择的四年制大学）的相关网站来了解它们的口述历史伦理审查政策。调查结果是令人失望的，在将近 95% 的大学网站中，它们只是提到口述历史受制于"快速审查"（1998 年联邦条例规定），大部分伦理审查委员会都拒绝接受口述历史排除审查的政策声明。另外，只有 11 个大学网站较为详细地讨论了 2003 年 9 月 22 日的政策声明，其中 9 个大学网站提到该项政策声明的具体内容，7 个大学网站提到 2003 年 10 月 30 日加州大学洛杉矶分校发布的备忘录，5 个大学网站提到 2004 年 1 月 8 日人类研究保护办公室赞同政策声明的重申意见。正是由于人类研究保护办公室在口述历史伦理审查问题上的相互冲突、矛盾的立场，使上述政策声明的实施情况变得相当糟糕。口述历史工作者被他们的专业组织告知其大部分研究可以排除审查，而事实上，大部分伦理审查委员会仍然无视或拒绝该声明，甚至有研究者（尤其是从事口述历史或利用保存在档案馆中的口述历史资料的学生）因为没

---

① Robert B. Townsend and Mériam Belli, "Oral History and IRBs: Caution Urged as Rule Interpretations Vary Widely", *Perspectives on History*, December 2004. 该文另载 *Oral History Association Newsletter*, Vol. 39, No. 1, Spring 2005, pp. 1 and 4-5.

有遵守联邦法规而遭受各种警告或惩罚。①

基于此，2005 年 11 月，罗伊·罗森茨维格代表美国历史协会致信人类研究保护办公室主任伯纳德·希维切（Bernard Schwetz），希望澄清联邦政府有关口述历史研究的伦理审查政策。除重申口述历史不是联邦法规所定义的研究类型及其理由之外，他催促人类研究保护办公室尽快发布有关该问题的正式书面指南（迈克尔·卡罗姆曾在 2004 年 1 月 8 日的电子邮件中承诺过）。而且，他还希望办公室能够将历史学界的意见汇报给人类受试者保护部长咨询委员会（Secretary's Advisory Committee on Human Subjects Protection），以及将 2003 年 9 月 22 日的政策声明纳入联邦法规并废除极易造成政策混乱的 2003 年 10 月 30 日备忘录。② 现有资料无法确定人类研究保护办公室是否答复罗伊·罗森茨维格的来信，不过在 2005 年 11 月 22 日，迈克尔·卡罗姆曾发布电子邮件澄清该问题。③ 此外，在 2006 年 11 月召开的美国医学科研公共责任组织（Public Responsibility in Medicine and Research，PRIM&R）会议上，迈克尔·卡罗姆重申了人类研究保护办公室在口述历史伦理审查问题上的政策立场。④ 从美国历史学界的反应来看，显然上述两次澄清并没有达成较为一致的意见，尤其是双方在联邦法规所定义的"研究"、"普遍性知识"与"系统性调查"等概念理解上存在差异，而且办公室坚持认为 2003 年 10 月 30 日的备忘录与 2003 年 9 月 22 日的政策声明并不冲突。因此，美国历史协会工作人员也失望地表示："考虑到我们过去与人类研究保护办公室之间的沟通与协议的有限影响，我们

---

① Robert B. Townsend, Carl Ashley, Mériam Belli, Richard E. Bond, and Elizabeth Fairhead, "Oral History and Review Boards: Little Gain and More Pain", *Perspectives on History*, February 2006; Robert B. Townsend, "History Association Tracks Status of IRB Oversight", *Oral History Association Newsletter*, Vol. 40, No. 1, Spring 2006, p. 9; Bernadette McCauley, "An IRB at Work: A Personal Experience", *Perspectives on History*, February 2006.

② Roy Rosenzweig, "Letter to the Director of the OHRP", *Perspectives on History*, February 2006.

③ Michael A. Carome, "Clarification of OHRP's Position on Oral History Information", November 22, 2005, http://www.utexas.edu/research/rsc/humansubjects/forms/michael_carome_updated.pdf, 2015 年 8 月 1 日访问。

④ E. Taylor Atkins, "Oral History and IRBs: An Update from the 2006 HRPP Conference", *Perspectives on History*, March 2007.

的期望是相当有限的。"①

　　的确如此，尽管以美国历史协会与口述历史协会为代表的专业组织仍然在积极推动口述历史伦理审查制度的改革，但收效甚微。2007 年 10 月 26 日，人类研究保护办公室就于 1998 年 11 月生效的联邦条例中符合伦理审查委员会"快速审查"的第五种研究类型的修改提议向社会征求书面意见②，回收的意见中涉及口述历史问题的共有 37 份。③ 作为美国历史协会的代表，该协会执行主任阿尼塔·琼斯（Arnita Jones）于 2007 年 12 月 20 日致信人类研究保护办公室，不仅强烈反对第五种研究类型的修改意见，而且要求将口述历史从"快速审查"类型（第七种研究类型）中删除并建议明确将口述历史排除在审查之外。④ 出于同样的目的，2011 年 7 月 26 日，美国健康与人类服务部就"共同规则"的可能性修改向社会发布法规制定预告通知并征求广泛意见。⑤ 在总共收到的 1142 份书面意见中，其中涉及口述历史伦理审查问题的大约占到 11%（笔者查询"oral history"共

---

　　① Robert B. Townsend, Carl Ashley, Mériam Belli, Richard E. Bond, and Elizabeth Fairhead, "Oral History and Review Boards: Little Gain and More Pain", *Perspectives on History*, February 2006.

　　② Department of Health and Human Services, "Protection of Human Subjects: Categories of Research That May Be Reviewed by the Institutional Review Board Through an Expedited Review Procedure", *Federal Register*, Vol. 72, No. 207, October 26, 2007, pp. 60848-60851; "Feds Invite Comments on IRB Rules Affecting Oral History", *Oral History Association Newsletter*, Vol. 41, No. 3, Winter 2007, p. 8.

　　③ Zachary M. Schrag (ed.), *Historians' Comments to OHRP*, October-December 2007, February 2008, https://web.archive.org/web/20080216010033/http://schrag.info/irb/historians_comments_to_ohrp.pdf, 2015 年 8 月 1 日访问。

　　④ "Arinita Jones's Letter to the Office for Human Research Protections", December 20, 2007, https://web.archive.org/web/20080216010032/http://www.historians.org/press/OralHistoryExclusion-Letter.pdf; Robert B. Townsend, "The Feds and IRBs: Your Opportunity to Weigh in", November 6, 2007, http://blog.historians.org/2007/11/the-feds-and-irbs-your-opportunity-to-weigh-in/, 上述访问时间为 2015 年 8 月 1 日。其他资料可参阅 Robert B. Townsend, "Historians Get Rare Opportunity to Comment on Federal Policy on Oral History", *Perspectives on History*, December 2007; Scott Jaschik, "Threat Seen to Oral History", *Insider Higher Education*, January 3, 2008.

　　⑤ Department of Health and Human Services, "Human Subjects Research Protections: Enhancing Protections for Research Subjects and Reducing Burden, Delay, and Ambiguity for Investigators", *Federal Register*, Vol. 76, No. 143, July 26, 2011, pp. 44512-44531; David Brown, "U. S. Proposes Rule Changes for Human-Subject Research", *The Washington Post*, July 23, 2011; Christopher Shea, "Historians and Human-Subjects Research", *The Wall Street Journal*, August 5, 2011.

检索到 127 条），足见美国口述历史学界对于该问题的关注程度。① 其中，
詹姆斯·格罗斯曼（James R. Grossman）和莉娜·本梅尔（Rina Benmay-
or）分别代表美国历史协会和口述历史协会于 2011 年 10 月致信人类研究
保护办公室主任杰里·曼尼科夫（Jerry Menikoff）提出反馈意见，他们一
致要求将口述历史完全排除在"共同规则"和伦理审查委员会的监管与审
查之外（修改意见仅仅指哪些研究类型可以豁免审查），并且对于联邦法
规有关限制信息风险（information risk）的规定表示担心，认为该规定将对
口述历史、档案保存与历史研究造成重大潜在伤害。② 上述美国历史协会
与口述历史协会两次要求排除审查的理由同之前的主张基本相同，无非
是强调"共同规则"并不适用于口述历史研究以及认为伦理审查委员会
的审查与监管制度极大地违背了口述历史研究的基本原则并侵犯了学术
自由。遗憾的是，这两次诉求没有得到美国健康与人类服务部或人类研
究保护办公室的任何答复，甚至这两个机构原先提出的修改意见也没有

---

① 详细内容可访问 http：//www. regulations. gov/#! docketBrowser；rpp = 25；po = 0；D =
HHS-OPHS-2011-0005，2015 年 8 月 1 日访问；Mary Larson，"Steering Clear of the Rocks：A Look at
the Current State of Oral History Ethics in the Digital Age"，*Oral History Review*，Vol. 40，No. 1，2013，
p. 40.

② "James R. Grossman's Letter to Jerry Menikoff"，October 24，2011，http://www. regulations. gov/
contentStreamer？ documentId = HHS-OPHS-2011-0005-0628&attachmentNumber = 1&disposition =
attachment&contentType = pdf；"Rina Benmayor's Letter to Jerry Menikoff"，October 25，2011，http：//
www. regulations. gov/contentStreamer？ documentId = HHS-OPHS-2011-0005-1010&attachmentNumber =
1&disposition = attachment&contentType = pdf. 其他相关资料还可参阅 Robert B. Townsend，"Getting Free
of the IRB：A Call to Action for Oral History"，August 1，2011，http：//blog. historians. org/2011/08/
getting-free-of-the-irb-a-call-to-action/；Robert B. Townsend，"Oral History and Information Risk：A Response to the Federal Proposal"，October 17，2011，http：//blog. historians. org/2011/10/oral-history-and-
information-risk-a-response-to-the-federal-proposal/；"Oral History，IRB and Information Risk：A Response
to the Federal Proposal"，October 18，2011，http：//www. oralhistory. org/wp-content/uploads/2011/12/
IRB-proposed-response. pdf；"AHA Reiterates Stance on Oral History Review and Cautions on Extension of
Privacy Rules"，October 25，2011，http：//blog. historians. org/2011/10/aha-reiterates-stance-on-oral-his-
tory-review-and-cautions-on-extension-of-privacy-rules/。除这两个组织之外，美国历史学家组织和美国
档案工作者学会（Society of American Archivists）也都致信杰里·曼尼科夫，建议完全排除口述历史
的伦理审查。详细内容参阅 "Historians and Archivists Comment on Oral History Review Rules"，ht-
tp：//historycoalition. org/2011/10/28/historians-and-archivists-comment-on-oral-history-review-rules/。 上
述访问时间为2015 年 8 月 1 日。

正式公布并生效。①

综上所述，在经过与联邦政府相关机构长达将近 20 年的沟通与斡旋之后，美国口述历史学界争取排除口述历史伦理审查的努力却陷入困境之中。口述史学在美国人文与社会科学中并不是主流的研究方法与领域，可是口述历史学界在抵制伦理审查制度向人文与社会科学的过度扩张方面所做的努力是有目共睹的，而且也受到其他领域众多学者的关注和赞赏。② 可是，为什么其效果仍然相当有限，究其原因，笔者以为主要有以下几点。

第一，联邦法规与政策的模糊性与矛盾性造成了解读与具体实施的混乱。有学者指出："令人吃惊的是，一个政府制定的简单的概念的模糊性（诸如'普遍性知识'）能够导致政府、伦理审查委员会与专业协会之间的管辖冲突。同样值得注意的是，这些冲突倾向于通过制定特别决议来解决。概念模糊不仅导致'任务蠕变'，而且常常传播着这些特别决议的串联。"③ 概念或政策的模糊性首先体现在"共同规则"对于"研究"的定义，而"研究"定义本身是决定研究计划是否接受伦理审查的前提。由于定义没有明确界定"普遍性知识"和"系统性调查"这两个核心概念，因而极易造成研究者、联邦监管机构与伦理审查委员会在理解与解读上的巨

---

① 笔者通过查询美国健康与人类服务部网站，发现最新的有关符合伦理审查委员会快速审查的联邦条例仍然是 1998 年 11 月生效的文件，2011 年提议的新规遭受搁置。详细内容可参阅 "Categories of Research That May Be Reviewed by the Institutional Review Board（IRB）through an Expedited Review Procedure"，http：//www. hhs. gov/ohrp/policy/expedited98. html，2015 年 8 月 1 日访问；Christopher Shea，"New Rules for Human-Subject Research Are Delayed and Debated"，*The Chronicle of Higher Education*，November 3，2014.

② Philip Hamburger，"The New Censorship：Institutional Review Boards"，*The Supreme Court Review*，Vol. 2004，2004，pp. 352-354；Rena Lederman，"The Perils of Working at Home：IRB 'Mission Creep' as Context and Content for an Ethnography of Disciplinary Knowledges"，*American Ethnologist*，Vol. 33，No. 4，2006，pp. 485-486.

③ Ronald F. White，"Institutional Review Board Mission Creep：The Common Rule，Social Science，and the Nanny State"，*The Independent Review*，Vol. 11，No. 3，2007，p. 553.

大差异，基本上是朝着有利于自己的方向进行合理性猜测与推论。① 因此，美国历史协会与口述历史协会以口述历史是为了"记录特定经历"、"解释特定过去"和"提供独特视角"为由来强调它并不是为了获得联邦法规所规定的"普遍性知识"，进而主张它不是联邦法规所定义的"研究"类型并因此可以排除伦理委员会的审查。可是在实践中，由于不同口述历史实践者在研究方法（生平式与主题式访谈）与研究目的上的差异，也无法排除有些研究者希望通过较为系统的口述历史访谈与研究来得出结论、为决策提供信息或总结发现结果，显然这些研究带有获得某种"普遍性知识"的可能性。② 基于此，迈克尔·卡罗姆在 2005 年澄清人类研究保护办公室关于口述历史伦理审查政策的电子邮件中就强调，口述历史活动本身并不构成联邦法规所定义的"研究"。他还举例指出，采集病史、抽血（为了检验血清生化指标）、胸透或脑部 CT 等活动一般而言都不包含人类受试者研究，可是当研究者利用这些程序进行非豁免的人类受试者研究时，这些研究（如果由美国健康与人类服务部执行或资助）必须接受伦理审查委员会的审查。③ 显然，从中可以看出，联邦监管机构确定口述历史活动是否接受伦理审查的标准取决于它如何操作及其应用目的。回顾美国主流口述历史学界要求排除口述历史伦理审查的理由，可以发现其主要是从口述历史本身的性质出发来强调其不是联邦法规所定义的"研究"类型。

作为美国口述历史学界努力排除审查的主要成果，2003 年 9 月 22 日的政策声明本身在关键术语使用上也是模糊不清的，声明中的"大多数"

---

① Caroline H. Bledsoe, Bruce Sherin, Adam G. Galinsky, Nathalia M. Headley, Carol A. Heimer, Erik Kjedgaard, James Lindgren, John D. Miller, Michael E. Roloff and David H. Uttal, "Regulating Creativity: Research and Survival in the IRB Iron Cage", *Northwestern University Law Review*, Vol. 101, No. 2, 2007, pp. 609-610. 正是如此，有学者主张联邦监管机构或伦理审查委员会应该为"普遍性知识"和"系统性调查"提供清晰定义。详细参阅 Jeffrey Cohen, "OHRP and Oral History", November 28, 2006, http://hrpp. blogspot. com/2006/11/ohrp-and-oral-history. html, 2015 年 8 月 1 日访问。

② 显然，2003 年 10 月 30 日备忘录所提供的第二个评估原则与范例就符合这一点，因此这样的口述历史计划需要接受伦理审查。

③ Michael A. Carome, "Clarification of OHRP's Position on Oral History Information", November 22, 2005.

和"一般而言"两个术语很难让研究者或伦理审查委员会判断哪些口述历史计划属于"非大多数"或"非一般"情况。不过，如上所述，真正造成该政策声明效果不佳的主要原因是人类研究保护办公室参与讨论并同意发布的与政策声明存在明显冲突、盾的 2003 年 10 月 30 日备忘录，该备忘录明确指出某些口述历史计划需要接受伦理审查，尽管其理由并不具有说服力。即使办公室随即于 2004 年 1 月 8 日发布电子邮件重新确认支持 2003 年 9 月 22 日的政策声明，可是已经造成比较明显的负面影响，当时就有学者指出："我们发现口述历史计划监管仍然是相当不同的政策与程序的令人混淆的拼凑。"① 就审查实践来看，绝大多数伦理审查委员会倾向于赞同备忘录的指导原则。

联邦法规与政策的模糊性与矛盾性还体现在联邦监管机构自身的言行不一，即 2004 年人类研究保护办公室在启动贝尔蒙特口述历史计划（Belmont Oral History Project）时就没有经过伦理审查委员会的审查与批准。该计划由伯纳德·希维切主任在内的人类研究保护办公室工作人员对国家保护生物医学与行为研究中的人类受试者委员会（National Commission for the Protection of Human Subjects of Biomedical and Behavioral Research）前成员与职员进行视频访谈，并将视频与抄本资料发布在办公室官方网站上。而且，部分访谈资料还被应用到一个纪录短片中，用来纪念和评价《贝尔蒙特报告》（Belmont Report）发布 25 周年。② 针对学者的质疑与追问，办公室于 2007 年做出回应，它们坚决宣称该口述历史计划并不属于联邦法规所定义的"研究"类型，因为它不是一项为了获得普遍性知识而进行的系统性调查。可是，有学者仍然强调该计划的网站（标题为"Oral History Ar-

---

① Robert B. Townsend and Mériam Belli, "Oral History and IRBs: Caution Urged as Rule Interpretations Vary Widely", *Perspectives on History*, December 2004.

② 该计划官方网站为 http://www.hhs.gov/ohrp/archive/belmontArchive.html#histArchive2，2015 年 8 月 2 日访问。有关《贝尔蒙特报告》的详细资料，请参阅 National Commission for the Protection of Human Subjects of Biomedical and Behavioral Research, *Belmont Report: Ethical Principles and Guidelines for the Protection of Human Subjects of Research*, Washington: U. S. Government Printing Office, 1979.

chive"）就像"一个为其他研究者提供研究资料的信息库"，而且办公室利用部分访谈资料制作的纪录片在某种程度上也具有为决策提供信息的功能。① 这些特征显然都符合 2003 年 10 月 30 日备忘录所提出的第二条和第三条原则，因而理论上需要接受伦理审查委员会的审查与批准，可是当时办公室却没有采取任何相关措施。

第二，伦理审查委员会的风险规避思维导致它们宁愿在监管程度上犯错误，也不愿意直接放弃对某些研究类型的审查权。如上所述，"共同规则"本身只适用于那些由 18 个联邦机构执行或资助的研究计划，而事实上，绝大部分大学或研究机构会将伦理审查委员会的审查扩展到所有研究类型，即使它们没有获得上述 18 个联邦机构的资助。② 正如有学者指出的那样，模糊的联邦政策以及管理者避免潜在诉讼或负面报道（因危险性或争议性研究所致）的本能培养了一种日益扩大的伦理审查委员会监管体制。因此，伦理审查委员会的风险规避思维导致审查范围不断扩大和审查要求日益严格；同时，也因为口述历史研究的不断发展与学术界的日益认可而引起其密切关注。③

伦理审查委员会要求审查口述历史主要基于两个方面的考虑：给受访者可能造成的心理伤害与保持受访者隐私的需要。④ 为避免心理伤害（甚至是人身危险），伦理审查委员会要求访谈者不能提问那些潜在的敏感问题。而口述历史学界认为，开放式的口述历史访谈很难预见是否或何时会涉及敏感主题；而且，与生物医学和行为科学研究中的人类受试者不同，

① Zachary M. Schrag, "'Generalizable' revisited", Institutional Review Blog, January 10, 2007, http://www.institutionalreviewblog.com/2007/01/generalizable-revisited.html, 2015 年 8 月 2 日访问; Zachary M. Schrag, *Ethical Imperialism: Institutional Review Boards and the Social Sciences, 1965-2009*, Baltimore: Johns Hopkins University Press, 2010, p. 158.

② 有学者之所以提出排除口述历史等人文科学领域的伦理审查要求，其重要理由是最可能资助人文科学研究的联邦机构美国国家人文科学基金会并不在"共同规则"监管范围之列。详细参阅 John A. Neuenschwander, *A Guide to Oral History and the Law*, Oxford and New York: Oxford University Press, 2009, p. 97.

③ "Institutional Review Boards Threaten Scholarly Work", *Oral History Association Newsletter*, Vol. 40, No. 3, Winter 2006, pp. 8-9.

④ Linda Shopes, "Negotiating Institutional Review Boards", *Perspectives on History*, March 2007.

具有高度自主性和能动性的受访者能够自我权衡敏感主题所可能造成的消极后果（访谈者也会适当提醒受访者予以注意）。甚至有学者强调，传闻和科学证据显示，有关敏感主题或创伤经历的访谈并不总是造成伤害，反而可能具有积极效果。① 至于隐私问题，伦理审查委员会要求受访者保持匿名（美国口述历史协会允许在极端情况下可以这样做），甚至要求在研究完成之后由研究者（受访者）保存资料或销毁它们。显然，这些做法都完全违背了口述历史研究的基本原则与目的，因为匿名资料在历史研究中缺乏可信性，而且对于绝大部分受访者而言，他们都为自己的经历能够成为历史记录的一部分而感到自豪因而希望可以公开自己的身份。正如美国口述历史协会前主席迈克尔·弗里斯科所说："简单而言，口述历史的核心目的常常是将有名字的人（named people）纳入历史记录当中，而不是掩饰或隐去姓名。"②

基于此，美国历史协会指出，如果公开的话，访谈当中的某些信息可能会给受访者带来名誉或财产损失，甚至让他们面临民事或刑事责任。但是，历史学家的更为重要的责任在于追踪证据所指引的方向，并在其所有复杂性当中认识与理解过去，而不是保护受访者免受他们过去的错误或罪行的可能性影响。③ 不过，在实践过程中，自 21 世纪以来，越来越多的口述历史计划涉及政治（社会）运动、内战（战争）、非法移民或创伤事件等敏感主题，同时数字化技术的发展使得口述历史资料的网络传播与使用变得更为容易与便捷，这些因素都使得口述历史工作所面临的法律与伦理

---

① 相关研究可参阅 Edward A. Walker, Elana Newman, Mary Koss, and David Bernstein, "Does the Study of Victimization Revictimize the Victims?" *General Hospital Psychiatry*, Vol. 19, No. 6, 1997, pp. 403-410; Elana Newman, Edward A. Walker, and Anne Gefland, "Assessing the Ethical Costs and Benefits of Trauma-Focused Research", *General Hospital Psychiatry*, Vol. 21, No. 3, 1999, pp. 187-196; Kari Dyregrov, Atle Dyregov, and Magne Raundalen, "Refugee Families' Experience of Research Participation", *Journal of Traumatic Stress*, Vol. 12, No. 3, 2000, pp. 413-26.

② Michael Frisch, "Comment on the Department of Health and Human Services (HHS) Notice: Human Subject Research Protections: Enhancing Protections for Research Subjects and Reducing Burden, Delay, and Ambiguity for Investigators", http://www.regulations.gov/#! documentDetail; D = HHS-OPHS-2011-0005-0751, 2015 年 8 月 2 日访问。

③ "Arinita Jones's Letter to the Office for Human Research Protections", December 20, 2007.

风险进一步加剧。当然，这些因素也直接导致了伦理审查委员会对于口述历史研究计划的审查程序与要求变得越来越严格。

显然，对于那些可能开展涉及危险或敏感主题研究的大学或机构管理者来说，波士顿学院口述历史传票案可能会让他们提高警惕，并要求伦理审查委员会加强对相关研究的审查与监管力度。同时，为避免引起不必要的法律纠纷或伦理风险，伦理审查委员会也习惯以"不怕一万，只怕万一"的心态要求审查所有以人为对象的研究计划，尽管某些计划根本没有研究风险可言。在某种程度上，这也能解释为什么大部分大学或研究机构并不赞同要求排除口述历史伦理审查的政策声明。

第三，将口述历史定位为不是联邦法规所定义的"研究"类型降低了其学术性，从而造成口述历史学界内部在伦理审查问题上的分歧。如上所述，美国历史协会与口述历史协会为了将口述历史排除在审查之外，主张口述历史并不是"共同规则"所定义的研究类型，当然它们并不是刻意贬低口述历史本身的学术性。但是，这种策略却引起了部分口述历史学家的激烈反对，前文提到的 E. 泰勒·阿特金斯就认为此举是不明智、自掘坟墓的。在他看来，任何希望在知名大学追求学术研究、终身教职或研究生学位的历史工作者都必须从事"研究"，即所谓的有助于获得普遍性知识的系统性调查。他进一步强调，如果从事的口述历史工作是没有经过审查的，将不能让他们获得预期的学术资历。① 加州大学伯克利分校地区口述历史办公室副主任马丁·米克尔（Martin Meeker）也指出："通过同意口述历史不能被定义为由诸如此类的资助机构所认定的研究类型，口述历史学家默认在学术层级体系中处于一种从属地位。……相对于一些过度扩张的伦理审查委员会来说，口述历史访谈在大学中的历史上和现在仍然延续的边缘化对这个领域的当前发展和未来

① E. Taylor Atkins, "Oral History and IRBs: An Update from the 2006 HRPP Conference", *Perspectives on History*, March 2007.

健康将带来更大风险。"①

的确，美国口述史学尽管已经有一定的社会影响力，可是其学术性（尤其是在职称晋升与学术资历评价方面）仍有待学术界认可。② 事实上，早在 2005 年美国口述历史协会就成立工作组来调查口述史学在学者专业评估中的作用，其中包括教职聘任、留任、晋升、终身教职授予、教学服务与社会服务等方面的评价与考核机制。③ 不过，这项工作一直没有任何进展，直到 2014 年 2 月，口述历史协会重启该项工作并准备起草一份有关"作为学术的口述史学"（Oral History as Scholarship）的文件。目前，口述历史协会正面向学术界广泛征求意见，最后的文件将在 2016 年协会年会上公布。④

基于此，如果口述历史学界为避免伦理审查而主张口述历史不是联邦法规所定义的研究类型，这种策略的确会影响口述历史的学术性与科学地位，甚至导致口述历史被其他领域的学者嘲笑为"非研究"（non-research）工作。显然，这并不是口述历史工作者愿意看到的，其实这个问题也促使他们不断调整策略，即不再过分关注口述历史与其他研究类型的性质差异，而是强调基于生物医学与行为研究伦理考量的联邦法规、政策与审查程序并不完全适用于口述历史。

---

① Martin Meeker, "The Berkeley Compromise: Oral History, Human Subjects, and the Meaning of 'Research'", in Claire Bond Potter and Renee C. Romano (eds.), *Doing Recent History: On Privacy, Copyright, Video Games, Institutional Review Boards, Activist Scholarship, and History that Talks Back*, Athens: University of Georgia Press, 2012, p. 131.

② 在大学终身教职评定中，很多口述历史工作者抱怨他们的工作被认为并非有价值和原创性的学术研究。详细参阅 Clifford Kuhn, "Considering Oral History as Scholarship: Comments Welcome", *Public History Commons*, June 17, 2015.

③ AHA Staff, "Oral History Association Task Force Calls for Reports", *Perspectives on History*, April 2005.

④ Clifford Kuhn, "OHA and Oral History at NCPH", H-OralHist, April 10, 2015; Clifford Kuhn, "OHA Document on Oral History as Scholarship", H-OralHist, June 22, 2015. 2014 年口述历史协会被美国学术团体委员会（American Council of Learned Societies）接纳为会员，也足见其学术性被逐步认可。详细内容可参阅 Clifford Kuhn, "Oral History Association Selected to ACLS", H-OralHist, May 12, 2014; "Focus on the Oral History Association", *ACLS News*, October 21, 2014, https://www.acls.org/news/08-21-2014/, 2014 年 8 月 2 日访问。

正是上述各种困境使得美国口述历史学界不断意识到联邦监管机构与伦理审查委员会根本不可能放弃审查权，即使符合豁免或排除条件，其决定权也属于伦理审查委员会而非研究者。作为口述历史排除审查的主要倡导者，琳达·肖普斯也承认他们的倡导活动在很大程度上是无效的，而且她也悲观地表示："口述历史学家不太可能从联邦监管机构那里获得许多让步。"① 的确，伯纳德·希维切尽管承认更为清晰的政策指南可能有助于让伦理审查委员会不那么具有干预性，但是他仍然坚决主张在非医学研究中也需要保护人类受试者免受任何危险。正如他所说："如果说不存在任何风险，我想那是天真的。"②

因此，众多学者提出口述历史学界真正需要的是采取一种更为积极主动的态度，而不是一味地抵制伦理审查委员会，其中最为关键的是教育与协商，③ 以期达成相互尊重与信任的和睦关系，并在此基础上与伦理审查委员会合作发展出真正适合口述历史的伦理审查政策与程序。

六　基于专业伦理的权责关系

波士顿学院口述历史传票案的另一个重要启示是促使我们思考如何更好地处理研究者（访谈者）、受访者与赞助（保存）机构之间的权利与责任关系，真正将研究参与者的利益作为优先考虑的目标。在此次事件中，莫洛尼与麦金太尔为保护受访者的利益而做的各种努力受到一些美国学术

---

① Linda Shopes, "Oral History, Human Subjects, and Institutional Review Boards", Oral History Association, 2009, http://www.oralhistory.org/about/do-oral-history/oral-history-and-irb-review/, 2015 年 8 月 2 日访问。

② Patricia Cohen, "Ethics Panels Expand Grip, No Field Is Off Limits", *New York Times*, February 28, 2007.

③ John A. Neuenschwander, *A Guide to Oral History and the Law*, Oxford and New York: Oxford University Press, 2009, p. 104.

与社会团体的大力赞赏与支持，他们很好地履行了口述历史实践中访谈者对于受访者所肩负的责任与义务。波士顿学院再次被指没有尽最大努力保护研究参与者（尤其是受访者）的利益，在面对法院的相关裁决时，不仅放弃了对于普莱斯口述历史资料的上诉请求，而且主动将其他大量口述历史资料交给法院。在面对麦金太尔要求转移口述历史资料保存地以尽可能保证其安全的请求时，波士顿学院予以断然拒绝。作为口述历史事业的核心，计划参与各方之间的信任与和睦关系的建立有赖于各方对于口述历史工作完整过程的充分了解与共识，需要通过签署具有法律效力的法律授权协议书、保密协议与知情同意书等文件来厘清和确定各方之间的权责关系。

除法律程序与手段之外，这种不同关系体之间权责关系的确立更需要建立在专业伦理基础之上。在60多年的长期实践中，美国口述史学界已经形成了一套较为完善的涉及各方关系的专业伦理规范，概括而言，主要涉及以下三个方面。

访谈者对于受访者应尽的责任：（1）必须告知受访者正在进行的口述历史计划的目的和程序，以及该计划所要实现的特定目标与预期用途；（2）必须告知受访者口述历史过程中的双方权益，例如编辑、使用限制、著作权、优先使用权、版税，以及口述历史记录的预期处置方式和各种传播方式；（3）必须告知受访者签署法律授权协议书的必要性，以及各种法律文件拟定与填写的具体细节；（4）必须告知受访者口述历史访谈中可能出现的危害第三者的情况，比如叙述的内容涉及诽谤与隐私权侵犯等可能；（5）访谈者必须特别注意访谈过程中受访者情绪的变化，并且根据受访者因年龄、性别、种族、民族、阶级、宗教信仰、社会地位和政见等因素的差异而及时调节访谈的节奏与方式；（6）访谈者必须尊重受访者有权拒绝讨论某些特定主题，并有权对访谈中某些内容的使用加以限制，如有必要甚至可以采取匿名方式；（7）访谈者必须珍惜受访者给予的信任，不能轻易地将受访者不愿被第三者知道的信息传播出去，以维护双方建立起来的和睦关系；（8）访谈者必须谨防向受访者做出一些自己无法实现的承诺；（9）在计划结束后，访谈者应该通过一定的方式向受访者表示感谢，并且无偿向受访者赠送一份口述历史抄本或以抄本为基础的任何出版物，以做纪念。

访谈者对于公众、赞助机构及专业本身应尽的责任：（1）访谈者在从事口述历史工作时，有责任维持最高的专业标准，具备熟练的访谈技巧和应变能力，并维护与口述历史相关的各类学科和专业的标准；（2）访谈者应与受访者共同努力，诚实、客观和完整地记录具有保存和研究价值的资料；（3）为提高口述历史资料的使用价值，受访者应该挑选那些对正在进行的计划最有帮助的受访者，并就受访者信息与历史背景知识积极做好各项准备工作；（4）为扩大口述历史资料的使用范围，访谈者应该努力说服受访者将访谈向公众开放；（5）为保护口述历史著作权所有者的利益，在向公众开放时，应该与保存机构或受赠机构做出必要的法律安排，以避免不必要的纠纷与诉讼；（6）使用者有责任维护口述历史资料的完整性，不能任意歪曲访谈内容，或者不顾前后脉络而任意摘用；（7）访谈者在接受赞助或委托机构的委托任务时，除坚持学术客观性与公正性之外，应该充分尊重赞助或委托机构的要求，尤其是必须履行双方签署的合作协议。

赞助与档案保存机构应尽的责任：（1）赞助机构应基于专业能力谨慎选择访谈者，并及时清楚地向访谈者说明计划的目标、程序及访谈所必须遵守的法律与伦理问题；（2）赞助机构在使用口述历史于商业用途时，应尊重受访者对某些访谈所设的限制条件，并根据双方协议向访谈者和受访者支付必要的经济报酬；（3）档案保存机构在口述历史的保存与维护上应保持最高的专业和伦理标准，有必要对访谈进行鉴别、编目和索引，并及时通过各种渠道向公众发布该机构所保存的口述历史资料信息，以最大限度地服务公众；（4）档案保存机构在利用口述历史于公开用途时，应明确注明该口述历史计划的赞助机构、访谈者与受访者等信息，以维护他们应有的署名权。①

　　综上所述，就波士顿学院口述历史传票案而言，尽管最终只需交出一小部分口述历史资料，且波士顿学院与莫洛尼和麦金太尔都认为这是一项重大的胜利。可是，该事件已经对美国口述史学发展产生了极其严重的消极影响，正如口述历史协会执行主任克利福德·库恩所说："对于波士顿学院和整个口述史学界来说，这个事件会成为一个不祥的先例。……口述史学已经被证明是一种记录当代世界战争、暴力与创伤的至关重要的手段。如果潜在的叙述者因为访谈会被泄露或承诺被打破而担心遭受报复，他们将不太可能参与这样的活动，结果就是我们都将陷入困境。我担心波士顿学院事件可能会像滚雪球一样，对口述史学事业产生一种真正的'寒蝉效应'。"② 而且，数字化时代的到来使得口述历史资料的网络传播与使用变得更加容易与便捷，而这些综合因素都将使美国口述历史工作所面临的法律与伦理风险进一步加剧，其前路可谓任重而道远。

---

　　① 上述内容总结自美国口述历史协会于 2009 年最新修订的《口述历史原则与最佳实务》（*Principles for Oral History and Best Practices for Oral History*），详细访问 http：//www. oralhistory. org/about/principles-and-practices/，2015 年 8 月 2 日。

　　② Affidavit of Clifford M. Kuhn, June 2, 2011, in Motion of the Trustees of Boston College to Quash Subpoenas, M. B. D. No. 11-MC-91078, United States District Court District of Massachusetts, June 7, 2011, p. 2.

结　　语

如上所述，在 1948 年美国现代口述史学诞生之前，将近 100 年前的美国著名流浪汉约瑟夫·古尔德就宣称要创作一部巨著《我们时代的口述历史》，记录他在街头巷尾所听到的人们的闲谈以及自己的生活经历与感受。尽管古尔德的宣称最终被证明是一场"骗局"，不过其历史遗产精髓却被过去 60 多年来的美国口述历史工作者所延续和践行。毫无疑问，作为个人视角的时代记忆与反思，口述史学已经成为一种记录、保存、传播与解释过去美国政治、经济、社会、文化乃至日常生活等领域的不同参与者的声音与历史记忆的重要方法与研究领域。正是如此，2012 年《纽约时报博客》（*New York Times Blogs*）上的一篇评论文章甚至宣称我们正在进入一个"口述历史的时代"。① 从"我们时代的口述历史"到"口述历史的时代"，美国口述史学发展的每个阶段都无不体现着时代与历史的互动关系。

在 20 世纪中叶，作为对技术变迁与侵袭造成历史记录重大缺漏的担忧，阿兰·内文斯在哥伦比亚大学率先开启这项影响深远和具有重要意义的现代口述史学试验。经过将近 20 年的艰辛努力，哥大口述历史研究室逐渐发展成为美国乃至世界著名的口述历史机构。而与此同时，它所开创的口述史学试验也演变成为一场席卷美国各地和不同领域的口述史学运动，其参与者包括大学（学院）、图书馆（档案馆、博物馆）、历史学会、专业协会、政府机构、非政府组织、公司（企业）、媒体、军事部门、医疗卫生机构及慈善组织等不同机构和独立研究者。

---

① John Williams, "The Age of Oral Histories", *New York Times Blogs*, March 2, 2012.

　　同样是为回应时代变迁与社会思潮冲击的需要，自 20 世纪 60 年代中期以来，美国口述史学界开始超越第一代口述史学家所主导的精英访谈模式而扩展口述历史的搜集范围与视野。正是如此，口述史学逐渐被广泛应用于少数族裔史、女性史、劳工史、同性恋史、移民史、家庭（家族）史、社区（社群）史与城市史等新社会史领域。美国口述史学的这种"新社会史转向"不仅为那些处于非主流社会的边缘人物与弱势群体记录和保存了大量原始资料，而且口述史学所具有的"民主动力"与"草根精神"很大程度上也挑战和改变了传统美国史学主要基于精英白人男性的传统书写模式。

　　而在政府机构与社会组织总体缩减口述历史计划资助经费的现实背景下，同时也因为跨学科理论与思潮的冲击与影响，进入 20 世纪 70 年代末以来，一些更具理论导向的美国口述历史学家呼吁重新思考口述历史的实践与解释方式。而以"记忆转向"、"叙事转向"和"口述历史关系反思"为主要表现形式的美国口述史学的理论转向很大程度上也是基于对口述历史生产过程复杂性的深度描述与全面反思，在越来越多的美国口述史学家看来，口述历史的功能不仅体现在它作为史料的证据价值，同时它也可以作为"文本"来理解意义的生成与诠释过程。当然，对于美国口述史学研究的理论过度问题，一些口述历史学家也表示要提高警惕，强调不能以纯理论研究来代替口述历史所记录和呈现的真实生活与经历。比如，面对美国女性口述历史深受后现代主义与后解构主义理论影响的严峻现实，一些主流学者开始强调女性口述历史的第一要务仍然在于"恢复、恢复、恢复"与"收集、收集、收集"，即如何更好地恢复、挖掘与记录女性自己的声音。①

---

　　① Susan Armitage and Sherna Berger Gluck, "Reflections on Women's Oral History: An Exchange", *Frontiers: A Journal of Women Studies*, Vol. 19, No. 3 (Problems and Perplexities in Women's Oral History), 1998, pp. 8, 10.

　　而作为时代变迁的重要表现与社会变革的重要动力，现代技术的发明、创新和应用与美国现代口述史学有着非常紧密的联系。如上所述，在某种程度上，阿兰·内文斯的口述史学试验是为了应对技术侵袭所造成的手写记录的进一步衰退。而随着录音机、缩微和计算机等技术手段的进一步发展，美国口述历史工作者日益意识到可以将口述史学运动看成一种利用技术的有意识的努力。而20世纪90年代以来以个人电脑、智能手机与互联网（包括电子邮件、网站、网络视频会议系统、网络摄像机、网络社交媒体与网络应用程序等）等计算机、网络通信、信息管理及多媒体技术为代表的数字化革命则给美国口述史学发展带来前所未有的机遇与挑战。

　　同样是基于对时代议题的积极关注，使得美国口述史学发展所面临的法律与伦理问题日益凸显。综观近十年来美国口述历史实践的新兴领域，我们可以发现口述史学被不断应用于战争与冲突、突发事件（比如自然灾难与恐怖袭击）、犯罪问题（比如毒品贸易与非法移民）与特殊疾病（比如艾滋病）等具有相当敏感性与争议性的当代议题。而发生于2011年的美国波士顿学院口述历史传票案更被认为是一个不祥的先例，在很多口述史学家看来，它将可能像滚雪球一样对美国口述史学事业产生影响深远的"寒蝉效应"。而数字化革命同样是一把双刃剑，它在给口述历史工作者带来机遇与便利的同时，跨越地理空间障碍的网络访问、传播与应用也使美国口述史学所潜藏的法律与伦理风险进一步加剧。

　　除法律与伦理问题之外，美国口述史学还面临学科定位与学术专业认可度等众多新兴分支学科和研究领域都同样存在的问题，但这些都不足以影响美国口述历史工作者对于口述历史记录与研究的热情与投入。简而言之，作为第二次世界大战后兴起的为数不多的兼具学术研究意义、社会行动议程与公共历史价值的研究方法与学科领域，在过去的60多年间，尽管遭到来自各方的挑战与质疑，不过在几代口述史学家的共同努力下，美国口述史学发展呈现出旺盛的生命力与独特的影响力。它被国际学术界公认为是现代口述史学的诞生地，在其辐射与影响下，口述史学在世界各地相继兴起（复兴）并蓬勃发展，成为收集原始资料、拓宽研究视野、更新研究方法、促进跨学科应用、推动教育改革、提供决策信息、促进社会正义与实现政治和解的重要手段与力量。

参考文献 *

一 英文

(一) 期刊

Oral History Association Newsletter（1967—）

Oral History（1972—）

Oral History Review（1973—）

Oral History Forum（1975—）

The Public Historian（1978—）

Oral History Australia Journal（1979—）

International Journal of Oral History（1980—1989）

Journal of American History（1987—2002，每年第 2 期都设"Oral History"专栏）

Oral History in New Zealand（1988—）

International Annual of Oral History（1990）

---

* 限于篇幅，在英文参考文献部分，这里只列出一些重要的学术期刊与专著（主要涉及理论与实践），相关论文请见正文；而中文部分则提供一些有关中国口述史学理论与方法研究的代表性作品（包括译著和港澳台作品），以供参考。为反映口述史学发展历程与趋势，所列参考文献根据出版时间排序，如同年出版则随机排列。

International Yearbook of Oral History and Life Stories （1992—1996）

Words and Silences （1997—）

International Oral History Association Newsletter （1998—）

Oral History Journal of South Africa （2013—）

（二）专著

Allan Nevins, *The Gateway to History*, New York: D. C. Heath and Company, 1938.

Columbia University, Oral History Research Office, *Compendium of the Columbia University Oral History Collection to August 1, 1957*, New York: Oral History Research Office, 1957.

Columbia University, Oral History Research Office, *The Oral History Collection of Columbia University*, New York: Oral History Research Office, 1960.

Columbia University, Oral History Research Office, *A Supplement to the Oral History Collection of Columbia University*, New York: Oral History Research Office, 1962.

Columbia University, Oral History Research Office, *The Oral History Collection of Columbia University*, New York: Oral History Research Office, 1964.

Columbia University, Oral History Research Office, *Oral History in the United States: A Report from the Oral History Research Office of Columbia University*, New York: Oral History Research Office, 1965.

Jan Vansina, *Oral Tradition: A Study in Historical Methodology*, Chicago: Aldine Publishing Company, 1965.

Malcolm X and Alex Haley, *The Autobiography of Malcolm X*, New York: Grove Press, 1965.

Jan Vansina, *Oral Tradition: A Study in Historical Methodology*, Chicago: Aldine Publishing Company, 1965.

Joseph Mitchell, *Joe Gould's Secret*, New York: Viking Press, 1965.

Columbia University, Oral History Research Office, *Oral History in the U-nited States: A Report from the Oral History Research Office of Columbia University*, New York: Oral History Research Office, 1966.

Columbia University, Oral History Research Office, *The Oral History Collection; Recent Acquisitions and A Report for 1966*, New York: Oral History Research Office, 1966.

Elizabeth I. Dixon (ed.), *The Oral History Program at UCLA: A Bibliography*, Los Angeles: University of California Library, 1966.

Donald J. Schippers and Adelaide G. Tusler (eds.), *A Bibliography on Oral History*, Los Angeles: Oral History Association, 1967.

Elizabeth I. Dixon and James V. Mink (eds.), *Oral History at Arrowhead: The Proceedings of the First National Colloquium on Oral History*, Los Angeles: Oral History Association, 1967.

Marion White McPherson, *Problems and Procedures on Oral Histories at the Archives of the History of American Psychology*, Akron: University of Akron, 1967.

Studs Terkel, *Division Street: America*, New York: Pantheon Books, 1967.

Thomas Milton Rivers and Saul Benison, *Tom Rivers: Reflections on a Life in Medicine and Science: An Oral History Memoir*, Cambridge: MIT Press, 1967.

Columbia University, Oral History Research Office, *Oral History, The First Twenty Years: Published Use 1948-1968, Recent Acquisitions Available for Use*, New York: Oral History Research Office, 1968.

Hilda Clarke Gallaghan, *An Introduction to Oral History*, Los Angeles: Oral History Program, UCLA, 1968.

Louis M. Starr (ed.), *The Second National Colloquium on Oral History*,

New York: Oral History Association, 1968.

Alfred Benjamin, *The Helping Interview*, Boston: Houghton Mifflin, 1969.

Columbia University, Oral History Research Office, *Oral History: Prospects in the 1970's: A Test: 100 Americans in the Oral History Collection: Review of 1968-1969*, New York: Oral History Research Office, 1969.

Gould P. Colman (ed.), *The Third National Colloquium on Oral History*, New York: Oral History Association, 1969.

Raymond L. Gorden, *Interviewing: Strategy, Techniques, and Tactics*, Homewood: The Dorsey Press, 1969.

T. Harry Williams, *Huey Long*, New York: Alfred A. Knopf, 1969.

Willa K. Baum, *Oral History for the Local Historical Society*, Stockton: Conference of California Historical Societies, 1969.

Gould P. Colman (ed.), *The Fourth National Colloquium on Oral History*, New York: Oral History Association, 1970.

Israel K. Katoke, *The Making of the Karagwe Kingdom: Tanzanian History from Oral Traditions*, Nairobi: East African Publishing House, 1970.

Lewis A. Dexter (ed.), *Elite and Specialized Interviewing*, Evanston: Northwestern University Press, 1970.

Studs Terkel, *Hard Times: An Oral History of the Great Depression*, New York: Pantheon Books, 1970.

William H. Banaka, *Training in Depth Interviewing*, New York: Harper and Row, 1970.

William Lynwood Montell, *The Saga of Coe Ridge: A Study in Oral History*, Knoxville: University of Tennessee Press, 1970.

Gary L. Shumway (ed.), *Oral History in the United States: A Directory*, New York: Oral History Association, 1971.

Joseph H. Cash and Herbert T. Hoover (eds.), *To Be an Indian: An Oral History*, New York: Holt, Rinehart and Winston, 1971.

Manfred J. Waserman (ed.), *Bibliography on Oral History*, New York: Oral History Association, 1971.

Willa K. Baum, *Oral History for the Local Historical Society*, Nashville: American Association for State and Local History by Special Arrangement with the Conference of California Historical Societies, new edition, 1971.

Columbia University, East Asian Institute, *The Chinese Oral History Project*, New York: Columbia University, 1972.

Eliot Wigginton (ed.), *The Foxfire Book*, Garden City: Doubleday, 1972.

Peter D. Olch and Forrest C. Pogue (eds.), *Selections from the Fifth and Sixth National Colloquia on Oral History*, New York: Oral History Association, 1972.

Pittsburgh Section, National Council of Jewish Women (ed.), *By Myself, I'm A Book! An Oral History of the Immigrant Jewish Experience in Pittsburgh*, Waltham: American Jewish Historical Society, 1972.

Victor N. Low, *Three Nigerian Emirates: A Study in Oral History*, Evanston: Northwestern University Press, 1972.

Alice Lynd and Staughton Lynd (ed.), *Rank and File: Personal Histories by Working-Class Organizers*, Boston: Beacon Press, 1973.

Elizabeth B. Mason and Louis M. Starr (eds.), *The Oral History Collection of Columbia University*, New York: Oral History Research Office, 1973.

Gary L. Shumway and William G. Hartley, *An Oral History Primer*, Salt Lake City: Primer Publications, 1973.

Gary L. Shumway, Richard D. Curtiss, and Shirley E. Stephenson (eds.), *A Guide for Oral History Programs*, Fullerton: California State University and

Southern California Local History Council, 1973.

Hayden White, *Metahistory: The Historical Imagination in Nineteenth-Century Europe*, Baltimore: Johns Hopkins University Press, 1973.

Kathy Kahn, *Hillbilly Women: Mountain Women Speak of Struggle and Joy in Southern Appalachia*, Garden City: Doubleday, 1973.

Jan Vansina, *Oral Tradition: A Study in Historical Methodology*, Harmondsworth: Penguin Books, 1973.

Peter Joseph, *Good Times: An Oral History of America in the Nineteen Sixties*, New York: Charterhouse, 1973.

Peter Parsons and Peter Anastas, *When Gloucester was Gloucester: Toward an Oral History of the City*, Gloucester: Gloucester 350th Anniversary Celebration, 1973.

Richard D. Curtiss, Gary L. Shumway and Shirley E. Stephenson (eds.), *A Guide for Oral History Programs*, Fullerton: Oral History Program, California State University, Fullerton, 1973.

Edward D. Ives, *A Manual for Field Workers*, Orono: Northeast Folklore Society, 1974.

Frank Freidel (ed.), *Harvard Guide to American History*, Cambridge: Belknap Press of Harvard University Press, revised edition, 1974.

Mike Steen, *Hollywood Speaks: An Oral History*, New York: Putnam, 1974.

Ronald J. Grele and Gaile A. Grele (eds.), *Oral History: An Annotated Bibliography*, Washington: National Institute of Education, U. S. Department of Health, Education and Welfare, 1974.

Studs Terkel, *Working: People Talk about What They Do All Day and How They Feel about What They Do*, New York: Pantheon Books, 1974.

Thomas J. Burns (ed.), *Accounting in Transition: Oral Histories of Recent*

U. S. Experience, Columbus: College of Administrative Science, Ohio State University, 1974.

Vivian Perlis, *Charles Ives Remembered: An Oral History*, New Haven: Yale University Press, 1974.

William W. Moss, *Oral History Program Manual*, New York, Praeger Publishers, 1974.

Alan M. Meckler and Ruth McMullin (eds.), *Oral History Collections*, New York: R. R. Bowker Company, 1975.

Manfred J. Waserman (ed.), *Bibliography on Oral History*, New York: Oral History Association, revised edition, 1975.

Peter Friedlander, *The Emergence of a UAW Local, 1936-1939: A Study in Class and Culture*, Pittsburgh: University of Pittsburgh Press, 1975.

Ramon I. Harris, Joseph H. Cash, Herbert T. Hoover, and Stephen R. Ward, *The Practice of Oral History: A Handbook*, Glen Rock: Microfilming Corporation of America, 1975.

Ronald J. Grele (ed.), *Envelopes of Sound: Six Practitioners Discuss the Method, Theory and Practice of Oral History and Oral Testimony*, Chicago: Precedent Publishing, 1975.

University of South Dakota (ed.), *American Indian Oral History Research Project*, Glen Rock: Microfilming Corporation of America, 1975.

Columbia University, Oral History Research Office, *Oral History: How to Use The Collection; Input/Output 1976: Toward a New Professionalism*, New York: Oral History Research Office, 1976.

David Kay Strate, *The Process of Oral History*, Dodge City: Cultural Heritage and Arts Center, 1976.

John A. Neuenschwander, *Oral History as a Teaching Approach*, Washington: National Education Association, 1976.

John Brady, *The Craft of Interviewing*, New York: Vintage Books, 1976.

John J. Fox, *Oral History: Window to the Past*, Salem: Salem State College, 1976.

Mary Jo Deering and Barbara Pomeroy, *Transcribing without Tears: A Guide to Transcribing and Editing Oral History*, Washington: Oral History Program, George Washington University Library, 1976.

Norman Michael Bock, *Chameleon Cloaks, Flying Tigers, and Missionary Ladies: The Oral History and Political Economy of Baltimore Chinatown and the China Relief Movement 1937-41*, Cambridge: Harvard University, 1976.

Oral History Guide: A Bibliographic Listing of the Memoirs in the Micropublished Collections, Glen Rock: Microfilming Corporation of America, 1976-1983.

Ann Rune (ed.), *Oral History Index: Washington State Oral/Aural History Program, 1974-1977*, Olympia: The Division, 1977.

Bruce M. Stave, *The Making of Urban History: Historiography through Oral History*, Beverly Hills: Sage Publications, 1977.

Bubberson Brownand Nick Lindsay, *An Oral History of Edisto Island: The Life and Times of Bubberson Brown*, Goshen: Pinchpenny Press, 1977.

Cullom Davis, Kathryn Back and Kay MacLean, *Oral History: From Tape to Type*, Chicago: American Library Association, 1977.

Gary L. Shumway, *An Oral History Primer*, Salt Lake City: Primer Publications, 1977.

Gwendolyn Safier, *Contemporary American Leaders in Nursing: An Oral History*, New York: McGraw-Hill, 1977.

Laurel Shackelford and Bill Weinberg (eds.), *Our Appalachia: An Oral History*, New York: Hill and Wang, 1977.

Oscar Lewis, Ruth M. Lewis, and Susan M. Rigdon, *Living the Revolu-*

tion: *An Oral History of Contemporary Cuba*, Urbana: University of Illinois Press, 1977.

Willa K. Baum, *Transcribing and Editing Oral History*, Nashville: American Association for State and Local History, 1977 and 1991.

Carl Oblinger, *Interviewing the People of Pennsylvania*: *A Conceptual Guide to Oral History*, Harrisburg: Pennsylvania Historical and Museum Commission, 1978.

Carol Fenichel, Cynthia S. Pomerleau, Regina Morantz, and Sarah Burke, *Oral History Collection on Women in Medicine*: *Catalogue*, Philadelphia: Medical College of Pennsylvania, 1978.

Claremont Graduate School, *Claremont Graduate School Oral History Program*: *A Bibliography*, Claremont: Claremont University Center, 1978.

Columbia University, Oral History Research Office, *Oral History*, *the First Thirty Years*: *Project on American Leaders*, *New Catalogue*, *Highlights 1948—78*, New York: Oral History Research Office, 1978.

Corinne Azen Krause, *Grandmothers*, *Mothers and Daughters*: *An Oral History Study of Ethnicity*, *Mental Health*, *and Continuity of Three Generations of Jewish*, *Italian*, *and Slavic-American Women*, New York: Institute on Pluralism and Group Identity, 1978.

Elizabeth Isichei (ed.), *Igbo Worlds*: *An Anthology of Oral Histories and Historical Descriptions*, Philadelphia: Institute for the Study of Human Issues, 1978.

Gus Richardson, et al. (eds.), *The Great War and Canadian Society*: *An Oral History*, Toronto: New Hogtown Press, 1978.

Joyce L. Kornbluh and M. Brady Mikusko (eds.), *Working Womenroots*: *An Oral History Primer*, Ann Arbor: Institute of Labor and Industrial Relations, University of Michigan-Wayne State University, 1979.

Neil V. Rosenberg (ed.), *Folklore and Oral History*, St. John's: Memorial University of Newfoundland, 1978.

Paul Thompson, *The Voice of the Past: Oral History*, Oxford and New York: Oxford University Press, 1978.

Shirley E. Stephenson, *Editing and Indexing: Guidelines for Oral History*, Fullerton: Oral History Program, California State University, Fullerton, 1978.

Benis M. Frank (ed.), *Marine Corps Oral History Collection Catalog*, Washington: History and Museums Division, Headquarters, U. S. Marine Corps, 1979.

Columbia University, Oral History Research Office, *Oral History, Looking to the 1980s: The New Catalogue, Where to Find It Input/Output, 1979, Sharing*, New York: Oral History Research Office, 1979.

Elizabeth B. Mason and Louis M. Starr (eds.), *The Oral History Collection of Columbia University*, New York: Oral History Research Office, 1979.

Georg G. Iggers and Harold T. Parker (eds.) *International Handbook of Historical Studies: Contemporary Research and Theory*, Westport: Greenwood Press, 1979.

George L. Mehaffy, Thad Sitton, and O. L. Davis, *Oral History in the Classroom*, Washington: National Council for the Social Studies, 1979.

Harry Maurer, *Not Working: An Oral History of The Unemployed*, New York: Holt, Rinehart, and Winston, 1979.

James Hoopes, *Oral History: An Introduction for Students*, Chapel Hill: University of North Carolina Press, 1979.

Milton L. Rakove, *We Don't Want Nobody Nobody Sent: An Oral History of the Daley Years*, Bloomington: Indiana University Press, 1979.

Ronald Fraser, *Blood of Spain: An Oral History of The Spanish Civil War*, New York: Pantheon Books, 1979.

Edward D. Ives, *The Tape-Recorded Interview: A Manual for Fieldworkers in Folklore and Oral History*, Knoxville: University of Tennessee Press, 1980.

Hubert Humphreys (ed.), *Louisiana Oral History Collections: A Directory*, Shreveport: Distributed by LSU-S Book Store, 1980.

Linda Shopes, *Using Oral History for a Family History Project*, Nashville: American Association for State and Local History, 1980.

Michael Kammen (ed.), *The Past Before Us: Contemporary Historical Writing in the United States*, Ithaca: Cornell University Press, 1980.

Oral History Evaluation Guidelines: Report of the Wingspread Conference, July 27-28, 1979, Racine, Wisconsin, as Amended and Approved by the Annual Business Meeting of the Oral History Association, October 27, 1979, East Lansing: Oral History Association, 1980.

Studs Terkel, *American Dreams: Lost and Found*, New York: Pantheon Books, 1980.

Suzanne B. Riess and Willa Baum (eds.), *Catalogue I of the Regional Oral History Office, 1954-1979*, Berkeley: Bancroft Library, University of California, Berkeley, 1980.

Theda Perdue, *Nations Remembered: An Oral History of the Five Civilized Tribes, 1865-1907*, Westport: Greenwood Press, 1980.

Archie Satterfield, *The Home Front: An Oral History of the War Years in America, 1941-1945*, New York: Playboy Press, 1981.

Al Santoli (ed.), *Everything We Had: An Oral History of the Vietnam War*, New York: Random House, 1981.

Barbara Allen William Lynwood Montell, *From Memory to History: Using Oral Sources in Local Historical Research*, Nashville: American Association for State and Local History, 1981.

Donald Denoon and Roderic Lacey (eds.), *Oral Tradition in Melanesia*,

Port Moresby: University of Papua New Guinea, 1981.

Howard Abadinsky, *The Mafia in America: An Oral History*, New York: Praeger, 1981.

James Bennett, *Oral History and Delinquency: The Rhetoric of Criminology*, Chicago: University of Chicago Press, 1981.

Kathryn Wrigley (ed.), *Directory of Illinois Oral History Resources*, Springfield: Oral History Office, Sangamon State University, 1981.

Stephen Humphries, *Hooligans or Rebels?: An Oral History of Working-Class Childhood and Youth, 1889-1939*, Oxford: Basil Blackwell, 1981.

Sylvia Rothchild (ed.), *Voices from the Holocaust*, New York: New American Library, 1981.

Thomas L. Charlton, *Oral History for Texans*, Austin: Texas Historical Commission, 1981 and 1985.

Audrey Olsen Faulkner, et al. (eds.), *When I Was Comin' Up: An Oral History of Aged Blacks*, Hamden: Archon Books, 1982.

Benjamin Appel, *The People Talk: American Voices from the Great Depression*, New York: Simon and Schuster, 1982.

Carol Gilligan, *In a Different Voice*, Cambridge: Harvard University Press, 1982.

David E. Kyvig and Myron A. Marty, *Nearby History: Exploring the Past around You*, Nashville: American Association for State and Local History, 1982.

David Henige, *Oral Historiography*, London: Longman, 1982.

Jeffrey A. Fadiman, *An Oral History of Tribal Warfare: The Meru of Mt. Kenya*, Athens: Ohio University Press, 1982.

Kenneth Griffith and Timothy E. O'Grady, *Curious Journey: An Oral History of Ireland's Unfinished Revolution*, London: Hutchinson, 1982.

Lynne Reid Banks, *Torn Country: An Oral History of the Israeli War of In-*

dependence, New York: Watts, 1982.

Patsy A. Cook (ed.), *Directory of Oral History Programs in the United States*, Sanford: Microfilming Corporation of America, 1982.

Regina Markell Morantz, Cynthia Stodola Pomerleau, and Carol Hansen Fenichel (eds.), *In Her Own Words: Oral Histories of Women Physicians*, Westport: Greenwood Press, 1982.

The Voices Project (ed.), *Oral History in the Classroom*, Boston: The Voices Project, Division of Curriculum and Instruction, Massachusetts Department of Education, 1982.

Alice Duffy Rinehart (ed.), *Mortals in the Immortal Profession: An Oral History of Teaching*, New York: Irvington Publishers, 1983.

Anthony Seldon and Joanna Pappworth, *By Word of Mouth: 'Elite' Oral History*, London: Methuen, 1983.

Ann Foley Scheuring (ed.), *Tillers: An Oral History of Family Farms in California*, New York: Praeger, 1983.

Ann L. Craig, *The First Agraristas: An Oral History of a Mexican Agrarian Reform Movement*, Berkeley: University of California Press, 1983.

Arthur R. Taylor, *Labour and Love: An Oral History of the Brass Band Movement*, London: Elm Tree Books, 1983.

Eileen Sunada Sarasohn (ed.), *The Issei, Portrait of a Pioneer: An Oral History*, Palo Alto: Pacific Books, 1983.

John H. Laub, *Criminology in the Making: An Oral History*, Boston: Northeastern University Press, 1983.

Lee Smith, *Oral History*, New York: Putnam, 1983.

Sherna Berger Gluck, *Rosie the Riveter Revisited: Women and the World War II Work Experience*, Long Beach: School of Social and Behavioral Sciences, Oral History Resource Center, California State University, 1983.

Thad Sitton, George L. Mehaffy, and O. L. Davis, Jr., *Oral History: A Guide for Teachers (and Others)*, Austin: University of Austin Press, 1983.

Belinda Hurmence (eds.), *My Folks Don't Want Me to Talk about Slavery: Twenty-one Oral Histories of Former North Carolina Slaves*, Winston-Salem: J. F. Blair, 1984.

David K. Dunaway and Willa K. Baum (eds.), *Oral History: An Interdisciplinary Anthology*, Nashville: American Association for State and Local History, 1984.

Edilberto N. Alegre and Doreen G. Fernandez, *The Writer and His Milieu: An Oral History of First Generation Writers in English*, Manila: De La Salle University Press, 1984.

Elizabeth Roberts, *A Woman's Place: An Oral History of Working-Class Women, 1890-1940*, New York: B. Blackwell, 1984.

John Tateishi (ed.), *And Justice for All: An Oral History of the Japanese American Detention Camps*, New York: Random House, 1984.

Peter Golenbock, *Bums-An Oral History of the Brooklyn Dodgers*, New York: Putnam, 1984.

Peter Read (ed.), *Down There with Me on the Cowra Mission: An Oral History of Erambie Aboriginal Reserve, Cowra, New South Wales*, New York: Pergamon Press, 1984.

Ron Strickland (ed.), *River Pigs and Cayuses: Oral Histories from the Pacific Northwest*, San Francisco: Lexikos, 1984.

Studs Terkel, *"The Good War": An Oral History of World War Two*, New York: Pantheon Books, 1984.

Tony Simpson, *The Sugarbag Years: An Oral History of the 1930s Depression in New Zealand*, Auckland: Hodder and Stoughton, second edition, 1984.

Wallace Terry (ed.), *Bloods, An Oral History of the Vietnam War*, New York: Random House, 1984.

William Luis (ed.), *Voices from Under: Black Narrative in Latin America and the Caribbean*, Westport: Greenwood Press, 1984.

Alfonso Griego, *Voices of the Territory of New Mexico: An Oral History of People of Spanish Descent and Early Settlers Born during the Territorial Days*, Albuquerque: A. Griego, 1985.

Claude Lanzmann, *Shoah*, Paris: Fayard, 1985.

Claude Lanzmann, *Shoah: An Oral History of the Holocaust*, New York: Pantheon Books, 1985.

Donald Knox, *The Korean War: An Oral History*, San Diego: Harcourt Brace Jovanovich, 1985-1988.

Eleanor Arnold (ed.), *Voices of American Homemakers*, Hollis: National Extension Homemakers Council, 1985.

Fran Leeper Buss (ed.), *Dignity: Lower Income Women Tell of Their Lives and Struggles: Oral Histories*, Ann Arbor: University of Michigan Press, 1985.

Ira Gitler, *Swing to Bop: An Oral History of the Transition in Jazz in the 1940s*, New York: Oxford University Press, 1985.

Jan Vansina, *Oral Tradition as History*, London: James Currey, 1985.

John A. Neuenschwander, *Oral History and the Law*, Denton: Oral History Association, 1985.

John Tullius, *I'd Rather Be a Yankee: An Oral History of America's Most Loved and Most Hated Baseball Team*, New York: Palgrave Macmillan, 1986.

Kings M. Phiri, *Oral History Research in Malawi since 1964*, Limbe: University of Malawi, Chancellor College, 1985.

Krzysztof M. Gebhard, *Community as Classroom: A Teacher's Practical*

Guide to Oral History, Regina: Saskatchewan Archives Board, 1985.

Lewis E. Weeks and Howard J. Berman, *Shapers of American Health Care Policy: An Oral History*, Ann Arbor: Health Administration Press, 1985.

Nigel Gray (ed.), *The Worst of Times: An Oral History of the Great Depression in Britain*, Totowa: Barnes & Noble, 1985.

Patricia Pate Havlice, *Oral History: A Reference Guide and Annotated Bibliography*, Jefferson: McFarland & Co., 1985.

Ronald J. Grele (ed.), *Envelopes of Sound: The Art of Oral History*, Chicago: Precedent Publishing, second edition, revised and enlarged, 1985.

Shirley E. Stephenson, *Oral History Collection, California State University, Fullerton*, Fullerton: Oral History Program, California State University, 1985.

Stewart Bird, Dan Georgakas, and Deborah Shaffer, *Solidarity Forever: An Oral History of the IWW*, Chicago: Lake View Press, 1985.

Susan E. Chaplin (ed.), *Fishing, Sand and Village Days: An Oral History of Frankston from the Early 1900s to 1950*, Frankston: Frankston City Library, 1985.

Sylvia Rothchild, *A Special Legacy: An Oral History of Soviet Jewish Emigrés in the United States*, New York: Simon and Schuster, 1985.

Ted Ferguson (ed.), *Sentimental Journey: An Oral History of Train Travel in Canada*, Garden City: Doubleday, 1985.

A. J. McClanahan, *Our Stories, Our Lives: A Collection of Twenty-three Transcribed Interviews with Elders of the Cook Inlet Region*, Anchorage: CIRI Foundation, 1986.

Al Barkow, *Gettin' to the Dance Floor: An Oral History of American Golf*, New York: Atheneum, 1986.

Alice Cornelison, Silas E. Craft, and Lillie Price, *History of Blacks in Howard County, Maryland: Oral History, Schooling, and Contemporary Issues*,

Columbia: Howard County, Maryland, NAACP, 1986.

Barbara J. Howe and Emory L. Kemp (eds.), *Public History: An Introduction*, Malabar: Krieger Publishing Company, 1986.

Carol Kammen, *On Doing Local History*, Nashville: American Association for State and Local History, 1986.

Catherine Johnson (ed.), *Looking Back at Liverpool: An Oral History of the Liverpool Region 1900-1960*, Liverpool: Liverpool City Council, 1986.

Eleni Fourtouni (ed.), *Greek Women in Resistance: Journals, Oral Histories*, New Haven: Thelphini Press, 1986.

Frederick J. Stielow, *The Management of Oral History Sound Archives*, Westport: Greenwood Press, 1986.

Joan Ringelheim and Esther Katz, *A Catalogue of Audio and Video Collections of Holocaust Testimony*, New York: Institute for Research in History, 1986.

John Miles Foley (ed.), *Oral Tradition in Literature: Interpretation in Context*, Columbia: University of Missouri Press, 1986.

John T. Mason, Jr. (ed.), *The Pacific War Remembered: An Oral History Collection*, Annapolis: Naval Institute Press, 1986.

Motlatsi Thabane, *Personal Testimony as an Historical Source in Lesotho: Some Methodological Guidelines*, Roma: National University of Lesotho, 1986.

Roy Rosenzweig (ed.), *Government and the Arts in Thirties America: A Guide to Oral Histories and Other Research Materials*, Fairfax: George Mason University Press, 1986.

S. J. T. Samkange, *Oral History: The Zvimba People of Zimbabwe*, Harare: Harare Publishing House, 1986.

Samuel Mullinsand Gareth Griffiths (eds.), *'Cap and Apron': An Oral History of Domestic Service in the Shires, 1880-1950*, Leicester: Leicestershire

Museums, Art Galleries & Record Service, 1986.

Steven P. C. Moyo, Tobias W. C. Sumaili, and James A. Moody (eds.), *Oral Traditions in Southern Africa*, Lusaka: Division for Culture Research, Institute for African Studies, University of Zambia, 1986.

Studs Terkel, *Hard Times: An Oral History of the Great Depression*, New York: Pantheon Books, 1986.

The People of Thurcroft, *Thurcroft, a Village and the Miners' Strike: An Oral History*, Nottingham: Atlantic Highlands, 1986.

William Greer with John A. Logan and Paul S. Willis, and Other Food Industry Leaders, *America the Bountiful: How the Supermarket Came to Main Street: An Oral History*, Washington: Food Marketing Institute in Cooperation with Beatrice Companies, 1986.

Bradford Heritage Recording Unit, *Destination Bradford: A Century of Immigration: Photographs and Oral History*, Bradford: Bradford Libraries and Information Service, 1987.

David Mas Masumoto, *Country Voices: The Oral History of a Japanese American Family Farm Community*, Del Rey: Inaka Countryside Publications, 1987.

Editors of Institutional Investor, *The Way It Was: An Oral History of Twenty Years of Finance*, New York: Institutional Investor, 1987.

George Ewart Evans, *Spoken History*, London: Faber, 1987.

Howard Williamson, *Toolmaking and Politics, The Life of Ted Smallbone: An Oral History*, Birmingham: Linden, 1987.

Kathryn Marshall, *In the Combat Zone: An Oral History of American Women in Vietnam, 1966-1975*, Boston: Little, Brown, 1987.

Kim Willenson, *The Bad War: An Oral History of the Vietnam War*, New York: New American Library, 1987.

Luisa Passerini, *Fascism in Popular Memory*: *The Cultural Experience of the Turin Working Class*, Cambridge: Cambridge University Press, 1987.

Paul Buhle (ed.), *Working Lives*: *An Oral History of Rhode Island Labor*, Providence: Rhode Island Historical Society, 1987.

Rina Benmayor, et al., *Stories to Live By*: *Continuity and Change in Three Generations of Puerto Rican Women*, New York: Hunter College, City University of New York, 1987.

Roberta Blaikie and Glenn Telfer, *Way to the Past*: *An Introduction to Oral History and Reminiscence Work*, Glasgow: Community Service Volunteers, 1987.

Ronnie Munckand Bill Rolston, *Belfast in the Thirties*: *An Oral History*, New York: St. Martin's Press, 1987.

Ruth Edmonds Hill and Patricia Miller King (eds.), *The Black Women Oral History Project*: *A Guide to the Transcripts*, Cambridge: Schlesinger Library, 1987.

Sherna Berger Gluck, *Rosie the Riveter Revisited*: *Women, the War, and Social Change*, New York: Twayne Publishers, 1987.

Stephen R. MacKinnon and Oris Friesen, *China Reporting*: *An Oral History of American Journalism in the 1930's and 1940's*, Berkeley: University of California Press, 1987.

Trevor Lummis, *Listening to History*: *The Authenticity of Oral Evidence*, London: Hutchinson Education, 1987.

Willa K. Baum, *Oral History for the Local Historical Society*, Nashville: American Association for State and Local History by Special Arrangement with The Conference of California Historical Societies, third edition, revised, 1987.

Zhang Xinxin and Sang Ye, *Chinese Lives*: *An Oral History of Contemporary China*, New York: Pantheon Books, 1987.

Al Santoli, *New Americans: An Oral History: Immigrants and Refugees in the U. S. Today*, New York: Viking, 1988.

Allen Smith, *Directory of Oral History Collections*, Phoenix: Oryx Press, 1988.

Anton Gill, *The Journey Back from Hell: An Oral History: Conversations with Concentration Camp Survivors*, New York: Morrow, 1988.

Barry A. Lanman and George L. Mehaffy, *Oral History in the Secondary School Classroom*, Los Angeles: Oral History Association, 1988.

Cynthia Stokes Brown, *Like It Was: A Complete Guide to Writing Oral History*, New York: Teachers and Writers Collaborative, 1988.

Dorothy E. Moore and James H. Morrison (eds.), *Work, Ethnicity, and Oral History*, Halifax: International Education Centre, St. Mary's University, 1988.

Jacqueline Sarsby, *Missuses and Mouldrunners: An Oral History of Women Pottery-Workers at Work and at Home*, Philadelphia: Open University Press, 1988.

Joe Smithand Mitchell Fink, *Off the Record: An Oral History of Popular Music*, New York: Warner Books, 1988.

Louise Douglas, Alan Roberts, and Ruth Thompson, *Oral History: A Handbook*, Boston: Allen & Unwin, 1988.

Max G. Manwaring and Court Prisk (eds.), *El Salvador at War: An Oral History of Conflict from the 1979 Insurrection to the Present*, Washington: National Defense University Press, 1988.

Paul Thompson, *The Voice of the Past: Oral History*, Oxford and New York: Oxford University Press, second edition, 1988

Peter Novick, *That Noble Dream: The "Objectivity Question" and the American Historical Profession*, Cambridge: Cambridge University Press, 1988.

Reflections on the Harvard Graduate School of Education 1948-1985: *An Oral History Recorded on the Occasion of Harvard's 350th Anniversary*, Cambridge: Harvard Graduate School of Education, 1988.

Stuart M. Archer and Nigel Shepley, *Witnessing History*: *Looking at Oral Evidence*, Cheltenham: Thornes, 1988.

Studs Terkel, *The Great Divide*: *Second Thoughts on the American Dream*, New York: Pantheon Books, 1988.

Susan Tucker, *Telling Memories among Southern Women*: *Domestic Workers and Their Employers in the Segregated South*, Baton Rouge: Louisiana State University Press, 1988.

Abraham J. Peck and Uri D. Herscher (eds.), *Queen City Refuge*: *An Oral History of Cincinnati's Jewish Refugees from Nazi Germany*, West Orange: Behrman House, 1989.

Anne Smith, *Women Remember*: *An Oral History*, London and New York: Routledge, 1989.

Belinda Hurmence (ed.) *Before Freedom*, *When I Just Can Remember*: *Twenty-Seven Oral Histories of Former South Carolina Slaves*, Winston-Salem: John F. Blair, Publisher, 1989.

Bob Blauner (ed.), *Black Lives*, *White Lives*: *Three Decades of Race Relations in America*, Berkeley: University of California Press, 1989.

Craig Etchison, *Maine Man*: *The Life and Times of a Down Easter*: *An Oral History of the Life of Ray Rice*, Santa Barbara: Fithian Press, 1989.

David Courtwright, Herman Joseph, and Don Des Jarlais, *Addicts Who Survived*: *An Oral History of Narcotic Use in America*, *1923-1965*, Knoxville: University of Tennessee Press, 1989.

Eric Hammel, *Khe Sanh*: *Siege in the Clouds*: *An Oral History*, New York: Crown Publishers, 1989.

Eva M. McMahan, *Elite Oral History Discourse: A Study of Cooperation and Coherence*, Tuscaloosa: University of Alabama Press, 1989.

Gerard Hutchinsonand Mark O'Neill, *The Springburn Experience: An Oral History of Work in a Railway Community from 1840 to the Present Day*, Edinburgh: Polygon, 1989.

Gerald R. Gioglio, *Days of Decision: An Oral History of Conscientious Objectors in the Military during the Vietnam War*, Trenton: Broken Rifle Press, 1989.

Harry Maurer, *Strange Ground: Americans in Vietnam, 1945-1975, an Oral History*, New York: H. Holt, 1989.

Henrietta Reifler (ed.), *Seattle Jews from China: Oral Histories*, Seattle: Washington State Jewish Historical Society, 1989.

Jeff Kisseloff, *You Must Remember This: An Oral History of Manhattan from the 1890's to World War II*, San Diego: Harcourt Brace Jovanovich, 1989.

Joel Makower, *Woodstock: The Oral History*, New York: Doubleday, 1989.

Johannes Steinhoff, Peter Pechel, and Dennis Showalter, *Voices from the Third Reich: An Oral History*, Washington: Regnery Gateway, 1989.

Personal Narratives Group (ed.), *Interpreting Women's Lives: Feminist Theory and Personal Narratives*, Bloomington: Indiana University Press, 1989.

Students in the Honors English Program at South Kingstown High School, *What Did You Do in the War, Grandma?: An Oral History of Rhode Island Women during World War II*, Linda P. Wood and Judi Scott, 1989.

Thomas Butler, *Memory: History, Culture and the Mind*, London: Basil Blackwell, 1989.

Zhila Rouhifar, *In Exile: Iranian Recollection*, London: Ethnic Communities Oral History Project, 1989.

Alice M. Hoffman and Howard S. Hoffman, *Archives of Memory*: *A Soldier Recalls World War II* , Lexington: University Press of Kentucky, 1990.

Anne Sells (ed.) *Remembering the Past*: *An Oral History Collection*, Melbourne: Victorian Branch of the Oral History Association of Australia, 1990.

Barbara Baird, *I Had One Too*: *An Oral History of Abortion in South Australia Before 1970*, Bedford Park: Women's Studies Unit, Flinders University of South Australia, 1990.

Cliff Kuhn, Harlon E. Joye and E. Bernard West, *Living Atlanta*: *An Oral History of the City*, *1914-1948*, Athens: University of Georgia Press, 1990.

David Steven Cohen (ed.), *America, the Dream of My Life*: *Selections from the Federal Writers' Project's New Jersey Ethnic Survey*, New Brunswick: Rutgers University Press, 1990.

David Thelen (ed.), *Memory and American History*, Bloomington: Indiana University Press, 1990.

Diane Manning, *Hill Country Teacher*: *Oral Histories from the One-room School and Beyond*, Boston: Twayne Publishers, 1990.

E. J. Alagoa (ed.), *Oral Tradition and Oral History in Africa and the Diaspora*: *Theory and Practice*, Nigeria: Centre for Black and African Arts and Civilization, Lagos for Nigerian Association for Oral History and Tradition, 1990.

Edward & Lois Schreiber (ed.), *Fish Creek Voices*: *An Oral History of a Door County Village*, Sister Bay: Wm Caxton, 1990.

Ellen S. Wasserman (ed.), *Oral History Index*: *An International Directory of Oral History Interviews*, Westport: Meckler, 1990.

Henry Hampton and Steve Fayer, *Voices of Freedom*: *An Oral History of the Civil Rights Movement from the 1950s through the 1980s*, New York: Bantam Books, 1990.

John T. Mason Jr. (ed.), *The Atlantic War Remembered: An Oral History Collection*, Annapolis: *Naval Institute Press*, 1990.

Judith Porter Adams, *Peacework: Oral Histories of Women Peace Activists*, Boston: Twayne Publishers, 1990.

Larry Engelmann, *Tears Before the Rain: An Oral History of the Fall of South Vietnam*, New York: Oxford University Press, 1990.

Marie-Noëlle Bourguet, Lucette Valensi, and Nathan Wachtel (eds.), *Between Memory and History*, New York: Harwood Academic Publishers, 1990.

Marilyn P. Davis, *Mexican Voices/American Dreams: An Oral History of Mexican Immigration to the United States*, New York: Henry Holt, 1990.

Michael Frisch, *A Shared Authority: Essays on the Craft and Meaning of Oral History and Public History*, Albany: State University of New York Press, 1990.

Michael P. Onorato, *Forgotten Heroes: Japan's Imprisonment of American Civilians in the Philippines, 1942-1945: An Oral History*, Westport: Meckler, 1990.

Michael V. Belok, Thomas H. Metos, and Nancy Lisherness, *The University President in Arizona, 1945-1980: An Oral History*, Lewiston: Mellen Press, 1990.

Neil MacMaster, *Spanish Fighters: An Oral History of Civil War and Exile*, New York: St. Martin's Press, 1990.

Oral History in Women Studies: Concept, Method, and Use, Bombay: Research Centre for Women's Studies, SNDT Women's University, 1990.

Paul Joseph Traver, *Eyewitness to Infamy: An Oral History of Pearl Harbor*, Lanham: Madison Books, 1990.

Paul Kenney and Sim Wentzell, *On the Beat: A Pictorial and Oral History* of the Royal Newfoundland Constabulary, St. John's: H. Cuff, 1990.

Raphael Samuel and Paul Thompson (eds.), *The Myths We Live By*, London and New York: Routledge, 1990.

Rhoda G. Lewin (ed.), *Witnesses to the Holocaust: An Oral History*, Boston: Twayne Publishers, 1990.

Robert Perks (ed.), *Oral History: An Annotated Bibliography*, London: British Library National Sound Archive, 1990.

Ron Strickland (ed.), *Whistlepunks and Geoducks: Oral Histories from the Pacific Northwest*, New York: Paragon House, 1990.

Rudolph Vecoli (ed.), *Voices from Ellis Island: An Oral History of American Immigration*, Frederick: University Publications of America, 1990.

Shelley Schreiner and Diane Bell (eds.), *This Is My Story: Perspectives on the Use of Oral Sources*, Geelong: Centre for Australian Studies, School of Humanities, Deakin University, 1990.

Stephen R. Fox, *The Unknown Internment: An Oral History of the Relocation of Italian-Americans During World War II*, New York: Twayne Publishers, 1990.

Alessandro Portelli, *The Death of Luigi Trastulli and Other Stories: Form and Meaning of Oral History*, Albany: State University of New York Press, 1991.

Bill McNeil, *Voices of a War Remembered: An Oral History of Canadians in World War Two*, Toronto: Doubleday Canada, 1991.

Corinne Azen Krause, *Grandmothers, Mothers, and Daughters: Oral Histories of Three Generations of Ethnic American Women*, Boston: Twayne Publishers, 1991.

Dick Irvin, *The Habs: An Oral History of the Montreal Canadiens, 1940-1980*, Toronto: McClelland and Stewart, 1991.

Eliot Wigginton (ed.), *Refuse to Stand Silently by: An Oral History of Grass Roots Social Activism in America, 1921-1964*, New York: Doubleday, 1991.

Eliot Wigginton and His Students (eds.), *Foxfire: 25 Years*, New York: Anchor Books, 1991.

Eugene Murdock, *Baseball Players and Their Times: Oral Histories of the Game, 1920-1940*, Westport: Meckler, 1991.

Feng Jicai, *Voices from the Whirlwind: An Oral History of the Chinese Cultural Revolution*, New York: Pantheon Books, 1991.

Joann Faung Jean Lee, *Asian American Experiences in the United States: Oral Histories of First to Fourth Generation Americans from China, the Philippines, Japan, India, the Pacific islands, Vietnam, and Cambodia*, Jefferson: McFarland & Co. , 1991.

John Tenhula, *Voices from Southeast Asia: The Refugee Experience in the United States*, New York: Holmes & Meier, 1991.

Karen Schwarz, *What You Can Do for Your Country: An Oral History of the Peace Corps*, New York: W. Morrow, 1991.

Richard Lourie, *Russia Speaks: An Oral History from the Revolution to the Present*, New York: E. Burlingame Books, 1991.

Robert C. Hardy, *One Hundred Years of Upstart Unitarianism in the Bible Belt: An Oral History of the First Unitarian Church of Oklahoma City*, Oklahoma City: First Unitarian Church, 1991.

Ronald J. Grele (ed.), *Envelopes of Sound: The Art of Oral History*, New York: Praeger Publishers, second edition, revised and enlarged, 1991.

Ruth Edmond Hill (ed.), *Black Women Oral History Project: From the Arthur and Elizabeth Schlesinger Library on the History of Women in America, Radcliffe College*, Westport: Meckler Publishing, 1991.

Sherna Berger Gluck and Daphne Patai (eds.), *Women's Words: The Feminist Practice of Oral History*, London and New York: Routledge, 1991.

Beatrice Rodriguez Owsley, *The Hispanic-American Entrepreneur: An Oral History of the American Dream*, New York: Twayne Publishers, 1992.

Ben Sidran, *Talking Jazz: An Illustrated Oral History*, San Francisco: Pomegranate Artbooks, 1992.

Elizabeth Tonkin, *Narrating Our Pasts: The Social Construction of Oral History*, Cambridge: Cambridge University Press, 1992.

Eric Marcus, *Making History: The Struggle for Gay and Lesbian Equal Rights, 1945-1990: An Oral History*, New York: HarperCollins, 1992.

Haruko Taya Cook and Theodore F. Cook, *Japan at War: An Oral History*, New York: The New Press, 1992.

J. T. Hansen, A. Susan Owen, and Michael Patrick, *Parallels: The Soldier's Knowledge and the Oral History of Contemporary Warfare*, Madden: Aldine de Gruyter, 1992.

Jacques Le Goff, *History and Memory*, New York: Columbia University Press, 1992.

James Thomas Baker, *Studs Terkel*, New York: Twayne Publishers, 1992.

John Bodnar, *Remaking America: Public Memory, Commemoration and Patriotism in the Twentieth Century*, Princeton: Princeton University Press, 1992.

John Shields (ed.), *All Our Labours: Oral Histories of Working Life in Twentieth Century Sydney*, Kensington: New South Wales University Press, 1992.

Julie Jones-Eddy, *Homesteading Women: An Oral History of Colorado, 1890-1950*, New York: Twayne Publishers, 1992.

Laurie Mercier and Madeline Buckendorf, *Using Oral History in Community History Projects*, Los Angeles: Oral History Association, 1992 (Carlisle: Oral History Association, 2007).

Luisa Passerini (ed.), *Memory and Totalitarianism*, Oxford and New York: Oxford University Press, 1992.

Mary Logan Rothschild and Pamela Claire Hronek, *Doing What the Day Brought: An Oral History of Arizona Women*, Tucson: University of Arizona Press, 1992.

Patricia Preciado Martin, *Songs My Mother Sang to Me: An Oral History of Mexican American Women*, Tucson: University of Arizona Press, 1992.

Peter Burke (ed.), *New Perspectives on Historical Writing*, University Park: Pennsylvania State University Press, 1992.

Phyllis K. Leffler and Joseph Brent (eds.), *Public History Readings*, Malabar: Krieger Publishing Company, 1992.

Reinharz Shulamit, *Feminist Methods in Social Research*, Oxford and New York: Oxford University Press, 1992.

Robert Perks, *Oral History: Talking about the Past*, London: The Historical Association and Oral History Society, 1992.

Ronald J. Grele (ed.), *International Annual of Oral History, 1990: Subjectivity and Multiculturalism in Oral History*, Westport: Greenwood Press, 1992.

Saad A. Sowayan, *The Arabian Oral Historical Narrative: An Ethnographic and Linguistic Analysis*, Wiesbaden: O. Harrassowitz, 1992.

Stephen E. Everett, *Oral History: Techniques and Procedures*, Washington: Center of Military History, United States Army, 1992.

Studs Terkel, *Race: What Blacks and Whites Think and Feel about the American Obsession*, New York: The New Press, 1992.

Tim Wells and William Triplett, *The Drug Wars: An Oral History from the Trenches*, New York: W. Morrow, 1992.

Vicki Jenkins, *Oral History as an Intergenerational Religious Education Program*, Malden: Unitarian Universalist Women's Heritage Society, 1992.

Andrew J. Dunar and Dennis McBride, *Building Hoover Dam: An Oral History of the Great Depression*, New York: Twayne Publishers, 1993.

Brett Harvey, *The Fifties: A Women's Oral History*, New York: Harper-Collins Publishers, 1993.

Daniel Bertaux and Paul Thompson (eds.), *Between Generations: Family Models, Myths, and Memories*, Oxford and New York: Oxford University Press, 1993.

Daniel McLaughlin and William G. Tierney (eds.), *Naming Silenced Lives: Personal Narratives and the Process of Educational Change*, London and New York: Routledge, 1993.

David Lemmon, *For the Love of the Game: An Oral History of First-Class Cricket*, London: M. Joseph, 1993.

Donald E. Miller and Lorna Touryan Miller, *Survivors: An Oral History of the Armenian Genocide*, Berkeley: University of California Press, 1993.

E. T. Wooldridge (ed.), *Carrier Warfare in the Pacific: An Oral History Collection*, Washington: Smithsonian Institution Press, 1993.

Edward Berger, *Basically Speaking: An Oral History of George Duvivier*, Metuchen: Scarecrow Press, 1993.

George Ewart Evans, *The Crooked Scythe: An Anthology of Oral History*, London: Faber and Faber, 1993.

Gerald S. and Deborah H. Strober, *Let Us Begin Anew: An Oral History of the Kennedy Presidency*, New York: HarperCollins Publishers, 1993.

James W. Tollefson, *The Strength Not to Fight: An Oral History of Conscien-*

tious Objectors of the Vietnam War, Boston: Little, Brown, 1993.

John A. Neuenschwander, *Oral History and the Law*, Albuquerque: Oral History Association, Revised Edition, 1993.

Justin Vitiello, *Poetics and Literature of the Sicilian Diaspora: Studies in O-ral History and Story-Telling*, San Francisco: Mellen Research University Press, 1993.

Kathleen Casey, *I Answer with My Life: Life Histories of Women Teachers Working for Social Change*, London and New York: Routledge, 1993.

Kim Lacy Rogers, *Righteous Lives: Narratives of the New Orleans Civil Rights Movement*, New York: New York University Press, 1993.

Linda Tamura, *The Hood River Issei: An Oral History of Japanese Settlers in Oregon's Hood River Valley*, Urbana: University of Illinois Press, 1993.

Mark Caruana and Barry York, *Oral History: A Practical Guide Based on Maltese Migration and Settlement in Australia (Including a Catalogue of Collec-tions)*, Canberra: Centre for Immigration and Multicultural Studies, Research School of Social Sciences, Australian National University, 1993.

Mary Kupiec Cayton, Elliott J. Gorn and Peter W. Williams (eds.) *Ency-clopedia of American Social History*, New York: Charles Scribner's Sons, 1993.

Martin J. Collins, *Oral History on Space, Science and Technology: A Cata-log of the Collection of the Department of Space History, National Air and Space Museum*, Washington: The Museum, 1993.

Martha K. Norkunas, *The Politics of Public Memory: Tourism, History, and Ethnicity in Monterey, California*, Albany: State University of New York Press, 1993.

Megan Hutching, *Talking History: A Short Guide to Oral History*, Welling-ton: Bridget Williams Books and Historical Branch, Department of Internal Af-fairs, 1993.

Michael E. Stevens (ed.), *Women Remember the War*, *1941—1945*, Madison: Center for Documentary History, State Historical Society of Wisconsin, 1993.

Myrna Katz Frommer and Harvey Frommer, *It Happened in Brooklyn*: *An Oral History of Growing up in the Borough in the 1940s*, *1950s*, *and 1960s*, New York: Harcourt Brace, 1993.

Normand Fortier (ed.), *Guide to Oral History Collections in Canada*, Ottawa: Canadian Oral History Association, 1993.

Patrick H. Hutton, *History as an Art of Memory*, Hanover: University Press of New England, 1993.

Peter Burke, *The Art of Conversation*, Ithaca: Cornell University Press, 1993.

Richard M. Stannard, *Infantry*: *An Oral History of a World War II American Infantry Battalion*, New York: Twayne Publishers, 1993.

Rosalie Riegle Troester (ed.), *Voices from the Catholic Worker*, Philadelphia: Temple University Press, 1993.

Rudy Tomedi, *No Bugles*, *No Drums*: *An Oral History of the Korean War*, New York: Wiley, 1993.

Shelton Stromquist, *Solidarity & Survival*: *An Oral History of Iowa Labor in the Twentieth Century*, Iowa City: University of Iowa Press, 1993.

Stacy Erickson, *A Field Notebook for Oral History*, Boise: Idaho Center for Oral History, second edition, 1993.

Stuart Rintoul, *The Wailing*: *A National Black Oral History*, Port Melbourne: W. Heinemann Australia, 1993.

The Sydney Film Festival, *An Oral History of the Sydney Film Festival*: *40 Years of Film*, Sydney: Sydney Film Festival, 1993.

Theda Perdue, *Nations Remembered*: *An Oral History of the Cherokees*,

Chickasaws, *Choctaws*, *Creeks*, *and Seminoles*, Norman: University of Oklahoma Press, 1993.

Vom Roy, *The Migration of Kenyah Badeng*: *A Study Based on Oral History*, Kuala Lumpur: Institute of Advanced Studies, Universiti Malaya, 1993.

Alec Bolton, *Interviewing for Oral History at the National Library of Australia*: *A Short Guide*, Canberra: National Library of Australia, 1994.

Alistair Thomson, *Anzac Memories*: *Living with the Legend*, Oxford and New York: Oxford University Press, 1994.

Clare Gillies and Anne James, *Reminiscence Work with Old People*, New York: Chapman & Hall, 1994.

Cornelia Heins, *The Wall Falls*: *An Oral History of the Reunification of the Two Germanies*, London: Grey Seal, 1994.

Diana Giese, *"All the Flavour of the Time Returns"*: *Using Oral History to Explore the Top End's Chinese Heritage*, Darwin: State Library of the Northern Territory, 1994.

Elaine Krasnow Ellison and Elaine Mark Jaffe, *Voices from Marshall Street*: *Jewish Life in a Philadelphia Neighborhood*, *1920-1960*, Philadelphia: Camino Books, 1994.

Elaine Latzman Moon, *Untold Tales*, *Unsung Heroes*: *An Oral History of Detroit's African American Community*, *1918-1967*, Detroit: Wayne State University Press, 1994.

Eva M. McMahan and Kim Lacy Rogers (eds.), *Interactive Oral History Interviewing*, Hillsdale: L. Erlbaum Associates, 1994.

Gerald S. Strober and Deborah H. Strober, *Nixon*: *An Oral History of His Presidency*, New York: HarperCollins, 1994.

Harry Maurer, *Sex*: *An Oral History*, New York: Viking, 1994.

Iwona Irwin-Zarecka, *Frames of Remembrance*: *The Dynamics of Collective*

Memory, New Brunswick: Transaction Publishers, 1994.

Jaclyn Jeffrey and Glenace E. Edwall (eds.), *Memory and History: Essays on Recalling and Interpreting Experience*, Lanham: University Press of America, 1994.

Jewell Fenzi and Carl L. Nelson, *Married to the Foreign Service: An Oral History of the American Diplomatic Spouse*, New York: Twayne Publishers, 1994.

Johannes Steinhoff, Peter Pechel, and Dennis Showalter, *Voices from the Third Reich: An Oral History*, New York: Da Capo Press, 1994.

John A. Benson, Jr. , *Oral Histories: American Board of Internal Medicine Chairmen*, *1947-1985*, Portland: Office of the ABIM Foundation Scholar, 1994.

John Peter, *The Oral History of Modern Architecture: Interviews with the Greatest Architects of the Twentieth Century*, New York: H. N. Abrams, 1994.

Julianne Lewis Adams, Thomas A. DeBlack, *Civil Obedience: An Oral History of School Desegregation in Fayetteville*, *Arkansas*, *1954-1965*, Fayetteville: University of Arkansas Press, 1994.

Jürgen Hesse (ed.) *Voices in Exile: Refugees Speak Out: An Oral History*, White Rock: Thinkware Publishers, 1994.

Kalman Jacob Mann, *Reflections on a Life in Health Care: An Oral History Memoir*, Jerusalem: Rubin Mass Ltd. , 1994.

Mike Parker, *Running the Gauntlet: An Oral History of Canadian Merchant Seamen in World War II* , Halifax: Nimbus, 1994.

Raphael Samuel, *Theatres of Memory: Past and Present in Contemporary Culture*, London: Verso, 1994.

Rina Benmayor and Andor Skotnes (eds.), *Migration and Identity*, Oxford and New York: Oxford University Press, 1994.

Rogan Taylor, Andrew Ward, and John Williams, *Three Sides of the Mersey: An Oral History of Everton, Liverpool and Tranmere Rovers*, London: Robson, 1993.

Roger J. Jones (ed.), *Back in Them Days: An Oral History of Preston*, Preston: Preston City Council, 1994.

Stephen Caunce, *Oral History and the Local Historian*, London: Longman, 1994.

Such a Long Story!: Chinese Voices in Britain, London: Ethnic Communities Oral History Project, 1994.

Sydney Lewis (ed.), *Hospital: An Oral History of Cook County Hospital*, New York: The New Press, 1994.

Ulric Neisser and Robyn Fivush (eds.), *The Remembering Self: Construction and Accuracy in the Self-Narrative*, Cambridge: Cambridge University Press, 1994.

Valerie Raleigh Yow, *Recording Oral History: A Practical Guide for Social Scientists*, Thousand Oaks: Sage Publications, 1994.

Alan Ward, *Copyright Ethics and Oral History*, Colchester: Oral History Society, University of Essex, 1995.

Ann Miller Morin, *Her Excellency: An Oral History of American Women Ambassadors*, New York: Twayne Publishers, 1995.

Barbara Weinberger, *The Best Police in the World: An Oral History of English Policing from the 1930s to the 1960s*, Aldershot: Scolar Press, 1995.

Bill Fawcett (ed.), *Hunters and Shooters: An Oral History of the U. S. Navy SEALs in Vietnam*, New York: W. Morrow, 1995.

Carl F. Kaestle, *Everybody's Been to Fourth Grade: An Oral History of Federal R&D in Education*, Madison: Wisconsin Center for Education, 1992.

Clara H. Friedman, *Between Management and Labor: Oral Histories of Arbi-*

tration, New York: Twayne Publishers, 1995.

Donald A. Ritchie, *Doing Oral History*, New York: Twayne Publishers, 1995.

E. T. Wooldridge (ed.), *Into the Jet Age: Conflict and Change in Naval Aviation, 1945-1975: An Oral History*, Annapolis: Naval Institute Press, 1995.

Edward D. Ives, *The Tape-Recorded Interview: A Manual for Field Workers in Folklore and Oral History*, Knoxville: University of Tennessee Press, second edition, 1995.

Elizabeth Roberts, *Women and Families: An Oral History, 1940-1970*, Oxford: Blackwell, 1995.

Ellen B. Basso, *The Last Cannibals: A South American Oral History*, Austin: University of Texas Press, 1995.

Gabrielle Morris, *Head of the Class: An Oral History of African-American Achievement in Higher Education and Beyond*, Boston: Twayne Publishers, 1995.

Jeff Kisseloff, *The Box: An Oral History of Television, 1920-1961*, New York: Viking, 1995.

Katrina R. Mason, *Children of Los Alamos: An Oral History of the Town Where the Atomic Age Began*, New York: Twayne Publishers, 1995.

Lisa Power, *No Bath but Plenty of Bubbles: An Oral History of the Gay Liberation Front, 1970-1973*, London: Cassell, 1995.

Marion Matters, *Oral History Cataloging Manual*, Chicago: Society of American Archivists, 1995.

Myrna Katz Frommer and Harvey Frommer, (eds.), *Growing up Jewish in America: An Oral History*, New York: Harcourt Brace & Co., 1995.

Paul Avrich, *Anarchist Voices: An Oral History of Anarchism in America*,

Princeton: Princeton University Press, 1995.

Robert Perks, *Oral History: Talking about the Past*, London: The Historical Association and Oral History Society, second and revised edition, 1995.

Rogan Taylor and Andrew Ward, *Kicking and Screaming: An Oral History of Football in England*, London: Robson, 1995.

Ruth R. Martin, *Oral History in Social Work: Research, Assessment, and Intervention*, Thousand Oaks: Sage Publications, 1995.

S. L. Sanger, *Working on the Bomb: An Oral History of WW II Hanford*, Portland: Portland State University, Continuing Education Press, 1995.

Studs Terkel, *Coming of Age: The Story of Our Century by Those Who've Lived It*, New York: The New Press, 1995.

Willa K. Baum, *Oral History for the Local Historical Society*, Walnut Creek: AltaMira Press, third edition, revised, 1995.

Willa K. Baum, *Transcribing and Editing Oral History*, Walnut Creek: AltaMira Press, 1995.

Yousuf Choudhury (ed.), *Sons of the Empire: Oral History from the Bangladeshi Seamen Who Served on British Ships During the 1939-45 War*, Birmingham: Sylheti Social History Group, 1995.

Veronica Lawlor (ed.), *I was Dreaming to Come to America: Memories from the Ellis Island Oral History Project*, New York: Viking, 1995.

Zorka Milich, *A Stranger's Supper: An Oral History of Centenarian Women in Montenegro*, New York: Twayne Publishers, 1995.

David K. Dunaway and Willa K. Baum (eds.), *Oral History: An Interdisciplinary Anthology*, Walnut Creek: AltaMira Press, second edition, 1996.

David D. Perata, *Those Pullman Blues: An Oral History of the African-American Railroad Attendant*, New York: Twayne Publishers, 1996.

David Richards and Tara Zachary (eds.), *Guide to Oral History Collections in Louisiana*, Baton Rouge: T. Harry Williams Center for Oral History, 1996.

Feng Jicai, *Ten Years of Madness: Oral Histories of China's Cultural Revolution*, San Francisco: China Books & Periodicals, 1996.

Heather T. Frazer and John O'Sullivan, *We Have Just Begun To Not Fight: An Oral History of Conscientious Objectors in Civilian Public Service During WWII*, New York: Twayne Publishers, 1996.

Janis Wilton (ed.), *Oral History in Australia: A List*, Sydney: Oral History Association of Australia (NSW Branch), 1996.

Larry Moffi, *This Side of Cooperstown: An Oral History of Major League Baseball in the 1950s*, Iowa City: University of Iowa Press, 1996.

Legs McNeil and Gillian McCain (eds.), *Please Kill Me: The Uncensored Oral History of Punk*, New York: Grove Press, 1996.

Leslie G. Kelen and Eileen Hallett Stone, *Missing Stories: An Oral History of Eight Ethnic and Minority Groups in Utah*, Salt Lake City: University of Utah Press, 1996.

Marat Moore, *Women in the Mines: Stories of Life and Work*, New York: Twayne Publishers, 1996.

Michael L. Gillette, *Launching the War on Poverty: An Oral History*, New York: Twayne Publishers, 1996.

Rick Halpern and Roger Horowitz, *Meatpackers: An Oral History of Black Packinghouse Workers and Their Struggle for Racial and Economic Equality*, New York: Twayne Publishers, 1996.

Ruth E. Wolman, *Crossing Over: An Oral History of Refugees from Hitler's Reich*, New York: Twayne Publishers, 1996.

Selma Leydesdorff, Luisa Passerini, and Paul Thompson (eds.), *Gender and Memory*, Oxford and New York: Oxford University Press, 1996.

Susan E. Johnson, *Lesbian Sex: An Oral History*, Tallahassee: Naiad

Press, 1996.

T. Lindsay Baker and Julie P. Baker (eds.), *The WPA Oklahoma Slave Narratives*, Norman: University of Oklahoma Press, 1996.

Trevor Blackwell and Jeremy Seabrook, *Talking Work: An Oral History*, London: Faber and Faber, 1996.

Alessandro Portelli, *The Battle of Valle Giulia: Oral History and The Art of Dialogue*, Madison: University of Wisconsin Press, 1997.

Andrew Shryock, *Nationalism and the Genealogical Imagination: Oral History and Textual Authority in Tribal Jordan*, Berkeley: University of California Press, 1997.

Benjamin Heim Shepard, *White Nights and Ascending Shadows: An Oral History of the San Francisco AIDS Epidemic*, Washington: Cassell, 1997.

Dan Rottenberg, *Middletown Jews: The Tenuous Survival of an American Jewish Community*, Bloomington: Indiana University Press, 1997.

David Cataneo, *Hornsby Hit One over My Head: A Fans' Oral History of Baseball*, San Diego: Harcourt Brace & Co. , 1997.

Dennis A. Trinkle and Scott A. Merriman (eds.), *The History Highway: A Guide to Internet Resources*, Armonk: M. E. Sharpe, 1997.

Edith Sizoo (ed.), *Women's Lifeworlds: Women's Narratives on Shaping Their Realities*, London and New York: Routledge, 1997.

Eric Foner (ed.), *The New American History*, Philadelphia: Temple University Press, revised and expanded edition, 1997.

James T. Sears, *Lonely Hunters: An Oral History of Lesbian and Gay Southern Life, 1948-1968*, Boulder: Westview Press, 1997.

John Howard (ed.), *Carryin' on in the Lesbian and Gay South*, New York: New York University Press, 1997.

Kim Marie Vaz (ed.), *Oral Narrative Research with Black Women*, Thousand Oaks: Sage Publications, 1997.

Legs McNeil and Gillian McCain (eds.), *Please Kill Me: The Uncensored Oral History of Punk*, New York: Penguin Books, 1997.

Lewis H. Carlson, *We Were Each Other's Prisoners: An Oral History of World War II American and German Prisoners of War*, New York: Basic Books, 1997.

Richard Stacewicz, *Winter Soldiers: An Oral History of the Vietnam Veterans against the War*, New York: Twayne Publishers, 1997.

Rita T. Kohn, William Lynwood Montell, and Michelle Mannering (eds.), *Always a People: Oral Histories of Contemporary Woodland Indians*, Bloomington: Indiana University Press, 1997.

Robert P. Grathwol, Donita M. Moorhus, and Douglas J. Wilson, *Oral History and Postwar German-American Relations: Resources in the United States*, Washington: German Historical Institute, 1997.

Susann Walens, *War Stories: An Oral History of Life Behind Bars*, Westport: Praeger, 1997.

Suzanne B. Riess and Willa Baum (eds.), *Catalogue II of the Regional Oral History office, 1980-1997*, Berkeley: Bancroft Library, University of California, Berkeley, 1997.

Alison Baker, *Voices of Resistance: Oral Histories of Moroccan Women*, Albany: State University of New York Press, 1998.

Andrés Torres and José E. Velázquez (eds.), *The Puerto Rican Movement: Voices from the Diaspora*, Philadelphia: Temple University Press, 1998

Bruce M. Stave, Michele Palmer, and Leslie Frank, *Witnesses to Nuremberg: An Oral History of American Participants at the War Crimes Trials*, New York: Twayne Publishers, 1998.

Deborah Hart Strober and Gerald S. Strober, *Reagan: The Man and His*

Presidency, Boston: Houghton Mifflin Co. , 1998.

Don Wallis (ed.), *All We Had Was Each Other: The Black Community of Madison, Indiana: An Oral History of the Black Community of Madison, Indiana*, Bloomington: Indiana University Press, 1998.

Filippo Salvatore, *Fascism and the Italians of Montreal: An Oral History, 1922-1945*, Toronto: Guernica, 1998.

Fred Moore, Paddy Gorman, and Ray Harrison, *At the Coalface: The Human Face of Coalminers and Their Communities: An Oral History of the Early Years*, Sydney: Mining and Energy Division of the Construction Forestry Mining and Energy Union, second edition, 1998.

James Robert Saunders and Renae Nadine Shackelford, *Urban Renewal and the End of Black Culture in Charlottesville, Virginia: An Oral History of Vinegar Hill*, Jefferson: McFarland & Co. , 1998.

Jean A. Boyd, *The Jazz of the Southwest: An Oral History of Western Swing*, Austin: University of Texas Press, 1998.

Kalyanee E. Mam, *An Oral History of Family Life under the Khmer Rouge*, New Haven: Yale Center for International and Area Studies, 1998.

Mary Chamberlain and Paul Thompson (eds.), *Narrative and Genre: Contexts and Types of Communication*, London and New York: Routledge, 1998.

Marylyn Addison (ed.), *King Island: A Time of Change: An Oral History of King Island*, King Island: Marylyn Addison, 1998.

Milton J. Nieuwsma, *Kinderlager: An Oral History of Young Holocaust Survivors*, New York: Holiday House, 1998.

P. Lim Pui Huen, James H. Morrison, and Kwa Chong Guan (eds.), *Oral History in Southeast Asia: Theory and Method*, Singapore: National Archives of Singapore and Institute of Southeast Asian Studies, 1998.

Patricia Burns, *The Shamrock and the Shield: An Oral History of The Irish in Montreal*, Montréal: Véhicule Press, 1998.

Penny Summerfield, *Reconstructing Women's Wartime Lives: Discourse and Subjectivity in Oral Histories of the Second World War*, Manchester: Manchester University Press, 1998.

Phil Pepe, *Talkin' Baseball: An Oral History of Baseball in the 1970s*, New York: Ballantine Books, 1998.

Robert Perks and Alistair Thomson (eds.), *The Oral History Reader*, London and New York: Routledge, 1998.

Steve Delsohn, *Talking Irish: The Oral History of Notre Dame Football*, New York: Avon Books, 1998.

William Lamont (ed.), *Historical Controversies and Historians*, London: University College London Press, 1998.

Bruce M. Stave, John F. Sutherland, and Aldo Salerno, *From the Old Country: An Oral History of European Migration to America*, Hanover: University Press of New England, 1999.

Chuck Foster, *Roots, Rock, Reggae: An Oral History of Reggae Music from Ska to Dancehall*, New York: Billboard, 1999.

David King Dunaway, *Aldous Huxley Recollected: An Oral History*, Walnut Creek: AltaMira Press, 1999.

David Pritchard and Alan Lysaght, *The Beatles: An Oral History*, St Leonards: Allen & Unwin, 1999.

James B. Gardner and Peter S. LaPaglia (eds.), *Public History: Essays from the Field*, Malabar: Krieger Publishing Company, 1999.

Jeff Kisseloff, *You Must Remember This: An Oral History of Manhattan from the 1890s to World War II*, Baltimore: Johns Hopkins University Press, 1999.

John Tateishi (ed.), *And Justice for All: An Oral History of the Japanese*

American Detention Camps, Seattle: University of Washington Press, 1999.

Judy Long, *Telling Women's Lives: Subject/Narrator/Reader/Text*, New York: New York University Press, 1999.

Judy Yung, *Unbound Voices: A Documentary History of Chinese Women in San Francisco*, Berkeley: University of California Press, 1999.

Kim Lacy Rogers, Selma Leydesdorff, and Graham Dawson (eds.), *Trauma and Life Stories: International Perspectives*, London and New York: Routledge, 1999.

Megan Hutching, *Long Journey for Sevenpence: An Oral History of Assisted Immigration to New Zealand from the United Kingdom, 1947-1975*, Wellington: Victoria University Press in Association with Historical Branch, Dept. of Internal Affairs, 1999.

Michael Keith Honey, *Black Workers Remember: An Oral History of Segregation, Unionism, and the Freedom Struggle*, Berkeley: University of California Press, 1999.

Patricia Cooper and Norma Bradley Allen, *The Quilters: Women and Domestic Art: An Oral History*, Lubbock: Texas Tech University Press, 1999.

Richard R. Vuylsteke (ed.), *Ties That Bind: Taipei American School, 1949-1999: An Oral History*, Taipei: Taipei American School, 1999.

Robert L. Leight and Alice Duffy Rinehart, *Country School Memories: An Oral History of One-Room Schooling*, Westport: Greenwood Press, 1999.

Russel Moldovan, *Martin Luther King, Jr. : An Oral History of His Religious Witness and His Life*, Lanham: International Scholars, 1999.

Stewart Emory Tolnay, *The Bottom Rung: African American Family Life on Southern Farms*, Urbana: University of Illinois Press, 1999.

Staughton Lynd, *Labor History, Oral History and May 4*, Kent: Kent State University, Libraries and Media Services, Department of Special Collections and Archives, 1999.

Studs Terkel, *The Spectator: Talk about Movies and Plays with Those Who Make Them*, New York: The New Press, 1999.

Teresa Barnett (ed.), *The UCLA Oral History Program: Catalog of the Collection*, Los Angeles: Oral History Program, Department of Special Collections, UCLA, third edition, 1999.

Alan B. Govenar, *African American Frontiers: Slave Narratives and Oral Histories*, Santa Barbara: ABC-CLIO, 2000.

Catherine Ward and Karen L. Westbrooks, *Oral Histories and Analyses of Nontraditional Women Students: A Study of Unconventional Strengths*, Lewiston: E. Mellen Press, 2000.

Daniel James, *Doña María's Story: Life History, Memory, and Political Identity*, Durham: Duke University Press, 2000.

Derek Matthews and Jim Pirie, *The Auditors Talk: An Oral History of a Profession from the 1920s to the Present Day*, New York: Garland Publishing, 2000.

Endel Tulving and Fergus I. M. Craik (eds.), *The Oxford Handbook of Memory*, Oxford and New York: Oxford University Press, 2000.

Hakeem B. Harunah, *Nigerian Oral Traditions and Oral History: Their Relevance to the Nation's Vision 2010 Programme*, Lagos: Nigerian Association for Oral History and Traditions (NAOHAT), 2000.

Jennie Ethell Chancey and William R. Forstchen (eds.), *Hot Shots: An Oral History of the Air Force Combat Pilots of the Korean War*, New York: W. Morrow, 2000.

Joanna Bornat, Robert Perks, Paul Thompson, and Jan Walmsley (eds.), *Oral History, Health and Welfare*, London and New York: Routledge, 2000.

Lois J. Einhorn, *The Native American Oral Tradition: Voices of the Spirit and Soul*, Westport: Praeger, 2000.

Michael C. Keith (ed.), *Talking Radio: An Oral History of American Radio in the Television Age*, Armonk: M. E. Sharpe, 2000.

Myrna Chandler Goldstein, *The Massachusetts Medical Society at 20th Century's Close: An Oral History of One Organization's Struggles in Support of Patient Care*, Waltham: Massachusetts Medical Society, 2000.

Nick Wilson, *Voices from the Pastime: Oral Histories of Surviving Major Leaguers, Negro Leaguers, Cuban Leaguers, and Writers, 1920—1934*, Jefferson: McFarland & Co. , 2000.

Paul Thompson, *The Voice of the Past: Oral History*, Oxford and New York: Oxford University Press, third edition, 2000.

Bonnie Brennen, *For the Record: An Oral History of Rochester, New York*, New York: Fordham University Press, 2001.

Debra L. Schultz, *Going South: Jewish Women in the Civil Rights Movement*, New York: New York University Press, 2001.

Forrest C. Pogue, *Pogue's War: Diaries of a WW II Combat Historian*, Lexington: University Press of Kentucky, 2001.

Geoffrey Roberts (ed.), *The History and Narrative Reader*, London and New York: Routledge, 2001.

Jaber F. Gubrium and James A. Holstein (eds.), *Handbook of Interview Research*, Thousand Oaks: Sage Publications, 2001.

Lisa Margonelli (ed.), *Stories of Survival: Three Generations of Southeast Asian Americans Share Their Lives*, San Francisco: Indochinese Housing Development Corp. , 2001.

Leland Cooper and Mary Lee Cooper, *The People of the New River: Oral Histories from the Ashe, Alleghany, and Watauga Counties of North Carolina*,

Jefferson: McFarland, 2001.

Luise White, Stephan F. Miescher, and David William Cohen (eds.), *African Words, African Voices: Critical Practices in Oral History*, Bloomington: Indiana University Press, 2001.

Myrna Katz Frommer and Harvey Frommer, *It Happened in Manhattan: An Oral History of Life in the City during the Mid-Twentieth Century*, New York: Berkley Books, 2001.

Ron Strickland (ed.), *Whistlepunks & Geoducks: Oral Histories from the Pacific Northwest*, Corvallis: Oregon State University Press, 2001.

Peter Burke (ed.), *New Perspectives on Historical Writing*, University Park: Pennsylvania State University Press, second edition, 2001.

Studs Terkel, *Will the Circle Be Unbroken: Reflections on Death, Rebirth and Hunger for a Faith*, New York: The New Press, 2001.

William H. Chafe, Raymond Gavins, and Robert Korstad (eds.), *Remembering Jim Crow: African Americans Tell About Life in the Segregated South*, New York: The New Press, 2001.

A. James Hammerton and Eric Richards (eds.), *Speaking to Immigrants: Oral Testimony and the History of Australian Migration*, Canberra: History Program and Centre for Immigration and Multicultural Studies, Research School of Social Sciences, the Australian National University, 2002.

Allen B. Weisse, *Heart to Heart: The Twentieth Century Battle Against Cardiac Disease: An Oral History*, New Brunswick: Rutgers University Press, 2002.

Barbara W. Sommer and Mary Kay Quinlan, *The Oral History Manual*, Walnut Creek: AltaMira Press, 2002.

Bernice Kazis, Elaine Bakal, Zelda Kaplan Swampscott, *Short Stories of A Long Journey: An Oral History of Russian Jewish Resettlement North of Boston*,

Massachusetts: Hand-In-Hand Oral History Project, 2002.

Chet Cunningham, *Hell Wouldn't Stop: An Oral History of the Battle of Wake Island*, New York: Carroll & Graf, 2002.

Dean E. Murphy, *September 11: An Oral History*, New York: Doubleday, 2002.

Elizabeth Mullener, *War Stories: Remembering World War II*, Baton Rouge: Louisiana State University Press, 2002.

Eric C. Wat, *The Making of A Gay Asian Community: An Oral History of Pre-AIDS Los Angeles*, Lanham: Rowman and Littlefield, 2002.

Eric Marcus, *Making Gay History: The Half-century Fight for Lesbian and Gay Equal Rights*, New York: Perennial, 2002.

Harry Spiller, *Pearl Harbor Survivors: An Oral History of 24 Servicemen*, Jefferson: McFarland & Co. , 2002.

J. Stuart Richards, *Pennsylvanian Voices of the Great War: Letters, Stories and Oral Histories of World War I* , Jefferson: McFarland & Co. , 2002.

Jim Fricke and Charlie Ahearn, *Yes Yes Y'all: The Experience Music Project Oral History of Hip-Hop's First Decade*, Cambridge: Da Capo Press, 2002.

John A. Neuenschwander, *Oral History and the Law*, Carlisle: Oral History Association, 2002.

Larry A. Sneed, *No More Silence: An Oral History of the Assassination of President Kennedy*, Denton: University of North Texas Press, 2002.

Lewis H. Carlson, *Remembered Prisoners of a Forgotten War: An Oral History of the Korean War POWs*, New York: St. Martin's Press, 2002.

Mary C. Wright (ed.), *More Voices, New Stories: King County, Washington's First 150 Years*, Seattle: Pacific Northwest Historians Guild, 2002.

Mary Chamberlain and Paul Thompson (eds.), *Narrative and Genre*, London and New York: Routledge, 2002.

Matthew Greenwald, *Go Where You Wanna Go: The Oral History of the Mamas and The Papas*, New York: Cooper Square Press, 2002

Megan Hutchingand Ian McGibbon (eds.), *Inside Stories: New Zealand POWs Remember*, Auckland: HarperCollins in Association with the History Group, Ministry for Culture and Heritage, 2002.

Mitchell Fink and Lois Mathias, *Never Forget: An Oral History of September II, 2001*, New York: Regan Books, 2002.

Paul Zollo, *Hollywood Remembered: An Oral History of Its Golden Age*, New York: Cooper Square Press, 2002.

Philippe Denis and James Worthington (eds.), *The Power of Oral History: Memory, Healing and Development*, Pietmaritzburg: University of Natal, 2002.

Richard Lally, *Bombers: An Oral History of the New York Yankees*, New York: Crown Publishers, 2002.

Russell Miller, *Behind the Lines: The Oral History of Special Operations in World War II*, London: Secker & Warburg, 2002.

Sean M. Maloneyand John Llambias, *Chances for Peace: Canadian Soldiers in the Balkans, 1992-1995: An Oral History*, St. Catharines: Vanwell Publishing, 2002.

Susan H. Armitage, Patricia Hart, and Karen Weathermon (eds.), *Women's Oral History: The Frontiers Reader*, Lincoln: University of Nebraska Press, 2002.

Alan Lysaght, *The Rolling Stones: An Oral History*, Toronto: McArthur & Co., 2003.

Alessandro Portelli, *The Order Has Been Carried Out: History, Memory, and Meaning of a Nazi Massacre in Rome*, New York: Palgrave Macmillan, 2003.

Barbara A. Mistral, *Theories of Social Remembering*, Buckingham: Open University Press, 2003.

Bruce M. Petty, *Voices from the Pacific War: Bluejackets Remember*, Annapolis: Naval Institute Press, 2003.

Carol Kammen, *On Doing Local History*, Walnut Creek: AltaMira Press, second edition, 2003.

D. Antonio Cantu and Wilson J. Warren, *Teaching History in the Digital Classroom*, Armonk: M. E. Sharpe, 2003.

David Katz, *Solid Foundation: An Oral History of Reggae*, London: Bloomsbury, 2003.

Deborah Hart Strober and Gerald S. Strober, *The Kennedy Presidency: An Oral History of the Era*, Washington: Brassey's, 2003.

Deborah Hart Strober and Gerald S. Strober, *The Nixon Presidency: An Oral History of the Era*, Washington: Brassey's, updated and revised edition, 2003.

Donald A. Ritchie, *Doing Oral History: A Practical Guide*, Oxford and New York: Oxford University Press, second edition, 2003.

Elias Kwaku Asiama, *Oral History and Cultural Practices of the Buem People*, Ghana, 2003.

Fiona C. Ross, *Bearing Witness: Women and the Truth and Reconciliation Commission in South Africa*, London: Pluto Press, 2003.

James F. Tent, *In the Shadow of the Holocaust: Nazi Persecution of Jewish-Christian Germans*, Lawrence: University Press of Kansas, 2003.

Jan Bender Shetler, *Telling Our Own Stories: Local Histories from South Mara, Tanzania*, Leiden: Brill, 2003.

Michael J. Chiarappaand Kristin M. Szylvian, *Fish for All: An Oral History of Multiple Claims and Divided Sentiment on Lake Michigan*, East Lansing:

Michigan State University Press, 2003.

Michelle Ferrari (ed.), *Reporting America at War: An Oral History*, New York: Hyperion, 2003.

Robert G. Thobaben (ed.), *For Comrade and Country: Oral Histories of World War II Veterans*, Jefferson: McFarland & Co., 2003.

Rustom Bharucha, *Rajasthan, An Oral History: Conversations with Komal Kothari*, New York: Penguin Books, 2003.

Sandy Polishuk, *Sticking to the Union: An Oral History of the Life and Times of Julia Ruuttila*, New York: Palgrave MacMillan, 2003.

Studs Terkel, *Hope Dies Last: Keeping the Faith in Difficult Times*, New York: The New Press, 2003.

Sucheng Chan (ed.), *Not Just Victims: Conversations with Cambodian Community Leaders in the United States*, Urbana: University of Illinois Press, 2003.

Timuel D. Black, Jr., *Bridges of Memory: Chicago's First Wave of Black Migration: An Oral History*, Evanston: Northwestern University Press, 2003.

Vincent M. Mallozzi, *Asphalt Gods: An Oral History of the Rucker Tournament*, New York: Doubleday, 2003.

William C. Wohlforth (ed.), *Cold War Endgame: Oral History, Analysis, Debates*, University Park: Pennsylvania State University Press, 2003.

Winona L. Fletcher and Sheila Mason Burton (eds.), *Community Memories: A Glimpse of African American Life in Frankfort, Kentucky*, Frankfort: Kentucky Historical Society, 2003.

Agnes Khoo, *Life as the River Flows: Women in the Malayan Anti-Colonial Struggle: An Oral History of Women from Thailand, Malaysia and Singapore*, Petaling Jaya: Strategic Information Research Development, 2004.

Anna Green and Megan Hutching (eds.), *Remembering: Writing Oral*

History, Auckland: Auckland University Press, 2004.

Astrid Tollefsen, *Following the Waters: Voices from the Final Norwegian Emigration: An Oral History & Personal Perspective on the Triumphs & Tragedies, Adventures & Lifestyles of Norwegian Emigrant Fishermen & Their Families during the Twentieth Century*, Cape Cod: Leifur, 2004.

Bureau of Arts and Culture, *Archaeological Inventory and Oral Histories Survey of Sonsorol State*, Koror: Historic Preservation Office, Ministry of Community and Cultural Affairs, Republic of Palau, 2004.

Callum G. Brown, Arthur J. McIvor and Neil Rafeek, *The University Experience, 1945-1975: An Oral History of the University of Strathclyde*, Edinburgh: Edinburgh University Press, 2004.

Carrie Papa, *A Mile Deep and Black as Pitch: An Oral History of the Franklin and Sterling Hill Mines*, Blacksburg: McDonald & Woodward Publishing Company, 2004.

Elizabeth A. Clark, *History, Theory, Text: Historians and the Linguistic Turn*, Cambridge: Harvard University Press, 2004.

Gerald L. Fetner, *Immersed in Great Affairs: Allan Nevins and the Heroic Age of American History*, Albany: State University of New York Press, 2004.

Glenn Whitman, *Dialogue with the Past: Engaging Students & Meeting Standards through Oral History*, Walnut Creek: AltaMira Press, 2004.

John Bennett and Susan Rowley (eds.), *Uqalurait: An Oral History of Nunavut*, Montreal: McGill-Queen's University Press, 2004.

Joseph Ribarow (ed.), *St Albans Oral History from the Tin Shed Archives*, St Albans: St Albans Community Youth Club, 2004.

Marilyn Beatonand Jeanette Walsh, *From the Voices of Nurses: An Oral History of Newfoundland Nurses Who Graduated Prior to 1950*, St. John's: Jesperson Publishing, 2004.

Mary Chamberlain and Paul Thompson (eds.), *Narrative and Genre*: *Contexts and Types of Communication*, New Brunswick: Transaction Publishers, 2004.

Max Arthur, *Forgotten Voices of the Second World War*, London: Ebury in association with the Imperial War Museum, 2004.

Megan Hutchingand Roberto Rabel (eds.), *A Fair Sort of Battering*: *New Zealanders Remember the Italian Campaign*, Auckland: HarperCollins in association with the Ministry for Culture and Heritage, 2004.

Melissa Walker (ed.), *Country Women Cope With Hard Times*: *A Collection of Oral Histories*, Columbia: University of South Carolina Press, 2004.

Meenakshie Verma, *Aftermath*: *An Oral History of Violence*, New York: Penguin Books, 2004.

Naomi Hirahara and Gwenn M. Jensen, *Silent Scars of Healing Hands*: *Oral Histories of Japanese American Doctors in World War II Detention Camps*, Fullerton: Center for Oral and Public History, California State University, 2004.

Neera Adarkar and Meena Memon, *One Hundred Years one Hundred Voices*: *The Millworkers of Girangaon*: *An Oral History*, Calcutta: Seagull Books, 2004.

Pascal Pinteau, *Special Effects*: *An Oral History*: *Interviews with 38 Masters Spanning 100 Years*, New York: Harry N. Abrams, 2004.

Patricia Preciado Martin (ed.), *Beloved Land*: *An Oral History of Mexican Americans in Southern Arizona*, Tucson: University of Arizona Press, 2004.

Paul Budra and Michael Zeitlin (eds.), *Soldier Talk*: *The Vietnam War in Oral Narrative*, Bloomington: Indiana University Press, 2004.

Robin McMillan, *Us against Them*: *An Oral History of the Ryder Cup*, New York: HarperCollins, 2004.

Rita Olsudong, Calvin T. Emesiochel (eds.), *Inventory of Cultural and*

Historical Sites and Oral History in Melekeok and Airai States, Republic of Palau: Bureau of Arts and Culture, Historic Preservation Office, Ministry of Community and Cultural Affairs, Republic of Palau, 2004.

Rita Olsudong, Calvin T. Emesiochel, and Errolfflynn T. Kloulechad (eds.), *Inventory of Cultural and Historical Sites and Oral History of Ngatpang State*, Republic of Palau: Bureau of Arts and Culture, Historic Preservation Office, Ministry of Community and Regional Affairs, 2004.

Samuel Iwry, *To Wear the Dust of War: From Bialystok to Shanghai to the Promised Land: An Oral History*, New York: Palgrave Macmillan, 2004.

Tom Weiner (ed.), *Voices of War: Stories of Service from the Home Front and the Front Lines*, Washington: National Geographic, 2004.

William B. Pickett (ed.), *George F. Kennan and the Origins of Eisenhower's New Look: An Oral History of Project Solarium*, Princeton: Princeton Institute for International and Regional Studies, Princeton University, 2004.

Benjamin D. Brotemarkle, *Crossing Division Street: An Oral History of the African-American Community in Orlando*, Cocoa: Florida Historical Society Press, 2005.

Brian Lockman (ed.), *World War II in Their Own Words: An Oral History of Pennsylvania's Veterans*, Mechanicsburg: Stackpole Books, 2005.

Chet Cunningham, *The Frogmen of World War II: An Oral History of the U. S. Navy's Underwater Demolition Teams*, New York: Pocket Star Books, 2005.

Chris Willis, *Old Leather: An Oral History of Early Pro Football in Ohio, 1920-1935*, Lanham: Scarecrow Press, 2005.

David Clark, Neil Small, Michael Wright, Michelle Winslow and Nic Hughes, *A Little Bit of Heaven for the Few? An Oral History of the Modern Hospice Movement in the United Kingdom*, Lancaster: Observatory Publications. 2005.

David Herman, Manfred Jahn, and Marie-Laure Ryan (eds.), *Routledge Encyclopedia of Narrative Theory*, London and New York: Routledge, 2005.

Della Pollock (ed.), *Remembering: Oral History Performance*, New York: Palgrave Macmillan, 2005.

Eoghan Rice, *We Are Rovers: An Oral History of Shamrock Rovers FC*, Stroud: Nonsuch, 2005.

Eric A. Johnson and Karl-Heinz Reuband, *What We Knew: Terror, Mass Murder and Everyday Life in Nazi Germany: An Oral History*, London: John Murray, 2005.

George T. Blakey, *Creating a Hoosier Self-portrait: The Federal Writers'Project in Indiana, 1935-1942*, Bloomington: Indiana University Press, 2005.

Gregorio Mora-Torres (ed.), *Californio Voices: The Oral Memoirs of José María Amador and Lorenzo Asisara*, Denton: University of North Texas Press, 2005.

Jayne K. Guberman (ed.), *In Our Own Voices: A Guide to Conducting Life History Interviews with American Jewish Women*, Brookline: Jewish Women's Archive, 2005.

Jo Ann Robinson, *Education as My Agenda: Gertrude Williams, Race, and the Baltimore Public Schools*, New York: Palgrave Macmillan, 2005.

John Sasso and Priscilla Foley, *A Little Noticed Revolution: An Oral History of the Model Cities Program and Its Transition to the Community Development Block Grant Program*, Berkeley: Berkeley Public Policy Press, Institute of Governmental Studies, University of California, 2005.

K. D. Richardson, *Reflections of Pearl Harbor: An Oral History of December 7, 1941*, Westport: Praeger Publishers, 2005.

Kazuo Tamayama. Houndmills, *Railwaymen in the War: Tales by Japanese Railway Soldiers in Burma and Thailand, 1941-1947*, New York: Palgrave Macmillan, 2005.

Kumud Sharma, *Memory Frames: Oral Narratives of Four First Generation Women's Studies Scholars*, New Delhi: Centre for Women's Development Studies, 2005.

Laura Homan Lacey, *Stay off the Skyline: The Sixth Marine Division on Okinawa: An Oral History*, Washington: Potomac Books, 2005.

Legs McNeil, Jennifer Osborne, and Peter Pavia, *The Other Hollywood: The Uncensored Oral History of the Porn Film Industry*, New York: Regan Books, 2005.

Lorne Holyoak, et al. , *Ethnographic and Oral History Survey of Aimeliik State, Republic of Palau*, Republic of Palau: Palau Bureau of Arts and Culture and Historic Preservation Office, Ministry of Community and Regional Affairs, 2005.

Robert K. Fitts, *Remembering Japanese Baseball: An Oral History of the Game*, Carbondale: Southern Illinois University Press, 2005.

Saidou Mohamed N'Daou, *Sangalan Oral Traditions: History, Memories, and Social Differentiation*, Durham: Carolina Academic Press, 2005.

Selma Leydesdorff, Luisa Passerini, and Paul Thompson (eds.), *Gender and Memory*, New Brunswick: Transaction Publishers, 2005.

Studs Terkel, *And They All Sang: Adventures of an Eclectic Disc Jockey*, New York: The New Press, 2005.

Studs Terkel, *Race: How Blacks and Whites Think and Feel about the American Obsession*, New York: The New Press, 2005.

Thomas Saylor, *Remembering the Good War: Minnesota's Greatest Generation*, St. Paul: Minnesota Historical Society Press, 2005.

Tom Wiener, *Forever A Soldier: Unforgettable Stories of Wartime Service*, Washington: Library of Congress, 2005.

Valerie Raleigh Yow, *Recording Oral History: A Guide for the Humanities and Social Sciences*, Walnut Creek: AltaMira Press, second edition, 2005.

Vivian Perlis and Libby Van Cleve, *Composers Voices from Ives to Ellington: An Oral History of American Music*, New Haven: Yale University Press, 2005.

Yap Historic Preservation Office, *The Japanese Era of Yap: The Elders Speak: Visualized Oral History*, Micronesia: Yap Historic Preservation Office, US National Park Service, 2005.

Ye Weiliand Ma Xiaodong, *Growing Up in the People's Republic: Conversations between Two Daughters of China's Revolution*, New York: Palgrave Macmillan, 2005.

Alison Parr (ed.), *The Big Show: New Zealanders, D-Day and the War in Europe*, Auckland: Auckland University Press in association with the Ministry for Culture and Heritage, 2006.

Allan Neuwirth, *They'll Never Put That on the Air: An Oral History of Taboo-Breaking TV Comedy*, New York: Allworth Press, 2006.

Barry A. Lanman and Laura M. Wendling (eds.), *Preparing the Next Generation of Oral Historians: An Anthology of Oral History Education*, Lanham: AltaMira Press, 2006.

Brad E. Lucas, *Radicals, Rhetoric, and the War: The University of Nevada in the Wake of Kent State*, New York: Palgrave Macmillan, 2006.

Bruce M. Petty, *At War in the Pacific: Personal Accounts of World War II Navy and Marine Corps Officers*, Jefferson: McFarland & Co. , 2006.

Daniel J. Cohen and Roy Rosenzweig, *Digital History: A Guide to Gathering, Preserving and Presenting the Past on the Web*, Philadelphia: University of Pennsylvania Press, 2006.

David P. Cline, *Creating Choice: A Community Responds to the Need for Abortion and Birth Control, 1961-1973*, New York: Palgrave Macmillan, 2006.

Donald Fixico, *Daily Life of Native Americans in the Twentieth Century*, Westport: Greenwood Press, 2006.

DoVeanna S. Fulton, *Speaking Power: Black Feminist Orality in Women's Narratives of Slavery*, Albany: State University of New York Press, 2006.

Elizabeth Shanks Alexander, *Transmitting Mishnah: The Shaping Influence of Oral Tradition*, Cambridge: Cambridge University Press, 2006.

Fay Vincent, *The Only Game in Town: Baseball Stars of the 1930s and 1940s Talk About the Game They Loved*, New York: Simon & Schuster, 2006.

Faith Eidse (ed.), *Voices of the Apalachicola*, Gainesville: University Press of Florida, 2006.

Gemma Romain, *Connecting Histories: A Comparative Exploration of African-Caribbean and Jewish History and Memory in Modern Britain*, London: Kegan Paul, 2006.

Gene Quigley, *Voices of World War II* , St. John's: Jesperson Publishing, 2006.

Jan Vansina, *Oral Tradition: A Study in Historical Methodology*, New Brunswick: Aldine Transaction, 2006.

Jana A. Brill, *Oral Traditions: When Did the French Stop Speaking Latin?* Lanham: University Press of America, 2006.

Jane Wehrey (ed.), *Voices from This Long Brown Land: Oral Recollections of Owens Valley Lives and Manzanar Pasts*, New York: Palgrave Macmillan, 2006.

John Rob, *Punk Rock: An Oral History*, London: Ebury Press, 2006.

Josh Frank and Caryn Ganz, *Fool the World: The Oral History of a Band*

Called Pixies, New York: St. Martin's Griffin, 2006.

Julian M. Pleasants, *Gator Tales: An Oral History of the University of Florida*, Gainesville: University of Florida, 2006.

Katharine Hodgkin and Susannah Radstone (eds.), *Memory, History, Nation: Contested Pasts*, New Brunswick: Transaction Publishers, 2006.

Kendall D. Gott (ed.), *Eyewitness to War: The US Army in Operation AL FAJR: An Oral History*, Fort Leavenworth: Combat Studies Institute Press, 2006.

Kim Lacy Rogers, *Life and Death in the Delta: African American Narratives of Violence, Resilience, and Social Change*, New York: Palgrave Macmillan, 2006.

Linda Barnickel, *Oral History for the Family Historian: A Basic Guide*, Carlisle: Oral History Association, 2006.

Max Brooks, *World War Z: An Oral History of the Zombie War*, New York: Crown, 2006.

Melissa Walker, *Southern Farmers and Their Stories: Memory and Meaning in Oral History*, Lexington: University Press of Kentucky, 2006.

Nannie Greene and Catherine Stokes Sheppard (eds.), *Community and Change in the North Carolina Mountains: Oral Histories and Profiles of People from Western Watauga County*, Jefferson: McFarland & Co. , 2006.

Olivia Bennett and Christopher McDowell, *Displaced: The Human Cost of Development and Resettlement*, New York: Palgrave Macmillan, 2012.

Paul Atkinson and Sara Delamont (eds.), *Narrative Methods: Oral History and Testimony*, Thousand Oaks: Sage Publications, 2006.

Peter L. Bergen, *The Osama bin Laden I Know: An Oral History of Al-Qaeda's Leader*, New York: Free Press, 2006.

Randy William Widdis, *Voices from Next Year Country: An Oral History of*

Rural Saskatchewan, Regina: University of Regina, Canadian Plains Research Center, 2006.

Robert F. Dorr, *Air Combat: An Oral History of Fighter Pilots*, New York: Berkley Caliber, 2006.

Robert Perks and Alistair Thomson (eds.), *The Oral History Reader*, London and New York: Routledge, second edition, 2006.

Sally French, John Swain, Dorothy Atkinson, and Michelle Moore (eds.), *An Oral History of the Education of Visually Impaired People: Telling Stories for Inclusive Futures*, Lewiston: E. Mellen Press, 2006.

Thom Loverro, *Hail Victory: An Oral History of the Washington Redskins*, Hoboken: J. Wiley, 2006.

Thomas L. Charlton, Lois E. Myers, and Rebecca Sharpless (eds.), *Handbook of Oral History*, Walnut Creek: AltaMira Press, 2006.

Thomas A. DuBois, *Lyric, Meaning, and Audience in the Oral Tradition of Northern Europe*, Notre Dame: University of Notre Dame Press, 2006.

Trish Wood (ed.), *What Was Asked of Us: An Oral History of the Iraq War by the Soldiers Who Fought It*, New York: Little, Brown and Co., 2006.

Damon DiMarco, *Tower Stories: An Oral History of 9/11*, Santa Monica: Santa Monica Press, expanded and second edition, 2007.

Diana Meyers Bahr, *The Unquiet Nisei: An Oral History of the Life of Sue Kunitomi Embrey*, New York: Palgrave Macmillan, 2007.

Francisco Cota Fagundes and Irene Maria F. Blayer (eds.), *Oral and Written Narratives and Cultural Identity: Interdisciplinary Approaches*, New York: Peter Lang, 2007.

Francisco Jiménez, Alma M. García, and Richard A. Garcia, *Ethnic Community Builders: Mexican Americans in Search of Justice and Power: The Struggle for Citizenship Rights in San José, California*, Lanham: AltaMira

Press, 2007.

Gennady Shubin (ed.), *The Oral History of Forgotten Wars*: *The Memoirs of Veterans of the War in Angola*, Moscow: Memories Publishers, 2007.

Geoffrey Cubitt, *History and Memory*, Manchester: Manchester University Press, 2007.

Gerald M. Oppenheimer and Ronald Bayer, *Shattered Dreams?*: *An Oral History of the South African AIDS Epidemic*, Oxford and New York: Oxford University Press, 2007.

Hal LaCroix, *Journey out of Darkness*: *The Real Story of American Heroes in Hitler's POW Camps*: *An Oral History*, Westport: Praeger Security International, 2007.

Huping Ling, *Voices of the Heart*: *Asian American Women on Immigration, Work, and Family*, Kirksville: Truman State University Press, 2007.

Jacob J. Podber, *The Electronic Front Porch*: *An Oral History of the Arrival of Modern Media in Rural Appalachia and the Melungeon Community*, Macon: Mercer University Press, 2007.

Jack Drescher and Joseph P. Merlino (eds.), *American Psychiatry and Homosexuality*: *An Oral History*, New York: Harrington Park Press, 2007.

Jeff Kisseloff, *Generation on Fire*: *Voices of Protest from the 1960s*: *An Oral history*, Lexington: University Press of Kentucky, 2007.

Julie Silver and Daniel Wilson, *Polio Voices*: *An Oral History from the American Polio Epidemics and Worldwide Eradication efforts*, Westport: Praeger, 2007.

Kenneth J. Bindas, *Remembering the Great Depression in the Rural South*, Gainesville: University Press of Florida, 2007.

Lois Gerber Franke, *J. Frank Torres*: *Crusader and Judge*: *An Oral History*, Santa Fe: Sunstone Press, 2007.

Lynn Salsi, *Voices from the North Carolina Mountains: Appalachian Oral Histories*, Charleston: History Press, 2007.

Mark Roberts, *Sub: An Oral History of U. S. Navy Submarines*, New York: Berkley Caliber, 2007.

Mary Ellen Mancina-Batinich, *Italian Voices: Making Minnesota Our Home*, St. Paul: Minnesota Historical Society Press, 2007.

Mary Muldowney, *The Second World War and Irish Women: An Oral History*, Dublin: Irish Academic Press, 2007.

Megan Hutching (ed.), *Last Line of Defence: New Zealanders Remember the War at Home*, Auckland: HarperCollins in association with the Ministry for Culture and Heritage, 2007.

Miguel Garcia and Charlene Riggins (eds.), *Forgotten Patriots: Voices of World War II Mexican American Veterans of Southern California*, Fullerton: Center for Oral and Public History, California State University, Fullerton, 2007.

Mike Hoyt and John Palattella (eds.), *Reporting Iraq: An Oral History of the War by the Journalists Who Covered It*, Hoboken: Melville House Publishing, 2007.

Nancy MacKay, *Curating Oral Histories: From Interview to Archive*, Walnut Creek: Left Coast Press, 2007.

Oral History Centre, National Archives of Singapore (ed.), *Memories and Reflections: The Singapore Experience: Documenting A Nation's History Through Oral History*, Singapore: Oral History Centre, National Archives of Singapore, 2007.

Pam Schweitzer, *Reminiscence Theatre: Making Theatre from Memories*, London: Jessica Kingsley Publishers, 2007.

Richard Holmes (ed.), *The World at War: The Landmark Oral History from the Previously Unpublished Archives*, London: Ebury, 2007.

Sally McBeth, *Native American Oral History and Cultural Interpretation in Rocky Mountain National Park*, Damascus: Penny Hill Press, 2007.

Sharlene Nagy Hesse-Biber and Patricia Lina Leavy (eds.), *Feminist Research Practice: A Primer*, Thousand Oaks: Sage Publications, 2007.

Studs Terkel, *The Studs Terkel Reader: My American Century*, New York: The New Press, 2007.

Studs Terkel, *Touch and Go*, New York: The New Press, 2007.

Thomas Saylor, *Long Hard Road: American POWs during World War II*, St. Paul: Minnesota Historical Society Press, 2007.

Wallace Terry, *Missing Pages: Black Journalists of Modern America: An Oral History*, New York: Carroll & Graf Publishers, 2007.

Askold Melnyczuk, *The House of Widows: An Oral History*, Saint Paul: Graywolf Press, 2008.

Carl Mirra, *Soldiers and Citizens: An Oral History of Operation Iraqi Freedom from the Battlefield to the Pentagon*, New York: Palgrave Macmillan, 2008.

Charles E. Trimble, Barbara W. Sommer and Mary Kay Quinlan, *The American Indian Oral History Manual: Making Many Voices Heard*, Walnut Creek: Left Coast Press, 2008.

Deborah Hart Strober and Gerald S. Strober, *Israel at Sixty: A Pictorial and Oral History of a Nation Reborn*, Hoboken: John Wiley & Sons, 2008.

George J. Billy and Christine M. Billy, *Merchant Mariners at War: An Oral History of World War II*, Gainesville: University Press of Florida, 2008.

Jane LaTour, *Sisters in the Brotherhoods: Working Women Organizing for Equalityin New York City*, New York: Palgrave Macmillan, 2008.

Joann Faung Jean Lee, *Asian Americans in the Twenty-first Century: Oral*

Histories of First-to Fourth-generation Americans from China, *Japan*, *India*, *Korea*, *the Philippines*, *Vietnam*, *and Laos*, New York: The New Press, 2008.

Karen Halttunen (ed.), *A Companion to American Cultural History*, Malden: Blackwell Publishing, 2008.

Larry Burke and Peter Thomas Fornatale, *Change Up: An Oral History of 8 Key Events that Shaped Modern Baseball*, New York: Palgrave Macmillan, 2008.

Laurence Armand French, *An Oral History of Southern Appalachia*, Lewiston: Edwin Mellen Press, 2008.

Manning Marable and Kristen Clarke (eds.), *Seeking Higher Ground: The Hurricane Katrina Crisis*, *Race*, *and Public Policy Reader*, New York: Palgrave Macmillan, 2008.

Mary Jo Maynes, Jennifer L. Pierce, and Barbara Laslett, *Telling Stories: The Use of Personal Narratives in the Social Sciences and History*, Ithaca: Cornell University Press, 2008.

Michael J. Galgano, J. Chris Arndt, and Raymond M. Hyser, *Doing History: Research and Writing in the Digital Age*, Boston: Thomson Wadsworth, 2008 and 2013.

Paula Hamilton and Linda Shopes (eds.), *Oral History and Public Memories*, Philadelphia: Temple University Press, 2008.

Philippe Denis and Radikobo Ntsimane (eds.), *Oral History in a Wounded Country: Interactive Interviewing in South Africa*, Scottsville: University of Kwa-Zulu-Natal Press, 2008.

Richard Stacewicz, *Winter Soldiers: An Oral History of Vietnam Veterans Against the War*, Chicago: Haymarket Books, 2008.

Sarah Shillinger, *A Case Study of the American Indian Boarding School Movement: An Oral History of Saint Joseph's Indian Industrial School*, Lewiston:

Edwin Mellen Press, 2008.

Studs Terkel, *P. S.* : *Further Thoughts from a Lifetime of Listening*, New York: The New Press, 2008.

Tamar Morad, Robert Shasha, and Dennis Shasha, *Iraq's Last Jews: Stories of Daily Life, Upheaval, and Escape from Modern Babylon*, New York: Palgrave Macmillan, 2008.

William Schneider, *Living with Stories: Telling, Re-Telling, and Remembering*, Logan: Utah State University Press, 2008.

Barbara W. Sommer and Mary Kay Quinlan, *The Oral History Manual*, Walnut Creek: AltaMira Press, second edition, 2009.

Catherine Fosl and Tracy E. K'Meyer, *Freedom on the Border: An Oral History of the Civil Rights Movement in Kentucky*, Lexington: University Press of Kentucky, 2009.

Claire Puccia Parham, *The St. Lawrence Seaway and Power Project: An Oral History of the Greatest Construction Show on Earth*, Syracuse: Syracuse University Press, 2009.

Cynthia Hart and Lisa Samson, *The Oral History Workshop: Collect and Celebrate the Life Stories of Your Family and Friends*, New York: Workman Publishing Company, 2009.

D' Ann R. Penner and Keith C. Ferdinand (eds.), *Overcoming Katrina: African American Voices from the Crescent City and Beyond*, New York: Palgrave Macmillan, 2009.

Donna M. DeBlasio, Charles F. Ganzert, David H. Mould, Stephen H. Paschen and Howard L. Sacks, *Catching Stories: A Practical Guide to Oral History*, Athens: Ohio University Press, 2009.

Fran Leeper Buss (ed.), *Moisture of the Earth: Mary Robinson, Civil Rights and Textile Union Activist: An Oral History*, Ann Arbor: University of

Michigan Press, 2009.

Greg Prato, *Grunge Is Dead: The Oral History of Seattle Rock Music*, Toronto: ECW Press, 2009.

Harvey Schwartz, *Solidarity Stories: An Oral History of the ILWU*, Seattle: University of Washington Press, 2009.

Joel Makower, *Woodstock: The Oral History*, Albany: State University of New York Press, 2009.

John A. Neuenschwander, *A Guide to Oral History and the Law*, Oxford and New York: Oxford University Press, 2009.

Jürgen Matthäus(ed.), *Approaching an Auschwitz Survivor Holocaust: Testimony and its Transformations*, Oxford and New York: Oxford University Press, 2009.

Kate Willink, *Bringing Desegregation Home: Memories of the Struggle Toward School Integration in Rural North Carolina*, New York: Palgrave Macmillan, 2009.

Liz Worth, *Treat Me Like Dirt: An Oral History of Punk in Toronto and Beyond, 1977-1981*, Montréal: Bongo Beat Books, 2009.

Lucinda McCray Beier, *Health Culture in the Heartland, 1880—1980: An Oral History*, Urbana: University of Illinois Press, 2009.

Luisa Del Giudice, *Oral History, Oral Culture, and Italian Americans*, New York: Palgrave Macmillan, 2009.

Marta Kurkowska-Budzan and Krzysztof Zamorski (eds.), *Oral History: The Challenges of Dialogue*, Amsterdam: John Benjamins Publishing Company, 2009.

Michi Kodama-Nishimoto, Warren S. Nishimoto, and Cynthia A. Oshiro (eds.), *Talking Hawaii's Story: Oral Histories of an Island People*, Mānoa: University of Hawaii Press, 2009.

Mike Heffernan, *Rig: An Oral History of the Ocean Ranger Disaster*, St. John's: Creative Publishers, 2009.

Nanci Adler, Selma Leydesdorff, and Mary Chamberlain (eds.), *Memories of Mass Repression: Narrating Life Stories in the Aftermath of Atrocity*, New Brunswick: Transaction Publishers, 2009.

Patricia Hill Collins, *Black Feminist Thought: Knowledge, Consciousness, and the Politics of Empowerment*, London and New York: Routledge, second edition, 2009.

Peter Molloy, *The Lost World of Communism: An Oral History of Daily Life Behind the Iron Curtain*, London: BBC, 2009.

Pranee Liamputtong, *Qualitative Research Methods*, Oxford and New York: Oxford University Press, third edition, 2009.

Roy Reed (ed.), *Looking Back at the Arkansas Gazette: An Oral History*, Fayetteville: University of Arkansas Press, 2009.

Stacy Enyeart (ed.), *America's Home Front Heroes: An Oral History of World War II*, Santa Barbara: Praeger/ABC-CLIO, 2009.

Sue Armitage and Laurie Mercier, *Speaking History: Oral Histories of the American Past, 1865-Present*, New York: Palgrave Macmillan, 2009.

Tracy E. K'Meyer and Joy L. Hart, *I Saw it Coming: Worker Narratives of Plant Closings and Job Loss*, New York: Palgrave Macmillan, 2009.

Xinran, *China Witness: Voices from a Silent Generation*, New York: Pantheon Books, 2009.

Alan Rosen, *The Wonder of Their Voices: The 1946 Holocaust Interviews of David Boder*, Oxford and New York: Oxford University Press, 2010.

Angela Zusman, *Story Bridges: A Guide to Conducting Intergenerational Oral History Projects*, Walnut Creek: Left Coast Press, 2010.

Anne Valk and Leslie Brown, *Living with Jim Crow: African American*

Women and Memories of the Segregated South, New York: Palgrave Macmillan, 2010.

Bahru Zewde (ed.), *Documenting the Ethiopian Student Movement: An Exercise in Oral History*, Addis Ababa: Forum for Social Studies, 2010.

Danke Li, *Echoes of Chongqing: Women in Wartime China*, Urbana: University of Illinois Press, 2010.

David King Dunaway and Molly Beer, *Singing Out: An Oral History of America's Folk Music Revivals*, Oxford and New York: Oxford University Press, 2010.

Diane Karper, *A Walk in My Shoes: Our Lives of Hope: An Oral History of the Artists of the "Made in Honduras Craft Co-op"*, Trujillo, Honduras, Chambersburg: Alan C. Hood & Co., 2010.

Gary Bruce, *The Firm: The Inside Story of the Stasi*, Oxford and New York: Oxford University Press, 2010.

Harvey Frommer, *Remembering Fenway Park: An Oral and Narrative History of the Home of the Boston Red Sox*, New York: Stewart, Tabori & Chang, 2010.

Heather Augustyn, *Ska: An Oral History*, Jefferson: McFarland & Co., 2010.

Ingo Cornils and Sarah Waters (eds.), *Memories of 1968: International Perspectives*, New York: Peter Lang, 2010.

J. P. Dudgeon, *Our Liverpool: Memories of Life in Disappearing Britain*, London: Headline Review, 2010.

J. Todd Moye, *Freedom Flyers: The Tuskegee Airmen of World War II*, Oxford and New York: Oxford University Press, 2010.

Jennifer Armstrong, *Why? Because We Still Like You: An Oral History of the Mickey Mouse Club*, New York: Grand Central Pub., 2010.

Jim Baker and Bernard M. Corbett, *The Most Memorable Games in Giants History: The Oral History of a Legendary Team*, Bloomsbury: New York, 2010.

Joanna Bornat and Josie Tetley (eds.), *Oral History and Ageing*, London: Centre for Policy on Ageing, 2010.

John C. Walter and Malina Iida (eds.), *Better than the Best: Black Athletes Speak, 1920-2007*, Seattle: University of Washington Press, 2010.

Ken Wharton, *Bloody Belfast: An Oral History of the British Army's War against the IRA*, Stroud: Spellmount, 2010.

Lynn Abrams, *Oral History Theory*, London and New York: Routledge, 2010.

Michael L. Gillette, *Launching the War on Poverty: An Oral History*, Oxford and New York: Oxford University Press, second edition, 2010.

Miki Ward Crawford, Katie Kaori Hayashi, and Shizuko Suenaga, *Japanese War Brides in America: An Oral History*, Santa Barbara: Praeger, 2010.

Mitchell G. Bard, *48 Hours of Kristallnacht: Night of Destruction/Dawn of the Holocaust: An Oral History*, Guilford: Lyons Press, 2010.

Nick Barratt, *Lost Voices from the Titanic: The Definitive Oral History*, New York: Palgrave Macmillan, 2010.

Nigel C. Hunt, *Memory, War, and Trauma*, Cambridge: Cambridge University Press, 2010.

Peter Friederici (ed.), *What Has Passed and What Remains: Oral Histories of Northern Arizona's Changing Landscapes*, Tucson: University of Arizona Press, 2010.

Philippe Denis, Radikobo Ntsimane and Thomas Cannell, *Indians versus Russians: An Oral History of Political Violence in Nxamalala (1987—1993)*, South Africa : Cluster Publications, 2010.

Robert Budd, *Voices of British Columbia: Stories from Our Frontier*, Vancouver: D&M Publishers, 2010.

Scott McConnell, *100 Voices: An Oral History of Ayn Rand*, New York: New American Library, 2010.

Suroopa Mukherjee, *Surviving Bhopal: Dancing Bodies, Written Texts, and Oral Testimonials of Women in the Wake of an Industrial Disaster*, New York: Palgrave Macmillan, 2010.

Susannah Radstone and Bill Schwarz (eds.), *Memory: Histories, Theories, Debates*, New York: Fordham University Press, 2010.

Tom Melchior, *Never Forgotten: Stories by Scott County, Minnesota, WWII Veterans*, Shakopee: Scott County Historical Society, 2010.

Twin Cities GLBT Oral History Project, *Queer Twin Cities*, Minneapolis: University of Minnesota Press, 2010.

Valentyna Borysenko, *A Candle in Remembrance: An Oral History of the Ukrainian Genocide of 1932-1933*, New York: Ukrainian National Women's League of America, 2010.

Zachary M. Schrag, *Ethical Imperialism: Institutional Review Boards and the Social Sciences, 1965-2009*, Baltimore: Johns Hopkins University Press, 2010.

Alessandro Portelli, *They Say in Harlan County: An Oral History*, Oxford and New York: Oxford University Press, 2011.

Alexander Freund and Alistair Thomson (eds.), *Oral History and Photography*, New York: Palgrave Macmillan, 2011.

Alison Owings, *Indian Voices: Listening to Native Americans*, New Brunswick: Rutgers University Press, 2011.

Angene Wilson and Jack Wilson, *Voices from the Peace Corps: Fifty Years of Kentucky Volunteers*, Lexington: University Press of Kentucky, 2011.

Bill Adair, Benjamin Filene, and Laura Koloski (eds.), *Letting Go?*: *Sharing Historical Authority in a User-Generated World*, Walnut Creek: Left Coast Press, 2011.

Bruce Granville Miller, *Oral History on Trial*: *Recognizing Aboriginal Narratives in the Courts*, Vancouver: University of British Columbia Press, 2011.

Carole Garibaldi Rogers, *Habits of Change*: *An Oral History of American Nuns*, Oxford and New York: Oxford University Press, 2011.

Charlene L. Martin & Maureen Ryan Doyle, *Voices of Worcester Women*: *160 Years after the First National Woman's Rights Convention*, Charleston: CreateSpace, 2011.

Christian F. Ostermann and James F. Person (eds.), *Crisis and Confrontation on the Korean Peninsula, 1968-1969*: *A Critical Oral History*, Washington: Woodrow Wilson International Center for Scholars, 2011.

Christian F. Ostermann and James F. Person (eds.), *The Rise and Fall of Détente on the Korean Peninsula, 1970-1974*, Washington: Woodrow Wilson International Center for Scholars, 2011.

Desiree Hellegers, *No Room of Her Own*: *Women's Stories of Homelessness, Life, Death, and Resistance*, New York: Palgrave Macmillan, 2011.

Donald A. Ritchie (ed.), *The Oxford Handbook of Oral History*, Oxford and New York: Oxford University Press, 2011.

Douglas A. Boyd, *Crawfish Bottom*: *Recovering a Lost Kentucky Community*, Lexington: University Press of Kentucky, 2011.

Eleanor Herz Swent, *Asian Refugees in America*: *Narratives of Escape and Adaptation*, Jefferson: McFarland & Co. , 2011.

Ellen Greenblatt (ed.), *Serving LGBTIQ Library and Archives Users*: *Essays on Outreach, Service, Collections and Access*, Jefferson: McFarland & Co. , 2011.

Evelyn S. Taylor, *Conducting Oral Histories: A Student's Guide to A Successful Interviewing Experience*, Bloomington: AuthorHouse, 2011.

Farina So, *The Hijab of Cambodia: Memories of Cham Muslim Women after the Khmer Rouge*, Phnom Penh: Documentation Center of Cambodia, 2011.

George Castle, *When the Game Changed: An Oral History of Baseball's True Golden Age, 1969-1979*, Guilford: Lyons Press, 2011.

Greg Prato, *Sack Exchange: The Definitive Oral History of the 1980s New York Jets*, Toronto: ECW Press, 2011.

Irum Shiekh, *Detained without Cause: Muslims' Stories of Detention and Deportation in America after 9/11*, New York: Palgrave Macmillan, 2011.

Jehanne M. Gheith and Katherine R. Jolluck, *Gulag Voices: Oral Histories of Soviet Incarceration and Exile*, New York: Palgrave Macmillan, 2011.

Jessica I. Elfenbein, Thomas L. Hollowak, and Elizabeth M. Nix (eds.), *Baltimore' 68: Riots and Rebirth in An American City*, Philadelphia: Temple University Press, 2011.

Joseph F. Rishel (ed.), *Pittsburgh Remembers World War II*, Charleston: History Press, 2011.

Komla Tsey, *Re-thinking Development in Africa: An Oral History Approach from Botoku, Rural Ghana*, Bamenda: Langaa Rpcig, 2011.

Lee Schweninger (ed.), *The First We Can Remember: Colorado Pioneer Women Tell Their Stories*, Lincoln: University of Nebraska Press, 2011.

Lucy Myersand Terri Unger, *People and Place: Oral Histories & Portraits of Ipswich Seniors*, United States: People and Place Project, 2011.

Malcolm D. Benally (ed.), *Bitter Water: Diné Oral Histories of the Navajo-Hopi Land Dispute*, Tucson: University of Arizona Press, 2011.

Mark Yarm, *Everybody Loves Our Town: An Oral History of Grunge*, New York: Crown Archetype, 2011.

Norman K. Denzin and Yvonna S. Lincoln (eds.), *The Sage Handbook of Qualitative Research*, Thousand Oaks: Sage Publications, fourth edition, 2011.

Paola Messana, *Soviet Communal Living: An Oral History of the Kommunalka*, New York: Palgrave Macmillan, 2011.

Patricia Leavy, *Oral History: Understanding Qualitative Research: Understanding Qualitative Research*, Oxford and New York: Oxford University Press, 2011.

Roy Rosenzweig, *Clio Wired: The Future of the Past in the Digital Age*, New York: Columbia University Press, 2011.

Sandra K. Schackel, *Working the Land: The Stories of Ranch and Farm Women in the Modern American West*, Lawrence: University Press of Kansas, 2011.

Shelley Trower (ed.), *Place, Writing, and Voice in Oral History*, New York: Palgrave Macmillan, 2011.

Angela Davis, *Modern Motherhood: Women and Family in England, 1945-2000*, Manchester: Manchester University Press, 2012.

Barney Hoskyns, *Led Zeppelin: The Oral History of the World's Greatest Rock Band*, Hoboken: John Wiley & Sons, 2012.

Carrie Hamilton, *Sexual Revolutions in Cuba: Passion, Politics, and Memory*, Chapel Hill: University of North Carolina Press, 2012.

Claire Bond Potter and Renee C. Romano (eds.), *Doing Recent History: On Privacy, Copyright, Video Games, Institutional Review Boards, Activist Scholarship, and History that Talks Back*, Athens: University of Georgia Press, 2012.

Craig Larkin, *Memory and Conflict in Lebanon: Remembering and Forgetting the Past*, London and New York: Routledge, 2012.

Daryl B. Hill, *Trans Toronto*: *An Oral History*, New York: William Rodney Press, 2012.

Dave Isay (ed.), *All There Is*: *Love Stories from StoryCorps*, New York: Penguin Press, 2012.

David Cartwright, Herman Joseph, Don Des Jarlais, *Addicts Who Survived*: *An Oral History of Narcotic Use in America before 1965*, Knoxville: University of Tennessee Press, 2012.

Donald J. Raleigh, *Soviet Baby Boomers*: *An Oral History of Russia's Cold War Generation*, Oxford and New York: Oxford University Press, 2012.

Elizabeth Kiely and Máire Leane, *Irish Women at Work*, *1930-1960*: *An Oral History*, Dublin: Irish Academic Press, 2012.

Fred Pelka, *What We Have Done*: *An Oral History of the Disability Rights Movement*, Amherst: University of Massachusetts Press, 2012.

Jason Weiss, *Always in Trouble*: *An Oral History of ESP-Disk'*, *the Most Outrageous Record Label in America*, Middletown: Wesleyan University Press, 2012.

John B. Holway, *Red Tails*: *An Oral History of the Tuskegee Airmen*, Mineola: Dover Publications, 2012.

Nina Howesand Eric Ferrara (ed.), *Lower East Side Oral Histories*, Charleston: The History Press, 2012.

Leontine Visser (ed.), *Governing New Guinea*: *An Oral history of Papuan Administrators*, *1950-1990*, Leiden: KITLV Press, 2012.

Louis Fairchild, *They Called It the War Effort*: *Oral Histories from WWII Orange*, *Texas*, Denton: Texas State Historical Association, second edition, 2012.

Mary Jo Festle, *Second Wind*: *Oral Histories of Lung Transplant Survivors*, New York: Palgrave Macmillan, 2012.

Michael L. Gillette, *Lady Bird Johnson: An Oral History*, Oxford and New York: Oxford University Press, 2012.

Michael S. Roth, *Memory, Trauma, and History: Essays on Living with the Past*, New York: Columbia University Press, 2012.

Michael Whorf, *American Popular Song Lyricists: Oral Histories, 1920s-1960s*, Jefferson: McFarland & Co. , 2012.

Mícheál Ó hAodha and John O'Callaghan (eds.), *Narratives of the Occluded Irish Diaspora: Subversive Voices*, New York: Peter Lang, 2012.

Miguel García-Sancho, *Biology, Computing, and the History of Molecular Sequencing: From Proteins to DNA, 1945-2000*, New York: Palgrave Macmillan, 2012.

Nan Alamilla Boyd and Horacio N. Roque Ramírez (eds.), *Bodies of Evidence: The Practice of Queer Oral History*, Oxford and New York: Oxford University Press, 2012.

Nur Masalha, *The Palestine Nakba: Decolonising History, Narrating the Subaltern, Reclaiming Memory*, London: Zed Books, 2012.

Peter Ephrossand Martin Abramowitz, *Jewish Major Leaguers in Their Own Words: Oral Histories of 23 Players*, Jefferson: McFarland & Co. , 2012.

Qiliang He, *Gilded Voices: Economics, Politics, and Storytelling in the Yangzi Delta since 1949*, Leiden: Brill, 2012.

Raphael Samuel, *Theatres of Memory: Past and Present in Contemporary Culture*, London: Verso, 2012.

Robert I. Weiner and Richard E. Sharpless, *An Uncertain Future: Voices of a French Jewish Community, 1940-2012*, Toronto: University of Toronto Press, 2012.

Rosalie G. Riegle (ed.), *Doing Time for Peace: Resistance, Family, and Community*, Nashville: Vanderbilt University Press, 2012.

Sean Field, *Oral History, Community and Displacement: Imagining Memories in Post-Apartheid South Africa*, New York: Palgrave Macmillan, 2012.

Sharon Doetsch-Kidder, *Social Change and Intersectional Activism: The Spirit of Social Movement*, New York: Palgrave Macmillan, 2012.

Steve Hochstadt, *Exodus to Shanghai: Stories of Escape from the Third Reich*, New York: Palgrave Macmillan, 2012.

Stuart Berman, *Too Much Trouble: A Very Oral History of Danko Jones*, Toronto: ECW Press, 2012.

Studs Terkel, *Hard Times: An Illustrated Oral History of the Great Depression*, New York: The New Press, 2012.

Abbie Reese, *Dedicated to God: An Oral History of Cloistered Nuns*, Oxford and New York: Oxford University Press, 2013.

Afe Adogame and Shobana Shankar (eds.), *Religion on the Move!: New Dynamics of Religious Expansion in a Globalizing World*, Leiden: Brill, 2013.

Alistair Thomson, *Anzac Memories: Living with the Legend*, Clayton: Monash University Press, 2013.

Amy Bhatt and Nalini Iyer, *Roots & Reflections: South Asians in the Pacific Northwest*, Seattle: University of Washington Press, 2013.

Amy Helene Forss, *Black Print with a White Carnation: Mildred Brown and the Omaha Star Newspaper, 1938-1989*, Lincoln: University of Nebraska Press, 2013.

Ann K. Ferrell, *Burley: Kentucky Tobacco in a New Century*, Lexington: University Press of Kentucky, 2013.

Anna Källén, *Making Cultural History: New Perspectives on Western Heritage*, Lund: Nordic Academic Press, 2013.

Anna Sheftel and Stacey Zembrzycki (eds.), *Oral History off the Record: Toward an Ethnography of Practice*, New York: Palgrave Macmillan, 2013.

Anthony Slaven and Hugh Murphy (eds.), *Crossing the Bar: An Oral History of the British Shipbuilding, Shipre pairing and Marine Engine Building in the Age of Decline, 1956-1990*, St. John's: International Maritime Economic History Association, 2013.

Bernadette Pruitt, *The Other Great Migration: The Movement of Rural African Americans to Houston, 1900-1941*, College Station: Texas A&M University Press, 2013.

Brian Lewis (ed.), *British Queer History: New Approaches and Perspectives*, Manchester: Manchester University Press, 2013

Catherine Carstairs and Nancy Janovicek (eds.), *Feminist History in Canada: New Essays on Women, Gender, Work, and Nation*, Vancouver: University of British Columbia Press, 2013.

Christine Allison and Philip G. Kreyenbroek (eds.), *Remembering the Past in Iranian Societies*, Wiesbaden: Harrassowitz Verlag, 2013.

Christopher Bell, *East Harlem Remembered: Oral Histories of Community and Diversity*, Jefferson: McFarland & Co. , 2013.

Dave Isayand Lizzie Jacobs (eds.), *Ties that Bind: Stories of Love and Gratitude from the First Ten Years of StoryCorps*, New York: The Penguin Press, 2013.

Dov Levin, *Historian's Testimony: Collection of Oral History Abstracts*, Jerusalem: Magnes, 2013.

Edward T. Linenthal, Jonathan Hyman, and Christiane Gruber (eds.), *The Landscapes of 9/11: A Photographer's Journey*, Austin: University of Texas Press, 2013.

Elizabeth Barlow Rogers, *Learning Las Vegas: Portrait of a Northern New Mexican Place*, Santa Fe: Museum of New Mexico Press in association with Foundation for Landscape Studies, New York City, 2013.

Eric Tagliacozzo, *The Longest Journey: Southeast Asians and the Pilgrimage to Mecca*, Oxford and New York: Oxford University Press, 2013.

Ernest Morrell, Rudy Dueñas, Veronica Garcia, and Jorge López, *Critical Media Pedagogy: Teaching for Achievement in City Schools*, New York: Teachers College Press, 2013.

Gay Wilgus (ed.), *Knowledge, Pedagogy, and Postmulticulturalism: Shifting the Locus of Learning in Urban Teacher Education*, New York: Palgrave Macmillan, 2013.

Ginandjar Kartasasmita, *Managing Indonesia's Transformation: An Oral History*, Singapore: World Scientific, 2013.

Gordon K. Mantler, *Power to the Poor: Black-Brown Coalition and the Fight for Economic Justice, 1960-1974*, Chapel Hill: University of North Carolina Press, 2013.

Hilda Kean and Paul Martin (eds.), *The Public History Reader*, London and New York: Routledge, 2013.

Isaac Hampton II, *The Black Officer Corps: A History of Black Military Advancement from Integration through Vietnam*, London and New York: Routledge, 2013.

Jack Dougherty and Kristen Nawrotzki (eds.), *Writing History in the Digital Age*, Ann Arbor: The University of Michigan Press, 2013.

Jack Sidnell and Tanya Stivers (eds.), *The Handbook of Conversation Analysis*, Malden: Wiley-Blackwell, 2013.

James Lough, *This Ain't No Holiday Inn: Down and Out at the Chelsea Hotel, 1980-1995: An Oral History*, Tucson: Schaffner Press, 2013.

Jason Lim, *A Slow Ride into the Past: The Chinese Trishaw Industry in Singapore, 1942-1983*, Clayton: Monash University Publishing, 2013.

Jessie L. Embry (ed.), *Oral History, Community, and Work in the Amer-*

ican West, Tucson: University of Arizona Press, 2013.

Joan Shelley Rubin and Scott E. Casper (eds.), *The Oxford Encyclopedia of American Cultural and Intellectual History*, Oxford and New York: Oxford University Press, 2013.

Joan Tumblety (ed.), *Memory and History: Understanding Memory as Source and Subject*, London and New York: Routledge, 2013.

John T. Shaw, *JFK in the Senate: The Pathway to the Presidency*, New York: Palgrave Macmillan, 2013.

Kah Seng Loh, Ernest Koh, and Stephen Dobbs (eds.), *Oral History in Southeast Asia: Memories and Fragments*, New York: Palgrave Macmillan, 2013.

Karen M. Dunak, *As Long As We Both Shall Love: The White Wedding in Postwar America*, New York: New York University Press, 2013.

Kerry McCluskey, *Tulugaq: An Oral History of Ravens*, Iqaluit: Inhabit Media, 2013.

Laurie Meijer Drees, *Healing Histories: Stories from Canada's Indian Hospitals*, Edmonton: University of Alberta Press, 2013.

Laurie R. Cohen, *Smolensk under the Nazis: Everyday Life in Occupied Russia*, Rochester: University of Rochester Press, 2013.

Linda Sandino and Matthew Partington (eds.), *Oral History in the Visual Arts*, London: Bloomsbury, 2013.

Loh Kah Seng, *Squatters Into Citizens: The 1961 Bukit Ho Swee Fire and the Making of Modern Singapore*, Singapore: Asian Studies Association of Australia in association with NUS Press and NIAS Press, 2013.

Lou Hernández, *Memories of Winter Ball: Interviews with Players in the Latin American Winter Leagues of the 1950s*, Jefferson: McFarland & Co., 2013.

Lynn Dumenil (ed.), *The Oxford Encyclopedia of American Social History*, Oxford and New York: Oxford University Press, 2013.

Mary Kay Quinlan, Nancy Mackay, and Barbara W. Sommer, *Community Oral History Toolkit* (five volumes), Walnut Creek: Left Coast Press, 2013.

Michael Honey, *Sharecropper's Troubadour: John L. Handcox, the Southern Tenant Farmers' Union, and the African American Song Tradition*, New York: Palgrave Macmillan, 2013.

Michael Kamber, *Photojournalists on War: The Untold Stories from Iraq*, Austin: University of Texas Press, 2013.

Mike Martin, *An Intimate War: An Oral History of the Helmand Conflict, 1978-2012*, London: Hurst and Company, 2013.

Nellie Carlson and Kathleen Steinhauer, *Disinherited Generations: Our Struggle to Reclaim Treaty Rights for First Nations Women and Their Descendants*, Edmonton: University of Alberta Press, 2013.

Norman K. Denzin and Yvonna S. Lincoln (eds.), *Collecting and Interpreting Qualitative Materials*, Thousand Oaks: Sage Publications, fourth edition, 2013.

Paul R. Gregory, *Women of the Gulag: Portraits of Five Remarkable Lives*, Stanford: Hoover Institution Press, 2013.

Peter Coleman, Daniela Koleva, and Joanna Bornat (eds.), *Ageing, Ritual and Social Change: Comparing the Secular and Religious in Eastern and Western Europe*, Burlington: Ashgate Publishing, 2013.

Philip F. Napoli, *Bringing It All Back Home: An Oral History of New York City's Vietnam Veterans*, New York: Hill and Wang, 2013.

Randall C. Jimerson, *Shattered Glass in Birmingham: My Family's Fight for Civil Rights, 1961-1964*, Baton Rouge: Louisiana State University Press, 2013.

Robin Morgan and Ariel Leve (eds.), *1963, The Year of the Revolution: How Youth Changed the World with Music, Art, and Fashion*, New York: it-books, 2013.

Rosalie G. Riegle, *Crossing the Line: Nonviolent Resisters Speak Out for Peace*, Eugene: Cascade Books, 2013.

Roxanne Dunbar Ortiz (ed.), *The Great Sioux Nation: Sitting in Judgment on America*, Lincoln: University of Nebraska Press, 2013.

Sabiyha Prince, *African Americans and Gentrification in Washington, D. C. : Race, Class and Social Justice in the Nation's Capital*, Farnham: Ashgate, 2013.

Scott Lewellen, *Funny You Should Ask: Oral Histories of Classic Sitcom Storytellers*, Jefferson: McFarland & Co. , 2013.

Semion Lyandres, *The Fall of Tsarism: Untold Stories of the February 1917 Revolution*, Oxford and New York: Oxford University Press, 2013.

Sue Sojournerand Cheryl Reitan, *Thunder of Freedom: Black Leadership and the Transformation of 1960s Mississippi*, Lexington: University Press of Kentucky, 2013.

T. Mills Kelly, *Teaching History in the Digital Age*, Ann Arbor: The University of Michigan Press, 2013.

Teng Siao See, Chan Cheow Thia, Lee Huay Leng (eds.), *Education-at-Large: Student Life and Activities in Singapore, 1945-1965*, Hackensack: World Scientific Publishing Company, 2013.

Teresa Barnett and Chon A. Noriega (eds.), *Oral History and Communities of Color*, Los Angeles: UCLA Chicano Studies Research Center Press, 2013.

Thomas J. Misa, *Digital State: The Story of Minnesota's Computing Industry*, Minneapolis: University of Minnesota Press, 2013.

Toni Weller (ed.), *History in the Digital Age*, London and New York: Routledge, 2013.

Vida "Sister" Goldman Prince, *That's the Way It Was: Stories of Struggle, Survival and Self-respect in Twentieth-century Black St. Louis*, Charleston: The History Press, 2013.

Wakako Higuchi, *The Japanese administration of Guam, 1941-1944: A Study of Occupation and Integration Policies, with Japanese Oral Histories*, Jefferson: McFarland & Co. , 2013.

Walter Hamilton, *Children of the Occupation: Japan's Untold Story*, New Brunswick: Rutgers University Press, 2013.

Wendy Pojmann, *Italian Women and International Cold War Politics, 1944—1968*, New York: Fordham University Press, 2013.

Yasmin Gunaratnam, *Death and the Migrant: Bodies, Borders and Care*, London: Bloomsbury Academic, 2013.

Alexander Aviña, *Specters of Revolution: Peasant Guerrillas in the Cold War Mexican Countryside*, Oxford and New York: Oxford University Press, 2014.

Alexander Freund, *Oral History and Ethnic History*, Ottowa: Canadian Historical Association, 2014.

Anne Balay, *Steel Closets: Voices of Gay, Lesbian, and Transgender Steelworkers*, Chapel Hill: University of North Carolina Press, 2014.

Ben Daley, *The Great Barrier Reef: An Environmental History*, London and New York: Routledge, 2014.

Benjamin Tromly, *Making the Soviet Intelligentsia: Universities and Intellectual Life under Stalin and Khrushchev*, Cambridge: Cambridge University Press, 2014.

Carol Kammen, *On Doing Local History*, Lanham: Rowman and Littlefield, third edition, 2014.

Catherine Krull (ed.), *Cuba in a Global Context: International Relations, Internationalism, and Transnationalism*, Gainesville: University Press of Florida, 2014.

Cathy A. Frierson, *Silence was Salvation: Child Survivors of Stalin's Terror and World War II in the Soviet Union*, New Haven: Yale University Press, 2014.

Clark A. Pomerleau, *Califia Women: Feminist Education Against Sexism, Classism, and Racism*, Austin: University of Texas Press, 2014.

Daniel Whitman (ed.), *Outsmarting Apartheid: An Oral History of South Africa's Cultural and Educational Exchange with the United States, 1960-1999*, Albany: State University of New York Press, 2014.

Dawn-Marie Gibson and Jamillah Karim, *Women of the Nation: Between Black Protest and Sunni Islam*, New York: New York University Press, 2014.

Devika Chawla, *Home, Uprooted: Oral Histories of India's Partition*, New York: Fordham University Press, 2014.

Dominick LaCapra, *Writing History, Writing Trauma*, Baltimore: Johns Hopkins University Press, 2014.

Donald A. Ritchie, *Doing Oral History*, Oxford and New York: Oxford University Press, third edition, 2014.

Donatella Della Porta (ed.), *Methodological Practices in Social Movement Research*, Oxford and New York: Oxford University Press, 2014.

Douglas A. Boyd and Mary A. Larson (eds.), *Oral History and Digital Humanities: Voice, Access, and Engagement*, New York: Palgrave Macmillan, 2014.

Emita Brady Hill and Janet Butler Munch (eds.), *Bronx Faces and Voices: Sixteen Stories of Courage and Community*, Lubbock: Texas Tech University Press, 2014.

Eric Eve, *Behind the Gospels: Understanding the Oral Tradition*, Minneapolis: Fortress, 2014.

Geraldine J. Clifford, *Those Good Gertrudes: A Social History of Women Teachers in America*, Baltimore: Johns Hopkins University Press, 2014.

Gül Öz ateşler, *Gypsy Stigma and Exclusion in Turkey, 1970: Social Dynamics of Exclusionary Violence*, New York: Palgrave Macmillan, 2014.

Hester Vaizey, *Born in the GDR: Living in the Shadow of the Wall*, Oxford and New York: Oxford University Press, 2014.

Hill Gates, *Footbinding and Women's Labor in Sichuan*, London and New York: Routledge, 2014.

Him Mark Lai, Genny Lim, and Judy Yung (eds.), *Island: Poetry and History of Chinese Immigrants on Angel Island, 1910-1940*, Seattle: University of Washington Press, second edition, 2014.

Ira Berkow, *Wrigley Field: An Oral and Narrative History of the Home of the Chicago Cubs*, New York: Stewart, Tabori & Chang, 2014.

Lisa Anderson Todd, *For a Voice and the Vote: My Journey with the Mississippi Freedom Democratic Party*, Lexington: University Press of Kentucky, 2014.

J. D. Zahniserand Amelia R. Fry, *Alice Paul: Claiming Power*, Oxford and New York: Oxford University Press, 2014.

Jackson Michael, *The Game Before the Money: Voices of the Men Who Built the NFL*, Lincoln: University of Nebraska Press, 2014.

JoAnna Poblete, *Islanders in the Empire: Filipino and Puerto Rican Laborers in Hawai'i*, Urbana: University of Illinois Press, 2014.

Joanne L. Goodwin, *Changing the Game: Women at Work in Las Vegas, 1940-1990*, Reno: University of Nevada Press, 2014.

John A. Neuenschwander, *A Guide to Oral History and the Law*, Oxford and New York: Oxford University Press, second edition, 2014.

John D' Emilio, *In a New Century: Essays on Queer History, Politics, and Community Life*, Madison: University of Wisconsin Press, 2014.

John Ernest (ed.), *The Oxford Handbook of the African American Slave Narrative*, Oxford and New York: Oxford University Press, 2014.

Joyce M. Bell, *The Black Power Movement and American Social Work*, New York: Columbia University Press, 2014.

JP Bean, *Singing from the Floor: A History of British Folk Clubs*, London: Faber and Faber, 2014.

Judith Flores Carmona and Kristen V. Luschen (eds.), *Crafting Critical Stories: Toward Pedagogies and Methodologies of Collaboration, Inclusion and Voice*, New York: Peter Lang, 2014.

Julia Hallam and Les Roberts (eds.), *Locating the Moving Image: New Approaches to Film and Place*, Bloomington: Indiana University Press, 2014.

Julie Shayne (ed.), *Taking Risks: Feminist Activism and Research in the Americas*, Albany: State University of New York Press, 2014.

Maria Gitin, *This Bright Light of Ours: Stories from the 1965 Voting Rights Fight*, Tuscaloosa: University of Alabama Press, 2014.

Mario T. García (ed.), *The Chicano Movement: Perspectives from the Twenty-first Century*, London and New York: Routledge, 2014.

Mark Cave and Stephen M. Sloan (eds.), *Listening on the Edge: Oral History in the Aftermath of Crisis*, Oxford and New York: Oxford University Press, 2014.

Maud Anne Bracke, *Women and the Reinvention of the Political: Feminism in Italy, 1968—1983*, London and New York: Routledge, 2014.

Meg Jensen and Margaretta Jolly (eds.), *We Shall Bear Witness: Life Narratives and Human Rights*, Madison: University of Wisconsin Press, 2014.

Melissa Morrone（ed.）, *Informed Agitation*: *Library and Information Skills in Social Justice Movements and Beyond*, Sacramento: Library Juice Press, 2014.

Michael Buffalo Smith, *Rebel Yell*: *An Oral History of Southern Rock*, Macon: Mercer University Press, 2014.

Michael Nelson and Barbara A. Perry（eds.）, *41*: *Inside the Presidency of George H. W. Bush*, Ithaca: Cornell University Press, 2014.

Munyaradzi B. Munochiveyi, *Prisoners of Rhodesia*: *Inmates and Detainees in the Struggle for Zimbabwean Liberation*, *1960-1980*, New York: Palgrave Macmillan, 2014.

Nancy Shoemaker（ed.）, *Living with Whales*: *Documents and Oral Histories of Native New England Whaling History*, Amherst: University of Massachusetts Press, 2014.

Patricia Leavy（ed.）, *The Oxford Handbook of Qualitative Research*, Oxford and New York: Oxford University Press, 2014.

Peipei Qiu, Su Zhiliang, and Chen Lifei, *Chinese Comfort Women*: *Testimonies from Imperial Japan's Sex Slaves*, Oxford and New York: Oxford University Press, 2014.

Peter Medway, John Hardcastle, Georgina Brewis and David Crook, *English Teachers in a Postwar Democracy*: *Emerging Choice in London Schools*, *1945-1965*, New York: Palgrave Macmillan, 2014.

Phyllis Leffler, *Black Leaders on Leadership*: *Conversations with Julian Bond*, New York: Palgrave Macmillan, 2014.

Robert Budd, *Echoes of British Columbia*: *Voices from the Frontier*, Madeira Park: Harbour Publishing, 2014.

Robert Wuthnow, *Rough Country*: *How Texas Became America's Most Powerful Bible-belt State*, Princeton: Princeton University Press, 2014.

Roberta Gold, *When Tenants Claimed the City: The Struggle for Citizenship in New York City Housing*, Urbana: University of Illinois Press, 2014.

Ronald E. Marcello, *Small Town America in World War Ⅱ : War Stories from Wrightsville, Pennsylvania*, Texas: University of North Texas Press, 2014.

Sarah Browne, *The Women's Liberation Movement in Scotland*, Manchester: Manchester University Press, 2014.

Sheree Scarborough, *African American Railroad Workers of Roanoke: Oral Histories of the Norfolk and Western*, Charleston: The History Press, 2014.

Stacey Zembrzycki, *According to Baba: A Collaborative Oral History of Sudbury's Ukrainian Community*, Vancouver: University of British Columbia Press, 2014.

Staughton Lynd, *Doing History from the Bottom Up: On E. P. Thompson, Howard Zinn, and Rebuilding the Labor Movement from Below*, Chicago: Haymarket Books, 2014.

Stefan Berger and Bill Niven (eds.), *Writing the History of Memory*, London: Bloomsbury Academic, 2014.

Steven High, *Oral History at the Crossroads: Sharing Life Stories of Survival and Displacement*, Vancouver: University of British Columbia Press, 2014.

Steven High, Edward Little, and Thi Ry Duong (eds.), *Remembering Mass Violence: Oral History, New Media and Performance*, Toronto: University of Toronto Press, 2014.

Suhi Choi, *Embattled Memories: Contested Meanings in Korean War Memorials*, Reno: University of Nevada Press, 2014.

Toby Smith, *Bush League Boys: The Postwar Legends of Baseball in the American Southwest*, Albuquerque: University of New Mexico Press, 2014.

Todd Wolfson, *Digital Rebellion: The Birth of the Cyber Left*, Chicago:

University of Illinois Press, 2014.

Tommy Dickinso, "*Curing queers*": *Mental Nurses and Their Patients, 1935-1974*, Manchester: Manchester University Press, 2014.

Una Mullally, *In the Name of Love*: *The Movement for Marriage Equality in Ireland*: *An Oral History*, Dublin: History Press Ireland, 2014.

Vic Hobson, *Creating Jazz Counterpoint*: *New Orleans, Barbershop Harmony, and the Blues*, Jackson: University Press of Mississippi, 2014.

Waskar Ari, *Earth Politics*: *Religion, Decolonization, and Bolivia's Indigenous Intellectuals*, Durham: Duke University Press, 2014.

Adrienne Jansen and Liz Grant, *Migrant Journeys*: *New Zealand Taxi Drivers Tell Their Stories*, Wellington: Bridget Williams Books, 2015.

Alexander von Plato, *The End of the Cold War?*: *Bush, Kohl, Gorbachev, and the Reunification of Germany*, New York: Palgrave Macmillan, 2015.

Anika Walke, *Pioneers and Partisans*: *An Oral History of Nazi Genocide in Belorussia*, Oxford and New York: Oxford University Press, 2015.

Anne J. Kershen (ed.), *London the Promised Land Revisited*: *The Changing Face of the London Migrant Landscape in the Early 21st Century*, Burlington: Ashgate Publishing Limited, 2015.

Arlene Alda, *Just Kids from the Bronx*: *Telling It the Way It Was*: *An Oral History*, New York: Henry Holt and Company, 2015.

Arn Keeling and John Sandlos (eds.), *Mining and Communities in Northern Canada*: *History, Politics, and Memory*, Calgary: University of Calgary Press, 2015.

Barbara W. Sommer, *Practicing Oral History in Historical Organizations*, Walnut Creek: Left Coast Press, 2015.

Blair Jackson and David Gans, *This is All a Dream We Dreamed*: *An Oral History of the Grateful Dead*, New York: Flatiron Books, 2015.

Carol McKirdy, *Practicing Oral History with Immigrant Narrators*, Walnut Creek: Left Coast Press, 2015.

Casey High, *Victims and Warriors: Violence, History, and Memory in Amazonia*, Urbana: University of Illinois Press, 2015.

Catherine Plum, *Antifascism after Hitler: East German Youth and Socialist Memory, 1949-1989*, London and New York: Routledge, 2015.

Celia Hughes, *Young Lives on the Left: Sixties Activism and the Liberation of the Self*, Manchester: Manchester University Press, 2015.

Christa Wirth, *Memories of Belonging: Descendants of Italian Migrants to the United Sates, 1884-Present*, Leiden: Brill, 2015.

Christian G. Appy, *American Reckoning: The Vietnam War and Our National Identity*, New York: Viking, 2015.

Christina D. Abreu, *Rhythms of Race: Cuban Musicians and the Making of Latino New York City and Miami, 1940-1960*, Chapel Hill: University of North Carolina Press, 2015.

Christina Robertson and Jennifer Westerman (eds.), *Working on Earth: Class and Environmental Justice*, Reno: University of Nevada Press, 2015.

D. W. Gibson, *The Edge Becomes the Center: An Oral History of Gentrification in the Twenty-first Century*, New York: The Overlook Press, 2015.

Danielle Fosler-Lussier, *Music in America's Cold War Diplomacy*, Oakland: University of California Press, 2015.

David Dean, Yana Meerzon, and Kathryn Prince (eds.), *History, Memory, Performance*, New York: Palgrave Macmillan, 2015.

Dionne Danns, Michelle A. Purdy, and Christopher M. Span (eds.), *Using Past as Prologue: Contemporary Perspectives on African American Educational History*, Charlotte: Information Age Publishing, 2015.

Dominic Johnson, *The Art of Living: An Oral History of Performance Art*,

New York: Palgrave Macmillan, 2015.

Eva M. McMahan, *Elite Oral History Discourse: A Study of Cooperation and Coherence*, Tuscaloosa: University of Alabama Press, 2015.

Faye Sayer, *Public History: A Practical Guide*, New York: Bloomsbury Academic, 2015.

George W. Noblit (ed.), *School Desegregation: Oral Histories toward Understanding the Effects of White Domination*, Rotterdam: Sense Publishers, 2015.

Harvey Schwartz, *Building the Golden Gate Bridge: A Workers' Oral History*, Seattle: University of Washington Press, 2015.

Hilary Orange (ed.), *Reanimating Industrial Spaces: Conducting Memory Work in Post-industrial Societies*, Walnut Creek: Left Coast Press, 2015.

Jason Zuidema (ed.), *Understanding the Consecrated Life in Canada: Critical Essays on Contemporary Trends*, Waterloo: Wilfrid Laurier University Press, 2015.

Jeffrey Meek, *Queer Voices in Post-war Scotland: Male Homosexuality, Religion and Society*, New York: Palgrave Macmillan, 2015.

Jennifer R. Nájera, *The Borderlands of Race: Mexican Segregation in a South Texas Town*, Austin: University of Texas Press, 2015.

Jennifer Ring, *A Game of Their Own: Voices of Contemporary Women in Baseball*, Lincoln: University of Nebraska Press, 2015.

John Darrell Sherwood, *War in the Shallows: U. S. Navy Coastal and Riverine Warfare in Vietnam, 1965-1968*, Washington: Naval History and Heritage Command, Department of the Navy, 2015.

Julia Brock, Jennifer W. Dickey, Richard J. W. Harker, and Catherine M. Lewis (eds.), *Beyond Rosie: A Documentary History of Women and World War II*, Fayetteville: University of Arkansas Press, 2015.

Kay Rippelmeyer, *The Civilian Conservation Corps in Southern Illinois*, *1933—1942*, Carbondale: Southern Illinois University Press, 2015.

Kristina R. Llewellyn, Alexander Freund and Nolan Reilly (eds.), *The Canadian Oral History Reader*, Montreal: McGill-Queen's University Press, 2015.

LaKisha Michelle Simmons, *Crescent City Girls: The Lives of Young Black Women in Segregated New Orleans*, Chapel Hill: University of North Carolina Press, 2015.

Leila J. Rupp and Susan K. Freeman (eds.), *Understanding and Teaching U. S. Lesbian, Gay, Bisexual, and Transgender History*, Madison: University of Wisconsin Press, 2015.

Lu Ann Jones (ed.), *A Directory of Oral History in the National Park Service*, Washington: National Park Service, U. S. Department of the Interior, third edition, 2015.

Maggie Rivas-Rodriguez, *Texas Mexican Americans and Postwar Civil Rights*, Austin: University of Texas Press, 2015.

Marilyn Barber and Murray Watson, *Invisible Immigrants: The English in Canada since 1945*, Winnipeg: University of Manitoba Press, 2015.

Mario T. García, *The Chicano Generation: Testimonios of the Movement*, Oakland: University of California Press, 2015.

Maureen Ryan Doyleand Charlene L. Martin, *In Her Shoes: A compilation of Inspiring Stories from the First Decade of the Worcester Women's Oral History Project*, Bermuda: CreateSpace Independent Publishing, 2015.

Merilyn Moos, *Breaking the Silence: Voices of the British Children of Refugees from Nazism*, New York: Rowman & Littlefield International, 2015.

Michael Gillen, *Merchant Marine Survivors of World War II: Oral Histories of Cargo Carrying Under Fire*, Jefferson: McFarland & Co. , 2015.

Monique Laney, *German Rocketeers in the Heart of Dixie: Making Sense of the Nazi Past during the Civil Rights Era*, New Haven: Yale University Press, 2015.

Natalia Khanenko-Friesen and Gelinada Grinchenko (eds.), *Reclaiming the Personal: Oral History in Post-socialist Europe*, Toronto: University of Toronto Press, 2015.

Noah Shenker, *Reframing Holocaust Testimony*, Bloomington: Indiana University Press, 2015.

Pauline Bermingham Scully (ed.), *Two Cigarettes Coming Down the Boreen: Oral Narratives from a South Galway Community*, Dublin: Arlen House, 2015.

Peter Hart, *Voices from the Front: An Oral History of the Great War*, London: Profile Books, 2015.

Rina Benmayor, María Eugenia Cardenal dela Nuez, and Pilar Domínguez Prats (eds.), *Memory, Subjectivities, and Representation: Approaches to Oral History in Latin America, Portugal, and Spain*, New York: Palgrave Macmillan, 2015.

Robert Perks and Alistair Thomson (eds.), *The Oral History Reader*, London and New York: Routledge, third edition, 2015.

Rosalyn Howard, *Recollection and Reconnection: Voices of the St. David's Islanders and Their Native American Relatives*, Bermuda: CreateSpace Independent Publishing, 2015.

Sandra Fahy, *Marching through Suffering: Loss and Survival in North Korea*, New York: Columbia University Press, 2015.

Simona Mitroiu (ed.), *Life Writing and Politics of Memory in Eastern Europe*, New York: Palgrave Macmillan, 2015.

Stephen M. Sloan, Lois E. Myers, and Michelle Holland (eds.), *Tattooed on My Soul: Texas Veterans Remember World War Ⅱ, College Station: Texas A&M University Press, 2015.

Steve Estes, Charleston in Black and White: Race and Power in the South after the Civil Rights Movement, Chapel Hill: University of North Carolina Press, 2015.

Steven High (ed.), Beyond Testimony and Trauma: Oral History in the Aftermath of Mass Violence, Vancouver: University of British Columbia Press, 2015.

Uriel Quesada, Letitia Gomez, and Salvador Vidal-Ortiz (eds.), Queer Brown Voices: Personal Narratives of Latina/o LGBT Activism, Austin: University of Texas Press, 2015.

Valerie Raleigh Yow, Recording Oral History: A Guide for the Humanities and Social Sciences, Lanham: Rowman and Littlefield, third edition, 2015.

Yuma Totani, Justice in Asia and the Pacific Region, 1945-1952: Allied War Crimes Prosecutions, Cambridge: Cambridge University Press, 2015.

Anna Clark, Private Lives, Public History, Melbourne: Melbourne University Press, 2016.

Craig S. Simpson and Gregory S. Wilson, Above the Shots: An Oral History of the Kent State Shootings, Kent: Kent State University Press, 2016.

Elizabeth Campisi, Escape to Miami: An Oral History of the Cuban Rafter Crisis, Oxford and New York: Oxford University Press, 2016.

Gregory W. Bush, White Sand Black Beach: Civil Rights, Public Space, and Miami's Virginia Key, Gainesville: University Press of Florida, 2016.

Howard B. Means, 67 Shots: Kent State and the End of American Innocence, Boston: Da Capo Press, 2016.

Jake Alimahomed-Wilson, Solidarity Forever?: Race, Gender, and

Unionism in the Ports of Southern California, Lanham: Lexington Books, 2016.

Janis Thiessen, *Not Talking Union: An Oral History of North American Mennonites and Labour*, Montreal: McGill-Queen's University Press, 2016.

Jerry McConnell (ed.), *The Improbable Life of the Arkansas Democrat: An Oral History*, Fayetteville: University of Arkansas Press, 2016.

Lynn Abrams, *Oral History Theory*, London and New York: Routledge, second edition, 2016.

Melanie Ilic and Dalia Leinarte (eds.), *The Soviet Past in the Post-Socialist Present: Methodology and Ethics in Russian, Baltic and Central European Oral History and Memory Studies*, London and New York: Routledge, 2016.

Michael Nelson, Barbara A. Perry, and Russell L. Riley (eds.), *42: Inside the Presidency of Bill Clinton*, Ithaca: Cornell University Press, 2016.

Michael T. Westrate, *Living Soviet in Ukraine from Stalin to Maidan: Under the Falling Red Star in Kharkiv*, Lanham: Lexington Books, 2016.

Miroslav Vaněk and Pavel Mücke, *Velvet Revolutions: An Oral History of Czech Society*, Oxford and New York: Oxford University Press, 2016.

Nancy MacKay, *Curating Oral Histories: From Interview to Archive*, Walnut Creek: Left Coast Press, second edition, 2016.

Natalie Thomlinson, *Race, Ethnicity and the Women's Movement in England, 1968-1993*, Basingstoke: Palgrave Macmillan, 2016.

Rodreguez King-Dorset, *Mandela's Dancers: Oral Histories of Program Participants and Organizers*, Jefferson: McFarland & Co., 2016.

Russell L. Riley, *Inside the Clinton White House: An Oral History*, Oxford and New York: Oxford University Press, 2016.

Steve Delsohn, *Cardinal and Gold: The Oral History of USC Trojans Football*, *New York: Crown Archetype*, 2016.

Svetlana Alexievich, *Secondhand Time: The Last of the Soviets*, New York: Random House, 2016.

Thomas Cauvin, *Public History: A Textbook of Practice*, London and New York: Routledge, 2016.

Timothy K. Blauvelt and Jeremy Smith (eds.), *Georgia after Stalin: Nationalism and Soviet Power*, London and New York: Routledge, 2016.

二 中文

唐诺·里奇:《大家来做口述历史》,王芝芝译,源流出版公司1997年版。

保尔·汤普逊:《过去的声音:口述史》,覃方明、渠东、张旅平译,(香港)牛津大学出版社1999年版、辽宁教育出版社2000年版。

游鉴明:《倾听她们的声音:女性口述历史的方法与口述史料的应用》,(台北)左岸文化事业有限公司2002年版。

梁妃仪、洪德仁、蔡笃坚合编:《协助社群认同发展的口述历史实践——结合理论与实务的操作手册》,(台北)唐山出版社2003年版。

肯·霍尔斯:《口述历史》,陈瑛译,(台北)播种者文化有限公司2003年版。

贝丝·罗伯森:《如何做好口述历史》,黄煜文译,(台北)五观艺术管理2004年版。

杨祥银:《与历史对话:口述史学的理论与实践》,中国社会科学出版社2004年版。

周新国主编:《中国口述史的理论与实践》,中国社会科学出版社2005年版。

唐纳德·里奇:《大家来做口述历史:实务指南》(第二版),王芝芝、姚力译,当代中国出版社2006年版。

当代上海研究所编:《口述历史的理论与实务:来自海峡两岸的探讨》,上海人民出版社2007年版。

陈旭清:《口述史研究的理论与实践》,中国社会科学出版社2010年版。

李向平、魏扬波:《口述史研究方法》,上海人民出版社2010年版。

定宜庄、汪润主编：《口述史读本》，北京大学出版社 2011 年版。

王宇英：《当代中国口述史：为何与何为》，中国大百科全书出版社 2012 年版。

李向玉主编：《众声平等：华人社会口述历史的理论与实务》，澳门理工学院 2013 年版。

陈墨：《口述历史门径（实务手册)》，人民出版社 2013 年版。

陈墨：《口述历史杂谈》，海豚出版社 2014 年版。

李卫民：《本土化视域下的口述历史理论研究》，上海人民出版社 2014 年版。

许雪姬主编：《台湾口述历史的理论实务与案例》，台湾口述历史学会 2014 年版。

杨祥银主编：《口述史研究》（第一辑），社会科学文献出版社 2014 年版。

陈墨：《口述史学研究：多学科视角》，人民出版社 2015 年版。

陈子丹：《少数民族口述历史档案研究》，云南大学出版社 2015 年版。

钱茂伟：《中国公众史学通论》，中国社会科学出版社 2015 年版。

徐雄彬、徐德源编著：《口述历史怎么做怎么样：齐红深的口述历史理论与实践》，新华出版社 2016 年版。

张李玺主编：《女性人生价值的诠释及口述史本土化探究》，中国妇女出版社 2016 年版。

网络资源①

9/11 Oral History Project，Pace University

http：//webpage. pace. edu/911oralhistoryproject/

12th Armored Division Oral History Project

http：//www. 12tharmoredmuseum. com/oral-history. asp

A Brief Guide to Basic Technology·Planning for Oral History Projects

http：//at. blogs. wm. edu/a-brief-guide-to-basic-technology-planning-

for-oral-history-projects/

A Guide to the Coleman-Fulton Pasture Company Oral History Collection，

Dolph Briscoe Center for American History，University of Texas at Austin

http：//www. lib. utexas. edu/taro/utcah/02501/02501-P. html

A Harlem Neighborhood Oral History Project，New York Public Library

http：//oralhistory. nypl. org/neighborhoods/harlem

Abraham Lincoln High School Oral History Project

http：//www. alhsoralhistoryproject. org/

Academic Health Center Oral History Project，University of Minnesota

http：//editions. lib. umn. edu/ahc-ohp/

ACT UP Oral History Project

http：//www. actuporalhistory. org/index1. html

---

① 这里罗列的口述历史网络资源以美国为主，部分涉及其他国家或地区，按照英文字母排序。所有网站访问时间为 2015 年 5 月—2016 年 10 月。

Ad Hoc Tribunals Oral History Project, Brandeis University

https：//www. brandeis. edu/ethics/internationaljustice/oral-history/

African American AIDS Activism Oral History Project

https：//afamaidsoralhistory. wordpress. com/

African Oral History, University of Portsmouth

http：//www. port. ac. uk/research/africanoralhistory/

Ahozko Historiaren Artxiboa/Archive of Oral History

http：//www. ahoaweb. org/

AIDS Activist History Project

http：//www. aidsactivisthistory. ca/

AIDS Oral History Project, New York Public Library

http：//www. nypl. org/voices/audio-video/oral-histories/aids

AIDS Oral History Projects, UCSF Library

https：//www. library. ucsf. edu/collections/archives/manuscripts/aids/oh

Alumni Oral History Project, Greensboro College

https：//www. greensboro. edu/museum-aohp. php

American Airpower Heritage Museum Oral History Program

http：//airpowermuseum. org/? page = cms/index&cms_ page = 95

American Life Histories: Manuscripts from the Federal Writers' Project, 1936 to 1940

https：//www. loc. gov/collections/federal-writers-project/

Alexandria Oral History Program

http：//www. alexandriava. gov/historic/info/default. aspx?id = 29666

Alive in Truth: The New Orleans Disaster Oral History and Memory Project

http：//www. aliveintruth. com/

Alumnae Oral Histories, Smith College

http：//www. smith. edu/libraries/libs/archives/collections/alumoralhistory

American Association for State and Local History

http: //www. aaslh. org/

American Memory, Library of Congress

http: //memory. loc. gov/ammem/index. html

An Era of Change: Oral Histories of Civilians in World War II Hawai 'i

http: //scholarspace. manoa. hawaii. edu/handle/10125/29796

An Oral History of the March on Washington

http: //www. smithsonianmag. com/history/oral-history-march-washing-

ton-180953863/? no-ist

Angling Oral History Project, Montana State University

https: //www. lib. montana. edu/trout/oral-histories/

Appalachian Food Ways Oral History, Berea College

http: //berea. libraryhost. com/? p = collections/controlcard&id = 158

Arab Immigration Oral History, University of Florida

http: //ufdc. ufl. edu/oharab

Archives for Oral History, White Plains Public Library

http: //whiteplainslibrary. org/tag/oral-history/

Archives of Lesbian Oral History

http: //alotarchives. org/

Arizona Queer Archives

http: //www. azqueerarchives. org/

Asian American Art Oral History Project, DePaul University

http: //via. library. depaul. edu/oral_ his/

Asocación de Historia Oral dela República Argentina (AHORA)

www. historiaoralargentina. org

Asociación Mexicana de Historia Oral

http: //iohanet. org/espa/home/documents/

Associaçao Brasileira de História Oral

www. historiaoral. org. br

Associazione Italiana di Storia Orale

http：//www. aisoitalia. it

Audio-Video Barn, Illinois State Museum

http：//avbarn. museum. state. il. us/

Australian Generations Oral History Project

http：//artsonline. monash. edu. au/australian-generations/

Baltimore's Forgotten Champions：An Oral History

http：//cnsmaryland. org/interactives/baltimore-stallions-oral-history/

Becoming Minnesotan：Stories of Recent Immigrants and Refugees, Minnesota Historical Society

http：//education. mnhs. org/immigration

Black Oral History Interviews(1972-1974), Washington State University Libraries

http：//ntserver1. wsulibs. wsu. edu/masc/finders/cass2. htm

http：//content. libraries. wsu. edu/cdm/landingpage/collection/5985/

Black Oral History Project, Villanova University

http：//www1. villanova. edu/villanova/diversity/timeline. html

Black Women at Virginia Tech History Project (Oral Histories)

http：//spec. lib. vt. edu/archives/blackhistory/oralhistory/

Black Women Oral History Project, Schlesinger Library, Harvard University

https：//www. radcliffe. harvard. edu/schlesinger-library/collection/black-women-oral-history-project

Born in Slavery: Slave Narratives from the Federal Writers' Project, 1936-1938

https：//www. loc. gov/collections/slave-narratives-from-the-federal-writers-project-1936-to-1938/

Boston College Subpoena News

https: //bostoncollegesubpoena. wordpress. com

Bridging Our Stories: Washington Heights and Inwood Oral History Project, New York Public Library

http: //oralhistory. nypl. org/neighborhoods/washington-heights-inwood

British Diplomatic Oral History Programme, Churchill College

www. chu. cam. ac. uk/archives/collections/bdohp

British Library Sounds

http: //sounds. bl. uk/

Buffalo Trace Oral History Project

www. nunncenter. org/buffalotrace

Capital Campus Oral History Program, California State University, Sacramento

http: //www. csus. edu/oralhist/

Captive on the U. S. Mainland: Oral Histories of Hawai'i-born Nisei

http: //scholarspace. manoa. hawaii. edu/handle/10125/23303

Capturing the Living Past: An Oral History Primer

http: //www. nebraskahistory. org/lib-arch/research/audio-vis/oral_ history/

Canadian Military Oral History Collection, University of Victoria

http: //contentdm. library. uvic. ca/cdm/landingpage/collection/collection13

Canadian Oral History Association

http: //canoha. ca/

Carnegie Corporation Oral History Project

http: //www. columbia. edu/cu/lweb/digital/collections/oral

_ hist/carnegie/

Center for Documentary Studies, Duke University

http：//documentarystudies. duke. edu/

Center for Oak Ridge Oral History

http：//cdm16107. contentdm. oclc. org/cdm/landingpage/collec-
tion/p15388coll1

Center for Oral History, Chemical Heritage Foundation

http：//www. chemheritage. org/research/institute-for-research/oral-his-
tory-program/index. aspx

Center for Oral History, University of Hawaii at Manoa

http：//www. oralhistory. hawaii. edu/

http：//scholarspace. manoa. hawaii. edu/handle/10125/21086

Center for Oral History and Cultural Heritage, University of Southern Mississippi

https：//www. usm. edu/oral-history

Center for Oral and Public History, California State University, Fullerton

http：//coph. fullerton. edu/

Center for Oral History Research, University of California, Los Angeles

http：//oralhistory. library. ucla. edu/

Center for the Study of History and Memory, Indiana University

http：//www. indiana. edu/~cshm/index. html

Center of Oral History, European University at St. Petersburg

http：//eu. spb. ru/en/history/projects/oral-history

Certificate in Oral History, Dublin City Council

http：//www. dublincity. ie/story/certificate-oral-history

Centre for Life History and Life Writing Research, University of Sussex

http：//www. sussex. ac. uk/clhlwr/

Centre for Oral History and Digital Storytelling, Concordia University http：//storytelling. concordia. ca/

Centre for Oral History and Tradition, University of Lethbridge

http：//www. uleth. ca/research/centres-institutes/centre-oral-history-and-tradition

Centre for Popular Memory, University of Capt Town, South Africa

http：//www. arc. uct. ac. za/the_ visual_ university/? lid = 262

Centre for Visual and Oral History Research, University of Huddersfield

https：//www. hud. ac. uk/research/researchcentres/cvohr/

Chicago Architects Oral History Project

http：//digital-libraries. saic. edu/cdm/landingpage/collection/caohp

Chicago Leather Archives and Museum Oral History Exhibit

http：//www. leatherarchives. org/oral. html

Children's Oral History Project, African American Museum of Iowa

http：//www. blackiowa. org/collections/childrens-oral-history-project/

Citadel Oral History Program

http：//www. citadeloralhistory. com/

Civil Rights Digital Library, University System of Georgia

http：//crdl. usg. edu/

Civil Rights Documentation Project, University of Southern Mississippi

http：//www. usm. edu/crdp/

Civil Rights History Project, Library of Congress

http：//www. loc. gov/collection/civil-rights-history-project/about-this-collection/

Civil Rights Movement in Kentucky Oral History Project

http：//205. 204. 134. 47/civil_ rights_ mvt/

Civil Rights Oral History Collection, Washington State University

http：//content. libraries. wsu. edu/cdm/landingpage/collection/cvoralhis

Cleveland Regional Oral History Collection, Cleveland State University

http: //engagedscholarship. csuohio. edu/crohc/

Closeted/Out in the Quadrangles: A History of LGBTQ Life at the University of Chicago

http: //gendersexuality. uchicago. edu/projects/closeted/

Colectivo de Historia Oral

http: //colectivohistoriaoral. wordpress. com

Collecting Memories: Oral Histories of American Folklorists

http: //www. afsnet. org/? page = OralHistory

http: //digital. lib. usu. edu/cdm/landingpage/collection/AFS

Colorado College Oral History Collections

https: //digitalcc. coloradocollege. edu/islandora/object/coccc%3A5978

Columbia Center for Oral History, Columbia University

http: //library. columbia. edu/locations/ccoh. html

Columbia Center for Oral History Research, Columbia University

http: //www. incite. columbia. edu/ccohr/

Commonwealth Oral History Project, Institute of Commonwealth Studies, University of London

http: //commonwealth. sas. ac. uk/research/cw-oral-history-project

Community Oral History Project, New York Public Library

http: //oralhistory. nypl. org/

Consortium for Oral History Educators

http: //www. coheonline. org/

Conversations with History, University of California, Berkeley

http: //conversations. berkeley. edu/

Conversations with Medical Informatics Pioneers: An Oral History Project

https: //lhncbc. nlm. nih. gov/project/medical-informatics-pioneers

Country Queers: A Multi-media Oral History Project

https：//countryqueers. com/

Crossing Borders, Bridging Generations, Brooklyn Historical Society

http：//cbbg. brooklynhistory. org/

Czech Oral History Association

https：//sites. google. com/site/czechoralhistoryassociation

D. C. Everest Oral History Project

http：//www. dceoralhistoryproject. org/

Dance Oral History Project, New York Public Library

http：//www. nypl. org/voices/audio-video/oral-histories/dance

Dartmouth College Oral History Project

https：//www. dartmouth. edu/~library/rauner/archives/oral_
history/

David and Barbara Pryor Center for Arkansas Oral and Visual History, University of Arkansas

http：//pryorcenter. uark. edu/

Dawson Oral History Project, Dawson College

https：//dohp. dawsoncollege. qc. ca/

Dayton and Miami Valley Oral History Project, Wright State University Libraries

http：//corescholar. libraries. wright. edu/history_ oral_ history/

Densho: The Japanese American Legacy Project

http：//www. densho. org/

Digital Audio Field Recording Equipment Guide

http：//www. vermontfolklifecenter. org/archive/res_ audioequip. htm

Digital Editing of Field Audio

http：//www. vermontfolklifecenter. org/archive/res_ digitalediting. htm

Digital Omnium

http：//digitalomnium. com/

Digital Oral History, Center for Lowell History, University of Massachusetts Lowell

http: //library. uml. edu/clh/OH/OrHist. htm

Documenting Lesbian Lives: Student Oral History Project, Smith College

http: //www. smith. edu/libraries/libs/ssc/lives/lives-intro. html

Documenting the American South

http: //docsouth. unc. edu/

Doug Boyd: Oral History, Archives, Music and Digital Technologies

http: //dougboyd. org/

Dreyer's Grand Ice Cream Oral History Project

http: //bancroft. berkeley. edu/ROHO/projects/dreyers/

East Midlands Oral History Archive, University of Leicester

https: //www. le. ac. uk/emoha/

Eastern Fine Paper Company Oral History Project, Maine Folklife Center

https: //umaine. edu/folklife/research-and-exhibits/research/eastern-fine-paper-company-oral-history-project/

Edmund S. Muskie Oral History Project, Bates College

http: //digilib. bates. edu/cgi-bin/library. cgi? site = localhost&a = p&p = about&c = muskieor&l = en&w = utf-8

Edward M. Kennedy Oral History Project

https: //www. emkinstitute. org/resources/oral-history-miller-center

Elizabeth Roberts' Working Class Oral History Archive, Lancaster University

http: //www. lancaster. ac. uk/users/rhc/resources/archive. htm

Ellis Island Oral History, National Park Service

www. nps. gov/elis/historyculture/ellis-island-oral-history-project. htm

ERA Oral History Project

http: //www. washingtonhistory. org/research/whc/oralhistory/

ERAOralHistory/

Ethnic Women of Cleveland Oral History Project

http：//www. clevelandmemory. org/ewc/

Everett L. Cooley Oral History Project, University of Utah

http：//content. lib. utah. edu/cdm/landingpage/collection/uu-elc

Exmoor Oral History Archive

http：//www1. somerset. gov. uk/archives/exmoor/

Family Oral History Using Digital Tools

http：//familyoralhistory. us/

Farmer Oral History Collection, College of Wooster

http：//openworks. wooster. edu/farmer_ oral_ history/

Fenn College Oral Histories

http：//flash. ulib. csuohio. edu/cmp/fenn/interviews. html

Field Recording in the Digital Age

http：//www. vermontfolklifecenter. org/archive/res_ digit-al-age. html

Finnish Oral History Network

http：//www. finlit. fi/en/research/research-networks/fohn-finnish-oral-history-network

Ford Reminiscences Oral Histories, Benson Ford Research Center

http：//cdm15889. contentdm. oclc. org/cdm/landingpage/collection/p15889coll2

Foreign Affairs Oral History Collections, Association for Diplomatic Studies and Training

http：//adst. org/oral-history/

Fortunoff Video Archive for Holocaust Testimonies, Yale University Library

http：//web. library. yale. edu/testimonies

Foxfire

http：//www. foxfirefund. org/

Frank Driggs Jazz Oral Histories Collection, Marr Sound Archives, University of Missouri-Kansas City

http：//library. umkc. edu/marr-collections/archival/driggs

Fundaçao Getulio Vargas, Programa de História Oral, Rio de Janeiro

http：//cpdoc. fgv. br/acervo/historiaoral

Gaelic Athletic Association Oral History Project, Boston College

http：//www. bc. edu/centers/irish/gaahistory/

George H. W. Bush Oral Histories

http：//millercenter. org/president/bush/oralhistory

George J. Mitchell Oral History Project, Bowdoin College

http：//digitalcommons. bowdoin. edu/mitchelloralhistory/

George W. Bush Oral Histories

http：//millercenter. org/president/gwbush/oralhistory

Getting Word Oral History Project

http：//www. monticello. org/getting-word

GLBT Historical Social Oral History Collection

http：//www. oac. cdlib. org/findaid/ark：/13030/ kt4779s1bc/entire_ text/

Goin' North, West Chester University

https：//goinnorth. org/oral-histories

Grand Rapids Oral History Collection, Gerald R. Ford Presidential Library

http://www. fordlibrarymuseum. gov/library/guides/findingaid/Grand_ Rapids_ -_ Oral_ Histories. asp

Greenwich Village Oral History Project, New York Public Library

http：//oralhistory. nypl. org/neighborhoods/greenwich-village

Groundswell：Oral History for Social Change

http：//www. oralhistoryforsocialchange. org/

Guide to Collecting Oral Histories, Grand Valley State University

http: //www. gvsu. edu/speaking/guide-to-collecting-oral-histories-7. htm

Guide to Oral Histories in Medicine and the Health Sciences, U. S. National Library of Medicine

https: //www. nlm. nih. gov/hmd/oral_ history/index. html

Guide to the Cornell University Oral History Program Records, 1961-1965

http: //rmc. library. cornell. edu/EAD/htmldocs/RMA01394. html

Guide to the Duke University Oral History Program Collection, 1973-1978, 1992

http: //library. duke. edu/rubenstein/findingaids/duohp/

Guide to the Oral History Collections, Virginia Polytechnic Institute and State University

http: //spec. lib. vt. edu/specgen/oralindx. htm

Guide to the Oral History of the American Left Collection, New York University

http: //dlib. nyu. edu/findingaids/html/tamwag/oh_ 002/

H-OralHist

https: //networks. h-net. org/h-oralhist

Hell's Kitchen Oral History Project, New York Public Library

http: //oralhistory. nypl. org/neighborhoods/hells-kitchen

Hellenic-American Oral History Project, Queens College, CUNY

http: //www. qc. cuny. edu/Academics/Degrees/DSS/Sociology/GreekOralHistory/

Historic Fulton Oral History Project, Virginia Commonwealth University

http: //dig. library. vcu. edu/cdm/landingpage/collection/ful

Historical Research Associates, Inc.

http: //hrassoc. com/

History Associates

https：//www. historyassociates. com/

History Factory

http：//www. historyfactory. com/

History through Memories and Stories: UW East Asia Library Oral History Project for Seattle Chinese Immigrants

http：//depts. washington. edu/oralhist/wordpress/

Holocaust Oral History Archives, Gratz College

http：//www. gratz. edu/pages/holocaust-oral-history-archive

Holocaust Oral History Project, University of California, Santa Barbara

http：//www. history. ucsb. edu/projects/holocaust/

Hong Kong Oral History Archives Project, University of Hong Kong

http：//sunzi. lib. hku. hk/hkoh/

Houston Oral History Project

http：//www. houstonoralhistory. org/

Hurricane Digital Memory Bank

http：//hurricanearchive. org/

Hurricane Sandy Oral History Interviews

http：//library. monmouth. edu/main/content/hurricane-sandy-oral-history-interviews

Hurricane Sandy Oral History Project, College of New Jersey

https：//hurricanesandy. pages. tcnj. edu/

Idaho Oral History Center, IdahoState Historical Society

http：//history. idaho. gov/oral-history

Impact Stories: An Oral History Project Gathering Stories from the California LGBT Community

http：//www. impactstories. org/aboutus. htm

Institute for Oral History, Baylor University

http：//www. baylor. edu/oralhistory/

Institute for Local and Oral History, Indiana University Southeast

https：//www. ius. edu/local-oral-history/

Institute of Oral History, University of Texas at El Paso

http：//digitalcommons. utep. edu/oral_ history/

Institute of Oral History, Wenzhou University

http：//oralhistory. wzu. edu. cn/

International Database of Oral History Testimonies

http：//www. ushmm. org/online/oral-history/detail. php? SurveyId = 241&letter = B&ord = 9

International Federation for Public History

http：//ifph. hypotheses. org/

International Oral History Association（IOHA）

http：//www. iohanet. org

International Women's Year Oral History Project

http：//www. washingtonhistory. org/research/whc/oralhistory/ IWYOralHistory/

Inventory of the Latvian Oral History Project Interviews

http：//www. oac. cdlib. org/findaid/ark：/13030/kt2t1nf0s7/entire_ text/

Iowa Women Artists Oral History Project

http：//www. lucidplanet. com/iwa/index. php

Iranian Oral History Project, Harvard University

http：//www. fas. harvard. edu/ ~ iohp/

Irish in Queens Oral History Project, Queens College

http：//www. qcirishstudies. org/new-page/

Italian-American Immigrant Oral History, Northern Michigan University

http：//www. nmu. edu/archives/node/103

Japan Oral History Association

http：//joha. jp

Jazz Oral History Project, Institute of Jazz Studies, Rutgers University

http：//newarkwww. rutgers. edu/IJS/OralHistory. html

John Foster Dulles Oral History Collection

http：//findingaids. princeton. edu/collections/MC017

Johns Hopkins University Oral History Collection

https：//jscholarship. library. jhu. edu/handle/1774. 2/37595

Judge David Edward Oral History, University of Denver

http：//www. law. du. edu/index. php/judge-david-edward-oral-history

June Mazer Lesbian Archives Youtube Channel

https：//www. youtube. com/user/mazerarchives/videos

Kennesaw State University Oral History Project

http：//archon. kennesaw. edu/? p = collections/controlcard&id = 202

Kent State Shootings Oral Histories Project, Kent State University

http：//omeka. library. kent. edu/special-collections/kent-state-shoot-
ings-oral-histories

Kentucky Oral History Commission

http：//history. ky. gov/kentucky-oral-history-commission/

Kodiak Oral History Project, Kodiak College

http：//www. koc. alaska. edu/students/library/virtual-collections/kodi-
ak-oral-history-project. cshtml

Koloa: An Oral History of a Kaua'i Community

http：//scholarspace. manoa. hawaii. edu/handle/10125/29783

Lafayette College Oral History Project

http：//sites. lafayette. edu/coeducation/oral-history/

Latah County Oral History Collection, University of Idaho

http：//digital. lib. uidaho. edu/cdm/landingpage/collection/latah

http：//www. lib. uidaho. edu/digital/lcoh/index. html

Latino Americans Memory Circles, New York Public Library

http: //oralhistory. nypl. org/neighborhoods/latino-americans

Legislative Oral History Project, Arizona State Archives

http: //azmemory. azlibrary. gov/cdm/landingpage/collection/legoral

Lesbian Herstory Archives, Herstories Audiovisual Collections

http: //herstories. prattsils. org/omeka/

LGBTQ Oral History Project, Vassar College

http: //lgbtq. vassar. edu/projects-initiatives/vassar-lgbtq-oral-history-project. html

LifeStories and Oral History, Museum of London

http: //www. museumoflondon. org. uk/collections/about-our-collections/what-we-collect/life-stories-and-oral-history-collection

Linda Garber Oral History Collection

http: //www. oac. cdlib. org/findaid/ark: /13030/c81z453d/

Listen and Tell: Oral History Projects, Jewish Women's Archive

http: //jwa. org/teach/profdev/webinars/oralhistory2013

Listening Project, British Library

http: //sounds. bl. uk/Oral-history/The-Listening-Project/

Living the Story: The Civil Rights Movement in Kentucky

http: //www. ket. org/itvvideos/offering/social/civilrights. htm

Louie B. Nunn Center for Oral History, University of Kentucky

http: //libraries. uky. edu/nunncenter

http: //www. kentuckyoralhistory. org/

Louis Armstrong Jazz Oral History Project, New York Public Library

http: //www. nypl. org/voices/audio-video/oral-histories/jazz

Macalester College Oral History Project

http: //digitalcommons. macalester. edu/macoralhist/

Magdalene Oral History Collection, Maynooth University

https：//www. maynoothuniversity. ie/iqda/collections/magdalene-oral-history-collection

Maria Rogers Oral History Program, Boulder, Colorado Public Library

http：//boulderlibrary. org/carnegie/collections/mrohp. html

Martha Ross Center for Oral History, University of Maryland, Baltimore County

http：//www. umbc. edu/mrc/index. html

Master Study Programme in Oral History and Contemporary History, Faculty of Humanities, Charles University

http：//fhs. cuni. cz/FHSENG-427. html

Mayors Oral History Series, Historical Society of Long Beach

http：//hslb. org/video/mayors-oral-history-series/

Memorial do Imigrante, História Oral, Sao Paulo

http：//memorialdoimigrante. org. br

Miami Valley College of Nursing and Health Oral History Project, Wright State University

http：//corescholar. libraries. wright. edu/nursing_ oral_ history/

Michigan Oral History Association

http：//www. michiganoha. org/

Midwest Oral Historians

http：//moh. library. okstate. edu/

Military Oral History Collection, Virginia Military Institute

http：//digitalcollections. vmi. edu/cdm/landingpage/collection/p15821coll13

Milwaukee Transgender Oral History Project

http：//collections. lib. uwm. edu/cdm/search/collection/transhist

Minnesota Dance Pioneer Oral History Project

https：//umedia. lib. umn. edu/taxonomy/term/825

Minnesota Immigrant Oral Histories

http：//collections. mnhs. org/ioh/

Moakley Oral History Project, Suffolk University

http：//www. suffolk. edu/moakley/moakleyoralhistory. html

Mormon Women's Oral History Project, Claremont Graduate University

http：//www. mormonwomenohp. org/

North Poudre Irrigation Company Oral History Collection, Colorado State U-
niversity

https：//dspace. library. colostate. edu/handle/10217/100160

http：//lib. colostate. edu/archives/findingaids/water/wnpi. html

Music at MIT Oral History

http：//libraries. mit. edu/music-oral-history/about-the-project/

Narrating Hurricane Katrina through Oral History, George Mason University

http：//hurricanearchive. org/collections/show/103

National Council on Public History

http：//ncph. org/

National Oral History Association of New Zealand

http：//www. oralhistory. org. nz/

National Science Foundation (NSF) Oral History Project

http：//ethw. org/Oral-History：National _ Science _ Foundation _
(NSF)

New England Association of Oral History

http：//www. oralhistory. uconn. edu/neaoh. html

New Orleans Oral History Initiative

http：//www. hnoc. org/programs/oral_ history. html

New York Chinatown Oral History Project

http：//ceoservices. wix. com/nycchinatownoralhist

New York City Trans Oral History Project

http：//www. nyctransoralhistory. org/

New York City Veterans Oral History Project, New York Public Library

http：//oralhistory. nypl. org/neighborhoods/veterans

New Zealand Oral History Awards, Ministry for Culture and Heritage

http：//www. mch. govt. nz/funding-nz-culture/ministry-grants-awards/
new-zealand-oral-history-awards

Newcomb Oral History Project

http：//newcomb. tulane. edu/blogs/oral-histories/

Northeast Archives of Folklore and Oral History, Maine Folklife Center, U-
niversity of Maine

https：//umaine. edu/folklife/archives/

Northwest Oral History Association

http：//northwestoralhistory. org/

Oberlin Oral History Project, Oberlin Heritage Center

http：//www. oberlinheritagecenter. org/researchlearn/oral_ histories

Office of Oral History, University of South Carolina Libraries

http：//library. sc. edu/socar/oralhist/

Oklahoma Oral History Research Program, Oklahoma State University

http：//www. library. okstate. edu/oralhistory/

Old Lesbian Oral Herstory Project

http：//www. oloc. org/projects/herstory. php

Oral Histories, Ball State University

http：//cms. bsu. edu/academics/centersandinstitutes/middletown/re-
search/deindustrialization/oral

Oral Histories, Center for Sacramento History

http：//www. centerforsacramentohistory. org/collections/oral-histories

Oral Histories, Charles Babbage Institute, University of Minnesota

http：//www. cbi. umn. edu/oh/

Oral Histories, Chicano Studies Research Center, UCLA

http: //www. chicano. ucla. edu/publications/oral-histories

Oral Histories, Dwight D. Eisenhower Presidential Library

http: //www. eisenhower. archives. gov/research/oral_ histories. html

Oral Histories, Georgia State University

http: //library. gsu. edu/search-collections/special-collections-archives/oral-histories/

Oral Histories, Hoover Institution, Stanford University

http: //www. hoover. org/library-archives/collections/oral-histories

Oral Histories, Jimmy Carter Presidential Library

http: //www. jimmycarterlibrary. gov/library/oralhist. phtml

http: //millercenter. org/president/carter/oralhistory

Oral Histories, Kentucky Digital Library

http: //kdl. kyvl. org/? f [format] [ ] = oral + histories

Oral Histories, Life Sciences Foundation

http: //biotechhistory. org/oral-histories/

Oral Histories, Lyndon B. Johnson Presidential Library

http: //www. lbjlibrary. net/collections/oral-histories/

http: //millercenter. org/scripps/archive/oralhistories/lbj

Oral Histories, Maryland Historical Society

http: //www. mdhs. org/library/oral-histories

Oral Histories, National Fire Heritage Center

http: //thenfhc. org/programs/oral-histories/

Oral Histories, National Press Club

https: //www. press. org/archives/oral-histories

Oral Histories, Office of NIH History, National Institutes of Health

https: //history. nih. gov/archives/oral_ histories. html

Oral Histories, Ohio State University Libraries

http：//library. osu. edu/find/collections/the-ohio-state-university-archives/buckeye-history/ohio-state-university-oral-history-program-2/

Oral Histories, Queer in Brighton

http：//www. queerinbrighton. co. uk/category/stories/oral-histories/

Oral Histories, Richard Nixon Presidential Library

http：//www. nixonlibrary. gov/forresearchers/find/histories. php

Oral Histories, Social Security Administration

https：//www. ssa. gov/history/orallist. html

Oral Histories, Southern Foodways Alliance

https：//www. southernfoodways. org/oral-history/

Oral Histories, University of Limerick

https：//ulir. ul. ie/handle/10344/1132

Oral Histories, University of Manchester

http：//www. racearchive. manchester. ac. uk/collections/oral-histories/

Oral Histories, University of Washington Special Collections

http：//content. lib. washington. edu/ohcweb/index. html

Oral Histories, Utah Valley University

https：//www. uvu. edu/library/archives/oral-histories. html

Oral Histories, Women's History Matters

http：//montanawomenshistory. org/oral-history/

Oral Histories: University of Virginia in the 20th Century, University of Virginia

http：//small. library. virginia. edu/collections/featured/oral-histories-u-va-in-the-20th-century/

Oral Histories about Super Storm Sandy, Monmouth University Library

http：//library. monmouth. edu/main/content/oral-histories-about-super-storm-sandy

Oral Histories and Interviews, Center for Legislative Archives,

U. S. National Archives and Records Administration

https：//www. archives. gov/legislative/research/special-collections/oral-history/

Oral Histories and Recollections, Austin History Center

http：//library. austintexas. gov/ahc/oral-historyaudio

Oral Histories Collection, Getty Research Institute

http：//www. getty. edu/research/special_ collections/oral_ histories/

Oral Histories Collection, Hogan Jazz Archive, Tulane University

https：//jazz. tulane. edu/collections/oral-history

Oral Histories Collection, LGBT Religious Archives Network

http：//www. lgbtran. org/OralHistory. aspx

Oral Histories Collection, University of California, Santa Barbara

http：//www. library. ucsb. edu/special-collections/oral-history

Oral Histories in Special Collections, J. Willard Marriott Library, University of Utah

http：//www. lib. utah. edu/collections/multimedia-archives/oralhistory. php

Oral Histories in the Gerald R. Ford Presidential Library

http：//www. fordlibrarymuseum. gov/library/oralhist. asp

Oral Histories in the Perry Library, Old Dominion University

http：//dc. lib. odu. edu/cdm/landingpage/collection/oralhistory

Oral Histories of the American South, University of North Carolina at Chapel Hill

http：//docsouth. unc. edu/sohp

Oral History, Auckland Libraries

http：//www. aucklandlibraries. govt. nz/EN/heritage/collections/oralhistorycollections/Pages/oralhistorycollections. aspx

Oral History, Billy Graham Center Archives

http：//www2. wheaton. edu/bgc/archives/oralhist. html

Oral History, British Library

http：//www. bl. uk/collection-guides/oral-history

Oral History, Brooklyn Historical Society

http：//www. brooklynhistory. org/blog/category/oralhistory/

Oral History, Centre for Archive and Information Studies, University of Dundee

http：//www. dundee. ac. uk/cais/programmes/modules/oralhistory/

Oral History, Engineering and Technology History Wiki

http：//ethw. org/Oral-History：List_ of_ all_ Oral_ Histories

Oral History, Faculty of Arts, University of Tasmania, Australia

http：//www. utas. edu. au/arts/oral-history

Oral History, Heritage Lottery Fund

https：//www. hlf. org. uk/oral-history

Oral History, Historical Archives of the European Union

http：//archives. eui. eu/en/oral_ history

Oral History, Making History, Institute of Historical Research

http：//www. history. ac. uk/makinghistory/themes/oral_ history. html

Oral History, Multicultural Canada

http：//multiculturalcanada. ca/LearningModules/OralHistory

Oral History, National Park Service

http：//www. nps. gov/parkhistory/oralhistory. htm

Oral History, Special Collections at Belk Library, Appalachian State University

http：//collections. library. appstate. edu/subjects/oral-history

Oral History, University of California, Riverside

http：//www. ucrhistory. ucr. edu/

Oral History, Washington State Legislature

http：//app. leg. wa. gov/oralhistory/

Oral History, Weeksville Heritage Center

http：//www. weeksvillesociety. org/oral-history/

Oral History, Writing Center, University of North Carolina at Chapel Hill

http：//writingcenter. unc. edu/handouts/oral-history/

Oral History, The A. V. Club

http：//www. avclub. com/features/oral-history/

Oral History (Certificate), New College of Interdisciplinary Arts and Sciences, Arizona State University

https：//newcollege. asu. edu/oral-history-certificate

Oral History: Techniques and Procedures, Center of Military History, U-
nited States Army

http：//www. au. af. mil/au/awc/awcgate/oralhist. htm

Oral History & Recorded Sound Collection, Australian War Memorial

https：//www. awm. gov. au/collection/sound/

Oral History/Audio, Austin History Center

http：//library. austintexas. gov/ahc/oral-historyaudio

Oral History and Community Memory Archive, California State University,
Monterey Bay

https：//csumb. edu/hcom/oral-history-community-memory

Oral History and Folklife Research, Inc.

http：//www. oralhistoryandfolklife. org/

Oral History and Folklore Collection, National Library of Australia

http：//www. nla. gov. au/what-we-collect/oral-history-and-folklore

Oral History Archive, University of Aberdeen

http：//www. abdn. ac. uk/historic/Oral_ history_ about_ archive

Oral History Archive, University of Hertfordshire

http：//www. herts. ac. uk/heritage-hub/oralhistoryarchive

Oral History Archive, Virginia Commonwealth University

http: //dig. library. vcu. edu/cdm/landingpage/collection/ohi

Oral History Archives, National September 11 Memorial Museum

http: //www. 911memorial. org/oral-history-archives-2

Oral History Association

http: //www. oralhistory. org/

Oral History Association of Australia (Western Australia Branch Inc.)

http: //www. ohaa-wa. com. au/

Oral History Association of South Africa

http: //www. ohasa. org. za/

Oral History at UCPL, University City Public Library

http: //ucitylibrary. org/Oral_ History

Oral History Australia

http: //www. oralhistoryaustralia. org. au/

Oral History Australia South Australia/Northern Territory

http: //oralhistoryaustraliasant. org. au/

Oral History Catalog, NASA's History Office

http: //history. nasa. gov/oralhistory/ohcatalog. htm

Oral History Catalogue, Air Force Historical Research Agency

http: //www. afhra. af. mil/documents/oralhistorycatalogue. asp

Oral History Catalogue, Claremont Graduate University

http: //web. cgu. edu/oralhistory/

Oral History Center, University of California, Berkeley

http: //www. lib. berkeley. edu/libraries/bancroft-library/oral-
history-center

Oral History Center, University of Louisville

http: //louisville. edu/library/archives/university/ohc

Oral History Centre, University of Winnepeg

http：//www. oralhistorycentre. ca

Oral History Centre, National Archives of Singapore

http：//www. nas. gov. sg/archivesonline/oral_ history_ interviews/

Oral History Collection, Cold Spring Harbor Laboratory Archives

http：//library. cshl. edu/oralhistory/

Oral History Collection, College of William & Mary

https：//digitalarchive. wm. edu/handle/10288/583

Oral History Collection, Computer History Museum

http：//www. computerhistory. org/collections/oralhistories/

Oral History Collection, Eastern Kentucky University

http：//www. library-old. eku. edu/new/content/archives/oralhist1. php

Oral History Collection, Fort Hays State University

http：//contentcat. fhsu. edu/cdm/landingpage/collection/p15732coll23

Oral History Collection, Gettysburg College

https：//www. gettysburg. edu/special _ collections/collections/oral _
history/

Oral History Collection, Hampshire College

https：//asteria. fivecolleges. edu/findaids/hampshire/mah025. html

Oral History Collection, Hope College

http：//digitalcommons. hope. edu/oral_ histories/

Oral History Collection, Houston Metropolitan Research Center, Houston
Public Library

http：//digital. houstonlibrary. org/cdm/search/collection/Interviews

Oral History Collection, Idaho State Historical Society

http：//idahohistory. cdmhost. com/cdm/landingpage/collection/
p15073coll1

Oral History Collection, Jacksonville State University

http：//www. jsu. edu/library/collections/oral_ history. html

Oral History Collection, Lakehead University

https：//www. lakeheadu. ca/academics/departments/indigenous-learning/resources/oral-history-collection

Oral History Collection, Millersville University

http：//digital. klnpa. org/cdm/landingpage/collection/mvsohist

Oral History Collection, Minnesota Historical Society

http：//sites. mnhs. org/library/content/oral-history

Oral History Collection, Oklahoma Historical Society

http：//www. okhistory. org/research/oralhist

Oral History Collection, Sophia Smith Collection

http：//www. smith. edu/libraries/libs/ssc/ohlist. html

Oral History Collection, University of Alabama at Birmingham

http：//contentdm. mhsl. uab. edu/cdm/search/collection/oralhistory

Oral History Collection, University of Illinois at Springfield

http：//library. uis. edu/archives/collections/oral/contents. html

http：//www. idaillinois. org/cdm/search/collection/uis

Oral History Collection, University of Maryland

http：//digital. lib. umd. edu/archivesum/rguide/oral. jsp

Oral History Collection, University of Maryland, Baltimore County

http：//library. umbc. edu/speccoll/findingaids/coll055. php

Oral History Collection, University of Texas at San Antonio

http：//digital. utsa. edu/cdm/landingpage/collection/p15125coll4

Oral History Collection, University of the Pacific Emeriti Society

http：//www. pacific. edu/Library/Find/Holt-Atherton-Special-Collec-tions/Digital-Collections/University-of-the-Pacific-Emeriti-Society-Oral-History-Collection. html

Oral History Collection, Walter P. Reuther Library, Wayne State University

http：//reuther. wayne. edu/memory

Oral History Collection, Westport Historical Society

http: //westporthistory. org/oh/

Oral History Collection, Wharton County Junior College

https: //www. wcjc. edu/Students/Library/Find-Books-DVDs/oral-histo-ry. aspx

Oral History Collection, Wisconsin Veterans Museum

http: //www. wisvetsmuseum. com/collections/oral_ history/

Oral History Collection, Youngstown State University

http: //www. maag. ysu. edu/oralhistory/oral_ hist. html

Oral History Collections, Brooklyn Historical Society

http: //brooklynhistory. org/library/wp/library-collections/oralhistory/

Oral History Collections, Center of Southwest Studies, Fort Lewis College

https: //swcenter. fortlewis. edu/finding_aids/inventory/OralHisto-ries. htm

Oral History Collections, Delta State University

http: //www. deltastate. edu/academics/libraries/university-archives-museum/guides-to-the-collections/oral-histories/

Oral History Collections, Howard University

http: //coas. howard. edu/msrc/manuscripts_ oralhistory. html

Oral History Collections, Loyola University Chicago

http: //www. luc. edu/archives/ohistories. shtml

Oral History Collections, Morehead State University

http: //research. moreheadstate. edu/special_ collections/oralhistories

Oral History Collections, Nashville Public Library

http: //www. library. nashville. org/localhistory/his_ spcoll_ coll_ orh-ist. asp

Oral History Collections, New York University

http: //www. nyu. edu/library/bobst/research/tam/oh_ collection. html

Oral History Collections, Pennsylvania State University

https: //libraries. psu. edu/about/collections/penn-state-university-park-campus-history-collection/penn-state-oral-history

Oral History Collections, Portland State University Library

https: //library. pdx. edu/research/special-collections-university-archives/oral-history-collections/

Oral History Collections, U. S. National Library of Medicine

https: //www. nlm. nih. gov/hmd/manuscripts/oh. html

Oral History Collections, University of North Carolina at Greensboro

http: //libcdm1. uncg. edu/cdm/oralhistory/

Oral History Collections, University of West Florida

http: //archives. uwf. edu/Archon/? p = collections/controlcard&id = 22

Oral History Collections, Weber State University

https: //library. weber. edu/collections/oral_ history

Oral History Collection Files, Howard University Libraries

http: //library. howard. edu/oral-history

Oral History Criminology Project, American Society of Criminology

https: //www. asc41. com/videos/Oral_ History. html

Oral History Division, Hebrew University of Jerusalem

http: //www. hum. huji. ac. il/english/units. php? cat = 4246

Oral History Division, Margaret Walker Center, Jackson State University

http: //www. jsums. edu/margaretwalkercenter/collections/oral-histories/

Oral History Guidelines, National WWII Museum

http: //www. nationalww2museum. org/learn/education/for-students/oral-history-guidelines. html

Oral History How-To Guide and Digital Best Practices

http: //www. fcla. edu/FloridaVoices/guidelines. shtml

Oral History Hub，LGBTQ History Digital Collaboratory

http：//lgbtqdigitalcollaboratory. org/oral-history-hub/

Oral History in Palliative Care，University of Sheffield

https：//www. sheffield. ac. uk/snm/research/oralhistory/main

Oral History in the Classroom

http：//www. learnnc. org/lp/editions/oralhistory2002/cover

Oral History in the Digital Age

http：//ohda. matrix. msu. edu/

Oral History in the Mid-Atlantic Region

https：//ohmar. org/

Oral History Interview Collection，Forest History Society

http：//www. foresthistory. org/Research/ohiguide. html

Oral History Interview Series，Alternative Farming Systems Information Center，United States Department of Agriculture

https：//www. nal. usda. gov/afsic/oral-history-interview-series

Oral History Interviews，American Institute of Physics

https：//www. aip. org/history-programs/niels-bohr-library/oral-histories

Oral History Interviews，Archives of American Art

http：//www. aaa. si. edu/collections/interviews

Oral History Interviews，Harry S. Truman Presidential Library

http：//www. trumanlibrary. org/oralhist/oral_ his. htm

Oral History Interviews，Institute for Latino Studies，University of Notre Dame

http：//latinostudies. nd. edu/library-archives/oral-history-interviews/

Oral History Interviews，National Associationof Music Merchants（NAMM）

https：//www. namm. org/library/oral-history/all

Oral History Interviews，New Mexico State University

http：//lib. nmsu. edu/depts/archives/oral_ history_ list. shtml

Oral History Interviews, The History Center

http：//historycenter. org/library/oral-history-interviews/

Oral History Journal of South Africa

https：//www. upjournals. co. za/index. php/OHJSA/index

Oral History Library, the Statue of Liberty & Ellis Island

http：//www. libertyellisfoundation. org/oral-history-library

Oral History Master of Arts Program, Interdisciplinary Center for Innovative
Theory and Empirics, Columbia University

http：//oralhistory. columbia. edu/

Oral History Metadata Synchronizer

http：//www. oralhistoryonline. org/

Oral History Network of Ireland

http：//www. oralhistorynetworkireland. ie/

Oral History NSW

http：//www. oralhistorynsw. org. au/

Oral History Queensland

http：//www. ohq. org. au/

Oral History Tasmania

http：//www. oralhistorytas. org. au/

Oral History of American Music, Yale University

http：//web. library. yale. edu/oham/about

Oral History of British Science, British Library

http：//www. bl. uk/historyofscience

Oral History of Houston, University of Houston

http：//www. uh. edu/class/ctr-public-history/research-projects/oral-
history/

Oral History of Irish America Project, New York University

http：//irelandhouse. fas. nyu. edu/page/oralhistoryproject

Oral History of Neuropsychopharmacology, American College of Neuropsychopharmacology

http：//www. acnp. org/programs/history. aspx

Oral History of Texas Architecture Project, University of Texas at Arlington

http：//www. uta. edu/cappa/research/dillon/oralhist. php

Oral History of the U. S. House of Representatives

http：//history. house. gov/Oral-History/

Oral History Office, University of Connecticut at Storrs

http：//www. oralhistory. uconn. edu/

Oral History Online, Alexander Street

http：//alexanderstreet. com/products/oral-history-online

Oral History Podcasts, Wexford County Council

http：//www. wexford. ie/wex/Departments/Library/OralHistoryPod-casts/

Oral History Portal, Columbia University Libraries

http：//library. columbia. edu/find/oral-history-portal. html

Oral History Portal, University of Illinois at Urbana-Champaign

http：//archives. library. illinois. edu/slc/oral-history-portal/

Oral History Primer, UC Santa Cruz

http：//library. ucsc. edu/reg-hist/oral-history-primer

Oral History Productions

http：//www. oralhistory-productions. org/

Oral History Program, Abraham Lincoln Presidential Library

https：//www. illinois. gov/alplm/library/collections/oralhistory

Oral History Program, Academy of Motion Picture Arts and Sciences

http：//www. oscars. org/oral-history

Oral History Program, Ah-Tah-Thi-Ki Seminole Indian Museum

http：//www. ahtahthiki. com/oral-history/

Oral History Program, American Bar Foundation

http: //www. americanbarfoundation. org/research/oralHistoryPro-gram. html

Oral History Program, Battleship New Jersey Museum and Memorial

http: //www. battleshipnewjersey. org/the-ship/oral-history/

Oral History Program, Charles Redd Center, Brigham Young University

https: //reddcenter. byu. edu/Pages/Oral. aspx

Oral History Program, California Secretary of State

http: //www. sos. ca. gov/archives/admin-programs/oral-history/

Oral History Program, California State University, Long Beach

http: //www. cla. csulb. edu/departments/history/oral-history-program/

Oral History Program, Claremont Graduate University

http: //www. cgu. edu/pages/663. asp

Oral History Program, Colorado State University-Pueblo

http: //library. csupueblo. edu/archives/oral. html

Oral History Program, Dixie State University Library

https: //library. dixie. edu/special_ collections/oral_ histories. html

Oral History Program, George Mason University

http: //sca. gmu. edu/oral. php

Oral History Program, Institute of Southern Jewish Life

http: //www. isjl. org/oral-history. html

Oral History Program, Jewish Buffalo Archives Project, State University of New York at Buffalo (University at Buffalo)

http: //library. buffalo. edu/archives/jbap/oral-histories/

Oral History Program, John F. Kennedy Presidential Library and Museum

https: //www. jfklibrary. org/Research/About-Our-Collections/Oral-his-tory-program. aspx

Oral History Program, Museum of Modern Art Archives

http：//www. moma. org/learn/resources/archives/oralhistory#aohi

Oral History Program, National Film and Sound Archive of Australia

http：//www. nfsa. gov. au/collection/oral-history/

Oral History Program, New Mexico Farm & Ranch Heritage Museum

http：//oralhistory. frhm. org/

Oral History Program, Oregon Health & Science University

http：//www. ohsu. edu/xd/education/library/about/collections/histori-cal-collections-archives/oral-history-program/index. cfm

Oral History Program, Roads and Maritime Services

http：//www. rms. nsw. gov. au/about/environment/protecting-heritage/oral-history-program

Oral History Program, Roman Catholic Archdiocese of Atlanta

http：//archatl. com/offices/archives/oral-history-program/

Oral History Program, Smithsonian Institution Archives

http：//siarchives. si. edu/research/oralvidhistory_ intro. html

Oral History Program, Stanford Historical Society

http：//historicalsociety. stanford. edu/ohistory. shtml

Oral History Program, State Historical Society of Missouri

http：//shs. umsystem. edu/oralhistory/index. html

Oral History Program, University of Alaska Fairbanks

http：//library. uaf. edu/oral-history

Oral History Program, University of Georgia Libraries

http：//www. libs. uga. edu/russell/collections/oralhistory. html

Oral History Program, University of Miami

https：//library. miami. edu/specialcollections/ohp/

Oral History Program, University of Nevada, Reno

http：//oralhistory. unr. edu/

Oral History Program, University of New South Wales, Sydney

https：//www. recordkeeping. unsw. edu. au/Collections/oral ＿ history. html

Oral History Program, University of North Texas

http：//oralhistory. unt. edu/

Oral History Program, University of South Florida

http：//guides. lib. usf. edu/ohp

Oral History Program, University of Wisconsin-La Crosse

https：//www. uwlax. edu/history/department-resources/oral-history-
program/

Oral History Program, University of Wisconsin-Madison

https：//www. library. wisc. edu/archives/archives/oral-history-pro-
gram/

Oral History Program, U. S. Food and Drug Administration

http：//www. fda. gov/AboutFDA/WhatWeDo/History/OralHistories/de-
fault. htm

Oral History Program, U. S. Naval Institute

http：//www. usni. org/heritage/oral-history

Oral History Program, Weber State College

http：//mwdl. org/collections/1861. php

Oral History Program, Wing Luke Museum, Asian Pacific American Experience

http：//www. wingluke. org/oral-history-program-1

Oral History Program, Winthrop University

http：//digitalcommons. winthrop. edu/oralhistoryprogram＿ overview/

Oral History Program, World Bank Group Archives

http：//oralhistory. worldbank. org/

Oral History Program Collection, Purdue University

http：//earchives. lib. purdue. edu/cdm/search/collection/oralhist

Oral History Project, American Institute for Conservation of Historic and Artistic Works

http://www. conservation-us. org/foundation/initiatives/oral-history-project#. VhnEJW71SII

Oral History Project, Arkansas State University

https://www. astate. edu/a/deltastudies/oral-history/

Oral History Project, Association for the Rhetoric of Science & Technology

http://www. arstonline. org/oral-history-project. html

Oral History Project, Audio Engineering Society Historical Committee

http://www. aes. org/aeshc/docs/oralhist/oral-history-project. html

Oral History Project, Augusta University

http://www. augusta. edu/education/tal/ohp/

Oral History Project, Bard College

http://www. bard. edu/archives/voices/oralhistoryproject/oralhist. php

Oral History Project, Center for the Study of War and Society, University of Tennessee, Knoxville

https://csws. utk. edu/oral-history-project/

Oral History Project, Citizens Archive of Pakistan

http://www. citizensarchive. org/projects/the-oral-history-project/

Oral History Project, College of Human Ecology, Cornell University

https://ecommons. cornell. edu/handle/1813/36303

Oral History Project, Country Music Hall of Fame and Museum

http://countrymusichalloffame. org/ContentPages/oral-history-and-collection

Oral History Project, Crestwood College

http://www. crestwood. on. ca/ohp/

Oral History Project, Finlandia University

http://www. finlandia. edu/oral-history-project. html

Oral History Project, Friends Seminary

http：//www. friendsseminary. org/page/alumni/connect/oral-history-project

Oral History Project, Greenwich Library

http：//www. glohistory. org/

Oral History Project, Indiana University South Bend

https：//www. iusb. edu/civil-rights/oral-history-project-and-archive/index. php

Oral History Project, Intrepid Sea, Air and Space Museum

http：//www. intrepidmuseum. org/OralHistoryProject

Oral History Project, Johnson Space Center, NASA

http：//www. jsc. nasa. gov/history/oral_ histories/oral_ histories. htm

Oral History Project, National Council of Jewish Women, University of Pittsburgh

http：//digital. library. pitt. edu/n/ncjw/

Oral History Project, New College of Florida

http：//www. sarasota. wateratlas. usf. edu/oral-history-project/

Oral History Project, Red Mountain Park

http：//redmountainpark. org/history/oral-history-project/

Oral History Project, San Francisco Conservatory of Music

http：//www. sfcm. edu/oralhistories

Oral History Project, School of Medicine, Washington University

http：//beckerexhibits. wustl. edu/oral/

Oral History Project, Society for Applied Anthropology

https：//www. sfaa. net/publications/oral-history-project/

Oral History Project, Society for Research in Child Development

http：//www. srcd. org/about-us/oral-history-project

Oral History Project, Southwest Texas State University

https：//www. eeoc. gov/eeoc/history/35th/voices/swt. html

Oral History Project, SUNY Buffalo Law School, University at Buffalo

https：//www. buffalo. edu/law125th/history/oral-history. html

Oral History Project, Texas Woman's University

http：//www. twu. edu/library/wc-oral-history-project-page. asp

Oral History Project, U. S. Senate Historical Office

http：//www. senate. gov/history/oralhistory. htm

Oral History Project, University of North Florida

https：//www. unf. edu/info/timeline/oralhistory/

Oral History Project, University of Puget Sound

http：//www. pugetsound. edu/about/offices-services/oral-history-pro-ject

Oral History Project, University of the Pacific

http：//www. pacific. edu/About-Pacific/AdministrationOffices/Office-of-the-Provost/About-the-Office-of-the-Provost/Emeriti-Society/Oral-History-Pro-ject. html

Oral History Project, University of West Georgia

https：//www. westga. edu/cph/index_ 6726. php

Oral History Project, University of Westminster Archive

https：//www. westminster. ac. uk/about-us/our-university/our-heritage/oral-history

Oral History Project, Vietnam Center and Archive, Texas Tech University

http：//www. vietnam. ttu. edu/oralhistory/

Oral History Project, Washington University School of Medicine

http：//beckerexhibits. wustl. edu/oral/

Oral History Project, Worcester Women's History Project

http：//www. wwhp. org/activities-exhibits/oral-history-project

Oral History Project, World Health Organization

http：//www. who. int/formerstaff/history/oralhistory/

Oral History Project：Trace the Memory of London Chinatown, Chinese Mental Health Association

http：//www. cmha. org. uk/projects/oral-history-project

Oral History Project in Labor History, Roosevelt University

http：//www. roosevelt. edu/Library/Locations/UniversityArchives/Oral-History. aspx

Oral History Projects, American West Center, University of Utah,

http：//awc. utah. edu/oral-histories/index. php

Oral History Projects, Center for Technology in Teaching & Learning, Rice University

http：//cttl. rice. edu/OralHistoryProjects/

Oral History Projects, Gerald R. Ford Presidential Library

http：//www. fordlibrarymuseum. gov/library/guides/findingaid/grfli-boh. asp

Oral History Projects, Millersville University

http：//blogs. millersville. edu/archivesandspecialcollections/oral-history/

Oral History Projects, Minnesota State University, Mankato

http：//lib. mnsu. edu/archives/oralh/intro. html

Oral History Projects, University of New Mexico

http：//libguides. unm. edu/route66/oralhistory

Oral History Projects, Washington State Historical Society

http：//www. washingtonhistory. org/research/whc/oralhistory/

Oral History Recordings Collection, University of Wollongong

http：//www. library. uow. edu. au/archives/collections/UOW095471. html

Oral History Research Center, University of Nevada, Las Vegas https：//www. library. unlv. edu/oral_ histories

Oral History Research Cluster, University of Bristol

http：//research-information. bristol. ac. uk/en/organisations/oral-histo-ry-research-cluster（d790ec40-16f3-40f4-8506-86870a0c900c）. html

Oral History Research Program, Chicago State College

http：//library. csu. edu/asc/findingaids/CSCOralHistoryResearchPro-grampapers. xml

Oral History Resources, Pennsylvania Historical & Museum Commission

http：//www. phmc. state. pa. us/portal/communities/oral-history/

Oral History Review

http：//ohr. oxfordjournals. org/

Oral History Section, Society of American Archivists

http：//www2. archivists. org/groups/oral-history-section

Oral History Series, Earthquake Engineering Research Institute

https：//www. eeri. org/products-publications/free-publications-and-re-ports/oral-history-series/

Oral History Series, Gerlind Institute for Cultural Studies

http：//www. gerlindinstitute. org/oralhistory. html

Oral History Series, University of Cincinnati

https：//www. libraries. uc. edu/winkler-center/resources/collections/o-ral-history. html

Oral History Society

http：//www. ohs. org. uk/

Oral History Summer School

http：//www. oralhistorysummerschool. com/

Oral History Team, York St John University

https：//yorkstjohnvoices. wordpress. com/

Oral History Techniques, Center for the Study of History and Memory, Indiana University

http：//www. indiana. edu/ ~ cshm/techniques. html

Oral History Transcript Editing Guidelines

http：//millercenter. org/oralhistory/styleguide

Oral History Transcripts, Central Arizona Project

http：//www. cap-az. com/about-us/oral-history-transcripts

Oral History Transcripts, Herbert Hoover Presidential Library

http：//www. ecommcode2. com/hoover/research/historicalmaterials/o-
ral. html

http：//millercenter. org/scripps/archive/oralhistories/hoover

Oral History Victoria

http：//www. oralhistoryvictoria. org. au/

Oral History Videos, Ohio Memory

http：//www. ohiomemory. org/cdm/landingpage/collection/
p15005coll37

Our Marathon: WBUR Oral History Project

http：//marathon. neu. edu/wburoralhistoryproject

Oxford Oral History Series

https：//global. oup. com/academic/content/series/o/oxford-oral-his-
tory-series-oralhis/? cc = us&lang = en&

Ozarks Oral History Project, Missouri State University-West Plains

http：//libraries. missouristate. edu/Ozarks-Oral-History-Project-MSU-
West-Plains. htm

Palestinian Oral History Archive, American University of Beirut

http：//aub. edu. lb/ifi/programs/poha/Pages/index. aspx

Palgrave Studies in Oral History, Palgrave Macmillan

http：//www. palgrave. com/series/Palgrave-Studies-in-Oral-History/
PSOH/

Panola Oral Histories Collection, Panola College

http: //cdm16076. contentdm. oclc. org/cdm/landingpage/collection/ p15279coll1

Pennsylvania Newspaper Journalists Oral History Program, Pennsylvania State University

http: //comm. psu. edu/research/centers/newspaper-journalists-oral-history-program

People & Stories: Oral History Project, White Plains Public Library

http: //whiteplainslibrary. org/local-history/people-stories/

Pioneers of American Landscape Design Oral History Project, Cultural Landscape Foundation

http: //tclf. org/pioneer/oral-history-project

Pioneers Oral History Project, Texas Woman's University

http: //www. twu. edu/oral-history/

Presidential Oral History Program, Miller Center of Public Affairs, University of Virginia

http: //millercenter. org/oralhistory

Programa de Historia Oral dela Universidad de Buenos Aires

http: //iigg. sociales. uba. ar/archivo-de-historia-oral

Project Jukebox, Digital Branch of the University of Alaska Fairbanks Oral History Program

http: //jukebox. uaf. edu/site7/

Public History Review, University of Technology, Sydney, Australia

http: //epress. lib. uts. edu. au/journals/index. php/phrj

Queer Oral History Project

http: //qohp. org/

Queer Oral History Project, Gender and Sexuality Center, University of Illinois at Chicago

https：//genderandsexuality. uic. edu/programs _ events/queer-oral-his-
tory-project/

Queer Newark Oral History Project

http：//queer. newark. rutgers. edu/

Race and Change Initiative, Florida Atlantic University,

http：//proteus. fau. edu/raceandchange/

Records of the Oakland University Chronicles Oral History Project

https：//library. oakland. edu/archives/finding-aids/collection. php?
collection = OU. HISTORY. CHR

Regional History Project, UC Santa Cruz

http：//library. ucsc. edu/regional-history-project

Regional Oral History Office (ROHO), University of California, Berkeley

http：//bancroft. berkeley. edu/ROHO

Reichelt Oral History Program, Florida State University

http：//ohp. fsu. edu/

Remembering Riverdale：Our Neighborhood Oral History Project, New
York Public Library

http：//oralhistory. nypl. org/neighborhoods/riverdale

Remembering the 20th Century：An Oral History of Monmouth County,
Monmouth County Library

http：//www. visitmonmouth. com/oralhistory/

Renee Garrelick Oral History Program Collection

http：//www. concordlibrary. org/scollect/fin_ aids/OralHistories. htm

Resource Guide to Oral History Interviews, University of Iowa Libraries

http：//www. lib. uiowa. edu/sc/archives/faq/faqoralhistory/

Resources for Digital Storytelling

http：//stories. umbc. edu/resources. php

Robert Rauschenberg Oral History Project, Robert Rauschenberg Foundation http：//www. rauschenbergfoundation. org/artist/oral-history

Rollins College Oral History

http：//lib. rollins. edu/olin/Archives/oral _ history/Updated% 20Pages/ Project_ Information. htm

Ronald Reagan Oral Histories

http：//millercenter. org/president/reagan/oralhistory

Roosevelt Junior College Oral History Project, Palm Beach State College

http：//www. palmbeachstate. edu/history/roosevelt-junior-college/rjc- project. aspx

Roy Rosenzweig Center for History and New Media, George Mason Univer- sity

http：//rrchnm. org/

Rutgers Oral History Archives, Rutgers University

http：//oralhistory. rutgers. edu/

Samuel Proctor Oral History Program, University of Florida

http：//oral. history. ufl. edu/

http：//ufdc. ufl. edu/oral

Science Fiction Oral History Association

http：//www. sfoha. org/

Scottish Oral History Centre, University of Strathclyde

http：//www. strath. ac. uk/humanities/research/history/sohc/

Sesquicentennial Oral History Collection, Oregon State University

http：//scarc. library. oregonstate. edu/oh150/index. html

Shenandoah Valley Oral History Project, James Madison University

https：//www. jmu. edu/history/shenandoah-valley-oral-history-pro- ject. shtml

Sinomlando Centre for Oral History and Memory Work in Africa, University of Kwa-Zulu Natal http：//sinomlando. ukzn. ac. za/

Sisterhood and After: The Women's Liberation Oral History Project, University of Sussex

http：//www. sussex. ac. uk/clhlwr/research/sisterhoodafter

Smithsonian Jazz Oral History Program

http：//americanhistory. si. edu/smithsonian-jazz/collections-and-ar-chives/smithsonian-jazz-oral-history-program

SoHo Stories: A Neighborhood Oral History Project, New York Public Library

http：//oralhistory. nypl. org/neighborhoods/soho

Somerset Voices Oral History Archive

http：//www. somersetvoices. org. uk/

Sounds and Stories: The Musical Life of Maryland's African-American Communities, John Hopkins University

http：//musiclibrary. peabody. jhu. edu/content. php？ pid ＝ 599119&sid ＝4940848

South Asian Oral History Project, University of Washington

http：//content. lib. washington. edu/saohcweb

South Dakota Oral History Center, University of South Dakota

http：//www. usd. edu/library/sdohc

Southern Oral History Program, University of North Carolina at Chapel Hill

http：//sohp. org/

http：//dc. lib. unc. edu/cdm/landingpage/collection/sohp

Southwest Oral History Association

http：//www. southwestoralhistory. org

Stapleton Speaks: Our Neighborhood Oral History Project, New York Public Library

http：//oralhistory. nypl. org/neighborhoods/stapleton

Step-by-Step Guide to Oral History, DoHistory

http: //dohistory. org/on_ your_ own/toolkit/oralHistory. html

Stories from the Line: Free Shakespeare in the Park, New York Public Library

http: //oralhistory. nypl. org/neighborhoods/shakespeare-in-the-park

StoryCorps

https: //storycorps. org/

Student Veteran Oral History Project, Monmouth University

http: //library. monmouth. edu/main/content/student-veteran-oral-history-project

Studs Terkel: Conversations with America

http: //conversations. studsterkel. org/index. php

Studs Terkel Radio Archive

http: //studsterkel. org/.

Suburban Oral History Project, Hofstra University

http: //www. hofstra. edu/academics/css/ncss_ suburban_ oralhistory. html

Suez Oral History Project, King's College London

http: //www. kingscollections. org/catalogues/lhcma/collection/s/xs80-001/

Suffolk University Oral History Project

http: //www. suffolk. edu/explore/26499. php

Sydney Oral Histories, City of Sydney

http: //www. sydneyoralhistories. com. au/

Syrian Oral History Project, International Coalition of Sites of Conscience

http: //www. sitesofconscience. org/2015/06/syrian-oral-history-project/

T. Harry Williams Center for Oral History, Louisiana State University

http: //www. lib. lsu. edu/services/oralhistory/

http：//cdm16313. contentdm. oclc. org/cdm/landingpage/collection/ p120701coll23/

Tell me Your Stories：An Oral History Curriculum

http：//www. tellmeyourstories. org/

Telling Their Stories, Urban School of San Francisco

http：//www. tellingstories. org/

Texas Oral History Association

http：//www. baylor. edu/toha

The HistoryMakers

http：//www. idvl. org/

http：//www. idvl. org/thehistorymakers/

The Hoover Company British War Children Oral History Collection

http：//cdm16722. contentdm. oclc. org/cdm/landingpage/collection/ p16722coll20

The Hoover Company Oral History Project

http：//cdm16722. contentdm. oclc. org/cdm/landingpage/collection/ p16722coll1

The Hopkins Oral History initiative, Johns Hopkins University

http：//retrospective. jhu. edu/our-initiatives/oral-histories

The Iraq and Afghanistan Veterans Oral History Project, University of Utah

http：//patrickthompson. me/awc/

The Katrina Experience

http：//thekatrinaexperience. net

The Keele Oral History Project, Keele University

http：//www. keele. ac. uk/thekeeleoralhistoryproject/

The Oral History Company

http：//theoralhistorycompany. com/

The Oral History of Homelessness

http：//ststephensmpls. org/oralhistory/

The Oral History Podcast

http：//theoralhistorypodcast. com/

The Race and Change Initiative, Florida Atlantic University

http：//proteus. fau. edu/raceandchange/

The Religious People of New York: A Digital Oral History Archive

https：//macaulay. cuny. edu/eportfolios/borja15/

The Schizophrenia Oral History Project

http：//www. schizophreniaoralhistories. com/

The Smithsonian Folklife and Oral History Interviewing Guide

http：//www. folklife. si. edu/education_exhibits/resources/guide/introduction. aspx

The Telling Lives Oral History Curriculum Guide

http：//incite. columbia. edu/storage/Telling_ Lives_ Curriculum_ Guide. pdf

The Whole World Was Watching: An Oral History of 1968

http：//cds. library. brown. edu/projects/1968/

Times Square Oral History Project, New York Public Library

http：//oralhistory. nypl. org/neighborhoods/times-square

Trade Union Women Oral History Project, Institute of Labor and Industrial Relations, University of Michigan and Wayne State University

http：//quod. lib. umich. edu/b/bhlead/umich-bhl-85223? rgn = main; view = text

Transgender Oral History Project

http：//transoralhistory. com/

Transgender Oral History Project, University of Minnesota Libraries

https：//www. lib. umn. edu/tretter/transgender-oral-history-project

Tsunamis Remembered: Oral Histories of Survivors and Observers in Hawai'i

http：//scholarspace. manoa. hawaii. edu/handle/10125/29800

Twin Cities Gay and Lesbian Community Oral History Project, Minnesota Historical Society

http：//collections. mnhs. org/voicesofmn/index. php/10002723

U. S. Army Guide to Oral History

http：//www. history. army. mil/books/oral. html

Under the Rainbow: Oral Histories of Gay, Lesbian, Transgender, Intersex and Queer People in Kansas

https：//kuscholarworks. ku. edu/handle/1808/5330

Union County Oral Histories, Eastern Oregon University

http：//library. eou. edu/ohgr/

United Nations Oral History Collection of the United Nations Dag Hammarskjöld Library

http：//www. unmultimedia. org/oralhistory/

United States Holocaust Memorial Museum

http：//www. ushmm. org/research/research-in-collections/overview/oral-history

United University Professions Oral History Project, University at Albany (State University of New York at Albany)

http：//library. albany. edu/speccoll/findaids/apap099. htm

University District Oral History Project, University of Washington Museology Graduate Program

http：//cdm200301. cdmhost. com/cdm/landingpage/collection/p15015coll7

University of Scranton Oral History

http：//digitalservices. scranton. edu/cdm/collectionguide/collection/oralhistory#collection-contents

University of York Oral History Project

https：//dlib. york. ac. uk/yodl/app/audio/oral-history

http：//www. york. ac. uk/borthwick/projects/oral-history/

Unspoken Memories： Oral Histories of Hawaii Internees at Jerome，
Arkansas

http：//scholarspace. manoa. hawaii. edu/handle/10125/33173

Untold Stories： The Leicester LGBT Centre Oral History Project

http：//www. lgbt-stories. org/

Upper East Side Story： Our Neighborhood Oral History Project，New York
Public Library

http：//oralhistory. nypl. org/neighborhoods/ues

USAHEC Senior Officer Oral History，US Army War College

http：//www. carlisle. army. mil/ahec/oralHistory. cfm

Utah Queer Oral Histories Collection

https：//heritage. utah. gov/apps/history/findaids/b1918/b1918. xml

UWAHS Oral History Portal，University of Western Australia

http：//www. web. uwa. edu. au/uwahs/oral-histories

Veterans' Oral History Project，Austin Peay State University

http：//vohp. lib. apsu. edu/

Veterans History Project，American Folklife Center，Library of Congress

http：//www. loc. gov/vets/

Veterans Oral History Project，Salem State University

https：//www. salemstate. edu/academics/schools/28907. php

Veterans Oral History Project，University of Oregon

http：//uovetsoralhistory. uoregon. edu/

Vietnam Era Veterans Oral Histories

http：//libx. bsu. edu/cdm/landingpage/collection/VtnmOrHis

Vietnam War Oral History Project

http：//www. vietnamwar. govt. nz/about

Vietnamese American Oral History Project, University of California, Irvine

http：//ucispace. lib. uci. edu/handle/10575/1614

http：//sites. uci. edu/vaohp/

Visible Lives: Oral Histories of the Disability Experience, New York Public Library

http：//oralhistory. nypl. org/neighborhoods/visible-lives

Visual History Archive, USC Shoah Foundation

https：//sfi. usc. edu/vha

Virtual Oral/Aural History Archive, CSULB

http：//www. csulb. edu/voaha

VOCES Oral History Project, University of Texas at Austin

http：//www. lib. utexas. edu/voces/

Voice/Vision: Holocaust Survivor Oral History Archive, University of Michigan-Dearborn

http：//holocaust. umd. umich. edu

Voice of Labor Oral History Project, Georgia State University

http：//research. library. gsu. edu/VoicesofLabor

Voice of Witness: Amplifying Unheard Voices

http：//voiceofwitness. org/

Voices from East of Bronx Park: An Oral History Project of the Allerton, Van Nest, Pelham Parkway and Morris Park Communities, New York Public Library

http：//oralhistory. nypl. org/neighborhoods/east-bronx

Voices from the Fisheries Oral History Project, National Oceanic and Atmospheric Administration

https：//www. st. nmfs. noaa. gov/humandimensions/voices-from-the-fisheries/index

Voices of Feminism Oral History Project, Smith College

https: //www. smith. edu/library/libs/ssc/vof/vof-intro. html

Voices of Homelessness Oral History Project, St. Catherine University

http: //sophia. stkate. edu/scuvoh_ audio/

Voices of Lycoming: Alumni Oral History Transcripts, Lycoming College

http: //www. lycoming. edu/library/archives/voicesTranscripts. aspx

Voices of the Holocaust, Illinois Institute of Technology

http: //voices. iit. edu

Voice of Witness

http: //voiceofwitness. org

Waikiki, 1910 - 1985: Oral Histories

http: //scholarspace. manoa. hawaii. edu/handle/10125/29790

Warwick Oral History Network, University of Warwick

http: //www2. warwick. ac. uk/fac/cross_ fac/ias/activities/supported/researchnetworks/oralhistory

Wesleyan University Oral History Project

http: //wesscholar. wesleyan. edu/oralhistory/

West Point Center for Oral History

http: //www. westpointcoh. org/

What Did You Do in the War, Grandma? South Kingstown High School

http: //cds. library. brown. edu/projects/WWII_ Women/tocCS. html

What Is Oral History? History Matters

http: //historymatters. gmu. edu/mse/oral/what. html

William J. Clinton Presidential History Project

http: //millercenter. org/president/clinton/oralhistory

Wexler Oral History Project, Yiddish Book Center

http: //www. yiddishbookcenter. org/collections/oral-histories

Women in Journalism, Washington Press Club Foundation

http：//wpcf. org/women-in-journalism/

Women in Politics

http：//digitum. washingtonhistory. org/cdm/search/collection/politics

Women of Central Washington University Oral History Transcripts

http：//digitum. washingtonhistory. org/cdm/landingpage/
collection/cwuoralh

Women of the Oklahoma Legislature, Oklahoma State University

http：//www. library. okstate. edu/oralhistory/digital/wotol/

Women's History Consortium Oral Histories Collection, Western Washington
University

http：//content. wwu. edu/cdm/search/collection/whc_ audio

Yad Vashem: The Holocaust Martyrs' and Heroes' Remembrance Authority, Jerusalem

http：//www. yadvashem. org

Yale Law School Oral History Series

http：//digitalcommons. law. yale. edu/ylsohs/

Year of China Oral History Project, Brown University

https：//www. brown. edu/about/administration/international-affairs/
year-of-china/china-brown/year-china-oral-history-project/year-china-oral-
history-project

York Oral History Society

http：//www. yorkoralhistory. org. uk/

索　引

A

阿道大·贝利（Adolf A. Berle）　60

阿兰·内文斯（Allan Nevins）　1, 2, 5—6, 30, 34, 44—45, 58—69, 70, 73, 83, 103—104, 107, 121, 138, 168, 227, 233—234, 244, 418

阿利桑乔·波特利（Alessandro Portelli）　29, 203—205, 207—208, 218, 223—224

阿利斯泰尔·汤姆森（Alistair Thomson）　24—25, 199, 212, 235

阿尼塔·琼斯（Arnita Jones）　405

艾伦·钱伯斯（Aaron Chambers）　148

艾伦·桑德勒（Alan L. Sandler）　397

艾米丽·索佩斯（Emily W. Soapes）　95

艾瑞克·霍尔德（Eric H. Holder）　364

艾滋病　11, 32, 185, 355, 420

埃德·莫洛尼（Ed Moloney）　360—368, 375, 378—382, 414, 417

埃德加·班克罗夫特（Edgar A. Bancroft）　64

埃德温·盖伊（Edwin F. Gay）　60

埃尔伍德·蒙德（Elwood R. Maunder）　72

埃里克·方纳（Eric Foner）　130, 135

埃里克·霍布斯鲍姆（Eric J. Hobsbawm）　130—131, 133

埃利奥特·威金顿（Eliot Wigginton）　339—340, 342, 344—345, 347

埃利诺·罗斯福（Eleanor Roosevelt）　84—85

埃斯特尔·夏普（Estelle B. Sharp）　71

爱德华·汤普森（Edward P. Thompson）　133

爱尔兰共和军　359—361, 363, 367, 376

爱尔兰临时新芬党　360

爱丽丝·弗莱彻（Alice C. Fletcher）　241

爱丽丝·霍夫曼（Alice M. Hoffman）　213

爱丽丝·科斯勒·哈里斯（Alice Kessler Harris）　202

爱丽丝·托克勒斯（Alice B. Toklas）　74

爱米尔·贝利纳（Emile Berliner）　240

安德烈·希夫林（André Schiffrin）　139, 141

安德鲁·詹森（Andrew Jenson）　40

安东尼·麦金太尔（Anthony McIntyre）　361—366, 368, 376, 378—380, 382, 414—415, 417

安妮·维科（Anne Vick）　344

奥柏林·史密斯（Oberlin Smith）　243

B

巴里·兰曼（Barry A. Lanman）　335, 337, 343, 348, 350—352

芭芭拉·特鲁斯德尔（Barbara Truesdell）　325

后　记

自 1999 年通过《美国历史杂志》（*Journal of American History*）首次接触 "Oral History"① 这个术语和概念以来，不知不觉间，我在口述史学领域的学习、实践与研究已经达 17 年之久。2004 年，我出版了国内较早的以口述史学基本理论、方法与发展现状为主要内容的口述史学专著《与历史对话：口述史学的理论与实践》②，粗线条地梳理了美国现代口述史学发展的基本历程。考虑到美国是现代口述史学的发源地且是世界上口述史学发展水平最高的国家，美国口述史学自然也一直是我关注与研究的焦点。对于该课题的系统研究则始于 2009 年，当年申报的 "美国现代口述史学研究"（项目批准号：09CSS001）获得国家社会科学基金青年项目立项。呈现在大家面前的这本同名专著便是过去 7 年的研究成果。本书对美国现代口述史学的起源、发展历程、国际背景、基本特征、理论研究、跨学科应用、口述历史教育与面临的主要挑战等问题做了较为全面而系统的梳理与研究。

需要特别指出的是，该项目的立项与后续研究对我而言具有非常重要的意义，尤其是为口述史学实践与研究平台的搭建提供了重要契机。作为国内高校较早的口述历史研究机构，温州大学口述历史研究所于 2008 年 11 月由温州大学批准成立。经过将近 8 年的发展，该所已经成为国内重要

① 通过查阅，笔者发现该杂志在 1987—2002 年间的夏季版都设有 "Oral History" 专栏，除特约编辑的《导读》之外，每期专栏大概有三篇文章。

② 杨祥银：《与历史对话：口述史学的理论与实践》，中国社会科学出版社 2004 年版。

的口述史学理论研究与实践机构，并享有一定的海内外知名度。除口述史学理论与方法研究之外，研究所确立了两大主要发展方向，即口述历史实践与学术传播平台建设。在口述历史实践方面，过去几年来，研究所与温州市委党史研究室、鹿城区归国华侨联合会和温州大学档案馆等机构合作，总共完成80多人的口述历史访谈工作（并且继续保持每年10—15位受访者的访谈规模）。这些涉及温州老领导老干部、温州改革开放先驱者、温州海外华侨和温州大学离退休教师与校友的口述历史计划搜集和保存了相当丰富的口述历史访谈稿、音视频资料以及照片与手稿等实物资料，我们的长远目标是建设一个以记录、保存与传播温州人历史与记忆为宗旨的"温州人口述历史数据库"。

为促进口述历史概念与实践在中国的发展与普及，研究所搭建了一个集学术集刊《口述史研究》、官方网站（http://oralhistory.wzu.edu.cn）、官方微博（@WZU口述史学）和微信公众平台"口述历史"（wzuoralhistory）于一体的学术传播与交流平台。其中，作为国内首份口述史学理论研究中文学术集刊，自2014年10月出版第一辑以来，《口述史研究》[1] 受到国内外同行的较高评价与认可，其中美国《口述历史协会通讯》（*Oral History Association Newsletter*）、《台湾口述历史学会会刊》、中国社会科学网、中国人民大学报刊复印资料《历史学文摘》和《北京晨报》等刊物和媒体都予以了专门报道和转摘。

回顾过去17年在口述史学领域的耕耘与努力，的确，它已经成为我学术生涯中最为重要的组成部分，我甚至经常跟人讲，我是将口述历史工作当成自己的事业来做。在此书即将出版之际，我要向那些给予我热心支持与帮助的老师、朋友、同行、学生以及家人表示衷心的感谢。首先，要特别感谢我的口述史学启蒙老师——美国米德威学院（Midway College）的克里斯蒂娜·米尼斯特（Kristina Minister）教授和威斯康星大学密尔沃基分校（University of Wisconsin-Milwaukee）历史系的迈克尔·格登（Michael

---

[1] 杨祥银主编：《口述史研究》（第一辑），社会科学文献出版社2014年版。

A. Gordon）教授。她们在我从事口述史学研究的初期给了我很大帮助，不仅热心解答我提出的各种问题，而且提供了大量宝贵的研究资料。特别难得的是，我跟格登教授至今仍然保持频繁的学术交流与联系。

我的口述史学研究贯穿本科、硕士与博士三个求学阶段，在吉林大学历史系（1997—2001）、中国社会科学院研究生院世界历史系（2001—2004）与香港中文大学历史系（2004—2007）的学习与生活时光给我留下了非常美好而深刻的记忆，有幸认识和得到众多知名学者和老师的热心指导与支持，在此一并致以诚挚的谢意，其中包括于沛、姜芃、叶汉明、郭少棠、刘德斌、王剑、张乃和、许兆昌、郝淑媛、聂洪凯、陈启能、吴英与梁元生等诸位师长。

2007 年 8 月进入温州大学人文学院工作以来，我的口述史学研究工作也得到了温州大学人文社科处与人文学院相关老师与领导的大力帮助与支持，在此一并表示感谢，其中包括叶世祥（1966—2013）、蔡贻象、李校堃、陈艾华、孙良好、王海晨、刘建国、张洁、尤育号、丁治民、黄涛、周湘浙、赵敏、吴静、夏雨禾、任映红、胡新根、刘玉侠、陈宝胜、郑春生、孙碧燕、孙鹏程、林玉双与周美琼等等。

当然，还要感谢众多海内外同行、师长与朋友给予的各种帮助与支持，他（她）们包括唐纳德·里奇（Donald A. Ritchie）、保罗·汤普森（Paul Thompson）、迈克尔·弗里斯科（Michael Frisch）、罗纳德·格里（Ronald J. Grele）、巴里·兰曼（Barry A. Lanman）、琳达·肖普斯（Linda Shopes）、阿利桑乔·波特利（Alessandro Portelli）、罗伯特·佩克斯（Robert Perks）、肖娜·格拉克（Sherna Berger Gluck）、达芬尼·帕泰（Daphne Patai）、阿利斯泰尔·汤姆森（Alistair Thomson）、道格拉斯·博伊德（Douglas A. Boyd）、克利福德·库恩（Clifford M. Kuhn，1952—2015）、维拉·鲍姆（Willa K. Baum，1926—2006）、理查德·史密斯（Richard Cándida Smith）、路易莎·帕萨里尼（Luisa Passerini）、约翰·博德纳（John Bodnar）、布鲁斯·斯蒂夫（Bruce M. Stave）、玛丽·克拉克

（Mary Marshall Clark）、玛丽·拉尔森（Mary Larson）、南茜·麦凯（Nancy MacKay）、乔安娜·博纳特（Joanna Bornat）、瑞贝卡·夏普莱斯（Rebecca Sharpless）、扎克利·施拉格（Zachary M. Schrag）、约翰·纽恩斯科范德尔（John Neuenschwander）、戴维·杜纳威（David K. Dunaway）、马克·特博（Mark Tebeau）、苏珊·阿米蒂奇（Susan H. Armitage）、林恩·阿布拉姆斯（Lynn Abrams）、瓦拉利·姚（Valerie Raleigh Yow）、亚历山大·柏拉图（Alexander von Plato）、杨立文、杨雁斌、钟少华、沈固朝、许雪姬、林发钦、古伟瀛、黄克武、游鉴明、黄文江、蔡笃坚、王惠玲、赖素春、左玉河、周新国、陈墨、王旭、陈红民、张连红、梁敬民、刘国柱、余新忠、马卫东、蒋蕾、陈新、陈恒、周兵、丁贤勇、李冈原、张藜、定宜庄、郭于华、赵小建、张英聘、刘大可、刘瑛华、张侃、郭平、王小平、金光耀、董正华、谢嘉幸、李丹柯、丁旭东、刘宇、林卉、李国武、张彦武、王宇英、李娜、李慧波、钱茂伟、唐建光、李丹青、徐阳、王玉敏、郭泽德、渠馨一、向晓静、熊春妹与李雅悠等。

作为老师而言，感到特别快乐和满足的是能够培养一批又一批自己的学生，自 2009 年开始招收硕士研究生以来，我共指导 14 位毕业和在读研究生，他（她）们分别是徐建伟、王少阳、王鹏、魏焕、甘慧、郑重、叶欣欣、欧阳程楚、常慧、张宁雅、刘美华、叶桦畅、曾富城与雷玉平。值得欣慰的是，他（她）们当中的一部分人已经和正在进入不断蓬勃发展的口述历史领域。

我还要感谢全国哲学社会科学规划办公室提供的经费支持以及多位匿名审稿专家对书稿提出的大量富有建设性的修改建议。当然，本书的出版还要感谢中国社会科学出版社副总编郭沂纹和责任编辑安芳，她们为本书的出版提供了诸多帮助与支持。尤其值得一提的是，郭沂纹副总编还是我的第一本口述史学专著《与历史对话：口述史学的理论与实践》一书的责任编辑。此外，还要特别感谢《历史研究》、《新华文摘》、《中国社会科学文摘》、《中国人民大学报刊复印资料》、《中国社会科学报》、《史学理论研究》、《社会科学战线》、《当代中国史研究》、《国外社会科学》、《史学集刊》、《社会科学辑刊》、《浙江学刊》、《华侨华人历史研究》、《江汉论坛》、《学习与探索》、《人民日报》（理论版）、《郑州大学学报》（哲学社会科学版）与《华中师范大学学报》（人文社会科学版）等刊物对于我的研究成果的关注与支持。

当然，作为口述历史工作的核心对象，我要特别感谢过去几年来接受我们访谈的 80 多位受访者，正是他（她）们的支持与配合才能使我们顺利完成各项口述历史计划，这些实践也不断促使我在理论与方法上进行自我反思与经验总结。在这里，还要感谢与我们进行多年合作的相关机构的领导与朋友，其中包括温州市档案局万邦联，温州市委党史研究室赵降英、赵万磊、张林、张林洁，鹿城区归国华侨联合会蒋晖、蔡喜莲，以及浙江中医药大学档案馆张坚君，等等。

最后，我要特别感谢我的家人，没有他（她）们的无私支持和付出是很难完成这本书的。尤其是我的父母和爱人为我分担了绝大部分的家庭职责，使我能够有更多时间和精力投入自己的研究工作当中。2009 年可爱儿子的出生更是给我带来了巨大的快乐与无比的幸福，更令我感到欣慰的是，随着他的渐渐长大，他也开始慢慢"懂得"我的研究工作，这很大程度上也是我在学术研究道路上继续前进的精神动力。回首过去十多年的实践与研究经历，尽管我在口述史学领域付出了相当多的心血与努力，但受时间和能力所限，书稿还存在诸多不足，希望以后有机会进一步完善与深化。

杨祥银

2016 年 11 月于茶山温州大学城